Court, Country, City

Studies in British Art 24

Court, Country, City: British Art and Architecture, 1660–1735

Edited by Mark Hallett, Nigel Llewellyn, and Martin Myrone

Published by
The Yale Center for British Art
The Paul Mellon Centre for Studies in British Art

Distributed by
Yale University Press, New Haven & London

Published by

The Yale Center for British Art
P.O. Box 208280
1080 Chapel Street
New Haven, CT 06520-8280
www.britishart.yale.edu

and

The Paul Mellon Centre for Studies in British Art
16 Bedford Square
London WC1B 3JA
United Kingdom
www.paul-mellon-centre.ac.uk

Distributed by

Yale University Press
P.O. Box 209040
302 Temple Street
New Haven, CT 06520-9040
www.yalebooks.com/art

Volume edited by Mark Hallett, Nigel Llewellyn, and Martin Myrone
Publication coordinated by A. Robin Hoffman at the Yale Center for British Art
Copyedited by Rose Bell
Index by Marcia Carlson

Designed by Anjali Pala, Miko McGinty Inc.
Set in Garamond by Tina Henderson
Separations by Professional Graphics, Inc., Rockford, IL
Printed in Italy by Conti Tipocolor S.p.A

Library of Congress Cataloging-in-Publication Data

Names: Hallett, Mark, 1965– editor. | Llewellyn, Nigel, 1951– editor. | Myrone, Martin, editor.
Title: Court, country, city : British art and architecture, 1660–1735 / edited by Mark Hallett, Nigel Llewellyn, and Martin Myrone.
Description: New Haven : Yale Center for British Art, 2016. | Series: Studies in British art ; 24 | Includes index.
Identifiers: LCCN 2016008925 | ISBN 978-0-300-21480-2 (hardback)
Subjects: LCSH: Art, British—17th century. | Art, British—18th century. | Architecture—Great Britain—History—17th century. | Architecture—Great Britain—History—18th century. | Art and society—Great Britain—History—17th century. | Art and society—Great Britain—History—18th century. | Architecture and society—Great Britain—History—17th century. | Architecture and society—Great Britain—History—18th century. | BISAC: ART / European. | ART / Criticism & Theory. | HISTORY / Europe / Great Britain. | HISTORY / Modern / 17th Century. | HISTORY / Modern / 18th Century.
Classification: LCC N6766 .C68 2016 | DDC 709.41/09032—dc23

A catalogue record for this book is available from the British Library.
10 9 8 7 6 5 4 3 2 1

This is the twenty-fourth in a series of occasional volumes devoted to studies in British art, published by the Yale Center for British Art and the Paul Mellon Centre for Studies in British Art.

Jacket illustrations: *(front)* Jan Griffier, *Millbank and the Horse Ferry* (detail), ca. 1706–10, oil on canvas. Museum of London; *(back)* George Bickham the Elder, published by John King and T. Slater, *Postscript to the Post-Boy*, 1706, engraving with hand-coloured etching, 16⅝ x 11 in. (42.3 x 27.9 cm). Worcester College, Oxford, George Clark Print Collection

Contents

KINGS, QUEENS, COMMANDERS

NETWORKS, SHARED PRACTICES, COMMUNITIES

Note to the Reader: Original spelling and punctuation have been preserved in the direct quotation of pre-twentieth-century sources. Editorial clarification within quotations has been kept to a minimum.

Acknowledgments

This book has its origins in the cross-institutional scholarly research project *Court, Country, City: British Art, 1660–1735*, which ran from 2009 to 2012. This collaborative project, which was developed and managed by the editors, was based at the University of York and Tate Britain and supported by the UK's Arts and Humanities Research Council. It was administered in York by Clare Bond, to whom we are especially grateful, and who brought her customary perceptiveness, clarity of thought, and sense of calm to every issue. Three post-doctoral researchers—Lydia Hamlett, Richard Stephens, and Claudine van Hensbergen—made enormous contributions to the project. We would like to thank them for their hard work, their art-historical insights, and their inspiring collegiality. The project also supported two doctoral studentships, which were held by Peter Moore and Caroline Good. They, too, brought a great deal of energy, insight, and creativity to our activities, which was much appreciated.

Court, Country, City featured three major conferences: *Revisiting British Art 1660–1735*, held at the University of York on 7 May 2010; *British Art 1660–1735: Close Readings*, held at Tate Britain on 20 May 2011; and *Histories of British Art 1660–1735: Reconstruction and Transformation*, held at the University of York on 20–22 September 2012. The project also generated the online database edited by Stephens, entitled *The Art World in Britain 1660 to 1735*, at http://artworld.york.ac.uk, and supported three temporary gallery displays at Tate Britain: *Court, Country, City: British Art 1660–1735*, in 2011; *Dead Standing Things: Still Life 1660–1740*, in 2012, with accompanying online resources; and *Sketches for Spaces: History Painting and Architecture 1630–1730*, in 2013–2014. The editors would like to offer their thanks to the many colleagues who made such important contributions to these different activities, and helped ensure that our discussions and debates were lively and informative. In addition to those mentioned elsewhere in these acknowledgments, we would like to thank Anne-Marie Akehurst, Malcolm Baker, Clare Barlow, David A. Brewer, Katherine Coombs, Margaret Dalivalle, Rudolf Dekker, Brett Dolman, Lauren Dudley, Jason Edwards, Charles Ford, Peter Forsaith, Matt

Fountain, Susan E. Gordon, Erin Griffey, Craig Ashley Hanson, Ailsa Hutton, Susan Jenkins, Sander Karst, Ruth Kenny, Arlene Leis, Peter N. Lindfield-Ott, Stephen Lloyd, Catharine MacLeod, Sarah Monks, Sarah Moulden, Darragh O'Donoghue, Lucy Peltz, Eleonora Pistis, Debra Pring, Anne Puetz, Kate Retford, Christine Riding, Greg Sullivan, Amy Todman, Simon Turner, Dror Wahrman, Roger Carr Whitworth, and Helen Wyld.

In addition, we would like to thank a number of colleagues at Tate Britain and York. Stephen Deuchar, the Director of Tate Britain when the project was first mooted, gave it his enthusiastic support, as did his successor Penelope Curtis. We are grateful for their recognition that such research projects can help stimulate and inform the work of a great public institution such as Tate Britain. Brian Cantor, Vice-Chancellor at the University of York during the life of the project, was similarly supportive, as was Mark Ormrod, the academic co-ordinator for the Arts and Humanities at the University. Other colleagues at both institutions collaborated closely with us on various aspects of the project. At Tate Britain, Tabitha Barber, Tim Batchelor, and Karen Hearn made important contributions on many levels; at York, we were especially grateful for the input of Caitlin Blackwell, Anthony Geraghty, Mark Jenner, Bill Sherman, Fiona Watson, and Andrew Wilkinson.

In helping us to translate part of the research generated by the project into a book of essays, we have, of course, been dependent on the labour, support, and enthusiasm of many other colleagues. First of all, we would like to thank the contributors to this volume. They have produced work of the highest calibre and—without exception—been warm and collaborative in their dealings with the editors and with each other. Thanks to their efforts, this has been a very happy and stimulating book to edit.

In putting this book together, we have also been hugely indebted to colleagues from the Yale Center for British Art. Eleanor Hughes, formerly Associate Director of Exhibitions and Publications at the Center, now Deputy Director for Art & Program at the Walters Art Museum in Baltimore, supervised the earlier stages of this volume's gestation and acted in effect as a fourth editor. Her astonishing energy and professionalism stimulated all aspects of this book's development. Meanwhile, Martina Droth, Nathan Flis, Matthew Hargraves (who also managed to find time to contribute an essay to our collection), and Scott Wilcox have been similarly collegial and collaborative. Particular thanks are due, moreover, to the two YCBA colleagues who brought this book to fruition. Robin Hoffman, who took over from Ellie in supervising the latter stages of the book's production, has been a wonderful editor, cheerfully and thoughtfully shepherding us through every stage of the process, and keeping an attentive eye out for even the smallest mishaps or stumbles; she has been a delight to work with. Shaunee Cole, Publications Assistant, has been a brilliant picture editor, working tirelessly to assist every contributor in finding the best possible images with which to illustrate their essays. Her efforts complement the characteristically thoughtful book design by Anjali Pala and the team at Miko McGinty, Inc. Rose Bell, our copyeditor, has cast an especially scrupulous and well-informed eye over the entire manuscript. She has been both patient and generous.

Mark Hallett would also like to thank his colleagues at the Paul Mellon Centre for Studies for British Art, to which he moved just a few days after the final *Court, Country, City* conference. In particular, he would like to thank his colleagues Ella Fleming, Sarah Turner, and Martin Postle for their efforts in ensuring the success of a special pre-publication workshop at the Centre, in which contributors had the chance to flesh out their ideas for the book. More generally, he would like to thank all the team at the Centre for making it such a conducive environment in which to pursue the work of co-editing this volume. In a similar vein, Nigel Llewellyn would like to acknowledge the work of his former colleagues in the Tate Research Department for their management of the AHRC award which supported the *Court, Country, City* project—in particular, Ailsa Roberts, the Research Manager, and Allie Biswas and Helen Griffiths, Tate's Research Administrators.

The series in which this book appears, *Studies in British Art*, has made a remarkable contribution to our understanding of all aspects of British art and architecture. We are very proud that our volume is part of such a rich and varied list of publications. This volume, however, will also be the last book to be published in the series in its present form; in future, it will live on in the rather different guise of special issues of the new online journal *British Art Studies*, which is jointly produced by the Paul Mellon Centre and the Yale Center for British Art. Even as we look forward to seeing the series moving forward in a fresh, digital form, we would like to use this moment of transition to pay appropriate tribute to the wonderful colleagues who, from London and New Haven, have guided *Studies in British Art* throughout its distinguished history: Brian Allen, Amy Meyers, and Duncan Robinson. All students and scholars of British art and architecture are in their debt.

Mark Hallett, Nigel Llewellyn, and Martin Myrone

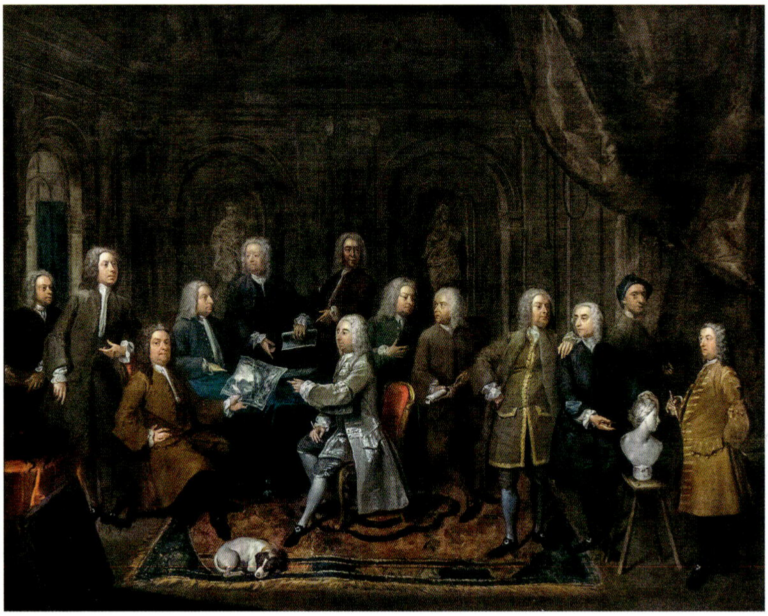

1. Gawen Hamilton, *A Conversation of Virtuosis at the King's Head*, 1734–35, oil on canvas, 34.5 x 43.9 in. (87.7 x 111.5 cm). National Portrait Gallery, London

symbolic of the thriving state of the arts in contemporary Britain. And, indeed, his notebooks of the period contain numerous entries that suggest a sense of satisfaction and excitement on his part regarding the modern history and future prospects of British art and architecture. On the one hand, he could look back with pride at the achievements of a figure like Sir James Thornhill, who, on his death in 1734, he described as "the greatest History [painter] this kingdom has ever produced", and whose "elaborate works in that noble structure of Greenwich Hospital [and] the Cupola of St. Paul's Cathedral" testified to the possibilities that had become increasingly available to native-born as well as immigrant artists since the restoration of the monarchy in 1660.[6] On the other hand, Vertue could celebrate the ever-increasing vibrancy of the art scene in the capital; thus, in 1732, he wrote that "Art flourishes more in London now than probably it has done 50 or 60 years before—in Numbers of artists. & works done."[7] A prime example of this burgeoning realm of practice was William Hogarth's innovative series of paintings and prints entitled *A Harlot's Progress*, which were publicly displayed in 1732, and which Vertue described as "the most remarkable Subject of painting that captivated the Minds of most People".[8] Another example of such enterprise, again involving Hogarth, was recorded by Vertue in the same year that Hamilton's painting was raffled: "this Winter 1735 an Academy for drawing from the Life sett up in St Martin's lane where several artists go to Draw from the life. Mr Hogarth principally promotes or undertakes it."[9]

A Conversation of Virtuosis chimes in with this sense of a flourishing metropolitan visual culture. Here, a group of five painters—including Gawen Hamilton himself, who looks out at us from his easel, the Swedish-born Michael Dahl, who sits on our left, and John Wootton, who stands with his arm resting on the shoulder of the Dutch-born sculptor John Michael Rysbrack—mix companionably with friends and colleagues from a range of other disciplines. There are two engravers—as well as Vertue, the canvas depicts the French-born reproductive engraver Bernard Baron, who is shown clasping a roll of paper in his right hand. There is a pair of architects, too—together with Gibbs, we find the less well-known figure of William Thomas, who sits listening to his colleague on the far side of the table. The picture also features the landscape architect Charles Bridgeman, who leans over to talk to Baron; the celebrated decorative painter and designer William Kent, who stands with a porte-crayon in his hand on the far right of the image; and a genteel amateur, Matthew Robinson, who is shown seated in the middle of the composition, pointing rather proudly to one of his own landscape watercolours.[10] Seen together, this grouping of figures offers a powerful ideal of gentlemanly dialogue between a variety of artistic practitioners, both professional and amateur, both foreign-born and local—one that speaks, we can suggest, of a wider spirit of collaboration, cosmopolitanism, and corporate pride amongst those who inhabited the art world of early Georgian Britain.

On closer investigation, however, both Hamilton's conversation piece and Vertue's writings can also be seen to reveal a far more competitive, fragmented, and, on occasion, troubled story of British art during the late Stuart and early Georgian periods. Tellingly, Hamilton's painting itself seems to have been commissioned and painted not simply as a celebration of artistic fraternity, as one might presume, but as an aggressive weapon in the marketplace for portraiture, designed in all probability to promote his practice over that of William Hogarth, who was also enjoying great success as the painter of small group-portraits—or "conversation pieces"—very like this one. As Vertue notes, "the proposition of his piece was to promote the interest of Mr Hamilton."[11] If the painting itself was thus in part the expression of artistic competition, and of the anxieties that attended such competition, the careers of the men it depicted were often framed by similar kinds of rivalry and unease. Vertue himself, for example, was someone who, as his writings make clear, continually fretted that his chosen profession of engraving was not treated with sufficient respect, and who looked upon the success enjoyed by Hogarth with a mixture of appreciation and distaste.[12]

In fact, Vertue's notebooks, as well as reporting on the artistic improvements of the era, teem with references to the factions and conflicts within British art, and to the miseries and failures of British artists. There is a dark side to his jottings, and to the stories they tell, which frequently record the diseased, poverty-stricken, or even suicidal fates of individual practitioners. Take, for example, his account of an old intimate of Dahl's, the portraitist Henry Tilson, who had misguidedly imagined that a rich female patron had fallen in love with him, and who, lovesick and suffering from "a distemper'd brain", had proceeded to kill himself: "he retird into his Closett. & with a pistol shot thro' the heart. aged about 36."[13] Or take his tale of the French painter Philippe Duval, who came to England soon after the Restoration and enjoyed the financial support of the experimental scientist Robert Boyle, but who, after the latter's death, fell into abject poverty: "his wants increased. disordered his mind & made him very unsociable. dyd poor & was buried in St Martins in the fields. about. 1709."[14] Or take, as one final example among many other narratives of artistic woe, Vertue's account of Christian Richter, a Swedish painter who, on his arrival in London at the beginning of the eighteenth century, had initially benefited from the encouragement he had been given by Dahl, his fellow countryman. Though he had proceeded to embark on a successful career as a copyist, Richter's prospects were hampered by the horrific effects of a sexually transmitted disease, which ravaged his face and thereby made him too gruesome to be contemplated by female sitters: "his face being no Agreable prospect for fine Ladys to see those scars were rather a motive of compassion than to inspire their graces & charms. such as always they expect shoud be represented by ye Painter—after a tedious indisposition & illness he dyd Nov. 1732 in St James Parish Westminster."[15] If, then, the modern history of British art could, from one perspective, be legitimately understood by the mid-1730s as a history of rapid development and success, and pictorially imagined in terms of a polite gathering of affluent and equable gentleman-artists in a well-appointed room, it could also be told as a story of repeated "disorders", false starts, and disappointments, and imagined far more bleakly through calling up the image—far more familiar to us, of course, from the Romantic period—of the diseased and dying painter lying in his closet.

Court, Country, City: British Art and Architecture, 1660–1735 offers a set of investigations into the expanding yet highly conflicted art world that Vertue recovered, reported upon, and lived through, and into the varied kinds of visual materials that he so often described within the pages of his notebooks. Focusing on the years bounded by the restoration of the monarchy in 1660—when artists and architects were suddenly faced with many new opportunities and challenges—and the founding of Hogarth's St Martin's Lane Academy in the winter of 1735—which marked one of the crucial stages in the development of a distinctive corporate identity for British art and artists—this collection of essays forgoes any attempt at a comprehensive or univocal art-historical narrative of the period, in favour of an approach which is more pluralistic, exploratory, even impressionistic in character. This approach testifies to the book's origins in a series of scholarly conferences on British visual culture of the period that took place at the University of York and Tate Britain between 2009 and 2012, and that were organized under the auspices of a major research project entitled *Court, Country, City: British Art, 1660–1735*, which was supported by the UK's Arts & Humanities Research Council.[16] Yet this approach also expresses the editors' sense that the art produced in Britain and its imperial territories during the years covered in this book, however comprehensively recorded by Vertue, remains remarkably open to a variety of interpretations, and has yet to be assigned the powerful meta-narratives that help shape debate on British art of earlier and later eras.

Indeed, this period, though focused upon in impressive detail by historians of British architecture, has been relatively under-studied—in the last few decades at least—by historians of painting, sculpture, and the graphic arts, certainly compared to the upsurge of such work on the mid-Georgian period and the steady interest in the artistic culture of earlier Stuart Britain. Until very recently, the last major scholarly survey of the art and architecture of the late Stuart and early Georgian eras remained Judith Hook's *The Baroque Age in England*, published some forty years ago.[17] The two other modern accounts to which one could turn for detailed information about the visual arts of the period were those found within Ellis Waterhouse's *History of British Art, 1530–1790*, published in 1953 as part of the Pelican History of Art series, and Margaret Whinney and Oliver Millar's *English Art, 1625–1714*, which was published as part of the Oxford History of English Art in 1957.[18] All three of these publications have great merits: Hook's *The Baroque Age* makes an eloquent case for the existence of a distinctive period style in England, while Waterhouse, Whinney, and Millar continue to provide a fund of facts and pithily expressed opinions on many of the era's leading artists. These and other authorities are, accordingly, referenced in the essays below, where a critical sense of the historiography of this period is regularly brought to the fore. Since the mid-twentieth century, however, new methodological approaches and a digitally led revolution in research methods have transformed the writing of art history in general, and writing on British art in particular.[19] These developments have opened up the possibility that the period covered by this book—which has often been overlooked in the rush to focus instead on a so-called "Age of Van Dyck" on the one hand or an "Age of Hogarth" on the other—can be systematically reinvestigated and newly appreciated, not only in relation to the histories with which it is typically bracketed in the literature, but also on its own terms and in its own right.[20]

Thankfully, this process of reappraisal has already begun happening and is being spearheaded—alongside the pioneering efforts of numerous other scholars—by many of the contributors to this book.[21] Christine Stevenson and Anthony Geraghty, for example, are leading a new wave of architectural historians who are producing innovative and original interpretations of the structures and spaces of late Stuart and early Georgian England.[22] Tabitha Barber and Diana Dethloff, who have long experience in the field, are continually enlarging our understanding of artists such as Mary Beale and Peter Lely, while newly emergent scholars such as Richard Johns, Helen Pierce, and Claudine van Hensbergen have produced a succession of important publications on the painting and sculpture of seventeenth- and early eighteenth-century Britain.[23] Pursuing a somewhat different mode of research, Richard Stephens has edited a remarkable online database entitled *The Art World in Britain, 1660–1735*, commissioned as part of the same scholarly project from which this book has emerged; this database rivals the notebooks of Vertue himself in the range and depth of information it provides to the contemporary scholar.[24] Most recently of all, David Solkin's newly published successor to Waterhouse's volume in the Pelican History of Art, *Art in Britain, 1660–1815*, incorporates an ambitious art-historical examination of our period that integrates painting and the graphic arts into the wider visual culture of the time, and that explores the relationship between these forms of artistic practice and the momentous political, social, and cultural developments that defined the era.[25]

This volume is very different in character from these various single-authored efforts, reflecting its genesis in an extended, collaborative research project. More particularly, it applies a variety of art-historical approaches to a series of five, loosely bounded areas of interest that emerged into prominence during our discussions. Accordingly, the first part of *Court, Country, City* focuses on a succession of highly charged spaces: the Palace of Westminster, which played a crucial role in the workings of the art market in our period; the rebuilt Royal Exchange, in which architecture and sculpture worked together to enact new narratives of imperial monarchy; the rebuilt livery halls of the City of London, which, after the devastation wreaked by the Great Fire in 1666, used a variety of architectural means to proclaim the continuing importance of the livery companies within the capital; the royal bedchamber, which played a crucial part in the performance of courtly identity; and Castle Howard, for which Nicholas Hawksmoor devised a Janus-faced design that sought to integrate very different forms of architectural symbolism.

Having set the scene in this way, this book moves on to investigate the portraiture of leading public figures from the period, and of a celebrated king from the past. Doing so allows a better appreciation of the complex visual and political work being done by such imagery, and of the variety of materials and genres that fed into the wider category of portraiture at this time. This second sequence begins with a grandiose allegorical portrait of King Charles II, which is used to investigate the work produced for the royal court by one of the period's most successful—if also most frequently neglected—artists, Antonio Verrio. It then moves on to investigate the various kinds of visual materials that were used to promote the public image of the celebrated military commander and political leader John Churchill, first Duke of Malborough, before looking in depth at a single, extremely elaborate example of such imagery, the great mural scheme painted by Louis Laguerre at Marlborough House. There then follow two essays on the ways in which Queen Anne was represented, both in the works of the famous portraitist Sir Godfrey Kneller and in a single, highly resonant example of sculpture. The section ends with an extended exploration into one of the most ambitious print projects of the early eighteenth century, which focused on a figure who continued to haunt the nation's historical imagination: Charles I.

The third part of *Court, Country, City* concentrates on the artistic networks and shared forms of practice that developed in this period, and on the conversations and controversies they stimulated. Again, the section begins with the early years of the Restoration, and with the kinds of artistic training—amounting to what seems to have been an informal academy of drawing—encouraged and supervised by Lely in and around his London studio. It then turns to the far less familiar figure of William Lodge, and to another urban site of artistic exchange and discussion, that of York, where a small group of virtuosi—provincial predecessors, in some ways, to those depicted by Hamilton—helped shape a distinctive visual culture for the city. This section proceeds to investigate the ways in which two particular genres—still life painting and portraiture—could also become highly charged sites of polemic. At the beginning of our period, still life painting found itself at the centre of animated debates concerning illusion, deception, and the relationship of artistic practice to scientific enquiry. Meanwhile, the death of Kneller in 1723, during the latter part of our period, prompted an intense discussion within the English capital's print culture, not only about his most appropriate successor as the King's Principal Painter, but also about the character and cast-list of the contemporary British school of portraiture.

Architecture and the visual arts shaped and defined a wide range of other environments operating beyond the capital, and beyond the great country houses and royal palaces that have, for understandable reasons, so often attracted scholarly attention. These include the gentry houses which served as important hubs of artistic patronage and practice in the period, and the far-flung territories that made up what has been described as the first British Empire.[26] The fourth part of this volume begins by taking the reader into the world of the estate prospects that served to celebrate and justify the land and activities of the rural gentry, and that constituted a complex subgenre of landscape painting and printmaking in their own right. It then moves on to a discussion of a remarkable topographical project that sought to document, in graphic form, a series of British forts on the African coast, before ending with a study of the ways in which, in the early eighteenth century, a "British" model of portraiture associated most closely with Kneller's work was translated, wholesale, within the mezzotint portraiture that was produced for the North American colonies.

The book's last section offers a series of meditations on the critical and theoretical texts about art and aesthetics that emerged during this era, and on the kinds of evaluative vocabulary used by connoisseurs and virtuosi. It begins with a study of a fascinating text on painting that was published on the eve of the Restoration, and that promoted a distinctly courtly and sensual critical aesthetics. It then turns to the ways in which—perhaps surprisingly to our eyes—the practice of copperplate engraving, thanks to the use of a burin to carve a succession of lines into the surface of the plate, could be understood as a branch of sculpture. A final discussion, of the ways in which tomb monuments were described and appreciated, moves from this particular topic to range across wider issues of periodization and methodology, and serves as an afterword to this book.

Though the twenty-one essays in this volume have been gathered together into these different groupings, their arguments and preoccupations enjoy resonances across the collection as a whole. For these reasons, we encourage readers not only to orient themselves according to the book's table of contents, but also to pursue their own paths through its assembled essays. This openness to different kinds of scholarly navigation, and this encouragement to criss-cross the book's pages in search of new linkages and overlaps between issues, objects, and approaches, seems appropriate when dealing with a period which is so ripe for reinterpretation and which challenges us to think outside familiar conceptual, periodic, and institutional frameworks. In this respect, it is worth mentioning that, when the research project that generated this volume was first conceived, the editors felt relatively confident that it would prove fruitful to look at the royal courts, the country houses, and the cities of the late Stuart and early Georgian period as three distinctive, and at least partially independent, cultural spheres. Over the course of the project itself, however, we became increasingly struck by, and interested in, the ways in which the artistic activities associated with such environments continually leaked into, or trespassed across, one another.

An interpretative openness on our and the reader's part, together with a focus upon artistic interaction and overlap, also seems appropriate when discussing an era in which different kinds of media and practice—architecture, sculpture, painting, graphic art, drawing, tapestry, and furniture making, to name just the most obvious—seem to have been so flexible and entwined in character. One of the recurrent terms—or neologisms—that emerged in our discussions was that of the *intermedial*, which testified to the amount of times we found ourselves looking at objects and environments which brought a variety of materials into intimate contact, or fused them together entirely. In fact, this interchange and identification between media might be said to be one of the defining characteristics of British art, architecture, and design in this period—one, indeed, that thoroughly blurred the boundaries *between* art, architecture, and design themselves.

These forms of exchange seem related to another characteristic of the visual culture of this era, or more particularly of the artistic community that serviced this culture: what we might describe as a kind of commonsensical or jobbing cosmopolitanism. From the Restoration onwards, the British art world was one in which native-born and immigrant European artistic professionals continually mixed and interacted; and though the balance between local and foreign artists undoubtedly shifted over this period, with Englishmen such as Thornhill and Hogarth claiming increasing power and prominence within the artistic community as a whole, it remained the case—as Hamilton's group portrait makes abundantly clear—that "British" art was in fact a realm of activity shaped by the contributions of individuals from Britain *and* from across Europe, and by the cross-fertilization that took place between the very different types of accomplishments and approaches they brought with them. It was not only that different kinds of media were being brought into distinctive and productive contact; it was also the fact that they were increasingly being reshaped by a pan-European range of conceptual, stylistic, and material skill sets.

As a consequence, the visual culture investigated in this book can appear, to the modern eye at least, a disturbingly confused and cluttered, if undoubtedly highly dynamic, mixture of different elements. To recap, it was one in which the boundaries between different cultural spheres seem to have been especially porous and uncertain. It was one in which artistic media were continually placed in intense and intimate dialogue. It was one in which practitioners drawn from different national "schools"—including Dutch still life painters, German and Swedish portraitists, French and Italian decorative history painters, and English architects—could find themselves, at different moments, working with or competing against each other in a crowded, relatively unregulated marketplace. And it was one in which, as Vertue's writings so powerfully demonstrate, the symbols of artistic success and progress—whether the knighthoods granted to Lely, Kneller, or Thornhill, the clubs and Academies that began forming from the Restoration period onwards, or the innovative new products that proliferated within the artistic marketplace—operated cheek-by-jowl with the signs of artistic crisis and failure.[27]

Famously, Vertue's notebooks, soon after his death, were acquired by the celebrated author and connoisseur Horace Walpole (1717–1797). Subsequently, Walpole used them as the basis for a far more structurally coherent, heavily edited, stylistically polished, and aristocratically inflected account of English art, published between 1762 and 1780 under the title *Anecdotes of Painting in England*.[28] But given those features of post-Restoration and early Georgian visual culture outlined above, it may well be that Vertue's original jottings and musings—precisely because of their kaleidoscopic, fragmented, improvised and sometimes contradictory character—offer us a more telling means through which to imagine the art of the period. Even as we increasingly move on from his notebooks, then, and draw instead on the historical materials and art-historical arguments being recovered and developed through new research, it will remain crucial to continue looking through Vertue's eyes, and through the distinctive interpretative lens provided by his writings.

1. For this painting, see Elizabeth Einberg, *Manners & Morals: Hogarth and British Painting, 1700–1760* (London: Tate Gallery, 1987), 85–86, and John Kerslake, *National Portrait Gallery: Early Georgian Portraits*, 2 vols. (London: HMSO, 1977), 1 (text): 340–42.
2. See Einberg, *Manners & Morals*; Kerslake, *National Portrait Gallery*; and George Vertue, "The Notebooks III", *Walpole Society* 22 (1934): 71–72.
3. For the Walpole Society transcriptions of the notebooks, see George Vertue, "Note-books", in the following volumes of the *Walpole Society*: "Note-books I", 18 (1930); "Note-books II", 20 (1932); "Note-books III", 22 (1934); "Note-books IV", 24 (1936); "Note-books V", 26 (1938); "Index to Vertue I–V", 29 (1942); "Note-books VI", 30 (1950 [1955]).
4. Vertue, "Note-books I", 6.
5. For a full identification of the individuals pictured in Hamilton's painting, see Kerslake, *National Portrait Gallery*, and Einberg, *Manners & Morals*.
6. Vertue, "Note-books III", 70.
7. Vertue, "Note-books III", 61.
8. Vertue, "Note-books III", 58.
9. Vertue, "Note-books III", 76.
10. For more on these figures, see Kerslake, *National Portrait Gallery*, and Einberg, *Manners & Morals*.
11. Vertue, "Note-books III, 72.
12. For Vertue's anxieties concerning the regard in which his profession was held, see Vertue, "Note-books III", 119. Meanwhile, his notebooks fuse generous praise for Hogarth's achievements with a sense of disgruntlement regarding the latter's "cunning" strategies of self-advancement and his habit of dismissing artistic predecessors and contemporaries. See, for example, Vertue, "Notebooks III", 155, 124.
13. Vertue, "Note-books I", 68.
14. Vertue, "Note-books I", 126.
15. Vertue, "Note-books III", 25.
16. This collaborative research project between the University of York and Tate Britain, which was developed

and managed by the three editors of this volume, with the much appreciated assistance of Clare Bond at the University of York, ran between 2009 and 2012. Over the course of its existence, the project—entitled *Court, Country, City: British Art, 1660–1735*—employed three post-doctoral researchers: Dr Lydia Hamlett, Dr Richard Stephens, and Dr Claudine van Hensbergen; it also supported two doctoral studentships, which were held by Peter Moore and Caroline Good. It featured three major conferences: *Revisiting British Art, 1660–1735*, held at the University of York on 7 May 2010; *British Art, 1660–1735: Close Readings*, held at Tate Britain on 20 May 2011; and *Histories of British Art, 1660–1735: Reconstruction and Transformation*, held at the University of York on 20–22 September 2012. The project also generated the online database edited by Dr Stephens, entitled *The Art World in Britain, 1660 to 1735*, at http://artworld.york.ac.uk, and supported three temporary gallery displays at Tate Britain: *Genres and Transformations: British Art, 1660–1730*, in 2011; *Dead Standing Things: Still Life, 1660–1740*, in 2012; and *Sketches for Spaces: History Painting and Architecture 1630–1730*, which was on view 14 October 2013–6 April 2014.

17. Judith Hook, *The Baroque Age in England* (London: Thames and Hudson, 1976).
18. Ellis Waterhouse, *Painting in Britain, 1530–1790* (London: Penguin, 1953); a 5th edition, with an introductory text by Michael Kitson surveying more recent scholarship on the same period, was published in 1994. Chapters 6–9 deal with the period covered in this book. Margaret Whinney and Oliver Millar, *English Art, 1625–1714* (Oxford: Clarendon Press, 1957).
19. An especially important development in the study of early eighteenth-century British art, for instance, has been the availability of such online databases as the *Eighteenth-Century Collections Online (ECCO)*, and the British Library's Burney Collection of newspapers. The online database of graphic materials from the British Museum's Prints and Drawings Room is proving equally revelatory for scholars of the period.
20. For a highly suggestive, if relatively brief, analysis of the period that sees it as one witnessing a crucial transition between more traditional and modern forms of British art, see Richard Humphreys, *The Tate Britain Companion to British Art* (London: Tate, 2002), 44–57.
21. Outstanding recent publications by authors who do not feature in this volume include: Joseph Monteyne, *The Printed Image in Early Modern London: Urban Space, Visual Representation, and Social Exchange* (Aldershot: Ashgate, 2007); Craig Ashley Hanson, *The English Virtuoso: Art, Medicine, and Antiquarianism in the Age of Empiricism* (Univ. of Chicago Press, 2009); Dror Wahrman, *Mr. Collier's Letter Racks: A Tale of Art & Illusion at the Threshold of the Modern Information Age* (New York and Oxford: Oxford Univ. Press, 2012); and Matthew C. Hunter, *Wicked Intelligence: Visual Art and the Science of Experiment in Restoration London* (Univ. of Chicago Press, 2013). Notable recent publications on the political and social histories of the period include: Anna Keay, *The Magnificent Monarch: Charles II and the Ceremonies of Power* (London: Continuum, 2008), and Steve Pincus, *1688: The First Modern Revolution* (New Haven and London: Yale Univ. Press, 2009).
22. For recent publications by both authors, see Christine Stevenson, *The City and the King: Architecture and Politics in Restoration London* (New Haven and London: Yale Univ. Press, 2013), and Anthony Geraghty, *The Sheldonian Theatre: Architecture and Learning in Seventeenth-century Oxford* (New Haven and London: Yale Univ. Press, 2013). Two other contributors to this volume—Anya Matthews and Emily Mann—have studied with Stevenson.
23. For a selection of publications by these scholars, see Tabitha Barber with Mary Bustin, *Mary Beale: Portrait of a Seventeenth-century Painter, her Family and her Studio* (London: Geffrye Museum, 1999); Diana Dethloff, "Reception and Rejection: Lely's Subject Pictures in an 'un-understanding land'", in *Peter Lely: A Lyrical Vision* (London: Courtauld Gallery, 2012), ed. Caroline Campbell, 41–61; Richard Johns, "'Those Wilder Sorts of Painting': The Painted Interior in the Age of Antonio Verrio", in *A Companion to British Art: 1600 to the Present*, ed. Dana Arnold and David Peters Corbett (Oxford: Wiley-Blackwell, 2013), 79–104; Helen Pierce, "Images, Representation, and Counter-representation", in *The Oxford History of Popular Print Culture*, vol. 1, *Britain and Ireland to 1660*, ed. Joad Raymond (Oxford Univ. Press, 2011), 263–79; and Claudine van Hensbergen, "Carving a Legacy: Public Sculpture of Queen Anne, c. 1704–12", *Journal for Eighteenth-Century Studies* 37, no. 2 (June 2014).

24. See *The Art World in Britain, 1660 to 1735*, at http://artworld.york.ac.uk.
25. David Solkin, *Art in Britain, 1660–1815* (New Haven and London: Yale Univ. Press, 2015), 3–93.
26. For a seminal account of the early phases of Britain's imperial expansion, see David Armitage, *The Ideological Origins of the British Empire* (Cambridge Univ. Press, 2000). For the standard accounts of British imperial expansion in this period, see Nicholas Canny, ed., *The Oxford History of the British Empire*, vol. 1, *The Origins of Empire: British Overseas Enterprise to the Close of the Seventeenth Century* (Oxford Univ. Press, 1998), and P. J. Marshall, Alaine Low, and William Roger Louis, eds., *The Oxford History of the British Empire*, vol. 2, *The Eighteenth-Century* (Oxford Univ. Press, 1998).
27. If we were to look for an art form that emblematizes the different characteristics outlined here—and that has the extra benefit of signalling the crucial role played by graphic art in binding together so many strands of contemporary visual culture—we might do worse than point to the medley prints that enjoyed a brief fashion in the first decade or so of the eighteenth century. For an example of one such image, see fig. 182 in this volume, which illustrates Martin Myrone's revisionist discussion of print culture in our period; for earlier discussions of such works, see Mark Hallett, "The Medley Print in Early Eighteenth-century London", *Art History* 20, no. 2 (June 1997): 214–37, or Hallett, *The Spectacle of Difference: Graphic Satire in the Age of Hogarth* (New Haven and London: Yale Univ. Press, 1999), 27–56.
28. See Horace Walpole, *Anecdotes of Painting in England*, 3rd ed., 5 vols. (London, 1782). For a recent consideration of Walpole's vision of and influence on English art, see Michael Snodin, ed., *Horace Walpole's Strawberry Hill* (New Haven: Yale Center for British Art, 2009).

SPACES, STAGES, ARENAS

The Palace of Westminster and the London Market for Pictures

Richard Stephens

Many characteristics of the London art trade in the period covered by this book are well established: public auctions, where prices were set in open competition, emerged as the dominant sale format for the resale market; art appreciation was part of the polite urban culture nurtured in the city's coffee houses, which frequently doubled as auction venues; pictures were priced to suit diverse budgets, and much of the supply at the cheap end was churned out by immigrant Dutch painter-dealers.[1] This suits a narrative of an art trade growing to serve a commercial and self-made public increasingly interested in painting in the decades around 1700; and Carol Gibson-Wood's thesis that picture ownership was "ubiquitous in London" by the turn of the century has gained widespread acceptance. However, this interpretation is in need of revision, for the reach of picture ownership into middling households has been overstated, and evidence for "a huge, and quite recent, demand . . . for modestly priced paintings with which middle-class Londoners could adorn their homes" is hard to find.[2] Gibson-Wood's own analysis of inventories found pictures in only a quarter of middling Westminster households, and in just over six in ten of the very affluent City households.[3] Instead, most picture selling was firmly targeted at the wealthy. Salesmen clustered themselves around their clientele, and almost all London picture sales in this period took place in the backyards of the nation's landowning, commercial, and legal elites: at the Palace of Westminster; the Inns of Court; the rich housing areas of Covent Garden and St James's Piccadilly; the fashionable taverns and shopping malls of the Strand; and the merchants' headquarters of the Royal Exchange. By and large, the few thousand people who frequented these places constituted London's art market.[4] The present essay, which offers a basic description of the art trade in and around the Palace of Westminster, also serves as a reminder of this essential fact.

In the late seventeenth and early eighteenth centuries, the Palace of Westminster was the home both of Parliament and the main law courts (fig. 2). It accommodated the government Treasury, state records, the Cottonian Library, and some

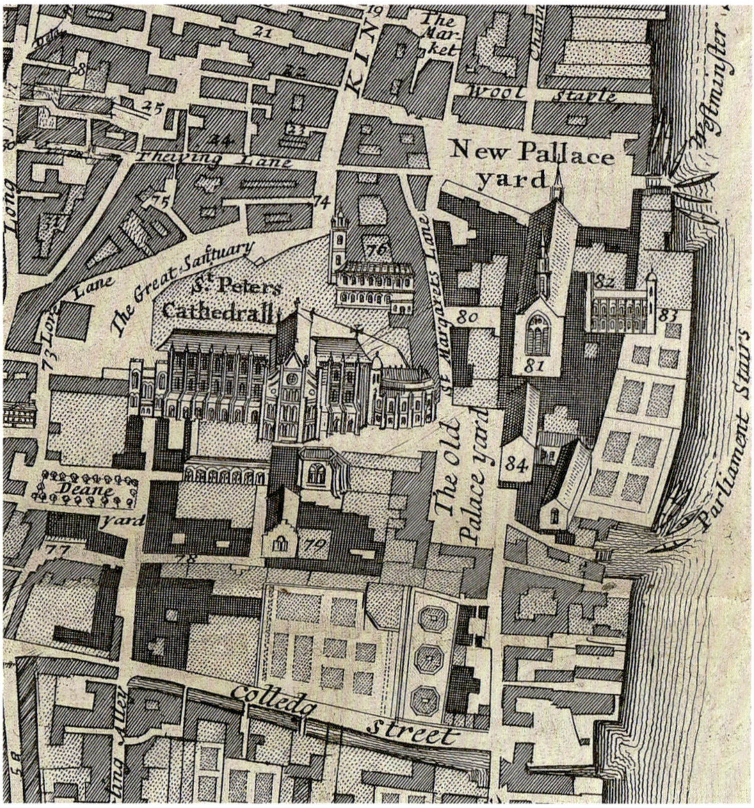

2. John Strype (engraver), "Plan of the Cities of London and Westminster," in John Stow, *A Survey of the Cities of London and Westminster: Containing the Original, Antiquity, Increase, Modern Estate and Government of those Cities…* (London: Printed for A. Churchill, J. Knapton, R. Knaplock, J. Walthoe, E. Home, B. Tooke, D. Midwinter, 1720), engraving. Beinecke Rare Book and Manuscript Library

housing for Crown servants. It was, in other words, the great meeting place of Britain's rulers: politicians, senior clerics and judges, office-holders and landowners. The palace and its accretions housed a wide array of commercial outlets that supplied these men with books, pamphlets, "toys"[5] and fine clothing, coffee and refreshment. Among all this, they could access almost the entire range of art services that the metropolis had to offer, including portraits, medals, old-master drawings, the latest mezzotints, grand imported history paintings, and contemporary decorative pictures. Buyers could make discreet private sales, attend public auctions, negotiate direct commissions, or buy lottery tickets. Catalogues for picture sales being held right across London were available for perusal at the palace's coffee houses and book stalls. Monuments, portrait busts, and other sculpture could be ordered nearby, at the yards that serviced Westminster Abbey over the road. Other painters and dealers were situated conveniently on nearby streets.

The palace had not been a royal residence since a fire in the early sixteenth century, so no serious investment was any longer made in it; it was just patched

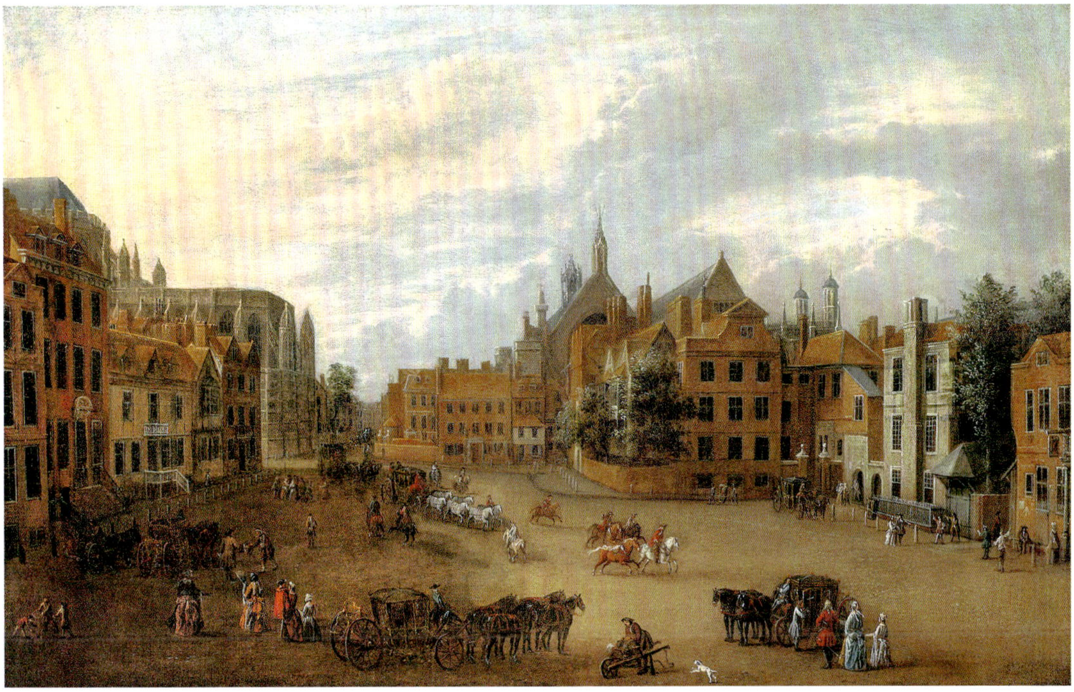

3. British School, *View of Old Palace Yard, Westminster, with the East End of Westminster Abbey with the Chapel of King Henry VII to the Left*, ca. 1700–20, oil on canvas, 23 x 36¾ in. (58.5 x 93.4 cm). Houses of Parliament, Westminster, London

up when things went wrong, and the bits of it that were no longer useful to the Crown were leased out to commercial tenants. The palace was in a poor parish, but the complex itself had excellent transport connections. It was at the western end of the great arterial road that ran from St Paul's Cathedral, and was by the River Thames, with access both from Parliament Stairs and the horse ferry at Millbank. An early eighteenth-century painting of Old Palace Yard draws attention to the extent to which the medieval palace had been overgrown by more recent building (fig. 3). It is a scene in which coaches bring peers to the House of Lords: some are still coming down St Margaret's Lane on the left, others have already arrived and are waiting, empty, for their masters to return. The top of the old palace is just visible over the cladding of more recent buildings that surrounded the medieval halls: in such buildings were the taverns where peers' servants waited while their masters attended Parliament, the coffee houses where MPs gossiped and plotted, and the studios and show rooms where painters and dealers lived and worked.

Visitors entering New Palace Yard faced Westminster Hall (fig. 4). The yard was dotted with houses and commercial premises which served now and again as venues for picture auctions, such as at the Long Dog in 1691.[6] More typically, though, they were used by picture sellers from Covent Garden, St James's, the Strand, and the Royal Exchange to promote their sales, as they were keen to interest the prime market that the palace's users represented. This meant that copies of catalogues for sales across London were available within the palace's coffee houses and book stalls—chiefly those in New Palace Yard and Westminster Hall, as well as Oliver's Coffee House, which fronted onto New Palace Yard. For instance, a 1689 sale of paintings, drawings, and prints at Tom's Coffee House near the Royal Exchange was promoted at the book stall of Matthew Gilliflower in Westminster Hall; Bird's Coffee House in New Palace Yard was the distribution point for catalogues of three picture sales at the Temple Change Coffee House in 1703–4.[7]

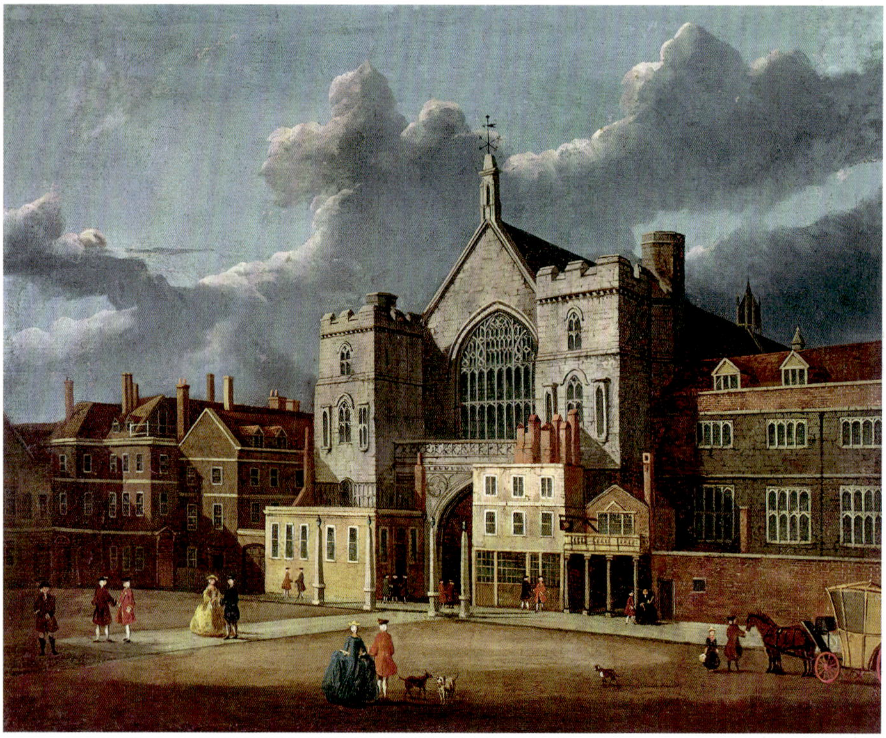

4. Attributed to Thomas Sandby, *Westminster Hall and New Palace Yard*, 18th century, oil on canvas, 23½ x 29½ in. (59.6 x 74.9 cm). Houses of Parliament, Westminster, London

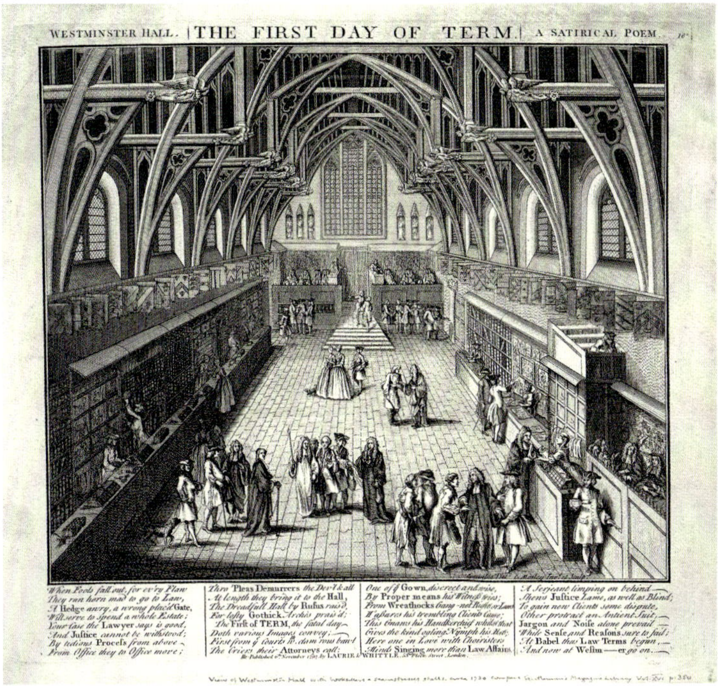

5a. Charles Mosley after Hubert Gravelot, *Westminster Hall: The First Day of Term: A Satirical Poem*, ca. 1750, etching and engraving, 12⅜ x 13½ in. (31.5 x 34.3 cm). British Museum, London

Westminster Hall was the major landmark and public space within the palace. It functioned as a series of courtrooms combined with a shopping mall containing forty-two small stalls lining the walls. Many of these, like Matthew Gilliflower's, were outposts of London's major booksellers and stationers, who maintained a precious foothold at Westminster but whose main premises were in St Paul's Churchyard.[8] There were also several picture sellers, the earliest documented of whom is Mr Roberts, "picture-seller in Westminster-Hall", who was mentioned in a 1684 newspaper advertising tickets for the annual Wiltshire Feast at Merchant Taylors' Hall.[9] If, as seems likely, he can be identified with the painter Edward Roberts, then he too maintained a base at St Paul's, and stocked an "abundance of good Pictures fit for Halls, Stair-Cases, Dining-Rooms, and Closet-Pieces" and "bound Books of Italian, French, and other Prints and Drawings".[10] Edward Luttrell was another painter who, though based outside, enjoyed access to Westminster Hall, for in 1710 "Mrs. Luttrell's Shop in Westminster-Hall" was displaying examples of his crayon portraits of historical personalities, which he intended to sell in a raffle at his house in nearby Channel Row.[11]

A later engraving of around 1730–50 portrays the hall looking busy on the first day of the legal term (fig. 5a). At the far left is the Court of King's Bench, Chancery

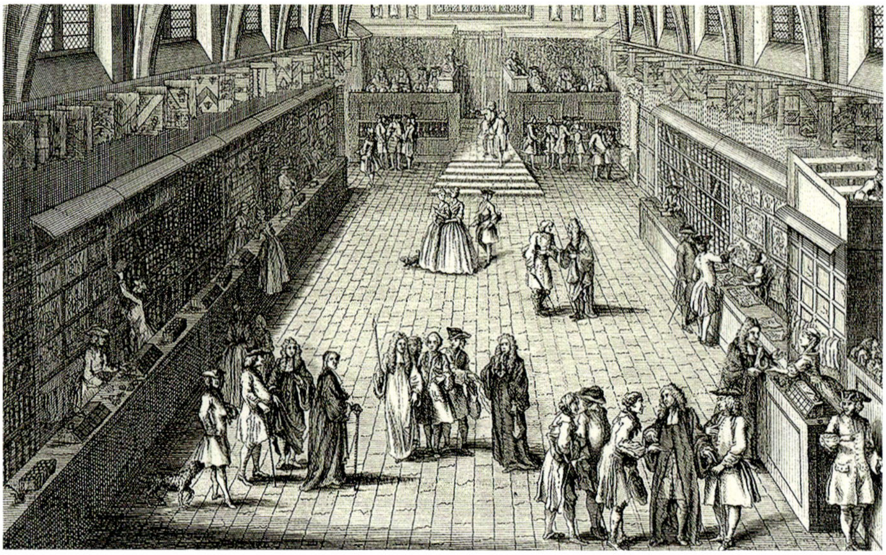

5b. Charles Mosley after Hubert Gravelot, *Westminster Hall: The First Day of Term: A Satirical Poem* (detail), ca. 1750, etching and engraving. British Museum, London

is at the far right, and in the extreme right foreground is the Court of Common Pleas. Several of the stalls have prints for sale and at least one was long-established, for in 1706 Pierce Tempest had been selling prints in partnership with the bookseller Robert Chilcott "next to the Court of Common Pleas", just where the engraving shows a print shop still in existence (fig. 5b). Tempest was selling Jan Griffier's prints of birds and beasts after Francis Barlow, Marcellus Laroon the elder's *Cryes of the City of London*, a print of St Clement Danes by Johannes Kip, and a new engraving of the west front of York Minster after a drawing by Francis Place.[12] Theirs was apparently not the main print shop, though, for "the great Print-shop in Westminster hall" was kept by Mrs Pitfeild, and offered "prints of French, Dutch and English, several mounted in gold and black frames and glazed with crown glass, consisting of a great many of the nobility and judges in metzotinto by Smith and the best masters". By stocking portraits of judges and peers, it is clear that Mrs Pitfeild knew her market; when it was all sold off after her death in 1711, customers were advised that they "may not have the like Opportunity to furnish their Parlors and Closets".[13] A third print seller in the hall around this time was Edward Fleetwood, active 1710–16 and trading "at the Parliament Stairs in Westminster Hall" according to newspapers, where he advertised the sale of a new set of world maps by Herman Moll and a book of ornaments engraved by G. Cole.[14]

In 1729, "John Marebeck, Printseller in Westminster Hall" stocked copies of an English translation of Claude Boutet's "Traité de la peinture en mignature".[15]

Westminster Hall was the place to go for a topical engraving, or to browse the book stalls for copies of auction catalogues; but the serious picture dealing happened beyond the steps at the far end of the hall, at the Court of Wards near the lobby of the House of Commons. The full sequence of its occupants can be established, and its continuous use suggests that it was an effective marketplace. The Court of Wards was in ruins between about 1680 and 1692, when it was renovated by Christopher Wren. Between 1694 and 1706 it was the address of John Kinsey; Captain Henry Turner was established there from 1708 until his death in 1714/15, and was succeeded by his widow Elizabeth; she sold the business around 1719 to Turner's former assistant Captain Henry Turner Broome, who continued dealing at the palace until his death in 1733, when his former assistant and relative John Roberts took over, until his own death in 1738/9.[16]

Kinsey's roots were in the book trade, but a contemporary classed him not as a bookseller but among the "ingenious auctioneers" that included the celebrated Edward Millington, who was transforming the book and picture markets around 1690.[17] So it is little surprise that the first record of Kinsey, in 1692, is as the manager of a picture auction near the Inner Temple.[18] Throughout his career Kinsey often worked in the coffee houses of Fleet Street and Cornhill; but, although only two or three picture auctions at the Court of Wards are known (1697/8), it was nevertheless his address from 1694 onwards.[19] In 1698 this was "Kinseys Auction in the Court of Wards, by Kistels Coffee House against the Lobby of the House of Commons"; in 1701 he was "at the Picture Auction in the Court of Wards, over against the Lobby of the House of Commons"; and in 1703 he was "the old Auctioneer John Kinsey, who is to be spoken with . . . over against the Parliament-House".[20] There is no record of Kinsey after 1706.[21]

Kinsey may have shared the Court of Wards with Captain Henry Turner, whose successor, Broome, claimed in 1730 that he and Turner had "Enjoy'd the Benefit [of the rooms] for upwards of 30 Years".[22] Turner was involved in the picture trade in the 1690s and after his death was said to have "dealt in Paintings for many Years".[23] However, it was not until 1708 that he set up shop permanently in the Court of Wards: on 23 March he signed a sixty-two-year lease on the "Picture or auction Room" and that same year he went abroad to hire two talented young Antwerp painters.[24] One, Peter Casteels, painted flower pieces and the other, his brother-in-law, Peter Tillemans, made "small peices of his own Composition. & copyd Bourgonione for Battles, which he did many & of his own designs very well. & landskips of other Masters coppyd extreamly well".[25] However, having arrived in London the pair soon absconded: both "Covenant Servants by the year to

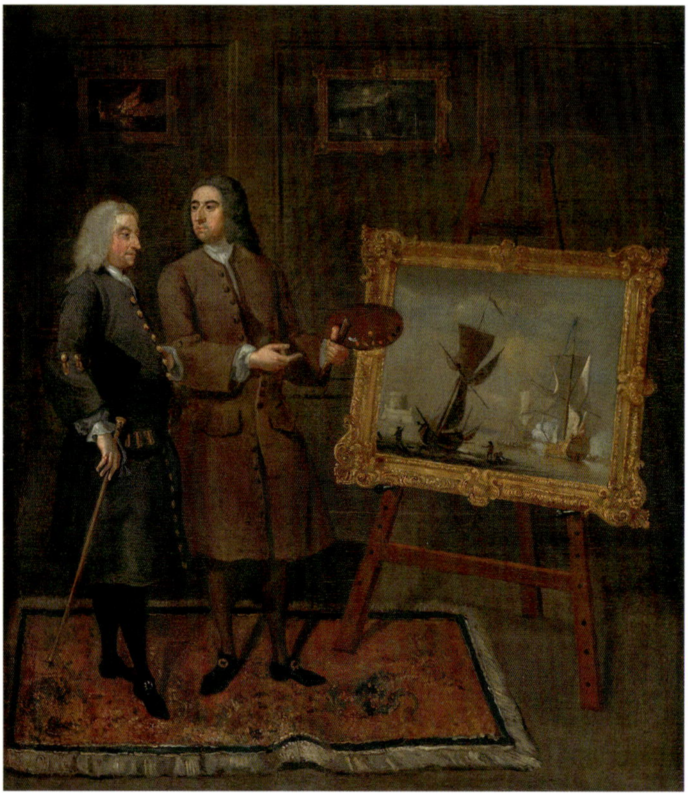

6. Gawen Hamilton, *Thomas Walker MP and Peter Monamy in his Showroom*, ca. 1735, oil on canvas, 24¼ x 21 in. (61.6 x 53.3 cm). Art Institute of Chicago, A. A. Munger Collection

Henry Turner in St Margarets-lane, Westminster; deserted their said Masters Service the 9th instant: This is to require that no Persons employ them, and that if any Person gives notice where they are, so that they may be seiz'd by a Constable, shall receive as a Rewards 5 l. for each."[26] It is unclear if either returned, but Broome's October 1714 contract with another foreign painter hired for the Court of Wards shop suggests that they had ample scope for complaint.[27] Either way, Tillemans's commission to paint the *House of Commons* (Palace of Westminster) and the *House of Lords* (Royal Collection) around this time indicates that he had come to the attention of the Court of Wards clientele, and in due course both he and Casteels became major picture dealers in their own right. Peter Monamy was a long-serving Court of Wards painter (fig. 6), and John Smibert also appears to have been employed there.[28]

Turner and Broome's "Great Picture-Room" aimed to meet the whole range of the elite's picture-related needs, and seems to have enjoyed great success. As well as high-quality furniture paintings "fit for Halls, Stair-Cases, Chimneys and Closets" produced on site by talented contractors, it also promised "constantly a fresh Supply of all manner of Paintings imported from beyond Sea, both Italian, Flemish and Dutch".[29] It stocked

> the greatest choice and variety of Foreign Prints, both as to size and value; Maps of the World from 1 sheet to the largest of 10 . . . all finely mounted and coloured, some in Guilt and Black Frames, others on Rolls and Leges: Globes of the World both Celestial and Terrestrial, from 9 inches Diameter to 22, all curiously mounted on Japan Frames; and at the same place is ready Money at all times, for all Pictures of good Masters, and for fine Prints and curious Drawings; as likewise for anything that is rare, whether its Natural or Artificial.[30]

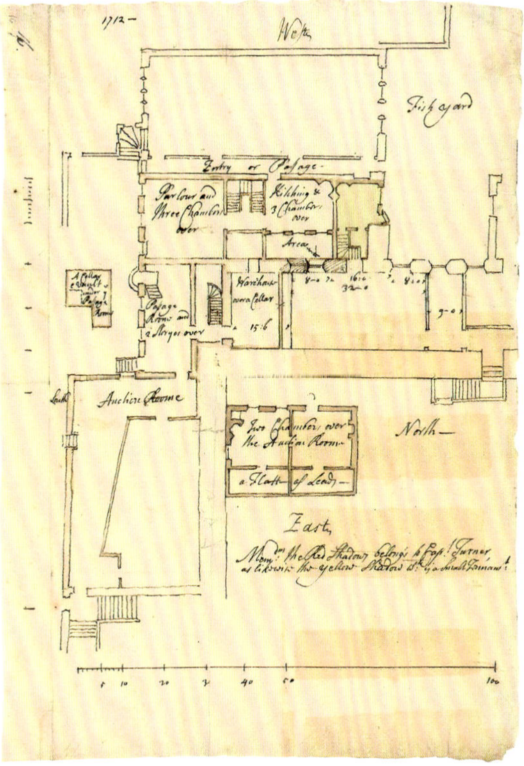

7. William Dickinson, *Survey Plan of Captain Turner's House, Westminster*, 1712, brown ink and coloured washes, 13⅛ x 9⅛ in. (33.3 x 23.3 cm). All Souls College, Oxford

A sceptical Vertue noted that pictures were repaired at the shop, too.[31] Not surprisingly, the premises were fairly extensive, comprising "one Parlour, a Kitchen & several Chamber Rooms, the use of the Passage Room, Rooms over the said. Passage Room, and the use of the Auction Room adjoining to the said. Passage Room" (fig. 7). In 1729–30 the Crown proposed to repossess the auction room for use as a waiting room for peers' footmen, and a Treasury committee considered the issue of compensation. In his submission, Broome claimed to have spent £1,000 on repairs and improvements, and demanded £500 for the lease.[32] What happened is unclear, for as late as 1737 Vertue attended a sale "at the picture sellers where Broome livd at Westminster. near the court of wards".[33] Wren Office plans show the auction room as a narrow space, bordered by a coffee house which was perhaps managed by John Roberts, Broome's assistant, who called himself a "coffee man".[34]

At his death in 1733 Broome was "one of the most considerable Dealers in Pictures in England . . . worth upwards of £20,000".[35] His stock was "well known to the curious" and it drew a clientele that included painters, dealers, and connoisseurs.[36] When in 1723 the painter and dealer Thomas Wright spotted a freshly imported painting by Thomas Blanchet (then attributed to Nicolas Poussin) at the Court of Wards, he snapped it up for his client, James Stanley, the tenth Earl of Derby; at £400, it was one of the largest sums ever paid in England for a picture. Wright's letters to Derby about this new prize show that London's leading artistic figures frequented the Court of Wards shop, including Jonathan Richardson junior; the Virtuosi of St Luke, London's top club of picture connoisseurs; and Peter Walton, Keeper of the King's Picture Collection. Wright relates that once he had paid a deposit, Broome allowed him to put the Blanchet in a room of its own and for Wright to place his own padlock on the door. Broome also undertook not to mention the price he'd agreed to anyone, though word of the sale did get out.[37] George Vertue, himself one of Broome's customers, evidently visited the Court of Wards in 1723, as his biographical sketches of Smibert, Monamy, and Tillemans (by then living nearby on Millbank) appear consecutively on the same page of the notebook he was using that year.[38] John Roberts was probably working for Broome by 1720, when he was mentioned as a stockist of a volume of maps "at the Picture-Room near the Lobby".[39] He succeeded Broome in 1733 but his master's great reputation cast a long shadow: even in 1738 Roberts was advertising a collection of pictures "at Captain Broome's Auction Room, near the Court of Request".[40]

The Court of Wards was at the east end of the Court of Requests, a large hall that at various points was itself used for selling pictures. Newspapers occasionally announced pictures or new engravings that could be bought in the toy shop or coffee houses located there. Its size made it possible to display large works, such as the "Nine Pieces of Gold and Silver Tapestry Hangings, which were the late Duke of Buckingham's, and are some of the richest that ever were in England" which were displayed for sale in 1703, and full-scale copies of the Raphael Cartoons which were hung there in 1720.[41] Just off the hall were the premises of John Fowler, a dealer in medals during the 1690s. Constantijn Huygens was introduced to him by the courtier and art collector William van Huls: "He had some medallions for sale, including an Alexander, a Lysimachus and a Phillipus Macedo, all gold and very beautiful and well-preserved. He was asking little more than twice the value of the gold for these. He told me how to find his house: 'You go downe out of the middle of the Court of Requests, to a Ground-Room on the left hand. My name is Howler.' He seemed to be a good man."[42]

Peers entered the Palace of Westminster from Old Palace Yard, and this made the nearby houses an attractive location for salesmen (see fig. 3). Among these was John Bullord, a respected bookseller whose usual base was the Old Black Bear in St Paul's Churchyard. Bullord's Westminster premises are usually described by reference to the Court of Requests, but he must have been near—or more likely in—the building fronting Old Palace Yard that was shortly afterwards occupied by Leonard Knyff and Mr Waghorn (see below). In 1690 this was called "Kistell's Coffee-House, adjoyning to the Court of Requests"; in 1692 it was "Wills Coffee-house at the West-end of the Court of Requests, over against the Painted chamber"; in 1693 it was "the New Auction Room next Vigures Coffee house in the Court of Requests"; and in 1696 Bullord held a book sale "at Mr. Knyff's house, over against the Painted Chamber, adjoyning to the Court of Requests".[43]

Along with Edward Millington and John Kinsey, John Bullord was one of a small number of booksellers who, in the late 1680s and early 1690s, attempted to colonize the London picture trade by applying the marketing techniques of the book auction. Bullord had already held several sales auctions in London by the time that he organized his first sale at the palace in October 1690, but the novelty of the move, as well as its experimental character in the context of his previous activities, is evident in an unusual preface that he wrote for the sale catalogue:

> How much the Art of Painting has been Honour'd, by the Greatest and Wisest of Princes, none in the least acquainted with History can be ignorant of: And the Generous Encouragement it has of late found in this Metropolitan City of LONDON, has excited the Undertaker to make this Collection of Pictures (of the best as well Ancient and Modern Masters) resolving to Expose the same to Sale, to oblige all the Ingenious Lovers of that Noble Art, not doubting of Reception suitable to the Merit of the Undertaking.[44]

Bullord remained very active at the palace until early 1693, but held only one more picture sale there after that. His grand words notwithstanding, Bullord—as befits a bookseller—began his period at Westminster by emphasizing the quantity of his stock. His October 1690 sale boasted "above 500 Paintings, by the most Eminent Ancient and Modern Masters"; in November there were "700 Pieces (most Originals)"; and in December "above 200 . . . being an Appendix to the late curious Collection".[45] Such claims did not appear again; apparently Bullord was on a steep learning curve.

The difficulties Bullord faced towards the end of his time at Westminster are revealed in a lawsuit. He was in partnership with another print- and bookseller, John Bullfinch, and a prominent draper, John Watson. These three had the capital to start up the sale of pictures but evidently lacked the necessary knowledge of painting, so they had approached two painters, Thomas Murray and Edward Roberts, to provide expert advice. According to the two artists, Bullord had "often pressed" them "to be concerned" with "the buying and disposing of Pictures . . . promising a just amount and affirming that it would be a thing of benefit". Things went wrong, and, in the ensuing court case, Bullord claimed that the painters still owed him money, and that it had been the painters who had approached him, not the other way around; they "being minded to lay out some mony in the buying of pictures or painting & designing to sell & dispose of the same againe to gaine ye profit thereby but not having monys sufficient". But the painters refuted Bullord's implication that they had enticed him to enter the picture trade, for "the said John Bullord had long before these Defendants had any thing to doe with them kept (or sould in) an Auction for Pictures at Westminster."[46]

Bullord's approach contrasts with that of Edward Davis, another picture seller nearby in Old Palace Yard. An engraver who developed a second career as a top-end picture dealer, Davis's clients included the Earls of Kent and Dorset.[47] While Davis was based chiefly at his "Auction-house for Pictures in St. Albans street" off Pall Mall, where he held auctions from 1682–97,[48] in November 1691 he opened an occasional second auction venue, at the Star in Old Palace Yard, which he operated until early 1696. The Star was a "House on the Right hand at the foot of the Stairs of the House of Lords" and "near the Back-Stairs of the House of Lords, leading down to the Water-side".[49] Probably this was "the House on the Right Hand of the Stairs going up to the House of Lords" where in 1707—long after Davis's time—prints and drawings from Remigius van Leemput's collection were offered for sale.[50] The value of Old Palace Yard was its proximity to a large and rich clientele, a fact which Davis acknowledged in the catalogue of his inaugural sale, which comprised pictures previously owned (he claimed) by Cardinal Antonio Barberini and Sir James Palmer, "all which shall be warranted originals to the nobility and gentry, &c. and for their accommodation are brought from the auction house in St Albans Street" to the Star. Davis had already attempted to sell the Palmer and Barberini collections in 1688–9 at St Alban's Street, so Old Palace Yard was a second outlet to re-present stock.[51] Perhaps space was limited, for the Barberini–Palmer catalogue lists only one hundred lots and his final sale numbered little over twenty; but scarcity also denotes quality.[52] The initial sale was organized in collaboration with the entrepreneurial bookseller–auctioneer (and Bullord's apparent book trade rival) Edward Millington, who is otherwise largely absent from the palace; but the partnership did not persist.[53] Perhaps Davis had overreached himself in the difficult art market of the mid-1690s.[54]

Davis's departure may have been hastened by the arrival, at the end of 1695, of a second painter, engraver, and picture dealer only a couple of doors away.[55] The Dutchman Leonard Knyff is recorded as living in Old Palace Yard until 1709, and may have returned towards the end of the 1710s. Knyff's house was "in the corner of the Old Palace-yard, Westminster; next door to the steps that go up to the House of Lords"; it was "at the Left Hand" of the House of Lords stairs (Davis was to the right of the stairs) and had "one Door in the Old Palace Yard, the other over against the Painted Chamber".[56] An advertisement of 1710 provides further detail: "Over Waghorn's Coffee-House, by the House of Lords, in the Old Palace Yard, are very large Rooms to be lett, being lately the Dwelling-House of Mr. Kniff the Limner; having a Door-way into the Court of Requests; and a very large Cellar, and Vault will hold 100 Butts of Beer."[57] In fact, Knyff had announced as early as 1707 that he would soon "withdraw himself from this into his native Country for the Recovery of his Health", and wished to sell all his pictures, prints, plates, household goods, and the house itself.[58] But he complained at the slow pace of the sale, and was still the rate payer in 1709; the picture sales that took place at Waghorn's in 1708 and 1709, which included a "Rolling Press for Printing, as good as new" were surely Knyff's own goods.[59]

In the 1680s, Knyff had occupied rooms in York Buildings near the Strand, and had been a major producer of pictures supplied to auctions taking place at Exeter Exchange and other nearby venues in the early 1690s.[60] These sales were attended by art collectors such as Philip Sidney, third Earl of Leicester; but Knyff's move to Old Palace Yard makes explicit his targeting of an elite clientele.[61] He began with a sale not of his own work, but with "an Extraordinary Collection of Original Pictures (never shewn before) by Italian, and other the best Masters of Europe".[62] Then in 1698 he announced a plan to draw and engrave "100 Noblemen and Gentlemens Seats", for which enterprise he was now very well situated, though subscriptions—at £10 each—trickled in slowly.[63] Although it seems to have ended up as a costly encumbrance, Knyff probably conceived the project as a means of

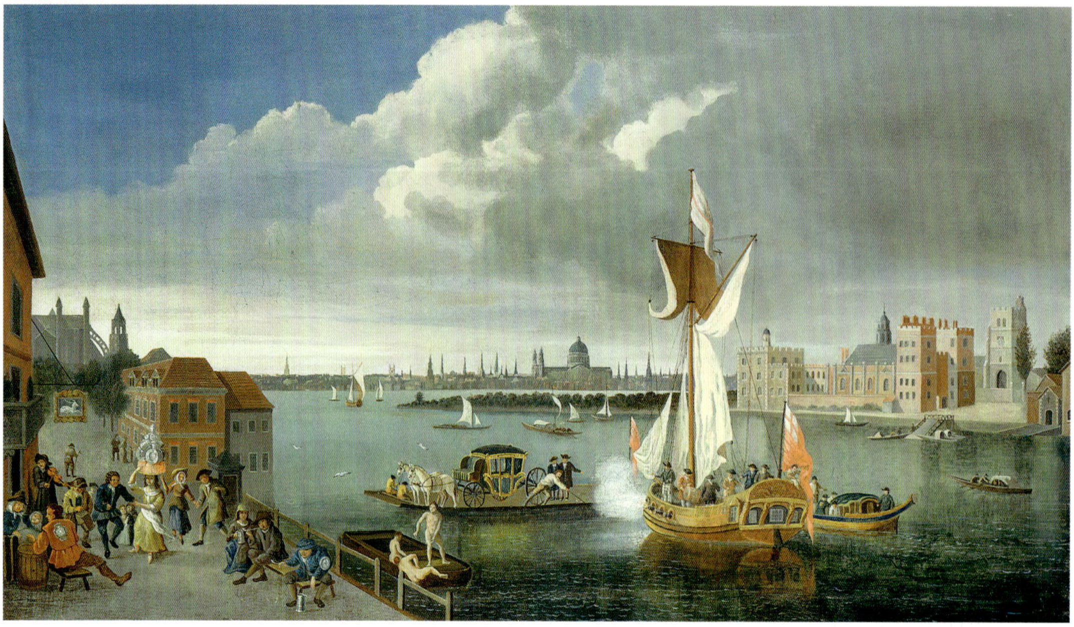

8. Jan Griffier, *Millbank and the Horse Ferry*, ca. 1706–10, oil on canvas, 23⅞ x 42¾ in. (60.6 x 108.7 cm). Museum of London

gaining wider custom from his subscribers, who were, of course, the richest landowners in England, whom he would visit in the parliamentary recess. Indeed, his letters of 1702–3 to Viscount Irwin's steward suggest how the prints were really just a way of opening a conversation with potential clients, whose substance was really about selling paintings.[64]

After Knyff left, it seems that Waghorn expanded the coffee house into Knyff's vacant upstairs rooms, establishing a dedicated space for auctions of pictures and books which saw use into the early 1720s.[65] Among the users of these premises in this phase was John or Edward Cooper, who offered a "curious Collection of foreign original Pictures of the most celebrated Masters . . . that was never expos'd before to Sale" in 1711.[66] Knyff himself may well have returned, for in 1719 he advertised another sale of pictures "at his House in the Old Palace Yard" which was, once again, in preparation for retirement, "he designing to go and live in the Country for his Health".[67]

In 1719 Knyff was hoping to retire to the country, but he cannot have travelled far, since at his death three years later he was living only a few hundred yards away on Millbank.[68] In fact, Millbank, which ran south from Old Palace Yard, attracted quite a few Dutch artists in the early eighteenth century; away from the noise of the city and with its river air and views of London, it must have been something like a poor-man's Twickenham. Certainly it was a convenient place both for river transport and to catch rich coach owners making their way on the horse ferry to

Surrey (fig. 8). Willem van de Velde the younger lived on Millbank from 1706 until his death the following year, when the house was taken over by his son-in-law.[69] From 1710 Van de Velde's painter son, Cornelius, was living a few doors away at the Green Balcony, where in July 1712 his pictures, drawings, and household goods were sold in preparation for his departure from England.[70] In about 1705, Jan Griffier moved to the Two Blue Balls, where he became in the "latter part of his time a great mimick of other masters both Italian & flemish. in which [he] succeeded & deceived very well. [and] livd somewhat retird towards his latter end".[71] After his death in 1718 his son Robert Griffier, also a painter and picture dealer, continued in the house, which was perhaps "near Peterborough-House" since that was where Griffier lost a gold chain in 1721.[72] As for Knyff, the rate book shows that he arrived on Millbank at midsummer 1720, where he lived at the Black Ball, five doors from Griffier.[73] The same year's rate book also shows Enoch Seaman living three doors from Griffier in the other direction and, three doors beyond him, Peter Tillemans (fig. 9).[74]

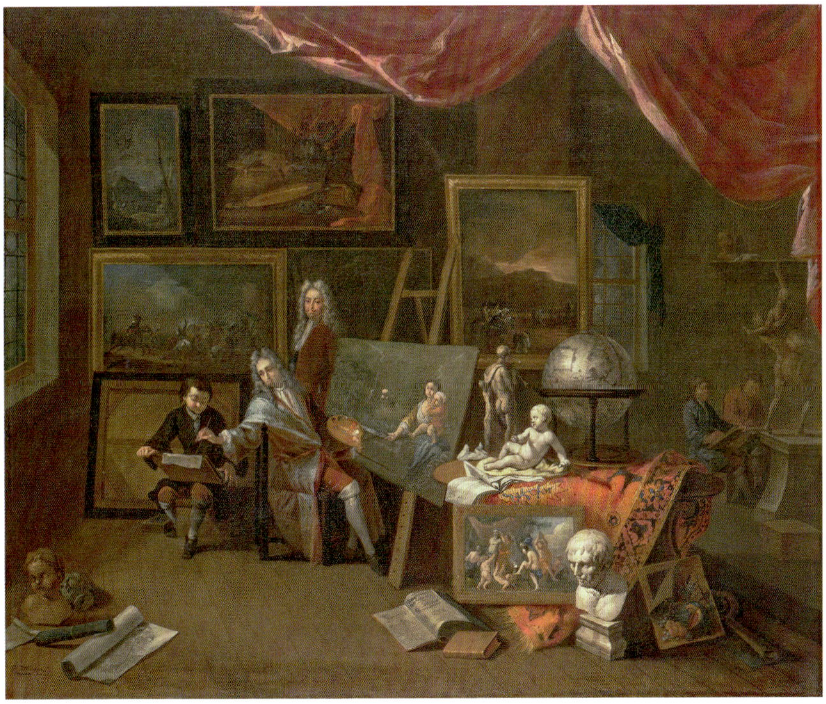

9. Peter Tillemans, *The Artist's Studio*, ca. 1716, oil on canvas, 26⅞ x 33⅛ in. (68.3 x 84 cm). Norwich Castle Museum and Art Gallery

Given the multiple functions of the Palace of Westminster, the art trade often had to make room for other activities. Westminster Hall was completely cleared of its sales booths for large ceremonial occasions, such as coronation feasts. The Court of Wards picture shop had to be dismantled too from time to time. After the death of Captain Turner, his widow planned to dispose of his stock, but was "prevented to go throw with the Sale, by the Trial of the Lord of Oxford" in the adjoining Westminster Hall.[75] As Broome explained to a Treasury Committee around 1730, "when it is made use of at a Coronation or the Tryal of Peers the partitions which are then taken down are put up again at the Governmts: charge", although on one occasion palace officials would not allow the picture shop to be set up again until a complaint was made to the Lord Chamberlain.[76]

The picture dealers of St James's and Covent Garden also had to be aware of palace business, for while it is obvious that picture sales organized at the palace were aimed at the people who frequented it, it was not very often stated explicitly that this audience was also the prime clientele for picture sellers more broadly across London. Even so, auctioneers would occasionally announce that "persons of quality" had asked for them to bring forward or delay their sales, and sometimes explained why. During the Jacobite invasion of 1715, for instance, Peter Motteux "having been desired by some Persons of Quality, to reserve the Nine last and best Pictures in his Sale on the 1st Instant, the Two Houses sitting late that Day", offered them instead a fortnight later.[77] Around the same time, a Mr James "did set up his collection of very curious pictures to be sold by auction . . . but the House of Lords and Commons then sitting, he did not dispose of them". Ignatio de Geer was due to raffle a picture at a Pall Mall coffee house on 16 May 1723, but he explained in a message to ticket holders that "few of the company met, the House of Lords sitting late, and the evening being very rainy."[78] The logistics of parliamentary sittings affected the art trade in one way, but the institution of Parliament was itself highly influential in quite another. Laws were made and enforced at Westminster, such as when the duty payable on the importation of pictures was changed in 1722, or when Hogarth's copyright act was passed in 1735. Now and again, the courts took a direct interest in London picture auctions, such as in 1714 when the House of Lords stopped the sale of the Earl of Winchelsea's pictures "till a Tryal depending before them is decided", or in 1689 when the Duke of Norfolk petitioned his peers to prevent Parry Walton from auctioning off his Arundel collection heirlooms.[79]

These occasional interruptions apart, the commercial routine was shaped chiefly by the regular stops and starts of the parliamentary and legal calendars, although their impact is not always clear. Generally though, picture sellers in the palace shut up shop when Parliament was not sitting. For instance, in 1714 pictures at Waghorn's would "continue to be sold during the remaining part of the session of Parliament".[80] Turner advertised a sale in 1712 that was "All to be dispos'd of before the Parliament is up, for after there will be no Attendance". Bullord's sale on 16 December 1690 "will conclude the Sale of Paintings at Westminster for this Season"; Parliament sat until 5 January 1691 and returned on 22 October; Bullord's sales began again on 27 October and ran until 22 February, 1692, two days before Parliament broke up once more.[81] Overall during the period 1690–1704, three-quarters of art auctions organized in and around the Palace of Westminster coincided with parliamentary sittings, compared with forty-two percent for auctions near the Royal Exchange at the other end of London. The legal calendar was also influential, especially in Westminster Hall itself where stallholders depended on the courts for customers. When Mrs. Pitfeild died in 1711, the advertisement stipulated that her stock "must be all sold off by the last Day of this Term".[82] A sale at Will's Coffee House began on 23 November 1692 and "will conclude the Sale for this Term".[83] And, in a sign of the pulling power of the palace as a marketplace, a watchmaker from Coventry announced in 1698 that "for the conveniency of those of his Customers in Westminster, in Term time, he will be at his Shop in Westminster-Hall till Twelve of the Clock in the Day."[84]

These schedules influenced the luxury retail trade all across London, of course, as once the Lords and Commons rose, its members not only dispersed from the Palace of Westminster but they left London altogether, to return to their country bases. Yet, while Parliament was its ultimate rationale, the attractions of London had energized this seasonal migration with its own tidal momentum. By 1720, picture sales in London—though happening year-round—were concentrated in a fairly dependable season that lasted, roughly, from November or December to May or June; usually, March was the peak month.[85] In 1720 more than 70 picture auctions took place in London; a decade later, the annual figure had exceeded 120.[86]

The foregoing sketch has been an attempt to provide some qualitative indication of the scale and diversity of London's art trade in just one of London's late seventeenth- and early eighteenth-century picture-selling zones. Future research on this and other centres of the capital's art market in this period will no doubt serve to enhance and modify the arguments and conclusions offered here. What already seems clear, however, is that this market—particularly the market for paintings—was dominated by a relatively circumscribed class of affluent buyers, itself catered to by a regularly replenished community of dealers and entrepreneurs—both British and foreign-born—who clustered around specific urban sites such as the Palace of Westminster.

1. For an art trade bibliography, see Carol Gibson-Wood, "Picture Consumption in London at the End of the Seventeenth Century", *The Art Bulletin* 84, no. 3 (Sept. 2002), n. 5. To this list could be added Peter Hecht, "Dutch Painters in England: Readings in Houbraken, Weyerman, and Van Gool", in *The Exchange of Ideas: Religion, Scholarship and Art in Anglo-Dutch Relations in the Seventeenth Century*, ed. Simon Groenveld and Michael Wintle (Zutphen: Walburg Pers, 1994), and Sander Karst, "Off to a New Cockaigne: Dutch Migrant Artists in London, 1660–1735", *Simiolus* 37, no. 1 (2013–14): 25–60. Much new primary material has been published by *The Art World in Britain, 1660 to 1735* at http://artworld.york.ac.uk, including transcripts of most of the sources cited in the present essay, such as newspaper advertisements and sale catalogues.
2. Gibson-Wood, "Picture Consumption in London", 495.
3. Based on analysis of probate inventories, Gibson-Wood estimated that 132,000 pictures were on display in 11,000 middling London households around 1700, but the calculation was made by extrapolating data on picture ownership in affluent urban areas across the entire suburban and rural metropolitan region. Furthermore, within the sample were titled office-holders and wealthy merchants, as well as the contents of painters' studios where, naturally, the incidence of pictures was atypical. Taking all this into account, the data actually suggests there were roughly 40,000 pictures shared between 3,000 to 4,000 houses in Westminster and the City of London. Gibson-Wood, "Picture Consumption in London", 493, 495.
4. London around 1700 contained about 3,000 to 5,000 households that Peter Earle called "families of the West End gentry, and what one may call upper middle-class", though, based on data from 1798, he acknowledged this was "largely a matter of guesswork". See Earle, *The Making of the English Middle Class: Business, Society, and Family Life in London, 1660–1730* (Berkeley: Univ. of California Press, 1989), 80–81.
5. In this context, the word "toy" was used to describe small decorative or scientific objects, often made of fine materials. For a recent discussion of this category of object, see Vanessa Brett, "Derided and enjoyed: what was a toy—what was a toyshop?" *History of Retailing and Consumption* 2, no. 1 (2015): 83–88.
6. *London Gazette*, 2 Nov. 1691, *Post Man*, 25 Nov. 1704.
7. Gilliflower was used frequently to distribute catalogues for auctions at Tom's Coffee House and the Barbados Coffee House in the period 1689–91.
8. H. R. Plomer, "Westminster Hall and its Booksellers", *The Library* 6, no. 24 (1905): 380–90.
9. *London Gazette*, 13 Nov. 1684.
10. Roberts's paintings were sold next door to Merchant Taylors' Hall: *Daily Courant*, 4 Aug. 1711, 23 Nov. 1711. The painter Henry Waggoner may also have had a stall at Westminster Hall.
11. *English Short-Title Catalogue* at http://estc.bl.uk (hereafter ESTC) T42988.
12. *Daily Courant*, 12 March 1706.
13. *Daily Courant*, 23 Nov. 1711.
14. *Daily Courant*, 10 Feb. 1710, *Post Man*, 12 April 1716. Fleetwood was also mentioned in George Vertue's address book "at the foot of the Parliament stairs", in George Vertue, *Notebook E.2.*, 1715–51, British Library Add MS 23095.
15. *Daily Post*, 16 May 1729 (ESTC N29989).
16. *Report of a Treasury Committee about the auction room and coffee house at the Court of Wards, Palace of Westminster*, ca. 1730, The National Archives (hereafter TNA) T 1/274.
17. John Dunton, *The Life and Errors of John Dunton Late Citizen of London* (London, 1705), 316 (ESTC T75140).
18. *London Gazette*, 20 Oct. 1692.
19. Kinsey was taxed at the palace in 1693/4, next to Charles Kistell, "coffee man". See Derek Keene, Peter Earle, Craig Spence, and Janet Barnes, eds., *Four Shillings in the Pound Aid 1693/4* (London: Centre for Metropolitan History, Univ. of London, 1992), online edition at http://www.british-history.ac.uk (accessed 26 July 2014). The catalogue for Kinsey's 8 February 1697 sale survives (ESTC R230644). Several book auctions were also advertised in 1701.
20. *Post Man*, 8 Feb. 1698, 20 March 1701, *Daily Courant*, 29 Nov. 1703.

21. The "Mr. John Kensey from the Parliament House" who held an auction of paintings at John's Coffee House near the Royal Exchange was presumably a son. *Daily Courant*, 2 April 1720.
22. *Report of a Treasury Committee about the auction room and coffee house at the Court of Wards, Palace of Westminster.*
23. On 8 June 1698 Joshua Bowes was indicted for stealing a picture from Turner. *The Proceedings of the Old Bailey, 1674 to 1913*, http://www.oldbaileyonline.org (accessed 11 Oct. 2011). Turner was doubtless the importer of picture frames and prints noted in *A Collection for Improvement of Husbandry and Trade*, 14 Sept. 1694.
24. *Daily Courant*, 6 June 1716, *Report of a Treasury Committee about the auction room and coffee house at the Court of Wards, Palace of Westminster.*
25. George Vertue, *Notebook A.f.*, transcribed in "The Note-books of George Vertue III", *Walpole Society* 22 (1934): 11, 14. Examples include a *Cavalry engagement*, signed and dated 1708, sold at Christie's, 22 Oct. 1982, lot 66; and an *Italianate harbour*, dated 1708, sold at Christie's South Kensington, 23 April 2004, lot 114.
26. *Post Man*, 16 April 1709.
27. Contract between Henry Turner Broome and Friedrich Hemeling, 1 Oct. 1714, transcribed in A. Bredius, "Archiefsprokkelingen", *Oud Holland* 49, nos. 1–6 (1932): 144. Hemeling was to work for a year "and will paint or copy any paintings" that Broome directed, in return for "free lodgings, food and drink, laundry and related things but also on top of this a sum of seventy guilders"—a mere £6 5s. 12d.
28. Vertue states that Smibert was occupied "coppying of paintings for dealers for 3 or 4 years" after coming to London around 1713, and probably this was at the Court of Wards, for Smibert's three-quarter portrait of Broome (now untraced) was a gift to the dealer—one of only two such gifts Smibert ever made, and the very last painting the Scottish artist completed in London before emigrating to Boston in 1728. Monamy lived in St Margaret's Lane and Fish Yard for twenty-five years, and he witnessed the will of John Roberts, Broome's successor, in 1738. Vertue states that Monamy's "works being done for dealers at moderate prices—kept him in but indifferent circumstances to his end". See Vertue, "Note-books III", 145; Rate book data cited at http://www.cichw1.net/pm19812.html (accessed 26 Dec. 2011); John Smibert, "Notebook", 1709–47, TNA EXT 11/94; and Will of John Roberts, 24 May 1738, TNA PROB 11/696.
29. *Daily Courant*, 15 Jan. 1720, in which Broome announced he had bought the rump of Turner's stock from his widow.
30. *Daily Courant*, 13 June 1712; *Post Man*, 9 March 1710; *Daily Courant*, 17 May 1717.
31. Broome advertised that if "any Gentleman that has a parcel of Paintings to dispose of, they may hear of a Purchasor, or if to be cleaned, lined, or framed, it will be well performed by the same Mr. Broome". But when a painting of Richard II from Westminster Abbey was repaired by Broome, Vertue remarked: "I doubt if they have been carefull enough to preserve the antient taste." *Daily Courant*, 15 Jan. 1720; George Vertue, *Notebook A.q.*, transcribed in "The Note-books of George Vertue IV", *Walpole Society* 24 (1936): 52–53.
32. *Report of a Treasury Committee about the auction room and coffee house at the Court of Wards, Palace of Westminster.*
33. George Vertue, *Notebook A.x.*, transcribed in "Note-books IV", 117.
34. All Souls College, Oxford, Wren III:10–16. Roberts's widow gave her address as Alice's Coffee House in Old Palace Yard. *London Daily Post*, 29 Nov. 1739. See Will of John Roberts, 24 May 1738, TNA PROB 11/696.
35. The report continued: "He was in good Health the Day before, and had given Orders to his Taylor to make him a new Suit of Cloaths." *Daily Journal*, 18 Oct. 1733.
36. *London Daily Post*, 25 March 1736. A catalogue of the second of Broome's posthumous sales survives (ESTC T211599).
37. Wright's letters survive in the Knowsley Hall Archive and have been published on *The Art World in Britain, 1660 to 1735* at http://artworld.york.ac.uk.
38. Vertue, *Notebook A.f.*, 14. Vertue bought a painting by Zoust that Broome had bought from his predecessor Captain Turner who had in turn bought it from another dealer, Joseph Partington.

39. *Post Boy*, 9 Feb. 1720. Perhaps he was a son of Edward Roberts, who had a son working in the picture trade as a copyist during the 1690s. *Chancery suit of John Bullord, John Bullfinch and John Watson vs Thomas Murray and Edward Roberts*, 1698, TNA C6/309/16. These papers are published on *The Art World in Britain, 1660 to 1735* at http://artworld.york.ac.uk.
40. Roberts's preface to the sale catalogue of the Countess of Spaur's pictures (ESTC T4412). After Roberts's death in 1738/9, his widow sold "At the Great Picture-Room near the Court of Requests . . . THE Genuine Collection of Original Pictures, &c. late of Mr. John Roberts, deceased, (Successor to Capt. Turner Broom) and by him imported from France, Flanders, Holland, &c. in 1738". *London Daily Post*, 29 Nov. 1739.
41. *London Gazette*, 25 Nov. 1703; *Post Boy*, 21 Jan. 1720; *Daily Courant*, 10 June 1721; *Daily Post*, 9 May 1727, 1 April 1728; *Daily Journal*, 3 Feb. 1730. James Sotheby bought two of Buckingham's tapestries. See National Art Library, *Notebook of James Sotheby*, MSL/1955/2717.
42. Constantijn Huygens, *Diaries*, 1688–96, National Library of the Netherlands, translated by Sanne van der Schee from Constantijn Huygens, *Journaal van 21 October 1688 tot 2 Sept. 1696* (Utrecht, 1876–77), entry for 3 March 1694 (British New Style); the English translation is published on *The Art World in Britain, 1660 to 1735* at http://artworld.york.ac.uk. Fowler also appears in Keene, Earle, Spence, and Barnes, eds., *Four Shillings in the Pound Aid 1693/4*.
43. *A collection of paintings of the most eminent ancient and modern masters* (London, 1690), ESTC R214268; *A curious collection of paintings by the best masters ancient and modern* (London, 1692), ESTC R214417; *London Gazette*, 16 Nov. 1693; *Bibliothecae Stawellianae pars secunda* (London, 1696), ESTC R184613. Despite the variations, it seems more likely that these are descriptions of the same place, using different terms, than that Bullord was moving from place to place within the same tiny locality. Both Charles Kistell and John Vigures are listed in a 1693/94 tax assessment in close proximity to Bullord. See Keene, Earle, Spence, and Barnes, eds., *Four Shillings in the Pound Aid 1693/4*.
44. *A collection of paintings of the most eminent ancient and modern masters* (1690).
45. *London Gazette*, 16 Oct. 1690, 24 Nov. 1690, 4 Dec. 1690.
46. *Chancery suit of John Bullord, John Bullfinch and John Watson vs Thomas Murray and Edward Roberts*, 1698.
47. Bedford and Luton Archives and Record Service L/34/1, Centre for Kentish Studies U269/A195/1–12.
48. *London Gazette*, 22 April 1689. Davis's widow Elizabeth, who was still living in 1714, continued his business for a few years.
49. Palmer–Barberini sale catalogue, "Auctio Davisiana, Pictuarum vere Originalium" (London, 1691), ESTC R214449, *London Gazette*, 10 Dec. 1694.
50. *Post Man*, 4 Dec. 1707. In 1727 the Star was "the late dwelling-house" of Thomas Lloyd, whose collection of pictures was being sold following his death. *Daily Post*, 6 Feb. 1727. Lloyd was also a rate payer in Old Palace Yard in 1714 "for a cellar". *St Margaret Westminster Rate Books*, 1714, Westminster Archives microfilm E231/979. Lloyd's position in the poor rate list makes it likely that he was occupying Leonard Knyff's former cellars, as Knyff disappears after 1709 to be replaced (by 1714) by Lloyd and Mary Waghorn.
51. Similarly, he offered the rump of General Tollemache's pictures at St Alban's Street in May 1695, and again in Old Palace Yard the following February. *London Gazette*, 6 May 1695, 10 Feb. 1696. The prime sale of Tollemache's collection took place in the Banqueting Hall in Whitehall in March 1695.
52. *London Gazette*, 10 Feb. 1696.
53. The next sale to take place at the Star after the Barberini–Palmer sale was, in fact, of Greek and Latin books. *London Gazette*, 4 Feb. 1692. Millington may well have been the organizer. The only other Millington sale at Westminster was of books, drawings, and prints "At Kistel's Coffee-house, near the Court of Requests" in 1696. *London Gazette*, 23 April 1696.
54. Davis announced "the last day of his Sale" in Old Palace Yard in early 1695, but he held further sales there at the end of that year and in early 1696. *London Gazette*, 28 Feb. 1695, 5 Dec. 1695, 2 Jan. 1696, 10 Feb. 1696.

55. Some kind of response to Knyff's arrival may be discerned in Davis's advertising in early 1696. When Knyff announced his inaugural sale at the end of 1695, boasting pictures "never shewn before", in the same paper Davis was also advertising a competing sale, more modestly described as "a most curious Collection of Pictures". Only weeks later, Davis upped his game with fresh pictures "which were never put to view or sold before" and paintings from the famous Tollemache collection. *London Gazette*, 5 Dec. 1695, 2 Jan. 1696, 10 Feb. 1696.
56. *Post Man*, 10 May 1698; *An extraordinary valuable collection of pictures to be seen, and sold out of hand, every day at Mr Knife's House* (ESTC T33932); *London Gazette*, 5 Dec. 1695.
57. *Post Boy*, 28 Oct. 1710. Another advertisement clarifies that direct access to the palace was through a "Door coming into the Passage leading into the Court of Request". *Daily Courant*, 25 Nov. 1708.
58. *Daily Courant*, 1 Feb. 1707. The sale of Knyff's picture collection began on 7 February but by late March was "not a quarter sold, and has been discontinued for some time". *Daily Courant*, 27 March 1707.
59. *St Margaret Westminster rate books*, 1709, Westminster Archives microfilm E323.2360, *Post Man*, 23 Nov. 1708.
60. *London Gazette*, 27 Oct. 1684. For details of these auctions, search "Knyff" and "Knife" at http://artworld.york.ac.uk.
61. For Lord Leicester's art purchases, see http://artworld.york.ac.uk/personView.do?personUrn=1.00086.
62. *London Gazette*, 5 Dec. 1695.
63. By mid-1701 Knyff had completed sixty views, but the subscription was not full; by the end of the year sixty-nine were finished; by 1707 he had "proceeded with design to compleat the whole set of 100; but for want of Subscriptions . . . is oblig'd to desist". *Post Man*, 31 May 1701; *Letter from Leonard Knyff*, 4 Dec. 1702, West Yorkshire Archive Service (reference unknown), cited in Hugh Honour, "Leonard Knyff", *The Burlington Magazine* 96, no. 620 (Nov. 1954): 337–38; *Daily Courant*, 1 Feb. 1707.
64. Knyff's correspondence, cited at note 62 above. James Sotheby also bought a picture from Knyff in 1702. See *Notebook of James Sotheby*, cited at note 41.
65. The coffee room was on the ground floor, and the auction space was "up one pair of Stairs (over the Coffee-Room)". *Daily Courant*, 10 May 1716. Perhaps Mr Waghorn discontinued his coffee house around the time that Knyff announced his departure, for several of Knyff's advertisements in 1707 refer to Waghorn's coffee house having "us'd to be kept" there (for example, *Daily Courant*, 16 June 1707). Waghorn then returned after the painter departed and Mary Waghorn, "who many Years kept Waghorn's Coffee-house in Old Palace Yard, adjacent to the House of Peers", died in 1743. *London Evening Post*, 12 March 1743.
66. *The Spectator* 44, Friday, 20 April 1711.
67. *Daily Courant*, 30 May 1719. It is uncertain, though, if Knyff's address in 1719 was the same as the earlier one.
68. There were three posthumous sales. In November 1722 his pictures were offered at Millbank; in May 1723 furniture pictures were sold at the Two Golden Balls in Covent Garden; and, finally, at the King's Arms Tavern in the Little Piazza, his prints, drawings, views of country mansions, and "a great Number of curious Plants and Flowers, which are dried and fixed on Paper" were sold in December 1723. *Daily Courant*, 22 Nov. 1722, 21 May 1723, *Daily Post*, 1 Dec. 1723.
69. Michael S. Robinson, *Van de Velde Drawings* (Cambridge Univ. Press, 1958), 26–27.
70. *Daily Courant*, 12 July 1712. It is unclear if he left, as in 1717 he was among a group of painters asked to review James Thornhill's work at Greenwich.
71. George Vertue, *Notebook A.j.*, transcribed in "The Note-books of George Vertue I", *Walpole Society* 18 (1930): 51.
72. *Daily Courant*, 28 Feb. 1719, *Daily Post*, 20 March 1729, 2 June 1721.
73. *Daily Courant*, 9 Nov. 1722.

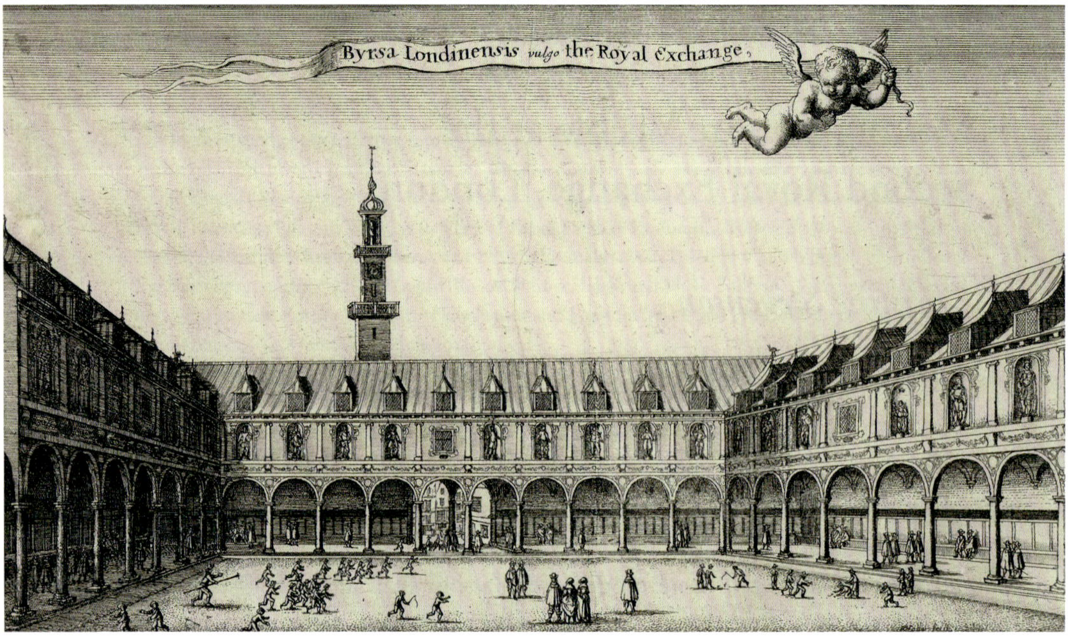

10. Wenceslaus Hollar, *Byrsa Londinensis vulgo the Royal Exchange*, ca. 1645–7, etching, 5⅞ x 10¼ in. (15 x 25.9 cm). British Museum, London

attendant upon territorial conquest.[4] For all its "Roman Habit", Gibbons's Charles II had an active part to play in this self-consciously modern redefinition of empire, at least for a while.[5]

SOVEREIGNS AND EMPIRES

The second Exchange considerably increased the number of retail spaces available at the location, but maintained the sixteenth-century building's arrangement of shops, which were little more than stalls. Those selling fancy goods were found on the upper floor, above series of shops on the ground floor that offered more masculine wares and services: pictures, tobacco, and mathematical instruments, scriveners and notaries.[6] All surrounded a rectangular courtyard that measured about 110 feet (33.5 metres) from column to column on the longest, east–west axis, within which the goods for sale were less tangible.[7] At fixed hours ("Exchange time"), merchants gathered in this space, enclosed but roofless, and in the open galleries—Edward Hatton called them "Ambulatories" or "Piazzas"—behind the arcading which lined the courtyard. They met in recognized but physically invisible "Walks" defined by their commercial spheres of interest: Canary Walk, Virginia

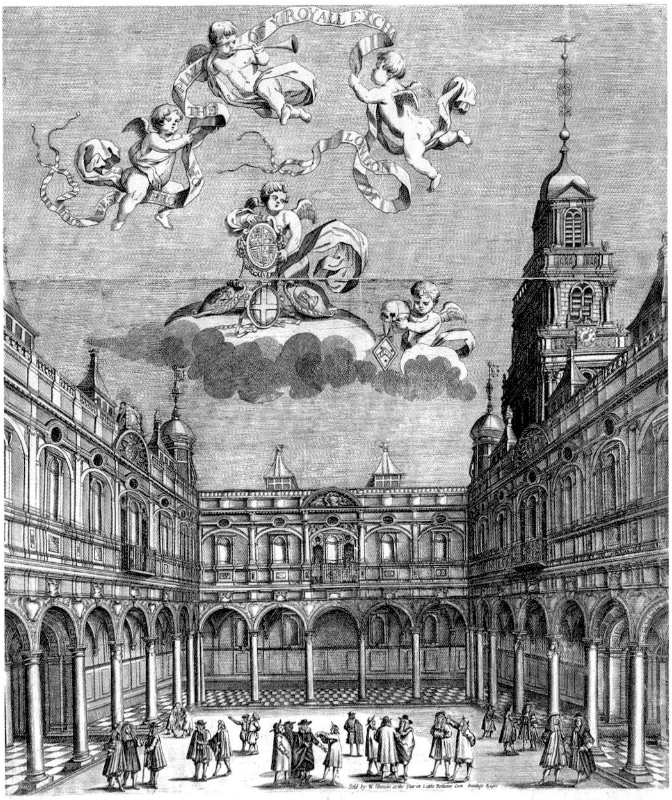

11. William Sherwin, *The West Prospect of the Piazza of ye Royall Exchange of London*, second state, 1674, engraving, 25½ x 22½ in. (65.0 x 57.3 cm). British Museum, London

Walk, Salters Walk, Irish Walk.[8] Hatton's *A New View of London* (1708) provided the first plan-diagram of the walks, but a visitor noted them in the 1570s: "Each nation has its own place [*quartier*] . . . so that those who have trade to do with them can find them with ease. . . . There also can usually be heard reports from many countries and regions" (fig. 12).[9]

Such galleries, or loggias, had characterized the Western exchange type—a place, that is, "where merchants could assemble out of the way of passing traffic and other impediments"—since the late thirteenth century. These buildings might serve particular nations or commodity trades, which, when united as they were at the Antwerp (1531), London (1569), and Amsterdam (1613) exchanges, found their own places in and around the loggias.[10] In London, this arrangement encouraged the trope whereby the Exchange becomes a map or microcosm, one reinvigorated by the Fire and subsequent rebuilding. It was a "Babel of Tongues", wrote Simon Ford: "the Universes Fair; / Where both Poles daily met, and what between / The vast extent of both the Poles is seen . . .".[11]

All this activity was overseen by a statue of the Exchange's original founder, Sir Thomas Gresham, in a niche on the rear wall of the gallery at both buildings' north-west corner, and by those of the English monarchs in their own "rooms", separated by Ionic pilasters, on the upper storeys: there were twenty-eight of these by 1666, the most recent being a Charles II, possibly carved by Caius Gabriel Cibber.[12] Gresham had stipulated their inclusion, and an engraving by Frans Hogenberg (ca.1570, a copy of which is incorporated into Nicholls's composite print, fig. 12) anticipates them. No one failed to note, in September 1666, that Gresham's statue had survived the fire; those of the monarchs, which began to be installed in the 1620s, had not.[13] Poets were positive that this accident was meaningful, but were uncertain about what, exactly, it meant.

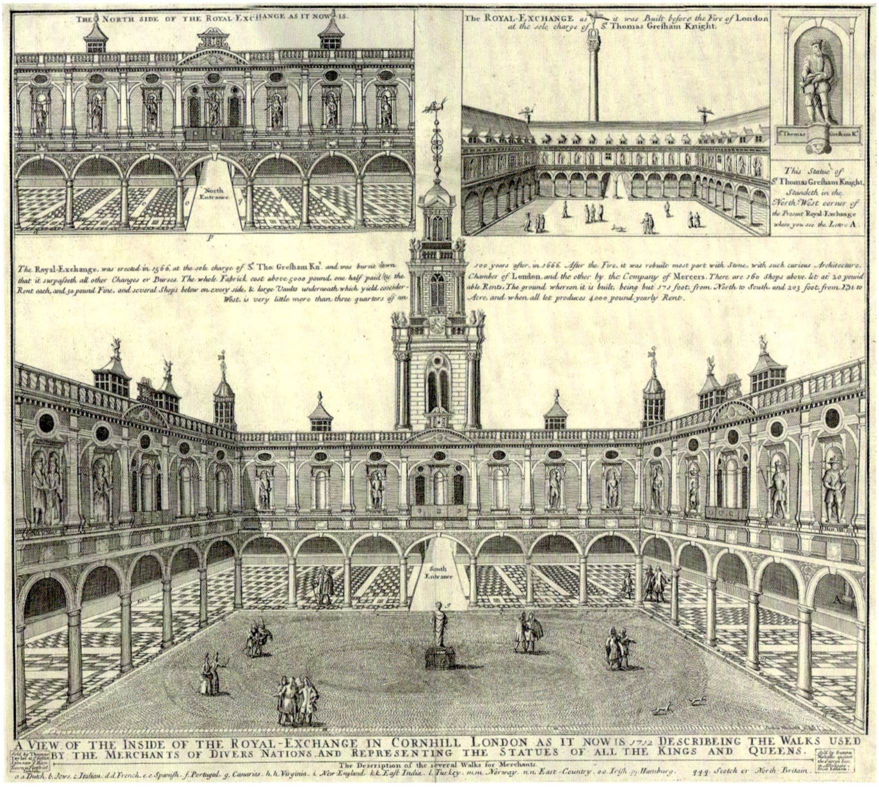

12. Sutton Nicholls, *A View of the Inside of the Royal-Exchange in Cornhill London as it Now is 1712 Describing the Walks Used by the Merchants of Divers Nations, and Representing the Statues of All the Kings and Queens*, 1712, etching and engraving, 19¼ x 22¼ in. (48.8 x 56.4 cm). British Museum, London

In December 1667, Edward Montagu, second Earl of Manchester and Lord Chamberlain of the royal household, wrote to the committee which had administered the Royal Exchange since 1597 and that was now managing its reconstruction. Manchester was recommending that the Gresham Committee appoint Cibber to replace the statues of the monarchs, beginning with Edward the Confessor, which had lined the upper storey of the old building's courtyard (fig. 10). The king, Manchester reported, had viewed with approval some "Modellos" for the work (of which two survive today), made by Cibber, recently sworn in as a royal Sculptor in Ordinary.[14] In principle the committee would have welcomed this royal interest: over the next few years both the conduct of this project and its outcome were made to exemplify an idealized relationship between a Charles II ever considerate for his merchants, and a trading community dedicated to burnishing the king's power, wealth, and glory. For the moment, however, its members replied that they were not yet in a position to consider the sculptures, having the "wholle Exchange to build first".[15]

The restoration of the line of monarchs was indeed a slow affair. A Charles I "(of Blessed Memory)" went up into its niche in 1683, though to little acclaim: "More for the Zeal than Workman's Labour prais'd".[16] Yet it was only after the publication, in November 1684, of a mayoral Precept urging the so-far uncommitted livery companies (which it names), and then the king's death fewer than three months later, that the statues began to go into their places systematically.[17] Their appearance coincided with a project at the Tower of London, where the Board of Ordnance began commissioning sculptors, including Gibbons, to create life-sized wooden kings and horses to carry its collection of historic armour (fig. 13). (This "Line of Kings" display reopened in 2013, advertised as the "longest running visitor attraction in the world".) Both programmes constituted attempts to give "visible backing", in the form of three-dimensional genealogies, to the monarchy of James II, whose right to take a place in any line of kings had been viciously disputed in the final years of Charles's reign.[18]

It was therefore before the replacement of these statues really got underway that the Exchange experienced a significantly new kind of intervention in May 1684, in the form of the statue of Charles II in a Roman-imperial incarnation. Though in 1669 it turned down the alderman Sir Robert Vyner's offer of an equestrian figure of Charles II for the middle of the courtyard, on the grounds that it would crowd the merchants and "hinder the prospect through both the doors", the Gresham Committee accepted, in 1682, the gift of another statue for this place, which had not been occupied at the old Exchange.[19] The Society of Merchant Adventurers, an old and prestigious though no longer powerful cloth-trading company based in Hamburg, grateful for "some great Favour received from the

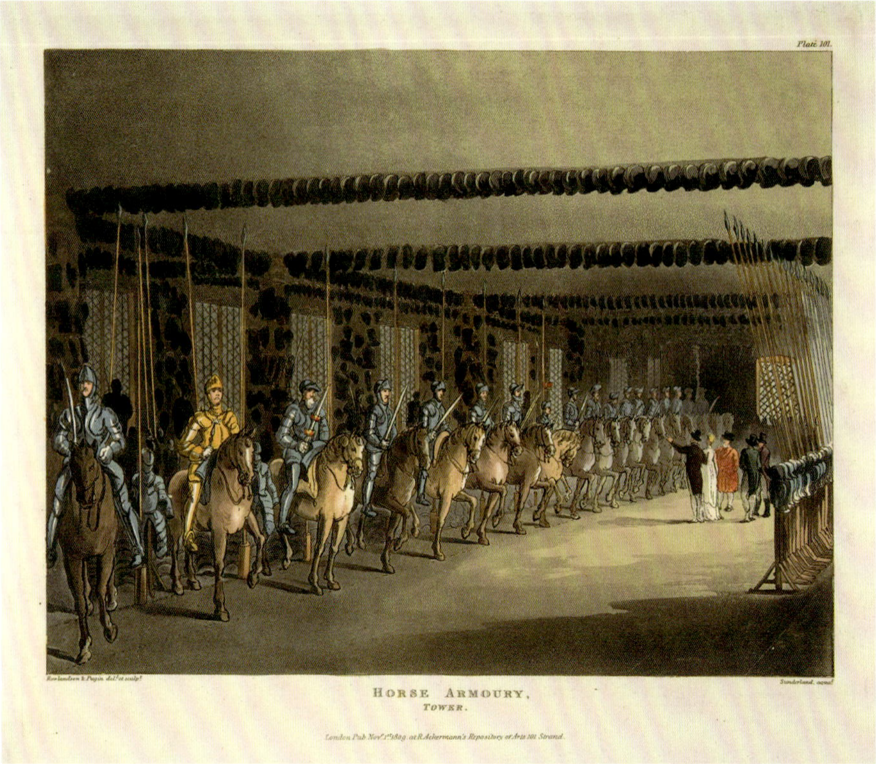

13. Thomas Sunderland after Thomas Rowlandson and Augustus Charles Pugin, *Horse Armoury, Tower of London*, 1809, etching and aquatint, hand-coloured, 7¾ x 10¼ in. (19.8 x 26 cm). The Metropolitan Museum of Art, New York

King", paid £500 (including pedestal) for the stone statue of Charles II. The favour is not known; I suspect it was related to the king's promise, in June 1683, to prosecute interlopers on the Adventurers' trade.[20]

Having weathered badly, the statue was replaced in 1791 by a completely new version (by John Spiller), which does survive.[21] Gibbons's bronze of Charles II at the Royal Hospital Chelsea, in London, which was made soon after the Exchange statue, does appear to be a close approximation of the original (fig. 14).[22] Strikingly, for contemporaries, both works showed the king "in the antient Roman Habit of their Cæsars", a costume that he favoured.[23] Writing at the end of the century, Martin Lister described how he had himself seen Charles II choose the "Roman Emperours Dress" for the bronze equestrian statue of himself at Windsor Castle, cast in 1679 after Gibbons's design.[24] Lister found the results faintly indecent, and preposterous.[25]

Facing south, the king stood on an 8-foot (almost 2.5 metre) pedestal, itself elaborately carved with the "Imperial Crown, Wings, Trumpets of Fame, Scepter and Sword, Palm-branches" and inscription visible in Peter Vandrebanc's engraving (fig. 15). On the pedestal's other sides, cupids supported shields with the arms of England and France, Ireland, and Scotland, "curiously done . . . all in Relievo".[26] This ornament telescoped a long evolution. By then, English monarchs had been represented wearing the closed or imperial crown, with the crossed bands on top, for three hundred years. "Imperial", that is, had and still meant, "sovereign".[27] However, the "Cæsari Britannico" addressed by the inscription, and the heraldry, was an emperor in the sense of ruler over contiguous territories, the Three Kingdoms of Britain and Ireland, and the Welsh principality (the claim to France was not abandoned until 1801). The inscription indicated still wider spheres of authority, though hazily: the king maintains peace across Europe ("Pacis Europæ Arbitro") and is the lord and protector of the seas ("Marium Domino ac Vindici"). One of the arches erected in 1661 by the City of London for Charles II's coronation had similarly identified him as the "British Neptune . . . at whose discretion the sea is open or closed".[28]

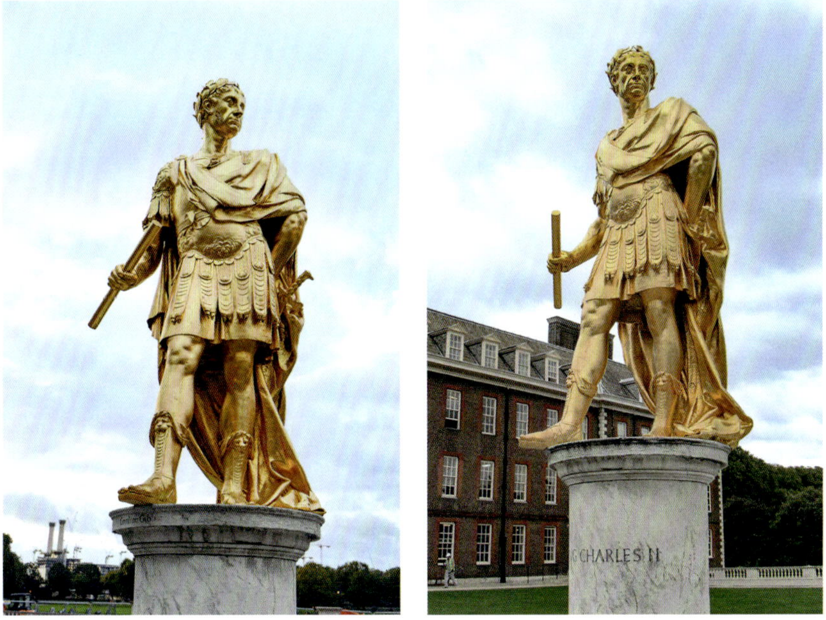

14. Grinling Gibbons, *King Charles II* (two views), ca. 1690, bronze, 88 in. (223.5 cm) [excluding pedestal]. Royal Hospital, Chelsea, London

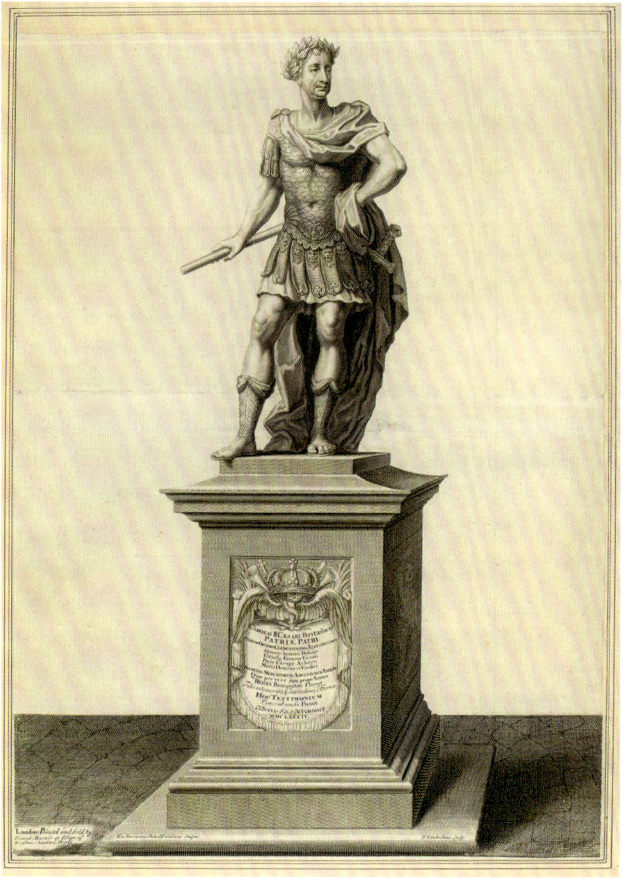

15. Peter Vandrebanc after Grinling Gibbons, *The Statue of Charles II at the Royal Exchange*, 1684, engraving, 25⅝ x 18⅞ in. (65.2 x 48 cm). British Museum, London

No jurist denied that the English monarch enjoyed sovereignty (*imperium*) over the island's surrounding waters, but in 1661 that still left open the question of whether this authority was attached to his person as opposed to the British empire, or state. The Commonwealth, after all, had claimed the same. Either way, the consensus admitted the "possibility of expanding the seas subject to sovereign control indefinitely when reason of state is expanded to include global trade". In that case, as the pedestal's inscription suggests, the seas could equally be open or closed: what mattered was the right to determine which.[29]

FAITHLESS LONDON

The Gresham Committee's reference to the hindrance of the "prospect" through the Exchange's north and south doors suggests that the enfilade was admired. In 1685 John Dryden described the setting for the first act of his *Albion and Albanius*:

> The Scene, is a Street of Palaces, which lead to the Front of the Royal Exchange; the great Arch is open, and the view is continued through the open part of the Exchange, to the Arch on the other side, and thence to as much of the Street beyond, as could, properly be teaken.[30]

Wenceslaus Hollar's small etching of the courtyard from his Four Views of London series gives something of the effect of the sight of "as much of the Street beyond", while the orthogonal elevations that began to be drawn in the early eighteenth century (always of the south, Cornhill front) suggest what the view in which Charles II was central looked like (see fig. 2.3).

Albion and Albanius, which is both a very early opera and a very late masque, begins with Mercury swooping down to regard, complacently, the Royal Exchange:

> Thou glorious Fabrick! stand for ever, stand:
> Well Worthy Thou to entertain
> The God of Traffique, and of Gain!
> To draw the Concourse of the Land,
> And Wealth of all the Main.

Yet something is wrong: "But where the shoales of Merchants meeting?"[31] Dryden's use of the fishy collective is nice: the Exchange is lapped on all sides by oceans bearing bounty, in an old figure ("though it be almost in the middle of the Citty", wrote Donald Lupton, decades earlier, "yet it Stands by the Sea") now thickened, for audiences, by the stage set's reminder of the view through the doors.[32] Like the island-nation itself, the Exchange is a place set apart, paradoxically, by its very porosity.

Mercury then interrogates Augusta (London) about this dismal, denatured Exchange, and she confesses that, seduced by "Faction" and "Zeal", she has been unfaithful to Albion (Charles I), with these disastrous results. The God of Traffic, or commerce, promises the restoration of Albion (now Charles II), in a neat encapsulation of a powerful, and novel, conception of British monarchy that had indeed attended the Restoration of 1660, as Blair Hoxby has shown. Unlike his Stuart predecessors, Charles was presented with a "fully developed vision of the Crown's... role in the advancement of trade", and unlike them, he was willing to accommo-

. . . the Joynts how firmly knit!
The well-wrought Muscles how they aptly swell,
And by their rise their springie Tendons tell.
How duely plac'd is e'ry branching Vein![42]

Martin Lister's report of Charles II's preference for this sinewy Augustanism is substantiated by the increasing number of sculptures which were then adopting it, and moreover in increasingly unadulterated forms; the long hair and moustaches of John Bushnell's otherwise imperial Charles I and Charles II (1670/1) on the Exchange's south, Cornhill front have disappeared, along with the latter's Garter.[43] However, for all its possible connotations of territorial conquest, this neoclassicism marked no departure from the king's self-presentation as ruler and protector of the seas.[44]

Like Philipps, the anonymous author of the *Poem upon the New Marble Statue* drew upon England's recent history to elucidate the statue's majesty. Both poems allude to the royal martyrdom of 1649 and subsequent "frantick Changes": "by remarkable Accident" the statue of Charles I, erected a year earlier, pointed at the future site of Gibbons's sculpture of his son.[45] Nahum Tate contrasted the tender naturalism of Gibbons's wood carvings with the Exchange statue, although he had trouble making the latter sound as enticing:

But stay—What Godlike Figure do I view?
Dare thy bold hand attempt th' Immortals too?
'Tis Cesar's Form with such Majestick grace,
As strikes a Sacred Rev'rence through the Place.[46]

The rhyme is tired, but the last line is not: Charles's presence in the Exchange courtyard did transform it in a way that the statues overlooking the courtyard did not, although they had their own potency.

EXCELLENT HARMONY

Gilbert Dugdale described, in 1604, how James I and VI, curious about preparations for his coronation cavalcade through London, attempted to "passe unknown" through the City to view them. He was spotted by the "wylie Multitude", but after taking refuge in the Exchange's upper floor was able to enjoy the sight of the merchants standing modestly and silently "like so many pictures"—that is, statues—in the courtyard beneath him.[47] The first of the monarchs' statues would not be installed for almost two decades, but the niches seem always to have been filled, in imagination. The story suggests, first, the way that at both Exchanges the monarchs' presence could be construed as admonitory, as they might be at Westminster Hall, at whose south end six royal statues still preside today: throughout the seventeenth century, as long before, they watched the deliberations of the Court of King's Bench and the Court of Chancery (fig. 16).[48] As Lupton jocularly wrote, at the Exchange the merchants "dissemble with, and cozen one another, though all the Kings that ever were since the Conquest, overlooked them".[49]

The story also connotes a specific power then being attributed to the king, of rendering rational, and profitable, the tumult of all this dissembling and dealing. James, Dugdale reported, commended those beneath him, saying that he was "never more delighted than seeing so many . . . divers and sundry on[e]s so well ord[e]red and so civill one with the other"—unlike the wily multitude outside.[50] Thomas Dekker described how, during the coronation entry, James passed from the triumphal arch built at the expense of the Italian merchant community to that erected by the "Belgians", Netherlanders, which stood near to the Exchange:

> The space of ground, on which their magnificent Arches were builded, being not unworthy to beare the name of the great Hall to this our Court Royal: wherein was to be heard & seene the sundry languages & habits of Strangers, which under Princes Roofes render excellent harmony.[51]

Finally, it reminds us of the sheer charm of overseeing. James looked down on the merchants through a window; what one poet called the "rich Balconies", both internal and facing outwards to busy Cornhill, on the Exchange's south side, were an innovation introduced at the second building which extended the privilege. From the balconies inside, "on peut voir le monde qui est à la Bourse d'en bas, qui sy' promene ou passe à travers" ("one can look down at everyone on the Exchange, walking or passing through"): again, the Exchange is a kind of clockwork model of the commercial world, one available, as commerce itself cannot be, for the apprehension of a single individual.[52]

Like his grandfather, Charles II was honoured, upon his coronation entry into London in 1661, by a great arch erected beside the Exchange (fig. 17). The location was significant: this arch was dedicated to the promotion of trade. The line between masonry and canvas-and-timber construction was further blurred by the composition of the new Exchange's south side, on which Bushnell's Charles I and Charles II were mounted in the positions occupied, on the arch, by Mars and Neptune, respectively; on both structures the royal coat of arms was large, high, and central (fig. 18).[53] Yet what was one entering, through that grand Cornhill front?

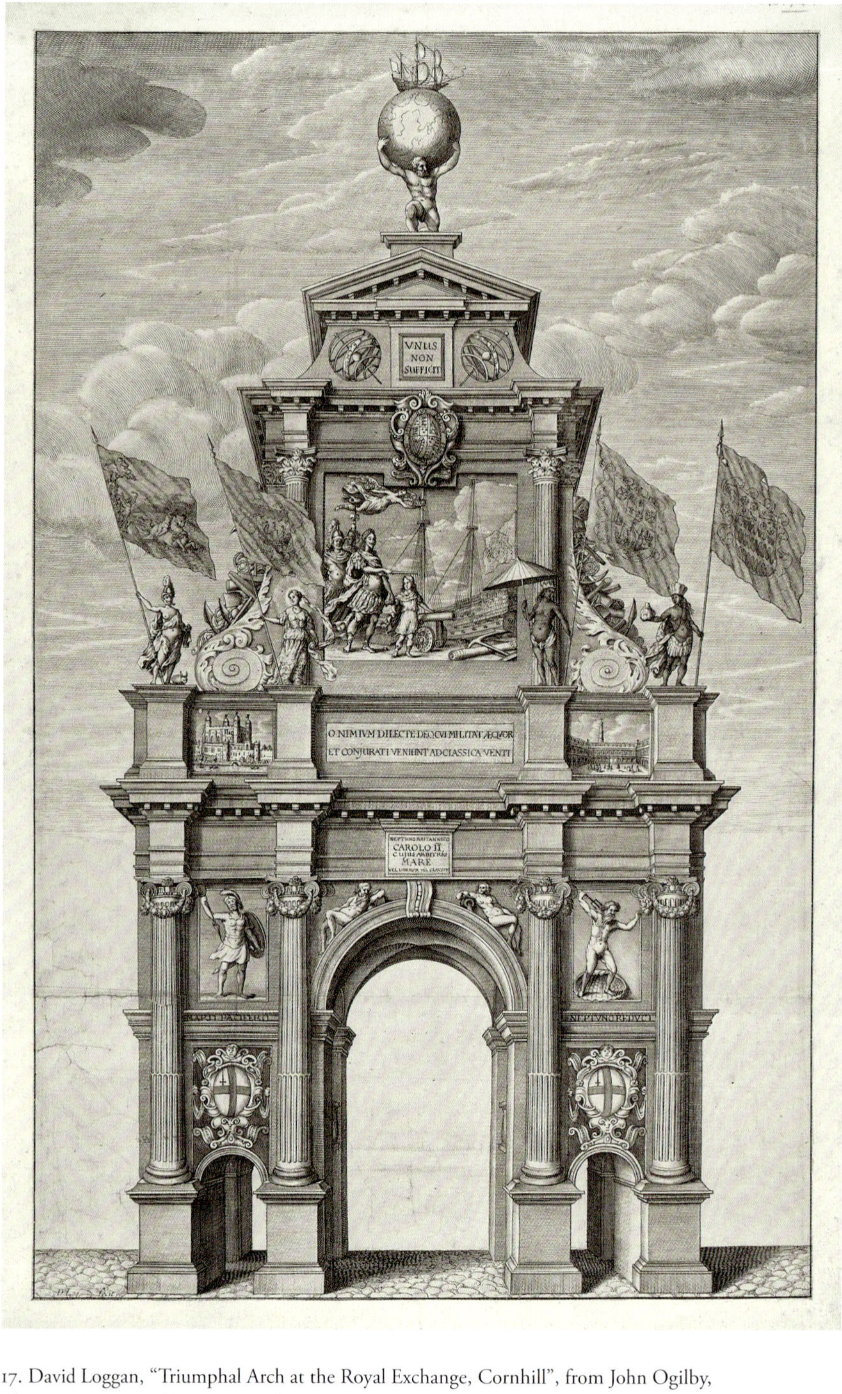

17. David Loggan, "Triumphal Arch at the Royal Exchange, Cornhill", from John Ogilby, *The Entertainment of his Most Excellent Majestie Charles II*, 1662, engraving, 16¾ x 11 in. (42.7 x 28.8 cm). Victoria & Albert Museum, London

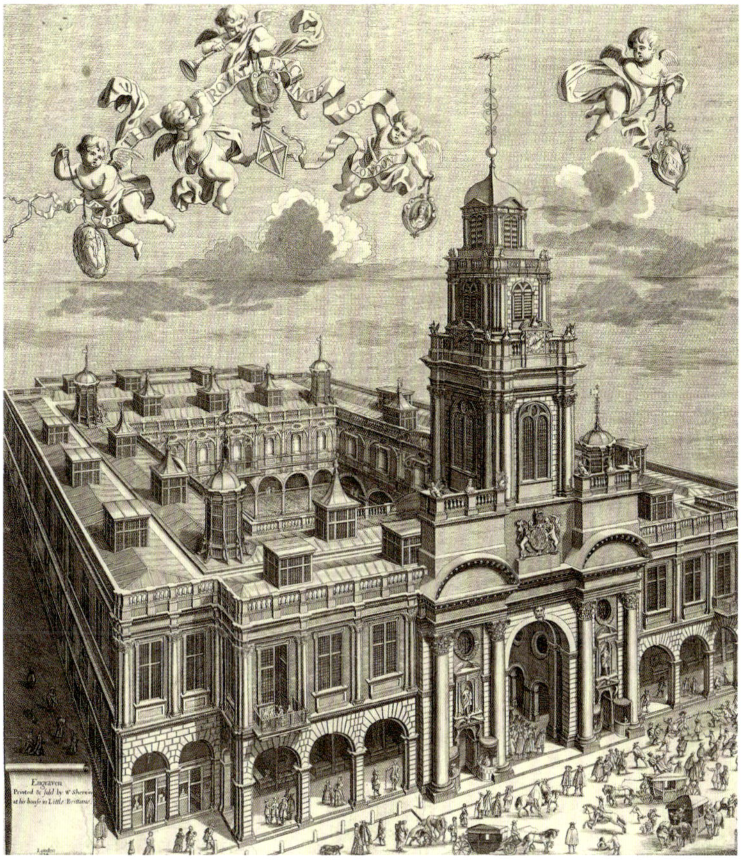

18. William Sherwin, *South-west Prospect of the Royal Exchange of London*, 1674, engraving, 26⅜ x 23½ in. (66.9 x 59.7 cm). British Museum, London

Writers mourning the Exchange's destruction in 1666 and celebrating the relatively swift rise of its successor addressed it as a "little Epitome, or rather Representative" of global trade, in a rhetorical habit encouraged by the naming of the walks.[54] Yet the Exchange was also an epitome, or abstract, of the island which was in turn the centre of an empire increasingly identified as an oceanic one, in terms of a global and heterogeneous collection of forts, stations, and marts servicing the ships which constituted the true imperial infrastructure. The River Thames ("his Garment Loose, and Flowing, . . . his Head crown'd with London Bridg[e], . . . his Beard long, Sea-green, and white") at Charles's second coronation arch praised "Your moving Forts, Your Floating Towns":

Though sev'ral Nations boast their Strength on Land,
Yet You alone the Wat'ry World command.[55]

Two years later, in an address *To the King's Most Sacred Majesty*, William Davenant efficiently disposed of France ("The Neighb'ring Monarch (wealthy and at ease) / Will build a City all of Palaces") in a conventional meditation on the frailty of human aspirations, save one:

Great Monsters, Cities, over-grown with Pow'r,
Do Neighb'ring Towns by hungry Trade devour.
You Cities build which not destructive be;
Ships grown to Fleets are Cities of the Sea.[56]

The characterization usefully distinguished this empire from the (former) Spanish, and the (modern) Dutch, French, and Ottoman presumptions to universal monarchy, and, as Hoxby suggests, Davenant was making another separation, too. In a "trading utopia of perfect collection and dispersion, there would be no need of urban concentrations" like great monster London, whose wealth and political power always threatened royal sovereignty.[57]

An admiring "Account of England" prepared for the Venetian Senate in 1671 explains that the "country has the Ocean for its territory where by the practice of navigation it carries on trade with the world or establishes its dominions by the mobile fortresses of its ships. These combining strength and speed, extend the glorious traffic of their own valour to the ends of the earth."[58] Like Davenant's poem, the report makes no distinction between ships hired by a Merchant Adventurer, say, and those of the Royal Navy. The correspondent Pietro Mocenigo went on to enumerate the "states in the four parts of the world" that England had acquired: Scotland, Ireland, New England, Virginia, Barbados, Newfoundland ("a great stretch of isolated territory towards the north"), Bombay, Tangiers, Hamburg, and the Guinea coast. His list conflates the monarchy's new property (Bombay and Tangiers arrived in 1663, along with Catherine of Braganza, Charles's Portuguese wife) with the Three Kingdoms; and both with territories, like Virginia, held by companies under royal patent, and with cities, like Hamburg, in which other companies (the Merchant Adventurers, in this case) continued to secure protection for their trade, both locally and back at home.

This empire thus operated at different removes, a condition which Mocenigo traced back to Elizabeth I: "The foundation upon which the queen built the trade of the country was the action of the companies, the people being encouraged to compete by the grant of privileges", in Muscovy, the Baltic, the Canaries, and the

East Indies. The events of the early 1680s, which turned on suspicion of the papal empire, now supposedly embracing James, Duke of York, left these privileges in peril; they had always depended on the will of monarchs, but never before en masse. It is notable that merchants cheating the Crown of customs incomes join the more familiar kinds of treasonable plotters in Dryden's poem "The Medal", published in the spring of 1682.[59] Yet corporate privileges were soon the gift of parliaments, not queens and kings. After the Glorious Revolution the monarchy's sovereignty no longer regularly included its subjects' "economic opportunity". Joint-stock companies like the Merchant Adventurers were increasingly subject to statute, and the lobbying that went with the passage of parliamentary Acts: the Adventurers lost their monopoly on the wool trade in one stroke, with the passage of the misleadingly titled "Act for the Better Preventing the Exportation of Woole" (I William & Mary, ca.32), only five years after the statue of the monarchs was erected in the Exchange.[60]

In the face of sustained opposition in the tiny territory that was the City, Charles II and his supporters, who included artists and writers, were, among other things, attempting to maintain a fiction of global empire turning, in part, on the way that monarchy rationalizes, unites, and protects the voices of a myriad of free and self-interested parties. Princes make harmony, as Dekker wrote about James I. In the version evolved by his grandson's panegyrists (bitter Dryden being the exception), imperial wealth does not take the form of customs dues. It is, rather, a natural by-product of the vigour of the seas and of the ships which sail them, or a gift freely offered. According to one of the 1684 poems celebrating Gibbons's "Skill Divine",

> . . . the World's united Treasure meet
> T'enrich Their [the Merchant Adventurers'] Bank, with each returning Fleet,
> Who lay their Hearts and Wealth at Caesar's Feet.[61]

Satisfactory gift-giving requires that the recipient, if a superior, condescends to receive the present. Such an exchange, of condescension in return for hearts and wealth, was conceivable only within the place created by Charles II's fully three-dimensional presence among the merchants on the ground (more or less: the pedestal was tall, and protected by a railing), as opposed to that made by his and his ancestors' surveillance from above.[62]

All this presumes viewers' identification of a statue with its subject, one made by the poem just quoted. We must also take into account the way that viewers identify themselves with statues. In the words of the cultural geographer Yi-Fu Tuan, an influential exponent of the differences between a culturally neutral

19. Gibson, "Kingdom's Marble Chronicle", 151, quoting the Repertories.
20. Gibson, "Kingdom's Marble Chronicle", 153, quoting Aurelian Cook's *Titus Britannicus* (1685), a posthumous biography of Charles II. She speculates about the "Favour" owed, but see the royal resolution that anyone trading contrary to the Adventurers' charters would be prosecuted by the Attorney General: proclamation issued under the name of John Nicholas, and beginning, *At the Court at Hampton Court, the Thirteenth of June 1683 Present, the Kings Most Excellent Majesty* (London: Printed by the assigns of John Bill [etc.], 1683).
21. Gibson, "Kingdom's Marble Chronicle", 157–58.
22. Gibson, "Kingdom's Marble Chronicle", 153–54.
23. Edward Chamberlayne, *The Second Part of The Present State of England*, 12th ed. (London: R. Bently, 1684), 301–2.
24. Martin Lister, *A Journey to Paris in the Year 1698*, 2nd ed. (London: Jacob Tonson, 1699), 28; Gibson, "Kingdom's Marble Chronicle", 154; Katharine Gibson, *The Cult of Charles II* (London: Royal Stuart Society, 1997), 10–11. The latter is cautious about the authorship of the Windsor statue (Gibson, "The Emergence of Grinling Gibbons as a 'Statuary'", *Apollo* 150, no. 451 [Sept. 1999]: 21–29, on 22–23), but John Dryden's *Albion and Albanius* (London: Jacob Tonson, 1685), 1, describes the first-act stage dressed with two gold equestrian statues: "one of these Statues is taken from that of the late King, at *Charing-Cross*; the other, from that Figure of his present Majesty (done by that noble Artist Mr. *Gibbons*) at *Windsor*."
25. Lister, *Journey to Paris*, 26–29.
26. Hatton, *New View of London*, 2: 616–17.
27. Armitage, *Ideological Origins of the British Empire*, 30–32 (on *imperium* as independent authority), 34–35 (on closed crowns).
28. "Neptuno Britannico, Carolo II, Cujus Arbitrio Mare vel Liberum, vel Clausum", in John Ogilby, *The Entertainment of His Most Excellent Majestie Charles II in His Passage through the City of London to His Coronation*, ed. Ronald Knowles (1662; Binghamton, NY: Medieval and Renaissance Texts and Studies, 1988), 51. Was he lord of the sea, or lord of the seas? I take the inscription from Hatton, *New View of London*, 2: 616 (invariably followed by later topographers); the engraving shows "Maris [genitive singular] Domino et Vindici", not "Marium Domino ac Vindici", while the *Poem upon the New Marble Statue*, 5, has "Maris Domino ac Vindici".
29. See Mark Somos, "Selden's *Mare Clausum*: The Secularisation of International Law and the Rise of Soft Imperialism", *Journal of the History of International Law* 14, no. 2 (2012): 287–330 (quotation on 288–89); Armitage, *Ideological Origins of the British Empire*, 113–21; and Blair Hoxby, "The Government of Trade: Commerce, Politics, and the Courtly Art of the Restoration", *ELH* 66, no. 3 (1999): 591–627 (609, 613).
30. Dryden, *Albion and Albanius*, 1.
31. Dryden, *Albion and Albanius*, 2.
32. Donald Lupton, *London and the Countrey Carbonadoed and Quartred into Severall Characters* (London: printed by Nicholas Okes, 1632), 26.
33. Hoxby, "Government of Trade", 593.
34. See note 24 above.
35. The opera was finally staged in June 1685, after rewriting to embrace Charles II's own death: James Anderson Winn, *John Dryden and His World* (New Haven and London: Yale Univ. Press, 1987), 394, 413.
36. Stevenson, *City and the King*, 291, quoting *An Appeal from the Country to the City* (1679) by Charles Blount ("Junius Brutus").
37. Jennifer Levin, *The Charter Controversy in the City of London, 1660–1688* (London: Athlone Press, 1969), 89–90.
38. Stevenson, *City and the King*, 81, 162–63.
39. *A Proclamation for Tryall of the King* (London: printed by Robert Ibbitson, 1648 [1649]). On Westminster Hall in this connection, see Gibson, "Kingdom's Marble Chronicle", 139; for public places, Stevenson, *City and the King*, 56–57.

40. In part, perhaps, because of contemporary scepticism about Gibbons's authorship of the work. David Esterly, *Grinling Gibbons and the Art of Carving* (London: V&A Publications, 1998), 208–9, follows George Vertue in attributing the Exchange statue to Arnold Quellin, but see Gibson, "Emergence of Grinling Gibbons", 24–27.
41. On Vandrebanc's engraving, see Antony Griffiths, *The Print in Stuart Britain, 1603–1689* (London: British Museum Press, 1998), 222–24, cat. no. 150 (quoting the *London Gazette* on 224).
42. Samuel Philipps, *To the Learned and Worthy Artist Mr. Grinsted* [sic] *Gibbons* (London: James Norris, 1684), 4.
43. Gibson, "Emergence of Grinling Gibbons", 24.
44. While the carvings on the Exchange statue's plinth denoted empire only in the restricted and long-established sense of the Three Kingdoms, that of Gibbons's earlier and equally *all'antica* Windsor statue bears panels of fat swags and artfully chaotic trophies of ships, shells, crustaceans, and fruit—and Mercury's caduceus (Gibson, "Emergence of Grinling Gibbons", 23). This is the bounty accruing from a maritime empire.
45. *Poem upon the New Marble Statue*, 3.
46. Nahum Tate, "To Mr. Gibbons on His Incomparable Carved Works", in *Poems Written on Several Occasions*, 2nd ed. (London: B. Tooke, 1684), 215–16.
47. Gilbert Dugdale, *The Time Triumphant, Declaring in Briefe, the A[r]rival of our Soveraigne Lieage Lord, King James into England* (London: printed by R. B[lower], 1604), fols. B1v–B2r. See Christine Stevenson, "Vantage Points in the Seventeenth-century City", *London Journal* 33 (2008): 217–32, on 217–18, with further references. On this meaning of "picture", see "picture, n.", *OED* Online. March 2014. Oxford Univ. Press. http://www.oed.com (accessed 1 April 2014).
48. Malcolm Hay, *Westminster Hall and the Medieval Kings* (London: British Museum Press, 1995), 2–3.
49. Lupton, *London and the Countrey Carbonadoed*, 25.
50. Dugdale, *Time Triumphant*, fol. B2r.
51. Thomas Dekker, *The Magnificent Entertainment Given to King James . . . Upon the Day of His Maiesties Tryumphant Passage . . . through His Honourable Citie (and Chamber) of London* (London: Tho. Man, 1604), fol. C1v.
52. "Theophilis Philalethes", *Great Britains Glory: Or, a Brief Description of the Present State, Splendor, and Magnificence of the Royal Exchange* (London : Jonathan Edwin, 1672), 19, François Colsoni, *Le Guide de Londres*, ed. Walter H. Godfrey (1693; [London]: London Topographical Society, 1951), 8.
53. The Charles I and Charles II statues survived the 1638 fire and are now at the Central Criminal Court (Old Bailey), London.
54. Samuel Rolle [Rolls], *Shalahvatih. Or, The Burning of London in the Year 1666: Commemorated and Improved in a CX. Discourses, Meditations, and Contemplations. Divided into Four Parts* (London: Nathaniel Ranew and Jonathan Robinson, 1667), 3:45.
55. Ogilby, *The Entertainment of His Most Excellent Majestie*, 43, 104.
56. William Davenant, *Poem to the King's Most Sacred Majesty* (London: Henry Herringman, 1663), 19, 20, ll. 277–78, 297–300. Hoxby's engaging analysis drew my attention to this poem: Hoxby, "Government of Trade", 616–19.
57. Hoxby, "Government of Trade", 617; Hoxby also links Davenant's fancy with the Thames's oration of 1661. For the general point, see Orr, *Empire on the English Stage*, and Armitage, *Ideological Origins of the British Empire*, 100–1.
58. Allen B. Hinds, ed., "Venice: June 1671, 1–10", *Calendar of State Papers Relating to English Affairs in the Archives of Venice, Vol. 37: 1671–1672*, British History Online, http://www.british-history.ac.uk/. My attention was drawn to this source by the discussion in Stein, "Tangier", 986.
59. "Customs to steal is such a trivial thing/ That 'tis their charter to defraud their king": "The Medal", in *John Dryden: Selected Poems*, ed. Steven N. Zwicker and David A. Bywaters (London: Penguin, 2001), ll. 195–96, Stevenson, *City and the King*, 303.

60. This was the summer of 1689. William A. Pettigrew, "Constitutional Change in England and the Diffusion of Regulatory Initiative, 1660–1714", *History* 99, no. 338 (2014): 839–63 (quotation on 863).
61. *Poem upon the New Marble Statue*, 4.
62. The statue was itself, of course, a gift, and in this way operated in another, more straightforward performance of the gift-exchange.
63. Yi-Fu Tuan, *Space and Place: The Perspective of Experience* (1977; Minneapolis: Univ. of Minnesota Press, 2011). Kindle edition.
64. Phrasing inspired by Hoxby's analysis of Davenant's and Dryden's fascination with the "perfect elasticity of trade", and "its power to concentrate even as it dispersed": Hoxby, "Government of Trade", 618, 620.
65. Joseph Roach, *Cities of the Dead: Circum-Atlantic Performance* (New York: Columbia Univ. Press, 1996), 87–88 (quotation on 87).
66. *The Spectator* 69, Saturday, 19 May 1711, in *The Royal Exchange*, ed. Saunders, 206–7 (quotation on 207).
67. Marie Sophie von La Roche, *Sophie in London, 1786, Being the Diary of Sophie v. La Roche. A Translation of the Portion Referring to England of "Tagebuch einer Reise durch Holland und England"*, trans. Clare Williams (London: Jonathan Cape, 1933), 222–23. La Roche quoted Addison and mentioned the line of kings, but not the Charles II statue.
68. "Ehver Kynd" (Henry Duke?), *Londons-Nonsuch, or, The Glory of the Royal Exchange* ([London]: s.n., 1668); Rolle, *Shalahvatih*, 3:45.

Honour, Ornament, and Frugality: The Reconstruction of London's Livery Halls after the Great Fire

Anya Matthews

IN 1666, John Dryden's *Annus Mirabilis*, a disaster occurred which was to precipitate the large-scale reconstruction of the City of London. The Great Fire, which raged from 2 to 5 September, destroyed a swathe of the City between the Tower of London and the Temple. The litany of buildings lost in the disaster rapidly became a feature of contemporary accounts of the event and remains a commonplace of modern histories of the fire: 13,000 houses, 400 streets, 87 churches, the City gates, the Royal Exchange, the Custom House, Blackwell Hall, Newgate prison, Bridewell, two debtors' prisons, the Sessions House, and all but the shells of the Guildhall and St Paul's Cathedral. At least forty-four halls belonging to the City's livery companies also lay in ashes when the last flames died down.[1] These were buildings which had in many cases, like "so many hives of bees", been the focus of uninterrupted guild activity for decades and sometimes centuries.[2] The halls were the headquarters of the City's guilds; corporate bodies that developed in the fourteenth and fifteenth centuries to regulate trades and crafts in and around the City, from the sale of salt and haberdashery, to the making of beer, cloth, and candles. Now, as John Evelyn noted on 6 September, "All . . . the Companies Halls, sumptuous buildings, arches, enteries, [were] all in dust."[3]

This essay explores the companies' response to the fire as architectural patrons and situates their hall-rebuilding projects in the more established historiography of the rebuilding of the City as a whole. It proposes a reappraisal of the halls' architecture, not on stylistic grounds, but with reference to the wide range of visual attributes that were considered relevant and important by those who commissioned, used, and first wrote about the buildings. In particular, the essay considers how the eclectic and elaborate ornament of the finished halls' external frontispieces, gates, and wainscotted interiors might have served the immediate corporate reputational need of the Restoration companies.

Though they were funded without any external assistance, livery halls were among the first buildings to be reconstructed in the City; a central problem will be to retrieve some of the concerns that drove the companies to rebuild speedily

some idea of the vacuum created by the Great Fire and the enormity of the task of rebuilding. The burnt area is represented by the almost entirely blank space in the centre; only the sites of major landmarks such as St Paul's and the City churches are marked out, and these are represented in crude plan form. Surrounding the flattened blank at the centre is the dense built-up area which escaped the fire, represented scenographically.[21] It is a contrast which is at once visually exciting and unsettling; the vacuum invites influx, repopulation, and speaks of opportunity but, as Joseph Monteyne has observed, it also represents an inversion of the relationship between the City and the suburbs.[22] This plan and others like it were not only mapping the trauma of the fire; they were also topographical chessboards inviting speculation about who was going to make the first move towards reconstruction.

THE HALLS AND THE WIDER RECONSTRUCTION OF THE CITY

In the immediate aftermath of the fire the companies were respectful of interventions made by the authorities to prevent unregulated building. Less than a week after the fire had ended, on 13 September 1666, King Charles II issued a proclamation blocking "hasty and unskilful building" in the immediate aftermath of the disaster so that proposals for reconstruction could be sifted and assessed, and surveying work accommodated.[23] This proclamation appears to have made a powerful impression on the Courts of the Tallow Chandlers' and Clothworkers' Companies, for example, both of which happened to meet that day. The former received petitions from their tenants asking for repayment of their leases but dismissed them, declaring:

> until his Majestie's pleasure shall be fully knowne how affaires between landlords and tenants shall be settled, and how buildings may be carried upp on demolished foundations; this Companie knows not how to give any Resolution.[24]

In line with the royal proclamation and precepts issued by the Court of Common Council, the companies did, however, start to clear their land of rubbish, secure their sites, and protect the integrity of surviving vaults and cellarage. The Clothworkers, for example, ordered that the materials of their ruined hall should be cleared and stored in the yard and vaults of their site.[25] Once they were sifted and secured, there was little to be done until the King's Commissioners and City Surveyors had made their surveys and decided on a model for reconstruction.

The various proposals advanced for rebuilding did not neglect the question of the livery halls. Both Christopher Wren and John Evelyn had envisaged manoeuvring and manipulating the halls in their celebrated plans for rebuilding the City submitted in the week following the fire. Even when these had been abandoned in favour of a more pragmatic approach to reconstruction, resiting the companies was still discussed in negotiations between the City authorities and the king. As T. F. Reddaway noted in what remains the definitive general survey of post-fire reconstruction, Charles II retained hope of influencing the overall design of the new City in the first months of 1667.[26] On 6 March a delegation of members of the Court of Common Council attended a council at Berkshire House in the presence of the king, the Duke of York, the Lord Chamberlain, the Lord Chancellor, and others. The City's account of this meeting includes the note: "His Matie doth recommend to their consideration that the lesser and meaner halls may be erected next to the Thames which will add much beauty to that place and the ground whereupon they stood will be applied to other uses."[27]

This intriguing vignette shows the king taking a direct and specific interest in the group of buildings with which we are concerned. The Court of Common Council declared its readiness to comply with Charles's wishes and to require "the said companies to build accordingly".[28] Thereafter the king's proposal for the new livery halls appears to have been dropped by the City. There is no evidence that the Lord Mayor (then William Bolton) relayed Charles's wishes to the companies, and the halls stayed resolutely on their pre-fire sites. The companies' records demonstrate undoubted awareness of and adherence to the wider legislative framework provided by the first "act for the rebuilding" which received royal assent on 8 February 1666/7, but few signs of outside interference. With two important exceptions, livery hall building projects proceeded with only minimal involvement from the King's Commissioner—or even from the City Corporation.[29]

REBUILDING THE HALLS

An inscription on the south face of the pedestal supporting the Monument erected to the fire, which was finished in 1677, declares rather optimistically: "Haste is seen everywhere, London rises again, whether with greater speed or greater magnificence is doubtful, three short years complete that which was considered the work of an age."[30] The relief sculpture by Caius Gabriel Cibber on the west face of the same structure depicts Charles II directing the reconstruction and the beleaguered figure of London being comforted by Time against a backdrop of smoking buildings. In reality what had been completed three years after the fire was the surveying of five thousand plots, the completion of four thousand houses, and the reconstruction of a single public building (the Royal Exchange). A great amount had been accomplished but nineteen public buildings, all of the churches, and thousands of houses remained unbuilt in 1669: their construction would continue well into the 1680s.[31] In *Londons Resurrection or the Rebuilding of London Encouraged, Directed and Improved*, published in 1668, Samuel Rolls despaired of the slow start to the reconstruction and what he called the "mixt face" of the City "while but some few houses are built in the midst of many ruinous heaps".[32]

The reconstruction of the livery halls did, however, justify some of the hyperbole of the Monument's inscription and deserve that double distinction of speed and magnificence. The vast majority of the companies chose to rebuild after September 1666.[33] Of the forty-four livery halls known to have burned down in the fire, eight had been rebuilt by 1669, ten had been more or less completed by 1670, and three-quarters were structurally complete by 1673.[34] Five of the first ten halls to be reconstructed benefited from the assistance of Edward Jerman (died 1668), one of the City's Commissioners for Rebuilding and a well-regarded master craftsman and surveyor, but a large cast of surveyors and craftsmen was employed overall by the companies in their rebuilding effort as part of a major mobilization of men and materials.[35]

The three competing constraints that hold most building projects in tension are quality of workmanship and materials, time, and cost: a low-cost building delivered quickly cannot be good quality, a good quality building delivered at low cost will take more time, and a good quality building delivered quickly will inevitably cost more. The companies were pulled in all three directions. The Stationers' Company expected "the best and speediest" carrying on of their new building in 1672, while two years later the Tallow Chandlers' Court were instructing their carpenter to see their hall "adorned & made ornamentall" yet "to performe the same with asmuch frugality for the Company as he can".[36] The companies were short of both money and time after the fire; however, an overriding concern with honour and its architectural expression meant that there was a certain quality of workmanship and materials below which damage to corporate reputation would start to exceed the benefits of completing reconstruction quickly or frugally. The potential damage to reputation of rebuilding shoddily or too slowly was real—but so, too, was the risk of losing credit by over-spending and being unable to pay debtors.

FINANCIAL DIFFICULTIES AND FUNDRAISING

That the livery companies were such sedulous builders is surprising given their financial situation. Whereas Parliament in its second Act for Rebuilding the City provided a formal funding mechanism for the reconstruction of public buildings and churches—an enhanced duty on coal—the quasi-public livery halls were funded entirely privately.[37] One could dismiss this as a task easily accomplished for rich guilds run by merchant princes and successful tradesmen, but civic grandees with significant disposable income—the picture buyers discussed in Richard Stephens's essay in this volume—formed by far the smallest component of the membership, even in the most senior companies.[38]

The fire had destroyed rental property across the City, robbing the companies of a vital source of income.[39] The first six decades of the seventeenth century had been financially challenging for the livery companies, too. Stuart royal policy towards the companies was antagonistic, coercive, and sometimes exploitative: an invitation from James I to invest in the plantation of Ulster was followed by a series of enforced loans under his successor, Charles I (as well as loans to Parliament during the Civil Wars).[40] At the Restoration, Charles II, like his predecessors, looked to the City for extraordinary income and again the livery companies collectively met the demands. Most recently they had helped the City loan the Crown £100,000 in 1664 and (grudgingly) funded the building of a ship called the *Loyal London* to be deployed in the second Anglo-Dutch war. These loans were meant to be repaid with interest but rarely were.[41] Such demands did not, of course, release the companies from expensive corporate civic duties: in May 1660 every company had been ordered by the Lord Mayor

> to be ready for Charles II's procession through London with twelve of their most tall and comely men well-horsed with best array and furniture of velvet plush or sattin and chaines of gold . . . railes, standings, clothes, banners and other ornaments of triumph belonging to the Companie.[42]

The companies' power and wealth had also been undermined by the growth of the suburbs outside the City walls where artisans, craftsmen, and tradesmen could evade their jurisdiction and the fees and fines that company membership entailed.[43]

If the historiography of the livery companies in the seventeenth century has occasionally been melodramatic in tone—the nineteenth-century historian William Herbert famously described the fire as "the consummation of their miseries", for example—the basic assessment that the companies were in straitened financial circumstances and feeling harried and harassed is correct.[44] It is worth our notice that while the Monument's relief sculpture places the personification of Fortitude and Justice in King Charles's entourage on the right, and puts the figures of Industry and Expedition in the manual arts firmly in the City's camp on the left, the figure of Plenty hovers non-committally over the two (fig. 20).[45] Where is the bounty she is so liberally pouring on the reconstruction enterprise supposed to be coming from? Plenty is shown conventionally supported by Peace, but the fire occurred in the midst of a war, another episode in the series of "interlocking traumas" that characterized the first decade of the Restoration.[46] For the companies at this time, plenty was elusive and the Court of the Brewers' Company spoke for most when, in 1667, it cursed "the destruccion & unsettledness of the tymes".[47]

Unlike the heralds at the College of Arms—also a corporate body rebuilding its headquarters in the City after the fire—the companies were not able to petition the king for permission to collect subscriptions from wealthy individuals outside the square mile.[48] They were, for the most part, limited to levying small subscriptions from freemen: the rank and file. However, they did this extremely effectively and assiduously. Evidence of these contributions can be found in a handful of surviving subscription and promissory books. An ordinary freeman might typi-

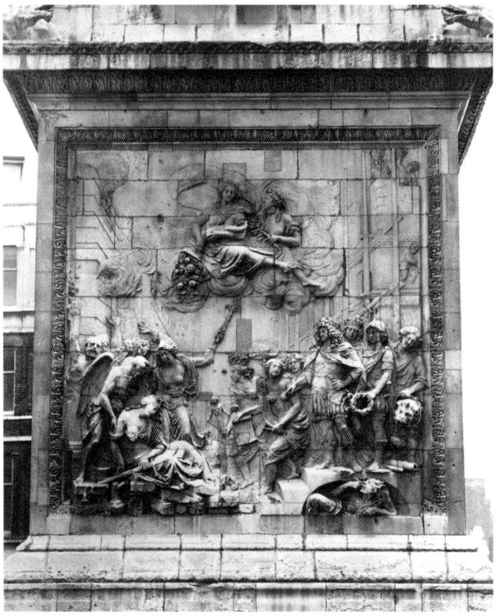

20. Caius Gabriel Cibber, *Charles II Coming to the Assistance of the City* (The Monument, London), 1673–1675, Portland stone (58 x 58 cm). Conway Library, The Courtauld Institute of Art, London.

cally contribute 20s., while liverymen, aware of their duty to lead by example, might donate a sum of £20. On 9 November 1670, for example, the Court of Assistants of the Tallow Chandlers' Company "being desirous to promote and encourage the rebuilding of this Companies Comon Hall did severally . . . and freely and voluntary subscribe" to the rebuilding of their Hall.[49]

Occasionally, a particularly wealthy or politically ambitious member of the livery offered to defray, or at least temporarily cover, the cost of wainscotting or plastering of a room. One notable example is that of Alderman Dennis Gauden (or Gawden) who, in December 1666, as the Clothworkers' Court was still struggling with loss of income and to recoup royal loans, offered to meet the cost of constructing the company's new parlour and kitchen until the company was in a position to repay him. He did so out "of the tender respects and kindness which hee hath for this Company and the greate sense . . . of their present condicion since ye late dreadfull fire".[50] As well as being a wealthy Court member of the Clothworkers, who held high office as a surveyor-general of victualling to the navy, Alderman Gauden was to become the following year both a knight and a member "of the Committee for building publique works of this Citty".[51] Such benevolence was a form of strategic patronage which gave Gauden an unusual degree of personal control over a building type usually built collectively: when the company were completing reconstruction they deferred to "Alderman Dennis Gauden for ye Orderinge & Contriving of the Rooffe and other concerns of this Companys Comon-hall as hee in his Judgmt shall thinke most fit & convenient".[52]

The Clothworkers were fortunate in Gauden's patronage and the loyalty of their rank and file but, with the shell of an average livery hall costing in the region of £5,000, for the most part the companies faced a shortfall which could only be met with high-interest loans.[53] Study of the fundraising methods employed by the companies shows firstly how dedicated they were to the rebuilding effort, and secondly that previous estimates of the cost of rebuilding the halls are seriously inaccurate. John Strype computed in 1720 that the cost of rebuilding the halls was £78,000 (or an average of £1,500 each).[54] Yet the Brewers' Company, for example, by no means one of the richest or most senior companies, spent nearly £6,000.[55]

The Brewers had been led to believe by Sir Samuel Starling, an Alderman and Past Master, that he would finance rebuilding in November 1666, but by December the Court was told that "his mind was altered."[56] The company was forced to adopt a series of painful fundraising methods: plate was sold for £116, but it was the compulsory subscriptions collected in "divisions" that brought in the sums needed. The diligence of the Wardens and Court of Assistants meant that £1,879 was soon collected in this way along with an in-kind offer of fifty thousand bricks.[57] Such importance was attached to the contribution of freemen to the rebuilding,

We see, in particular, a return to the "rhetoric of antiquity". For example, on completion of their new hall the Vintners made "preparations for election day according to antient custome".[77] Most interestingly, while the halls might be "new rebuilded", as far as the companies were concerned they were still somehow "ancient" in essence. In December 1669 the Pewterers' Company gave thanks that they had been restored to the building "which not long since lay in Ashes". The following summer the whole livery

> was acquainted that in as much it hath pleased Almighty God to restore the Company to their *auntient habitacon* they should according to *auncient Custome* appeare at ye hall this day seavenight in the fore noon being the day appointed for the Masters feast decently Apparrelled in their Livery Gouns from whence they are to goe to hear a Sermon And to return thanks to God for his abundant mercies in restoring the Company to almost all their estate which they had before the Late dreadfull fire.[78]

For liverymen, the completed halls possessed a "double historicity": the buildings were newly constructed but also "tokens" in a chain of "substitutable replicas". As Alexander Nagel and Christopher Wood have argued, to the pre-modern mind "new buildings were understood as reinstantiations, through typological association, of prior structures".[79] As we shall see, the halls were the product both of a powerful conservatism and a willingness to innovate. The former impulse was expressed in the new buildings' traditional spatial arrangement, which provided stability and continuity with the past. The latter found an outlet in decoration and ornament.

"COSTLY WITHOUT, BUT RICHLIER INLAID": THE ARCHITECTURE OF THE POST-FIRE HALLS

Twentieth-century writers—where they considered the post-fire livery halls at all—tended to consider them in purely stylistic terms and to subsume them in the general category of vernacular classicism or "artisan mannerism".[80] This pejorative label, invented by John Summerson, denotes the supposedly debased classicism of buildings executed by City craftsmen in the middle decades of the seventeenth century. Notable motifs now associated with this category, which occurred on buildings in a variety of combinations from ca. 1620–75, include: segmental pediments breached by or filled with decorative tablets, cartouches or shields; balustraded balconies; eared or "lugged" architraves, half pilasters and scrolls around windows, doors, and chimneypieces; columns or pilasters of the giant order; mixed window sizes and shapes on a single elevation; deep eaves-cornices; sculpted gables; string courses; and heavy use of rubbed brickwork.[81]

For those who subscribe to the term—and it is one that architectural historians continue to use—"artisan mannerism" was the product of builders and craftsmen not skilled or educated enough to assimilate the classicizing principles of architecture introduced to England by Inigo Jones.[82] It is a category which Summerson applies to all of the post-fire halls, bar the Fishmongers', which he allows "something of the new Dutch influence".[83] For Summerson, the halls were "regular City architecture" by which he meant buildings of a "vigorous but impolite character" that, despite their later date, appear "mannered and coarse" when compared with Inigo Jones's earlier exercises in Palladian classicism, and even the "purer type of Artisan classicism" of his master mason Nicholas Stone, builder of the pre-fire Goldsmiths' Hall (1635–38).[84] At most, the Restoration halls are permitted a kind of "trim, dolls house charm".[85]

In an influential article, Elizabeth Chew challenged this hierarchical and anachronistic interpretation of seventeenth-century architecture, arguing that writers such as Summerson were guilty of imposing "twentieth-century ideas of quality" on buildings such as Raynham Hall (1622–37) or Lindsey House (1640) "without considering whether such judgements had any relevance to the people who commissioned and lived" in them.[86] Chew argues convincingly that the early modern contrivers of such buildings were not simply incapable of replicating Jonesian classicism, as the earlier writers would have it, but were knowingly mixing forms, motifs, and references borrowed from diverse sources. The eclectic and inventive approach to the design and ornamentation of buildings that later writers found "mannered" and "coarse" was a way of conveying the many complex associations and references a patron required, Chew explained.[87] Suddenly artisans and craftsmen started to appear more advanced, for, as J. Mordaunt Crook has observed, "eclecticism is the vernacular of sophisticated societies."[88]

A more nuanced and balanced appraisal of the halls' architecture can be achieved by combining visual analysis with a consideration, in line with Chew's methodology, of what was relevant to the corporate patrons who commissioned and used the buildings as well as the craftsmen and surveyors who undertook design and construction on their behalf. Just as Palladian classicism was merely one of a range of available stylistic options, "style" in the seventeenth-century City was merely one visual attribute of many: quality of materials and workmanship and richness of ornament were as important as the consistent use of certain motifs.[89] It is this difference of emphasis which explains how the same City classicism classified as coarse "artisan mannerism" by twentieth-century writers was described more approvingly by contemporaries as "richly adorn'd".[90]

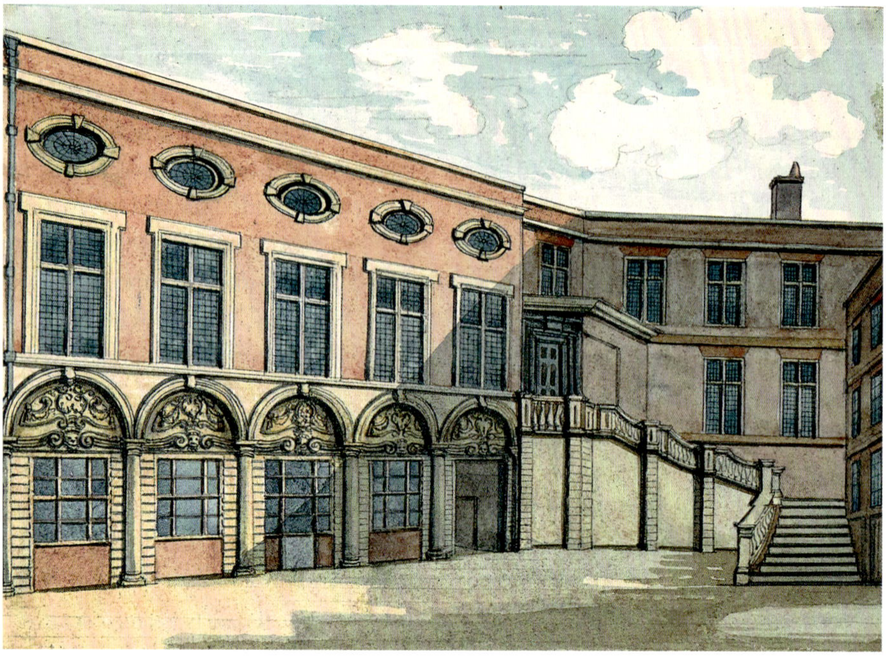

24. Samuel Ireland, "Brewers' Hall," prepared for *Picturesque Views with an Historical Account of the Inns of Court in London and Westminster*, between 1794 and 1800, watercolour, graphite, and pen and black ink on paper, 5 x 7 in. (12.7 x 17.8 cm). Yale Center for British Art, Paul Mellon Collection

The result was a *cour d'honneur*; a building around "three sides of a Quadrangle" separated from Thames Street by the brick wall mentioned above.[94] Entry was through an iron gate flanked by freestone piers topped with a Bacchus sitting on three tuns, a device found on the company's coat of arms. The Mercers' Hall had always enjoyed a powerful presence on Cheapside; here, shops at ground level were combined with a highly ornamental carved stone frontispiece (fig. 25). Though Fishmongers' Hall was also rebuilt around a courtyard, its riverside plot—unique among the companies—provided the opportunity for an uncompromised principal elevation.

When the street range of a hall was rebuilt, decisions had to be made about which ornaments and marks of distinction should appear there, and which should be reserved for the inner complex—the "facing" and "inlaying" referred to in the poem above. Obscurity was a risk; however, spending vast sums on adorning an entire elevation comprising shops or tenements was not necessarily a sensible course of action, given limited resources. The result, in most cases, was a degree of focused investment on the street range, with the remainder of the ornamental display reserved for the exterior of the main hall range and, in particular, the interiors. It is this paradox of recessive display that led Strype to observe of the post-fire halls that many were "little inferior to some Princes Palaces" but "lie for the most part backwards, and cannot be taken notice of by strangers".[95]

The requirement that street ranges be primarily functional, income-generating structures placed an additional symbolic burden on the hall gates that stood at their centre and which were the natural pinch point in the plan which led to the courtyard and hall range. Gates and doorcases to the street had to be designed with maximum impact and so scrollwork, festoons, swags, garlanded Ionic capitals, swan-necks, over-sized coats of arms under shell hoods or breaching segmental pediments, and other ornaments were deployed.[96] Sometimes the architectural emphasis given to a hall's door or gate extended the full height of an otherwise plain brick elevation, creating a vertical "sliver of splendour".[97] Such frontispieces operated as an index of what lay beyond. Indeed Strype, invoking an ancient maxim of proportionality, likened the relationship of livery gates to livery hall to the way "Hercules' Body may be judged by his Foot."[98]

The joiner Thomas Whiting's early design for a frontispiece for the Brewers' Company indicates how the dexterous contrivers of some post-fire halls were

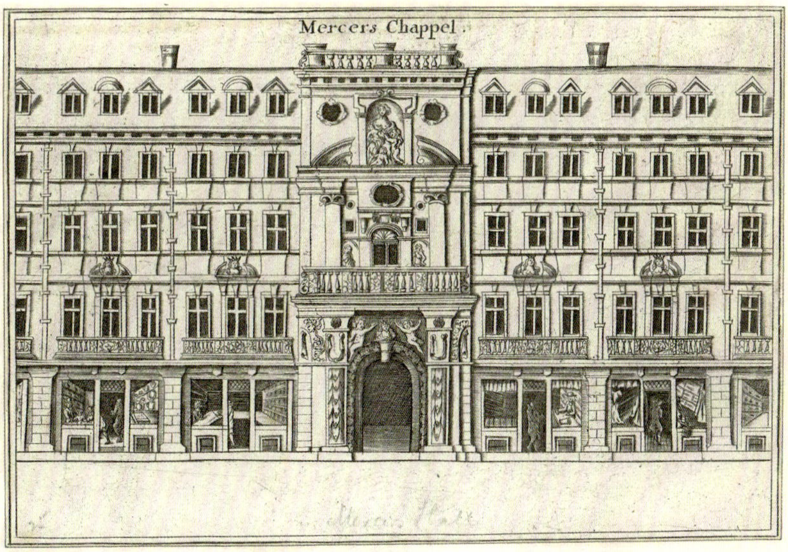

25. English School, *Mercer's Chappel; Cheapside; London*, 17th century, engraving. Private collection

forced to think vertically and to pile up ornament on the street range. Financial necessity and the awkwardness of City plots constrained innovation as far as the plans of the post-fire halls were concerned, but the design and decoration of these frontispieces provided an outlet for invention. At street level, a fleshy cartouche bearing the company's arms fills a segmental pediment flanked by pilasters topped with foliage capitals. At the next stage is a tripartite window which appears to be a mullioned and transomed adaptation of a Serliana, pierced by a keystone carved with a head, flanked by leafy scrolls, and topped with two horizontal scrolls which support the Moorish woman device of the Brewers.[99] The third stage holds another tripartite window flanked by festoons of carved fruit and topped by palm fronds which hold a cartouche bearing the numerals "1669". Surmounting the whole composition is a pedimented dormer window above a parapet flanked by two large squashed volutes. Whiting's design would be labelled "coarse", "mannerist", and "untutored" according to the dominant construction of seventeenth-century architecture in Britain, but, as we have seen, its logic was driven by context and the needs of the City patron. It combines the concise legibility of the heraldic device with the rhetorical power of sculptural ornament to convey information to and create an effect on the viewer; a category which included the citizenry, other liverymen, senior office holders in the City Corporation, and royal officials.

"RICHLIER INLAID": THE DESIGN AND DECORATION OF THE HALLS

Aside from the gates and frontispieces described above, hall exteriors were often relatively unadorned, made up of plain brick with stone architraves and quoins. The companies invested instead in interior decoration. In particular, their buildings were lined with very fine wainscotting and wood carving, ranging from the elaborate screens which towered over the lower end of the hall room to the intricate chimneypieces which adorned parlours and Court rooms. This non-structural, ornamental medium allowed the combination of a seemingly infinite variety of motifs. Company devices and symbols could be incorporated in imaginative and surprising ways; a fact which did not escape Hatton's notice.[100] One notable joiner of the post-fire halls was John Symes, whose work at both the halls of the Vintners and the Tallow Chandlers is extant.[101] The Court room of the former and the hall and parlour of the latter are richly adorned with carved festoons, swags, volutes, and classical ornament. The Tallow Chandlers' parlour wainscotting, completed in 1674 as the gift of Sir Joseph Sheldon, includes a carved bay-leaf architrave around the fireplace (a favourite feature of Symes's), an acanthus frieze, and an overmantel crowned with the Stuart royal arms and foliage festoons.[102] Sheldon's arms are included in a cartouche over a sham door at the room's eastern end. Symes had also been employed at Brewers' Hall once that building was structurally complete in early 1672 and the job of decorating and ornamenting began. In October of that year he was paid £355 to wainscot their hall room (fig. 26).[103] The wainscot reached to just beneath the oval top lights, and the festooned shields in each of the six frontispieces on both sides of the hall held the arms of a benefactor to the rebuilding. The arms and names of the wardens for the year 1673 were included over the pedimented door in the north side. At the west end behind the Master's chair was wainscotting surmounted with the carved figure of a Moorish woman flanked by Neptune, Jupiter, and sea-horses. The screen, dated 1673, included elaborate carved spandrels and a large broken pediment holding the company's arms and the company's Moorish woman crest again. On either side sat carved putti astride the barrels of the brewing trade. Elsewhere in the City, the Joiners' Hall—rather unsurprisingly—had a fine display of wainscotting and carving, as Hatton noted:

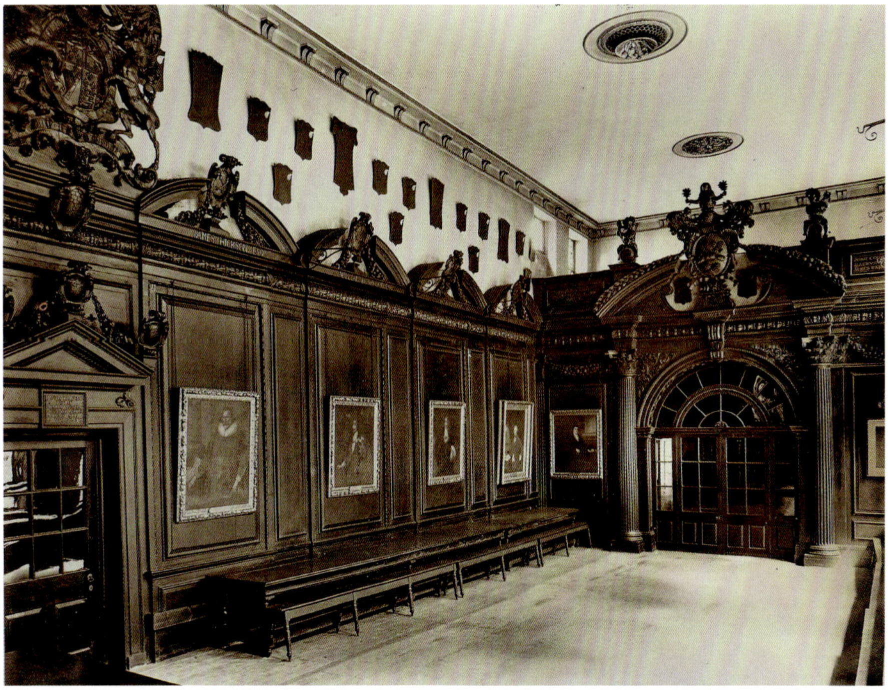

26. Interior of the Brewers' Hall wainscotted by John Symes, 1672–3. London Metropolitan Archives

> This Hall is remarkably curious for a magnificent Screen (as you enter the Hall) having demy Savages and other variety Enrichments well carved in right Wainscot, and the great Parlour is wainscotted with Cedar.[104]

Thomas Whiting was working there, too, between 1673 and 1675, and the leading joiner William Cleare was paid in the region of £200 for carving in the main hall in 1675 and 1676.[105] The Mercers also invested heavily in wainscotting and carving. Between 1676 and 1682 the carvers Richard Cleare, Ralph Morice, John Miller, and John Baker worked to produce fine examples of their craft for the premier City company. Though demolished in 1829, an early survey drawing indicates that the wainscotting of the post-fire Goldsmiths' Hall was also highly elaborate, with fluted Corinthian pilasters at its centre and two entries surmounted with festooned cartouches similar to those at Brewers' Hall.

Plaster ceilings offered another field for the display of ornament in post-fire hall interiors, though Hatton noted them less often. An outstanding (though non-extant) ceiling was that in the Court room of the repaired Goldsmiths' Hall (1669), recorded in a survey drawing by the architect Philip Hardwick made just prior to its demolition in 1829. This had a graceful pattern of beams with a central quatrefoil whose soffits were covered with swirling foliage. The coved edge was decorated with swags and scrolls and a procession of unicorns and putti. Similarly, the ceiling of the master's parlour at Pewterers' Hall was one of the most ornate elements in this otherwise fairly plain building by John Wildgos on Lime Street (1668). The elaborate design followed the irregular pentagonal shape of the room and included high-relief panels with the figure of St Catherine and grotesque work incorporating the company's crest of two arms holding erect a dish.

ORNAMENT AND HONOUR

We have seen how the distribution and concentration of ornament on the exterior and, to a greater extent, the interiors of the halls was undertaken with great care by rebuilding committees of liverymen and the craftsmen they commissioned. The halls' reconstruction involved a continual renegotiation between the need for architectural distinction on one hand and frugality on the other; between the desire for honourable external display and the reticence which favoured inward adornment. This tension between allowable magnificence and superfluous luxury was common to much architectural discourse in the early modern period and earlier. The notion of decorum, and of *ornatus* as a manifestation of *dignita*, was developed by Leon Battista Alberti (1404–1472), who advised: "we should erect our

building naked, and let it be quite complete before we dress it with ornaments"; ornaments which, "like clothes, should reveal the social status of their owner-occupier".[106] The appropriate degree of architectural restraint and external disposition of ornament was something each company had to resolve for itself, but the guiding principle, as the post-fire poet put it, was to build halls that were "Costly without, but richlier inlaid". The tension between ornament and plainness, dignity and restrained frugality, was a constant theme in the reconstruction of the halls after the fire: the proper degree of ornament was determined not just by the availability of funds but by a sense of what was appropriate for the honour and credit of the company.

Some of these tensions and paradoxes appear to be characteristic of corporate building projects more generally in early modern society. The Renaissance Venetian *scuole* parallel the early modern London companies in many important ways, operating, as they did, on a particular competitive model which involved a number of confraternities, the largest corporate bodies in the city after the government itself, "competing to be equal".[107] Patricia Fortini Brown has argued that the pursuit of corporate honour and the honour of the Republic allowed these Venetian confraternities to reconcile architectural splendour with a reputation for religious piety and virtue:

> Such display caused no qualms, for magnificence was necessary for the honor—and, by extension, the protection—of the city . . . For the private citizen, the principal problem with ostentatious patronage, even if inspired by the most pious of motivations, was the accusation of pride and vainglory. Lay groups . . . offered a solution. Rather than a sign of personalized vainglory or cause of personal shame, collective ostentation was a means to gain divine favor for the polity and honor for the individuals now gathered into a sponsoring group.[108]

In this way, the confraternities of Venice came to regard conspicuous and elaborate architectural patronage as a necessity. The highly ornamental, sculpted façades of the Renaissance *scuole grandi* make all but the Mercers' post-fire hall appear frugal indeed by comparison, but, by investing in the central frontispieces and gates of their street ranges, the London companies were, in a more restrained way, also claiming their share of honour—and honouring the City of which they were part. As John Evelyn remarked in 1664, properly ornamented buildings could become ornaments themselves, adorning and adding "lustre" to the Commonwealth.[109]

1. Walter George Bell, *The Great Fire of London in 1666* (London: Bodley Head, 1923), 338, Appendix IV, lists the halls known to have been destroyed in the fire as well as the seven that escaped the flames. It is unclear whether some of the very smallest companies such as the Farriers and Hatmakers had halls of their own before the fire or merely rented other companies' halls or accommodation elsewhere in the City. A few of the smallest companies may have decided not to rebuild.
2. James Howell, *Londinopolis: An Historical Discourse or Perlustration of the City of London, The Imperial Chamber, and Chief Emporium of Great Britain* (London, 1657), 41.
3. E. S. De Beer, ed., *The Diary of Sir John Evelyn*, 6 vols. (Oxford Univ. Press, 1955), 3: 460.
4. On the general validity—and pitfalls—of the term, see Keith Wrightson, *Earthly Necessities: Economic Lives in Early Modern Britain* (New Haven and London: Yale Univ. Press, 2000), 289–90.
5. John Summerson, *Georgian London* (London: Pleiades Books, 1948), 43.
6. On the book's context, reception, and impact, see Michela Rosso, "Georgian London Revisited", *London Journal* 26, no. 2 (2001): 35–50.
7. S. R. Epstein and Maarten Prak, eds., *Guilds, Innovation and the European Economy, 1400–1800* (Cambridge Univ. Press, 2008). See, for example, George Unwin, *The Guilds and Companies of London* (London: Methuen, 1908), and S. Kramer, *The English Craft Guilds: Studies in their Progress and Decline* (New York: Columbia Univ. Press, 1927).
8. See, for example, Michael Berlin, "Guilds in Decline? London Livery Companies and the Rise of a Liberal Economy, 1600–1800", in *Guilds, Innovation and the European Economy*, ed. Epstein and Prak, 316–41.
9. Mark Knights, "A City Revolution: The Remodelling of the London Livery Companies in the 1680s", *English Historical Review* 112, no. 449 (Nov. 1997): 1143.
10. Ian Gadd and Patrick Wallis, eds., *Guilds, Society & Economy in London, 1450–1800* (London: Centre for Metropolitan History, Univ. of London, 2002), 5.
11. The Custom of London meant that members of the livery companies could practise any trade in the City. A citizen might be free of the Tallow Chandlers by patrimony, for example, but work as a joiner or bricklayer. Company members were not always, therefore, united by their occupation.
12. Ann Rosalind Jones and Peter Stallybrass, *Renaissance Clothing and the Materials of Memory* (Cambridge Univ. Press, 2000), 6, 20.
13. See, for example, the Tallow Chandlers' Company Court Book for 13 Sept. and 18 Oct. 1666. Guildhall Library, London (hereafter GL), MS 6153/3, fols. 116r, 117v.
14. Cynthia Wall, *The Literary and Cultural Spaces of Restoration London* (Cambridge Univ. Press, 1998), 6.
15. GL MS 7090/6, 18 Sept. 1666. The Clothworkers' Account Book for that year records 8s. "paid att the Bull Inn in Bishopsgate streete when the Committee met about Rebuilding" and another payment for meeting at the "Castle Taverne in Breadstreete". See Clothworkers' Company, London (hereafter CC), CL/D/5/10, fol. 9v.
16. GL MS 3111/1, fol. 54r.
17. See, for example, the Barber-Surgeons' Account Book which notes a payment of £3 "for carrying of the Companyes goods by Porters to Moore Fields . . . and carrying thence to Holborne Bridge". Barber-Surgeons' Company, London (hereafter BC), D/2/2, Warden's Accounts, 1666–7.
18. The acquisition of barges and barge-houses began to preoccupy Courts from the early part of the century and in several instances seems to have coincided with hall-building activity. The Tallow Chandlers' procured theirs in 1668, shortly before they began re-erecting their hall after the Great Fire. See GL MS 6153/4, fol. 10r.
19. Ian Archer, "Discourses of History in Early Modern London", *Huntington Library Quarterly* 68, nos. 1–2 (2005): 205–26.
20. Gary S. De Krey, *London and the Restoration, 1659–1683* (Cambridge Univ. Press, 2005) provides the most comprehensive account of the highly complex political landscape following the restoration of monarchical government in 1660 (and the City of London's role as an arena for opposition within it).
21. Joseph Monteyne, *The Printed Image in Early Modern London: Urban Space, Visual Representation, and Social Exchange* (Aldershot: Ashgate, 2007), 140.

22. Monteyne, *Printed Image*, 140.
23. See John E. N. Hearsey, *London and the Great Fire* (London: John Murray, 1965), 181, and Michael Cooper, "*A More Beautiful City": Robert Hooke and the Rebuilding of London after the Great Fire* (Stroud: Sutton, 2003), 106.
24. GL MS 6153/3, fol. 116r.
25. GL MS 6153/3, fol. 116r.
26. T. F. Reddaway, *The Rebuilding of London after the Great Fire* (London: Jonathan Cape, 1940), 105.
27. London Metropolitan Archives (hereafter LMA), Journal of the Court of Common Council, Journal 46, 1665–9.
28. LMA, Journal 46. See also Reddaway, *Rebuilding of London*, 105.
29. The Fishmongers' Hall technically breached the first "act for the rebuilding" which prohibited building within forty feet of the river between the Tower and Temple. Special dispensation was required from Sir Christopher Wren, the King's Surveyor. In 1668, three men sympathetic to the Anglican settlement joined the Court of the Stationers' Company by order of the king and Sir Roger L'Estrange, surveyor of the imprimery, as part of a royal campaign to suppress the proliferation of seditious books and pamphlets. These Tory intruders became members of the committee for rebuilding Stationers' Hall; a project in which Charles II took a special interest.
30. As translated from the Latin in Charles Welch, *History of the Monument* (London: Corporation of the City of London, 1893), 32.
31. Bell, *Great Fire of London*, 265, Reddaway, *Rebuilding of London*, 244.
32. Samuel Rolls, *Londons Resurrection, or the Rebuilding of London Encouraged, Directed and Improved in Fifty Discourses* (London, 1668), 91.
33. Reddaway, *Rebuilding of London*, 252, 254.
34. Bell, *Great Fire of London*, 273; Reddaway, *Rebuilding of London*, 255; Stephen Porter, *The Great Fire of London* (Stroud: Sutton, 1996), 131.
35. Helen Collins, *Edward Jerman: The Metamorphosis of a Master-Craftsman, 1605–1668* (Cambridge: Lutterworth Press, 2004), 20. The glass-painter and City surveyor John Oliver, the joiner and surveyor Thomas Whiting, and the carpenter John Wildgos, are among those craftsmen who figured prominently in hall rebuilding projects. See Howard Colvin, *A Biographical Dictionary of Architects, 1600–1840*, 3rd ed. (New Haven and London: Yale Univ. Press, 1996), 714–15, 1045, 1052.
36. GL MS 6153/4, fol. 85v, 7 Oct. 1674.
37. Reddaway, *Rebuilding of London*, 183.
38. Keith Wrightson, "Degrees of People", in *English Society 1580–1680*, ed. Wrightson (London: Routledge, 2002).
39. Reddaway, *Rebuilding of London,* 250–56. The Goldsmiths, for example, lost property worth £1,000 per annum and were left with only £231 of unburnt rents: Porter, *The Great Fire of London*, 131.
40. Valerie Pearl, *London and the Outbreak of the Puritan Revolution* (Oxford Univ. Press, 1961), 75, Robert Ashton, *The City and the Court, 1603–43* (Oxford Univ. Press, 1979), 70.
41. See, for example, the Clothworkers' Company's resolution to borrow £550 to cover an additional payment for the *Loyal London* so that "His Majesty's ship" could be "ready for this sommers expedicion" in July 1666, followed by unsuccessful attempts in December of that year to reclaim a loan of £2,000 to Charles II in 1664 at "interest 6 p cent". CC CL/B/1/10, fols. 12v, 19r, 43r.
42. Precept recorded in the Court Book of the Society of Apothecaries, MS 8200/2, fol. 56r.
43. Gadd and Wallis, *Guilds, Society & Economy in London*, 12. See also N. G. Brett-James, *The Growth of Stuart London* (London: London and Middlesex Archaeological Society, 1935).
44. William Herbert, *The History of the Twelve Great Livery Companies of London* (London, 1834), 176.
45. The figures as identified in the key of a print representing Cibber's work made by John Bowles around 1676 (British Museum Crace Collection).
46. De Krey, *London and the Restoration*, 69.

47. GL MS 5445/20, fol. 21r.
48. The College of Arms took the decision to rebuild its premises just to the south of St Paul's on St Benet's Hill in 1670 after several livery halls were already rebuilt. The king gave the heralds a commission to collect donations from armigerous families towards the estimated £5,000 cost. In the end, however, only £700 was collected this way and building was not finished until 1688. See Mark Noble, *History of the College of Arms* (London: Printed for J. Debrett and T. Egerton, 1804), 269, and Walter H. Godfrey and Anthony Wagner, *An Account of the College of Arms in Queen Victoria Street* (London: London Survey Committee, 1963), 11–15.
49. GL MS 6153/4, fol. 37v.
50. CC CL/B/1/10, fol. 45r.
51. LMA, Repertory of the Court of Aldermen, COL/CA/01/01/077, fol. 24r, J. R. Woodhead, *The Rulers of London, 1660–1689: A Biographical Record of the Aldermen and Common Councilmen of the City of London* (London: London and Middlesex Archaeological Society, 1965), 75.
52. CC CL/B/1/10, fol. 65r, 6 Aug. 1667. For other examples of strategic artistic and architectural patronage by City grandees in the period, see Mireille Galinou, ed., *City Merchants and the Arts, 1670–1720* (London: Corporation of London, 2004).
53. The Blacksmiths rebuilt for the frugal amount of £2,100 while the Drapers, one of the Great Twelve, spent £13,000; analysis of more than twenty companies' accounts suggests £5,000 was a more typical sum.
54. John Strype, *A Survey of the Cities of London and Westminster* (London, 1720), 1, 227.
55. GL MS 5502, "The Accompt of Receipts & Payments relateing to the building of Brewers Hall" for Dec. 1669–Jan. 1673/4 records the final "discharge" as £5,673 16s. 6d.
56. GL MS 5445/20, fol. 8r, 22 Nov. 1666, fol. 10v, 19 Dec. 1666; Woodhead, *Rulers of London*, 156. Starling, Alderman of Portsoken Ward, translated to the Drapers' Company from the Brewers' Company in 1668 and became Lord Mayor in 1669. He had been Master of the Brewers' Company in 1661. A staunch Tory, the MS *Account of Alderman* of 1672 describes Starling as a vigorous persecutor of "phanatics".
57. GL MS 5445/20, fol. 242r, 8 March 1669/70.
58. GL MS 5445/21, fol. 131r, 4 Dec. 1672.
59. GL MS 5445/20, fol. 36v, 6 Dec. 1671.
60. Woodhead, *Rulers of London*, 147. Alderman Sheldon, another Tory who did "passionately love" the king's interest, served with Starling on the Court of Aldermen's committee for public works after the fire. He was Master of the Tallow Chandlers in 1667 and, like Starling, translated to the Drapers' Company ahead of his mayoralty in 1676. Sheldon also paid for the parlour of his adopted company hall to be wainscotted.
61. GL MS 6221, MS 6153/4, fol. 5r, 29 April 1668.
62. L. H. Cust, "Morgan, Sylvanus (1620–1693)", rev. Colin Lee, *Oxford Dictionary of National Biography* (Oxford Univ. Press, 2004), http://www.oxforddnb.com/view/article/19235.
63. Ian Gadd, "Early Modern Printed Histories of the London Livery Companies", in *Guilds, Society & Economy*, ed. Gadd and Wallis, 42.
64. Gadd, "Early Modern Printed Histories", 42.
65. Andrew Hopper, "Honour, Reputation, and the Self-fashioning of Elite Side-changers", in *Turncoats and Renegadoes: Changing Sides during the English Civil Wars*, ed. Hopper (Oxford Univ. Press, 2012).
66. Susan E. Whyman, "Land and Trade Revisited: The Case of John Verney, London Merchant and Baronet, 1660–1720", *London Journal* 22, no. 1 (1997): 16, Galinou, *City Merchants and the Arts*, xi.
67. Thomas Hobbes, *Leviathan or the Matter, Forme, and Power of a Commonwealth. Ecclesiasticall and Civill* (London, 1651), 1: 10.
68. Craig Muldrew, *The Economy of Obligation: The Culture of Credit and Social Relations in Early Modern England* (London: Macmillan, 1998), 156.
69. GL MS 5445/20, fol. 326r.
70. Muldrew, *Economy of Obligation*, 149, 151–52.
71. On kinds of capital and the relationship between credit and reputation, see also Wrightson, *Earthly Necessities*, 300–1.

72. On demarcation disputes between the Carpenters and Joiners, for example, see Jasper Ridley, *A History of the Carpenters' Company* (London: Carpenters' Hall, 1995), 61–62.
73. GL MS 7151/1, 1 Feb. 1660/1, fol. 414r.
74. CC CL/D/5/10, fol. 9v.
75. British Library, London, M985/45, 5 Aug. 1672.
76. GL MS 6153/4, fol. 54r, 30 Oct. 1671.
77. GL MS 15201/5, fol. 263v, 17 June 1675.
78. GL MS 7090/6, 11 Aug. 1670; my italics.
79. Alexander Nagel and Christopher S. Wood, "Interventions: Towards a New Model of Renaissance Anachronism", *Art Bulletin* 87, no. 3 (2005): 405.
80. John Summerson, *Architecture in Britain, 1530–1830*, 9th ed. (New Haven and London: Yale Univ. Press, 1993), 190.
81. Summerson, *Architecture in Britain*, 142–44.
82. See, for example, Lee Prosser, "Kew Palace: A Seventeenth-century Villa Rediscovered", *Transactions of the Ancient Monuments Society* 51 (2007): 25. Prosser sticks to the term though uses it in a more neutral, less pejorative sense: "Artisan Mannerism was by its very nature individualistic, excessive, and not subject particularly to rules that we can readily delineate."
83. Summerson, *Architecture in Britain*, 190.
84. Summerson, *Georgian London*, 43–44, Summerson, *Architecture in Britain*, 151, 188.
85. Summerson, *Georgian London*, 44.
86. Elizabeth V. Chew, "'A Mockery of the Surveyor's Style'? Alternatives to Inigo Jones in Seventeenth-century Elite British Architecture", in *Articulating British Classicism: New Approaches to Eighteenth-century Architecture*, ed. Barbara Arciszewska and Elizabeth McKellar (Aldershot: Ashgate, 2004), 65.
87. Chew, "Mockery of the Surveyor's Style", 80.
88. J. Mordaunt Crook, *The Dilemma of Style: Architectural Ideas from the Picturesque to the Post-Modern* (London: John Murray, 1987), 11.
89. On the difficulties associated with fixing an iconography of architectural style in seventeenth-century England, see Christine Stevenson, *The City and the King: Architecture and Politics in Restoration London* (New Haven and London: Yale Univ. Press, 2013), 53.
90. Stevenson, *City and the King*, 177.
91. For "curious" we should understand fine, delicate, skilled, exquisite, choice, and excellent.
92. The hall was a room or range as well as a description of the overall hall complex, which contained many other rooms besides (typically a parlour, Court room, armory, kitchen, and beadle's office and accommodation).
93. GL MS 15201/5, fol. 165r, 20 Feb. 1672/3.
94. Edward Hatton, A *New View of London: Or an Ample Account of that City* (London, 1708), 621. The Vintners adorned their three-sided hall with a stone balustrade from York House, home of the Dukes of Buckingham on the Strand, purchased in early 1674 as that building was demolished. The Court of Assistants spent 5d. per foot on the "railes and bannisters" which, they decided, would "bee proper for the coapeing of the front walles". See GL MS 15201/5, fol. 209v, 29 Jan. 1673/4.
95. Strype, *Survey*, 1: 235.
96. Such devices were popularized by the publisher Robert Pricke's folio volumes of engraved ornament, including *The Ornaments of Architecture* (London, 1674). See Eileen Harris, *British Architectural Books and Writers, 1556–1785* (Cambridge Univ. Press, 1990), 36, 380.
97. Stevenson, *City and the King*, 28.
98. Strype, *Survey*, 1: 235.
99. For further discussion of this hybrid window type common to a number of the post-fire halls and to urban vernacular architecture of this period more generally, see Howard Colvin, "Thorpe Hall and its Architect", in *Essays in English Architectural History*, ed. Colvin (New Haven and London: Yale Univ. Press, 1999), 164.

100. Wainscot is mentioned in nearly all of Hatton's hall accounts and sometimes dwelt on for longer than any other single element of the building, as in his entry for Vintners' Hall in *New View*, 621, which notes "the Walls richly Wainscotted with right Wainscot enrich'd with Fruit Leaves, & c. finely carved, as is more especially the noble Screen at the E. end".
101. Symes appears to have been free of the Tallow Chandlers' Company rather than the Joiners' Company. GL MS 6153/4, fol. 79r, 9 July 1674.
102. GL MS 6153/4, fol. 77r, 10 Dec. 1673.
103. GL MS 5502, "Deed of Articles with John Symes, Joiner, for wainscotting the Hall, October 1672".
104. Hatton, *New View*, 610.
105. For William Cleare or Cleere, see Colvin, *Biographical Dictionary*, 252; G. W. Beard, *Craftsmen and Interior Decoration in England, 1660–1820* (New York: Holmes & Meier, 1981), 251; and Pete Smith, "William Cleere, Master Joiner", *The Georgian Group Journal* 18 (2010): 8–34.
106. Christine Stevenson, "Buildings and the Body", in *The Oxford Companion to the Body*, ed. Colin Blakemore and Sheila Jennett (Oxford Univ. Press, 2001), 128.
107. Patricia Fortini Brown, "Honor and Necessity: The Dynamics of Patronage in the Confraternities of Renaissance Venice", *Studi veneziani* 14 (1987): 183–84. See also David Thomson, *Renaissance Architecture: Critics, Patrons, Luxury* (Manchester and New York: Manchester University Press, 1993).
108. Fortini Brown, "Honor and Necessity", 183–84.
109. John Evelyn, *An Account of Architects and Architecture, in an Historical and Etymological Explanation of Certain Tearms particularly Affected by Architects; with Leon Baptista Alberti's Treatise Of Statues, by John Evelyn, Esq.* (London, 1664), 120.

Fashioning and Furnishing for Performance: The Rise and Fall of the State Bedchamber in the English Royal Palace

Sebastian Edwards

INTRODUCTION: THE FIRST STATE BEDCHAMBERS OF CHARLES II

IF IT IS axiomatic for the period covered by these studies that enormous social and political shifts were the catalyst for great changes in the arts, then we might expect to see some of the greatest effect on the spaces created for the monarchs of the period. This essay considers the space and domestic object most intimately associated with the royal person: the state bedchamber and its great bed, during a time when this domestic setting became the focus of the royal palace and when the forms of personal rule displayed there were being questioned in the decades leading up to the "Glorious Revolution" of 1688.

There has been a great deal of revisionist thought in the related areas of seventeenth- and eighteenth-century court history, which can be drawn on to help understand the substantial change that occurred in the state bedchamber, a crucial aspect of the royal court. This essay benefits from recent studies in political biography, material culture, social and domestic history, and, in particular, the relatively new subject area of court studies, which have hugely expanded our understanding of this era.[1] It also draws upon the great wealth of unpublished archival material associated with the late Stuart and early Hanoverian palaces from the records of the Royal Wardrobe and Office of Works, which has yet to be explored systematically. It also engages with modern scholarly debates on the exchange of influences and ideas between the city palaces and the great houses of the leading courtiers, which held a mirror up to the royal court and on occasion even exceeded the splendour of the king's residences.

Unlike more portable works of art, the survival rate for these complex decorative interiors and spaces is very low. No royal state bedchambers created before 1688 remain intact, while only a handful of royal beds survive, which may explain the relative paucity of reliable studies in this area until recently. To give some sense of the significance of this single aspect of the royal household in terms of expenditure, it is notable that during the reign of Charles II alone (1660–85) well over fifty royal beds were commissioned and about twenty bedchambers either built or remodelled.[2] Although none of the English monarchs of the period had much opportunity to build anew on the ambitious scale of their European, absolutist rivals, Charles II and James II could each choose from a number of palaces and houses in which to live and in which to perform the different aspects of their royal duties: governmental business, ambassadorial receptions, greeting their people, familial events, or sporting pursuits. The two monarchs also decided where to sleep and to meet their court, and regularly did so on the basis of personal preference or historical accident (such as the devastating fire at Whitehall in 1698) rather than simply following tradition.

The desire to create new state apartments with a new form of bedchamber at their heart, in which the monarch could hold more personal audiences, had its origins in the courts of late sixteenth-century France and their later imitators, which were created for absolute monarchs who, like the later Stuarts, needed to reassert their personal power. This progression from an essentially late medieval form of bedchamber saw the space becoming characterized by a location at the end of a sequence of state rooms and by larger dimensions, improved security, and an increasingly sizeable and magnificent bed: all indications of a greater and more formal access to a previously private space. When these state bedchambers first appeared in France or other northern European states is not entirely clear, but they still seem to be relatively uncommon even in Paris until Louis XIV reached his majority at the end of the 1650s.[3] Beyond the royal palaces themselves, the arrangement of these apartments also became highly influential upon the architectural planning of high-ranking courtiers' country houses in England and Scotland. The Tudor practice of regular court progresses, during which whole households were expected to be handed over to royal guests, had been succeeded during the early seventeenth century by the equally or sometimes more costly provision of one or even two royal apartments. From the 1660s onwards, up and down the country courtier-houses contained magnificent, but empty, bedchambers, which rarely, if ever, received a visit from the king or queen to justify their great expense.

THE STATE BEDCHAMBER: NEW FORM AND FUNCTION

When King Charles II arrived back in England after the Interregnum, ambitious to establish his reign and bringing with him the latest French fashions, from his pencil-moustache to the rituals of the *Grand Lever* and *Coucher* (the formal ceremonial rising and retiring), the prospects for radically reforming the royal bedchamber were limited because of the political demands on his time and a much depleted treasury.[4] The principal palace from which he would assert his rule was Whitehall, the rambling and largely Tudor complex of Henry VIII and Elizabeth I, where the trappings of power within had of course been dispersed during the Interregnum.[5]

Charles II quickly set about creating a new state bedchamber based on models from France and the Hague, which he knew well from his time in exile during the 1650s.[6] The essential architectural and decorative language of these early state bedchambers (known as "chambres de parade" in France), which were separated from the monarch's sleeping lodgings close by, comprised several key elements: a markedly large room in a prominent position that was connected to preceding receiving-chambers by at least one ante room; a canopied (or "tester") bed, placed opposite the room's formal entrance; the physical separation of the bed from the main room space, which was achieved with a bed alcove, a balustrade, or both; doorways at the bed-end of the room leading to private closets, or often a small oratory; and significantly, the presence of high-status figural and architectural decoration with which to emphasize the importance of the room's occupant.

At the heart of this space, the state bed itself derived from a successful model that had developed from the middle of the sixteenth century, when luxury textiles began to become the defining characteristic of beds described in royal inventories.[7] Rich plain velvet, ornamented with gold and silver "lace" or embroidered with metal thread, occurs repeatedly in Charles's many orders for new beds. The form of the bed—a tall, box-like four-poster with a headcloth and curtains all round, and valances (short hangings) above and below the curtains—had not changed at all from the beds of Charles I, some of which his son found remaining at Hampton Court Palace, where they had been retained for Cromwell's own use.[8] The new state beds required by the restored king also conformed to precedent in their well-established choices of colour, with crimson or green beds predominating in the royal warrants. What mattered at this crucial time was that the state bed presented the king in a magnificent setting that once more reflected on the royal person, his clothes, and personal belongings. At the Restoration, continuity of form and materials appear to have been more important than fashion.

All of Charles II's bedchambers and probably most of the beds at Whitehall, including the rebuildings that had taken place during his reign, were destroyed in the devastating fire of 1698 that ended the palace's life as the principal administrative centre for the monarchy. Without the benefit of any contemporary visual records or detailed first-hand descriptions, nor indeed any inventory of contents apart from a list of the paintings, their layout and appearance have been specula-

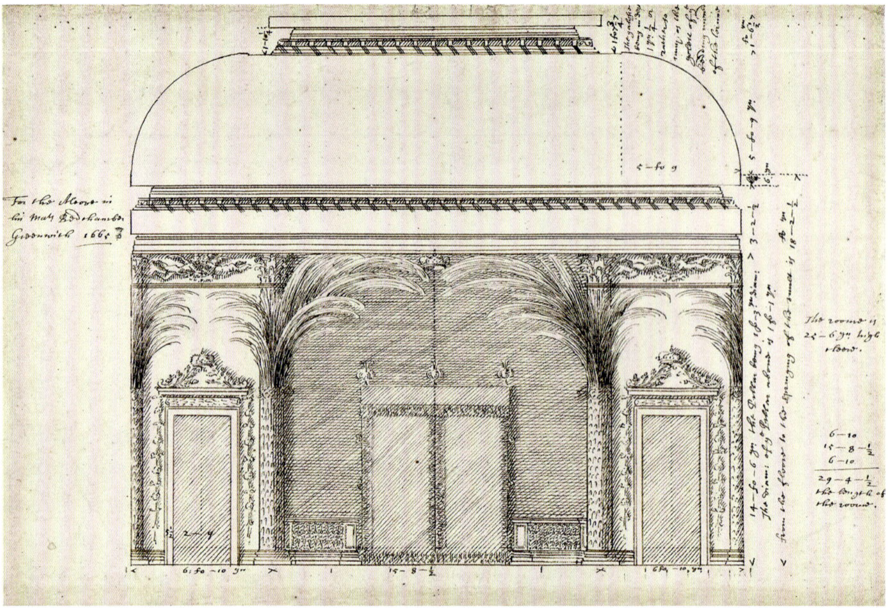

27. John Webb, Design for Charles II's alcove bedchamber in the new palace at Greenwich, London, ca. 1666, drawing, 11½ x 17⅛ in. (29 x 43.5 cm). Royal Institute of British Architects, London

tively reconstructed by Simon Thurley and Anna Keay.[9] One of the things that this makes clear is that almost immediately after the Restoration, the king refitted the existing bedchamber with the first known alcove in this country, which, it has been noted, was similar to a surviving design published by Inigo Jones's former assistant John Webb for a projected new palace at Greenwich (fig. 27). This space was abandoned as an empty shell by the end of the 1660s.[10] The new bedchamber at Whitehall was of slightly smaller dimensions, with an alcove nineteen feet wide and twelve feet deep (5.9 x 3.6 m), and we can assume that the chamber itself was proportionately larger to accommodate the king's "company", consisting of bedchamber staff, ministers, and invited guests who came to meet him at his rising or retiring. There were two doors leading to closets on either side of the bed: these created the alcove, and the floor here was raised to form a dais like the one under the Cloth of Estate in the Presence Chamber, the preceding royal chamber, which by tradition was used to affirm the status of the king and to delineate his personal space. Etiquette, in the form of well-established household ordinances, which were regularly reissued and revised from reign to reign, were used to ensure that the behaviour of those present respected the king's body within these spaces. At Whitehall, the clear separation of the bed and the "royal body" on display was given

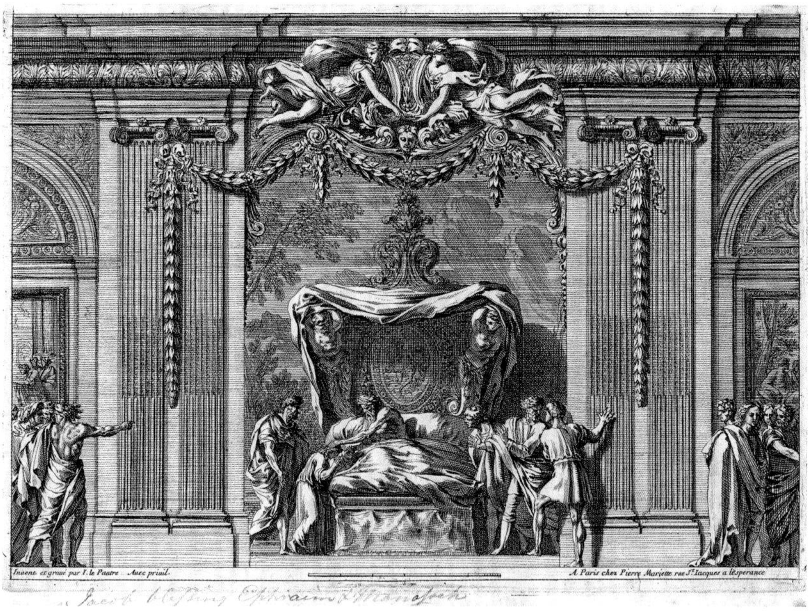

28. Jean Le Pautre, *Design for a Bed Alcove, Paris*, ca. 1650, etching, 5¼ x 7½ in. (13.4 x 19.3 cm). British Museum, London

greater emphasis by two further features: the alcove's parquet floor, a luxurious feature rarely found in England, where the use of matting on floors still prevailed, and a bed rail or "balustrade".[11]

Webb's unexecuted design for the bedchamber at Greenwich was, if not quite fantasy, beyond Charles's means. This featured a highly original carved palm tree alcove, which was a hubristic allusion to the Temple of Solomon in this secular space.[12] However, the first alcove built at Whitehall was much more in keeping with contemporary European designs, which were being circulated by that time.[13] The Office of Works accounts for the room describe a feature similar to those found in influential interiors such as those made by Jean Le Pautre in France from the 1650s, which were imported and even occasionally republished in England (fig. 28). Furthermore, Charles and his entourage, some of whom had accompanied him into exile, would have had first-hand experience of such models in Paris, encountered when he stayed at the Palais du Louvre in the company of the young Louis XIV after the unrest of the Fronde in 1652.[14] Early in 1661, William Dickson, the principal carver, was paid £40 for making "two great draperies with two flying boys . . . holding up the drapery before his Majesty's Alcove . . . with the two great Eagles and a Shield with a head upon it".[15] There was also a carved oak tree above

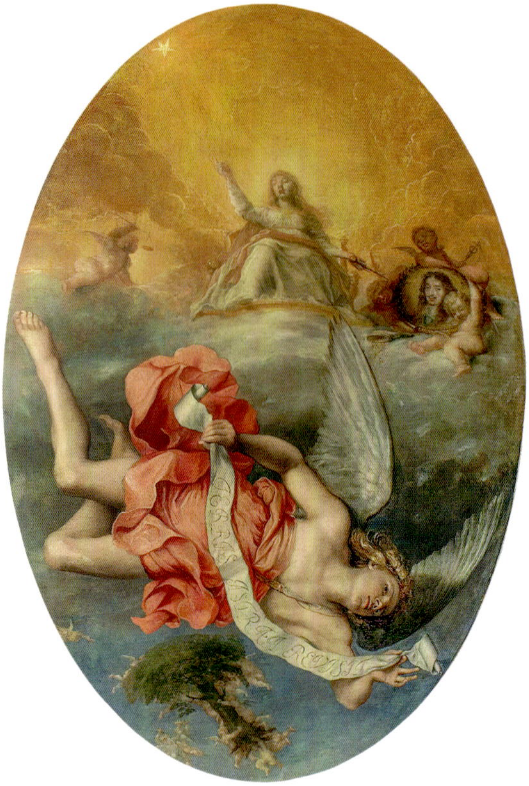

29. John Michael Wright, *Astraea Returns to Earth* (Charles II's Restoration) from the King's Bedchamber ceiling, Whitehall Palace, ca. 1662, 90 x 56 in. (228.6 x 142.2 cm). Nottingham City Museums and Galleries

the alcove, a reference to Charles's dashing escape at the Battle of Worcester when he hid in the celebrated oak tree at Boscobel House, a story that soon became an important feature of his personal iconography. This archetypal royal symbol of strength and renewal was also prominently featured in John Michael Wright's ceiling painting of Astraea heralding the king's new Golden Age, which remarkably survived the fire (fig. 29).

THE BEDCHAMBER AS A STAGE

A telling comparison can be made between the design of the king's new bed alcoves, used to present the king at the commencement of his *lever*, and contemporary designs for his theatre's proscenium, the first new royal theatre to be built since the Restoration (fig. 30). Both share the same square framing device over a raised stage, surmounted by royal arms which are supported by angels or putti,

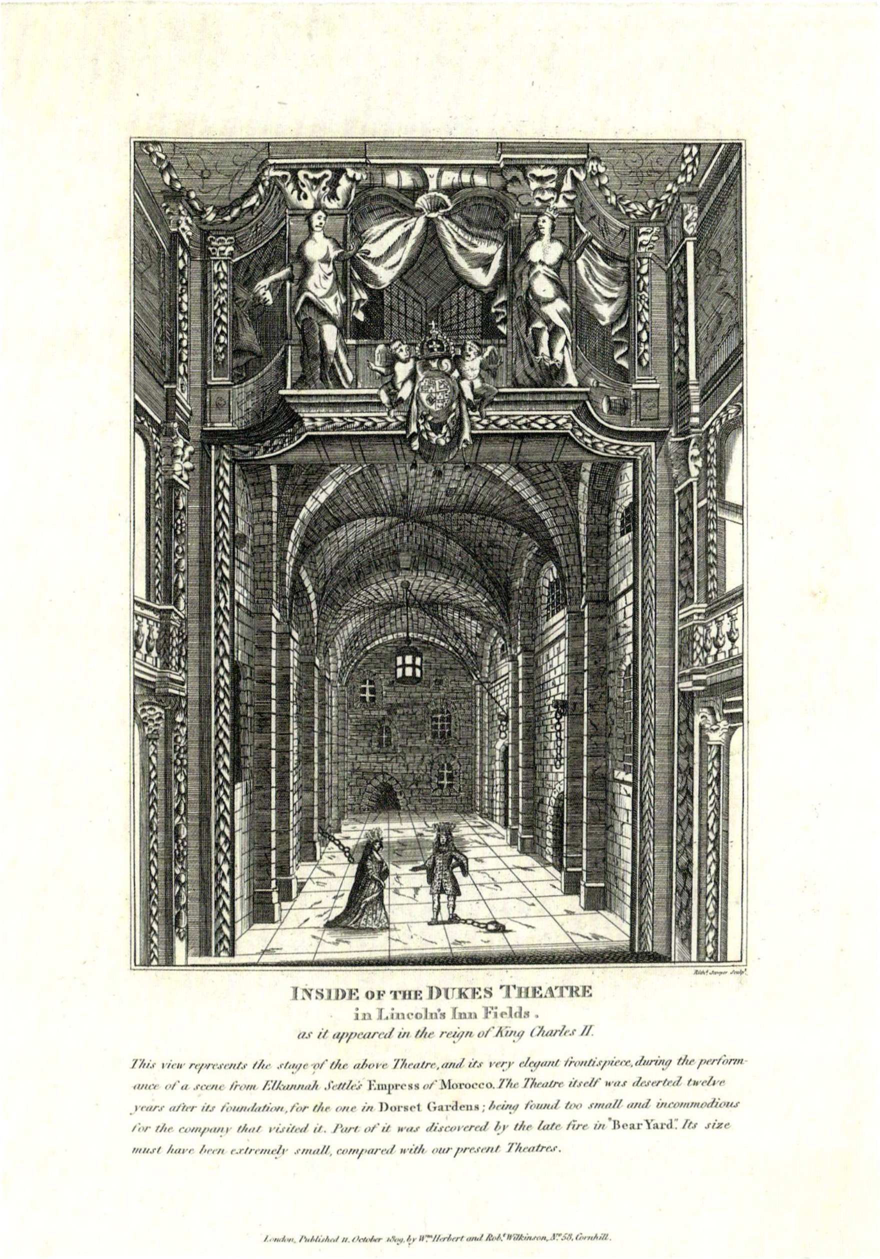

30. William Sawyer, *Inside of the Duke's Theatre in Lincoln's Inn Fields*, ca. 18th century, engraving, 11⅞ x 8⅜ in. (30.1 x 21.4 cm). Victoria & Albert Museum, London. This rare image of a Restoration royal stage is engraved after an earlier print representing a performance of "The Empress of Morocco" of 1673.

tied-back curtains or drapery—in the one case often sculpted, in the other actual—and doors set forward on each side for either the monarch's retreat to his closets in the bedchamber or the actors' entrance on to the forestage.[16] These similarities are perhaps serendipitous but it should be remembered that Charles's bedchamber and the official royal theatre, The King's Theatre, which was newly established after the Restoration, were intimately connected in more ways than one. His theatre manager and playwright, Thomas Killigrew, was an old companion from exile and had been made a Groom of the Bedchamber. Furthermore, the dramatist and infamous friend of the king, the Earl of Rochester, was given the senior position of Gentleman of the Bedchamber; two of the king's mistresses were chosen from among the first professional actresses; and the Master Carpenter of the King's Works, John Davenport, also worked on the new King's Theatre in Drury Lane in 1661. This blurring of lines between publicly staged dramas and ceremony at court can be traced back further to the court masques of Charles I, where the king and his family were both audience and participants at the same time. Some of the creators of those performances like Davenport (ca. 1593–1668) were still employed by the new king after the Restoration, although this very individual art form had been transformed into a much more passive spectacle.[17] While the English king's actual *lever* never developed into a fully delineated ceremony, with a pattern of ritualistic phases not dissimilar to the scenes in a performance—as happened at the court of Louis XIV—it did include theatrical elements, which fit in with the notion of a "stage".[18] From the king's bedchamber curtains being drawn in the morning, to the human chain of bedchamber staff who delivered and put on his clothes, and to the gilt ewer held up for him to wash his hands, there was a strongly theatrical, at points almost liturgical aspect to this daily performance.

The second new feature in Charles II's bedchamber was the bed rail, which served to protect the bed, and by extension the royal body itself, from the surrounding company. These are not known to have been used by either James I or Charles I before the Restoration, although they were associated with Charles I's queen, Henrietta Maria, who had first-hand experience of them during her early years in France.[19] These elaborate barriers, decorated with gold or silver leaf (silver being often used for the queen), were entered through a pair of gates. This offered a parallel to the way that, in a more overtly religious context, a priest approached the Host on the altar. Indeed the design of such bed rails shared much in common with the rails protecting church altars. This may well have been a conscious adaptation of church ceremonial and liturgical furniture, given the quasi-divine status of the king's body that was upheld by most Roman Catholic monarchs of the time, including Charles II and his brother James.[20] It should also be borne in mind that private prayer was a daily practice in most bedchambers, and though largely unremarked on by visitors to the English court, was observed as an integral part of the French ritual at the very start and end of the day.[21]

The bed rail was almost exclusively a royal feature in England, with a few notable exceptions in the houses of ambitious courtiers who were very close to the monarch.[22] According to custom, it enclosed a pair of armchairs and a set of "back stools" for guests, a contemporary term that emphasized their lower status. Apart from the senior body servants, there are scant references to even the most honoured guest actually entering this most intimate space alongside the king, although it may have been more commonplace according to personal preference. The monarch would occupy the bed alcove or, *ruelle* as it was called in France, in a state of undress, aided by his gentlemen and grooms of the bedchamber. This moment in the *lever* marked his transformation, as he changed from the human and vulnerable "body natural" in nightshift, to his vest and hose, and began to assume the guise of the spiritual and durable "body politic", resplendent in silks and gold trimmings that were the equal in magnificence to his richly appointed furnishings.[23] Sir John Reresby recalled the intimate morning and evening ceremonies that took place in such surroundings: "I was at the King's going to bed. There were but four present . . . he was that night two hours putting off his clothes, and it was halfe an hour past one before he went to bed."[24]

IMAGERY AND MESSAGE IN THE STATE BEDCHAMBER

When it came to employing representational art in the bedchamber, Charles's choice for Whitehall of a blatantly triumphalist and politically charged ceiling painting, with the subject of Astraea, Greek goddess of justice, heralding a new Golden Age, added to the setting's sense of drama (see fig. 29). This aerial but rather literal vision of Charles's Restoration may well have appealed to the theatre-loving members of the king's close retinue who were familiar with the elaborate "deus ex machina" which continued in use as one legacy of the genius of Inigo Jones's pre-Commonwealth masques. It is probable that Charles took a close interest in the choice of imagery around him at court, and this extraordinary composition, which merges conventional classical iconography with this king's highly personal imagery, may also have evoked Rubens's expansive, heavenly image of *The Apotheosis of James I* in the nearby Banqueting House, thus providing another continuity with the spaces used by the king's father.[25] The choice of ceiling painting in this more personal space is far more overtly political than his father's commemoration of James I's achievements. Wright's painting also prefigured Charles's long-term patronage of Antonio Verrio (see Richard Johns's essay in this volume), who would further develop a very personal, though sometimes loosely programmed iconography in the mural paintings for Windsor Castle, where the new state bedchamber in the building campaign of 1674–8 provided the culmination of a series of painted ceilings depicting the Four Continents, led by the figure of France, offering their riches to a god-like King Charles. The choice of this highly optimistic scene for his state bedchamber supported the king's need to assert his personal opposition to the French after his previous disastrous alliance with them against the Dutch.

The king's choice of easel paintings for the spaces in which he wielded most personal control was another opportunity to provide such performative spaces with narratives that could be read by those present. The inventory of paintings at Whitehall made early in his reign around 1666 provides the only detailed view of how Charles personally supervised the hanging of his bedchamber.[26] This picture hang consisted of portraits of members of the king's immediate family, a number of which are ascribed to Anthony van Dyck, along with that artist's late masterpiece, *Cupid and Psyche* (Royal Collection), which almost certainly hung over the chimney piece. At Whitehall the modish approach of hanging a collection of paintings on crimson damask in the bedchamber, rather than the more familiar use of history tapestries, must only have drawn attention to the very personal message the king wished to convey in this room.

As for the beds themselves, it has been noted by Keay that Charles II did conduct a genuine *coucher* in the evening on a regular basis, and slept in his great bed on occasions, rather than retiring to the privy bedchamber—another innovation at the Restoration court.[27] He seems to have preferred to commission and install a conventional "French bed" in several of his bedchambers, a contemporary term which could refer to its box-shape but also to the lavishly upholstered four-poster beds occasionally imported from France, such as those supplied by Jean Peyrard in 1671 and 1673.[28] However, the Royal Wardrobe accounts show that this was not invariably the case, especially in the creation of private beds or the field beds used on royal progresses. To give one example from many, for his new privy lodgings at Whitehall in 1677, Charles chose a striking sky-blue, gold, and black velvet bed, lined with cherry-colour satin. To complete this vibrantly sensuous effect, this intimate room also had songbirds in cages.[29]

James II's short reign brought no real departures in either the use or display of his bedchambers. As Duke of York, he had lavishly entertained his own court at his brother's expense in his own well-appointed apartments and had shared Charles's royal craftsmen and suppliers. If anything, he leaned more towards the absolutist French court than Charles, and had no need to reset the stage that he inherited. Little did he know that he would soon be enjoying these French fashions

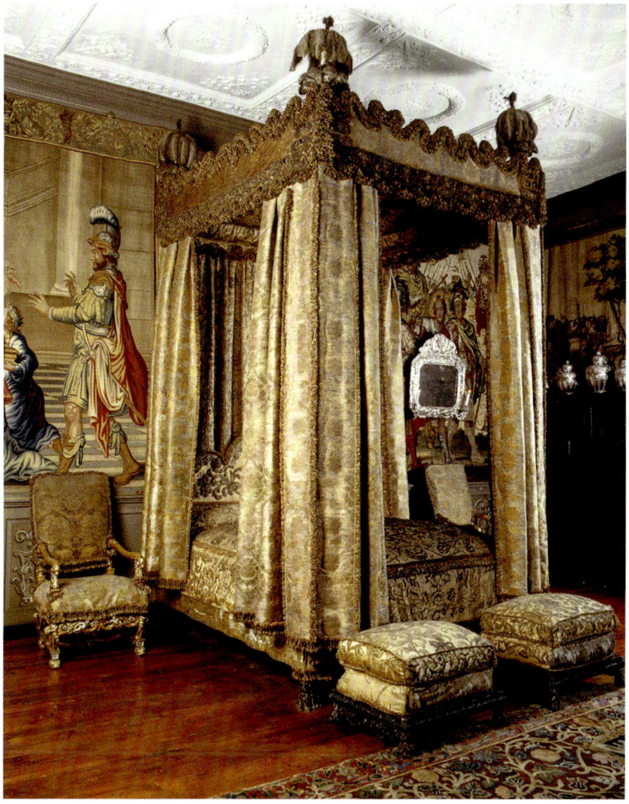

31. "King's bed" made for the Duke of York, now at Knole, ca. 1673, with wood, gold and silver thread, 90⅝ x 84⅛ in. (230 x 214 cm). National Trust Kent, UK

at first-hand once more.[30] James's II's most relevant legacy is a couple of rare, surviving royal state beds, which give a real sense of the richness and extravagance of the materials used in the most important bedchambers, where the upholstery could often be worth more than the silver plate or paintings. The finer of the two is the magnificent "King's bed" hung with gold and silver lampas, which was later displayed as a Lord Chamberlain's perquisite at Knole in Kent. This was ordered by James around 1673, perhaps as his marriage bed at St James's Palace (fig. 31).[31]

THE LATER STUARTS: REACTION AND CONTINUITY

Greater changes in both the appearance and the use of the royal bedchamber followed the dynastic rupture of the 1688 revolution and the arrival on the throne of a very different Stuart king, William III. Although he is often characterized as being dour and introverted with no taste for pomp, in contrast to his uncle

Charles II, we should not overlook the fact that he was brought up with the expectation of reuniting his princely House of Nassau with the governing position of Stadholder in the United Provinces, and therefore had long held aspirations to rule as a monarch within a republic. He also appreciated and understood the new court style of his enemy, Louis XIV, and was prepared to employ leading French architects like Daniel Marot to help design his palaces in the latest style. Ironically, following the "Glorious Revolution", William was given considerable opportunities to build on a scale denied to his more ambitious predecessors, even though he was far more accountable to Parliament as effectively an elected king.[32]

William, with his co-ruler Mary, decided to rebuild their country palaces, rather than live at Whitehall, which was too public a place for their needs. In the state apartments at Hampton Court we can see the ideal palace that he and Mary developed with the most progressive architects of their generation, Christopher Wren, Nicholas Hawksmoor, and William Talman. It has been noted how little the actual layout of the completely new state apartment had developed since the time of Henry VIII, the only significant new space being the intermediary Withdrawing Room, which had been introduced by the early Stuarts as a last resort before admitting more people into the bedchamber.[33] William's most important innovation was to make the King's Great Bedchamber a much larger room, with the Little Bedchamber and Gentlemen of the Bedchamber's room conveniently placed immediately adjacent, providing the king with access to the privy lodgings beyond, instead of the warren of subsidiary rooms that sprawled at Whitehall (fig. 32). The bed alcove—with all of its associations with personal rule—was rejected as an impractical experiment in English kingship, and although there remained a bed rail, it was of a relatively new form. Here it was a kind of fence made from leaves carved of cedar wood inset with gilt wire, which could be readily dismantled and stored. This design suggests it was intended for occasional ceremonial use, which would have suited William, as he was only prepared to put up with English formality when it was demanded of him.[34] Around the same time as he was completing this apartment at the turn of the century, Louis XIV was also about to move, and greatly enlarged his own state bedchamber at Versailles, placing it at the very centre of his vast palace.[35] This was done in order to accommodate the great crowds who attended him daily. He too eschewed the more limited space of the deep bed alcove in favour of a rail across the room, but for quite different reasons.[36] In contrast to Louis's busy *levers*, which required two sessions, scant references remain as to how William III used his bedchambers. Of course, lack of evidence for the mundane routines of courtly life should not be accepted as lack of proof that they took place, but it would seem that William was uncomfortable with the personalized ceremony of his predecessors. The new king did however, on

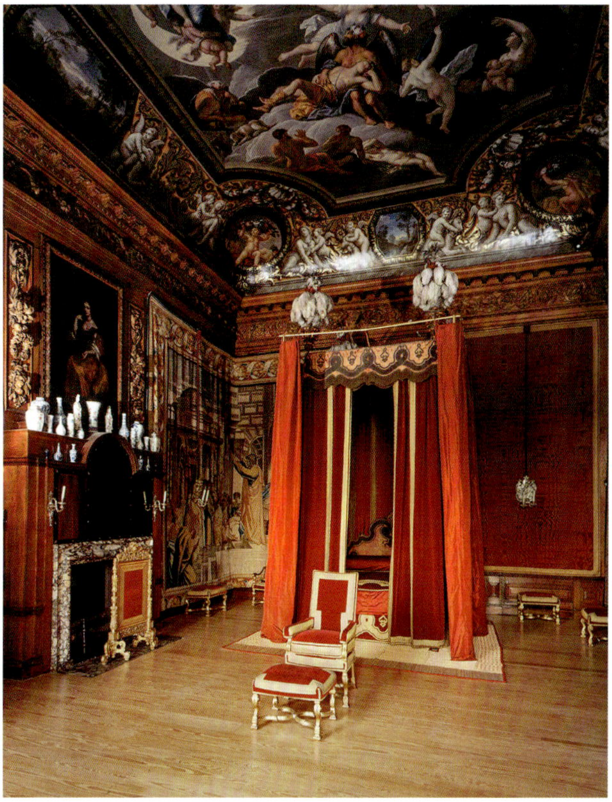

32. William III's Great Bedchamber and State bed. Hampton Court Palace, Historic Royal Palaces

occasion, receive important visitors in his bedchamber, such as the French minister Count Tallard, who recalled how he "arrived at Newmarket . . . and went to the King of England's lever. I approached him when he had finished undressing, and . . . still ventured to ask him for an audience."[37] However, it seems clear from various contemporary sources that the need for a highly staged audience in the bedchamber was already beginning to wane, as power shifted to the Council Chamber and ultimately to the Palace of Westminster.

In rejecting the stage-like setting of the bed alcove and balustrade, William was returning to a much simpler use of his bedchamber, more akin to the time of Charles I, but with one key difference: his large room was decorated with more personal imagery and possessions aimed at a larger and perhaps less public audience. The ceiling was painted by Antonio Verrio with the story of *Diana and Endymion*, and the choice of other objects for the room appears quite individual and non-political in comparison to those of Charles and James. The painted scene of the Moon goddess's doomed love for a mortal must surely refer to the king's recently deceased and much-loved queen, Mary, who had been painted as a young princess by Peter Lely in the same persona. This probably also explains the choice of his mother-in-law, Anne Hyde, for the subject of the only easel painting in the room, which avoided any politically charged portraits of his predecessors, or else the religious subjects, which would have inflammatory associations for most Protestants. In another return to more conventional decoration in the bedchamber, William hung the walls with tapestries and selected the Old Testament story of Joshua from Henry VIII's fine set: a safe choice, but one which also affirmed his success as a military leader, as found in so much of the imagery around his palaces. More advanced taste was displayed around the hearth, the second social focus of a bedchamber, where the monarch could invite an important guest to sit with him in comfort. Here the king displayed shelves of Chinese and Japanese export porcelain from Queen Mary's collection in a very Dutch manner. This was an art form in which the king himself took no great aesthetic interest; perhaps this too can be regarded as part of this bedchamber's covert function as a highly personal memorial to his queen.[38]

THE ROYAL BEDCHAMBER: KING AND COURTIERS

One of the possible explanations for this change in pattern of use and display may have been William's upbringing in the much smaller and more informal Dutch court. Equally significantly, he was an active soldier-king who spent even more time abroad during his short reign than George I would do in Hanover. This meant that he actually spent very little time getting to know his adopted country. William's knowledge of England and his English courtiers' great houses was therefore quite limited, and yet he seems to have assimilated the fashions of his new country quite readily. Until her death in 1694, this was largely due to Queen Mary's management of their households (where she exercised her own very individual taste in her private bedchambers). However, in October 1695 William decided to make his first—and only—progress to celebrate victory over Louis at the Siege of Namur, and to gain much-needed support in a forthcoming general election. During a six-week tour of central England he inspected several of the Whig nobility as they were completing their new houses or rebuilding their ancestral homes. The royal progress included a visit to his former French ambassador and then current Master of the King's Wardrobe, the Earl of Montagu, at Boughton, Northamptonshire. Montagu showed the king around his barely finished state apartment and the king was reported to reply in his typically down-to-earth manner that, "twas not too good for One to set ones Heart on any of them, for neither He nor his lordship should be there in Forty years to see them."[39] The house was incomplete, and Louis Chéron's ceiling paintings may not have been very far advanced; however, this and other stops on the tour—including great Baroque houses such as Welbeck and Burghley—clearly influenced the style and arrangement of the king's new apartments at Kensington and at those completed at Hampton Court six years later. The accounts of this relatively late royal progress provide first-hand evidence of the exchange of ideas, artists, and craftsmen between the monarch and the houses of the leading courtiers across the country, during a period of change when it was important for members of the new ruling class to assert their position through their possessions as much as their actions. These new state apartments, replete with their royal bedchambers, continued to be a potent symbol of royal power across the country, and a number of loyal aristocrats were prepared to outdo the king himself in the quality and magnificence of the state apartments they incorporated within their new homes.

MOVING BACKSTAGE: A SOVEREIGN QUEEN

The accession of Queen Anne in 1702 heralded many changes both at court and in the city, given her unique position as the first single female sovereign for a century and also the fact that she bore the burden of the Hanoverian succession as the last reigning Stuart. As a woman she was of course not expected to perform the *lever* and *coucher* as a public ceremony in her bedchamber. Instead she would engage in the politics of court directly through her Privy Council and in closet meetings with ministers or with a wider circle at her "drawing rooms". Nevertheless the room remained politically significant, because her chosen bedchamber ladies were also the wives of those powerful men, under the very effective, sometimes manipulative control of Anne's Groom of the Stole, Sarah, Duchess of Marlborough.[40]

There were a number of reasons why Anne had no pressing need to transform the royal bedchamber. One immediate challenge was to curtail royal expenditure during a period of European warfare; this at a time when her brother-in-law's newly improved palaces were readily available for her use. It was therefore relatively straightforward for her to occupy the old king's bedchambers, leaving those that had been finished for the late queen to be occupied by her consort, George, Prince of Denmark. Anne was by nature painfully shy and eschewed the public display so readily embraced by her father and uncle. However, in time her perennial ill-health and her natural reticence encouraged her to abandon etiquette and admit male courtiers into her state bedchamber. The poet Jonathan Swift, always seeking preference at court, provides us with a glimpse of such an occasion in her later life:

> There was a drawing room today at Court; but so few company, that the Queen sent for us into her bedchamber, where we made our bows, and stood about twenty of us round the room, while she looked at us round with her fan in her mouth, and once a minute said about three words to some that were nearest to her, and then she was told dinner was ready, and went out.[41]

Although the queen spent relatively little on her state apartments during her reign, and was even prepared to re-use her much loathed brother-in-law's beds, she rather inexplicably started to restore her state apartment at Windsor Castle during the final month of her life, at the beginning of August 1714.[42] This great refurnishing of Catherine of Braganza's old rooms, costing some £2,726 (the value of a large London house), would be all but forgotten but for the survival of her great bed, decorated with rich multi-coloured velvet and attributed to the Huguenot weavers of London's Spitalfields district (fig. 33).[43] The bed, with its accompanying furnishings, takes the conventional form of a high four-poster with a large architectural cornice, where the emphasis is typically on the richness of its textiles, and there is no evidence that its making was allied with any other alterations to the bedchamber. What is significant is Anne's act of ordering such an extravagant bed and its timing. Beset by serious illnesses, Anne knew she was living on borrowed time—although she did not know that she only had weeks to live. With no surviving children, she had reluctantly come to accept the Hanoverian succession, which had been firmly settled: she held no further hope that Prince Charles Stuart, "The Old Pretender", might return as a Protestant king.[44] It therefore seems very probable that she planned her new apartment in preparation for her own final illness and death, when it was likely that she would be forced to spend increasing periods of time attended by ministers at her bedside before her inevitable demise. Could the ordering of the bed even be regarded as her final act of defiance at the hands of fate, driven by an irrational hope for a revival of great audiences at court where her frail body would be displayed in as great a splendour as her uncle Charles II's body had once been? An alternative explanation is that she was preparing a magnificent setting for her successor, George, Elector of Hanover, the man whom she refused to meet in England during the latter part of her life, but this seems implausible, given Anne's stubborn and often unforgiving nature. In the end fate dealt her one more cruel hand. Anne was never to present herself—dead or alive—in this great bed: she died at Kensington, suddenly and without much dignity, as her gaggle of doctors ineffectively tended her failing body.

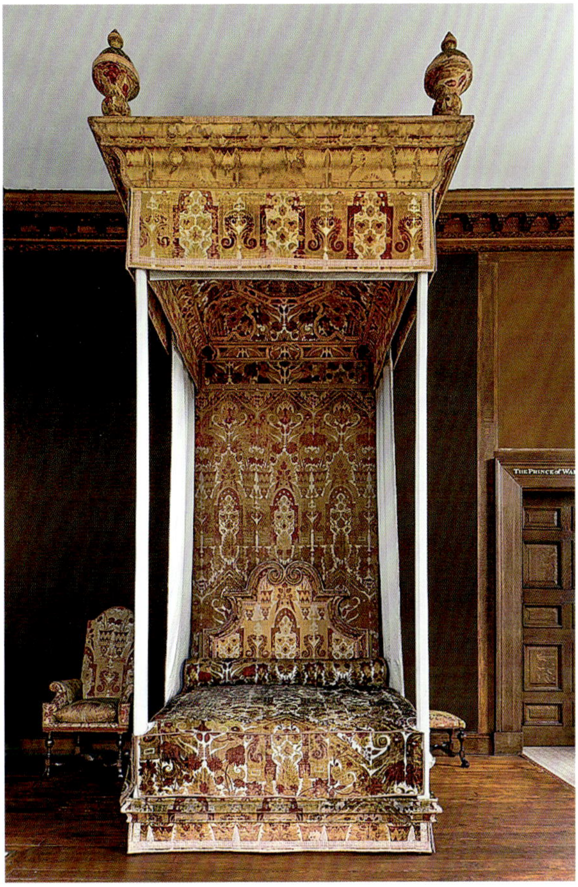

33. Queen Anne's bed from Windsor Castle, now at Hampton Court Palace, ca. 1714, 180 in. (457.2 cm). Historic Royal Palaces

THE FINAL CURTAIN: CONSTITUTIONAL CHANGE AND THE DEMISE OF THE STATE BEDCHAMBER

The last Stuart monarch's death and the enactment of the Hanoverian succession meant that the demise of the state bedchamber was only going to be a matter of time. Although a virtual absolutist ruler in his homeland of Hanover, George I had little interest or use for the *lever* and *coucher*, wisely leaving British politics to his British ministers. He also had far less opportunity to build or modify his inherited palaces than William III, except where expedient. So it was that the last great functioning state bedchambers in England were created out of necessity, rather than any ambition of the king to continue using such spaces as the settings for politically charged ceremonial. George I had to complete the bedchamber at Hampton Court, left unfinished on the death of Queen Mary, for his son George,

Prince of Wales, and for Princess Caroline, because he reluctantly required them to represent him as "Guardians of the Realm" during his regular absences in Hanover (fig. 34). The room is another magnificent survival, with James Thornhill's ceiling painting of Aurora and the royal upholsterers' crimson bed. However, in this instance, the German monarchs were simply following the English pattern and protocol for the bedchamber, as they quickly learned through political necessity to conform to their new country's traditions.[45]

A few years later George I was obliged to rebuild the core of Kensington Palace, which was falling down. At what was a secondary palace, it took him five years to complete his own state bedchamber, since George was by inclination as reluctant to perform in court rituals as Queen Anne had been. Any innovation here was down to his young protégé, William Kent, who both charmed and took advantage of his new patron. In this bedchamber Kent is known to have created one of three Inigo Jones-inspired grotesque ceilings. This, unfortunately, has not survived, nor has any trace of its design or iconography. However, there is no evidence for this king using this impressive room for regular audiences, as was no doubt intended to be the case.[46] In contrast, his son, George II, was the last English king to maintain the *lever* in public, using his father's bedchambers. The second King George was a great lover of etiquette and display, but equally, he understood that he needed to follow his father's adherence to English ceremonial and traditions. His use of the bedchamber was thus more conventional and, in terms of wielding direct political power, largely redundant.[47] However, it is worth noting that the actions and decisions that did take place in George II's chamber now revolved around personal or, increasingly, party political loyalty, rather than displays of personal monarchical authority.

With George II's death in 1760 the bedchamber ceased to be the centre of personal rule that had once made it the *ne plus ultra* of a palace. These great rooms, with their huge and costly beds, gradually became curiosities for antiquarians and early tourists, whom the royal Housekeepers were happy to entertain with unreliable tales. The *lever* became a less-ritualized audience, which took place wherever monarchs preferred to receive personal guests, before it gradually fossilized within the court etiquette of the following century.[48] With undoubted relief, owners of country houses ceased building royal apartments, and occasional royal visitors were now more likely to be greeted with venerable antique beds on retiring at night.

But over the century from 1660, a period of intense political and far-reaching social change, the state bedchamber became one of the most important and highly visually charged spaces in England. It began as the setting for very personalized state ceremonial, social exchange, and as a space in which the people—or rather

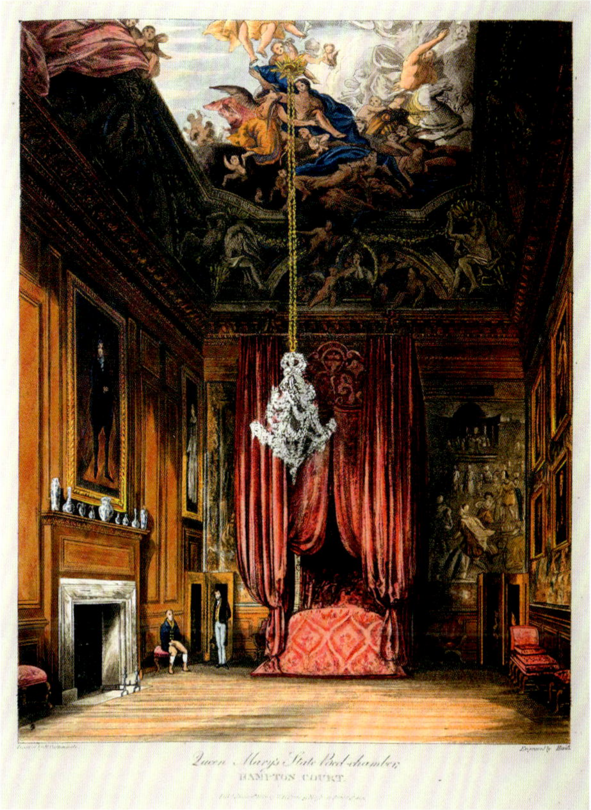

34. Richard Cattermole, *Queen Mary's State Bedchamber* [later George, Prince of Wales's bedchamber and state bed], 1715, coloured engraving or watercolour, 10⅛ x 8¼ in. (25.8 x 21 cm). Historic Royal Palaces

the elite that mattered—could come to gauge the health and fecundity of their monarch. The template for the visual appearance and use of this space was adopted from the absolutist courts of Europe, most especially from France. This was in tune with the Restoration monarchy's attempts to cling on to vestiges of Charles I's personal rule. However, their successors' personal styles of ruling and the changes demanded in their conduct by Parliament caused them to adapt the character and decoration of the state bedchamber continually, up until the point it ceased to have any real political relevance. For the period of this volume the royal bedchamber remained a unique space for the performance of monarchy and a place where all the arts could be orchestrated to create a unique setting for the royal body.

The background to this essay and papers given at the conferences of the *Court, City, Country: British Art, 1660–1735* research project was a lengthy period of conservation of the remarkable surviving collection of early royal beds in the Royal Collection and the Historic Royal Palaces, and an exhibition in 2013 at Hampton Court Palace. I would like to thank colleagues at HRP and in particular Dr Olivia Fryman for their generosity in sharing information and new research.

1. This essay builds on the handful of recent studies that have examined the Restoration palaces in detail, most notably those of Simon Thurley on Whitehall and Anna Keay on Charles II (cited in notes 5 and 9), and introduces further documentary material from the Lord Chamberlain's and Office of Works' departments of the Royal Household, which are deposited in The National Archives, London. Surviving material evidence from the palaces is reconsidered in the light of contemporary documentation and descriptions. Some new ideas are suggested based on recent biographical histories of the monarchs concerned here, and studies in other cultural fields that relate to the courts under discussion. However, there has yet to be published a critical, general history of early beds and bedchambers in English. For reliable and thoughtful earlier studies, see Peter Thornton, "The Royal State Bed", *Connoisseur* 195 (Jan. 1977): 137–47; John Fowler and John Cornforth, *English Decoration in the 18th Century*, 2nd ed. (London: Barrie and Jenkins, 1978); Peter Thornton, *Seventeenth-century Interior Decoration in England, France, and Holland* (New Haven and London: Yale Univ. Press, 1981), chap. 7; Gervase Jackson-Stops and others, eds., *The Fashioning and Functioning of the British Country House: Studies in the History of Art Symposium Series 25* (Washington, DC: National Gallery of Art, Center for Advanced Studies in the Visual Arts, 1989); and Geoffrey Beard, *Upholsterers and Interior Furnishing in England, 1530–1840* (New Haven and London: Yale Univ. Press, 1997). There are several important recent articles on individual state beds: Geoffrey Beard and Annabel Westman, "A French Upholsterer in England: Francis Lapiere, 1653–1714", *The Burlington Magazine* 135, no. 1085 (Aug. 1993): 515–24; Annabel Westman, "A Royal Bed at Chatsworth: The Puzzle of the 4th Duke's Perquisite", *Apollo* 167, no. 555 (June 2008): 68–75; Tessa Murdoch, "Fit for a King: The State Bed from Melville House, Fife", *Apollo* 155, no. 479 (June 2002): 3–9; Nicola Gentle, "Lord Rochester's Bed", *Furniture History* 45 (2009): 35–54; and Lucy Wood, "A Royal Relic: The State Bedroom Suite at Warwick Castle", *Furniture History* 67 (2012): 45–103.
2. Olivia Fryman at Historic Royal Palaces has compiled a database of detailed Royal Wardrobe accounts for seventeenth-century royal beds, based on the Lord Chamberlain's records in The National Archives, London. She has kindly shared this work in progress, the results from which are being prepared for eventual publication.
3. This is in part due to the destruction of many earlier European royal apartments with their associated documentation. For references to early alcoves in Paris, see Louis Hautecoeur, *L'Histoire des château du Louvre et des Tuileries* (Paris: G. Vanoest, 1927), 8 (plan 3), 19, 50, and Pierre Quoniam and Laurent Guinamard, *Le Palais du Louvre* (Paris: Nathan, 1988), 91–100.
4. See Kevin Sharpe, *Rebranding Rule: The Restoration and Revolution Monarchy, 1660–1714* (New Haven and London: Yale Univ. Press, 2013), introduction and chap. 1; and for an insightful view of Charles's rival Louis XIV's evolving bedchamber, see David Gallo, "Royal Bodies, Royal Bedrooms: The Lever du Roy and Louis XIV's Versailles", *Cahiers du dix-septième: An Interdisciplinary Journal* 12, no. 1 (2008): 99–118. I am grateful to Olivia Fryman for this citation.
5. See Simon Thurley, *Whitehall Palace: An Architectural History of the Royal Apartments, 1240–1690* (New Haven and London: Yale Univ. Press, 1999), chap. 7. On the reclamation of royal goods after the Restoration, see Andrew Barclay, "Recovering Charles I's Art Collection: Some Implications of the 1660 Act of Indemnity and Oblivion", *Historical Research* 88, no. 242 (Nov. 2015): 636, 646.
6. See Hautecoeur, *L'Histoire des château du Louvre*, 8, 50, and Henry Havard, *Dictionnaire de l'ameublement et de la décoration depuis le XIIIe siècle jusqu'à nos jours* (Paris: Ancien Maison Quantin, 1887–90), 1: 46. The earliest detailed evidence for a king using an alcove appears to date from the early reign of Louis XIV.
7. See Maria Hayward, "Repositories of Splendour: Henry VIII's Wardrobes of the Robes and Beds", *Textile History* 29, no. 2 (1998): 141–44.

8. See Lee Prosser, "Writings and Sources XII: The Inventory of 1659", *Cromwelliana* 6 (2009): 61–93.
9. See Thurley, *Whitehall Palace*, 106–14, and Anna Keay, *The Magnificent Monarch: Charles II and the Ceremonies of Power* (London: Continuum, 2008), 95–102.
10. Simon Thurley, "A Country Seat Fit for a King: Charles II, Greenwich and Winchester", in *The Stuart Courts*, ed. Eveline Cruickshanks (Stroud: Sutton, 2000), 214–40.
11. See Thurley, *Whitehall Palace*, 106, and for a parquet floor at Whitehall, see Simon Thurley, *Somerset House: The Palace of England's Queens, 1551–1692* (London: London Topographical Society, 2009), 109.
12. See John Bold, *John Webb: Architectural Theory and Practice in the Seventeenth Century* (Oxford: Clarendon Press, 1989), 144.
13. See Thornton, *Seventeenth-century Interior Decoration*, 294, 403, and Keay, *Magnificent Monarch*, 96, n. 11. Keay points out that Charles II reversed the early French practice of reserving the alcove as a sleeping or private bedchamber. See also Gallo, "Royal Bodies", and Antony Griffiths, *The Print in Stuart Britain, 1603–1689* (British Museum Press, London 1998), 19, 27, 266.
14. For the creation of Louis XIV's bedchamber in 1654–5, see Hautecoeur, *L'Histoire des château du Louvre*, 50.
15. The National Archives (hereafter TNA) Work 5/1, fols. 163v, 196v, 198v.
16. See Edward A. Langhans, "The Theatre", in *The Cambridge Companion to English Restoration Theatre*, ed. Deborah Payne Fisk (Cambridge Univ. Press, 2000), chap. 1.
17. See Dawn Lewcock, *Sir William Davenant, the Court Masque, and the English Seventeenth-century Scenic Stage, c.1605–1700* (Amhurst, NY: Cambria Press, 2008), 112, and Thurley, *Whitehall Palace*, 117.
18. For a detailed account of Louis XIV's bedchamber rituals, see Beatrix Saule, *Versailles Triomphant: une journée de Louis XIV* (Paris: Éditions Flammarion, 1996), chap. 3.
19. For the earliest appearance of bed rails in England, see Jean Puget de la Serre, *Histoire de l'entree de la Reyne Mere du Roy Tres-Chrestien [Mary de'Medici, Queen Consort of Henry IV] dans la Grande Bretaigne, etc.* (London: J. Raworth, 1639), unpaginated; Oliver Millar, "The Inventories and Valuations of the King's Goods, 1649–51", *Walpole Society* 43 (1970–72): 121, 124, 412; and Thurley, *Somerset House*, 46. I am grateful to Erin Griffey (University of Auckland) for kindly providing references in TNA royal accounts cited in these references for the supply of Queen Henrietta Maria's bed rails in the 1630s.
20. For the belief in divine authority expressed early in the century by James I see, for example, King James I, "Speech to Parliament, March 1609", in *King James VI and I: Selected Writings*, ed. Neil Rhodes, Jennifer Richards, and Joseph Marshall (Aldershot: Ashgate, 2003), 327, where he claims that, "even God calls kings gods."
21. For Louis XIV's *lever* and *coucher* see Saule, *Versailles Triomphant*, chap. 3, which includes private prayer.
22. For the occasional appearance of bed rails in courtiers' houses from as early as 1635, see Simon Jervis, "Furniture for the First Duke of Buckingham", *Furniture History* 33 (1997): 48; Peter Thornton and Maurice Tomlin, "The Furnishing and Decoration of Ham House", *Furniture History* 16 (1980): 141–48; and Christopher Rowell, ed., *Powis Castle* (London: The National Trust, 2000), 16.
23. The modern notion of the king's two bodies was first evinced in Ernst H. Kantorowicz, *The King's Two Bodies: A Study in Mediaeval Political Theology* (1957; Princeton Univ. Press, 1998).
24. John Reresby, *The Memoirs of Sir John Reresby*, ed. Andrew Browning, 2nd ed. (London: Royal Historical Society, 1991), 208.
25. See Sara Stevenson and others, *John Michael Wright: The King's Painter* (Edinburgh: National Galleries of Scotland, 1982), 67, and Keay, *Magnificent Monarch*, 96.
26. Inventory of Charles II's pictures etc. at Whitehall, "O.M. 16", fol. 15, Surveyor of the Queen's Picture's Office, Royal Collection Trust, St James's Palace, London. This was discussed by Erin Griffey (University of Auckland), in her paper "Art and Display at the Court of Charles II" at the *Histories of British Art, 1660–1735* conference, 20–22 September 2013, University of York, held in preparation for this volume.
27. Anna Keay, "The Ceremonies of Charles II's Court" (PhD diss., Queen Mary Univ. of London, 2004), 23–48.

28. TNA LC5/140, 31, 122, 237; Christopher Rowell, "The King's Bed and its Furniture at Knole", *Apollo* 160, no. 513 (Nov. 2004): 58–65. For a note on the etymology of "French Bed", see Lucy Wood, *The Upholstered Furniture in the Lady Lever Art Gallery*, 2 vols. (New Haven and London: Yale Univ. Press, 2009), 1: 2, n. 10.
29. TNA LC5/142, 124.
30. Thurley, *Whitehall Palace*, 124, 132.
31. Rowell, "King's Bed", Olivia Fryman, "Rich Pickings: The Royal Bed as a Perquisite, 1660–1760", *Furniture History* 50 (2014): 125.
32. See Simon Thurley, "Kensington Palace: An Incident in Anglo-Dutch Architectural Collaboration?", *The Georgian Group Journal* 17 (2009): 5–7, for a European perspective on William III's palaces.
33. Simon Thurley, *Hampton Court: A Social and Architectural History* (New Haven and London: Yale Univ. Press, 2003), 153, 186, Robert O. Bucholz, "Going to Court in 1700: A Visitor's Guide", *The Court Historian* 5, no. 3 (Dec. 2000): 196–211.
34. TNA LC5/125 loose folio, 30 June 1700, and LC9/281, fol. 49. Thurley, *Hampton Court* suggested this was Charles II's surviving bed rail, but close correlation between warrant and bill more likely refers to a wire bed "screen". For a contemporary description, see Christopher Morris, ed., *The Journeys of Celia Fiennes* (London: Cresset Press, 1949), 280. There is no evidence that William fitted rails or alcoves in any of his palaces.
35. See Gallo, "Royal Bodies".
36. See Saule, *Versailles Triomphant*, chap. 3.
37. Paul Grimblot, ed., *Letters of William III and Louis XIV and of their Ministers* (London: Longman, 1848), 1: 419.
38. Evidence for these rooms is discussed in Simon Thurley, ed., "The King's Apartments, 1689–1702, Hampton Court Palace", *Apollo* 140, no. 390 (Aug. 1994). William previously gave away the majority of Mary's ceramic collection to his favourite, the Earl of Albemarle.
39. Anon., *The Royal Progress . . . or, a Diary of the King's Journey* (London, 1695). This is discussed in Stefan van Raaij and Paul Spies, *The Royal Progress of William & Mary* (Amsterdam: D'Arts, 1988), trans. P. K. Graafland, cited in Sharpe, *Rebranding Rule*, chap. 11, n. 84.
40. Robert O. Bucholz, *The Augustan Court: Queen Anne and the Decline of Court Culture* (Stanford Univ. Press, 1993), 242–48.
41. Jonathan Swift, *Journal to Stella*, ed. Harold Williams (Oxford: Clarendon Press, 1948), 1: 328.
42. Thurley, *Hampton Court*, 213; Wood, "A Royal Relic".
43 Hans Christoph Ackermann, *Textilsammlung der Abegg-Stiftung*, vol. 2, *Seidengewebe des 18. Jahrhunderts I Bizarre Seiden* (Riggisburg, Switzerland: Abbeg-Stiftung, 2000), 76–80.
44. See Anne Somerset, *Queen Anne: The Politics of Passion* (London: Harper Press, 2012), chap. 15, for a recent study of Anne's final months.
45. Cécile Brett, "Revealing Thornhill's Mythological Scene at Hampton Court", *British Art Journal* 13, no. 3 (Winter 2012/13): 3–8.
46. TNA Work 4/2, fols. 110v, 143v; Work 6/7, fols. 320, 358; Work 6/15, fol. 15. There are no known contemporary descriptions of George I's *levers*.
47. For the move from personal to parliamentary placements in George II's bedchamber, see Jean McGinnis, "The Bedchamber in the Reign of George II" (PhD diss., Univ. of Northern Colorado, 1977).
48. John Brooke, *King George III* (London: Constable, 1972), 293–95.

Castle Howard and the Interpretation of English Baroque Architecture

Anthony Geraghty

The phenomenon that we now call English Baroque architecture sits exactly within the chronological range of this book—1660 to 1735. It was in the years immediately following the Restoration of Charles II that Christopher Wren first put pen to paper as an architect, and it was in 1736 that a gouty and embittered Nicholas Hawksmoor passed over the Styx into Hades, in effect bringing the curtain down on the English Baroque. This was a period of intense architectural activity, and buildings such as Wren's Greenwich Hospital, Sir John Vanbrugh's Blenheim Palace, and Hawksmoor's Stepney churches are extensively documented and justly celebrated. But the period as a whole remains one of the least understood episodes in British architectural history. For a century, now, it has been characterized as "Baroque", and therefore in relation to Continental Europe. But the comparative method that accompanies this classification only takes us so far, and few scholars have attempted a general explanation in the fifty years since John Summerson's *Architecture in Britain, 1530–1830* and Kerry Downes's *English Baroque Architecture*.[1]

In this essay, I want to suggest some new ways of thinking about English Baroque architecture. I do so via Castle Howard, the spectacular house in the North Yorkshire countryside that was designed by Sir John Vanbrugh for Charles Howard, third Earl of Carlisle, in the first decades of the eighteenth century (fig. 35).[2] And I write about Castle Howard via a brief description of the house that was made at the end of our period, in October 1734. The passage occurs in a letter by Hawksmoor, who assisted Vanbrugh on the design of the house from the outset. By 1734, however, Vanbrugh was dead, and Hawksmoor was deeply concerned at the unfinished state of the house—the northwest wing was still unbuilt, thirty-five years after the start of work. He therefore wrote to Carlisle, who was by then more interested in his landscape than his house, to beseech him to finish it:

> It must (or shoud) be observed that Your Lordships Seat, so expensively Built, and the situation so greatly improved, engages a great deal of consid-

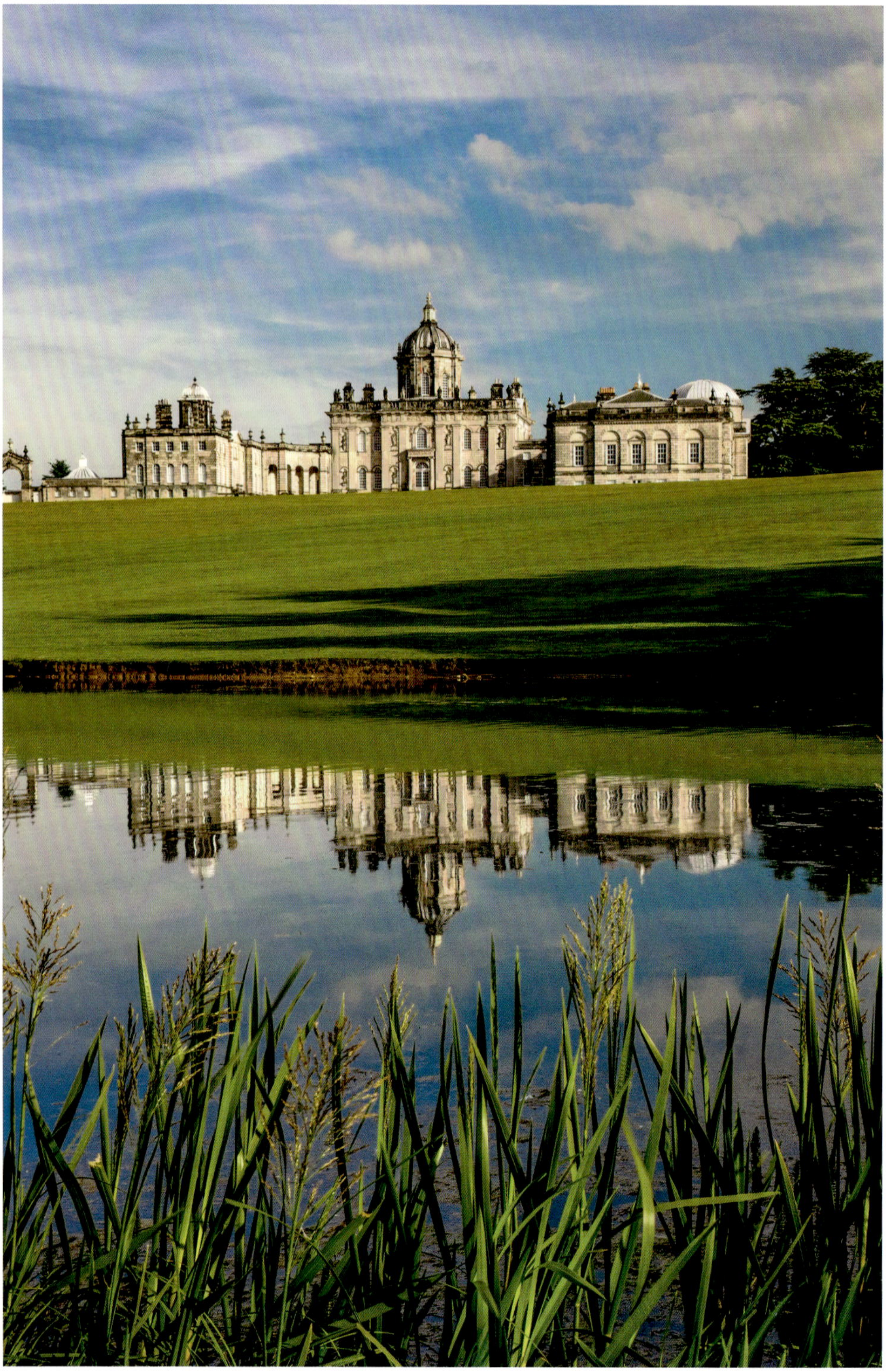

35. Castle Howard exterior from north. Photograph courtesy of Mike Kipling, 2010

eration. It is the seat of one of [the] chief nobles of Britain, it is both a Castle and Pallace conjoyn'd, and claims more Regard, than one of Palladios humble Villas in the Vicentine, or Veronese—or than sundry of the Chateaus in France, or such familiar sites, as we see in England, this I am offering because I think the great access not answering the Dignity of Castle Howard—must needs be a great Blemish and disappointment.[3]

The particular statement I want to confront is Hawksmoor's claim that Castle Howard is "both a Castle and Pallace conjoyn'd". Taken at face value, this is challenging, for Castle Howard is ostensibly neither of these things, however one chooses to define an architectural typology, architecturally or socially. But Hawksmoor's statement is emphatic—Castle Howard "is . . . a Castle and Pallace conjoyn'd". What did he mean by this, and why did he say it? By addressing these questions, and by exploring the design of Castle Howard in relation to the typologies of palace and castle, I hope to shed some new light on the nature of English Baroque architecture.

Castle Howard is certainly "conjoyn'd". As is well known and often commented upon, the front and back of the house are markedly different in their architectural expression (in discussing the building, I do so with reference to the original design (figs. 36–38), which, as we have already seen, remained unfinished at Vanbrugh's death, and which was finished to a very different set of architectural ideals a generation later). This difference starts and finishes with the articulation of the main block. The front has a Doric order (fig. 38a), while the garden front is Corinthian (fig. 38b). The front façade is textured with channelled masonry, while the garden front is predominantly smooth. Not only does this give different characters to the same building, but it undermines the integrated relationship between the architectural ornament and the underlying fabric—between the elevation and the section—that is implicit in classical articulation. This is especially so on the main block, where the front and garden façades come closest to each other, but are awkwardly segregated by the neutral treatment of the side façades.

Hawksmoor felt compelled to defend this arrangement, and in a second letter to Carlisle, also dating from 1734, he wrote as follows: "The South side, and North front of your Ldships house cannot be seen together at the same Time, nor at any time upon the Diagonall (or angular view)."[4] His justification—that the subjectivity of the beholder is the final sanction—is very telling. It suggests an attitude to articulation that is grounded less in the structural reality of the building as an object than an ambition to impart general information about the building as a project. This rhetorical emphasis, with its playful expectation of a beholder, is indeed apparent in the building itself. For example, on both sides of the house,

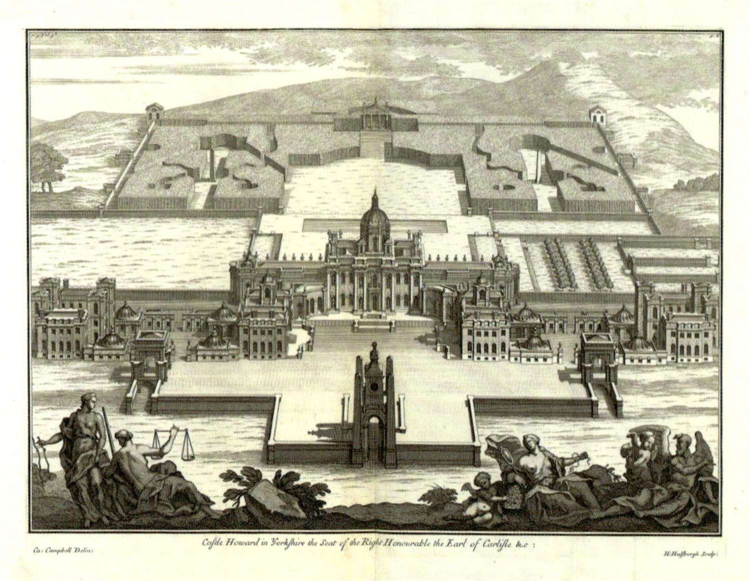

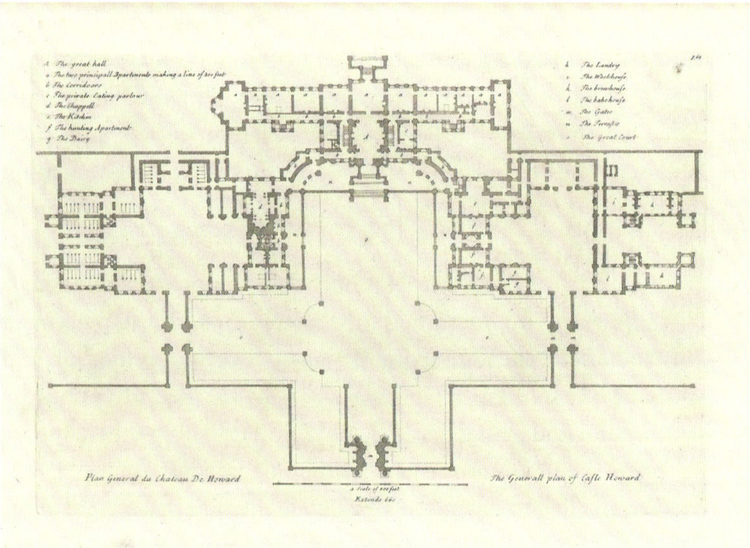

36. Colen Campbell, "Castle Howard in Yorkshire the Seat of the Right Honourable the Earl of Carlisle &c:", from *Vitruvius Britannicus, or The British Architect*, London, vol. III, plates 5–6, 1715–25, engraving. Yale Center for British Art, Paul Mellon Collection

37. Colen Campbell, "The Generall Plan of Castle Howard", from *Vitruvius Britannicus, or The British Architect*, vol. I, plate 63, London, 1715–25, engraving, Beinecke Rare Book and Manuscript Library

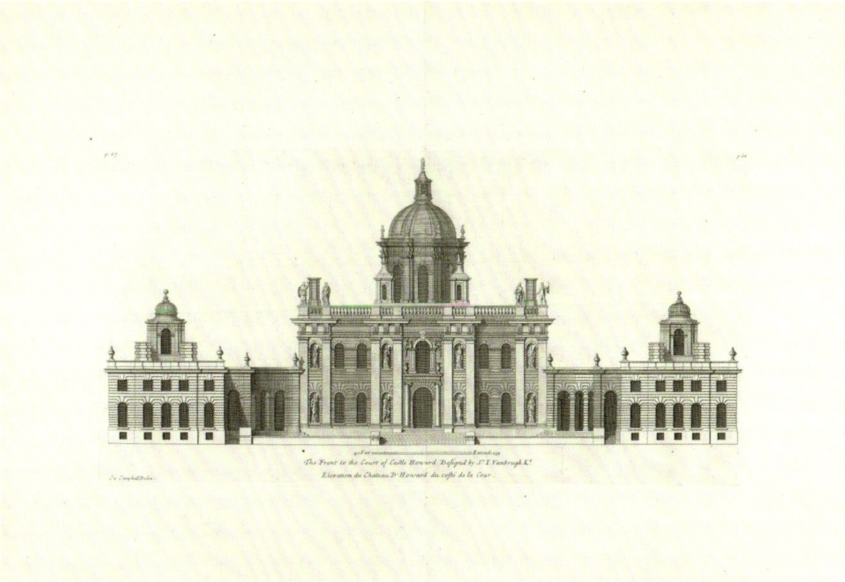

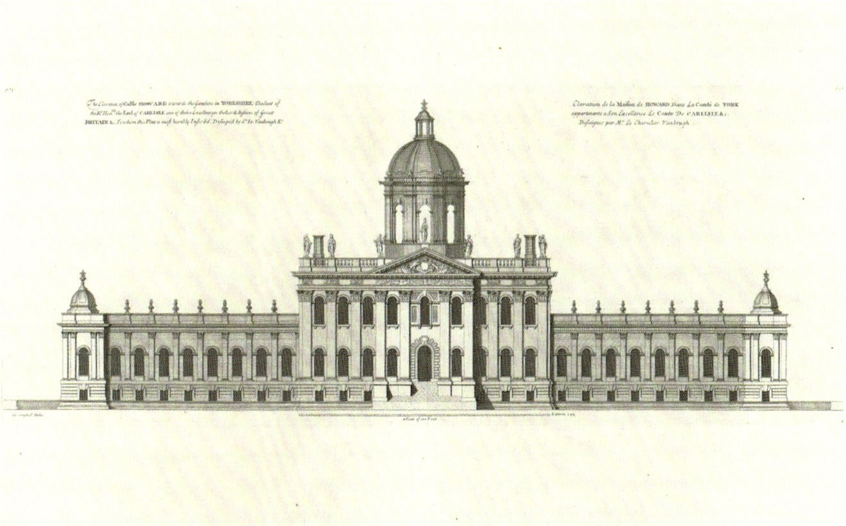

38a. Colen Campbell, "The Front to the Court of Castle Howard", from *Vitruvius Britannicus, or The British Architect*, vol. I, plates 67–8, London, 1715–25, engraving. Beinecke Rare Book and Manuscript Library

38b. Colen Campbell, "The Elevation of Castle Howard towards the Gardens in Yorkshire", from *Vitruvius Britannicus, or The British Architect*, London, vol. I, plates 69–70, 1715–25, engraving. Beinecke Rare Book and Manuscript Library

the extent of the articulation is determined by the beholder's field of vision. Thus on the north side, the channelled masonry of the main block is continued round the quadrant arcade, then across the fronts of the family wing, before wrapping around the end façade. But at that point, at the far return angle of the family wing, it is abruptly discontinued (fig. 39). Something similar happens on the garden front, where the articulation of the main block is continued, albeit more diminutively, across the low wings. This is then continued all the way round the end pavilions, where it is halted. The back façades of the four wings are therefore treated as voids, but as the celebrated bird's-eye view in Colen Campbell's *Vitruvius Britannicus* (fig. 36) demonstrates, these are largely, though not entirely, invisible to the beholder, whether this be a human standing in the forecourt or garden, or

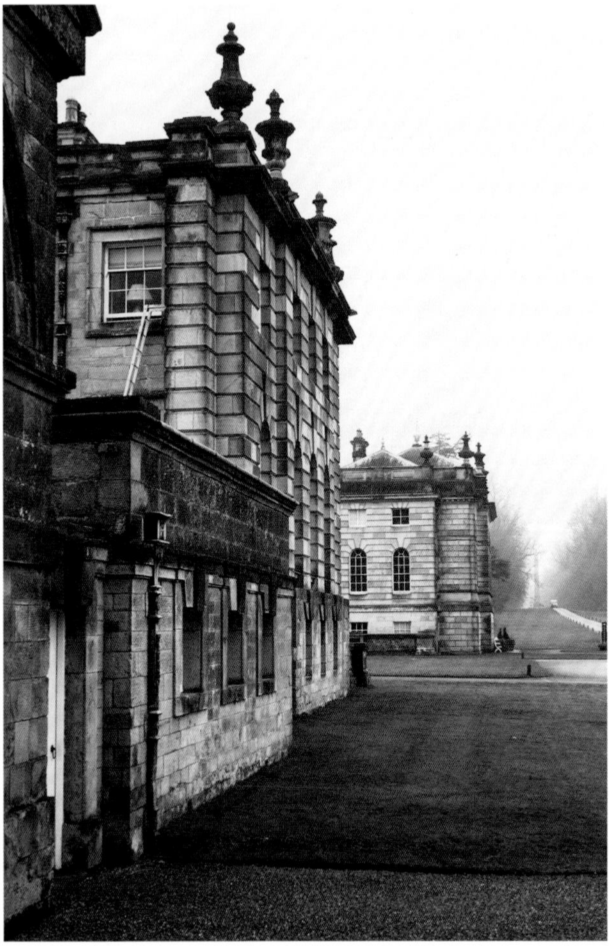

39. Castle Howard, northeast corner of northeast wing, looking west. Photograph courtesy of Anthony Geraghty

a bird flying through the sky.[5] The effect, however, depends on an orthogonal, or nearly orthogonal, viewpoint, hence the unusually symmetrical format of the bird's-eye view.

But we should not presume that the building sets out to deceive, for the visitor to Castle Howard does not have to look very hard or far to see the limits of the articulation. *Pace* Hawksmoor, the edges of both façades *are* visible from certain angles (from Ray Wood, for example), while the rear façade of the family wing, with its subgrade ashlar, could easily be seen from within the front court while it existed. In short, the building acknowledges its discontinuities: it suspends its unrealities because its notion of articulation is primarily rhetorical.

Hence the front and the back of the same building are made to say different things (figs. 38a and 38b). But do they speak of castle and palace? What, if anything, does Castle Howard borrow from these typologies? Strictly speaking, the house is of course neither of these things. Rather, its actual function—as Hawksmoor says in the first of the letters quoted above—is to be "the seat of one of [the] chief nobles of Britain". And as the "seat" of a peer, it sits within the mainstream of elite country house design in late Stuart England. This is especially apparent on the entrance side of the house, where the two-storey bulk of the central block is prefaced by low service wings joined by quadrant arcades, a formula first introduced to English architecture by Inigo Jones at Stoke Bruerne Park in Northamptonshire in 1629, and then popularized at the Restoration by Hugh May at Berkeley House, Piccadilly.[6] Immediately associated with Italy and Palladio, this forecourt arrangement (or something like it) was taken up on the grandest scale at the end of the century: at Kiveton Park in the West Riding of Yorkshire for the Duke of Leeds from 1694; at Lowther Castle in Cumbria for Viscount Lonsdale at about the same time; at Burley-on-the-Hill in Rutland for the Earl of Nottingham from 1696; at Castle Howard from 1699; and at Buckingham House in London for the Duke of Buckingham shortly thereafter.[7] Vanbrugh's use of the giant order is likewise consistent with these houses. His early drawings for the entrance front, moreover, show a Corinthian rather than a Doric order, in keeping with most of the above.[8]

Moving inside the house, we again find features consistent with late Stuart country house design. The main block belongs ostensibly to the two-storey, double-pile type introduced by Roger Pratt in the 1650s and common thereafter, but with the roof-scape suppressed after the example of Chatsworth. The internal disposition of the rooms is likewise typical, if more rigorously symmetrical, with a hall-cum-vestibule located in the middle of the plan and matching dog-leg stairs to either side. By rising through the full height of the house, the Entrance Hall reveals the two-storey section of the interior, dramatizing the entrances to the

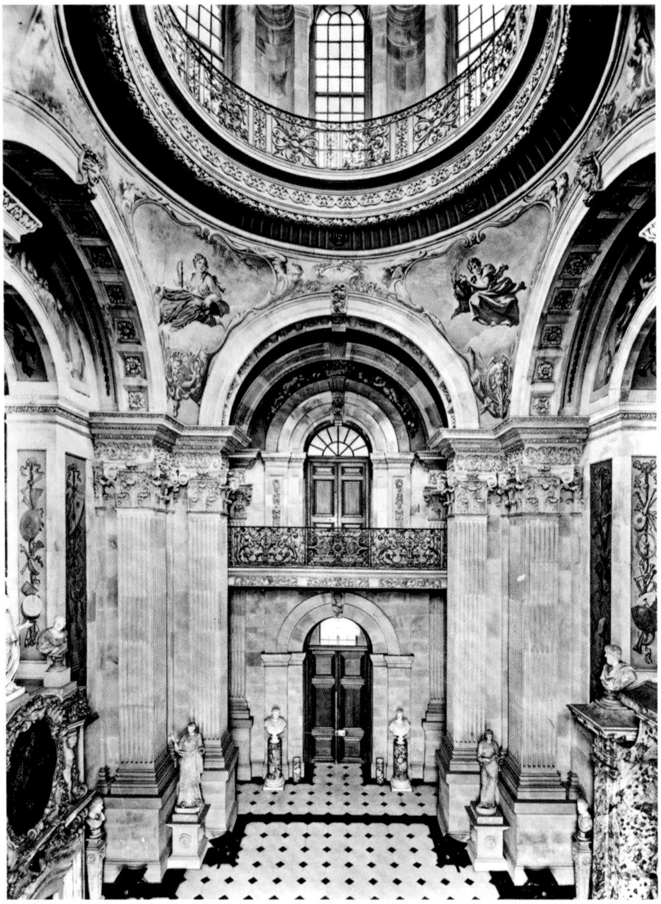

40. Interior of the Great Hall at Castle Howard, ca. 18th century. Country Life Picture Library

principal spaces beyond: Garden Hall below, High Saloon above (fig. 40). This arrangement recalls Inigo Jones's Queen's House at Greenwich and Roger Pratt's Coleshill in Berkshire,[9] and most of the essential features of the interior would have been familiar and comprehensible to an elite British visitor.

But it is of course impossible to talk about Castle Howard—inside or outside—without acknowledging the one feature that departs most radically from country house design: the dome. For the dome lies at the very heart of Castle Howard—conceptually, structurally, and spatially (fig. 41). Roger Pratt had popularized the cupola as the terminating feature of the country house, but his modest structures were small in comparison, almost always built of timber, and seldom if

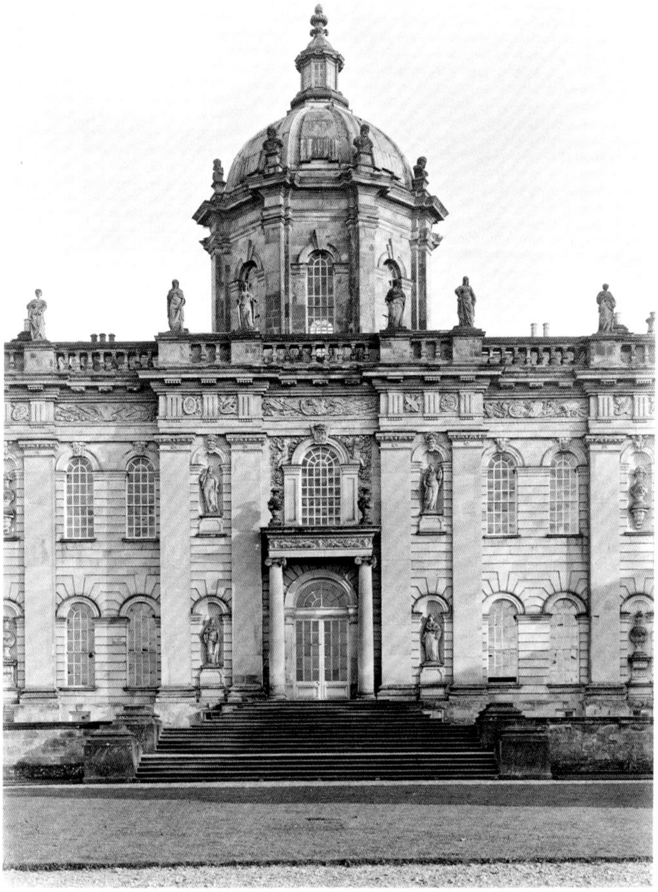

41. Central portion of north front at Castle Howard, with dome above. Country Life Picture Library

ever related to the interior spaces below. Vanbrugh's dome, in scale and purpose, sits within a very different tradition.

CASTLE HOWARD AS A "PALLACE"

The Castle Howard dome, with its masonry drum, hemispherical cupola, and glazed lantern, relates to late seventeenth-century palace design and the design aspirations of the Office of Works (fig. 41). For nearly half a century, the Stuart monarchy had dreamed of building a symmetrical palace surmounted by a dome.

These ambitions began in the 1660s, when John Webb prepared designs for a new palace at Greenwich.[10] Only a portion of this was executed, the King Charles block, but as originally envisaged it was to have included a central range surmounted by a massive cupola.[11] The section is not recorded, but the plans imply that it was to have risen directly from an octagonal great chamber located on the first floor. The plans also show flanking staircases, as at Castle Howard. In the second of his letters to Carlisle, Hawksmoor explicitly states that Webb's design was a source of inspiration for Castle Howard[12] and we should remember that he and Vanbrugh were engaged upon the transformation of Greenwich into the Royal Hospital for Seamen, Hawksmoor from the outset, Vanbrugh from 1703.

After Webb, the dome is next encountered in the palace designs produced by Sir Christopher Wren in the 1680s, first for Winchester in about 1682,[13] and then for Hampton Court in 1689.[14] Wren's most emphatic statement of the theme, however, occurs in 1695, in the first and grandest of the preliminary designs for Greenwich Hospital, the so-called "central dome scheme".[15] Though Greenwich was now being developed as a hospital rather than a palace, the commission was still a royal one, and the institution was conceived with, in the words of Nicholas Hawksmoor, a "fixt Intention for Magnificence".[16] This too remained on paper, but following the decision to retain the central vista to the Queen's House, Wren and Hawksmoor introduced the bravura idea of twin domes, one crowning the hall vestibule, the other (eventually) the chapel vestibule. The first of these was begun in the mid-1690s, and its design, in form and concept, relates very closely to the Hall at Castle Howard.

The association between the dome and the palace was widely understood in seventeenth-century England. In their respective notes on palace design, for example, both Roger Pratt and Roger North include the dome as princely symbol.[17] These associations were probably derived from France, where the secular dome was particularly associated with gateways to royal chateaux, as at the Palais du Luxembourg in Paris.[18] But the Stuarts probably derived the idea from the Tuileries palace in Paris, where the central staircase was originally surmounted by a dome, which, in its general outline, bore a striking kinship to Castle Howard.[19] The idea of the vestibule dome was still current in the 1660s, when François Mansart produced a series of domed entrances to the Louvre.[20] Vanbrugh and Hawksmoor could never have known these last examples, but the basic idea of the vestibule surmounted by a dome was almost certainly the catalyst for Webb's Greenwich designs. Charles II of course knew the Tuileries from his years of exile, and we should not forget the dynastic connections (through his mother, Queen Henrietta Maria) that underpin these architectural relationships. The dome as princely symbol was therefore understood internationally as an ingredient of court architecture.

The internal treatment of the Great Hall at Castle Howard (fig. 40) can be associated with a more recent development in French architecture: the vogue for double-height rooms surmounted by domes. These were called *salons à l'Italienne*, as the form was derived from, and continued to be associated with, Italy.[21] Such spaces were described in the 1684 *Dictionnaire de l'Académie Française* as a "room in an *appartement* which is much higher than the other rooms, and which is usually domed and enriched with architectural ornaments and painting",[22] and it was this idea, I suspect, that Vanbrugh imported to England, together with the aesthetic of internal masonry and decorative painting that accompanied it. The most famous example exists at Vaux-le-Vicomte, where the domed salon, originally open to the elements, provides access to André Le Nôtre's garden.[23] This lofty space, and others like it, was ultimately inspired by Palladio's Villa Rotonda, where the double-height salon rises to a dome.[24] But the Hall at Castle Howard differs from these precedents in one key respect: the dome rises not from a cylindrical basis, but over a square space articulated with a giant order. This necessitated the introduction of pendentives, which bring an element of structural complexity to Castle Howard that is seldom if ever found in French or Italian domestic architecture. The pendentives also explain why the design has so often been associated with ecclesiastical, as opposed to secular, domes. Wren, and therefore probably Hawksmoor, was aware (at second hand) of the domes on pendentives in the Topkapi Palace in Constantinople.[25]

But the design of Castle Howard ultimately takes us beyond single precedents. As Hawksmoor's letter confirms, it introduces elements derived from English country house design, from the chateaux of France, and from the villas of Italy. And in so doing it trumps them all. It also introduces the royal symbol of the dome, and does so with an unprecedented complexity and magnificence. And this was surely the point: to create a princely magnificence through the fusion of diverse typologies and national schools.

The introduction of the dome, and the structural challenge of supporting it within the two-storey conventions of the double-pile house, probably accounts for the second feature at Castle Howard that departs from the norms of late seventeenth-century country house practice: the introduction of low projecting wings on the south front (fig. 38b). These wings attracted attention from the outset, and Vanbrugh proudly recorded the reaction of the Duke of Devonshire, whom he visited at Chatsworth in the summer of 1699:

> I have been this Summer at my Ld Carlisle's, and Seen most of the great houses in the North, as Ld Nottings: Duke of Leeds Chattesworth &c. I stay'd at Chattesworth four or five days the Duke being there. I shew'd him

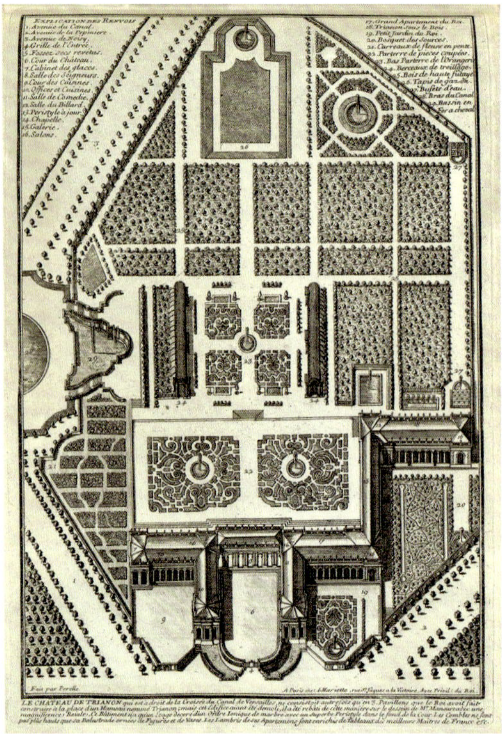

42. Gabriel Perelle or Perelle family, *Trianon de marbre, Versailles*, late 17th century, engraving, 13⅝ x 9⅛ in. (34.5 x 23.2 cm). Reunion des Musées Nationaux-Grand Palais, Chateau de Versailles, France

> all my Ld Carlisle's designs, which he said was quite another thing, than what he imagin'd from the Character yr Ldship gave him on't; He absolutely approved the whole design, particularly the low Wings, which he said wou'd have an admirable effect without doors as well as within, being adorn'd with those Ornaments of Pillasters and Urns, wch he never thought of, but concluded 'twas to be a plain low building like an orange house.[26]

The two "low Wings" originally contained the principal apartments of the house, to left and right of the Garden Hall, and they originally accommodated a state apartment on the west and a private apartment on the east (fig. 38b).

The massive substructure of the dome, needed to counter the lateral forces of the four arches upon which it sits, encroaches upon the rectangular volume of the main block. This probably explains the network of subsidiary spaces that flank the main square of the hall: stairs to left and right, corridors to front and back (fig. 37). The latter in particular, with their dense sequence of lateral arches, allowed Vanbrugh to brace and stabilize the dome, while providing convenient access to the four corners of the plan. A significant portion of the plan, then, was given over to the structural integration of the dome.

It was probably for this reason that Vanbrugh introduced the two low wings that project laterally from the south edge of the main block and create the impressive length of the garden frontage. The basic silhouette of this façade is without precedent in English architecture, and the single-storey wings are the second basic element at Castle Howard that can be associated with princely architecture. In particular, they probably relate to the Europe-wide vogue for single-storey pleasure pavilions, initiated by Louis XIV at the Grand Trianon at Versailles in 1687,[27] which was built as a retreat from the formalities of court life and constructed just before Vanbrugh was imprisoned in France (fig. 42).[28] Trianon was the name of the village that occupied the site, but the word quickly became affixed to a new kind of building typology—the single-storey pleasure pavilion in a garden location. Imitations sprang up across Europe, and in 1699—in other words, at exactly the time Vanbrugh was designing Castle Howard—King William resolved to build one.[29] This was never executed, but in his enthusiasm for the project he obtained copies of Jules Hardouin Mansart's drawings for the Trianon at Versailles. John Talman produced a series of unexecuted designs for a Trianon at Hampton Court at about this time, possibly for himself, but more likely for the king.[30] The idea, then, was very much in the air at exactly the moment Carlisle and his architects were conceiving Castle Howard. The Trianon at Versailles has no central pavilion, but it does have a forecourt flanked by wings and a garden front with apartments stretching to either side of a central feature. Its relationship to Castle Howard may not be so direct, but we can nevertheless characterize the latter as a diminutive garden palace.

One final word about these suggested sources of inspiration: they exemplify, in very general terms, architectural knowledge, and it was surely Vanbrugh's knowledge of French architecture—or, more likely, an exaggerated pretence to such knowledge—that made his employment at Castle Howard credible.[31] Vanbrugh, in the words of Swift—and it is impossible to write about Vanbrugh without quoting them—famously turned to architecture "without Thought or Lecture".[32] But he *had* been to France, and everyone knew it, for he had been imprisoned in the Bastille. Paris might not be Rome, but it was home to the *Académie royale de l'architecture*, and, as such, the centre of architectural discourse. This is why, Swift aside, Vanbrugh's involvement at Castle Howard probably seemed more credible to his contemporaries than it does to us.

CASTLE HOWARD

Mention of the Bastille brings us back to castles, and the question of whether—or rather how—Castle Howard is a castle. The name itself—Castle Howard—suggests that it was understood as such, and the house that we see today replaced a castle, Henderskelfe Castle, formerly on the site. Vanbrugh, describing his proposed alterations to Kimbolton Castle, famously thought it "absolutly best, to give it Something of the Castle Air, tho' at the Same time to make it regular",[33] and there is indeed something of the "Castle Air" in the approach to Castle Howard (fig. 44), especially in its treatment of thresholds—walls and gateways—all of which, and this is no coincidence, acknowledge and articulate the pre-existing landscape. But what about the house itself, which was designed a good decade before the name Castle Howard came into common usage? Does this too, in spite of its Italianate forms, evoke a "Castle Air"?

I would like to suggest that it does, and, in positing this claim, initiate a discussion about the operation of meaning in English Baroque architecture. I am primarily referring to the north front (fig. 41), which, as we saw above, effects a deliberate, if deferred, contrast to the sunny garden side. If we return to the second of Hawksmoor's explanatory letters, we find a lengthy analysis of both façades. Much of his analysis therein is conventional, grounded as it is in the classical theory of decorum, and in Vitruvius especially. But a more original idea, one directly relevant to our purpose, can also be inferred. The letter therefore merits quotation at length:

> I humbly observe to yr Lordship touching the North front that it was intended, much in the same Style as Mr Inigo Jones, and Mr Webb intended the Kings pallace at Greenwich (now Turned into an hospitall) vizt That ye Basment and Grand plinth, upon which all the Superstructure was to be deposited, should be plain, and appear one solid stone (or Rock) the better to distinguish the upper order as well as to sustain it.
>
> The South side, and North front of your Ldships house cannot be seen together at the same Time, nor at any time upon the Diagonall (or angular view.) And tho ye South front is Rusticated in the Basment yet the order upon it is plain, but divided into a perpetuall Arcade, supported with a Range of pilasters, by which the contrast and dispar, between the Basment and the order, become more visibly remarkable. and it is most certain, that when a machine is composed of different parts, Limbs, or members, one would not have them, blend and melt into one mass, so as not to be able, to distinguish ye Noble parts from the inferior, the Basment, from the order,

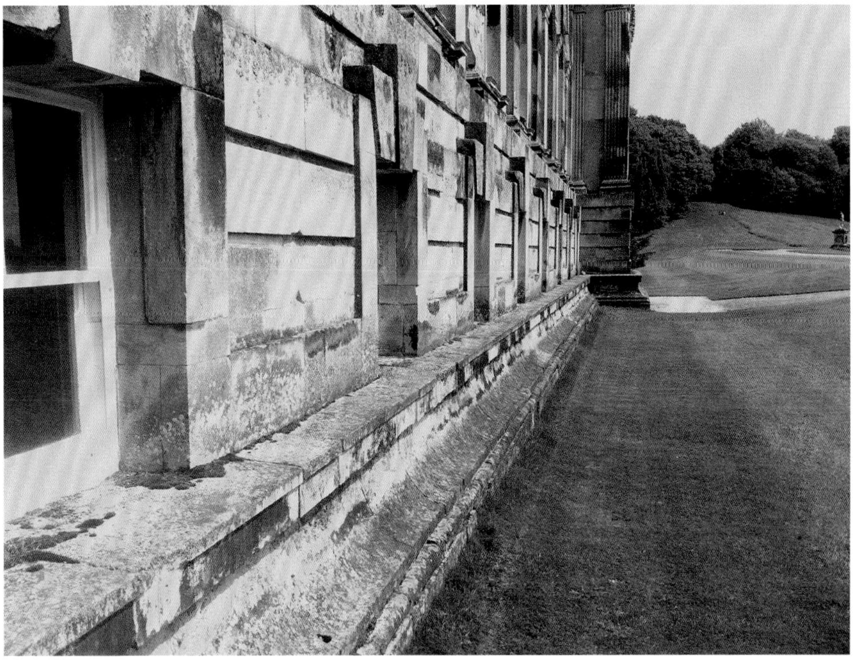

43. Castle Howard, south front, detail of basement. Photograph courtesy of Anthony Geraghty

> that rests upon it. or as in human bodys, the Trunck from the Limbs. The North front is of the Dorick order Rusticated except in the Basment, which is plain and represents (or intended so to do) a grand entire plinth made out of one solid Rock of Stone and ought not to be Subdivided, and cannot, without hurting ye Beauty and Strength of ye Building.[34]

Hawksmoor was writing to a purpose: to oppose a plan, recently suggested to the Earl, to decorate the basement of the entrance front with rusticated stonework. This explains why Hawksmoor's letter is less about the contrast between the front and back of the house, than it is about the contrast between the top and bottom of each façade. Hawksmoor begins with the south front, probably because it exemplifies the more conventional arrangement: the basement, he carefully recounts, is "Rusticated", while the "order" above is "plain" (fig. 38b).[35] This was of course standard practice, and Hawksmoor had himself deployed it at Easton Neston in Northamptonshire. On the north front, however, this arrangement is reversed (fig. 38a): "the Dorick order [is] Rusticated except in the Basment, which is plain."

This is a more unusual arrangement, but one which, Hawksmoor reveals, was based on John Webb's work at Greenwich.[36] Hawksmoor's rationale for these contrasts is multi-layered. The first step in his argument is familiar from Vitruvius and the Renaissance theorists: "the contrast and dispar[ity], between the Basment and the order" visualizes the relative importance of the levels—they "become . . . visibly remarkable". This process of differentiation is then likened, in the standard Vitruvian way, to the human form, with its hierarchy of "parts, Limbs, or members", which likewise "distinguish ye Noble parts from the inferior". But the system depends on more than arbitrary difference, since each element has to be structurally appropriate to its hierarchical function, and it is here that Hawksmoor's thinking assumes a secondary level of metaphor directly relevant to our purpose. Moving beyond the analogy of the human form, he expounds the architectural detailing of the house in natural philosophical terms: as building materials hewn from the earth—rocks and stones—and subject to the statical properties of the material universe. He repeatedly describes the plain basement on the north front of the house as a rock: as "one solid stone (or Rock)", as "a grand . . . plinth made out of one solid Rock of Stone", and as "a sollid rock quit plain". And as such, he writes, the basement, or "plinth", is equipped to receive the "deposited" "Superstructure" of the house itself (fig. 38a).

Of course, in reality, the plinth is no such thing and serves no such purpose: it is a wall composed of separate stones (but with the mortar joints suitably effaced), and beyond it lies an elevated basement, hence the windows set into the plinth, something that Hawksmoor conveniently omits to mention. He does, however, acknowledge this displacement between appearance and reality: the plinth, he writes, should "*appear* one solid stone"; similarly, it "*represents* . . . a grand . . . plinth made out of one solid Rock". In other words, the architectural ornament of the north front is a *pictorial representation* of a non-existent architectural structure—but it is nevertheless informed by the material and tensile properties of the structure it implies. As such, it is free to exaggerate, and it is the exaggeration of structure, I would like to suggest, that is the dominant idea of English Baroque architecture. As Hawksmoor says at end of the passage quoted above, a building must be strong as well as beautiful.

Strong architecture is also to be found on the garden side of the house, where the plinth's status as supporting member level is brilliantly exaggerated (fig. 43). The thickness of the wall is dramatically amplified, firstly with channelled masonry and then, below and in front of this, with a deep buttress-like moulding which stretches the footprint of the building by an additional two feet. The windows to the basement are located in the same plane as the upper "order", but they are framed by deep surrounds, comprised of unadorned mullions to left and right, and triple keystones above. The latter motif was a favourite of Hawksmoor and Vanbrugh, and is one that, more than any other, encapsulates the basic thesis I am arguing. For the elemental purpose of the keystone is that of a wedge, which holds a series of stones in tension and stasis, and by introducing three of these rather than one, by projecting them beyond the plane of the window, and above all by overscaling them so egregiously, they draw attention to this elemental purpose and to the role it performs in the maintenance of a lintel.[37] In between these surrounds, the intervening stretches of wall are thickened by stretches of channelled masonry. The treatment of these is again very telling: each course of masonry is dropped firmly into place between the window surrounds, like a pile of massive slabs. On the side wings, this effect is heightened by the omission of an upper channel, which serves to reveal, and thereby express, the thickness of the projection. Under the main block of the house, however, the channelled masonry is continued all the way up to the top of the basement, doubtless to suggest an even greater level of support for the two stories that are superimposed above. As in Hawksmoor's letter, then, we see an ornamental vocabulary that draws attention to (1) the volumetric shape of the stones and (2) the structural consequences of their superimposition. At this stage in his career, Vanbrugh equated the presumed strength of the ornament to the structural function it purports to fulfil. But in his later houses he reconfigures the relationship, tipping the balance in favour of weight. At Seaton Delaval, for example, his treatment of the basement suggests the *inability* of the basement to support the intense weightiness of the house. The channelled masonry is now pulvinated, as if compressed by the gravitational forces of the House.

In drawing attention to this strand of Hawksmoor's thinking, I am not saying anything we do not already know: from Vitruvius onwards, and probably before, classical articulation has been understood as a representation of building, and one, moreover, that bears a limited relationship to the structural reality of the building it articulates (think of Vitruvius on the Doric entablature). Moreover, *firmitas* is one of the three elements of architecture as defined by Vitruvius. I draw attention to this aspect of classical ornament, however, because it assumes a particular centrality in the architecture of Vanbrugh, Hawksmoor, and the English Baroque.

All of which brings us back to the idea of the castle. I would like to suggest that the forms of the north front, by virtue of the meanings just outlined, are indicative of strength. This begins with the Doric pilasters, an unprecedented choice of order for a high-status house (fig. 41). There are eight of these, grouped as four pairs. They are exquisitely smooth, and, if we follow Hawksmoor's conceptualization of the building, they were meant to be understood as giant monoliths. They are set against channelled masonry, the meaning of which I have already discussed. At Chatsworth and Easton Neston, the pilasters alternate with windows and articulate the solidity of the intervening wall masses. But at Castle Howard, the widest and stockiest of the classical orders is arranged in pairs, creating, in effect, four identical units, each composed of two pilasters surmounted by projecting sections of entablature. The effect is powerfully architectonic, grounded in the same elemental trabeation as the trilithons of Stonehenge. The effect of four massive supporting members is further suggested by the treatment of intervening bays, which are dragged forward and held within the clutches of the pilasters. They accommodate not windows but niches, which express the depth and therefore the solidity of the wall. Similarly, the triglyphs of the frieze are limited to the four "piers", which, to a viewer versed in Vitruvius, suggests that it is the four piers, and they alone, that support the cross members of the roof.

Once again, this powerful expression of architectural structure has a limited relationship to the reality that lies beyond it. In the middle of the façade, the four central pilasters are boldly projected, so that the outer pilasters stand proud of the main plane by two feet, as square piers. This projection is indeed very solid, and, as such, probably does buttress the outward thrusts of the dome and Great Hall. It also enables the visitor to Castle Howard to enter the house through a remarkable thickness of wall, and it means that, at the upper level, Vanbrugh was able to insert circulation corridors into the wall, in a fashion strikingly like an actual castle. At the edges of the façade, however, the clusters of pilasters are purely pictorial, with next to no relationship to the building's section, but they suggest a massive solidity to the edges of the house. This discrepancy is true all the way up the façade, as the entablature projections to either end of the design in actual fact front a mezzanine of attic rooms (these are lit by oval windows, tucked away on the side façades).

All of these forms, then, are grounded in architectural values, and it is these values that allow them to mean something quite specific at Castle Howard: that this is an impregnable building. They are therefore appropriate to the conceit of the house as a castle. The martial conceit of the building is likewise apparent in the decorative carving of the north front.[38]

The question of why Carlisle wanted a house that evoked a castle is a subject for another occasion, for my concern in this essay is not why, but how, Castle Howard means what it does.[39] But we are faced with a challenge all the same: the challenge of a castle that does not look like a castle. The fact that this is so, however, reveals something of the anachronistic nature of our thinking about English Baroque architecture. For our notions of appropriateness—of how decorum is effected—remain steeped in historicist notions of style, by which I mean the direct correlation of specific architectural forms (and sets of forms) to particular historical moments and periods.

Elsewhere at Castle Howard, we find forms that, it must be admitted, do suggest, by virtue of their form, a medieval origin—the Carrmire Gate, for example, designed by Hawksmoor in 1730 (or thereabouts), with its crenellated walls and tower (fig. 44). But even here we need to strip architectural forms from the historical moment of their invention: it is what the forms do—or pretend to do—that accounts for their inclusion. If we ask not when or where the forms originate, but focus instead on the role they perform in context, or pretend to perform, then the design of the gateway becomes an entirely plausible proposition.[40] We might take a single motif: the small pyramids that cluster around the central opening. These may or may not derive from Porsenna's Tomb, but even if they do it is not this origin that activates their deployment; rather, it is the role they perform as a buffer to the opening that accounts for their inclusion. The fusion of Roman and medieval sources at the Carrmire Gate (if this is indeed how Hawksmoor understood them) become unified and reconciled in purpose.

Hawksmoor and Vanbrugh were, of course, aware that such forms have their origins in history. But the point I want to emphasize is that it was their relevance to the requirements of the moment that activated their appropriateness and continues to make them so. Indeed, the notion of *the present* is absolutely fundamental to the theory and practice of architectural decorum, and it is primarily the ahistorical fundamentals of architectural construction that make Vanbrugh and Hawksmoor's designs so enduringly appropriate. We too are subject to these physical norms, which is why English Baroque architecture retains its expressive capacity.

Finally, what makes this ahistoricism so fascinating at Castle Howard is the way it was brought to bear, and indeed still is, on the larger purpose of the place, which is basically an affirmation of aristocracy—of landownership, and the ways in which landownership fuels an ever-deepening legitimacy, as past and present move forward into future.[41] This is why ancestry and progeny are so explicitly articulated at Castle Howard—through the overlaying of a historic landscape, with park and castle at its heart; and through the erection, in that very landscape, of pyramid and mausoleum, representative, respectively, of ancestry and progeny. The larger challenge of Castle Howard, then, is to understand how these political ideas—ideas grounded in temporal notions of past, present, and future—were expressed through an architectural system that operated through a primarily ahistorical understanding of architectural agency.

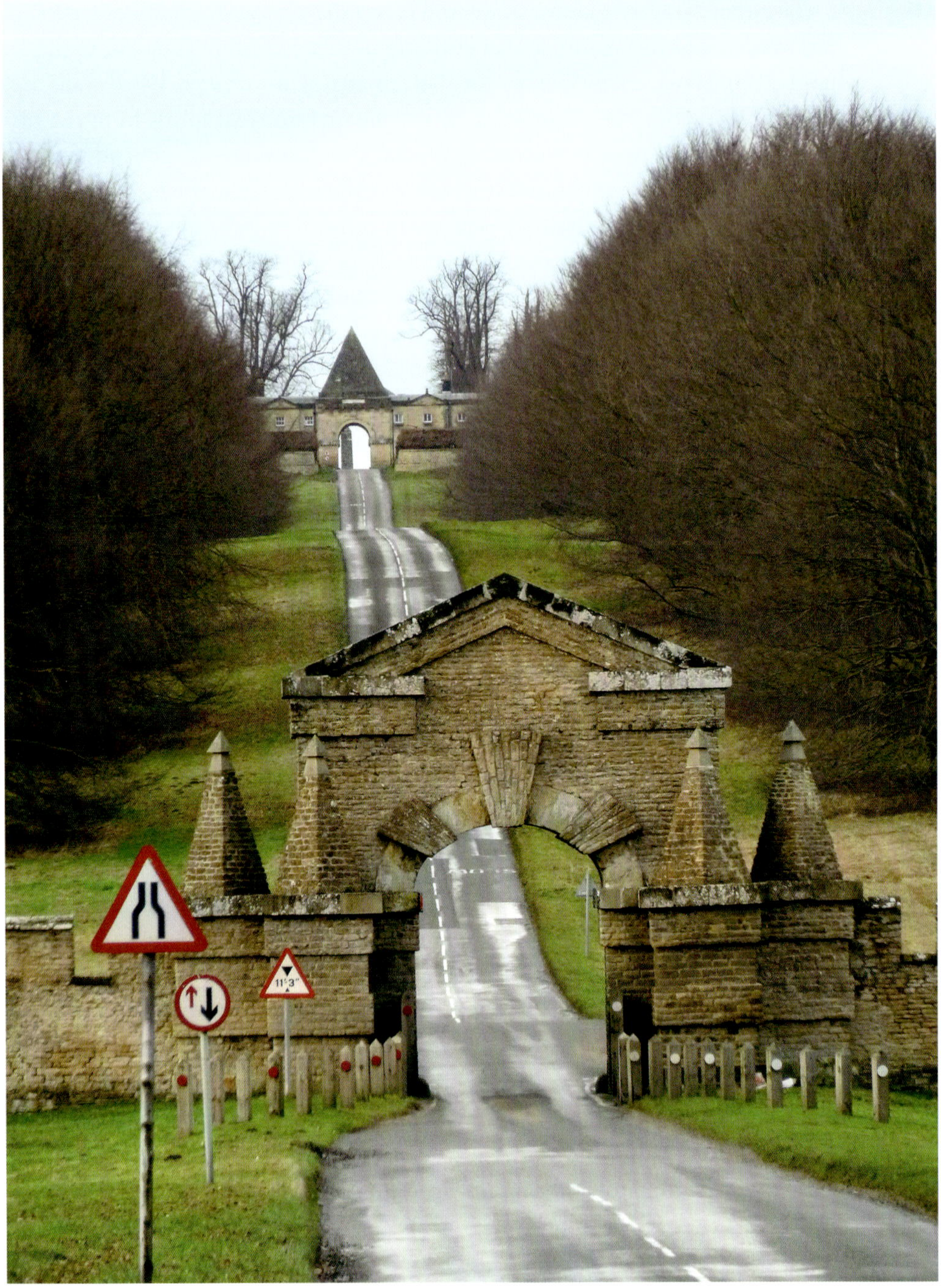

44. The Carrmire Gate (detail), Castle Howard. Photograph courtesy of Amanda Lillie

CONCLUSION

In this essay I have emphasized two aspects of the design of Castle Howard. Firstly, the ambition with which it engages with architectural precedent: as Hawksmoor's letter confirms, Castle Howard "engages a great deal of consideration" because, as a country house, it is more than "such familiar sites, as we see in England" and "claims more Regard, than one of Palladios humble villas in the Vicentine . . . or than sundry of the Chateaus in France". But, as we have seen, it brings elements of these three architectural traditions into a grandiloquent synthesis, and combines them with additional elements drawn from European palace design. Hawksmoor's letter, then, suggests that the architects of Castle Howard thought about their creation in terms of typology, and that it was by combining these typologies that they created a house as magnificent as a palace. Secondly, we have seen how the exterior articulation of the house exemplifies a set of meanings grounded in architectonic values, and that these values communicate a powerful sense of structural solidity, thereby imbuing the house with the "air", if not necessarily the appearance, of a castle. Hawksmoor's characterization of the house as "Castle and Pallace conjoyn'd" alludes, then, to these two fundamental priorities of English Baroque architecture. This essay has prioritized the writings of Hawksmoor, but in conclusion I would like to quote from Vanbrugh himself, referring to Blenheim Palace in 1710 and the properties that such a house ought to exemplify: "Beauty[,] Magnificence, and Duration".[42] This reworking of the Vitruvian triad (Beauty, Utility, Strength) epitomizes the features I have been describing: the magnificence of the palace, and the duration of the castle. Therein lies the beauty.

1. John Summerson, *Architecture in Britain, 1530–1830*, 9th ed. (New Haven and London: Yale Univ. Press, 1993), Kerry Downes, *English Baroque Architecture* (London: A. Zwemmer, 1966). The key exception is Judith Hook, *The Baroque Age in England* (London: Thames and Hudson, 1976).
2. Kerry Downes, *Vanbrugh* (London: A. Zwemmer, 1977), 26–39, Charles Saumarez Smith, *The Building of Castle Howard* (London: Faber and Faber, 1990).
3. Geoffrey Webb, "The Letters and Drawings of Nicholas Hawksmoor relating to the Building of the Mausoleum at Castle Howard, 1726–1742", *Walpole Society* 19 (1931): 154 (Letter 45).
4. Kerry Downes, *Hawksmoor* (London: A. Zwemmer, 1959), 254.
5. Colen Campbell, *Vitruvius Britannicus*, III (1715), plates 5–6.
6. Oliver Hill and John Cornforth, *English Country Houses: Caroline, 1625–1685* (London: Country Life, 1966), 30, 61–64, Summerson, *Architecture in Britain*, 129–30, 174.
7. James Lees-Milne, *English Country Houses: Baroque, 1685–1715* (London: Country Life, 1970), 15, 112–18, 278.
8. Laurence Whistler, *The Imagination of Vanbrugh and his Fellow Artists* (London: Art & Technics, 1954), 40–50.
9. Hill and Cornforth, *English Country Houses*, 51–56, 90–96.

10. John Bold, *John Webb: Architectural Theory and Practice in the Seventeenth Century* (Oxford: Clarendon Press, 1989), 126–46, Bold, *Greenwich: An Architectural History of the Royal Hospital for Seamen and the Queen's House* (New Haven and London: Yale Univ. Press, 2000), 77–82.
11. John Harris and A. A. Tait, *Catalogue of the Drawings by Inigo Jones, John Webb & Isaac de Caus at Worcester College Oxford* (Oxford: Clarendon Press, 1979), 37, Anthony Geraghty, *The Architectural Drawings of Sir Christopher Wren at All Souls College Oxford* (Aldershot: Lund Humphries, 2007), 123–25.
12. Downes, *Hawksmoor*, 254.
13. Kerry Downes, *Sir Christopher Wren* (London: Whitechapel Art Gallery, 1982), 92.
14. Simon Thurley, *Hampton Court: A Social and Architectural History* (New Haven and London: Yale Univ. Press, 2003), 156–59. See also Gordon Higgott's online catalogue of *English Baroque Drawings* at Sir John Soane's Museum in London. http://jeromeonline.co.uk/drawings/.
15. Geraghty, *Architectural Drawings of Sir Christopher Wren*, 128–30. See also Gordon Higgott's online catalogue of *English Baroque Drawings* cited in note 14 above.
16. Bold, *Greenwich*, 104.
17. R. T. Gunther, *The Architecture of Sir Roger Pratt* (Oxford Univ. Press, 1928), 194–95, Howard Colvin and John Newman, eds., *Of Building: Roger North's Writings on Architecture* (Oxford: Clarendon Press, 1981), 150–51. See also Charles Ford, *Roger North's Scientific Manuscripts*, [n.d.], http://discovery.ucl.ac.uk/1403234
18. Nathan T. Whitman, "Fontainebleau, the Luxembourg, and the French Domed Entry Pavilion", *Journal of the Society of Architectural Historians* 46, no. 4 (Dec. 1987): 356–73.
19. Guillaume Fonkenell, *Le Palais des Tuileries* (Arles: Éditions Honoré Clair, 2010), 49–69. The sixteenth-century dome was replaced by Jacques Lemercier in the mid-seventeenth century. Prints of it, however, remained available.
20. Allan Braham and Peter Smith, *François Mansart*, 2 vols. (London: A. Zwemmer, 1973), 1: 120–49; 2: plates 463–539, Jean-Pierre Babelon and Claude Mignot, *François Mansart: le génie de l'architecture* (Paris: Editions Gallimard, 1998), 241–55.
21. See the discussion of the chambres "à l'italienne" in Alexandre Cojannot, *Louis Le Vau et les nouvelles ambitions de l'architecture française, 1612–1654* (Paris: Editions A. et J. Picard, 2012), 56–60.
22. Mark Girouard, *Life in the French Country House* (London: Cassell, 2000), 135.
23. Jean-Marie Pérouse de Montclos, *Vaux le Vicomte* (London: Scala Books, 1997).
24. Andrea Palladio, *The Four Books on Architecture*, trans. Robert Tavernor and Richard Schofield (Cambridge, MA, and London: MIT Press, 1997), 94–95.
25. Lydia M. Soo, *Wren's "Tracts" on Architecture and Other Writings* (Cambridge Univ. Press, 1998), 163.
26. *The Complete Works of Sir John Vanbrugh*, ed. Bonamy Dobrée and Geoffrey Webb, 4 vols. (Brooklyn, NY: AMS Press, 1967), 4: 4–5.
27. Raphaël Masson, "Trianon de marbre", in *Jules Hardouin-Mansart, 1646–1708*, ed. Alexandre Gady (Paris: Éditions de la Maison des sciences de l'homme, 2010), 282–97, Bertrand Jestaz, *Jules Hardouin-Mansart: Vie et oeuvre*, 2 vols. (Paris: Picard, 2008), 1: 251–56.
28. Vanbrugh was released in 1693 and briefly at liberty to explore French architecture. See Kerry Downes, *Sir John Vanbrugh: A Biography* (London: Sidgwick and Jackson, 1987), 75–76.
29. Historic Manuscripts Commission, *Marquis of Bath*, III (1908), 309, 311, 312, 315, 321, 325, 326, 329, 332, 333, 334.
30. John Harris, "William and John Talman: Architecture and a Partnership", in *John Talman: An Early-Eighteenth-Century Connoisseur*, ed. Cinzia Maria Sicca (New Haven and London: Yale Univ. Press, 2008), 97–125 (103–14).

31. I use the work "credible" intentionally, to evoke the recent work of Matthew Walker, who, borrowing his terminology from a historian of science (Steven Shapin), has argued that design credibility in late seventeenth-century England was grounded not in professional training—for no such training was available—but in a knowledge of Continental design, preferably acquired at first hand, but failing that, from printed sources. Matthew Walker, "*Architectus Ingenio*: Robert Hooke, the Early Royal Society, and the Practices of Architecture" (unpublished PhD diss., Univ. of York, 2009).
32. Quoted in Downes, *Sir John Vanbrugh*, 202.
33. Vanbrugh, *Complete Works*, 4: 14. Vanbrugh's use of the word "air" is difficult to focus, but its meaning probably corresponds with the following definition in the OED: "expressing the character, quality, or (usually abstract) thing of which another gives the impression" (IV.13.a). In other words, Kimbolton has the "air" of a *castle* because it is first and foremost a *house*.
34. Downes, *Hawksmoor*, 254.
35. Hawksmoor uses the term "order" to refer to the upper level as a whole, and not the pilaster articulation.
36. The plinth level is more apparent in Webb's drawings than it is in reality. See Bold, *John Webb*, 138, fig. 92, which is annotated by Hawksmoor.
37. The introduction of what is, in effect, a flat arch suggests that Vanbrugh and Hawksmoor understood the arch itself as a strong form, owing to the compression of its voussoirs. This interpretation of the arched window, which was seldom used in post-medieval English secular architecture before Castle Howard, is further suggested by the voussoirs over the main windows on the north front and the keystones over the main windows on the south front.
38. See Vaughan Hart, *Sir John Vanbrugh: Storyteller in Stone* (New Haven and London: Yale Univ. Press, 2008), 129–35.
39. The question of why Carlisle wanted a house that evokes a castle has yet to be answered, but an answer would require a detailed consideration of the residual chivalric elements of late seventeenth-century aristocratic culture. For a preliminary discussion of post-medieval chivalry and its bearing on English architecture, see John Goodall, *The English Castle, 1066–1650* (New Haven and London: Yale Univ. Press, 2011), 489–91.
40. My thinking is indebted to Quentin Skinner, "Meaning and Understanding in the History of Ideas", in Skinner, *Visions of Politics, Vol. 1: Regarding Method* (Cambridge Univ. Press, 2002), 57–89.
41. Smith, *Building of Castle Howard*.
42. Vanbrugh, *Complete Works*, 4: 45.

KINGS, QUEENS, COMMANDERS

Antonio Verrio and the Triumph of Painting at the Restoration Court

Richard Johns

In the spring of 1996 one of Europe's largest auction houses advertised for sale a late seventeenth-century portrait of the Holy Roman Emperor Leopold I (1640–1705), attributed to an unidentified follower of the Flemish artist Jan Thomas.[1] The life-size painting (fig. 45) presents its royal subject against a sun-infused sky, wearing a rejuvenating wig and laurel crown, and swathed in layers of rich fabric—all befitting one of the seventeenth century's most powerful princes. On closer inspection, however, the conventions of the regal head-and-shoulder type portrait are visibly disrupted by the artist's loose painterly style (especially noticeable in the casual approach to detail in the lace cravat) and by a flash of lead white that cuts diagonally across the sitter's body, suggestive of the silky lining of the ceremonial blue velvet mantle that covers his shoulders. While the artist's broad-brush technique suggests that the painting may have been conceived with a more distanced kind of viewing in mind, the dynamic open-armed gesture signalled by the exposed layers of red, white, and blue fabric indicates that the image once revealed far more about its royal subject than its present dimensions permit.

Following the auction in 1996, the painting was bought for the British Royal Collection from a sharp-eyed London art dealer who, recognizing the jowly portrait as a more convincing likeness of Charles II, had bid successfully for the oil-on-plaster painting and reattributed it as a fragment of the long-vanished ceiling of St George's Hall, Windsor Castle, by the Italian artist Antonio Verrio (ca. 1636–1707).[2] That the true identity—including the nationality—of both sitter and artist could be so easily forgotten, only to be rediscovered when the painting surfaced on the art market, is a useful reminder of the interchangeability of the visual codes of kingship adopted by the competing courts of early modern Europe (not to mention the conditional status of any pictorial likeness). That Verrio's portrait should have been removed from its original context in the first place, cropped, then framed, suggests something rather different about the unstable critical fortunes of a kind of painting which, more than any other, shaped the visual experience of the Restoration court.

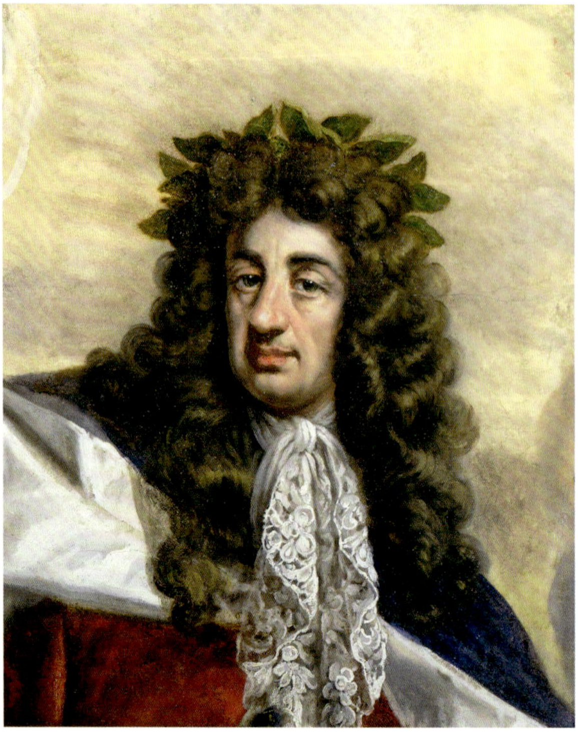

45. Antonio Verrio, *Charles II*, ca. 1684, oil on plaster, 32⅝ x 27 in. (82.8 x 68.7 cm). Private collection

Despite a resurgence of interest in the artist in recent years, Verrio remains a fairly marginal figure in the history of British art.[3] He arrived in London from Paris in 1672, an experienced painter in his mid-thirties, under the protection of Ralph Montagu, Charles II's ambassador to the court of Louis XIV. During a long and prestigious career in England that spanned several decades, he worked for four successive monarchs as well as several of the country's most powerful aristocratic patrons. In 1684, after completing the ceiling of St George's Hall, Verrio was made "chief and first painter" to the king (a position previously held by Peter Lely and, before him, Anthony van Dyck), and years later he died in the palatial surroundings of Hampton Court, where he had lived and worked with a generous pension from Queen Anne.[4] More than any other artist, Verrio was responsible for introducing English audiences to the forms and fancies of decorative history painting—a distinctive mode of grand-scale allegorical wall and ceiling decoration that dominated new courtly, country, and elite city interiors during the late seventeenth and early eighteenth centuries. From the royal palaces of Windsor and Hampton Court to the great houses of Chatsworth and Burghley, Verrio flattered and gave pleasure to his employers with exuberant schemes that brought together a fantastical array of mythological and historical characters, often extending across several rooms. In doing so, he set a standard against which, for better or worse, the work of a new generation of painters that included Louis Laguerre and James Thornhill would be judged.

The decoration of St George's Hall (1682–4) marked the culmination of a long-term project to refashion Windsor in accordance with Charles II's decision to make the medieval castle his principal royal residence outside London.[5] Beginning in 1673, the king's architect Hugh May made the exterior of the medieval castle more uniform, but largely preserved the monumental, castellated silhouette of the fourteenth-century buildings. More noticeably, he rebuilt the courtyard of the north range, creating a new and expansive interior comprising two very grand state apartments, a large chapel, and a great hall. The decoration of these royal spaces with a sequence of religious, mythological, and historical subjects occupied Verrio and a small team of assistants for the best part of ten years, eventually reaching across twenty rooms and three staircases. The result was a painted environment of unprecedented grandeur, in which the king and his consort, Catherine of Braganza, featured repeatedly in an all-encompassing display of royal taste and power.[6] The new palace attracted enthusiastic praise, much of it parcelled with loyal reflections on the reign of Charles II, who died within a year of its completion. John Evelyn thought the hall "stupendous", as good as anything he had seen abroad; and in 1686, Aphra Behn described Windsor as "the most glorious Palace in the Christian World", and predicted that Verrio's painting, together with the woodcarving of Grinling Gibbons, would remain forever as a monument to its royal patron, "to tell succeeding Ages, that all Arts and Learning were not confin'd to antient Rome and Greece, but that England too could boast its mightiest Share".[7]

Verrio successfully navigated the political turbulence of the later 1680s, but within a few years of his death in 1707, his reputation began a precipitous decline. As the eighteenth century progressed, Verrio's work fell foul of an evolving cultural hegemony—articulated in the influential writing of Anthony Ashley Cooper, third Earl of Shaftesbury, and by other taste-makers of the period including Alexander Pope and Horace Walpole—which characterized his allegorical inventions as artless and derivative, and condemned his methods as crude and overbearing. Within this Augustan "republic of taste", with its emphasis on polite physical and moral restraint, Verrio's kind of painting was quickly identified as the epitome of poor taste.[8] The intellectual and physical rejection of Verrio's painting culminated in the 1820s with the wholesale destruction of his work at Windsor, when all but three of the ceilings that had first brought the artist fame and fortune were pulled down by Jeffry Wyatville in a bid to return the castle to an imagined Gothic past.[9] Ever since, Verrio has been defined as a peripheral, even preposterous, figure within the history of British art, operating somewhere at the fag-end of a Continental Baroque tradition.

As a counterpoint, this essay reconsiders the circumstances of Verrio's extraordinary artistic success during the 1670s and 1680s. It asks how an itinerant altarpiece painter from the south of Italy rose to become one of the most prominent and highly remunerated artists in England. Rather than focus on why Verrio's efforts subsequently became synonymous with bad art, it seeks to explain why his trademark combination of allegory, unrestrained colour, and flamboyant composition came to be looked upon as exemplary. The purpose is not to rescue a neglected painter from obscurity—still less to persuade modern viewers of the timeless quality of his work—but to explore the shifting, socially determined nature of artistic value in the period covered by this book. The contingencies of taste and aesthetic value are foregrounded when the focus of attention is a type of art that historically has been identified as an aberration, or an afterthought (one, moreover, associated exclusively with elite culture and the strategies of panegyric). Issues of conservation and destruction come into play when studying a body of art that has such a low survival rate, and for which there is often little or no visual record. And conventional disciplinary constraints are challenged when examining a type of site-specific imagery that cannot easily be defined by the traditional categories of either painting or architecture, but which clearly intrudes on both. In other words, I am interested in Verrio's work, in part, because I think it can tell us as much about the structures and narratives of British art that have attempted to exclude it, as it can about the cultural and political environment in which that work was conceived and first assigned value.

In the alternative narrative of late seventeenth-century art that follows, Verrio features as a leading artist—perhaps *the* leading artist—in the creation of a Restoration courtly visual culture. Its focus is not an immersive decorative scheme of the kind for which Verrio became best known, but a large allegorical portrait, approximately seven feet high (two metres), that has remained in the Royal Collection since it was completed for Charles II in 1674. The *Sea Triumph of Charles II* (fig. 46) is among the earliest surviving works that Verrio produced following his arrival in England two years earlier. He eventually received £70 for the painting, a relatively modest sum for such a large canvas, but as a prospectus for further royal patronage it proved to be of far greater value.[10] George Vertue later remarked that the *Sea Triumph* had been "well approvd of", and that this favourable reception had persuaded the king to entrust Verrio with the far more extensive and lucrative

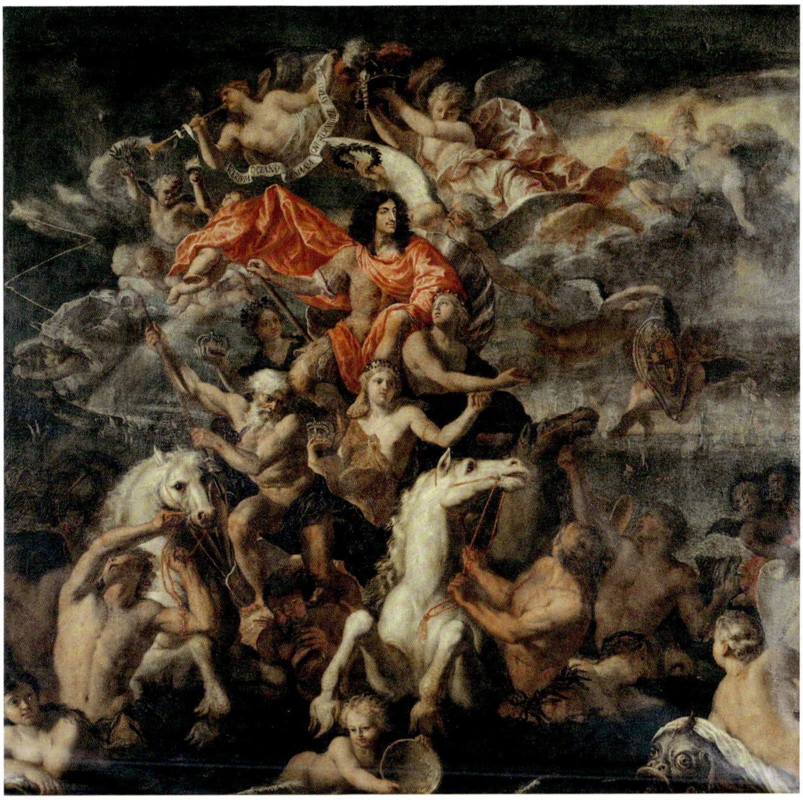

46. Antonio Verrio, *Sea Triumph of Charles II*, ca. 1674, oil on canvas, 88⅜ x 91 in. (224.5 x 231 cm). Royal Collection Trust, London

task of decorating the new state apartments at Windsor Castle.[11] It thus marks a beginning, of sorts, and so it is to this image that we turn for a closer understanding of what once made Antonio Verrio the painter of choice.

A *SEA TRIUMPH*

Charles II careers triumphantly towards us, resplendent in red and gold as he is carried in a sea chariot driven by Neptune and drawn by four powerful sea horses. Three garlanded female figures, embodying the kingdoms of England, Scotland, and Ireland, each offers her sovereignty (and, it seems, her body) to the king. A grey-haired figure of Time presents a laurel crown and Victory a plumed helmet, as two winged infants rise up bearing an olive branch and a flaming torch, signifying Peace and Love. Further to the left of the picture, the contorted body of Envy is struck by lightning as two more putti cook up a storm of wind and rain. In the distance, a fragment of coastline with shipping is illuminated by the arc of a rainbow that appears to radiate from the monarch's head. Behind the king to the right, a fleet of Royal Navy ships lies at anchor in a fair breeze, as a group of Olympian deities including Minerva, goddess of wisdom, war, and commerce, and Juno, protector of the state, look on approvingly from above. Meanwhile, Fame unfurls a Virgilian epithet that equates the king's dominion with the unlimited earthly power of Julius Caesar: *Imperium oceano, famam qui terminet astris* ("Whose empire ocean, and whose fame the skies alone shall bound").[12]

The *Sea Triumph of Charles II* was the most emphatic portrayal of the restored monarch as ruler of the waves ever attempted, but the idea, at least, was already established by the time Verrio arrived in England. Among the temporary structures erected for the king's coronation procession in 1661 was a naval arch replete with maritime symbolism, including a living personification of the Thames, and an inscription that identified the restored monarch as *Neptuno Britannico*.[13] Four years later, Charles appeared as a Neptune-like figure driving a sea chariot beneath the motto *Et pontus serviet* ("The sea too shall be subject") on the reverse of a portrait medal struck by Thomas Simon to commemorate the Battle of Lowestoft (1665) and the outbreak of the second Anglo-Dutch war.[14] The corresponding military context for Verrio's elaborate maritime panegyric was most likely the Treaty of Westminster of February 1674—a settlement that signalled an end to the third (and final) contest between the English and Dutch navies, and which initiated a territorial exchange that consolidated English colonial control over the east coast of North America. It doesn't seem far-fetched to imagine Verrio fingering Simon's silver medal while contemplating how best to commemorate England's most recent conflict with the United Provinces, or leafing through John Ogilby and David Loggan's published account of the king's coronation entertainments, and appreciating how in both the interplay of image and text fused a personal mythology of kingship with an aggrandizing narrative of maritime and imperial supremacy.[15]

While recognizing *Neptuno Britannico* as a recurring theme of Restoration visual culture, a privileged group of contemporary viewers may also have noticed parallels between Verrio's painting and the ambitious iconographic programme dedicated to the personality cult of Louis XIV then unfolding at Versailles. There is a revealing comparison to be made, for example, between Verrio's *Sea Triumph* and the characterization of Neptune and Amphitrite in a near-contemporary French allegory of *Water*—one of a series of Gobelins tapestries representing the four elements that Charles Le Brun designed in the early 1660s for Versailles. Le Brun's *Elements* were engraved by Sébastien Le Clerc for André Félibien's *Tapisseries du Roi* in 1670 (fig. 47), and he went on to develop the theme for the south end of the painted ceiling of the Galerie d'Apollon at the Louvre, at precisely the time

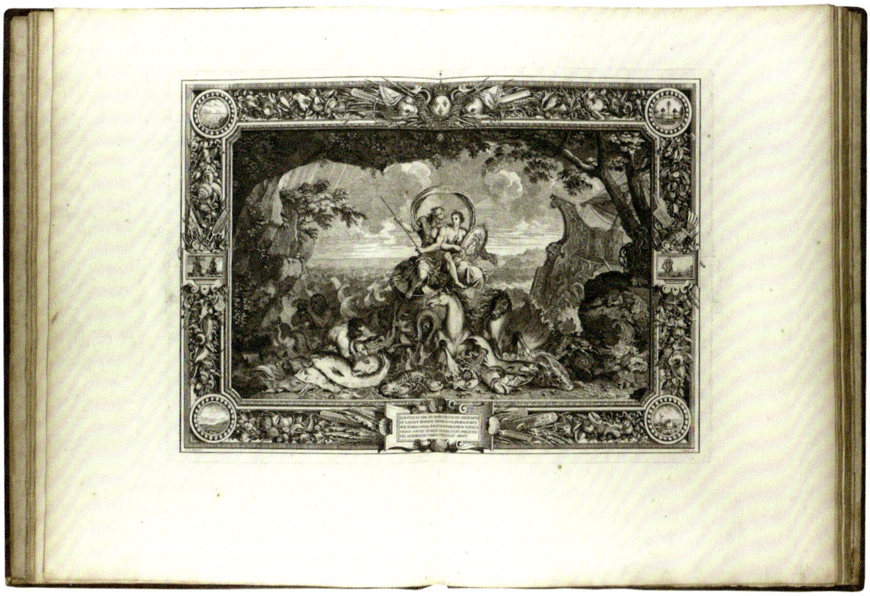

47. Sébastien Le Clerc after Charles Le Brun, "Water," in André Félibien, *Tapisseries du Roi, où sont représentés les quatre élémens & les quatre saisons* (Paris, 1670), engraving. Beinecke Rare Book and Manuscript Library

of Verrio's stay in Paris.[16] It is hardly conceivable that Montagu and Verrio did not encounter these important decorations for the French king. Indeed, Montagu later commissioned his own set of Le Brun's *Elements* for Montagu House.[17]

Verrio's role in the cultural alignment of the Stuart and Bourbon courts also becomes apparent when considering the *Sea Triumph* alongside a later allegorical portrait of the French king by Antoine Coypel, painted in the light of the Truce of Ratisbon in 1684. Like Verrio's painting, Coypel's *Glory of Louis XIV* (fig. 48) marshals a complex pictorial allegory to commemorate an inconclusive and unpopular territorial war as an unimpeachable royal triumph. Both monarchs wear a variation of imperial Roman military dress: they are Caesars, enthroned, swathed in scarlet, and surrounded by a constellation of allegorical figures, exposed limbs, and emblems that endow every aspect of their appearance—their age, complexion, physical abilities, even the style of their hair—with a contemporary political urgency. While certain structural and figural similarities raise the possibility of a direct correspondence between these various images, we can be even more confident in concluding that all three artists shared a commitment to the classical

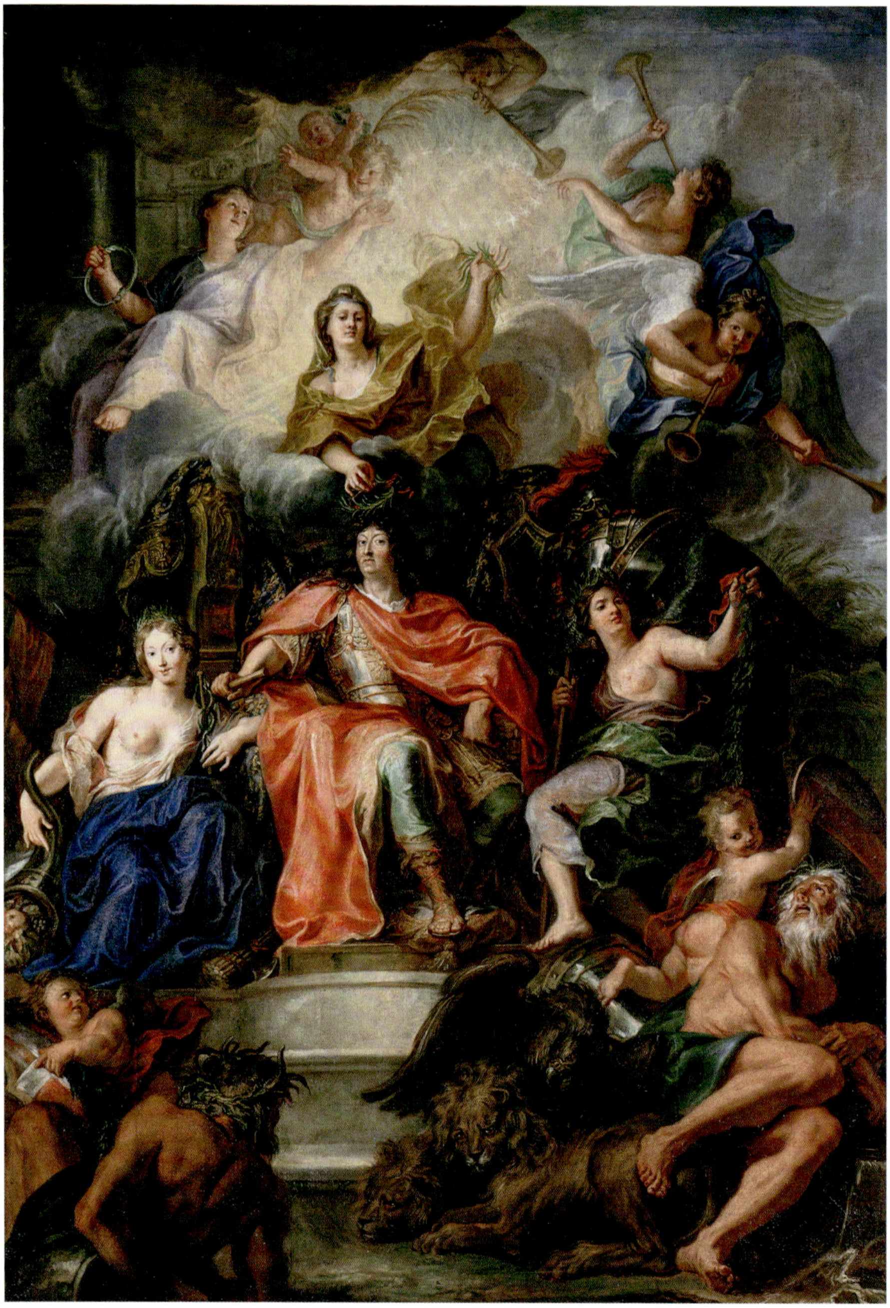

48. Antoine Coypel, *The Glory of Louis XIV*, ca. 1686, oil on canvas, 77¾ x 53 ½ in. (197.5 x 136 cm). Chateau de Versailles, France

language of imperial conquest that was being institutionalized and promoted within the French Académie royale de peinture et de sculpture under the direction of Jean-Baptiste Colbert.

Verrio was one of several Catholic painters who forged a successful career at the Restoration court after travelling to England via Paris and the Académie. Others included Benedetto Gennari, who painted devotional pictures for the queen and erotic mythological subjects for the king, and Henri Gascar, whose high-saturation portrayal of the Duke of York as a Roman naval commander (fig. 49) rivals the *Sea Triumph* as a display of Restoration grandiloquence and maritime pomp. The apparent ease with which Verrio moved from the French capital to London as part of Ralph Montagu's diplomatic entourage, before going on to

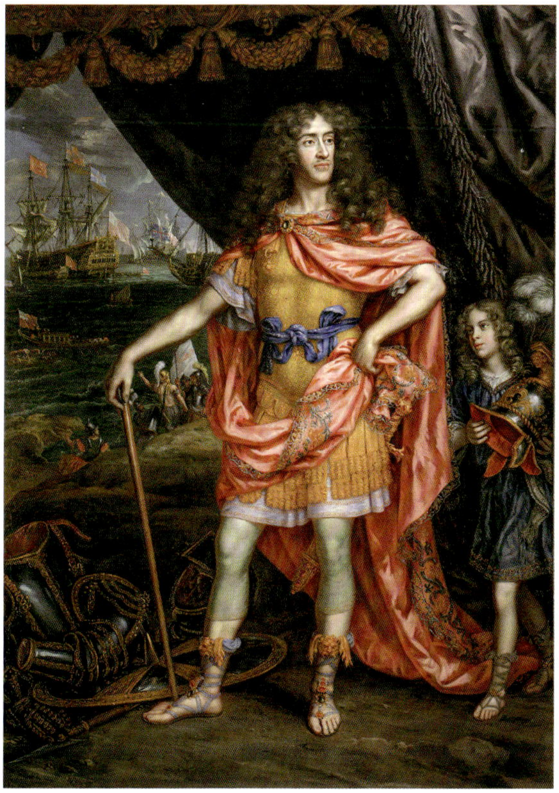

49. Henri Gascar, *James, Duke of York*, 1672–3, oil on canvas, 90 x 64 in. (228.6 x 162.5 cm). National Maritime Museum, Greenwich, London, Greenwich Hospital Collection

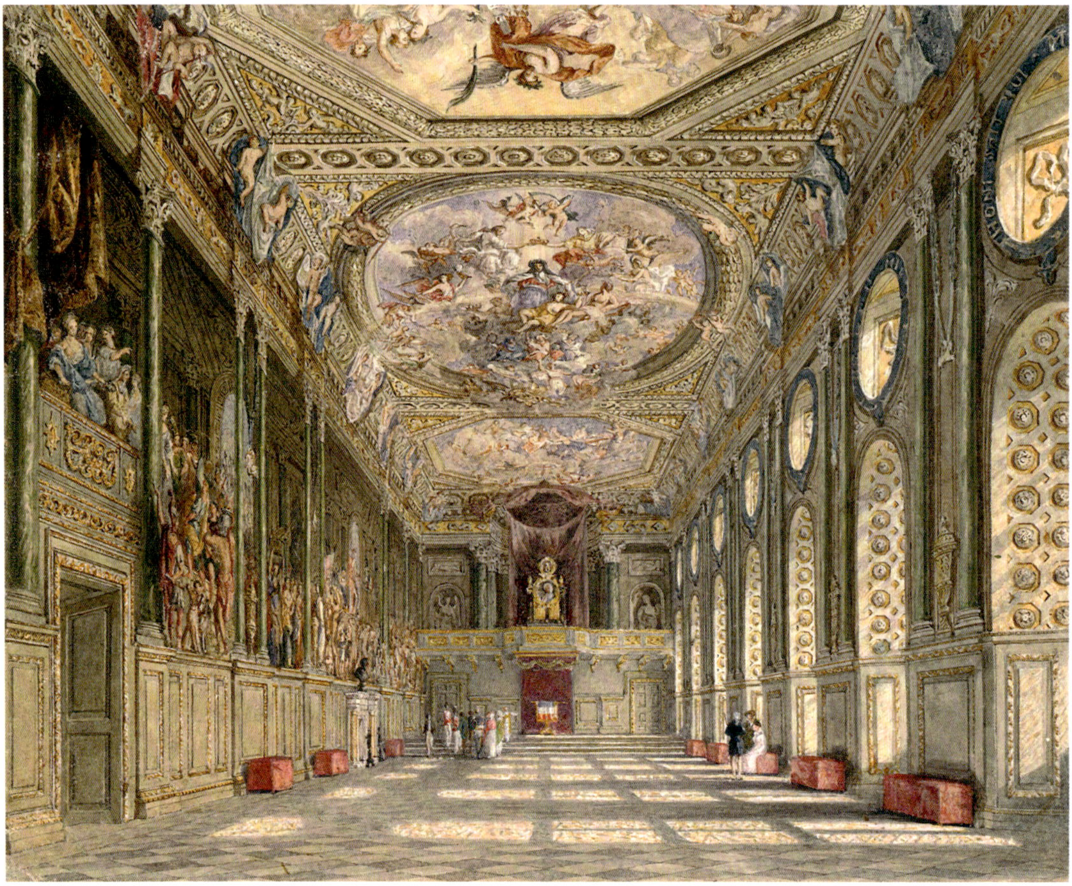

53. Charles Wild, *St. George's Hall, Windsor Castle*, ca. 1816, watercolour, 8 x 10 in. (20.2 x 25.4 cm). Royal Collection Trust, London

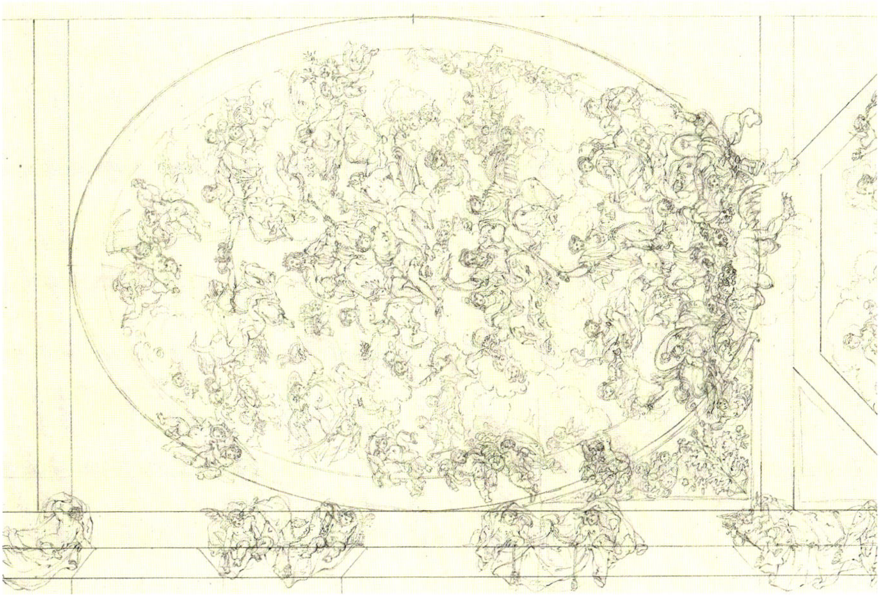

54. Attributed to John Francis Rigaud, *North Wall and Part of the Ceiling of St George's Hall, Windsor Castle* (detail), ca. 1800, pencil on paper, 17¼ x 23¾ in. (43.9 x 60.2 cm). Royal Collection Trust, London

At Windsor, Charles II was surrounded on the ceiling by a wealth of symbolic objects and bodies, all of which referred to the potency of his reign. In an important essay on the decoration of St George's Hall, Katharine Gibson has drawn attention to the ways in which the materiality of Restoration politics encroached upon the symbolism of the ceiling. She observes, for example, the variety and significance of the ceremonial headwear that encircled the body of Charles II, each item a clearly rendered marker of the political aspirations of the Restoration monarchy: an ostrich-plumed hat of the Order of the Garter; a warrior's helmet presented by a winged Victory; the St Edward's crown, made for Charles's coronation, held aloft by two female figures.[32] These and other details of Verrio's ceiling can be gleaned from two nineteenth-century images, both made just a few years before the palace was remodelled by Wyatville. The first is a watercolour made by Charles Wild for William Henry Pyne's *Royal Residences* (1816–19; fig. 53); the second a pencil drawing, attributed by Gibson to John Francis Rigaud, that was probably made around 1805, when the artist was employed at Windsor (fig. 54).[33] Where Wild's colourful watercolour hints at the lost grandeur of the room, and the illusionistic effects of Verrio's horizontal perspective, Rigaud's scale drawing offers a more detailed, if partial, trace of the ceiling and adjacent north wall as they appeared more than a

1. Dorotheum, Vienna, 6 March 1996, lot 156. The painting sold for €8,420.
2. Historical Portraits, "Portrait of King Charles II (1630–85) 1684 by Antonio Verrio": www.historicalportraits.com/Gallery.asp?Page=Item&ItemID=583 (accessed 1 May 2015). The painting is one of three portrait fragments by Verrio. One other, removed from the King's Presence Chamber, is also in the Royal Collection. A third, taken from the ceiling of the King's Withdrawing Room, is in the collection at Packwood House, Warwickshire (National Trust).
3. The most extensive recent work on Verrio, published in Italian and French, focuses on the artist's early career on the Continent: Raffaele De Giorgi, *"Couleur, Couleur!" Antonio Verrio: un pittore in Europa tra Seicento a Settecento* (Edizione Firenze, 2009), and Axel Hémery, ed., *Antonio Verrio: Chroniques d'un peintre italien voyageur (1636–1707)* (Toulouse: Musée des Augustins, 2010). Notable among a handful of recent essays on the artist's career in England is Brett Dolman, "Antonio Verrio (c.1636–1707) and the Royal Image at Hampton Court", *British Art Journal* 10, no. 3 (Winter 2009): 18–28.
4. "Entry Book: June 1684, 26–30", in *Calendar of Treasury Books*, vol. 7: *1681–1685*, ed. William A. Shaw (London: HMSO, 1916), 1184–1188; also at British History Online, http://www.british-history.ac.uk/cal-treasury-books/vol7/pp1184-1188 (accessed 1 May 2015). As is so often the case for British art of this period, much of what is known about Verrio's career in England is derived from the writings of George Vertue. A fuller, modern account was set out by Edward Croft-Murray in his landmark study *Decorative Painting in England, 1537–1837*, 2 vols. (London: Country Life, 1962–70). More recently, the details of the artist's professional life have been revisited and refined by Cécile Brett in "Antonio Verrio (c.1636–1707): His Career and Surviving Work", *British Art Journal* 10, no. 3 (Winter 2009): 4–17.
5. The iconography of Verrio's painting in St George's Hall is examined by Katharine Gibson in "The Decoration of St George's Hall, Windsor, for Charles II: 'too resplendent bright for subjects' eyes'", *Apollo* 147, no. 435 (May 1998): 30–40. The architectural components of Verrio's painting in the hall are the focus of a more recent essay by Wolf Burchard, "Illusion and Involvement: The Lost Baroque Architecture of St George's Hall at Windsor Castle", *Immediations* 2, no. 4 (2011): 98–119.
6. See Croft-Murray, *Decorative Painting in England*, 1: 240–42. Andrea MacKean offers an extended analysis of the decorated state apartments at Windsor in "The Shaping of Identity in Public Places: An Examination of Subjective Identification in British Decorated Interiors, 1630–1800" (PhD thesis, Univ. of Manchester, 1999), 104–77.
7. Behn's description belongs to Iris, heroine of her *La montre, or, The lover's watch* (London, 1686), 154–55. Evelyn made several visits to Windsor to see Verrio's work in progress. See, for example, 13 June 1683 and 6 Sept. 1685, in *The Diary of John Evelyn*, ed. E. S. De Beer, 6 vols. (Oxford Univ. Press, 1955), vol. 4. For other contemporary responses, see Gibson, "Decoration of St George's Hall", esp. 30.
8. For a fuller analysis of Verrio's critical demise at the hands of Shaftesbury and others, see Richard Johns, "'Those Wilder Sorts of Painting': The Painted Interior in the Age of Antonio Verrio", in *A Companion to British Art: 1600 to the Present*, ed. Dana Arnold and David Peters Corbett (Oxford: Wiley-Blackwell, 2013), 79–104.
9. For an account of Wyatville's intervention, see Derek Lindstrum, *Sir Jeffry Wyatville: Architect to the King* (Clarendon Press: Oxford, 1972), esp. 166–200. Verrio's ceilings survive in the King's Dining Room, and in the Queen's Audience Chamber and Presence Chamber.
10. Pipe Office declared accounts (money for special uses, 1673–75), The National Archives E 351/39, cited in Katharine Gibson, "'Best Belov'd of Kings': The Iconography of King Charles II" (PhD thesis, Courtauld Institute of Art, Univ. of London, 1997), 135.
11. George Vertue, "The Note-books of George Vertue II", *Walpole Society* 20 (1932): 132.
12. Virgil, *Aeneid* 1: 391–92, in *The Works of Virgil*, trans. John Dryden (London: Jacob Tonson, 1697), 213. Modern scholars disagree over whether the passage in question is a reference to Julius Caesar or Augustus Caesar, although for seventeenth-century audiences the distinction between the two figures was, in any case, often blurred. For a summary of modern interpretations, see James J. O'Hara, *Death and the Optimistic Prophecy in Vergil's Aeneid* (Princeton Univ. Press, 1990), esp. 155–62.
13. See John Ogilby, *The Entertainment of his most excellent majestie Charles II* (London, 1662), 43–110.

14. George Vertue, *Medals, Coins, Great Seals, and Other Works of Thomas Simon*, 2nd ed. (London, 1780), 63–64 and pl. XXXVII. See also, British Museum G3,EM.334.
15. Loggan produced a large engraving of each of the four coronation arches for Ogilby's *The Entertainment of his most excellent majestie Charles II*.
16. Geneviève Bresc-Bautier, ed., *La galerie d'Apollon, au palais du Louvre* (Paris: Gallimard/Musée du Louvre, 2004).
17. Montagu commissioned the *Elements* from John Vanderbank sometime around 1689. They now hang in the Great Hall at Boughton. For details (including a discussion of the likely date of the commission), see Wendy Hefford, "Ralph Montagu's Tapestries", in *Boughton House: The English Versailles*, ed. Tessa Murdoch (London: Faber and Faber, 1992), 96–107 (esp. 106–7) and 221.
18. Ronald Hutton, "The Making of the Secret Treaty of Dover, 1668–1670", *The Historical Journal* 29, no. 2 (June 1986): 297–318. In fact, Verrio's tacit involvement in Anglo-French affairs had already begun. In 1671, the subject chosen for his Académie reception piece was an allegory of Louis XIV's peaceful conquest of Dunkirk, a strategically important port town that Charles II had sold to his French cousin in 1662 for 5 million livres. See Anatole de Montaiglon, ed., *Procès-verbaux de l'Académie royale de peinture et de sculpture, 1648–1793* (Paris: J. Baur, 1875–92), 1: 362–63.
19. Michael S. Robinson, *A Catalogue of the Paintings of the Elder and the Younger Willem van de Velde*, 2 vols. (London: Sotheby's, 1990).
20. Royal Collection Trust, "Three Mortlake tapestries depicting scenes from the Battle of Solebay": www.royalcollection.org.uk/collection/1145/the-battle-of-solebay (accessed 1 May 2015).
21. Hefford, "Ralph Montagu's Tapestries", 96–107.
22. The tapestries are represented in situ in an early eighteenth-century painting by Peter Tillemans in the Royal Collection, *Queen Anne addressing the House of Lords* (ca. 1708–14). The most detailed visual record, however, is a series of prints by John Pine (with borders engraved by Henri Gravelot), published in 1738 as *The Tapestry Hangings of the House of Lords*.
23. The shipping in the background of the painting illustrated (one of three known variations) indicates that the wooden panel was either partially repainted or copied anew in the context of the naval wars of the later 1600s. For issues surrounding the dating of the painting, see Catharine Macleod, "Dynasties: London, Tate Gallery", *The Burlington Magazine* 138, no. 1114 (Jan. 1996): 41–43 (43), and Pieter van der Merwe, "The Shardeloes 'Armada Portrait'", *The Burlington Magazine* 138, no. 1118 (May 1996): 329.
24. Virgil, *Eclogue* 4: 17. The translation here is Pope's, from *The Works of Mr. Alexander Pope* (London, 1717), 41–42.
25. Jonson's text appeared in print a few weeks after the event as *Loves triumph through Callipolis. Performed in a masque at court 1630* (London, 1630 [1631]).
26. The single performance cost £600 to stage, with an additional £300 for costumes. See Stephen Orgel and Roy Strong in the preface to *Inigo Jones: The Theatre of the Stuart Court*, 2 vols. (London: Sotheby Parke Bernet, 1973), 1: 405.
27. Jonson, *Loves triumph through Callipolis*, 1–2.
28. Jonson, *Loves triumph through Callipolis*, 5–6.
29. See, for example, J. Douglas Canfield, "The Significance of the Restoration Rhymed Heroic Play", *Eighteenth-Century Studies* 13, no. 1 (Autumn 1979): 49–62, and Nancy Klein Maguire, *Regicide and Restoration: English Tragicomedy, 1660–1671* (Cambridge Univ. Press, 1992), esp. 83–101. Issues of narrative and nostalgia are discussed in relation to a very different set of Restoration images in a crucial essay by David H. Solkin, "Isaac Fuller's *Escape of Charles II*: A Restoration Tragicomedy", *Journal of the Warburg and Courtauld Institutes* 62 (1999): 199–240.
30. Initially published by Edward Cooper and Richard Thompson in the mid-1680s, the two-plate image was reissued by John Bowles in the mid-1700s under the new title *The Restoration of King Charles the Second*, with an explanatory inscription that was not part of the original edition.
31. Other emblematic references to the Order of the Garter featured throughout. For a more detailed description of Verrio's painting in the hall, see Gibson, "Decoration of St George's Hall".

32. Gibson, "Decoration of St George's Hall", 34–35.
33. Gibson, "Decoration of St George's Hall", 30–31.
34. Both images incorporate changes that Verrio made to the north wall around 1700, in a partial attempt to introduce William III into the scheme. An oil sketch relating to those alterations, formerly in the collection of Edward Croft-Murray, was offered for sale in 2009 (Christie's, South Kensington, 23 April 2009, lot 184; bought in). See Brett, "Antonio Verrio", 11 and fig. 8; and Hémery, *Antonio Verrio*, 112–13.
35. Charles II's sexual conduct and reputation are elegantly summarized and contextualized by Kevin Sharpe in *Rebranding Rule: The Restoration and Revolution Monarchy, 1660–1714* (New Haven and London: Yale Univ. Press, 2013), esp. 170–72. See also Harold M. Weber's literary analysis of the king's "profane body" in *Paper Bullets: Print and Kingship under Charles II* (Lexington: Univ. Press of Kentucky, 1996), esp. 88–127.
36. John Wilmot, second Earl of Rochester, "A Satyr on Charles II", ca. 1673, in *The Complete Poems of John Wilmot, Earl of Rochester*, ed. David M. Vieth (New Haven and London: Yale Univ. Press, 1962), 60–61. Vieth reads the poem's comparison between Charles II and Louis XIV as an allusion to the third Anglo-Dutch war and, more specifically, the Treaty of Westminster that signalled an end to the latest Anglo-French military alliance.
37. Weber, *Paper Bullets*, esp. 97–101.
38. John Dryden, *Absalom and Achitophel*, cited and discussed by Weber in *Paper Bullets*, esp. 88–92. See also Stephen Zwicker, *Lines of Authority: Politics and English Literary Culture, 1649–1689* (Ithaca: Cornell Univ. Press, 1993), esp. 130–72.
39. Rachel Weil, "Sometimes a Sceptre is only a Sceptre: Pornography and Politics in Restoration England", in *The Invention of Pornography*, ed. Lynn Hunt (New York: Zone Books, 1993), 125–53, Weber, *Paper Bullets*, esp. 126–27.
40. Catharine MacLeod and Julia Marciari Alexander, eds., *Painted Ladies: Women in the Court of Charles II* (New Haven and London: National Portrait Gallery, 2001); and MacLeod and Alexander, eds., *Politics, Transgression, and Representation at the Court of Charles II* (New Haven and London: Yale Univ. Press, 2007).

The Public Image of John Churchill, First Duke of Marlborough, 1702–1708

Matthew Hargraves

IN the autumn of 1703, the German-born medallist John Croker struck a new medal to celebrate the allied army's recent campaign in Flanders (fig. 55).[1] The allies, under Marlborough's command, had taken three towns in French hands: Bonn, Limbourg, and Huy. These small victories only highlighted the overall lack of success enjoyed by the allies. Even Marlborough acknowledged that his achievements had been modest, admitting to the Lord Treasurer, Sidney Godolphin, that capturing these towns would "make very little noise in the world".[2] But with the war already becoming unpopular and critics longing to see a humbled Marlborough recalled home, the ministry attempted to turn small victories into triumphs.

It was Marlborough and the Earl of Godolphin who headed the ministry that had plunged England back into war with France in 1702, and both were in severe political difficulty by the end of 1703. It was the political legacy of William III that

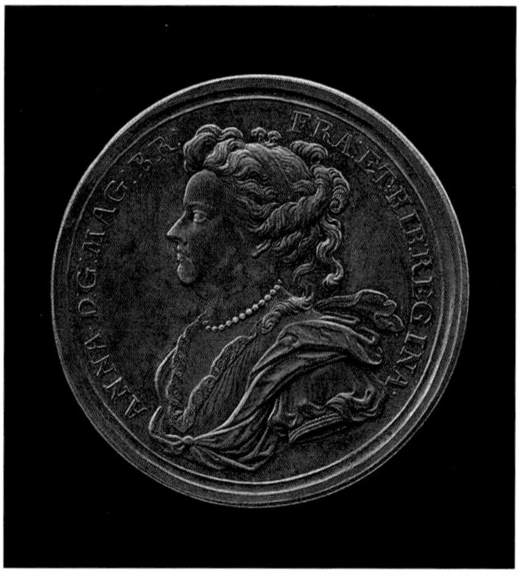

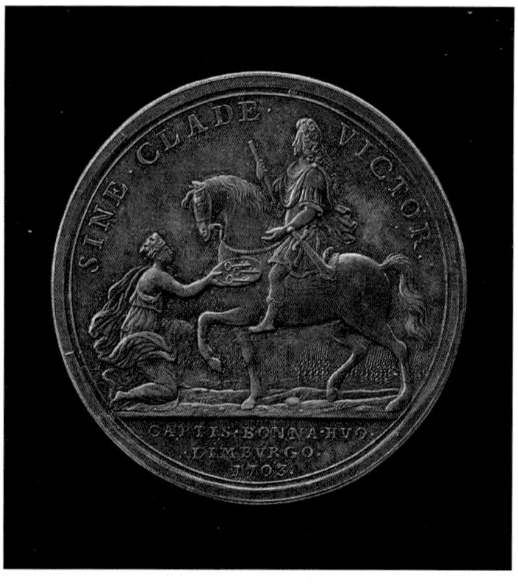

55. John Croker, *Sine Claude Victor* Medal, 1703, silver, 1⅝ in. (4.2 cm). British Museum, London

committed Anne to maintaining the Grand Alliance against Louis XIV when she became queen, but without clear victories and with the threat of a quick French triumph, the Tories increased their opposition, seeking to end England's involvement in Continental land campaigns. To the Tories, the government's reliance on financiers to fund its wars had put the power of the landed interest under increasing threat; for them, it would be better instead to abandon land campaigns and trust in England's navy when fighting the French. Facing this opposition, Marlborough and Godolphin sought to cast the conflict as a glorious enterprise in the tradition of King William's wars using whatever means lay at their disposal. Central to the ministry's strategy was to define an official image for Marlborough as a popular hero, someone who had taken on the mantle of the late king as the scourge of Louis XIV. But the ministry was not blind to the obstacles it faced. Aside from Marlborough's troublingly close relationship to the queen, his heroism and martial prowess were doubted. Tories never forgot his betrayal in deserting James II, the man to whom he owed everything, for which William rewarded him with an earldom in 1689. Moreover, Marlborough's actual military experience was extremely limited, since William had dismissed him from all offices in 1692 for intriguing with the Jacobite court. The choice of Marlborough as Captain-General in 1702 owed more to his status as Queen Anne's favourite and a lack of other candidates acceptable to the allies than to any proven expertise.[3] Worse still, Marlborough's wife, Sarah, had been Anne's intimate confidante since as early as 1673, and although the Duke's sympathies were moderately Tory, Sarah had a reputation for being a zealous Whig whose proximity to the throne aroused both anxiety and resentment among the opposition. So close were the Churchills to the queen that they even created nicknames for one another: Anne was Mrs Morley and the Churchills were Mr and Mrs Freeman. William Legge, first Earl of Dartmouth, later recalled that in William III's reign John and Sarah Churchill were said to have so much influence on Princess Anne that Marlborough would one day rule her as king.[4] To compound these fears, memories of recent military fiascos by royal favourites remained fresh in many minds. Charles I had placed his trust in the Duke of Buckingham and been humiliated by the failed siege of the island of Ré, off La Rochelle, in 1627. Precedents such as these did nothing to strengthen Marlborough's position.

But history aside, the overarching problem for the ministry was the advent of party politics, a free press, and the emergence of what can be called public opinion.[5] Every one of Marlborough's successes, no matter how trivial, had to be cast as a great victory if the war against the French was to continue, providing one reason behind the decision to strike a medal in 1703. William III had established the vogue for these celebratory military medals in the previous decade; in accordance with the iconography that he had established for these earlier works, the obverse of Anne's medal depicts her bust-length in an iconic profile.[6] The medal's reverse, however, broke with all precedent. At first glance it appears traditional enough. A male figure on horseback, dressed in the guise of a Roman commander, receives the humble surrender of the three captured towns represented by a crouching female figure. William III's medals had customarily depicted him in just this fashion. His 1690 medal recording the pacification of Ireland, for instance, showed the king's profile on one side, and his equestrian portrait as the army's commander-in-chief on the other.[7] The novelty of Anne's medal was that the equestrian figure on the reverse was no monarch, but her Captain-General, Marlborough himself. A Latin inscription running round the medal's edge, beginning *Sine Clade Victor*, styles the Duke as a magnanimous conquering hero. In full translation it reads: "A Conqueror Without Slaughter. Bonn, Huy, and Limbourg taken, 1703".

Croker sold these medals in gold for £7 each, but cheaper versions were available in silver and copper for 12s. and 4s. respectively; the large number still surviving suggest that this medal was a popular example.[8] Nevertheless, in some circles Croker's representation of Anne and Marlborough on two sides of the same medal was swiftly condemned as a breach of all decorum. March 1704 saw the appearance of some satirical verses *On the New Medal with the Queen on one side and the General on Horseback on the other with this motto Sine Clade Victor*.[9] The author attributes the medal's genesis to Godolphin and begins by protesting that Marlborough won a victor's medal cheaply, without even deigning to raise his sword. How different, he argues, to "Good Queen Besse's days" when generals earned their laurels from bravery and bloodshed on the battlefield. For the satirist, Marlborough's image on the reverse of Anne's medal indicated either that the queen was giving her Captain-General too much licence, or that he was taking liberties with his sovereign. Again citing the precedent of Elizabeth I, the author argues that "Good Queen Besse herself would always ride/ And scorn'd to lett her subjects get astride."[10]Alluding to Marlborough's alleged sexual indiscretions, he pointed out that even Elizabeth's Treasurer, unlike Godolphin, never "durst attempt so daring a design/ To stamp his Queen and Cuckold on one coin".[11] The contrast between the Elizabethan era and the present state of the nation under Queen Anne highlighted two principal complaints: first, that the Continental land campaign was a fruitless charade led by an amateur general; second, as inferred from the medal, that the Duke was becoming an overmighty subject seeking parity with the queen herself.

If the medal provoked outrage in some quarters it was not entirely Croker's fault. The satirist neatly exploited the fact that the queen was unable to lead her armies personally into battle. Her husband, Prince George of Denmark, held the ranks of Generalissimo and Lord High Admiral but these were purely honorific titles. He was, after all, the man of whom Charles II said: "I've tried him drunk, and I've tried him sober, and there's nothing in him."[12] The ineffectual Danish Prince left Marlborough with the title of Captain-General and *de facto* control of the allied forces. It was Marlborough, then, who took on William III's role as the nemesis of Louis XIV, Catholicism, and arbitrary government.[13] Yet as a subject filling a void created by the death of a sovereign, Marlborough was left in a position that required the deployment of a whole new set of representational strategies. One reason for the medal's hostile reception lay in the fact that the ministry had blundered by not taking this on board. Its initial attempts to represent the Duke as hero were based on the wholesale appropriation of the iconography of the late king who had been both monarch and general. Moreover, the controversy surrounding the Croker medal demonstrates that what was intended to commemorate one specific incident in Marlborough's career was taken instead as evidence of the general relationship subsisting between him and the queen. The unfortunate result was to play into the hands of Marlborough's enemies by making him, as another satire put it, "the shadow of a king".[14]

The Tory satire on Croker's medal reflects a mood of optimism within the party that reached its height in the spring of 1704. Tories revelled in Marlborough's lack of real success, pointing out the folly of continuing with an expensive land campaign and ridiculing the apparently feeble favourite.[15] By the summer of 1704 Marlborough's impeachment was threatened in Parliament before Blenheim silenced the critics. The allied army's spectacular victory over a superior French force on 13 August 1704 saved Marlborough and the administration from ruin. Having just debated impeaching him, Parliament now fought over how a grateful nation could best honour its victorious Captain-General. Yet no amount of military success could resolve the constitutional complexities of a male Captain-General serving a female sovereign. Even in his moment of triumph, problems of decorum arose in regard to Marlborough's representation. One suggestion was for a square to be laid out in London to be named after the Duke and furnished with two statues, one of him and one of the Queen. Having been stung by the criticism of the Croker medal, Godolphin baulked at this suggestion. As he told his fellow minister Robert Harley:

> I am not fond of the proposal of two statues, one for the Queen and th' other for the Duke of Marlborough. What merit soever a subject may have I am doubtful that may set him upon too near an equality with one upon the throne. My own opinion inclines most to an anniversary thanksgiving by Act of Parliament for so entire a victory, as the most public, the most decent, and the most permanent record of it to posterity.[16]

Croker's medal had been grist to the opposition's mill that Marlborough aspired to rule over the queen; Godolphin would not make that mistake again. Rather than a direct tribute to the Duke, it was better to institute a regular and extravagant national celebration to swing opinion behind the war. Nevertheless the queen demanded some personal tribute to her favourite and Parliament finally obliged by granting Marlborough the royal manor of Woodstock in February 1705.[17]

John Closterman (1660–1711) presumably began his equestrian portrait of Marlborough when the conquering hero came home in triumph after Blenheim (fig. 56). Although the early history of the painting is entirely undocumented, George Vertue recorded that "the Duke of Marlbro sat for his own picture for the great picture on horseback", adding a description of it in 1731 as "a large Picture on Horseback. With Aligoricall [*sic*] figures".[18] Sadly Vertue adds nothing more of substance so we remain in the dark about the circumstances of the portrait's com-

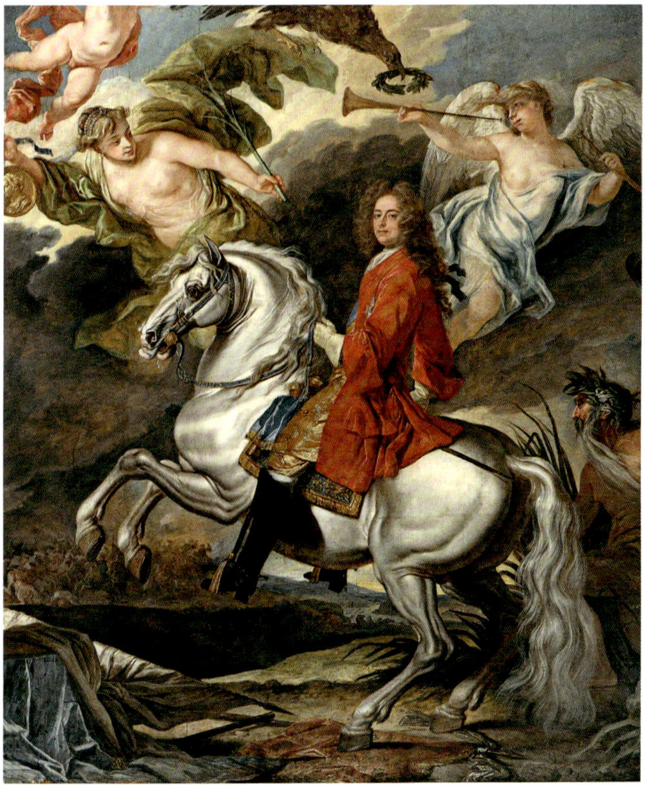

56. John Closterman, *The Triumph of John, 1st Duke of Marlborough*, ca. 1705, oil on canvas, 133⅞ x 106¼ in. (340 x 270 cm). Royal Hospital, Chelsea, London

mission. Closterman certainly conceived it on a vast scale; despite having been cut down it still measures some twelve feet by ten (3.6 x 3 m).[19] The Duke, dressed in a scarlet jacket over a waistcoat embroidered with gold, sits astride a rearing white horse. His left hand, clad in a silver glove, holds the reins of his fiery steed. An indistinct battle is raging in the distance with a turbulent black sky casting a lengthy shadow across the canvas. A river god is seen crouching behind the horse, gazing across to the battle, while the sky around the Duke is filled with a host of Vertue's "aligoricall figures". To the right flies a winged figure of Fame blowing her trumpet, above which hovers a victory eagle carrying the hero's laurels. In the top left is another figure representing Victory, shown clad in a billowing green dress and holding a victor's palm in her left hand. In her right is a golden medal struck with a profile portrait of Queen Anne.

Such equestrian portraits had been a customary way of representing leaders, whether of sovereigns or military commanders, since classical times.[20] Ironically, it seems that Closterman based both the painting's composition and iconography on Rubens's now lost portrait of George Villiers, Duke of Buckingham, then owned by Sir Francis Child and hanging at Osterley Park.[21] Given that Buckingham was a notorious favourite of Charles I and militarily incompetent, the comparison was not altogether felicitous. Even if his model was somewhat risky, Closterman, unlike Croker, took care to incorporate certain elements that helped to diffuse the tensions surrounding the commemoration of a male Captain-General serving under a female sovereign.

If the painting was indeed made after Blenheim, then it was surely intended to depict that battle rather than a general moment of the campaign. Not only does the river god suggest the Danube, the river by which Marlborough won his victory, but the Duke's scarlet coat and white mount correspond to contemporary reports of his appearance on that famous day.[22] Thus in the midst of battle the Duke is represented as supremely composed. The similarity, for instance, between the horse's flowing mane and the Duke's wig invites comparison between the rider and his steed's strength and dynamic energy. But where the horse spits and glares wildly in apparent confusion and anxiety, the Duke's countenance is calm and serene, casting a nonchalant eye out to the spectator. The courageous Duke, unlike his horse, is in full command of his passions, and brings the unruly horse into a purposeful levade.

There are notable parallels between Closterman's glorification of Marlborough and Joseph Addison's poem *The Campaign: A Poem, to His Grace, the Duke of Marlborough*, first published in 1705. This panegyric was part of Godolphin's campaign to promote the war and earned the author instant government office. Addison's verses offer a textual equivalent to the painter's celebration of Marlborough's bravery and strength:

Twas then Great Marlbro's mighty Soul was prov'd,
That, in the Shock of Charging Hosts unmov'd,
Amidst Confusion, Horror and Despair,
Examin'd all the Dreadful Scenes of War;
In peaceful Thought, the Field of Death survey' d . . .
Calm and Serene he drives the furious blast . . .
Rides in the Whirl-wind, and directs the storm.[23]

Like Closterman, Addison hails Marlborough's serenity in the midst of danger. Contrary to Tory jibes, both poet and painter seek to demonstrate that Marlborough is no coward. Moreover, both representations make great play of the Duke's countenance. In the Closterman painting his features are handsome and youthful, belying the fact that Marlborough was already fifty-four years old by the time he fought Blenheim. Such outward beauty, heightened by contrast to the ruddy complexion of the hoary river god, suggests a comparable moral virtue. Likewise, Addison's poem parallels Closterman's representation of Marlborough's polished visage: "Such Fire with so much Sweetness mixt!/ Such easie Greatness, such a graceful Port,/ So turn'd and finish'd for the Camp or Court!"[24]

For Addison and Closterman, the Captain-General's grace and sangfroid under fire betray the dispassionate character—the courtly *sprezzatura*—that defines him as the perfect gentleman.[25] But however composed Marlborough might be, Closterman's image is also about martial ardour, about devotion to duty in the midst of the hot and tumultuous battle. Readers would have detected Addison's borrowing from Sir Philip Sidney in his lines. In Sidney's *Defence of Poesy* he related the opinion of John Pugliano that "soldiers were the noblest estate of mankind, and horsemen the noblest of soldiers. He said they were the masters of war and ornaments of peace, speedy goers and strong abiders, triumphers both in camps and courts."[26] The ministry was borrowing more than just Sidney's ideas; it was appropriating the whole idea of the courtly Elizabethan knight as a representational precedent for the Captain-General. In the early eighteenth century Philip Sidney was still revered as the chivalric defender of European Protestantism, the polished courtier, soldier, and poet. Moreover, his death in a skirmish at Zutphen in 1586 fighting against Spain, provided the ministry with a model of military heroism and courtly refinement based on the chivalrous ideal of loyal service rather than villainous self-service. Although parallels between Anne and Elizabeth I were rather strained—they shared the motto "Semper eadem", but Anne was no Virgin Queen with an extravagant cult of devotion from her male courtiers—they did provide one possible solution to the problems of representing Marlborough that had dogged Croker's representation in 1703.[27] Closterman's portrait introduced this concept of devoted service to negotiate the complex relationship between the Duke and his female monarch. Although such a vast portrait was necessarily an extravagant celebration of Marlborough himself, decorum was maintained by the inclusion of a golden medal with a profile portrait of Queen Anne in the top left corner. The medal points the way for the Duke to follow, reminding the viewer that the nature of the Duke's soldiery is service, not the pursuit of personal glory. Addison too had written of Marlborough, "Thou lives not for thyself; thy QUEEN demands/ Conquest and Peace from thy Victorious Hands."[28] Closterman's bravura play of direct light and Rubensian reflected highlights further reinforce the message of service.[29] The light source is at the painting's top left where a patch of clear sky breaks through the tempestuous clouds. Here the golden medal passes through the sky like a sun, clearing away the dark clouds and spreading light across the scene below. Thus the Captain-General basks not in the praise of his own merits, but in the reflected glory of Queen Anne.

The language in which Marlborough's official image was configured was therefore that of heroism, both moral and military, and of an ardent masculinity, restless in the defence of the queen. Nevertheless, "in the Augustan period", as J. R. Jones has put it, "popular heroes were not yet in vogue, nor had media been developed specifically to project spectacular images of heroes."[30] Heroism, particularly military heroism, was generally regarded as a virtue exemplified only by princes, so that William III, for instance, could adopt the persona of Hercules to represent himself.[31] Some Tory thinkers even maintained that military men were essentially devoid of virtue since their "heroism" was based more on the pursuit of personal glory than public liberty. Even the Whig Earl of Shaftesbury felt compelled to acknowledge that for every Hercules or William III there was a Julius Caesar or a Cromwell who forfeited the claim to heroic virtue by misplaced ambitions. "By a small mis-guidance of the Affection", he wrote, "a Lover of Mankind becomes a Ravager: A Hero and Deliverer becomes an Oppressor and Destroyer."[32] Marlborough's political intentions had already aroused suspicion and the memories of Cromwell remained fresh in people's minds. The government could use the media to promote Marlborough but, try as it might, the free press and organized political opposition denied it complete authority over his representation. The ministry's opponents were free to deploy the very same resources to define a contrasting image of Marlborough.[33] "Since this nation is unhappily divided into parties", Defoe reasoned, "every side ought to have an equal advantage in the use of the press."[34]

Nevertheless, it was Marlborough's loyal and heroic service to the queen in the Elizabethan tradition that was vigorously promoted by the ministry. The public was treated to a series of ostentatious thanksgiving services at St Paul's Cathedral after each of the Duke's victories, complete with elaborate triumphal processions through London. John Evelyn records the first on 7 September 1704 to celebrate Blenheim:

> This day was celebrated the thanksgiving for the late greate victory, with the utmost pomp and splendor by the Queene, Court, greate Officers, Lord Mayor, Sheriff, Companies, &c. The streets were scaffolded to Temple Bar . . . the Queene in a rich coach with 8 horses, none with her but the Dutchess of Marlborough in a very plain garment, the Queene full of jewels.[35]

With the Duke away on campaign, the Duchess acted as his proxy, her modest appearance compared to Anne's magnificence representing Marlborough's subordinate position in relation to his sovereign. Evelyn's account continues:

> Music and Trumpets at every City Company. The greate Officers of the Crown, Nobility, and Bishops, all in coaches with 6 horses, besides innumerable servants, went to St. Paul's where the Dean preach'd . . . the City Companies feasted all the Nobility and Bishops, and illuminated all night.[36]

These tactics worked. When military victories were combined with public spectacles the appetite for all things Marlborough grew apace, and his image quickly become widely reproduced on a commercial basis. A half-length mezzotint portrait based on Closterman's equestrian portrait was published by J. Simon and available from 1705 along with scores of other portraits. Despite reducing Closterman's painting to a mere head and shoulders, the print still captures something of the clamour of battle through the fluttering wig and dramatic chiaroscuro. But interest in the Duke was not just confined to mere portraits. Maps of Marlborough's movements, plans of his engagements, and engravings of the national thanksgiving services were all soon available from print-sellers.[37] Even potters found a ready market for Marlborough imagery on commemorative tin-glazed dishes and plates.[38]

Probably only a year after Closterman's portrait was completed, Godfrey Kneller (1646–1723) received a commission to produce his own allegorical painting of Marlborough (fig. 57). Only a sketch survives and it is unlikely that Kneller ever proceeded beyond this stage. On the back of the sketch is an inscription recording: "His Grace the Duke of Marlborough/ Painted by Sr Godfrey Kneller/ soon after the Battle of Ramillies". Ramillies was the Duke's second great victory. After decisively beating the French army on 23 May 1706, Marlborough was con-

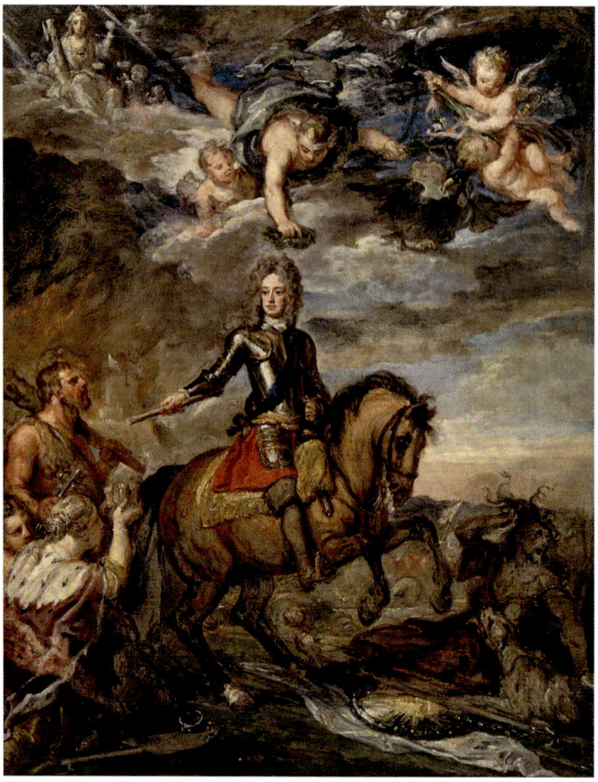

57. Sir Godfrey Kneller, Bt, *John Churchill, 1st Duke of Marlborough*, ca. 1706, oil on canvas, 36½ x 29 in. (92.7 x 73.7 cm). National Portrait Gallery, London

fident that a lasting peace could now be negotiated. On returning home the general was even permitted to ride in triumph through London at the head of the army, depositing the banners captured from the French at Westminster Hall and the Guildhall.[39] It is tempting to suppose that Kneller was commissioned to paint what Marlborough believed would be the final portrait of the war, a picture suitable for display in the enormous house John Vanbrugh was building at Woodstock. Marlborough had just been given Anthony van Dyck's portrait of *Charles I on Horseback* (National Gallery, London) and it is not inconceivable that the Kneller portrait was commissioned to act as some kind of pendant to that painting at Blenheim.[40]

Like Closterman, Kneller depicted Marlborough on horseback and employed much of the same iconography. A figure of Mercury or Victory swoops down from the clouds to crown him with laurels, while an indistinct figure of Fame flies off to the right trumpeting Marlborough's name. The crowned eagle also reappears overhead, but is here accompanied by two putti who gather flowers to throw down onto the hero. Despite these similarities, there are some key differences between Kneller and Closterman's representations. Where Closterman pushed Marlborough's horse up close to the picture plane, Kneller set it deeper into space, thereby increasing the significance of the allegorical components and making the Captain-General interact with the surrounding figures. On the left stands Hercules, emblem of heroic virtue, gazing admiringly up at the Duke and clutching his club and the keys to an enemy city. Next to him kneels a female figure clad in ermine, who offers up a conquered fortress or town to the commander. The broken manacle alongside the rudder of state at her side casts Marlborough as liberator, freeing the oppressed from tyranny. On the opposite side are a terrified figure of Discord and a howling Dog of War about to be crushed under the feet of Marlborough's horse. Strewn on the ground in the foreground are military trophies, including the prominent standard of the French *Corps du Roi* with its characteristic fleurs-de-lys, and a shield with the Sun King's own device upon it. In the sky high above sits Astraea, the goddess of Justice, indicating that behind all Marlborough's actions lies the cause of right.

Astraea had been one of Elizabeth I's allegorical guises and it is conceivable that Kneller intended the figure in his sketch to suggest Queen Anne herself, the distant yet overriding authority behind the Captain-General. Nevertheless, Kneller's composition raises some of the same difficulties as Croker's *Sine Clade Victor* medal of three years earlier. Both portrayed the Duke on horseback receiving the supplication of a crouching female figure, a format that highlighted the unusual relationship between him and Anne.[41] The repetition of this dominant male over submissive female motif risked allowing viewers to extend the representation to the actual state of affairs between the Captain-General and his queen. While imagery such as this was intended to glorify Marlborough, it risked playing into the hands of those political enemies who regarded him as a dangerously over-mighty and grasping subject, something which may in part explain why it never got beyond the sketch stage. To complicate his status even further, the Holy Roman Emperor created Marlborough an Imperial Prince in 1705 with Mindelheim his principality.

In 1708 Kneller received a second commission to produce a major Marlborough painting. This time it was the queen who ordered an allegorical painting of herself delivering the plans of Blenheim Palace to her Captain-General, to hang at the palace itself, then under construction (fig. 58).[42] According to Kneller:

> The Queen sent her orders to me by the Duke of Shrewsbury (Then Lord Chamberlain) to design a Large Picture Twelve foot high and Eight foot broad for the upper end of the Long Gallery at Blenheim. The Duke of Marlborough (who was then present) desired that no person should be represented by the life Except the Queen's Majesty But that the whole Picture should be Allegoricall.[43]

Marlborough, who won his third great victory at Oudenarde in July 1708, was clearly acutely aware of the dangers of *lèse-majesté*, for it was he who advocated replacing his own portrait with an allegorical figure, leaving the queen in a position of unrivalled supremacy as the only living person on view. Marlborough was to be represented in the guise of a "warlike Vigorous Figure representing Millitary Meritt", embodying precisely those virtues considered unattainable by a woman such

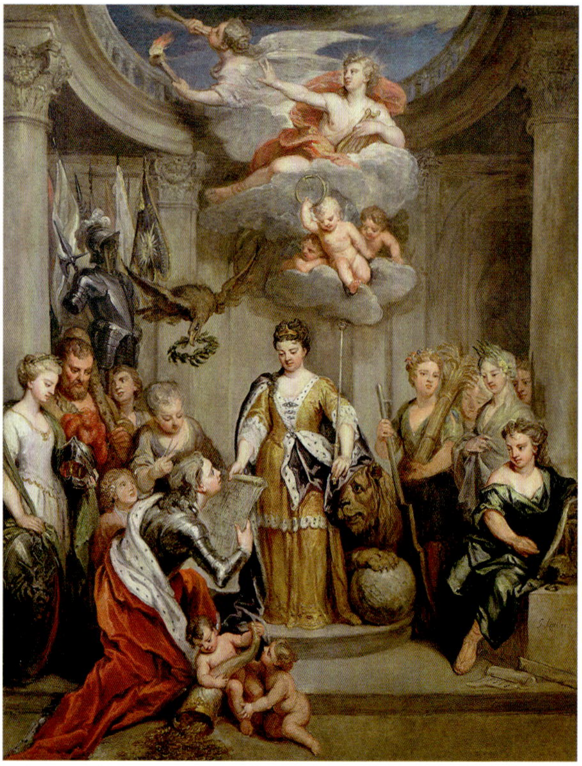

58. Sir Godfrey Kneller, Bt, *Queen Anne Presenting Plans of Blenheim to Military Merit*, 1708, oil on canvas, 50 x 40 in. (127 x 101.5 cm). Blenheim Palace, Oxfordshire

as Anne.[44] Once again circumstances conspired to prevent Kneller getting beyond a sketch, though he produced a far more detailed modello than he had for the Duke's equestrian portrait.

We are fortunate to have what is reported as Kneller's own account of the content of this allegory. "The Queen", he states, "is represented by the Figure of Generosity holding in her Left hand her Scepter with the Eye of Providence on the Top resting on a Lyon, with a Globe of the World under his Paw, the Emblem of Power and Strength."[45] The figure of "Millitary Meritt" intended for Marlborough is shown genuflecting at Anne's feet, clad in full cuirass armour and a resplendent red ermine-trimmed mantle. Above him "an Eagle Descends holding an Imperiall Lawrell Crown in his Talon", while to his left Hercules looks benignly upon the hero. Alongside Hercules, Victory rests her right hand on the shield of Minerva—the goddess of war and protector of heroes—and holds the helmet of Mars in her left. Behind them is a collection of the "Trophys of conquered Countreys" with the Sun King's personal banner prominent among them, ironically emblazoned with his own motto "Nec Pluribus Impar" (Not Unequal to Many). On the right-hand side are figures representing the benefits of Marlborough's labours, "Plenty both by Sea and Land with other Nimphs of Rivers", Kneller explains.[46] Above Anne, Apollo rests on a cloud directing Fame's trumpets. The central action, however, is Anne passing Marlborough "a Model of Blenheim drawn on paper" with Architecture looking on, and at his feet "is the Golden Cornucopia Shead by her Majesty's Affections".[47]

Given Marlborough's own concerns about propriety, Kneller depicts the figure of Military Merit as an idealized portrait, disregarding the commander's advanced years. Not only has Kneller abstracted the Duke, he has also shown him kneeling before his queen, reversing the representation of gender and authority in the earlier Ramillies sketch. Here Marlborough is not the Imperial Prince but the humble knight faithfully obeying his monarch. The youthful "vigour" once again connotes an ardent masculinity, though it is one that is safely channelled into military service. The gilded cornucopia and the plan of Blenheim Palace are presented as just rewards from the sovereign to a man of heroic virtue. At root the design is an extravagant protest of Marlborough's loyalty to Anne, a denial that his rank and ambitions threatened her authority. This charge had become all the more acute in 1708 when the death of Anne's consort and Generalissimo, Prince George, left Marlborough the closest male to the queen. Hence the Elizabethan references come ever more to the fore; consciously anachronistic armour, plumed helmets, and antiquated halberds all hark back to an earlier age of military service to a female sovereign. Kneller's sketch chimed with Matthew Prior's post-Ramillies *Ode, Humbly Inscrib'd to the Queen*, written in imitation of Edmund Spenser, in

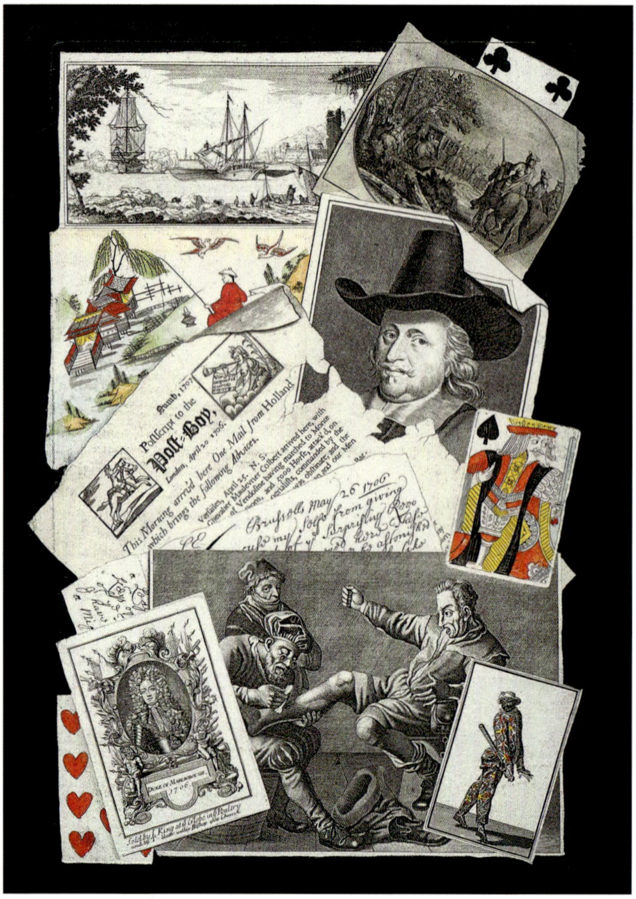

59. George Bickham the Elder, published by John King and T. Slater, *Postscript to the Post-Boy*, 1706, engraving with hand-coloured etching, 16⅝ x 11 in. (42.3 x 27.9 cm). Worcester College, Oxford, George Clark Print Collection

which Marlborough was cast as an ardent Spenserian knight, eternally loyal to Anne. The poem begins with an evocation of the dying William III anointing Marlborough his military heir by handing on his sword. Prior writes:

> He took the Gift; Nor ever will I sheath,
> He said, (so *Anna*'s high Behests Ordain)
> This Glorious gift, unless by Glorious Death
> Absolv'd, 'till I by Conquest fix your Reign.
> Returns like these Our *Mistress* bids us make.[48]

While Kneller's sketch appears to represent the extraordinary extent of Anne's favour to Marlborough, the reality was rather different. By 1708 Anne's feelings towards the war were growing decidedly lukewarm. The elation of Blenheim and Ramillies gave way to pangs of conscience after she heard about the carnage at Oudenarde. As her commitment to the war waned she turned increasingly to her Tory ministers who sought to end the war. Worse for the Captain-General, Anne's relationship with Sarah had cooled considerably. Taken together these circumstances weakened Marlborough despite his former successes. The ambiguity of his position became increasingly apparent as did more vocal attacks upon his character. George Bickham the elder's hand-coloured medley print, *Postscript to the Post-Boy* (fig. 59) of 1706 had already explored the various ways in which the Duke could be viewed. On the surface this engraving is an illusionistic representation of the different prints that John King, who published the medley, had on sale at that time.[49] In the lower left corner Bickham included a half-length portrait of Marlborough dressed in armour and surrounded by cannon and martial banners. Elsewhere the sheet features references to the latest campaign: the first page of an edition of the *Postscript to the Post-Boy* records the defeat of the Habsburg army in Italy, while a hand-written dispatch announces Marlborough's triumph at Ramillies.[50] But there were also more ambiguous inclusions. For instance, a portrait of John Pym, the parliamentary leader in the early years of the English Civil War, is prominently displayed along with the King of Spades from a pack of cards and a print of a charlatan. By the early eighteenth century, Pym was regarded by Whigs as a hero who had struggled for the rights of Parliament against a tyrannical Crown, just as Marlborough humbled French ambitions.[51] To Tories, however, Pym was the instigator of the rebellion against his anointed king, and had raised a rebel army to overturn the proper order of the realm just as they feared Marlborough might if left unchecked.[52] Such medley prints were inherently ambiguous; juxtaposing Marlborough with Pym was especially so. Who is the king, and who is the charlatan?[53] That the engraving could represent Marlborough simultaneously as Tory villain *and* Whig hero was a measure of both the uncertainties of Marlborough's position and the ministry's inability to establish an absolute and affirmative image of the Captain-General in an age of free press, party politics, and the unconstrained debate of the coffee house. As such, Bickham's medley print offers an eloquent distillation of the wider ambiguities and tensions surrounding the representation of early eighteenth-century Britain's greatest military hero.

The origins of this essay are found in my MA thesis "'Great Man' or 'Knave?': The Disputed Public Image of the Duke of Marlborough: 1702–1736" (Courtauld Institute of Art, Univ. of London, 2000). I am grateful to David Solkin for his original supervision and continued encouragement. Since that time my understanding of Marlborough has benefited greatly from discussions with Julia Marciari Alexander, Mark Hallett, and Robert Wellington.

1. For Croker, see George F. Hill, *A Guide to the Exhibition of Historical Medals in the British Museum* (London: British Museum, 1924), 64.
2. William Coxe, *Memoirs of John, Duke of Marlborough*, 3 vols. (London: Henry G. Bohn, 1847), 1: 127.
3. Marlborough had served under the Duke of Monmouth in France in the 1670s as well as commanding a force in Flanders in 1692 during the Nine Years' War before his dismissal.
4. Dartmouth's account is found in his notes on Bishop Burnet's *History of His Own Time.* Burnet recorded a suggestion that there was a plan afoot late in William's reign to deny Anne's right of succession and transfer the crown direct to the House of Hanover. Dartmouth notes: "The dukes of Bolton and Newcastle both proposed it to me, and used the strongest argument to induce me to come into it, which was, that it would be making Lord Marlborough king, at least for her [Anne's] time, if the princess succeeded; and that I had reason to expect nothing but ill usage during such a reign." Lord Dartmouth in Bishop Burnet, *History of His Own Time: with Notes by the Earls of Dartmouth and Hardwicke, Speaker Onslow, and Dean Swift*, 6 vols., 2nd ed. (Oxford Univ. Press, 1833), 4: 553.
5. After the Restoration the "printed word . . . [was] essential to the transmission of ideas and values, the figuration of authority and power". Harold Weber, *Paper Bullets: Print and Kingship under Charles II* (Lexington: Univ. Press of Kentucky, 1996), 8. J. R. Jones argues: "one can talk of 'politics' and 'public opinion' after 1667 in an almost modern sense." Jones, *Charles II: Royal Politician* (London: Allen and Unwin, 1987), 5.
6. For the use of the medal in early modern propaganda, see Mark Jones, *The Art of the Medal* (London: British Museum, 1979), 83–88.
7. See Edward Hawkins, *Medallic Illustrations of the History of Great Britain and Ireland to the Death of George II*, vol. 2, ed. Augustus W. Franks and Herbert A. Greuber (London: British Museum, 1885), 722. In this medal William is shown as joint monarch with Queen Mary. However, the superimposition of his profile over hers established his masculine dominance.
8. See Helen Farquhar, *Portraiture of our Stuart Monarchs on their Coins and Medals, Part 6: Anne* (London: Harrison and Sons, 1914), 220, and Hawkins, *Medallic Illustrations*, 246.
9. British Library (hereafter BL) Add MS 40060, fol. 50. This poem is taken from a collection of predominantly Tory satires from the early years of the eighteenth century. Edmund Curll attributed the text to Richard Gwinnett in his edition of *Pylades and Corinna: or, the memoirs of the lives, amours, and writings of Richard Gwinnett Esq.* (London, 1731), 1: 52. See also Richard Johns, "'The British Caesar': John Churchill, 1st Duke of Marlborough, and the Visual Arts", in *Marlborough: Soldier and Diplomat*, ed. John B. Hattendorf, Augustus J. Veenendaal, Jr., and Rolof van Hövell tot Westerflier (Rotterdam: Karwansaray Publishers, 2012), 332.
10. BL Add MS 40060, fol. 50.
11. BL Add MS 40060, fol. 50.
12. Christopher Hibbert, *The Marlboroughs: John and Sarah Churchill, 1650–1744* (London: Viking, 2001) 27.
13. W. A. Speck, *The Birth of Britain: A New Nation, 1700–1710* (Oxford: Blackwell, 1994), 194.
14. The lines read in full: "Accept My Lord of this small glittering thing/ Tis like thy self the shadow of a king." *On the Sword given by the K: of Sp: to the Generall*, Feb. 1704, BL Add MS 40060, fol. 50.
15. One satire of July 1703 provided a spoof catalogue of Marlborough's library. Item 15 has the title, "The Whole art of War, of Encamping, Entrenching, retreating, running away &c by the Duke of Marlborough dedicated to Barron Obdam-n-". *A Catalogue of Books to be Sold by auction at ye D: of Mrs. [Marlborough's] lodgings at St. James's on Sunday the 25 of July 1703*, BL Add MS 22267, fol. 131.
16. Historical Manuscripts Commission, *Bath Papers* i.63, cited in Winston Churchill, *Marlborough: His Life and Times* (London: George G. Harrap & Co., 1934), 2:518. Robert Harley, the future Earl of Oxford, was brought into government in 1702, forming a triumvirate with Marlborough and Godolphin.

17. David Green, *Blenheim Palace* (London: Country Life, 1951), 38. Ruth Smith points out that Anne did not reveal her intention of paying for a house on the site to Parliament until 1707. See Ruth Smith, "Sarah, Duchess of Marlborough: An Analysis of Her Relationship with Architecture" (unpublished MA diss., Courtauld Institute of Art, Univ. of London, 1998), 21.
18. See Malcolm Rogers, "John and John Baptist Closterman: A Catalogue of their Works", *Walpole Society* 49 (1983): 254, and George Vertue, "The Note-books of George Vertue II", *Walpole Society* 20 (1932): 139. For its later history, see A. H. Johnson, *The History of the Worshipful Company of Drapers of London*, 5 vols. (Oxford: Clarendon Press, 1922), 3: 445.
19. Rogers, "John and John Baptist Closterman", 253, J. Douglas Stewart, *Sir Godfrey Kneller and the English Baroque Portrait* (Oxford: Clarendon Press, 1983), 74.
20. For a succinct discussion of the tradition of equestrian portraiture, see Roy Strong, *Van Dyck: Charles I on Horseback* (London: Penguin, 1972), 49.
21. For a full discussion of the precedents for Closterman's portrait, see Douglas Stewart, *Sir Godfrey Kneller*, 74. As Malcolm Rogers argues, the traditional anecdote that the Duke of Buckingham commissioned the portrait is more likely to be a confusion with the painting's pictorial source. See Rogers, "John and John Baptist Closterman", 254.
22. For his costume, see Hibbert, *The Marlboroughs*, 148. The Duke of Marlborough's military regulations, codified in 1711, stipulate "That ye Officers be all Cloath'd in Redd Plain and uniforme, wch is expected they shall wear on all marches, & other Dutys as well as days of review". *The Military Regulations of the Duke of Marlborough*, BL Add MS 29477, fol. 117. Malcolm Rogers suggests that the river god could conceivably be a representation of the Moselle to mark the campaign in that region in 1705. See Rogers, "John and John Baptist Closterman", 254.
23. Joseph Addison, *The Campaign: A Poem, to His Grace, the Duke of Marlborough* (1705; London, 1710), 11.
24. Addison, *The Campaign*, 15.
25. That Marlborough's greatness was inscribed upon his face was a standard trope among his supporters. Prince Vaudemont is alleged to have told William III in the early 1690s that "there is something in the Earl of Marlborough that is inexpressible, all those Virtues seem to be united in his single Person; and I have lost my wanted knowledge of physiognomy, if any Subject you have can ever attain to such a Height of Military Glory, as this Combination of sublime Perfections must one Day or other advance him to." Anon., *The Lives of the Two Illustrious Generals, John, Duke of Marlborough, and Francis Eugene, Prince of Savoy* (London, 1713), 30.
26. Sir Philip Sidney, *An Apology for Poetry: or, The Defence of Poesy*, ed. Geoffrey Shepard (London: T. Nelson, 1965), 81.
27. "Queen Anne, for obvious reasons, was . . . closely identified with Elizabeth. She adopted Elizabeth's '*Semper Eadem*' motto and made her first parliamentary appearance in 1702 in robes modelled on a portrait of her female predecessor . . . Poets celebrating the victories of Ramillies and Blenheim made much of the Britomart side of Elizabeth's personal mythology to eulogize Anne." Christine Gerrard, *The Patriot Opposition to Walpole: Politics, Poetry, and National Myth, 1725–1742* (Oxford: Clarendon Press, 1994), 152.
28. Addison, *The Campaign*, 8.
29. For the use of Rubensian lighting in military portraits, see Desmond Shawe-Taylor, *The Georgians: Eighteenth-century Portraiture and Society* (London: Barrie and Jenkins, 1990), 38.
30. J. R. Jones, *Marlborough* (Cambridge Univ. Press, 1993), 7.
31. See Stefan van Raaij and Paul Spies, *The Royal Progress of William & Mary*, trans. A. P. K. Graafland (Amsterdam: D'Arts, 1988), 67.
32. Anthony Ashley Cooper, third Earl of Shaftesbury, "Sensus Communis; an Essay on the Freedom of Wit and Humour", in *Characteristicks of Men, Manners, Opinions, Times* (1709; London, 1732), 1:113.
33. For similar difficulties faced by Charles II, see Paul Hammond, "The King's Two Bodies: Representations of Charles II", in *Culture, Politics and Society in Britain, 1660–1800*, ed. Jeremy Black and Jeremy Gregory (Manchester Univ. Press, 1991), 41–42.

34. Daniel Defoe, *An Essay on the Regulation of the Press* (London, 1704), 13.
35. *The Diary of John Evelyn*, ed. William Bray, 4 vols. (London: Bickers and Son, 1906), 4: 168–69.
36. Evelyn, *Diary*, 4: 168–69.
37. As Clayton puts it, the "appetite for plans and views of Marlborough's sieges and battles was fed during the war by a steady output of prints . . . each new incident in the war continued to be illustrated by maps, plans and views of various sizes and prices." Timothy Clayton, *The English Print, 1688–1802* (New Haven and London: Yale Univ. Press, 1997), 79.
38. Anthony Ray, *English Delftware Pottery in the Robert Hall Warren Collection, Ashmolean Museum, Oxford* (London: Faber and Faber, 1968), 106–7.
39. Corelli Barnett, *Marlborough* (London: Book Club Associates, 1974), 183.
40. Cited in Douglas Stewart, *Sir Godfrey Kneller*, 68. Douglas Stewart suggests that the sketch was later in the collection of Henrietta, Duchess of Marlborough, the daughter of the Captain-General. If so, this might imply that Marlborough himself had a hand in commissioning the painting, though there is no firm evidence for such a supposition.
41. The composition of the sketch also recalls the one Kneller made in preparation for the Hampton Court portrait of William III in 1697, underlining that precedents for Marlborough's representation were most easily found in those of the former king. The sketch was formerly in the Gatchina Palace, St Petersburg, but was destroyed in the Second World War. See Douglas Stewart, *Sir Godfrey Kneller*, cat. no. 843.
42. George Vertue recorded the sketch being in Dr Mead's collection. "This picture", he noted, "being a design for a large painting was done by Sr. Godfrey being historicall and when done much commended for his skill—afterwards the Duke being out of favour this picture came into the possession of Dr. Meade." "The Note-books of George Vertue V", *Walpole Society* 26 (1938): 88.
43. Green, *Blenheim Palace*, 298. Green fails to identify the manuscript other than being among the Blenheim papers. I have been unable to trace it in the papers transferred to the British Library. Douglas Stewart likewise cites the manuscript from Green's book.
44. Kneller in Green, *Blenheim Palace*, 298.
45. Kneller in Green, *Blenheim Palace*, 298.
46. Kneller in Green, *Blenheim Palace*, 298.
47. Kneller in Green, *Blenheim Palace*, 46.
48. Matthew Prior, *An Ode, Humbly Inscrib'd to the Queen. On the Late Glorious Success of Her Majesty's Arms. Written in Imitation of Spencer's Stile* (London, 1706), 7. Gerrard writes: "Prior used Marlborough's recent victories at Ramillies as an excuse for producing this barely disguised piece of Stuart dynastic glorification celebrating Anne-as-Elizabeth through a fulsome revival of Spenser's Brutus-Troynovant-Arthur myth, whence 'TUDOR's hence, and STUART's Off-Spring flow.'" Gerrard, *Patriot Opposition to Walpole*, 167.
49. See Clayton, *English Print*, 6.
50. I have been unable to obtain the issue of *The Postscript to the Post-Boy* illustrated in Bickham's print, but the date of the issue and the visible text reveal it to record the defeat of the Habsburg forces in Italy by Marshal Vendôme's French army.
51. As Linda Colley notes, John Pym had earned a place among the "martyrs in the Whig pantheon who had suffered in the struggle against arbitrary power". Colley, *Britons: Forging the Nation, 1707–1837* (1992; London: Vintage Press, 1996), 117.
52. As one contemporary noted, "the Whigs . . . are Enemies to all Monarchy, Rebels, Deposers of Kings, and Republicans." Thomas Burnet, *A Certain Information of a Certain Discourse That happen'd at a Certain Gentleman's House, In a Certain County. Written by a Certain Person then present, to a Certain Friend now at London. From Whence you may Collect the great Certainty of the Account*, 2nd ed. (London, 1712), 62.
53. Hallett argues that medley prints precluded "any real interpretative closure, satiric or otherwise . . . the medley's satire is deliberately ambiguous rather than polemically strident". Mark Hallett, *The Spectacle of Difference: Graphic Satire in the Age of Hogarth* (New Haven and London: Yale Univ. Press, 1999), 42–45.

Rupture through Realism: Sarah Churchill and Louis Laguerre's Murals at Marlborough House

Lydia Hamlett

Louis Laguerre (1663–1721) was one of the most in-demand grand-scale mural artists of his time.[1] His subjects were almost always allegorical, frequently celestial, and often mythological, with the figures of his patrons being placed among the gods. The arrival of Laguerre in England in 1684 has provided art historians with a convenient starting date for the development of the European-style "baroque" mural in the British Isles—"baroque" here being used to evoke the general aesthetic of the (largely) ecclesiastical murals of late sixteenth- and early seventeenth-century Italy and its translation into the highly politicized art of Louis XIV's France.[2] That Laguerre was a godson of the French king only further reinforces this identification between the painter and this genre. Yet Laguerre was also responsible for what was in many ways the most unusual mural scheme of the period, a project which manipulated and departed from Continental precedents to precise political ends. His murals at Marlborough House in St James's, the London home of John and Sarah Churchill, Duke and Duchess of Marlborough, executed around 1712, rejected allegory and instead represented recent historical events in an uncharacteristically direct and detailed style. They represent an anomaly in Laguerre's career and, more importantly, a significant rupture in the development of the genre as a whole. Nothing comparable was attempted again by Laguerre or anyone else.

Edward Croft-Murray's remark that the Marlborough House murals are "interesting as contemporary military documents, but apart from that they have little merit", typifies a traditional prejudice against the genre of mural painting, much aggravated by the routine but anachronistic description of them as "decorative" painting (contemporary usage designated such works as "history").[3] If ill-founded, the prejudice has a powerful historical origin in the contemporaneous dismissal of frescoes in the Earl of Shaftesbury's *Tablature of Hercules* (1713).[4] This essay takes a different course. It considers the murals themselves and how they were to be experienced; the significance of their form within the rest of Laguerre's work; the circumstances around their commission and the motivations for their production; and their meaning within a broader political, cultural, and historical context. Crucially, it makes the case that the Marlborough House murals represent a unique example of a peculiarly English sublime, shaped by contemporary discourse on the representation of war.

Marlborough House is located directly next to the royal palace of St James's, and was built from scratch on land granted by the monarch in 1708, a mere four years before the murals were completed.[5] This location placed the Marlboroughs at the physical heart of the court. Although it has never been the subject of a comprehensive monographic study (unlike the Marlboroughs' most famous home, Blenheim Palace in Oxfordshire), and is rarely accorded more than a paragraph in the myriad biographies of the Duke and Duchess, the house nonetheless had an important part to play in both their lives. It functioned as a place of political assembly for Whigs and Tories and for the entertainment of British and foreign royals, as well as a domestic hub for the Marlboroughs themselves, where key rites in the lives of the family unfolded, including marriages and the deaths of both its patrons.[6] But, if the house has not received the scholarly attention it properly deserves, its murals have received even less: if they are mentioned at all it is only incidentally in relation to the machinations of architectural construction.[7] Their subject, the victorious battles of the Duke in the War of the Spanish Succession, has, perhaps, seemed self-explanatory to historians of the house and its owners, and art historians have been swayed by the old aesthetic prejudices noted above.

Those prejudices have perhaps been reinforced by the physical histories of the murals. They have been heavily restored and cleaned on numerous occasions over the centuries since they were painted.[8] Kenneth Clark remarked worryingly on seeing the murals in 1936 that they should be treated "like furniture which indeed they are" and cleaned with a mop.[9] Yet despite this history of abuse they still convey a credible sense of space and topographical detail and, most extraordinarily, remain vivid as depictions of human suffering on an unsettling scale. This last characteristic is most striking given the fact that they occupy the very core of the house, being painted onto the walls of what was once the main entrance hall for guests waiting for an audience with the Marlboroughs, and the staircases to either side of it.[10] These three spaces were united from the start through a shared iconography, each depicting the course of famous battles unfolding in continuous narratives on their major walls. The Duke's first battle won under Queen Anne, Blenheim (1704), was depicted in the hall; Ramillies (1706) in the west staircase, and Malplaquet (1709) in the east staircase.[11]

Until recently, scholars have seen these battle scenes in the context of other contemporary images of leaders on the battlefield, including the tapestries commissioned by the same patrons for Blenheim Palace (*The Art of War*, 1705, and the

Victories, 1708, though only delivered years later).[12] Croft-Murray playfully suggested that, so similar were they to the extensive artistic programme mobilized for Laguerre's former patron, Louis XIV, they put the artist in danger of being accused of treachery to his country of birth. Certainly, the murals share some of the tropes of seventeenth- and early eighteenth-century Continental battle scenes: the French showcasing of war heroes on the battlefield; the Dutch interest in the minute documentation of battle, including apparently unflinching depictions of death and dying. This could be reckoned unsurprising given the climate of intimate artistic exchange that characterizes the period, and the fact that Laguerre was briefly in the studio of Charles Le Brun and likely studied under the king's *peintre de batailles*, Adam Frans van der Meulen.[13] More recently, however, scholarship has rightly begun to emphasize the contrast between the Marlborough House murals and such pictorial precedents, drawing attention instead to the ways in which these images are experienced in their architectural setting.[14] The mass of minute detail typical of seventeenth-century Dutch battle canvases is blown up to life-size at Marlborough House, and the violent skirmishes brought to the fore by artists such as Van der Meulen, Joseph Parrocel, Lambert de Hondt (in the cavalry combats at Dresden and Schleissheim), and Jan van Huchtenburg (in the ten contemporary battle canvases for Marlborough's great ally, Prince Eugene), are strategically placed within the architecture so as to meet our gaze confrontationally.[15] Ascending and descending both staircases, the spectator is forced into eye-level contact with these imposing scenes of carnage. At each turn, we have no choice but to confront individual dramas: turning on the landing of the west staircase going up, we stare directly into the terrified eyes of a wounded horse (fig. 60); going down, we are faced with the dead body of Colonel Bingfield. On the landing of the east stairs, which shows the famously bloody and controversial Battle of Malplaquet, we are forced to walk past a sustained display of dead soldiers being stripped of their garments; are plunged into undergrowth littered with the debris of war, dead bodies, and discarded weapons; and are compelled to act as witnesses to yet another gruesome act of human violence (fig. 61).[16]

The immediacy of these battle scenes is enhanced by the mural technique, with the paint being directly applied to the walls, rendering the images integral to the experience of architectural space. Furthermore, the Marlborough murals operate without the prominent allegorical borders that characterize tapestries or the broad decorative surrounds that are a feature of such works as Van der Meulen's battles on Louis Le Vau's Versailles staircase, which provide a decisive boundary around the image (fig. 62).[17] Even the relatively plain painted frames and surrounds that are visible around the large swathes of the principal scenes (they each measure several metres across) are likely to be later additions rather than part of

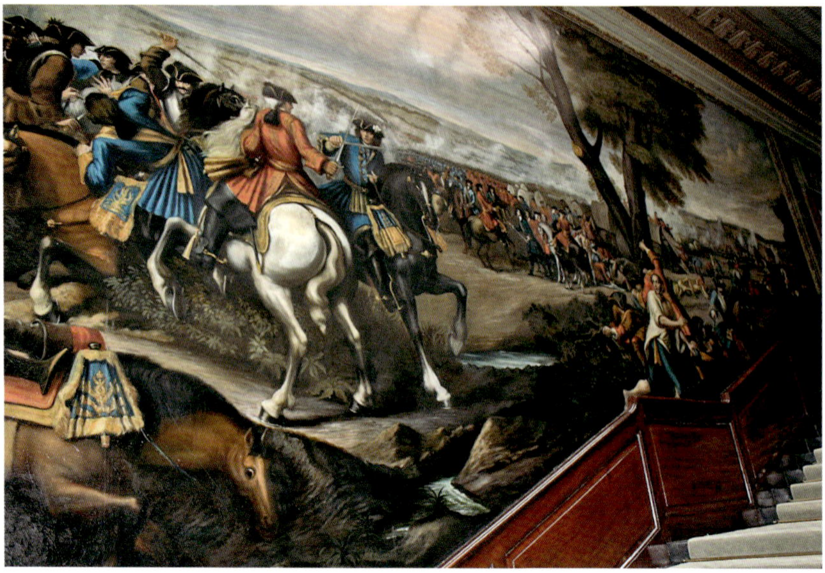

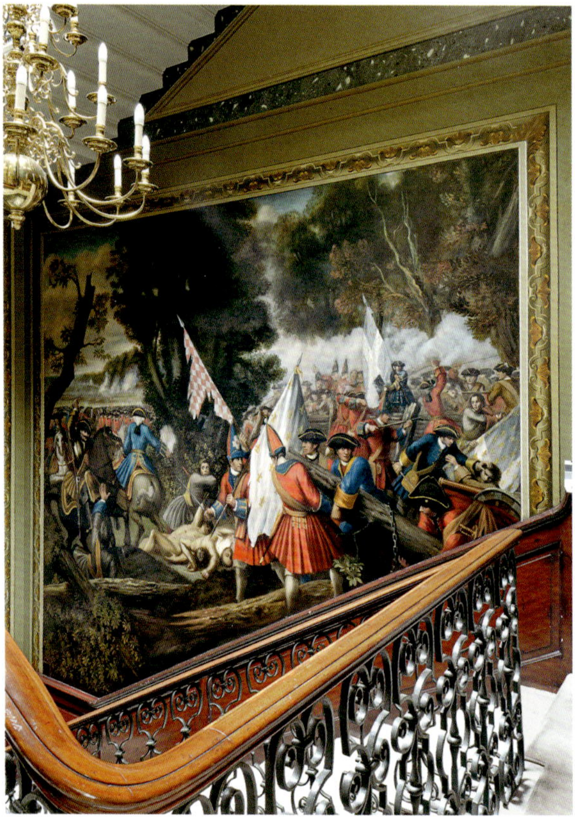

60. Louis Laguerre, *Battle of Ramillies, 23 May 1706, Evening*, ca. 1713, oil on plaster, 172 x 334¼ in. (437 x 849 cm). Royal Collection Trust, London

61. Louis Laguerre, *Battle of Malplaquet (Taniers Wood), 11 September 1709*, ca. 1713, oil on plaster, 160¾ x 180¾ in. (408.2 x 459 cm). Royal Collection Trust, London

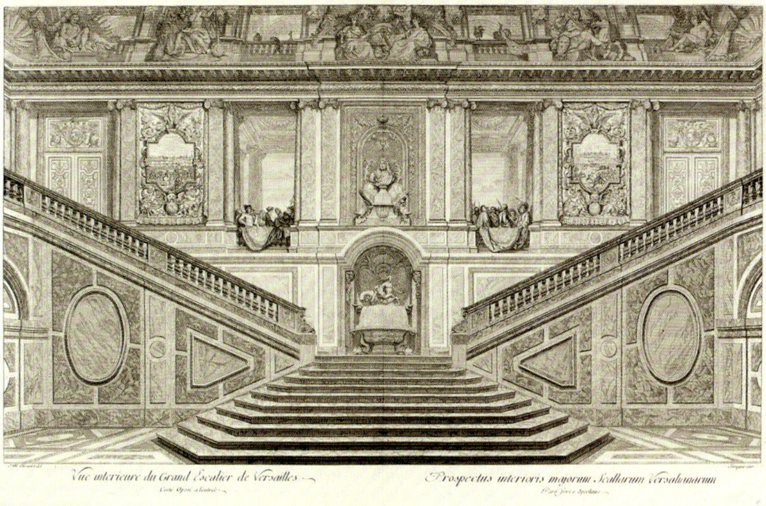

62. Louis De Surugue after Jean Michel Chevotet, *View of the Ambassador's Staircase, Versailles*, 1720, engraving, 20⅝ x 30⅜ in. (52.5 x 77 cm). Victoria & Albert Museum, London

Laguerre's original conception.[18] These now appear to break the continuity of the main scenes, most obviously on the west and north walls of the Malplaquet staircase, which are joined as one in the various eighteenth-century prints and painted copies associated with the murals: they also cut out thin vertical slithers of the composition. It could be that the frames on the main scenes date from the late eighteenth or early nineteenth centuries, when extra storeys were added to the house, requiring extra flights on the Malplaquet staircase. This may also account for the omission of the town of Malplaquet from its proper position in the left distance, an area of the composition now in darkness below these stairs. The absence of emphatic framing here means that a sense of continuity and vividness is retained, a quality that was surely intended as a key feature of Laguerre's scheme. The original idea, then, appears to have been that the viewer, rather than being removed to a point of safety, as so often in Continental murals—for example in the staircase at Versailles where illusionistic spectators watch from a balcony, a device later re-used by Laguerre himself at the dining room at Blenheim Palace (ca. 1719)—is cast directly into the midst of the battlefield.

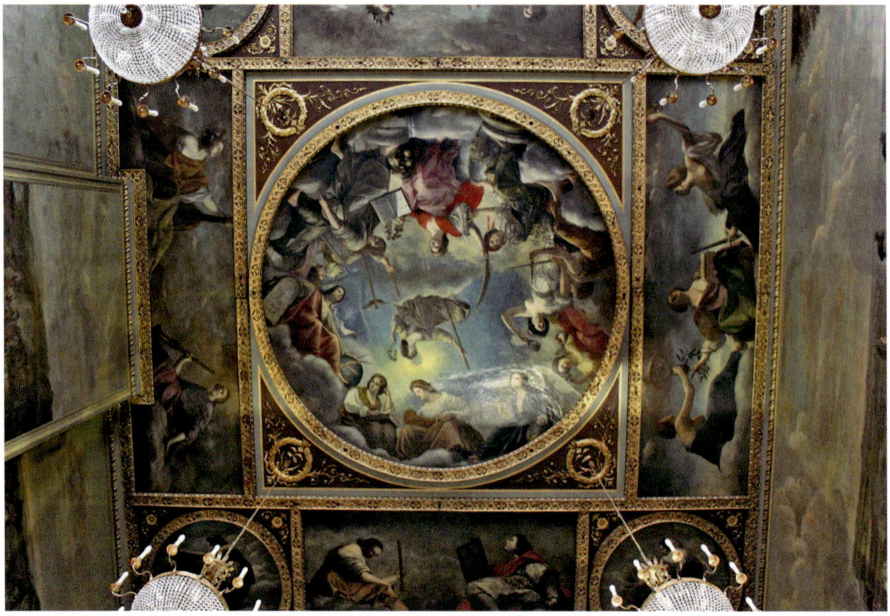

63. Orazio Gentileschi, *An Allegory of Peace and the Arts*, ca. 1635–38, oil on canvas, mounted on board, diameter: 188⅝ in. (479 cm). Royal Collection Trust

Furthermore, the kind of weaponry that decorates the borders of the *Victories* tapestries for Blenheim, woven by the De Vos workshop after designs by Philippe de Hondt—including the jutting spearheads in *Bouchain I,* or the canons and barrels in *The Surrender of Lille*—are at Marlborough House brought diagetically into the main scenes on the south wall of the hall and the north wall of the Malplaquet staircase.[19] In the tapestries, idealized arrangements of foliage, carefully placed groups of objects such as standards and kettle-drums and even allegorical figures, such as the reclining river god in *Oudenarde,* are foregrounded. In the murals weapons are shown damaged, foliage destroyed, and there is a total absence of allegory within the main scenes.[20]

The form in which the person of the Duke of Marlborough is represented also diverges starkly from the precedent set by the depiction of Louis XIV in his battle scenes, and in the tapestries and murals at Versailles; it also departs from the celestial allegories that were to be found at Blenheim Palace. In Le Brun's galéries des Glâces ceiling, for example in *The Franche-Comté Conquered for the Second Time* (begun 1678), the monarch is presented as a deity, illuminated, ethereal, and set apart from the human action. In the murals at Blenheim Palace, meanwhile, the compositions exploit the type of soaring effect possible in painted ceilings. There, James Thornhill's *Hero entering the Temple of Fame* (1716) in the hall and Laguerre's allegory of *War and Peace* in the dining room (1720) are intended to impress upon the viewer below the gloriously elevated figure of the Duke.[21] The murals in the hall at Marlborough House work quite differently. Here Marlborough and his battles are confined to the realm just below the ceiling's threshold, while an earlier allegory of Peace by Orazio Gentileschi and its decorative surround, transferred from the Queen's House at Greenwich on the orders of the Duchess in 1711, fill the vault.[22] Laguerre's murals were therefore undoubtedly planned with the juxtaposition of Gentileschi's earlier canvases in mind, not only thematically but also formally, as the colour and composition of both the skies blend seamlessly (fig. 63). The ceiling provides an allegorical counterpoint that underscores the relatively life-like depictions of war below but also serves to suggest that this brutal apprehension of violence could coexist alongside a hope for peace. This was a period filled with what the Marlboroughs viewed as underhand negotiations with the French that eventually led to the Peace of Utrecht in 1713.[23] What the ceiling and wall murals communicated together was that, far from being anti-peace *per se*, or simply "pro-war", the Marlboroughs were rather against the nature of the discussions that not only excluded them but also disregarded what the Duke had been, and still was, fighting for.[24]

The image of the Duke in Laguerre's murals also differs substantially from that in the *Victories* tapestries, which consistently place him at the front of the scene. These ultimately derived in their format from the series that defined the contemporary military tapestry, the *Histoire du Roi* of Louis XIV, produced after designs by Le Brun and Van der Meulen. Alan Wace describes the image of the king presented there as one that shows him "in his glory, usually on a prancing steed, surrounded by a glittering staff and occupying the place of honor in the foreground, while the actions which give their name to the tapestries are relegated to a small scale in the distance".[25] Though he is recognizable within each of the Marlborough murals, the Duke's position within them is more nuanced. His presence is important but not overbearing, and the spectator is obliged to consider his enemies, both of high rank and low, and to appreciate their dignity and pain. This is partly because the topography of the murals offers a faithful rendition of the flat landscapes where the fighting took place, rather than one which has been doctored, as in the *Histoire du Roi* or *Victories* tapestries, to feature an elevation from which Louis or the Duke look down on the panorama of battle in the lower distance. Rather than placing the Duke apart from the action, protected by an imaginary landscape repoussoir, the murals offered a more immediate depiction of the realities of risk and sacrifice, while at the same time emphasizing Marlborough's

est foreign enemy.[51] That the Duchess was so closely involved before and during the murals' execution renders it inconceivable that Laguerre would not have discussed presentation pieces with the Duchess prior to beginning painting and agreeing his and his workmen's fees; it is entirely probable, therefore, that she would have had a hand in their content and design before she left to join her husband abroad.[52]

Steered by the Duchess, the murals functioned as a pictorial pamphlet writ large, their topical narrative immediately recognizable through the representation of the Duke's sublime magnanimity and vivid depictions of very recent historical events.[53] In this brief period, described by Frances Harris as one of "paper wars", the murals were legible as ripostes to the barrage of hostile literature—famously including Jonathan Swift's *The Conduct of the Allies* (1711)—intent on ruining the Duke's reputation. They visualized not only the dangers in which the Duke continued to place himself, and the original reasons for his elevation, but also attempted to persuade the spectator of the contention that the Crown continued to rely heavily on his type of military valour. This was also the purpose of the Duchess's book, *An Account of the Conduct of the Dowager Duchess of Marlborough, from her first coming to Court, to the Year 1710*, which focuses on these years (though it was only published much later, in 1742).[54] The *Account* described the early 1710s as a critical time for the couple as they tried to retain their influence in court: the Duchess had been stripped of her offices after the Tory victories and had recently lost favour with Queen Anne, while the Duke had offended the monarch by presuming to request the position of Captain-General for life.[55] Its tone is one of utter indignation at the perceived poor treatment of both husband and wife and the lack of recognition for the sacrifices they had made for the nation.

In the event, the construction and interiors of Marlborough House embodied and promoted the Duchess's political stance more immediately than did the *Account*, with its protracted publication schedule.[56] The Dutch-style simplicity of the house's architecture, contrasting with the French-inspired opulence of Blenheim Palace, has been noted often enough, and parsimony is often suggested as the reason for the Marlboroughs' choice of architecture, as well as for that of mural painting over tapestry.[57] Though economy may have played its part in the decision-making process, parsimony was, for the Duchess, a grand gesture in itself. She not only wanted to showcase a different, more humble, image of her husband at a time when criticism of him relied heavily on the charge of avarice, but also, more broadly, wanted to propose a new visual language that was deliberately set against the courtly elegance of Blenheim Palace and its bespoke artworks (including the *Victories* tapestries). While constantly expressing a lack of interest in the state-funded Blenheim, a project which she appeared to view with suspicion—indeed, almost as a decoy from the real politics of the situation—the Duchess chose instead to concentrate her efforts on her town house, largely funded from within the family and pointedly far closer to the royal palace at St James's.[58] The lack of obvious grandeur in both the architecture and the murals was part of a plan to contrast her house with the royal dwellings from which she had recently been expelled.[59] Furthermore, mural painting had the advantage of being relatively expeditious to produce and—given that it was executed in situ—easy to manage, thus giving the Duchess more immediate control over its execution than would have been the case for tapestries produced offsite or even abroad.

The murals belonged to a period of propaganda in various media, both for and against the Duke, in which the Duchess was heavily embroiled.[60] At around the same time as the murals were commissioned there appeared an anonymous pamphlet that seems to have shared their purposes. Entitled *A Short Narrative of the Life and Actions of His Grace John, D. of Marlborough* (1711), it has been identified by certain scholars as likely to have been written by Daniel Defoe.[61] The text's central conceit is that it is penned by a loyal but anonymous soldier, whose sole interest is to bolster the professional reputation of the Duke by referring to his remarkable qualities both as a military leader and as a person. These encomia to the Duke are included alongside scrupulously detailed descriptions of the author's experiences at the Battles of Blenheim and Ramillies, so as to verify his standing as a witness. Although scholars have pointed to similarities in the text's interests and style with those of Defoe, it is worth pointing out that he produced many authored pamphlets regarding the Duke at around this time, most of which were by no means as one-sided as the pamphlet, which is powered by a seemingly intimate acquaintance with Marlborough and by an unusual ardour for him. The intimacy it betrays, as well as the author's relentless tone of indignation, are more reminiscent of the actions and writings, both public and private, of the Duchess.[62]

The sublime personal qualities that were embodied by the Duke—such as empathy, charity, politeness, and good-breeding—are all described by the Duchess as being important; however, it was characteristics that enjoyed more political potential—such as his lack of wastefulness—that she most emphasized in these years, and communicated via her literary, architectural, and artistic commissions. Most important of all, in the pamphlet as well as in the murals, is the trope of regarding sympathetically one's comrades and enemies.[63] The pamphlet concentrates on the appreciation that the Duke's own soldiers had for his humanity and piety, and describes the magnanimity that he showed towards his enemy, exemplified by the surrender at Blenheim depicted in the murals and described above. The most graphic description is one of a common soldier's rain-sodden march and siege, which is worth quoting in full:

> . . . if they did but see them in a Rainy Season, when the whole Country about them is trod into a Chaos, and in such intolerable Marches, Men and Horses dying and dead together, and the best of them glad of a bundle of Straw to lay down their wet and weary Limbs: If they did but see a Siege, besides the daily danger and expectation of Death, which is common to all, from the General to the Centinel; the Watches, the Labours, the Cares which attend the greatest; the ugly Sights, the Stinks of Mortality, the Grass all wither'd and black with the Smoke of Powder, the horrid Noises all Night and all Day, and Spoil and Destruction on every side; I am sure they would be perswaded, that a State of War, to those who are engag'd in it, must needs, be a state of Labour and Misery; and that a great General, I mean such a one as the Duke of Marlborough, weak in his Constitution, and well stricken in Years, would not undergo those eating Cares, which must be continually at his Heart; the Toils and Hardships which he must endure, and the often Sorrows which must prick his Heart for ugly Accidents, if he has the least Spark of humane Commiseration, I say, he would not engage himself in such a Life, if not for the sake of his Queen and Country, and his Honour.[64]

The description of the appalling conditions, alongside the anguish that they caused the Duke, tries to persuade the reader that far from being war-hungry, the Duke was in fact driven by duty to his country rather than any self-serving motive.

Such words, of course, are strongly reminiscent both of the reality of the horrors that are depicted in the murals but also of the passages of correspondence which passed between the Duke and Duchess during these years. The Duchess frequently tried to imagine the life in the trenches endured by her husband, a man to whom she was famously close but from whom she had been parted for much of the previous decade.[65] Her imagination was fuelled by regular descriptions of the frontline of battle from her husband's own hand. In 1709, the Duke wrote to her about his queasiness at the state of the trenches, which were soon to be depicted with unusual frankness in Laguerre's murals: "It is not to be imagined the ill weather we have, in so much that the poor soldiers in the trenches are upto their knees in durt, which gives mee the spleen to a degree that makes me very uneasy, and consequently makes me languish for retirement."[66]

It seems possible that the Duchess would have played a part in the pamphleteering of the time, though if she did she would not, as a woman, have been able to put her name to any production that she might have had a hand in.[67] That must remain speculation; what is certain is that it is through the murals at Marlborough House that her challenge to the intolerable criticism of her husband is communicated. Laguerre's murals served to keep an idea of the reality of close combat at the forefront of the minds of the Duchess and visitors to her house.[68] The political programme motivating the scheme pushed Laguerre towards uncharacteristic innovations, which, judged against the standards of the allegorical or mythological history painting of the time, might appear deviant or confrontational. The accumulation of visual detail in the murals—what Roland Barthes would term the "reality effect"—and the organization of the space to make those details insistently present to visitors, often at eye level, as they move around, forces the question of their physical and mental distance from realities on the ground.[69]

The murals, like the 1711 pamphlet, worked hard to provoke a sense of gratitude from what the Duchess viewed as an ungrateful nation. Her primary concern during this period was to keep her husband's sacrifices at the forefront of the minds both of those in power and a wider public; her house provided the Duchess with one platform to do precisely this. By dramatizing the Duke's suffering and humanity, Sarah sought to challenge those partaking in armchair politics, described in the pamphlet as men "whose Mouths go off smartly with a Whiff of Tobacco, and fight Battles, and take Towns over a Dish of Coffee".[70] She maintained that such distant viewers had no idea of the Duke's actual predicament, of the sublimity of combat, but merely revelled in domestic infighting. Backscheider concludes about the pamphlet that, "written in the interim between two foreign policies when so many momentous plans were proceeding backstage, [it] mirrors the age."[71] The same could be said of the murals: taking elements of history paintings that had been intended to glorify Louis XIV through a typological alignment with an ancient hero, Alexander, Laguerre transformed them into a new type of topical mural painting that sought to persuade with graphic urgency.

The troubled physical history of the murals, the low status given to the genre in art-historical literature, and, perhaps, a reluctance to acknowledge the prominent role played by a female patron—all have meant that Laguerre's scheme at Marlborough House has received little scholarly attention. The scheme's significance for the history of painting in England, for our understanding of the highly particular interplay between art and politics, print and paint, at the very dawn of the eighteenth century and the new polite society, has thereby been obscured. When the Marlboroughs returned to England and George I was crowned, the new monarch was hosted at Marlborough House and a new era began. While the murals had polemical force at an important political moment, they nonetheless also contained a fundamental message about the Duke and his particular brand of military valour that their medium allowed to be immortalized, and that continued to be communicated throughout the Duke's retirement and up until the death of the Duchess in 1744. Their subsequent obscurity should not overshadow the vital and complex role they played in that earlier historical moment.

17. On Le Vau's staircase, see Lydia Beauvais, *Charles Le Brun, 1619–1690: Célébration du tricentenaire de la mort de l'artiste: le décor de l'escalier des Ambassadeurs à Versailles* (Paris: Éditions de la Réunion des musées nationaux, 1990).
18. For precise measurements, see Walker, *Marlborough House*. The frames as well as the painted and gilt surrounds in all three spaces are likely to have been embellished due to extensive architectural and decorative additions to the house since the eighteenth century. Major architectural changes that we know of include the addition of the balcony in the hall, and the addition of extra storeys to the house from the late eighteenth and nineteenth centuries, which necessitated an extra flight of stairs in the east. The mahogany panels on both staircases are certainly nineteenth-century additions. Some decorative changes, for example those that occurred under Edward, Prince of Wales, and Princess Alexandra from 1863–1903, are commemorated by an inscription on the hall mirror. It would take a separate study to address the precise architectural and decorative evolution of the spaces with which this essay is concerned; but a case study that unearthed the original setting for the murals would be invaluable.
19. On the Blenheim Palace tapestries, see Alan Wace, *The Marlborough Tapestries at Blenheim Palace* (London and New York: Phaidon, 1968), and Jeri Bapasola's catalogue entry in *Tapestry in the Baroque: Threads of Splendor*, ed. Thomas P. Campbell and others (New Haven and London: Yale Univ. Press, 2007), 471–77.
20. On the allegorical figures and decorative details, for example on the north wall of the Ramillies staircase, see the inventory in Walker, *Marlborough House*.
21. Thornhill does not go so far as to name the Duke explicitly in his *Explanation of the Painting* written for the Duchess, but the parallel with the patron and victor commemorated is clear. James Thornhill, *The Explanation of ye Painting in ye Oval of the Great Hall at Blenheim*, BL Add MS 61354, fols. 38r–39v. The inexplicit naming of the patron was also an issue in Godfrey Kneller's design for a large allegorical painting of Queen Anne granting Blenheim Palace to a man. On the Kneller painting and the murals at Blenheim in general, see David Green, *Blenheim Palace* (London: Country Life, 1951).
22. This is clear from a letter of 23 April 1711 to the Duchess from Christopher Wren's son, who managed the project on his father's behalf. In it he states that the paintings had to be cut down because their large size did not leave enough space for the required level of framing, and also that the method of arranging them had been personally approved by the Duke. BL Add MS 61357, fols. 55r–56r.

    That the lower layer of the room's artistic programme remains a mystery is unfortunate; the tapestries currently occupying this space of peasants merry-making in idealized pastoral scenes could not have been a part of the original commission, as they only came into the Royal Collection when they were presented by the Corporation of the City of London to King George V and Queen Mary on their marriage in July 1893 (source: The Royal Collection). No tapestries are mentioned as being in the hall in an inventory of 1744 (BL Add MS 61473, fol. 11r).
23. For example, Harris, *Passion for Government*, 185–87.
24. See also Hargraves, "'Great Man' or 'Knave'?", 29.
25. Wace, *Marlborough Tapestries*, 19.
26. I am grateful to Robert Wellington for suggesting this link to me. Further investigations into Laguerre's French background and experience may shed further light on the reasons for certain aesthetic inspirations. On Parrocel's murals, see Joëlle Barreau and others, *Peintures murales aux Invalides: l'oeuvre révélé de Joseph Parrocel* (Dijon: Éditions Faton, 2005), and Jérôme Delaplanche, *Joseph Parrocel, 1646–704: la nostalgie de l'héroïsme* (Paris: Arthena, 2006).
27. The effect today is quite different from what was originally intended, with the distraction of subsequent architectural alterations, including the addition of an ornate balcony on the south wall in 1862. Charlton, *Marlborough House*, 18 (1962), 22 (1978).
28. Quoted in David McNeil, *The Grotesque Depiction of War and the Military in Eighteenth-century Military Fiction* (Newark: Univ. of Delaware Press, 1990), 72. I am indebted to my conversations with David McNeil for prompting me to look further into this link: this is just one of many topics relating to the Marlborough House murals which could benefit from further, in-depth study.

29. This scene was also included in sculptural relief on the Marlboroughs' tomb monument at Blenheim, designed by William Kent in close collaboration with the Duchess and sculpted by John Michael Rysbrack.
30. Anon. [Richard Steele], *The Englishman's Thanks to the Duke of Marlborough*, London, 1 Jan. 1712.
31. Andrew Lincoln, "War and the Culture of Politeness: The Case of *The Tatler* and *The Spectator*", *Eighteenth-Century Life* 36, no. 2 (2012): 60–79.
32. Richard Steele in *The Tatler* 209, Thursday, 10 Aug. 1710.
33. Joseph Addison's *The Campaign* of 1705 is emblematic of this. For an excellent account of poetry during the period, see Abigail Williams, *Poetry and Creation of a Whig Literary Culture, 1681–1714* (Oxford Univ. Press, 2005).
34. Bainbrigg Buckeridge, *On her Majesty's Grant of Woodstock Park, &c. to His Grace the Duke of Marlborough, 1704. In a letter to Signior Antonio Verrio at Hampton-Court* (London, 1705).
35. Richard Blackmore, *Instructions to Vander Bank, A Sequel to the Advice of the Poets: A Poem, Occasion'd by the Glorious Success of Her Majesty's Arms, under the Command of the Duke of Marlborough, the last Year in Flandres* (London, 1709).
36. On the goriness of the murals in a Swiftian context, see David McNeil, *The Grotesque Depiction of War*. On the sublime, see passages from William Smith's translation of Longinus, *On the Sublime* (London, 1739), VII, 15; XVIII.
37. William Harison, *Woodstock Park, A Poem* (London, 1706), 8–9.
38. For example, in Matthew Prior, *Letter to Monsieur Boileau Depreaux occasion'd by the Victories at Blenheim* (London, 1704), 4.
39. Croft-Murray, *Decorative Painting in England*, 1: 64.
40. For example, in a letter of 1713 published in Sarah Churchill, Duchess of Marlborough, *Letters of Sarah Duchess of Marlborough now first published from the original manuscripts at Madresfield Court* (London: J. Murray, 1875), 78–79, no. 22.
41. Hannah Smith, "'Last of all the Heavenly Birth': Queen Anne and Sacral Queenship", *Parliamentary History* 28 (2009): 137–49.
42. Smith, "Last of all the Heavenly Birth". See also Hargraves, "'Great Man' or 'Knave'?"
43. Smith, "Last of all the Heavenly Birth", 147.
44. See documents published in Snyder, ed., *Marlborough–Godolphin Correspondence*, 2: nos. 1007, 1023, 1121; 3: nos. 1294, 1414, as well as those in Churchill, *Letters*, nos. 7, 22, 24, 32. On the exile, see Edward Gregg, "Marlborough in Exile, 1712–1714", *The Historical Journal* 15, no. 4 (1972): 593–618.
45. Gregg, "Marlborough in Exile", 596.
46. In a letter to Jennens of 7 May 1714, in Churchill, *Letters*, 96–97, no. 29. A month later the Duchess says not to worry about making any alterations, as more well-placed judges—including a certain "Mr Degmar"—thought that none were necessary, the smaller figures being visible enough (no. 33).
47. Churchill, *Letters*, 104–6, no. 33.
48. Churchill, *Letters*, 81–84, no. 24.
49. Churchill, *Letters*, 78–79, no. 22.
50. Horace Walpole, *Anecdotes of Painting in England*, 4 vols. (Twickenham: Printed for Thomas Farmer at Strawberry-Hill, 1762–71), 3: 114.
51. The Duchess acknowledges the irony of her choice in a letter from Frankfurt (17 June 1713); Churchill, *Letters*, 40–42, no. 7.
52. Churchill, *Letters*, 103–4, no. 32. It is unclear which paintings connected with the murals would have been the presentation pieces, if any. Laing surmises that they are likely to be the larger, more sketchy ones, three of which are now at Grimsthorpe Castle, Lincolnshire. More work needs to be done on this topic. On the various types and the status of painters involved (though with an ambiguous use of the word "decorative"), see Iain Pears, *The Discovery of Painting: The Growth of Interest in the Arts in England, 1680–1768* (New Haven and London: Yale Univ. Press, 1988), 115–16. That the duchess was pleased by the end result is indicated by the fact that soon after, Laguerre worked for her close friends Lord and Lady Cowper, painting their staircase murals

to being uncomfortable with the concept of divine right, requesting that the term be removed from an address to her from the City of London),[6] it is argued here that it is surely an error to seek straightforward evidence for this seminal historical shift in the queen's painted image. Rather, although a new conception of and language about monarchy was emerging by Anne's reign, Kneller's images can in fact be situated within a relatively stable tradition of representation. Similarly, although recent scholarship on the construction of Queen Anne's image, particularly as found in prose and verse, in sermons, laudatory panegyric, and plays, has demonstrated an ideological struggle over the royal image that was governed by party politics and self-interest,[7] it is questionable whether this had any impact on her painted state portrait. In text Anne was presented over her reign variously as Pallas Athena, Deborah, and Britannia as a way of harnessing her person—a female monarch in an age of war—to military success; and at her accession in 1702, the court presentation of the queen was as the "nursing mother" of her people, a firm Protestant defender of the Church of England who appropriated Elizabeth I's motto "Semper eadem" as her own, and whose heart was "entirely English". These various formulas for viewing the queen are absent from Kneller's official state portraits, however. Instead, it is a phrase in Queen Anne's own speech to Parliament on 11 March 1702, and to the House of Lords on 30 March 1702, which perhaps best encapsulates their intention and purpose. In her addresses she stressed the necessity of giving just regard to maintaining "the Honour and Dignity of the Crown", thus projecting a self-consciousness about the traditions of monarchy and her status as sovereign, and the need for grandeur and spectacle of ceremony that that entailed. While, as parliamentary sovereign, she may have been disinclined to embrace the sacral element of monarchy, what remained was the need for her public image to embody both her personal majesty and authority, and the dignity and authority of the nation.

The queen's extension over private and public worlds, so acutely observed by Sir John Clerk, was also a feature of the code of friendship with which Anne was familiar and by which she conducted her private and public relationships. With its roots in classical texts and expressed in countless treatises and conduct manuals, friendship was an integral element of early modern culture.[8] Identified by Jeremy Taylor in *A Discourse of the Nature, Offices and Measures of Friendship* (1657) as the "greatest bond in the world", [9] it was a code that governed not only affectionate, personal relationships but also political patronage and kinship alliances and diplomatic "friendships" between nations. Friendship, as Taylor and others argued, demanded mutual love, support and trust, and an openness and honesty between equals. It was expressed in exaggerated, passionate language, not only privately but at the international diplomatic level to affirm allegiance; and gifts of portraits, both in the private and public sphere, were seen as symbolic expressions of friendship. As princess, Anne had commissioned portraits of her intimate friend Sarah, Duchess of Marlborough, in which she had sought "true" likeness. She was "mighty fond of for ye likness sake" one particular portrait, and had an enamel miniature made after it so she would never be without it. It would last forever, Anne said, "& I can allways have it about me to look on when you are out of my sight".[10] The queen gave her own image to friends, ministers, and loyal servants, and circulated it abroad as a gift to fellow sovereigns, a gesture interpreted both as a personal token of regard but also emblematic of national alliance. This duality of public and private coloured every element of the queen's life. She was a private person, yet symbolized a nation; she yearned for a quiet life of privacy, in easy clothes, and in the company of a close circle of friends, but was conscious of the public demands that came with sovereignty; she conducted a sincere and heartfelt friendship with the Duchess of Marlborough, corresponding with her as "Mrs Morley" to "Mrs Freeman" to effect equality, yet was attuned to her privilege of rank; and she inhabited a physically frail body that was at huge variance with public expectations of majesty.

Kneller's role as the Queen's Principal Painter—what his commissions were, and for whom—will here be reconsidered through an examination of the warrants, petitions, and accounts in the Treasury papers,[11] as well as diplomatic correspondence in the State papers. The same evidence allows us to rethink how his portraits performed and were received on the stage for which they were intended. In painting the queen, Kneller's task was to draw closer together her private reality with public expectation, and to create an image of majesty that was both "true" and "like" but which presented to the world her monarchical authority. Never was this more important than in an age dominated by war. The War of the Spanish Succession (1701–14) consumed Anne's reign and the royal image, used within the conventions of international diplomacy, performed an important role as a diplomatic tool in the forging and confirmation of political alliances. Conceived within the established tradition of the royal state portrait, Queen Anne's image was intended to convey her royal command and to be understood both at home and, crucially, by an international audience.

The familiar art-historical assessment of Kneller's relationship with Queen Anne is that it was poor. Kneller, it is said, suffered disappointment, humiliation, and slights during her reign, which saw the suspension of his annual salary of £200 and commissions that should have been his being awarded to others.[12] Documentary evidence in the Treasury and State papers would suggest otherwise. The papers do not tell the complete story, as the survival of bills and accounts is incomplete and minute book entries, particularly in the early part of the reign, are scanty. In addition, because there was insufficient income to settle the civil list, and particularly the household, expenses claims for payment for the same pictures were frequently resubmitted, sometimes over several years, so distinguishing new from old commissions can be difficult. What emerges, however, is not that Kneller was neglected or bypassed by the queen, but that he was kept busy for the duration of the reign with recorded commissions covering the period 1702 until at least 1713, the year before her death.

The office of Principal Painter fell under the auspices of the royal household department of the Lord Chamberlain. Kneller had held the position since 1689, at first jointly with John Riley and then, following Riley's death in 1691, as the sole office holder. He was reconfirmed in his position in the new reign in 1702. In 1705 an administrative oversight came to light, that had resulted in Kneller and other office holders not having been paid for their services since the accession. Letters and warrants rectifying the situation are also of interest, however, as they clarify the role of the Principal Painter. It was, they state, to draw "her Majesty's picture for embassadors and for all the plantations . . . the price for each picture at whole length 50ll".[13] The fee of £50 for a full length (and £30 for a three-quarter length) was the same remuneration that Kneller had received under William III. After deducting the Lord Chamberlain's office and Exchequer fees (both charged 6d. per pound) that are attached to most bills, it is clear that the price paid by the Crown remained constant throughout the queen's reign.

Payment for at least thirty-one portraits of the queen, most of them full lengths, can be extracted from the Treasury papers. The earliest reference occurs in May 1703 in Kneller's petition for payment for several pictures, including the great equestrian portrait of William III.[14] The queen's airy dismissal ("Her Majesty does not care for the picture of £350") is sometimes taken as evidence of her attitude towards Kneller, but in fact it has more to do with her need for financial retrenchment. As the editor of the Treasury papers commented, "the claim that 'the King never dies' does not appear to have applied to the debts of the kingly office": Kneller's was one of many claims left unpaid by William that were declined to be liquidated.[15] The queen did, however, pay for "several pictures of her Majesty" in the same petition. Warrants for payments to Kneller were usually for multiple portraits. On 16 January 1706, for example, he was to be paid for nine full lengths; on 27 March 1710 for seven; and in 1713–14 for five full lengths and three three-quarter lengths.[16] In cases where the intended recipient is named (and in conjunction with evidence gleaned from diplomatic correspondence in the State papers), it can be confirmed that the majority of portraits were intended either as diplomatic gifts to foreign heads of state, or for British extraordinary ambassadors to have with them when negotiating terms of peace, for example at the allied negotiations at The Hague in 1709 and the international congress at Utrecht in 1712–13.

A handful were gifts to household officers. The 1710 payment for seven full lengths, for example, included two for the Prussian court, one each for Lord Marlborough and Lord Townshend, the queen's ambassador plenipotentiaries at The Hague in 1709, and two further pictures associated with diplomatic business, for "the Swiss" and for "Lord Galloway", presumably Lord Galway, ambassador to Britain's key ally, the King of Portugal. The seventh portrait was for Thomas Coke, the queen's Vice Chamberlain. The Treasury papers make no specific mention of portraits for the "plantations" but references can be picked up in the Colonial papers. For example, on 23 February 1703 the colonial government of Virginia requested the queen's picture, "as hath bin usual to all her Majesties Colonys", and on 25 February the Council of Trade and Plantations advised the queen that it was customary for her picture to be sent to all Provinces for display in their Council Chambers.[17] Also not included in the Treasury papers are the numerous portraits of the queen needed by ordinary ambassadors for their embassies abroad, for which they were given money from the Exchequer to commission themselves.[18] By contrast, Michael Dahl, who is often written about as the artist favoured over Kneller by the queen, received commissions on only two occasions: in 1707 for two full lengths, which seem to have been personal gifts from the queen;[19] and in 1712 for a full length for John Robinson, Bishop of Bristol, one of the diplomats at the Utrecht peace conference.[20] Given that Robinson had previously been British Envoy to Sweden, the choice of a Swedish artist for his portrait was surely not accidental. Rather than suffering slights during her reign, it is clear that Queen Anne used the services of her Principal Painter both extensively and, according to the expectations of that appointment, correctly.

The face pattern of the queen established by Kneller was used in all official contexts that necessitated her visual image. This included the coinage, commemorative medals, illuminated charters and letters patent, as well as her state portrait. Civic authorities, Inns of Court, universities, and private individuals could, of course, commission whichever artist they chose for a portrait of the queen. While many chose Kneller, whose studio produced a vast number of repetitions, in the absence of direct access to the queen artists such as Thomas Murray based their portraits of her on Kneller's pattern.[21] Kneller's working method for royal sitters, certainly the method he had used for William III, was to wait on the monarch at one of the royal palaces to make an *ad vivum* sketch, from which he produced a finished portrait in his studio.[22] On 4 April 1702 it was reported in the *Postman* that the queen had had her picture drawn by Kneller for the official coronation medal,[23] presumably the profile portrait used as a model by the Royal Mint (Royal Collection, London). Kneller may have taken the opportunity to take a frontal likeness at the same time, but the first mezzotint after Kneller of Anne as queen,

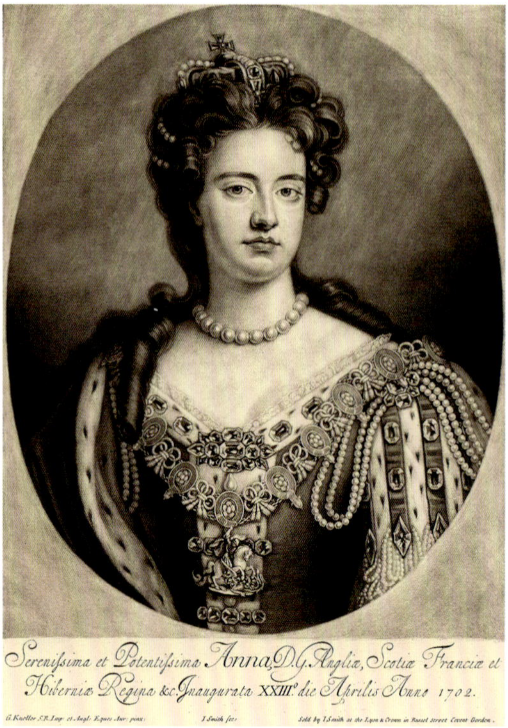

68. John Smith, after Sir Godfrey Kneller, Bt, *Queen Anne* [Chaloner Smith 5, state 1], 1702, mezzotint, 13½ x 9¾ in. (34.4 x 24.7 cm). British Museum, London

issued by John Smith in 1702 (fig. 68), seems to be based on Kneller's face pattern of Anne as Princess of Denmark, with a crown added and state robes borrowed from his portrait of Mary II. Clearly it was an image hurried out by Smith in response to immediate demand for the new queen's image. The second and third states of the print show the queen with a more thick-set face, and then with considerably fuller hair, perhaps adjusted in light of Kneller's fresh access to his sitter and her actual appearance at the coronation (although the depiction of the state robes was not corrected until 1706).

Whether Kneller had access to the queen to update her image as the reign progressed is a vexed question, as is the precise date of creation of the four different portrait types he produced of her, here designated as types A–D. Type A shows the queen standing in coronation robes. Unsurprisingly, it is dated to 1702, evidence for which is the portrait at the Inner Temple (fig. 69) that was commissioned in

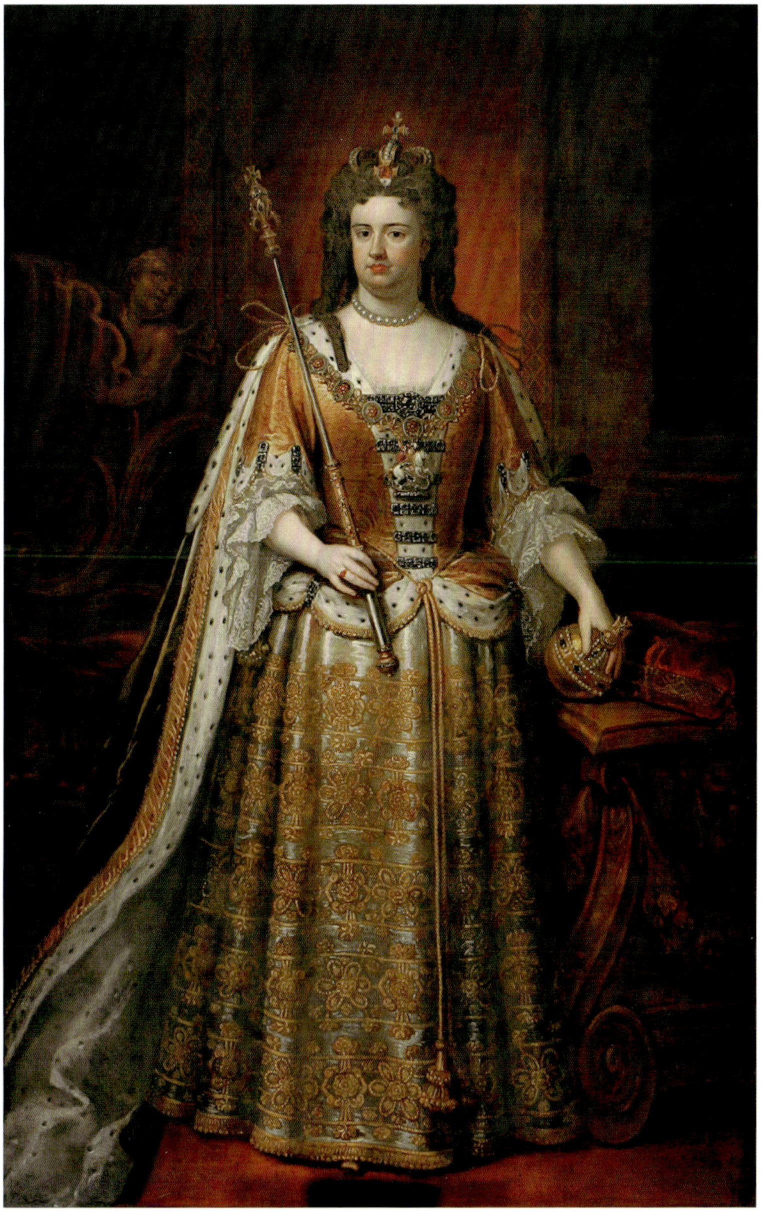

69. Sir Godfrey Kneller, Bt, *Queen Anne* [Type A], 1702/3, oil on canvas, 90½ x 54⅜ in. (230 x 138 cm). The Honourable Society of the Inner Temple, London

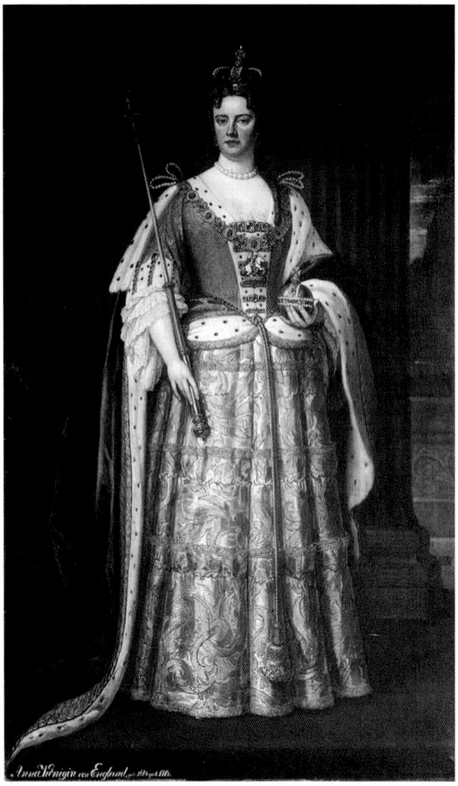

70. Sir Godfrey Kneller, Bt, *Queen Anne* [Type B], 1709, oil on canvas, 91⅜ x 52¾ in. (232 x 134 cm). Stiftung Preußische Schlösser und Gärten, Berlin-Brandenburg

1702 and paid for on 28 January 1703.[24] The queen wears the crown, holds the sceptre and rests her hand on the orb, placed on a nearby table. Type B (fig. 70) is a variant of A, but shows the queen holding the orb, with her velvet and ermine robe arranged differently and with a column and view onto a garden beyond. Type C (fig. 71) is markedly different, and shows the queen seated on a dais in a simplified gold gown and an ermine-lined cloak that sweeps dramatically down the raised steps. The crown and regalia appear on a table to the left and she raises a graceful hand to touch the jewelled Garter badge, or Lesser George, that hangs from the blue riband round her neck, perhaps an allusion to her coronation having taken place on St George's Day, as well as to her being head of the Order of the Garter. Kneller's composition deliberately enhances a sense of majesty and authority by the queen's high placement, with the viewer having to look up at her from below. Figure 71 shows the portrait of this type at Wrest Park. Enlarged at a later date on either side, it is signed and dated 1705 and is said to have been a gift from the queen to the Duke of Kent (her Lord Chamberlain, appointed 1704).[25] The date does not necessarily reflect the date of the portrait's inception, although the portrait of the Duchess of Marlborough (Woburn Abbey) that deploys the same composition is also dated 1705. Type D also shows the queen seated on an elabo-

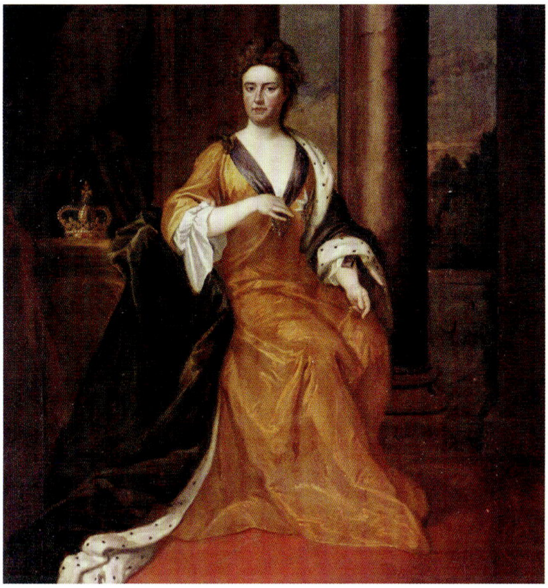

71. Sir Godfrey Kneller, Bt, *Queen Anne* [Type C], 1705, oil on canvas, 92⅛ x 79⅞ in. (234 x 203 cm). English Heritage, Wrest Park

rately carved chair of state, but dressed more formally in state robes and wearing the Garter Collar and Greater George (fig. 72). The crown appears on the table to the right but the queen rests the orb on her knee. Variants of type C show Anne in state robes; and sometimes in type D she appears with the Lesser George rather than the Garter Collar, and rests her feet on a large crimson velvet cushion. The type D face pattern was not issued in print until 1709, and the queen, perhaps, appears slightly aged. But despite references to the queen sitting, and being requested to sit, for her portrait in 1707–8, which will be discussed below, some hesitation is needed in assigning this later date to type D, since a payment of 1706 can perhaps be connected to a portrait of this type at Drumlanrig.[26] In summary, these types do not necessarily succeed one another. In fact, all Kneller's portrait types could ultimately be derived from the same sitting, and rather than being used successively, as they were created, they appear to have been in circulation simultaneously.

Kneller's state portraits of the queen, either standing, gracious and poised, or enthroned, with the insignia of royalty—the symbols of monarchical authority—prominently displayed, were conceived wholly within the traditions of the English state portrait. They represent a continuation of that tradition, not a break from it, and would have conveyed an image of monarchical power within the visual con-

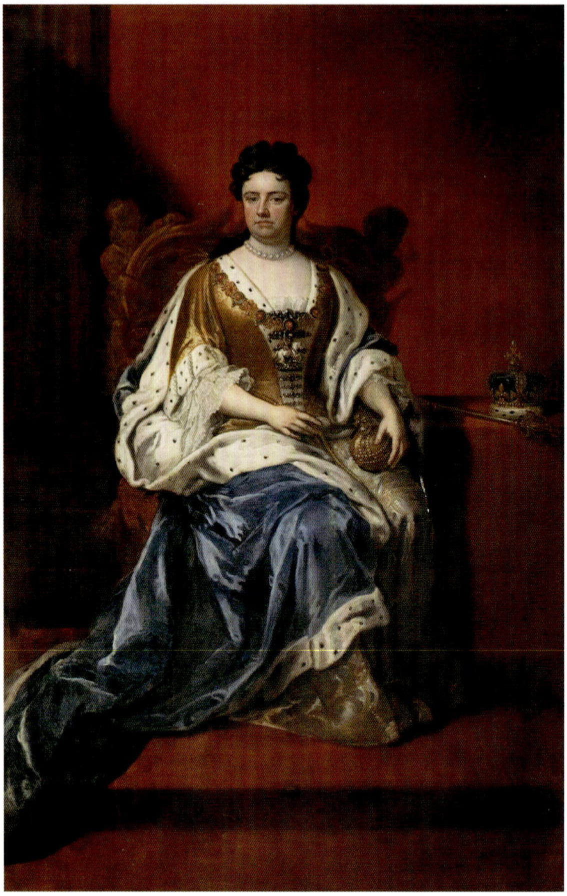

72. Sir Godfrey Kneller, Bt, *Queen Anne* [Type D], ca. 1706 or later, oil on canvas, 90½ x 54⅜ in. (230 x 138 cm). The Duke of Buccleuch, Drumlanrig Castle

vention expected of them by their international audience. Yet however much they were formulated according to traditional principles, Kneller's public images conveyed not simply a manipulated ideal of monarchy but were grounded in the reality of the queen's appearance. However, Anne's episodes of chronic invalidism meant that the reality of her physical presence was unpredictable. At her accession Lord Godolphin noted to Lord Harley her unwieldy lameness; she was without the use of her limbs for periods, and had to be aided when she walked, or carried in a chair. Looking back on her reign, the Duchess of Marlborough noted how "exceeding gross and corpulent" she became. She was also naturally bashful. Jonathan Swift described the desultory nature of her drawing rooms, with the queen looking about the room with her fan in her mouth and uttering "about three words" to those nearest to her before withdrawing to dinner.[27] But the queen could also rise to the occasion, and understood her obligation for grandeur. The Duchess of Marlborough conceded that there was "something of majesty in her look", and on state occasions, such as thanksgiving services at St Paul's Cathedral and ceremonial receptions of ambassadors, the queen could put on a fine public show. The impact of majesty was not lost on Celia Fiennes, who witnessed the queen at her coronation wearing a richly embroidered robe of gold tissue and silver lace, and diamonds in her hair "which at the least motion brill'd and flamed".[28] In the coronation portrait (fig. 69), the coronation regalia, their jewels, and the lustrous shimmer of the queen's gold and silver dress are carefully captured by Kneller, as is the Garter worn tied to her left arm. The queen had consulted several people on the correct etiquette for this, there being no precedent for a woman wearing it (the idea that this motif was borrowed from a portrait of Elizabeth I is incorrect).[29] Kneller also shows the queen's extraordinarily full hair, some of it false, that had been created for her coronation. Mrs Ducaila was paid £12 for a "head of hair with long locks and puffs" as well as 2s. 6d. for a "pair of favourites" (two curls) which are shown on either side of her temple.[30] Kneller's portrait types A and B clearly incorporate these documented elements of the queen's physical appearance, and combine a knowledge of her actual person with an idealized vision of majesty.

There were two aspects to the use of the queen's portrait in an international context: first, there was the possession and symbolic display of her image by ambassadors, to lend them authority as the monarch's representatives abroad; and second, the gift of, or equally the request for her portrait to and by heads of state as expressions of personal and political friendship. Such gifts and requests were part of diplomatic convention, and were used to forge and cement bonds of alliance.

The royal portrait was part of an ambassador's necessary equipage paid for by the Exchequer, which included a state coach for the required grand formal entrance to a city on appointment, elaborate plate as a fitting reflection of the honour and dignity of the monarch he represented, as well as a rich chair and canopy of state. Hung in the embassy audience chamber in conjunction with the latter two items, the royal portrait became a powerful embodiment of the monarch's sovereignty and authority.[31] This concept of the portrait as the visual stand-in for the absent monarch is evident in John Michael Wright's account of Lord Castlemaine's embassy to Rome in 1685. A portrait of James II, very similar in nature to Wright's powerfully illusionistic enthroned Charles II (Royal Collection, London), showing the King "as big as the life, sitting Crown'd on his Throne, and clad in his Regal Habit", can be seen in an accompanying engraving to the publication. Shown placed in the middle of the wall, under a canopy of state, the portrait was the first

he thought it would improve the quality of the portrait, whether saying that the portrait had been taken from life would impress, or whether the request was simply a calculated form of flattery, is not known. The portrait Raby received is most likely the one now at the Royal Hospital Chelsea,[42] a standard repetition of the coronation portrait, type A, and most unlikely to have been "touched" in the royal presence. But on 26 January 1706 its impact in Berlin was recorded by Raby: "the King last thursday dined with me", he wrote, "& seeing the Queens Picture made me promis to write again that he might have one."[43] In September 1708 the picture had still not been received. In a letter to Boyle (Harley's successor) Raby says that in a private audience with the king, following Raby's delivery of the queen's personal letter to him, and a mutual exchange of compliments in which Frederick I gave "the utmost assurance of his firm friendship & adherence to her Maty & her interest", the king "asked me immediately if I had braught the Queens picture with me, & chid me for not doing it, since he waited for it with great impatience seing he heard the Queen had been so good to set for it several times". Raby reported that he had assured the king that he expected it "every post by Hambourg", but asked Boyle to speak to the Lord Chamberlain to hasten it.[44] The final reference to the picture is a month later, in a letter to Lord Sunderland.[45] Raby had let the king know that the queen would sit again to have the picture "finished out of hand", with which the king was pleased, "& desired me to make twenty Compliments to the Queen upon it". The request for one picture, however, had turned into two, one for the king and one for his son. Raby advised that "tho a bagatelle", there should be a distinction between the two portraits as they would be "observed at this court".

This extended exchange over several years raises questions. While it is clear that portraits could be used as a prompt to exchange compliments, and that the flattering request for a portrait could either precede or conclude pertinent political business, and was thus used as a way of exerting pressure and a sense of reciprocal obligation among allies, why was it that Frederick I's portrait took so long to be delivered? In fact, he was not the only one to be kept waiting. On 15 May 1708 Lord Galway wrote to Sunderland from Lisbon hoping that the portrait of the queen for King John V of Portugal would "come soon";[46] and in August 1707 Lord Marlborough had written to his wife in frustration that a portrait of the queen promised to Count Wratislaw, a key diplomat and minister at the Imperial court, had not only not arrived but had not even been begun, because Kneller needed a Lord Chamberlain's warrant.[47] Despite this hint at administrative inefficiency, what this must also suggest is that the request for a portrait was sometimes interpreted as a symbolic gesture of friendship that was sufficient in itself, without always requiring the production of an actual portrait.

Raby's dismissal of the queen's portrait as a "bagatelle", suggestive of a superfluous trifle, may partly have been a reference to its comparatively low financial value, but its symbolic value was worth considerably more. Its possession was certainly valued by Raby himself, who tried to extract another one on his diplomatic transfer from Berlin to The Hague in 1711 (he was refused on the grounds that his current one could not possibly be "worn out").[48] In 1703 Sophia of Hanover lavished extravagant praise on what the Duchess of Marlborough described as "a very ill copy" of the queen's portrait, which she had procured, on Marlborough's instructions, not through the Lord Chamberlain but directly from Kneller's studio, in response to Sophia's request for the queen's image. The portrait, Sophia told Sarah, was worth more than the universe itself, and she sent her £3,000 worth of tapestry and £3,000 for plate in thanks.[49] The possession of the queen's image, and what it advertised in terms of allegiance to those who would see it displayed, was clearly worth more to Sophia than the picture's aesthetic merit.

In other letters, the issue of the queen actually sitting for her portrait is frequently mentioned. This implies that a likeness taken from a life sitting, and not simply a repetition or copy of a portrait, was not only valued by contemporaries but was regarded as a particular compliment to the recipient. In Marlborough's 1707 letter to his wife concerning Wratislaw's portrait of the queen, the contents of which he knew would be passed on to Anne, he writes that not only had Wratislaw "set his heart on the honour" of receiving the queen's portrait, but that "Sir Godfrey might order it so that her majesty need not have the trouble of sitting but once." Sitting only once would demonstrate Marlborough's consideration in inconveniencing the queen as little as possible, while at the same time honouring Wratislaw with a true likeness. But Marlborough goes on to make a further flattering and calculated gesture of friendship. Next year, he says, "I must beg the favour of the queen that she will allow Sir Godfrey to come three or four times to draw her's and the prince's pictures for Blenheim; if I am ever to enjoy quietness, it must be there, so that I would have nothing in my sight but my friends." In requesting three or four sittings, Marlborough was impressing on the queen their mutual, special, and intimate friendship; by saying the portraits were for Blenheim he was being deliberately mindful of the queen's great gift to him; and by desiring the portraits at all he was attempting to repair the fractured relationship between his wife, himself, and the queen. The references to the queen actually sitting for her portrait for Frederick I could well have been fiction. The two portraits requested by the Prussian court were eventually dispatched (they are listed in Kneller's group of seven to be paid for in 1710, as is the King of Portugal's). A portrait of Queen Anne, until 1945 in the collection of the Stiftung Preußische Schlösser, and thought to bear the date 1709, is presumably one of them (fig. 70).[50] It is type B, the variation on the coronation portrait that Marlborough had with him in The Hague in the same year. Of a substantial size, and signed "G Kneller Eques", it may have been a painting that Kneller took more care over than other standard repetitions. What the other Prussia portrait looked like—whether, as recommended by Raby, there was a difference between the two, and whether it (or type B even) was a new portrait type—is not known.

While Kneller was the Queen's Principal Painter, she also employed a painter in enamel. Charles Boit (1662–1727) had held the office under William III until 1699 when he went abroad, not to return until after the queen's accession. His name first appears in the Treasury books on 26 May 1708, and the first reference to him as her Majesty's "painter in enamel" occurs in 1709.[51] Exactly when he was appointed is not clear, but his undated petition to the queen for preferment to the post survives among the State papers. In it he proposes painting in enamel "on large Plates" histories and battle scenes, and specifically the "great Actions of this last Glorious Campaign" (presumably Blenheim, 1704). The queen's encouragement, he says, would "cause him to bend all his Thoughts towards filling your Majesties Closett with Master-pieces of the Art, and your Majesties Name will be Renowned to Posterity as the Great Patroness of this Art, which will most Effectually represent your Majesties Astonishing Successes to all after Ages".[52] The queen never employed Boit to glorify the military victories of her reign.[53] Instead, the official duty of the office holder was the production of enamel portrait miniatures of the queen to be presented by her as gifts (see, for example, figs. 73–74). Based on the likeness of the queen established by Kneller, they were bestowed as rewards for loyalty and service, and to foreign princes and diplomats as tokens of her regard and friendship.

The intimate nature of the portrait miniature had been utilized by English monarchs in international diplomacy since the reign of Henry VIII.[54] As a gift from sovereign to sovereign, or from a sovereign to a departing foreign ambassador, it symbolized official gratitude and friendship but, by virtue of the nature of the object, on a particularly personal and private level. Presumably it was hoped that the gift of such a thing from the queen to a foreign ambassador would foster goodwill, and stimulate the diplomat's willingness and obligation to advocate the queen's, and the nation's, interest back at home.[55] A vivid illustration of the persuasive power the gift of a miniature had on the recipient occurs in Daniel Defoe's fictitious (but utterly believable) memoirs of Nicolas Mesnager, the French agent in London in 1711 delegated to construct secret terms of peace with Britain, without the knowledge of Britain's allies, prior to the international peace congress at Utrecht. Mesnager had an evening audience with the queen's close personal servant, her Keeper of the Privy Purse, Abigail Masham:

> She told me she had it in Charge to let me know how well I was with the Queen, and how agreeable it was to her Majesty to hear that I was to be at *Utrecht*: And going to her Cabinet, she called me to her, and presented me in a Purse of Crimson Velvet, made up like a Case, and fastn'd with a Gold Clasp, her Majesty's Picture set round with Diamonds. I started back a little, and offered to receive it on my Knee, which she understood immediately, but would not suffer me: *For, Sir*, says she, *I do not tell you that the Queen presents you, but you may be assur'd* BY IT, *says she, how satisfactory your Visits have been*, and how much I think it my Honour to hand this Present to you.[56]

With the praise and compliments of the queen still fresh in his mind, and with her personal, jewelled image in his possession as both confirmation and a reminder of their mutual understanding and obligations, Mesnager set out to the Utrecht peace negotiations.

As with the queen's state portrait, references to miniatures in the Treasury books are presumably incomplete. From the extant evidence, and through cross-referencing and supplementing it with information contained within money warrants to the jewellers who mounted the miniatures in gold and set them with diamonds, it is possible to conclude that the queen used her image primarily as her official departure gift to foreign diplomats. International diplomatic protocol dictated a hierarchical treatment of foreign agents, both in the ceremonial surrounding their reception and in the nature and value of gifts exchanged and bestowed.[57] The queen did not, therefore, give her image to all foreign agents but only to extraordinary ambassadors, and sometimes envoys, who represented particular nations. This reflected status according to diplomatic grade, the level of respect that had to be observed for certain nations, and also careful management of relationships with Britain's key international allies. In 1702, for example, when representatives of foreign powers were in London to congratulate the new queen on her accession and coronation, Frederick van Reede and Willem van Haren, the two extraordinary ambassadors from the States General of the United Provinces, and Johann Quintin, Count Jörger, the Emperor's envoy—representatives of Britain's key allies in the Treaty of Grand Alliance—received enamel miniatures of the queen surrounded by diamonds, each worth £1,000. Envoys from other nations received only diamond rings, worth either £400, £350, or £300 according to a carefully calibrated hierarchy of status.[58] This strict observance of hierarchy and protocol, and the value of gifts awarded by one nation to another as befitting their dignity, was noted at national level, in the press, and also by individuals. In the

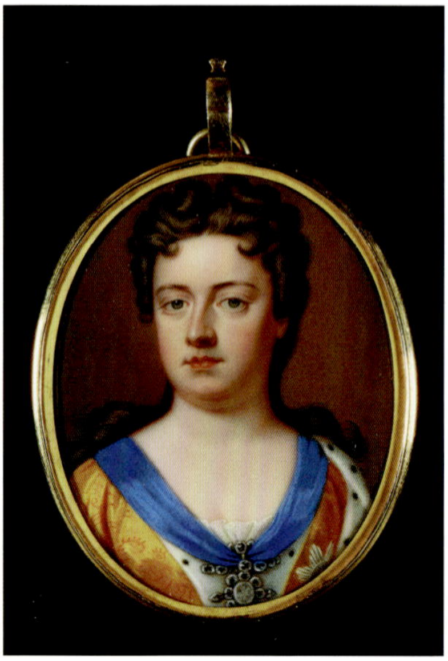

73. Charles Boit, *Queen Anne*, ca. 1705, enamel, 1¾ x 1⅜ in. (4.4 x 3.6 cm). Royal Collection Trust, London

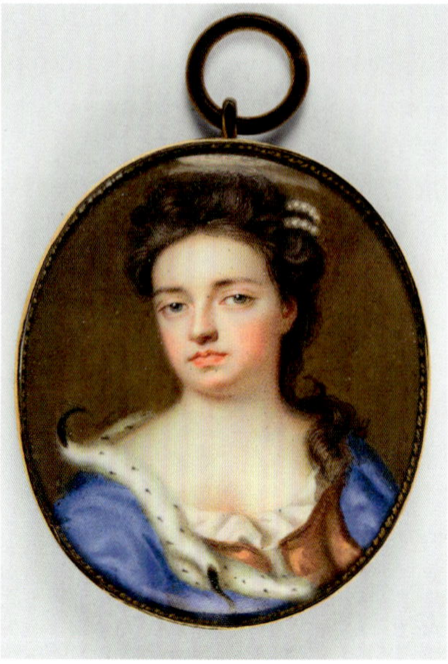

74. Attributed to Jean-Louis Petitot, *Queen Anne*, enamel, 1½ x 1¾ in. (3.8 x 4.5 cm). Portland Collection, Welbeck Abbey

Post Boy, for example, it was reported that on departing Vienna on 10 August 1709, Sir Philip Meadows, the British envoy extraordinary, had received "his Imperial Majesty's Picture, set with diamonds";[59] and on his departure from Berlin in July 1709 it was reported that Lord Raby had received at his audience of leave a diamond-encrusted buckle worth 6,000 crowns.[60] On 29 April 1707 Lord Marlborough privately reported to his wife that on leaving the court of Sweden he had been promised the king's picture which was to be sent to The Hague, and that the King of Prussia had "forced" a ring on him, worth £1,000.[61] The queen herself inspected the quality of the diamonds surrounding a miniature of herself intended as a gift to Princess Anne of Hanover.[62] The giving of her image and costly jewels was thus part of an international convention of gift-giving, where the value and nature of the gift both flattered and satisfied the honour of the receiver, and oiled the wheels of international relations.

Of the miniatures of Queen Anne that survive today, the majority are by Boit. No name is given in the Treasury papers for the artist who produced the miniatures given to diplomats in 1702, and the only other miniaturist mentioned is Petitot, presumably Jean-Louis Petitot (1652–1730), who produced two enamel miniatures in 1710.[63] Boit's recorded commissions, once unravelled from the numerous resubmissions for payment for the same items over several years, included in 1708 enamel miniatures of the queen for the Venetian extraordinary ambassadors, Erizzo and Erani, and probably one "to be sent to Switzerland"; in 1709 miniatures for Pedro da Sousa, Marquis das Minas, the King of Portugal's representative, and Francesco Cornaro, the departing Venetian ordinary ambassador; and on 4 June 1713 there was a warrant for payment of £100 for miniatures ordered by the queen "for presents for divers persons"—perhaps as tokens of thanks and friendship to foreign delegates or her own ministers for securing the Treaty of Utrecht. Having been set with diamonds the miniatures were individually worth between £800 and £1,000, but Boit received somewhat less than £20 for each enamel image.[64]

None of the miniatures by Boit known today can be specifically linked to a particular royal diplomatic gift, which leaves open the question as to what form they took, and whether that form was of the same type as miniatures presented as gifts to loyal servants and friends. In 1710, for example, Boit produced a miniature as a gift, perhaps a wedding gift, to Mrs Coke, the queen's former maid of honour and the new wife of her Vice Chamberlain.[65] Boit's miniature is based on Kneller's type D state portrait. Boit has removed the blue ermine-lined robe but has retained the gold, ermine-edged dress and the queen wears the Lesser George on a riband round her neck. Other miniatures, for example in the Royal Collection (fig. 73) and the National Portrait Gallery, show variations to the costume, but this head and shoulders format, with the queen presented without the regalia (which in the Kneller portrait were displayed on a table, and the orb on her knee) seems to have been the standard one distributed both at home and internationally.[66] Such a miniature is shown in portraits of Colonel Daniel Parke (fig. 75), who requested and was given by the queen her image as a reward for delivering to her the great news of the victory at Blenheim.[67] Set with diamonds, it is proudly displayed as he habitually wore it, hanging from a red ribbon round his neck. Parke's gift seems close in format to a miniature of the queen historically ascribed to Petitot (fig. 74). Traditionally identified as the former gift of friendship from Anne to the Duchess of Marlborough, in April 1713 it became party political news because of Sarah's ill treatment of it.[68] Jonathan Swift, a dinner guest at Lord Oxford's, was shown "a small picture, enamelled work, and set in gold, worth about twenty pounds; a picture, I mean, of the Queen, which she gave to the Duchess of M------gh". On preparing to leave England, her friendship with the queen over, and both herself and the Duke of Marlborough dismissed from their posts, Sarah had stripped the miniature of its valuable diamonds and given it to a Mrs Higgins to sell to some

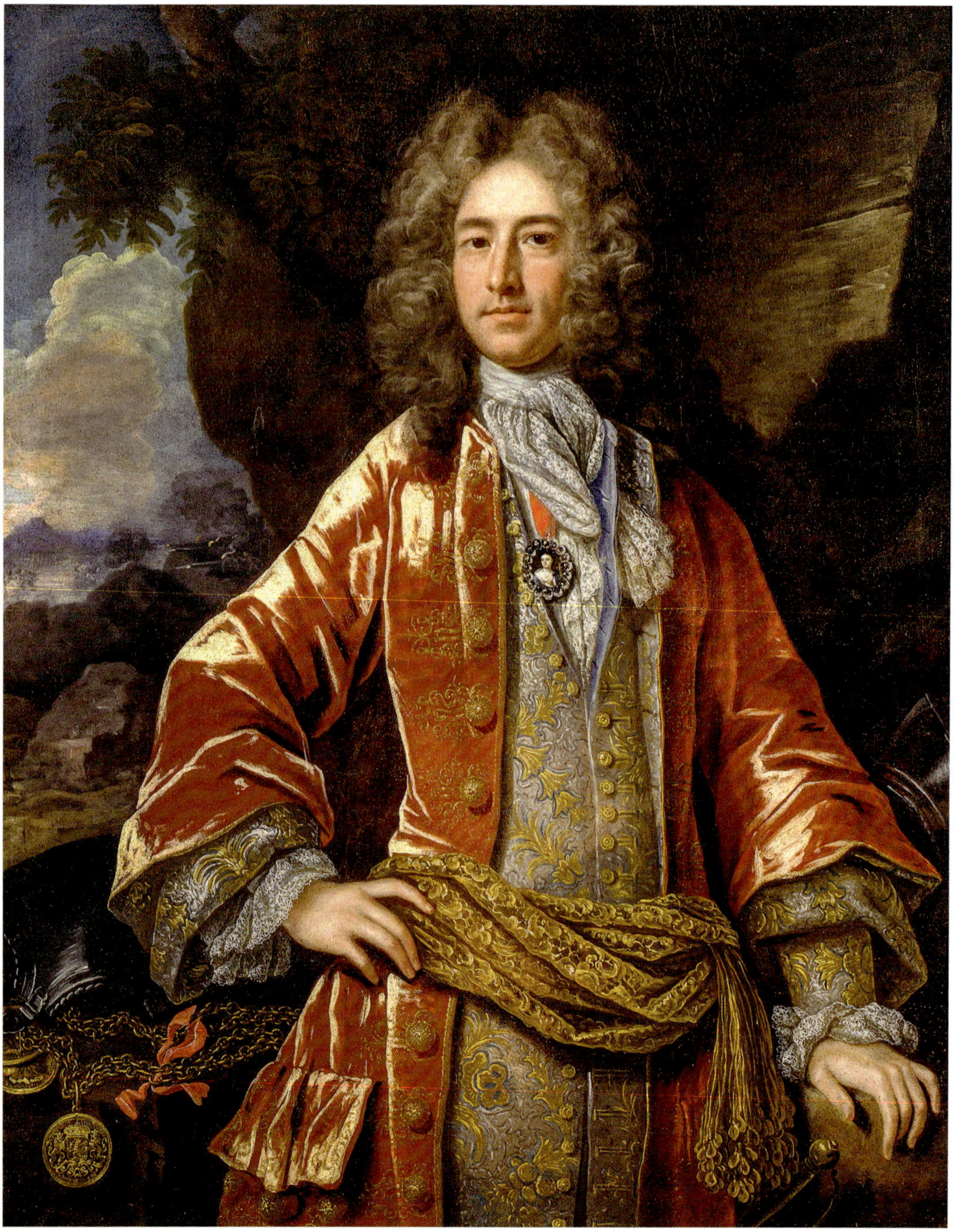

75. John (or John Baptist) Closterman, *Daniel Parke (1664/5–1710)*, ca. 1705, oil on canvas, 56 x 47 in. (142.2 x 119.4 cm). Virginia Historical Society

"flattering fool" if she could. This casual and shocking casting aside of the image of the queen was news that circulated. Worse, Lord Dartmouth told Bishop Burnet that the miniature showed the queen as Princess of Denmark, when Anne and Sarah's friendship was at its most intense. "She takes off the diamonds, and gives away the picture to an insignificant woman, as a thing of no consequence; and gives it to her to sell, like a piece of old-fashioned plate", wrote Swift, adding that the Whigs "will not believe it".[69]

This episode highlights the confused and blurred boundaries that existed between the queen's private and public lives. Her miniature image, given as a private token of affection, was now symbolic, through the manner of its being discarded, of an abuse of her honour, out of which people sought to make party political capital. It also underlines, however, the important symbolic value attached to the queen's image. As a gift it was a powerful gesture, both private and public, of her friendship, favour, and goodwill, and its distribution and request were important elements in the performance of international diplomacy, with its carefully crafted reciprocal exchanges of regard. Rather than embodying a wholly new view of monarchy, however, Kneller's state portraits of Anne deploy the traditions and conventions of the royal state portrait. They were conceived as a continuation of traditional representational modes and were expected to perform according to the established functions of the art to convey and represent the queen's monarchical authority. It was a tradition that endured, as is demonstrated by looking at the portraits of Queen Anne's successor, George I. Kneller continued in his post as Principal Painter and produced, as he had done for William III and Anne, and for the same fee, standing and seated state portraits of the king in state robes, displaying the royal regalia as symbols of his authority. Shortly after his succession, Kneller was being paid for numerous repetitions of the king's image, to be sent to ambassadors, the plantations, German princes, and key ministers. Despite the passing of the Stuart era, and in the new world of parliamentary monarchy, very little had changed. As William III and Anne's portraits had been, George I's were methodically repeated and dispatched abroad to convey the king's and the nation's authority around the world.[70]

1. John M. Gray, ed., *Memoirs of the life of Sir John Clerk of Penicuik* (London: Roxburghe Club, 1895), 62, Edward Gregg, *Queen Anne* (1980; New Haven and London, Yale Univ. Press, 2001), 231–32.
2. See Ernst Kantorowicz's influential book, *The King's Two Bodies: A Study in Medieval Political Theology*, first published in 1957 (Princeton Univ. Press, 1998).
3. Kevin Sharpe, *Rebranding Rule: The Restoration and Revolution Monarchy, 1660–1714* (New Haven and London, Yale Univ. Press, 2013), 589, 671.
4. Sharpe, *Rebranding Rule*, xvi–xix.

5. Kevin Sharpe, *The Personal Rule of Charles I* (New Haven and London, Yale Univ. Press, 1992), 181–82.
6. She considered the claim "unfit to be given to anybody". See Gregg, *Queen Anne*, 306 and 402 for Anne's views on divine right, and J. C. D. Clark, *English Society, 1660–1832: Religion, Ideology and Politics during the Ancien Régime* (Cambridge Univ. Press, 2000), 87, for the view that Anne at least thought it imprudent to use the doctrine politically.
7. See most recently James Anderson Winn, *Queen Anne: Patroness of Arts* (Oxford Univ. Press, 2014); *Journal for Eighteenth-Century Studies* (Tercentenary Commemorative Special Issue on Queen Anne and British Culture, 1702–14) 37, no. 2 (June 2014); Sharpe, *Rebranding Rule*, 509–681; and Robert Bucholz, "The 'Stomach of a Queen,' or Size Matters: Gender, Body Image, and the Historical Reputation of Queen Anne", in *Queens and Power in Medieval and Early Modern England*, ed. Carole Levin and Robert Bucholz (Lincoln, NE: Univ. of Nebraska Press, 2009).
8. For early modern friendship, see Alan Bray, *The Friend* (Chicago Univ. Press, 2003); Keith Thomas, "Friendship and Sociability", in Thomas, *The Ends of Life: Roads to Fulfilment in Early Modern England* (Oxford Univ. Press, 2009), chap. 6; and Frances Harris, *Transformations of Love: The Friendship of John Evelyn and Margaret Godolphin* (Oxford Univ. Press, 2002), 75–81.
9. Jeremy Taylor, *A Discourse of the Nature, Offices and Measures of Friendship: With Rules of Conducting It* (London, 1657).
10. Anne to Sarah, Campden House, Friday, 7 May ?1697. See Margaret Toynbee, "Princess (Afterwards Queen) Anne as Patroness of Painters", *The Burlington Magazine* 112, no. 804 (March 1970): 149–53, 152.
11. The following have been consulted: *The Calendar of Treasury Books* (hereafter CTB), vols. 17–29 (1702–15), ed. William A. Shaw, and William A. Shaw and F. H. Slingsby (London: HMSO, 1936–57), and *Calendar of Treasury Papers* (hereafter CTP), vols. 3 and 4 (1702–14), ed. Joseph Redington (London: HMSO, 1874). Also at British History Online, http://www.british-history.ac.uk.
12. J. Douglas Stewart, *Sir Godfrey Kneller and the English Baroque Portrait* (Oxford: Clarendon Press, 1983), 60–61, 68.
13. CTP 3 (March 1702–Dec. 1707): 340, 27 April 1705; CTB 20: 298, Warrant Book, 17 June 1705. The oversight had been the omission to give the Lord Chamberlain the authority to sign warrants for "customary allowances". Kneller's "customary allowance" was the fee for each portrait. The rectification was backdated to 24 June 1702.
14. CTB 18: 50, Minute Book, 19 May 1703.
15. Joseph Redington, preface, CTP 3 (March 1702–Dec 1707): x.
16. CTB 20: 546, Warrant Book, 16 Jan. 1706 (according to a warrant dated the previous November); CTP 4 (Jan. 1708–July 1714): 172–73, 27 March 1710 (the same portraits may have remained unpaid for until November 1712); CTB 28: ccvi, Declared Accounts: Civil List, 22 Sept. 1713–4 Nov. 1714. Although the latter accounting period falls partly within George I's reign, Kneller is referred to as the Queen's Principal Painter, and the pictures were for "the Queen's service".
17. Cecil Headlam, ed., *Calendar of State Papers Colonial, America and West Indies*, vol. 21, *1702–1703* (London: HMSO, 1913). In 1706 the Province of Massachusetts Bay was reproved for not acknowledging receipt of their portrait.
18. Helen Jacobsen, *Luxury and Power: The Material World of the Stuart Diplomat, 1660–1714* (Oxford Univ. Press 2011), 27.
19. CTB 22: ccxcvii, Declared Accounts (29 Sept. 1706–29 Sept. 1707). Dahl is referred to as "Dalb". The original warrant, dated 24 Jan. 1707, specifies that the portraits were for the Rt Hon. The Lady Hide and Mrs How. See Wilhelm Nisser, *Michael Dahl and the Contemporary Swedish School of Painting in England* (London: Bodley Head, 1927), 111.
20. CTP 4 (Jan. 1708–July 1714), 15 May 1712; CTB 26: 541, Warrant Book, 13 Dec. 1712; CTB 28: 326–27, Warrant Book, 28 June 1714. The latter makes it clear that the original warrant was dated 16 May 1712. Like Kneller, Dahl received £50 for a full length, clearly the Crown's standard rate.

21. Edmund Lilly had a great trade in images of the queen and other members of the royal family (see the notice of his sale of stock, *The Tatler*, 23 Dec. 1710, in *The Art World in Britain, 1660 to 1735*, at http://art-world.york.ac.uk) but there is no evidence that he received direct royal patronage. Michael Dahl's portraits of the queen need to be examined in relation to George of Denmark's patronage, and in the context of private, as opposed to state, patronage.
22. Oliver Millar, *The Tudor, Stuart and Early Georgian Pictures in the Collection of Her Majesty the Queen* (London: Phaidon, 1963), 23 and 142.
23. Agnes Strickland, *Lives of the Queens of England*, 12 vols. (London, 1840–48), 12: 55.
24. F. A. Inderwick, ed., *A Calendar of the Inner Temple Records* (London, 1902), 3: lxxxviii, 377.
25. My thanks to Laura Houliston and Esmé Whittaker of English Heritage for this information.
26. The portrait at Drumlanrig can possibly be connected to a payment in 1706 of £3 4s. 6d. to the Lord Chamberlain's secretary for "the dues of the warrant to Sir Godfrey Kneller for drawing the Queen's picture". This reference, taken from account books at Shambellie, occurs as an ink annotation in a copy of the *Catalogue of the Pictures at Drumlanrig Castle* (privately printed, 1909), 16, in the Heinz Library and Archive, National Portrait Gallery, London.
27. Recounted by Swift in 1711, see Gregg, *Queen Anne*, 330.
28. Cited in Winn, *Queen Anne*, 266–69.
29. When Anne attended Parliament for the first time on 11 March 1702, Count Wratislaw reported that she wore the heavy crown of England over a red velvet cap, a long red velvet robe lined with ermine and trimmed with gold, the Garter collar and Greater George, and the Garter ribbon on her left arm. He believed she had modelled her costume on a portrait of Queen Elizabeth I. Cited in Winn, *Queen Anne*, 282. No such portrait of Elizabeth conforming to this description is known, however, and it would appear that Anne was simply wearing Parliament robes. For the placement of the Garter ribbon on the left arm being particular to Anne, see Peter J. Begent and Hubert Chesshyre, *The Most Noble Order of the Garter: 650 Years* (London: Spink, 1999), 159.
30. David Green, *Queen Anne* (London: Collins, 1970), 95–96.
31. Jacobsen, *Luxury and Power*, 27–29.
32. Michael Wright, *An Account of his Excellence Roger Earl of Castlemaine's Embassy* (London, 1688), 54.
33. Patricia Bonomi, *The Lord Cornbury Scandal: The Politics of Reputation in British America* (Chapel Hill: Univ. of North Carolina Press, 2000), 15.
34. Marlborough to the Duchess of Marlborough, The Hague, 19 May 1709, in William Coxe, ed., *Memoirs of John, Duke of Marlborough, with his Original Correspondence*, 3 vols. (London, 1818–19), 3: 32.
35. Christopher Tilson, Treasury Chambers, to Lord Townshend, 24 May (OS) 1709, MS of the Marquis of Townshend, HMC 11th Report, Appendix, part IV, 49–50.
36. At Raynham Hall until sold at the Townshend Heirloom sale, Christie's, 7 March 1904, lot 176; purchased by Lord Luke and given to the Drapers' Company in 1955.
37. A drawing after this portrait type, formerly attributed to Kneller and with an Edward Byng provenance, shows the palm fronds and olive branches more clearly. British Museum 1888,0719.69
38. For diplomatic friendship, see Tracey Sowerby, "'A memorial and a pledge of faith': Portraiture and Early Modern Diplomatic Culture", *English Historical Review* 129 (April 2014), and Evgeny Roshchin, "The Concept of Friendship: From Princes to States", *European Journal of International Relations* 12, no. 4 (2006).
39. Sowerby, "A memorial and a pledge of faith", 296.
40. The National Archives (hereafter TNA), State Papers, SP 90/3, fol. 403.
41. TNA, State Papers, SP 90/3, fol. 415.
42. Purchased from the Wentworth Castle sale, 1949.
43. TNA, State Papers, SP 90/4, fol. 21.
44. TNA, State Papers, SP 44/242, fol. 45.
45. TNA, State Papers, SP 90/4, fol. 763.
46. TNA, State Papers, SP 89/20/9, fol. 22.

47. Marlborough to the Duchess of Marlborough, Meldert, 4 Aug. 1707, in Coxe, ed., *Memoirs of John, Duke of Marlborough*, 2: 292.
48. Jacobsen, *Luxury and Power*, 28.
49. Marlborough to Raby, Camp at Hanneff, 22 June 1703; Marlborough to the Electress Dowager of Hanover, 2 Oct. 1703; David Green, *Sarah, Duchess of Marlborough* (London: Collins, 1967), 91.
50. Stiftung Preußische Schlösser, inv. no. GK I 5271, 232 x 134 cm, signed and dated "G Kneller. Eques / 1709 (?)". http://lostart.de. My thanks to Katrin Herbst for her help in trying to trace the Prussian portraits.
51. CTB 22, 26 May 1708; and CTB 23, Warrant Book, 11 Nov. 1709.
52. TNA, State Papers, SP 34/35, fol. 53.
53. The commission for the astonishingly costly and never completed enamel, originally intended to glorify Marlborough's military victories, was instigated by Prince George of Denmark. After his death his promise to Boit of £2,000 was honoured by Queen Anne but in staged payments on evidence of progress. See CTB 24: 239, Warrant Book, 18 April 1710, and payments thereafter until 1713. The large enamel double portrait of the queen and Prince George, dated 1706 (Royal Collection, London) was most likely a private rather than a state commission—whether the queen's or George of Denmark's is not known.
54. Sowerby, "A memorial and a pledge of faith", 315–16.
55. For the importance of private friendship between international diplomats, see Daniel Riches, *Protestant Cosmopolitanism and Diplomatic Culture: Brandenburg–Swedish Relations in the Seventeenth Century* (Leiden and Boston: Brill, 2013), 111–19, 158. See also Sowerby, "A memorial and a pledge of faith", 318.
56. [Daniel Defoe], *Minutes of the Negotiations of Monsr. Mesnager* (London, 1717), 1736 edition consulted, 286.
57. Maija Jansson, "Measured Reciprocity: English Ambassadorial Gift Exchange in the 17th and 18th Centuries", *Journal of Early Modern History* 9, nos. 3–4 (2005): 348–70; Anna Keay, *The Magnificent Monarch: Charles II and the Ceremonies of Power* (London: Hambledon Continuum, 2008), 102–12.
58. CTB 17: 429, Treasury Warrant, 24 Dec. 1702 to Sir Stephen Evance, Her Majesty's Jeweller; CTB 18, 399, Warrant Book, money warrant to Evance, 10 Sept. 1703.
59. *Post Boy*, 20–23 Aug. 1709.
60. *Post Boy*, 30 July–2 Aug. 1709.
61. Marlborough to Sarah, Duchess of Marlborough, The Hague, 29 April 1707, in *Private Correspondence of Sarah, Duchess of Marlborough*, 2 vols. (London: Henry Colburn, 1838), 1: 69.
62. Gregg, *Queen Anne*, 140.
63. He is referred to as Thomas, and later as Francois and Francis. His bill of £32 was eventually paid in 1711. CTB 23: 386, Warrant Book, 7 Oct. 1709; ccxcvi, Declared Accounts: Civil List 1709; CTB 25: 497, Warrant Book, 10 Oct. 1711 (which clarifies that the commission dated back to 10 June 1708).
64. In 1708 Boit was to receive £57 5s. 0d. for three miniatures; in 1709 £61 5s. 6d. for three more; and on 11 Nov. 1709 £34 8s. 0d. for two more. It is not clear if these figures include fees.
65. The cost of £27 17s. 6d. most likely included the gold case and fees. CTB 24: 163, Warrant Book, 3 Feb. 1710 mentions that the picture was "set in a gold case"; CTB 25: 497, Warrant Book, Oct. 1711 makes it clear that the original warrant was dated 30 Jan. 1709–10. In 1711 the jeweller Arnold Vanbeck was charging £6 for a gold case (CTB 25: 143, Warrant Book, 20 Jan. 1711).
66. Royal Collection, RCIN 421098, National Portrait Gallery, London, NPG 6282.
67. As well as the Closterman (fig. 75), Parke is shown wearing his miniature of Queen Anne in portraits by Kneller, sold Sotheby's, 14 Nov. 1990 (lot 26), and Dahl, sold Christie's, London, 16 Dec. 2010 (lot 72). I am grateful to James Mulraine for bringing the Dahl to my attention.
68. Richard W. Goulding, "The Welbeck Abbey Miniatures belonging to His Grace the Duke of Portland: A Catalogue Raisonné", *Walpole Society* 4 (London, 1916): cat. 99, 103–4. With thanks to Gareth Hughes, Curator, Welbeck Abbey, for information concerning this miniature.
69. John Hawkesworth, ed., *Letters, Written by the late Jonathan Swift . . . and several of his friends from the year 1703 to 1740*, 4 vols. (London, 1766–68), 1: 177.
70. CTB 29: clx, Declared Accounts, 1 Aug.–30 Sept. 1714; 734, Warrant Book, 13 Sept. 1715.

Public Sculpture of Queen Anne: The Minehead Commission (1715)

Claudine van Hensbergen

In Wellington Square in Minehead, a small town on the north Somerset coast, a statue of Britain's last Stuart monarch, Queen Anne, shelters under an ornate Victorian temple canopy (fig. 76). This work, attributed to Francis Bird (1667–1731), the leading British sculptor of the age, is remarkably well preserved in comparison with much other public sculpture of the period. Yet, despite this, the statue has attracted little critical interest beyond mere reference to its existence. This is not an unusual state of affairs: in his 1969 study of sculptural designs, John Physick noted how "today sculpture of the later 17th century and afterwards, is frequently treated with contempt."[1] Over four decades on, Physick's reflection remains pertinent. Whilst the sculptural productions of the years 1660–1735 were many and varied, as illustrated by the major British sculptural surveys which cover the period, sculpture has continued to occupy a marginalized position within art-historical studies of the eighteenth century.[2] Malcolm Baker has suggested that this situation is a result of historical eventualities, since this marginalization has been exacerbated by the lack of the sustained contemporary critical discourse that exists for painting from the 1730s onwards:

> The absence of any sustained discussion of sculpture in contemporary texts has meant that the reading of sculpture, like painting, as registers of ideological and social concerns has until recently been little done because the bridge that such discussions provided (in the case of painting) between the visual image and social political ideas was lacking.[3]

In recent years Baker has been at the forefront of attempts to reinstate sculpture's importance within the art-historical record. Yet Baker's focus, like all other substantial studies that have emerged in recent decades, begins an analysis of eighteenth-century sculpture with the elite works that emerged from the 1720s and 1730s onwards in the hands of leading migrant sculptors such as John Michael Rysbrack (1694–1770), Peter Scheemakers (1691–1781), and Louis François Roubiliac (1702/05–1762).[4]

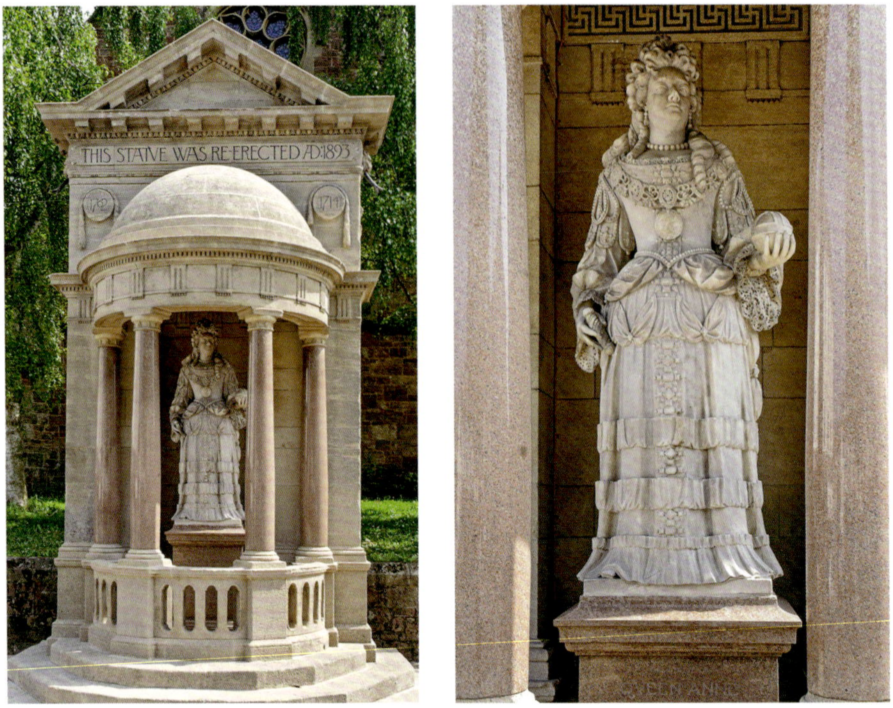

76. Francis Bird, *Queen Anne* (with detail), 1715, alabaster, 22½ x 22⅞ x 73¼ in. (57 x 58 x 186 cm). Wellington Square, Minehead, Somerset

Indeed, scholars are yet to gain a complex understanding of the field of sculptural productions from the years 1660–1735. Research into sculpture of this period is made difficult by a number of factors that pose less of an issue for an analysis of the works that emerged in the hands of Rysbrack and his contemporaries from the 1720s onwards, not least the frequently poor survival state of individual works, and the recurrent absence of any archival traces. A further issue lies with the fact that the professions of sculptor and stonemason were often conflated at this time, with many of the leading sculptors of the age heavily involved in major architectural projects, such as the reconstruction of the City of London following the Great Fire of 1666. It was, as Matthew Craske reminds us, only in the 1720s and 1730s that the elite sculptors of the age "assumed the title of 'statuary', as opposed to 'mason' or 'sculptor', indicating their special skills in the production of statues in the classical manner".[5] Yet perhaps the biggest issue posed is that of attribution. The autographing of sculptural works does not seem to have been a common practice at the turn of the eighteenth century, making attribution a frequently problematic process. The implications of this are most apparent in the major British sculptural surveys which cover the period, all three of which are biographically arranged, meaning that no sculptural works of unknown attribution are included; even the roughest estimation based upon consultation of the photographic surveys held in the Courtauld Institute's Conway Library would suggest that a vast swathe of sculptural works are therefore excluded from these surveys, providing us with, at best, a partially distorted view of the "many thousands of monuments and other sculpture" that Physick notes were erected in the seventeenth and eighteenth centuries.[6]

Reflecting on the art-historical tendency to approach eighteenth-century sculpture through a focus on biographies of individual sculptors and a restricted range of well-known works, Baker notes how this has skewed our understanding of the field, providing "a view of sculpture that largely ignores its public functions".[7] Sculpture was, after all, one of the most public of art forms, and was a key means by which Britain's emerging political system and social ideologies were given physical expression within the nation's landscape. Contemporaries certainly did not ignore the public functions of sculpture, and research into the period will often reveal cultural responses to these works in the form of poems, pamphlets, guides, diary entries, sketches, and engravings. These sources, frequently disseminated in print, help us to glimpse the ways in which the public understood and interacted with sculpture displayed on the streets and squares of the nation.[8] It is likely that the statue of Queen Anne at Minehead has received so little critical attention because, unlike some of its sister statues of the queen, it does not seem to have prompted a range of public responses, at least none that have survived to us; furthermore, it was a provincial work, rather than one displayed in the capital. Yet it was a public work, and as such we can surmise that it was produced to convey a set of meanings that contemporaries would have well understood. The following essay therefore acts as a case study of the ways in which we might begin to recover the history of an individual sculptural work for which little archival or contemporary traces remain. To achieve this, the essay explores the apparent reasons behind the Minehead statue's commission and resituates it within its original artistic and historical contexts. The statue's history is a fascinating one which reveals the political and personal motivations behind its creation and points to the connections between provincial and urban sculptural projects. But it also foregrounds many of the wider questions that arise when conducting research into sculpture of the period: issues of attribution, dating, design, and setting.

SCULPTURE OF QUEEN ANNE

The Minehead statue is just one of at least twenty public statues of Queen Anne executed during her reign and in the years that followed.[9] This figure appears to mark a significant reinvestment in public sculpture of the monarch. Whilst many statues of Charles I and II were produced during the Restoration, including the magnificent oversized figures by John Bushnell now housed in the Old Bailey (1636–1701), relatively few statues were erected of their successors: a small number were raised of James II during his brief reign, and only one to William III was executed during his thirteen years on the throne.[10] In contrast, as Nicola Smith details, Anne's sculpted image proved a "fashionable ornament" from the outset of her reign in 1702, and was subsequently "promoted as a symbol of unity, first in the wake of the Union of England and Scotland in 1707 and then in celebration of national military victories in the War of Spanish Succession".[11] Anne tacitly indicated her approval of this sculptural programme when, about 1710–11, she ordered that the necessary marble for Francis Bird's sculpture of her for St Paul's Cathedral be supplied from the royal store yard.[12] Despite the relatively high number of statues commissioned of Anne, there is no evidence to suggest that these were mass-produced works of the type pioneered by John Nost the elder (died 1729), and from 1738 by John Cheere (1709–1787), from their respective statuary workshops at Hyde Park Corner. Each surviving statue of the queen appears to differ in some respect from its sister sculptures, suggesting the individual commissioning and execution of each work.

Public statuary of Anne shared much in common with that of her immediate Hanoverian successors. In studying the public sculpture of George I and George II, Charlotte Chastel-Rousseau has noted the distinctly British nature of the general mode of commission:

> A close study of the commissions of royal public monuments reveals the crucial role played by municipal corporations and private patrons in the glorification of George I and George II. Most striking is the absence of the king or of his representatives in the process, a feature distinctly British in eighteenth-century Europe. In a parliamentary regime the king had in fact a very limited budget to spend personally. Moreover, royal self-glorification could be interpreted as an inappropriate absolutist device.[13]

Statues of Anne were, similarly, not the product of a state-funded and organized programme and were likewise commissioned by a range of patrons including the Church, guildhalls, Oxford colleges, and private individuals. And, as with statues

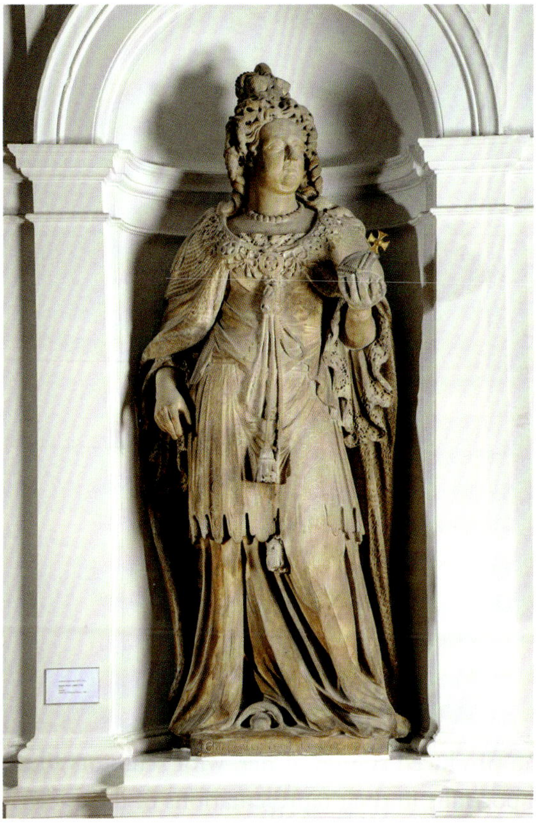

77. Andries Carpentière, *Queen Anne*, 1712–13, white marble, 78 in. (198 cm). Leeds Museum and Galleries

of George I and George II, the "iconographical programme of the statues and the way they were displayed in the public space were . . . often elaborated locally in an intricate network of influences and competences. As a result, those monuments seemed disappointing and surprisingly modest to many eighteenth-century observers."[14] The overall design of sculpture of Anne proved formulaic, with each statue portraying the queen in coronation robes holding the orb and sceptre: the most significant variations in design are found in Andries Carpentière's statue for the Moot Hall in Leeds (fig. 77) which depicts Anne wearing a Roman skirt over her gown—an addition that mirrors the Roman dress in which Grinling Gibbons (1648–1721) sculpted her predecessors James II and Charles II—and two unattributed statues in Oxford, at University College and Christ Church College (fig. 78), both depicting Anne in a more active and triumphant pose, brandishing a sword of which now only the hilt remains.[15] Despite such minor variations in design, statuary of the queen conformed to the standard mode of the representation of Anne's royal image. There is no evidence that Anne personally sat for sketches

nurturing mother. This idea was disseminated from the time of Anne's coronation, for which she selected Isaiah 49 as the foundation verse for Archbishop Sharp's sermon ("Kings shall be thy nursing Fathers, and their Queens thy nursing Mothers"), and was enforced thereafter through various means.[23] By the time the Minehead statue was commissioned, the concept of Anne as nursing mother had already taken on physical sculptural expression through the position of the aforementioned scheme designed by Bird for St Paul's Cathedral, in which Anne's statue, presented in full royal regalia, sat in an elevated position over radiating allegories of Britannia, France, Ireland, and America at the foot of the cathedral's west door. Occupying this key position at the cathedral's main public entrance, the scheme created a direct axis with the altar at the cathedral's east end. Thus, whilst its design stressed Anne's rule over foreign and domestic dominions, the scheme's position emphasized her maternal role as protector of the spiritual heart of the Anglican Church.[24]

At St Paul's, Anne's statue carried overt Anglican associations, but it was also publicly visible to the thousands of subjects of diverse beliefs who passed through this central space within the City's square mile. At Minehead, the statue's public audience was more restricted, with Anne's figure accessible only to those who entered into the church's interior. This privileging of the statue for the town's Anglican parishioners probably played into local concerns over growth in religious dissent. As in London, where the Anglican Church was taking steps to counter the expansion of dissenting communities, Minehead was home to an expanding Quaker population which counted many local prosperous merchants and their families amongst its members. The position of Anne's statue inside St Michael's may therefore be understood as an attempt to emphasize the idea that the town's Anglican worshippers were the queen's true and loyal subjects. Indeed, whilst David Bindman reminds us that "monuments in a church occupied a public space, and all levels of society were notionally allowed habitual and regular access to them", religious denomination was a factor that surely restricted access to "public" statues such as the Minehead figure of the queen.[25]

The statue was evidently valued by the Minehead parishioners, as some expense was taken to clean the work in the decades following its erection, with the modest 1s. 6d. required to underwrite this task in 1723 rising to 22s. by 1742.[26] The statue's original position in St Michael's was recorded by the antiquarian John Collinson in 1791:

> Within an iron railing at the east end of the north aile is an elegant statue of Queen Anne, in white alabaster, on a pedestal four feet high, holding the globe and sceptre. Thereon is this inscription:—"This statue was given

> by Sir Jacob Banks, and erected in 1719. He represented this borough in parliament sixteen years, and during this time was a benefactor to it on all occasions."[27]

The railings encircling the statue were installed at considerable expense soon after its arrival, and may have been inspired by the St Paul's scheme, which was surrounded by railings made by the French Huguenot master ironworker Jean Tijou (active in England 1688–1712).[28] At St Paul's these railings served a protective function; in light of the Minehead statue's presumably secure interior location, these railings were surely intended to enforce the status of Anne's statue. Further parallels between the schemes are notable. As at St Paul's, the Minehead statue was carved in the round, and displayed on a plinth that, whilst elevating the work, kept it at an accessible height for the statue's detail to be properly appreciated. The majority of the other statues made of Anne were produced for display in elevated architectural niches, making their function more that of an architectural decoration rather than an individual monument. The parallels between the Minehead statue and the St Paul's scheme are surely not the product of coincidence, with the latter work likely providing a key source of inspiration for the former. In his capacity as MP for Minehead, Bancks would have been in attendance at the St Paul's sculpture's unveiling, a celebratory event which took place at the state occasion of the thanksgiving service for the Peace of Utrecht on 7 July 1713. Furthermore, the approximate dates of the Minehead statue's commission support such a theory: as the work was erected in 1715, it is likely the statue would have been ordered about 1713–14.

As we have seen, Bancks surely commissioned the statue with ambitious ideas in mind, as one inspired by the production of the St Paul's monument and mirroring its religious associations. Yet in commissioning the statue, Bancks, as an MP, must have been aware that the work would also complement the efforts of a wider sculptural scheme then unfolding in the capital. The City Churches Commission (1711–27), a natural successor to the work completed at St Paul's in 1711, was created by an Act of Parliament that same year to oversee the completion of fifty new city churches. The project to build the churches was given life by Anne herself with the drafting of royal letters to the newly elected Parliament in 1710 that called for them to put at the head of their agenda "the drawing up of a representation of the present state of religion among us, with regard to the late excessive growth of infidelity, heresy, and profaneness".[29] Anne's personal interest and involvement in the city churches project is evident from her proviso that the commissioners were to submit regular updates directly to her, and the minutes recorded at their meetings contain details of the queen's feedback on their progress. Two years into the project, with work on the churches underway, attention was turned to the ways in which sculpture of the queen might be deployed to advantage, as it had been at nearby St Paul's. Accordingly, on 25 June 1713, the commissioners introduced two items to their agenda:

> 8. A statue of Queen Anne, "made by the best hands", to be set up "in the most conspicuous and convenient part" of each new church.
> 9. Mr Bird and Mr Gibbons to be desired to provide designs and estimates for such statues.[30]

These instructions were introduced at a time when Bird's completed sculptural scheme of Anne for St Paul's was on the cusp of its unveiling, an event which took place within the fortnight. The "conspicuous" positions ordained by the church commissioners for the statues of Anne mirror the entirely conspicuous position of the statue at St Paul's, and it was from this work that they surely took their cue, naming Bird as one of the two sculptors to tender for the work. The plans suggest a desire to promote further a new religious aesthetic in which Anne's leadership and responsibility for the national church was to be made visually and publicly clear through the medium of sculpture. An even more ambitious development was to follow when this scheme was replaced, on 29 April 1714, with an initiative to erect a fifty-foot column outside St Mary le Strand, with a statue of Anne at its top:

> Instead of statues to be put in the fifty new churches, a steeple in form of a pillar to be built at west end of the church near the Maypole in the Strand, with the Queen's statue on top, with bases for inscriptions to perpetuate the memory of the building of the fifty new churches.[31]

James Gibbs won the tender for the column, bidding against Nicholas Hawksmoor's rival design;[32] the Italian sculptor Giovanni Battista Foggini was commissioned to make the ten-foot-high bronze statue of the queen for the column's top.[33] Initial construction of the column soon began, although work was abandoned in the wake of Anne's death on 1 August that year. Even though the column was never completed, it is within this context of a profound sculptural investment in statuary of the queen that we should understand Bancks's decision to commission the work for his Minehead parish. Such designs give us a good sense of the intended status of public statues of the queen, and help us to understand the impetus behind many of the smaller-scale sculptural projects undertaken in the provinces.[34]

THE STATUE'S COMMISSIONER, SIR JACOB BANCKS, MP

As we have seen, the Minehead statue of Queen Anne can be understood as a work responding to broader projects in the capital and as promoting a specifically Anglican agenda. However, the statue should also be understood within a further context, chiefly in terms of how it served the personal and political agenda of its commissioner, Sir Jacob Bancks. The only known surviving portrait of Bancks is a silver medal cast in 1703 by the Swedish medallist Bengt Richter (1670–1735), now in the collections of the National Maritime Museum, Greenwich (fig. 81). This medal is referenced by Vertue in his notebooks and portrays Bancks in profile wearing a long wig, with the reverse depicting a ship dropping anchor accompanied by the motto "*tandem*" ("at last").[35] It was produced as one of a group of medals made by Richter, who was visiting London that year, and cast to commemorate the English and Swedish members of a London gentlemen's club that included amongst its members the court painter Michael Dahl (1659–1743).

The present inscription on the Minehead statue's plinth conceals Bancks's Swedish origins through an anglicized spelling of his name. Jacob Bancks, son of Lorens and Christina Bancks, was born at Stockholm in 1662. In 1681, Bancks travelled to England, accompanying his uncle, John Birkman, Count of Leyenburgh, then the Swedish ambassador. Bancks joined the Royal Navy and in 1690 gained a commission as a captain, serving on the ships *Carlisle*, *Russell*, and *Cambridge*. Bancks's naval career was to come to an abrupt end when, in 1696, he

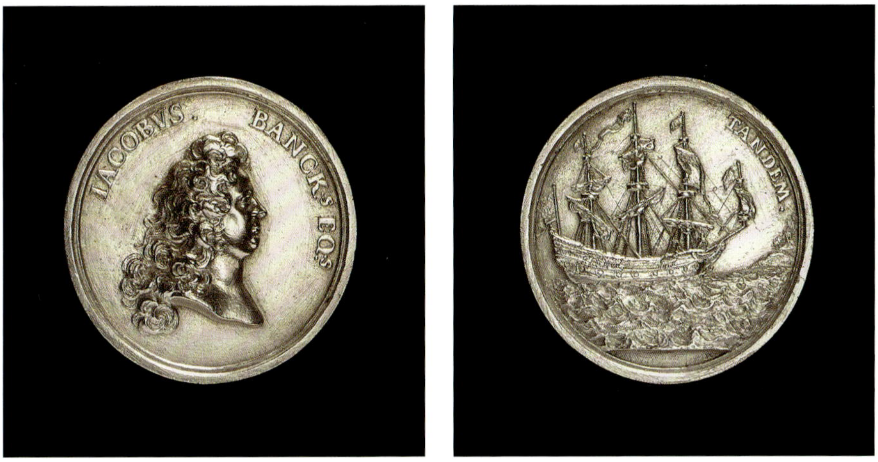

81. Bengt Richter, *Medal Commemorating Sir Jacob Bancks*, 1703, silver, 2. x 2 in. (5.1 x 5.1 cm). National Maritime Museum, Greenwich, London

withdrew from active naval service, a result of his failure to win favour under William III's pro-Whig administration. Forced into retirement, Bancks took the prudent decision to marry a wealthy and well-connected young widow, Mary Luttrell (née Tregonwell). Reports survive, possibly apocryphal, that romance between Bancks and Mary had blossomed when the gallant captain rescued the beautiful widow from a devastating fire that had destroyed her London home in St James's Street. However true such accounts may be, it is impossible to ignore the more strategic motives Bancks harboured, with the marriage bringing him the land, money, and status necessary to embark on a career as a Tory politician. First on the agenda was the small matter of naturalization, which was achieved on 1 February 1697 after Bancks's name had been added to an amended draft drawn up by the House of Lords. The following year Bancks was elected alongside Mary's brother-in-law, Henry Luttrell, as MP for Minehead; shortly after, in 1699, he was made a baronet.

Bancks's political loyalties were unswervingly Tory, Anglican, and Stuart. He is listed amongst those who voted against the Succession Act in 1702, he retired from politics upon the Hanoverian succession, and just two years later he was implicated in the Jacobite conspiracy of the Gyllenburgh plot (1716–17). Bancks was to prove both a prominent and controversial politician.[36] His election as MP in 1698 caused a minor controversy when John Sandford, who lost his seat to Bancks, petitioned the House of Commons to overturn his rival's victory, which he claimed was won through "Bribes" and "other undue Means of *Jacob Banks* Esquire, a Foreigner, and his Agents . . . contrary to the Law; and prejudicial to the Privileges of the said Borough".[37] In July 1703 Bancks found himself at the centre of a public scandal when William Colepeper accused him of assault at Windsor Castle, where Colepeper had been petitioning the queen on behalf of Daniel Defoe.[38] Yet Bancks's political ideology was nowhere made clearer than in an infamous speech he gave to his Somerset constituents in 1710, on the eve of the collapse of the Whig administration amidst the public riots caused by the trial of the Tory churchman, Dr Henry Sacheverell. The Duke of Ormond presented a copy of Bancks's speech to the queen, claiming it showed concern for her throne by drawing attention to the dangerous spread of a Whiggish "Republican Principle of Resistance".[39] This speech swiftly became known as "the Minehead Doctrine", and spawned a wave of satirical pamphlets in response.[40] Soon after, Bancks became a leading figure within the October Club, which had formed in 1711 as a splinter group within the Tory party, attempting to challenge Lord Harley's administration in a bid for party reform. In early 1714 Bancks was elected President of the Club, although it lost all influence later that year with Anne's death and the collapse of the Tory administration. Bancks retired from politics shortly after.

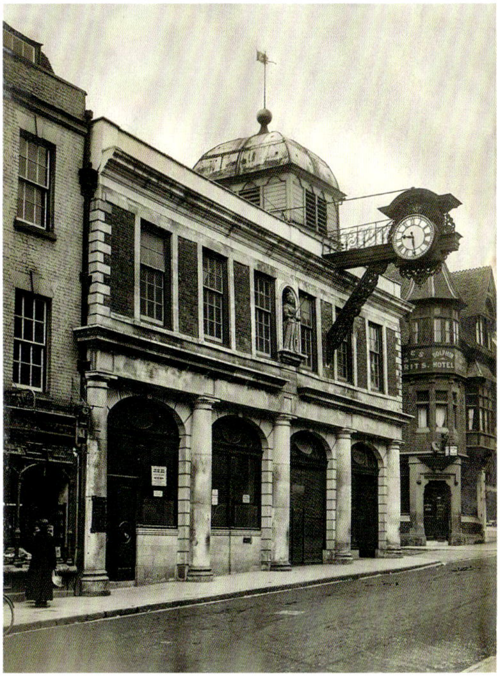

82. Old Guildhall, Winchester [ca. 1934]. Winchester City Council

The brief biographical sketch given above suggests that Bancks's decision to commission a statue of the queen derived in part from a wish to make a lasting public monument to commemorate his active role in Tory politics and allegiance to Anne. We can find a clear parallel for this type of commemorative display in Alderman William Milner's decision to commission an expensive marble statue of the queen from Andries Carpentière for display in the Moot Hall, Leeds (see fig. 77). Yet sculpture was not only employed to commemorate individual loyalties, but also to embody political rivalries across the nation. For example, the city of Oxford erected statues of all of the nation's Stuart monarchs yet not one of a Hanoverian king, a move seen as reflecting the city's Jacobite sensibilities.[41] A further, more immediate, example of the partisan uses of sculpture of Queen Anne is found in a statue that remains in situ in Winchester (fig. 82). This work was presented to the city's corporation in March 1714 by the Whig politician Colonel George Brydges of Avington, at a time when he was running for the Winchester seat in a by-election. This public display of loyalty to Crown and country paid off, with Brydges winning the seat. The statue was displayed in a niche on the façade of the old Guildhall, and stands testament to Brydges's Whig victory. However, the partisan associations of the work were soon disrupted when the statue was eclipsed by a giant clock presented to the city by Lord William Paulet, Brydges's local political rival. Such works provide a context for further understanding the motivations behind the positioning of the Minehead commission inside St

Michael's Church, and show how those on both sides of the party political divide attempted to claim Anne's image for their own cause. As noted, Minehead was home to a growing and highly influential Quaker community. Worryingly for Bancks, the Minehead Quakers were allied closely with local Whig interests and politics. The statue's location thus seems to have been one that intentionally aligned loyalty to the queen with loyalty to the Anglican Church, and in so doing excluded the local Whig-allied Quaker populace from Anne's presence. It is easy to underestimate the power of the royal image at the turn of the eighteenth century, and the resonances and meanings it conveyed. But statues of Anne were surely interpreted by the public as her proxies, and conveyed a sense of royal authority even when they were commissioned by private individuals such as Bancks, who carried their own agendas. In this way, the royal image was used as a propaganda tool in countering local political concerns.

In her study of the public sculpture of George I and II, Charlotte Chastel-Rousseau reflects upon the critical tendency to ignore the complexity of individual commissions: "The viewing of the few royal monuments that are still in place today does not give any idea of the intricate negotiations and clashes of interest at stake during their erection."[42] Indeed, Bancks's motivations likely lay beyond a mere display of political loyalty and statement of partisan rivalry, as events taking place during the timeframe of the statue's commissioning show. In 1712 Bancks sent a petition to Lord Harley, Anne's chief minister, requesting a redress of his position with the navy; this was followed by a further appeal addressed to Anne herself, "To the Queen's Most Excellent Maj.^{tie}: The humble Memorial of S^{r}. Jacob Bancks".[43] In his petition Bancks claimed that in the 1690s he had been unfairly placed on half-pay since he had never actually retired from naval service, but had rather been forced out by the Whig administration. He therefore requested reinstatement in the navy and to be paid the salary arrears owed to him. Bancks must have believed he stood a good chance of success in this appeal since Thomas Wentworth, the Earl of Strafford, was acting as Bancks's chief contact in pursuing his case: Bancks was a close friend of Strafford, then First Lord of the Admiralty (1712–14), and had acted as his proxy at Strafford's installation as a Knight of the Garter at Windsor on 4 August 1713. The Minehead commission could therefore be considered as a further act, or financial investment, taken at this time to aid Bancks's appeal, acting as a sculptural "memorial" to the queen and serving as a display of loyalty which surely merited reward.

We might also infer that the commissioning of the Minehead statue was an act that served, in some ways, to create a public identity and legacy for Bancks that smoothed over his foreign origins, showing him to be a true English gentleman loyal to Crown and country. Whilst Bancks retained links to his native Sweden—

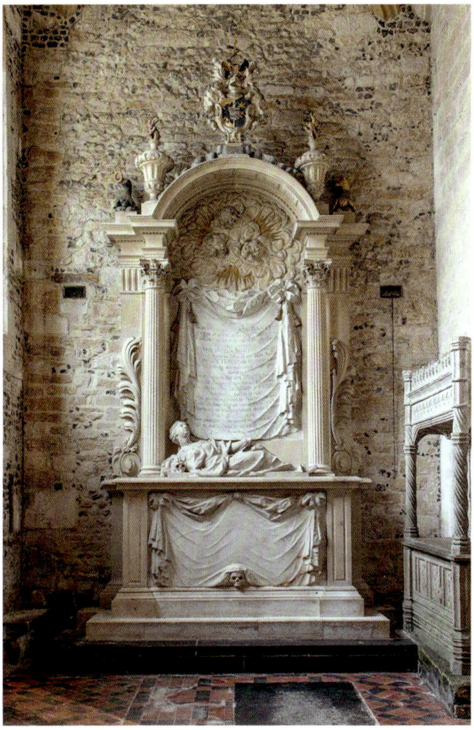

83. Unknown sculptor, *Bancks Family Memorial*, ca. 1703–4, Portland stone with drapery in white marble. Milton Abbey, Dorset

as the commissioning of Richter's 1703 medal shows—his Swedish origins exposed him to political attacks that labelled him a foreigner and outsider. This issue had come to the fore in 1710 through Benson's attacks on Bancks's "Minehead Doctrine". In his retaliatory pamphlet, Benson claimed that Bancks's political arguments were especially incomprehensible in light of his Swedish origins: surely a politician who had emigrated from absolutist Sweden and become a citizen of Britain's constitutional monarchy should recognize the pitfalls of passive obedience.[44] Indeed, even when Bancks was an established MP, having served more than twelve years in Parliament, one political observer was to emphasize his foreign extraction, describing him as "a Swede, one of the most violent Tories in the House. He procured one of the highest addresses last summer . . . He has a good estate, and he is very forward to speak in the House, though no foreigner speaks worse English."[45]

Bancks's funeral monument (fig. 83), an impressive sculptural work which remains in situ in Milton Abbey, Dorset, reveals his desire to emphasize and commemorate his Englishness. He commissioned this work for his family following the death of his wife, Mary, in March 1702, and was later interred here also. The tomb carries a carved epigraph in Latin above Mary's effigy which details her life, accompanied by an inscription added later detailing Jacob's own:

> *Hic situs est Jacobus Bancks, eques, suedus natione, Anglia autem donatus, vereque Anglicanus, sincerus hujus insulae ecclesiaeque amator, in omni statu fidus utriusque defensor, in classe fortiter, in senatu diligenter, provinciam administrans, ob. 22 Decembris, 1724, aetat. sexagesimo quarto.*
> [Here lies Jacob Bancks, knight, Swedish by birth, but devoted to England and truly Anglican, a sincere lover of this island and church, in every circumstance faithful and a defender of both, bravely in naval service and diligently in parliament discharging his duty. He died 22 December 1724 in his sixty-forth year.][46]

In commissioning Mary's monument, Bancks was simultaneously commissioning his own monument, and thinking about the ways in which he wanted posterity to remember the first English generation of the Bancks family. The inscription acknowledges Bancks's Swedish origins, but speaks to his desire to claim and commemorate a specifically English identity, emphasizing his service to the state and, above all, his loyalty to the Anglican Church. In light of this, we might understand the commissioning of the Minehead statue of Queen Anne as a complementary investment, one that also commemorated his loyalty to the state and, above all, to the national church. Sculpture, after all, provided Bancks with a means of attempting to control how posterity would remember him.

CONCLUSION

Malcolm Baker has reflected on the critical indifference to the majority of eighteenth-century sculpture, which, "with its limited range of conventions and monochrome—and apparently so undifferentiated—surfaces has been perceived as not having that complexity and subtlety that attracts academic curiosity or invites searching or speculative interpretation".[47] Viewing the Minehead statue today, it is easy to underestimate the significance of this provincial work, which was one made with grand ambitions in mind. Some of those ambitions were no doubt to further the reputation and interests of the notorious foreign naval captain turned Tory politician, Sir Jacob Bancks. But the statue also served as a mirror for a wider London-based programme that used sculpture of Anne to conflate ideas of loyalty to the Crown with loyalty to the Church, and its existence points to the wide reach that, for a few brief years, this programme had. By resituating the Minehead statue within its original setting and historical context we can begin to glimpse the dynamic and complex role sculpture played in the life of the nation, both in the provinces as well as in the capital. Whilst the statue is just one of the many sculptures of Anne erected in the period, it offers a rare example of a relatively intact work, and is in far better condition than Bird's original sculpture of the queen completed for the West front of St Paul's Cathedral.

The tercentenary of Anne's death in 2014 was accompanied by the beginning of a shift in our historical understanding of Anne's relationship to the arts. In their sustained studies of her reign, Kevin Sharpe and James Anderson Winn have argued that Anne engaged with the arts more actively than historians have previously suggested; essays published to mark the tercentenary have likewise offered new research into Anne's engagement with British culture.[48] In this way, the pervasive image of Anne as a gouty, awkward, and culturally disinterested monarch is starting to be tempered by a new understanding of the way her image was promoted and understood by her subjects. The Minehead statue provides one example amongst many of the types of varied resonances Anne's image came to hold, and the ways in which her subjects promoted their own, as well as national interests in raising statues to the queen. But the statue also serves as a reminder of the wider theoretical issues involved in the study of public sculpture of the period, not least the dearth of the kinds of criticism needed to situate and understand these works. Indeed, as Baker aptly surmises, "through its concern with the biographies of individual artists and its emphasis on a restricted range of sculpture, the literature (along with those displays that have made its narratives visible) presents us with an account of sculpture produced in Britain rather than sculpture to be seen in eighteenth-century Britain."[49] Admittedly, historians of sculpture are missing the same types of contemporary theoretical frameworks extant for painting, but this simply necessitates a new way of approaching the material. As the Minehead statue shows us, in the case of public sculpture from 1660 to 1735, the relevance of original setting, identity of patron, and links to wider sculptural programmes all provide key contexts for interpreting such works. A more authoritative attribution to Bird would, of course, help to strengthen many of the arguments made here about the Minehead statue's importance, but Bird's biography is far from being the only or perhaps even the most important context we can bring to bear in our understanding of the work.

The author would like to thank Sue Sanders of Minehead Town Council and Douglas Carpenter of Cliveden Conservation for sharing the Minehead statue's 2010 treatment report.

1. John Physick, *Designs for English Sculpture, 1680–1860* (London: HMSO, 1969), 16.
2. See Rupert Gunnis, *Dictionary of British Sculptors, 1660–1851*, rev. ed. (London: Abbey Library, 1968); Margaret Whinney, *Sculpture in Britain, 1530–1830* (Harmondsworth: Penguin, 1988); and Ingrid Roscoe, Emma Hardy, and M. G. Sullivan, *A Biographical Dictionary of Sculptors in Britain, 1660–1851* (New Haven and London: Yale Univ. Press, 2009).
3. Malcolm Baker, *Figured in Marble: The Making and Viewing of Eighteenth-century Sculpture* (London and Los Angeles: V&A Publications and J. Paul Getty Museum, 2000), 9.
4. See, for example, David Bindman and Malcolm Baker, *Roubiliac and the Eighteenth-century Monument: Sculpture as Theatre* (New Haven and London: Yale Univ. Press, 1995); Baker, *Figured in Marble*; Cinzia Sicca and Alison Yarrington, eds., *The Lustrous Trade: Material Culture and the History of Sculpture in England and Italy, c.1700–1860* (Leicester Univ. Press, 2000); Matthew Craske, *The Silent Rhetoric of the Body: A History of Monumental Sculpture and Commemorative Art in England, 1720–1770* (New Haven and London: Yale Univ. Press, 2007); and Malcolm Baker, *The Marble Index: Roubiliac and Sculptural Portraiture in Eighteenth-century Britain* (New Haven and London: Yale Univ. Press, 2015).
5. Craske, *Silent Rhetoric*, 5.
6. Physick, *Designs for English Sculpture*, 15.
7. Baker, *Figured in Marble*, 9.
8. For an example of the varied cultural responses to individual sculptures of Queen Anne, see Claudine van Hensbergen, "Carving a Legacy: Public Sculpture of Queen Anne, c.1704–12", *Journal for Eighteenth-Century Studies* (Tercentenary Commemorative Special Issue on Queen Anne and British Culture, 1702–14) 37, no. 2 (June 2014): 229–44, and Marcia Pointon, "Material Manoeuvres: Sarah Churchill, Duchess of Marlborough and the Power of Artefacts", *Art History* 32, no. 3 (June 2009): 484–515.
9. For a list of known executed statues of Queen Anne, see Terry Friedman, "Foggini's Statue of Queen Anne", in *Kunst des Barock in der Toskana: Studien zur Kunst unter den letzten Medici*, ed. Klaus Lankheit (Munich: Bruckmann, 1976), 52, n. 64.
10. For a survey of public sculpture of the later Stuart monarchs, see Nicola Smith, *The Royal Image and the English People* (Aldershot: Ashgate, 2001), 119–41. See also Kevin Sharpe's discussion of the propagandistic role of public sculpture of the later Stuart monarchy in Sharpe, *Rebranding Rule: The Restoration and Revolution Monarchy, 1660–1714* (New Haven and London: Yale Univ. Press, 2013).
11. Smith, *Royal Image*, 134.
12. For a detailed history of the St Paul's sculpture of Queen Anne, see Philip Ward-Jackson, *Public Sculpture of the City of London* (Liverpool Univ. Press, 2003), 374–81.
13. Charlotte Chastel-Rousseau, "Royal Public Statues and the Legitimisation of the Dynasty of Hanover in Georgian Britain, 1714–1760", in *Power and Persuasion: Sculpture in its Rhetorical Context*, ed. Urszula Szulakowska and Peter Martyn (Warsaw: Instytut Sztuki, PAN, 2004), 109.
14. Chastel-Rousseau, "Royal Public Statues", 109–10.
15. Roscoe, Hardy, and Sullivan, *Biographical Dictionary*, 114, attribute the University College statue of Anne and an accompanying one of her sister, Mary, to Francis Bird, and date these works to 1720. However, the antiquarian Thomas Hearne records the arrival of Anne's statue at the college on 4 October 1709 as a gift of "Mr. Ward". There is no surviving evidence in the college archives to support the attribution to Bird in either case. See *The Remarks and Collections of Thomas Hearne*, ed. by C. E. Doble (Oxford: Clarendon Press, 1886), 2: 273.
16. E. Beresford Chancellor, *The Lives of the British Sculptors* (London: Chapman & Hall, 1911), 96–98.
17. *Universal Spectator* 126, 6 March 1731.

18. The Minehead statue is attributed to Francis Bird in Roscoe, Hardy, and Sullivan, *Biographical Dictionary*, 114. This attribution appears to be based upon a brief reference to the statue in Whinney's earlier survey, in which Whinney lists the Kingston-upon-Thames (1706) and Minehead (1715) statues as variants "evidently ordered" of the St Paul's statue; Whinney, *Sculpture in Britain*, 152. This assertion ignores the fact that the Kingston statue predates the St Paul's scheme by several years. In Gunnis, *Dictionary of British Sculptors*, the Minehead statue is not attributed to Bird.
19. Fergus Cannan, "Alabaster", in *The Making of Sculpture: The Materials and Techniques of European Sculpture*, ed. Marjorie Trusted (London: V&A Publications, 2007), 113.
20. In 1880 the statue was moved out of St Michael's Church due to restoration works, and placed inside the newly built Town Hall (now the Old Hospital). In 1893 it was re-erected in its current location.
21. The History of Parliament Online (http://www.historyofparliamentonline.org/volume/1690-1715/member/banks-jacob-1662-1724, accessed 23 July 2015) gives Bancks's birth date as 22 Aug. 1662. However, various birth dates for Bancks have been recorded, ranging from 1633 to 1662. James Savage records it as 1633 in *The History of the Hundred of Carhampton* (Bristol: W. Strong, 1830), 638. Bancks's tombstone states that he died aged sixty-four in 1724, suggesting (but not stating) his birth date to be ca. 1660.
22. Account Books, 1712–99, Minehead St Michael and St Andrew Parish Records, Somerset Heritage Centre, D/P/m.st.m./4/1/2.
23. For a discussion of the ways in which this idea was fostered, see Sharpe, *Rebranding Rule*, 558–67.
24. For further discussion of the St Paul's sculpture of Queen Anne, see Friedman, "Foggini's Statue"; Van Hensbergen, "Carving a Legacy"; and Ward-Jackson, *Public Sculpture*.
25. David Bindman, "Public Space and Public Sphere: From Parish Church to Westminster Abbey", in Bindman and Baker, *Roubiliac and the Eighteenth-century Monument*, 9.
26. Lois Lamplugh, *Minehead and Dunster: A History* (Chichester: Phillimore, 1987), 50.
27. John Collinson, *The History and Antiquities of the County of Somerset, collected from Authentick Records, and an Actual Survey made by the Late Mr. Edmund Rack*, 3 vols. (Bath, 1791), 2: 32.
28. These railings are visible in old photographs of the church interior: Lamplugh, *Minehead and Dunster*, 50.
29. M. H. Port, ed., *The Commissions for Building Fifty New Churches: The Minute Books, 1711–27, A Calendar* (London: London Record Society, 1986), x.
30. Port, ed., *Commissions for Building Fifty New Churches*, 21.
31. Port, ed., *Commissions for Building Fifty New Churches*, 32.
32. The designs by Gibbs (BM 1913,1216.9) and Hawksmoor (BM 1881,0611.161) survive in the British Museum's collections.
33. Terry Friedman and Francesco Freddolini have both traced the sculptural strand of the city churches project, which took several turns before its eventual abandonment a full year after Anne's death. See Friedman, "Foggini's Statue" and Francesco Freddolini, "John Talman in Florence: The Court, the Courtiers and the Artists", in *John Talman: An Early Eighteenth-century Connoisseur*, ed. Cinzia Maria Sicca (New Haven and London: Yale Univ. Press, 2009), 127–57.
34. For example, it seems likely that the inspiration behind the fifty-foot commemorative column to Queen Anne, topped with her statue and commissioned for Cirencester Park by the Earl of Bathurst in 1741, may well have been indebted to the abandoned Gibbs scheme.
35. Vertue refers to this set of medals in his notebooks: Manuscripts comprising the autograph collections of George Vertue, the engraver, 1713–54, vol. 5, British Library (hereafter BL) Add MS 23072.
36. For a brief biography of Bancks, see Paula Watson and A. A. Hanham, "Banks, Jacob (1662–1724), of Milton Abbas, Dorset and Somerford, Hants.", in *The History of Parliament: The House of Commons. 1690–1715* (Cambridge Univ. Press, 2002), 3: 128–29.
37. British History Online (http://www.british-history.ac.uk/report.aspx?compid=39688, accessed 21 Aug. 2014), *House of Commons Journal* 12, no. 22 (Dec. 1698).

38. Colepeper claimed that Bancks's attack should be prosecuted as one directly on the queen's person as Anne was present at court when it happened, and in light of this Bancks was ordered to appear before a magistrate at the Quarter-Sessions in Berkshire: no conviction followed.
39. Kenneth White, *The Wisdom of Looking Backward* (London, 1715), 37.
40. The most notable of these response pamphlets was William Benson's *A Letter to Sir J– B–, Concerning the Late Minehead Doctrine* (London, 1711). Benson, a Whig architect and critic, entered into a personal rivalry with Bancks, with Benson standing against Bancks in the 1713 election: Bancks retained the Minehead seat.
41. See Smith, *Royal Image*, 136.
42. Chastel-Rousseau, "Royal Public Statues", 101.
43. Bancks to Oxford, 24 Feb. 1712–13, BL Add MS 70279; Bancks's memorial to the queen, May 1712, BL Add MS 70317.
44. In 1680 Charles XI of Sweden had re-established absolute rule, a development confirmed by the Riksdag of the Estates in 1693. Benson portrayed the weakening of the Swedish empire under absolutism as an example of how British success depended upon the monarchy's willingness to consult with and take advice from Parliament.
45. Watson and Hanham, "Banks, Jacob (1662–1724)", 129.
46. I am grateful to Dr Scott Scullion of Worcester College, University of Oxford, for kindly providing this literal translation of Bancks's tombstone.
47. Baker, *Figured in Marble*, 11.
48. See Sharpe, *Rebranding Rule*; James Anderson Winn, *Queen Anne: Patroness of Arts* (Oxford Univ. Press, 2014); and *Journal for Eighteenth-Century Studies* (Tercentenary Commemorative Special Issue on Queen Anne and British Culture, 1702–14) 37, no. 2 (2014).
49. Baker, *Figured in Marble*, 9.

The English Revolution and the Revolution of History Painting: The Bowles Brothers' "Life of Charles I"

David H. Solkin

In an important recent study of J. M. W. Turner, Leo Costello has written persuasively of how the painting of contemporary historical subjects operated as a significant cultural front in the battle for political representation that dominated British public life during the late eighteenth and early nineteenth centuries.[1] The first person to make this connection, as Costello quite rightly points out, was John Galt in his biography of Benjamin West (1820), where he credits West's *Death of General Wolfe* (1770; National Gallery of Canada, Ottawa) with having "occasion[ed] a revolution in the art"—thus implying that the painter had somehow anticipated subsequent developments in the political sphere, starting with the American War of Independence later in the same decade.[2] Galt's evocative phrase went on to enjoy an exceptionally fruitful twentieth-century afterlife, thanks in large part to Edgar Wind: in a famous article of 1938 entitled "The Revolution of History Painting", Wind argued that the "mitigated realism" exemplified by the *Death of General Wolfe* spoke for a democratic challenge to established authority, which he saw as an expression of the artist's American origins (and of his antimonarchical sympathies).[3] While the specific claims made on behalf of West's picture and its author have long since been overturned, there is still a case to be made, as indeed Costello has done, for the link between revolutionary politics on the one hand, and the invention of history painting in modern dress on the other.[4]

This essay aims to shed new light on the origins of this relationship, and on the whole question of the "revolution of history painting", by taking a close look at the first painted and engraved sequence of historical pictures ever to be planned in Britain, representing the *Most Remarkable Transactions of the Reign of Charles I*.[5] Issued in 1728 as a set of ten large engravings, all but one of which were based on oils commissioned especially for the purpose between around 1721 and 1727, the *Life of Charles I* (as it has come usually to be called) was one of the most complex publishing projects of its era, involving the collaboration of no fewer than thirteen English, French, and Flemish artists and engravers. Their efforts were orchestrated by the print-selling partnership of Thomas and John Bowles, who as commercial patrons of historical art began a trend that would culminate in the late eighteenth century with the far more celebrated endeavours of John Boydell, Thomas Macklin, Robert Bowyer, and the like.[6]

The world of print will have an important role to play in my story, especially when I come to talk about the hybrid stylistic character of the *Charles I* series, which incorporates extensive use of historically informative detail (*à la* West's *Death of General Wolfe*) alongside significant vestiges of an older, and arguably more prestigious system of representation. But in part because these images remain remarkably little known—despite their acknowledged importance in the history of English printmaking—I will begin by introducing the individual scenes one after another, and considering briefly the story that they collectively set out to tell.[7] As we shall see, the way in which they construct the life and character of their royal protagonist bears eloquent witness to the restrictive ideological conditions under which the British monarchy found itself in the decades following the Hanoverian succession, in circumstances which increasingly placed the king's body at the service of an emerging public sphere. How this same shift in the balance of power left its mark on the formal language of the Bowleses' series is a question I shall simply pose for now, holding the complex issues it raises in abeyance for the time being.

In what will prove to be a significant harbinger of events to come, the opening act of the *Life* omits its named protagonist: although the scene is entitled *The Marriage of the King*, Charles himself does not appear; instead it is his proxy, the Duke of Buckingham, accompanied by the god Hymen, who is shown exchanging vows with Henrietta Maria (fig. 84). Conducting the ceremony is Cardinal Richelieu, whose presence takes on a somewhat malevolent significance when read in the light of the caption on the engraving of Louis Chéron's oil, which provides the only direct explanation in the entire series for all the catastrophes to follow. Here, in a passage lifted almost word for word from Laurence Echard's *History of England*, the viewer is informed that "This Marriage notwithstanding it was carried on with the unanimous Consent of the last Parliament, was against the main bent and Genius of the People, and proved one great Occasion of the future Calamities of the Nation."[8] The clear implication is that Charles I's problems arose in the first instance from his alliance with a French Catholic princess, never mind the fact that the match may have been necessitated by political imperatives and fully sanctioned under British law. As far as any other "Occasions" are concerned, the king's absence from his own wedding may have invited the inference—confirmed in the subsequent plates—that he would bring the "future Calamities" of his reign upon himself, by ceding too much of his rightful authority to others.

Closely based on the marriage scene (and the image of another royal wedding by proxy) in Rubens's famous Marie de' Medici cycle, Chéron's design for the

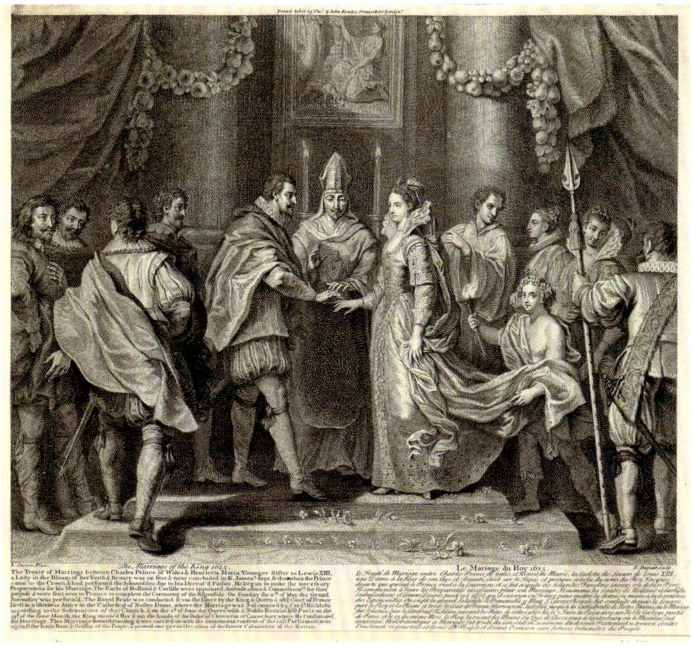

84. Nicolas-Gabriel Dupuis after Louis Chéron, *The Marriage of the King 1625*, 1728, engraving with etching, 16¼ x 18⅛ in. (41.2 x 46 cm). Royal Collection Trust, London

initial plate in the series honours Charles I in the pictorial language of early seventeenth-century courtly art, while at the same time highlighting his dynastic connection with one of the great royal houses of Europe (Henrietta Maria being the daughter of Marie de' Medici and Henri IV). Such grandeur, however, does little more than act as a dramatic foil for the precipitous fall that, in the series, immediately follows. The period of fifteen-plus years of relative stability that followed Charles's marriage in 1625 is simply passed over—not a surprising omission, perhaps, given that this was the era of his involvement with a parade of widely despised favourites—Buckingham, the Earl of Strafford, Archbishop Laud—and of his flawed and ultimately abortive attempt at personal rule. Yet even if the Bowles brothers may have been reluctant to showcase the absolutist tendencies of a monarch in whom they had invested such a great deal, the same editorial process also effectively downplayed Charles's own agency; indeed, at no point in the series is he depicted in a position of unchallenged command.

Quite the contrary. The second scene, commissioned from the French battle painter Charles Parrocel, jumps forward to the year 1642, to the first moment in the Civil War when Charles met with outright public defiance of an expressly delivered command. In *Hull Summoned by the King* (fig. 85) we see a monarch humiliated in full sight of his people, as his request to be allowed entry into the city (which held a royal arsenal full of much-needed weaponry) meets with a courteous but nonetheless absolute refusal by its governor, Sir John Hotham.

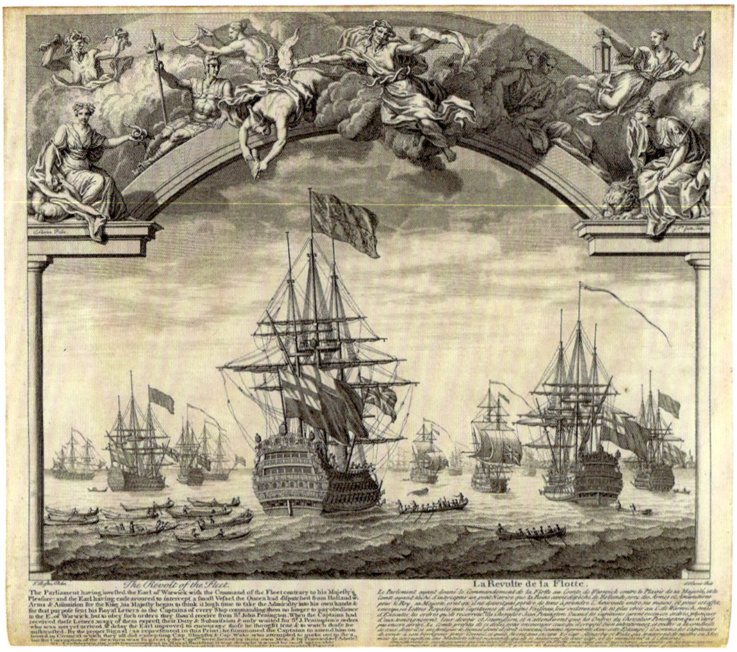

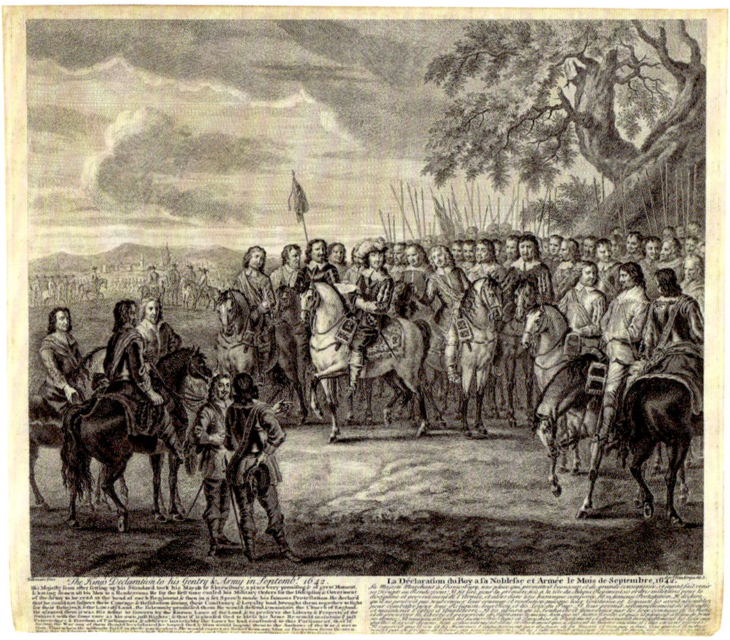

86. John Harris and Gerard Vandergucht after Thomas Baston and Louis Chéron, *The Revolt of the Fleet*, 1728, engraving with etching, 16⅜ x 18¾ in. (41.5 x 47.5 cm). Ashmolean Museum, University of Oxford

87. Gerard van der Gucht after Peter Tillemans, print made by, *The King's Declaration to his Gentry & Army in September 1642*, 1728, engraving with etching, 16⅜ x 18½ in. (41.7 x 47 cm). Ashmolean Museum, University of Oxford

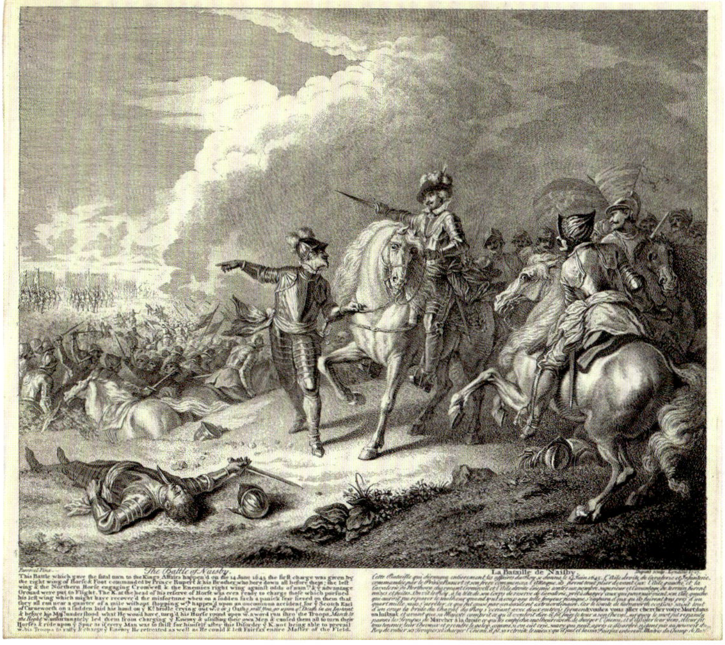

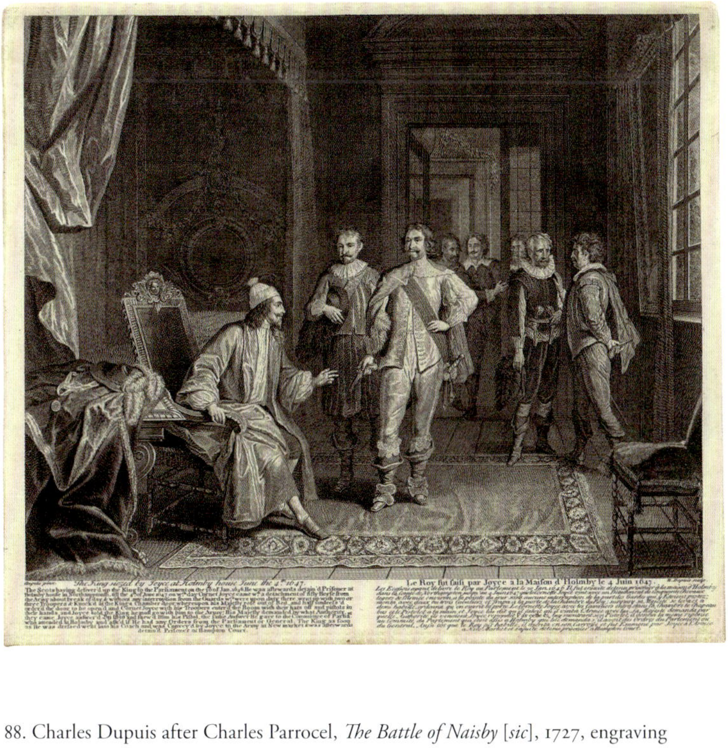

88. Charles Dupuis after Charles Parrocel, *The Battle of Naisby* [*sic*], 1727, engraving with etching, 16⅛ x 18¾ in. (41 x 47.5 cm). Ashmolean Museum, University of Oxford

89. Bernard Baron after Peter Angellis, *The King Seized by Joyce at Holmby House, June the 4th 1647*, 1728, engraving with etching, 15⅛ x 18¾ in. (40.5 x 47.6 cm). Ashmolean Museum, University of Oxford

Charles does recover his position somewhat in the seventh plate, also designed by Angelis, which shows him making plans for what turned out to be an abortive escape from his confinement at Hampton Court (fig. 90). Given its singularly undramatic character, the Bowleses' choice of this particular episode seems rather hard to explain; perhaps they wanted the series to include at least one representation of the king in his "natural habitat", encircled by retainers in the opulent setting of a royal palace. Moreover, in its appearance of calm normality the Hampton Court scene provides the narrative with an important point of contrast with the king's preceding trials and humiliations, and the even more tragic events to follow. The portrayal of Charles as he "really" was also points to certain aspects of his character which historians felt had contributed to his sorry situation. Thus one imagines that an early eighteenth-century audience could have read two distinct but overlapping meanings into the pictures and ornate vessels that feature so prominently in Angelis's composition, seeing these either as markers of the king's magnificence and his devotion to the arts, and/or as more problematic signs of a tendency to luxurious self-indulgence. Further indicators of the latter are provided by his sartorial splendour and the mirror on the table, which in their conjunction might have prompted associations with vanity. In any case, it seems most unlikely that any effective plan of action could ever be devised by so fashionable and delicate a gentleman-king; and the caption offers a brief summation of the plot's calamitous results, stressing the failure of Charles's chosen confederates to act either wisely or effectively on his behalf.

From Hampton Court the narrative then moves on to Westminster Hall and *The Tryal of the King* (fig. 91). Aside from the Garter Star on his voluminous cloak, the accused bears no traces of his former glory; indeed the relative simplicity of his dress makes him look humbler than his assembled subjects, as well as humbled by them. Angelis's design presents the king as the isolated focus of a staged spectacle, where he is subject not only to the frowns and stares of the army's "Officers and Creatures" (John Bradshaw most prominent among them), but also to the varied glances—some sympathetic, others not—of the men and women who tower above him on either side. A secondary point of interest is supplied by the figure of Lady Fairfax, shown midway up on the left: where the other members of the audience are content simply to watch or to talk among themselves, she alone stands up to express her contempt for the proceedings of this court, denying its claim to be acting on behalf "of all the good People of England". Her gesture also stands in pointed contrast to the king's own passivity, as he quietly awaits his fate. Referring to a curious accident that many contemporary observers took as a portent, the gold head of his cane is shown dropping spontaneously to the floor, foreshadowing its owner's own decapitation and offering a poignant reminder of his fashionable past.

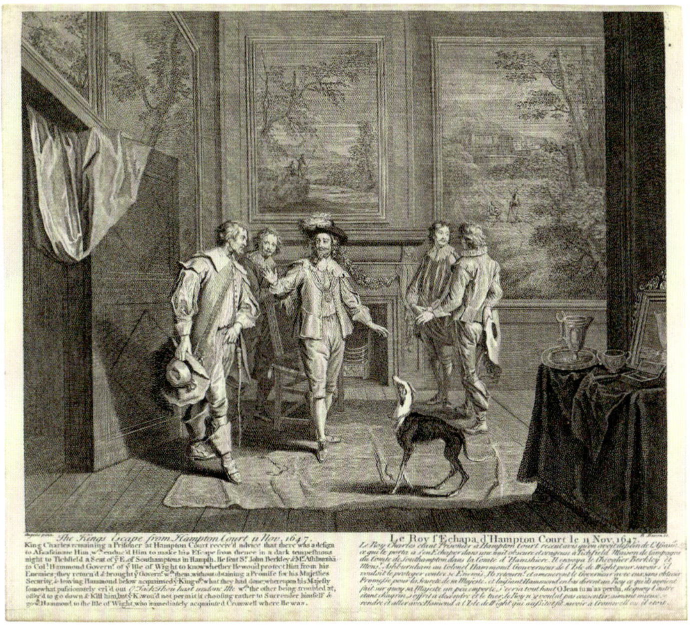

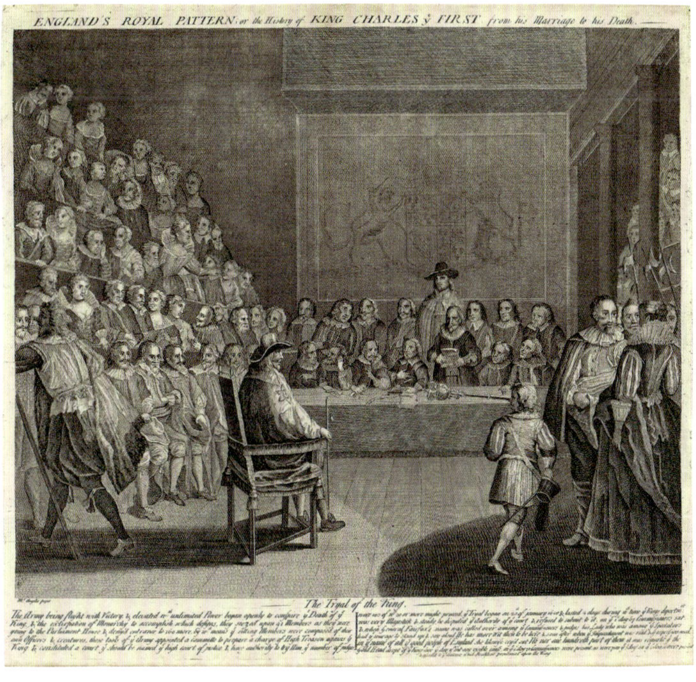

90. Bernard Baron after Pieter Angellis, *The King's Escape from Hampton Court*, 1728, engraving with etching, 16⅜ x18½ in. (41.6 x 47 cm). Ashmolean Museum, University of Oxford

91. Claude Dubosc after Pieter Angellis, *The Tryal of the King*, 1728, engraving with etching, 16 x 18¼ in. (40.7 x 46.2 cm). Ashmolean Museum, University of Oxford

The caption details Charles's repeated denials of the court's right to try the nation's duly anointed sovereign; but in the image the indefensibility of judging a king in the name of the king is implied only by the "CR" flanking the British coat of arms above the heads of his judges. A study in dignified resignation—the text beneath describes him as "very Majestick and Steady" throughout his ordeal—Charles does, or is seen to do, nothing, having by now lost any power whatsoever to affect the course of his own life.

But in his final hours he still remains committed to acting as a positive influence on the lives of others, or so at least the ninth plate in the Bowles series would have us believe. With *King Charles Taking Leave of his Children* (fig. 92) we reach the emotive climax of the narrative; even John Oldmixon, who had little love for the Stuarts, felt compelled to admit that

> The Interview between the King and his Children the Day before Execution is so moving, that there is not a tragick Scene in any Drama, which can affect one like it. The Tenderness of it is exquisite, and much easier to be conceiv'd, or to be felt, than to be express'd.[11]

To try and convey the dramatic character of this poignant episode, the French painter Jean Raoux produced a composition that was clearly meant to look like a stage tragedy, with his actors' facial expressions and hand gestures designed for maximum impact and legibility. As befits the most intimate scene in the series, the viewer is placed exceptionally near to the pictured space, in a position which invites close scrutiny of the figures: the tears of Princess Elizabeth, the heartfelt concern of the more stoic Duke of York, and the attentive posture of the eight-year-old Duke of Gloucester, each child responding in his or her different way to the calming words of their condemned father. The caption informs us that he is speaking to his youngest son of the implications of his own impending execution, counselling him to refuse any offers to assume the throne as long as his older brothers remain alive: "I Charge you do not be made a King by them [the Parliamentarians], at which the child sighing said I will be torn in pieces first; which falling from one so young exceedingly pleas'd the King."

Although his talk is all of political pressures and beheadings, there are no signs of violence or anger in Charles's face, which instead invokes a contrary character of melancholic sweetness. In this we may read the outward sign of that mildness of temperament which, according to Clarendon, made Charles "the best Master, the best Friend, the best Husband, the best Father, and the best Christian"—though perhaps not the best of monarchs.[12] Clarendon's basic case for Charles I was that his virtues made him ideally suited to play a part in private life, but were

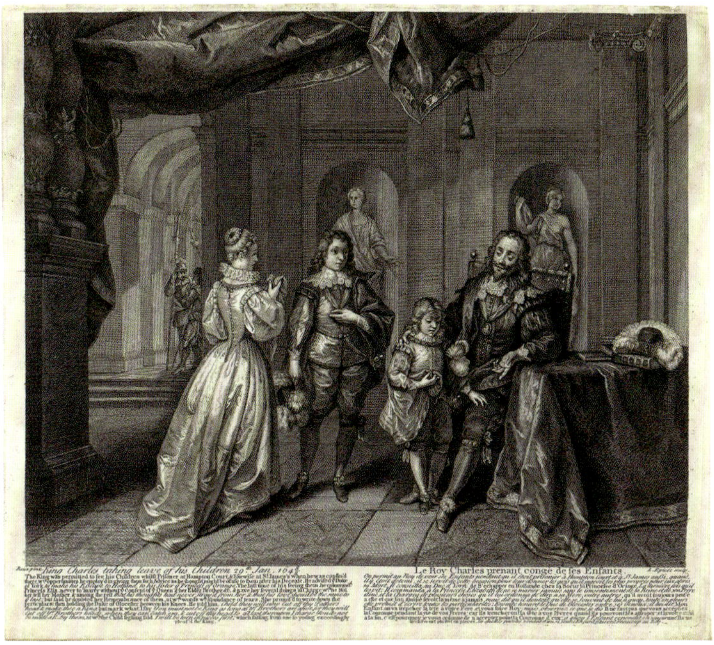

92. Bernard Lépicié after Jean Raoux, *King Charles Taking Leave of his Children*, 1728, engraving with etching, 16⅜ x 18¾ in. (41.5 x 47.6 cm). Ashmolean Museum, University of Oxford

largely responsible for his downfall as a king. Other early commentators, however, were considerably less charitable. For Bishop Burnet, for example, Charles's

> reign both in peace and war was a continual series of errours: So that it does not appear that he had a true judgment of things. He was out of measure set on following his humour, but unreasonably feeble to those whom he trusted, chiefly to the Queen. He had too high a notion of the regal power, and thought that every opposition to it was rebellion. He minded little things too much, and was more concerned in the drawing of a paper, than in fighting a battle.[13]

Was it Clarendon's or Burnet's Charles I whom early eighteenth-century viewers saw in Raoux's *King Charles Taking Leave of his Children*? One thing they surely would have noticed is the clothing of the figures, which in the context of the series here reaches an apogee of delicacy and richness. While such splendour speaks volumes for the nobility of the participants in this sorrowful drama, it also reminds us of the questions that historians had raised about the king's judgment—in particular his inflexible insistence upon the prestige of the monarchy in the face of all challenges to its authority, as well as his preoccupation with small matters of appearance instead of larger issues of substance. That he had devoted so much time and money to glorifying himself through the arts, but had signally failed in politics and arms, had also become a commonplace in the criticisms of his reign. There were certain unfortunate tendencies in Charles's character, in other words, which could be (and often were) held at least partially responsible for the disastrous fate that befell him—tendencies toward lavish self-presentation and arrogant self-aggrandizement which had to be counted, too, among his various legacies to his children. It may have been in order to convey a point of this sort that Raoux made the single most dramatic departure from historical truth in the entire Bowles series, by anachronistically introducing the figure of the Duke of York (who had actually found safety on the Continent some months prior to January 1648/49) into the scene of the king's final leave-taking. The Duke, of course, would later ascend the throne as James II, whose stubborn insistence on the exercise of his royal prerogatives would prove a decisive factor in his political undoing, and the ultimate collapse of the Stuart line. Raoux's image goes out of its way to stress the close resemblance in appearance between Charles I and his admiring second son, who clasps his medallion of St George as the marker of his dynastic status; in hindsight it may not have been difficult to conclude that James had inherited more from his father than a similar taste for opulent dress.[14]

In the final scene, however, of *The Apotheosis or Death of the King* (fig. 93), Charles rises above worldly splendour to embrace eternal glory in the company of angels. John (or Moses?) Vanderbank's design places the dead sovereign's elevation to heaven against the background of his execution on the scaffold that had been placed in front of his own palace at Whitehall—thus conjuring up both the heights and the depths of his troubled earthly existence.[15] Of all the images in the Bowles set, the *Apotheosis* most fully embraces the basic precepts of the cult of the royal martyr, which took its founding articles of faith from Charles I's own *Eikon Basilike*. Likewise, the conventions used by Vanderbank for his portrayal of the king—one hand clasped to his chest, his eyes raised skywards—find their obvious point of origin in William Marshall's famous frontispiece to the *Eikon*. The caption on the Bowles print, paraphrasing Echard's *History of England*, details the sentence of execution before going on to describe the exemplary manner of the king's conduct on the scaffold. If Vanderbank's composition illustrates a specific text, it is that supplied by Charles's final conversation with his confessor, Bishop Juxon:

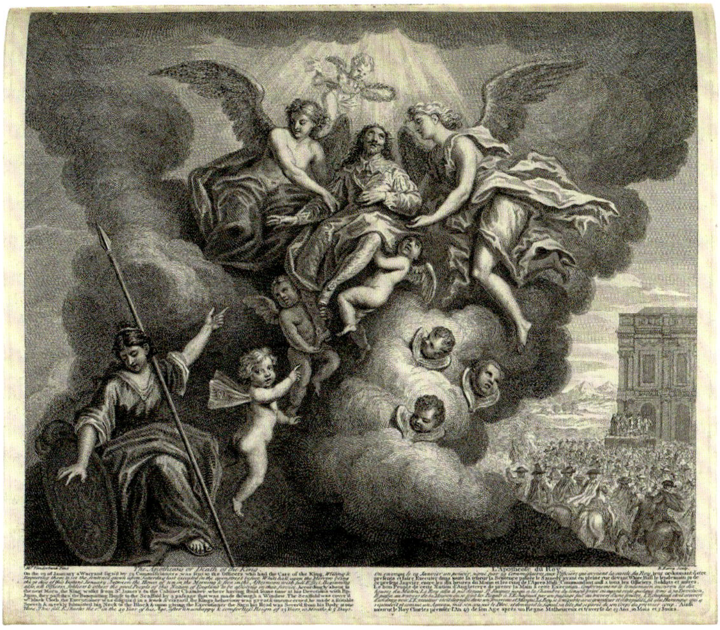

93. Bernard Baron after John (or Moses?) Vanderbank, *The Apotheosis or Death of the King*, 1728, engraving with etching, 16⅛ x 18¾ in. (41.1 x 47.7 cm). Ashmolean Museum, University of Oxford

> The Bishop alluding to his private Discourse with him concerning the several Stages of Man's Life, said, *There was but one Stage more; which tho' turbulent and troublesome, would carry him a very great way, from Earth to Heaven, where he should find the desired Prize, a Crown of Glory.* To which the King adjoyn'd, *I go from a corruptible to an incorruptible Crown, where there can be no disturbance; a happy Exchange*, as the Bishop reply'd.[16]

No wonder that Bishop Burnet wrote of Charles that "he died greater than he lived; and shewed, that which has often been observed of the whole race of the *Stewards*, that they bore misfortunes better than prosperity."[17] In the manner of the king's death, numerous clergymen discovered a model of Christian fortitude and forgiveness, which, especially in the annual sermons commemorating the regicide, often prompted comparisons with Christ himself.[18]

The final plate, as Alan Ide has noted, confirms the dependence of the Bowles set as a whole on previous painted and/or engraved cycles portraying the life of Christ. Not only do Charles's sorrowful features look more and more Christ-like

is only shown without it in the *Apotheosis* and in the *Tryal* scene, where he has adopted plain garb suited to the gravity of the occasion (in *The Marriage* and *The Revolt of the Fleet,* we remember, he does not appear at all). Though feathered headgear can occasionally be found in seventeenth-century portraits of English royalty (albeit, with the exception of the Prince of Wales, more often of female than of male sitters), kings, when not shown bare-headed, are typically depicted either with crowns or helmets. The Bowleses' Charles, by contrast, wears his distinctive combination of soft felt and plumage even in circumstances of war (see fig. 11.3), or when he addresses his troops (see fig. 11.5). In two other images (see figs. 11.3 and 11.6) the same article of clothing occupies the table-top space usually reserved for a crown in representations of enthroned monarchs; and we again encounter the same hat as a central point of interest in the lavish interior of Hampton Court (see fig. 11.7).

A clue as to the likely meaning of this sartorial detail is provided by the last-mentioned scene, where the king's posture and aspects of his clothing are clearly based on an early seventeenth-century French fashion plate by Abraham Bosse, which an English engraver had subsequently adapted for use as an emblem of Pride (fig. 94). In drawing upon this source, Angelis and the other artists employed on the Bowles project may have been striving to achieve some degree of historical accuracy in the matter of period costume, but the fact that they chose the Bosse or its pirated copy in preference to contemporary likenesses of Charles himself (by Anthony van Dyck, for example) suggests another, more complicated set of motives. One of these must have been to prompt viewers to recognize the king's interest in French customs and manners as a key issue for the series as a whole. For Charles's biographers, Frenchness was not simply a matter of fashionability—on the contrary, it raised questions of grave political importance, given the nationality and religion of his queen, and the persistent criticisms that his excessive dependence on Henrietta Maria had subjected him to the corrupting influence of foreign absolutism. Absolutist tendencies, furthermore, were widely understood as an extension and expression of royal pride, which early eighteenth-century historians identified as one of the principal causes of Charles's ruin.

Taken as a metonym for the king's inner character, Charles's feathered hat—that doubled sign of Frenchness and vanity—speaks also of flightiness and inconstancy, of delicacy to the point of weakness, and of susceptibility to even the very slightest of external influences. These are qualities which early eighteenth-century viewers would have identified with effeminacy, a term held to be broadly synonymous with the corruption of the individual or the state. But before we rush to place too exclusive an emphasis on this negative reading of the *Life*, we need to remind ourselves that there was at the same time much in this Charles I for

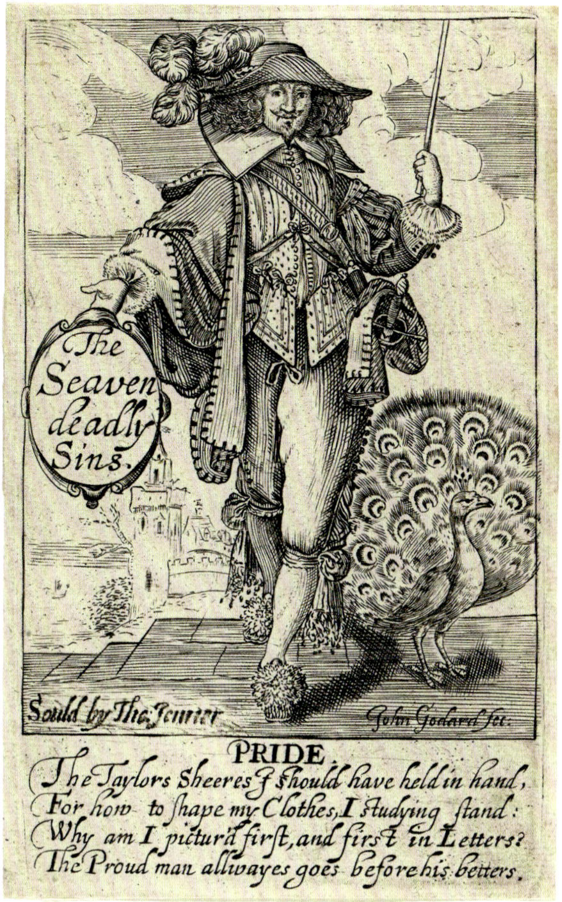

94. John Goddard after Abraham Bosse, published by Thomas Jenner, *The Seaven Deadly Sins: Pride*, 1639–50, engraving, 5⅞ x 3⅝ in. (14.9 x 9.cm). British Museum, London

the Bowleses' audience to admire—and especially in the sympathetic figure of the last three plates.

The large Overton and Hoole composite copy of the original series (fig. 95), which may date from the early 1730s, offers immediate visual confirmation that the king was judged to be most worthy of praise only after his cause had been utterly lost.[27] Because they have been given such disproportionate prominence in relation to all of the other scenes, here the *Tryal* and the *King Charles Taking Leave of his Children* operate as dominant companion-pieces, working in tandem to

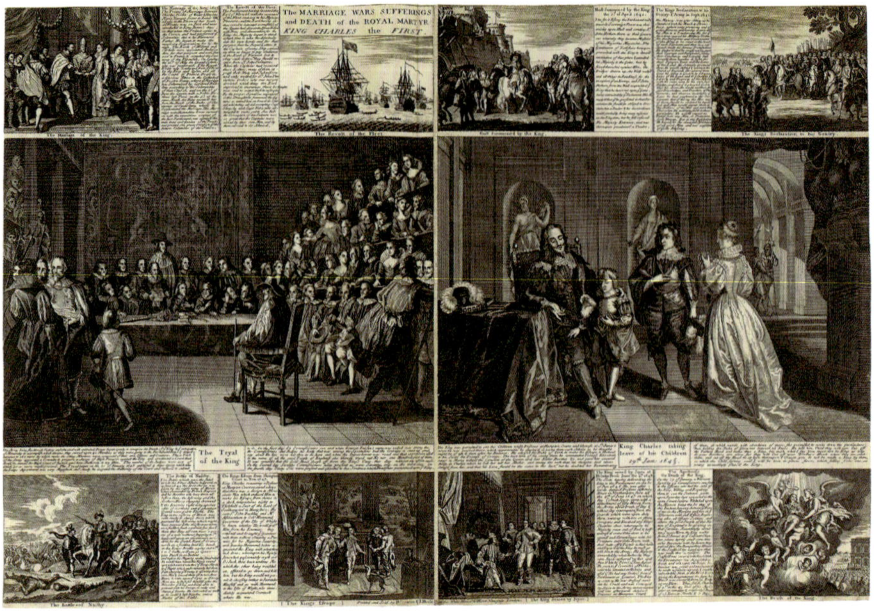

95. Unknown engraver after various artists and engravers, *The Marriage, Wars, Suffering and Death of the Royal Martyr, King Charles the First*, ca. 1730–35, engraving, 22⅛ x 34¼ in. (58.3 x 87 cm). Ashmolean Museum, University of Oxford

encapsulate the essential meanings of THE MARRIAGE WARS SUFFERINGS AND DEATH OF THE ROYAL MARTYR KING CHARLES THE FIRST. Where that title indicates a sequence of dramatic, even violent events, the two scenes singled out for special attention are emphatically tranquil in nature. Charles, too, is given the character of a man of peace; indeed, it might justifiably be argued that he is made to look like just the sort of king who could have been custom-tailored to suit the ideological requirements of eighteenth-century polite society. Calm in the face of provocation, obedient to his own reason, and respectful of authority, he personifies Christian fortitude and patience as he listens passively to the judgment of the hostile tribunal. But if the king's public world is one of trials and tribulations, his personal life offers a contrasting refuge of familial intimacy, where he fully comes into his own. Charles's uxoriousness, his sentimental attachment to his children, his piety, his highly cultured tastes—such qualities defined a privately oriented masculinity that was decorous and virtuous, refined yet chaste, and given to demonstrations of tenderness; qualities that may not have been best suited to support the exercise of regal authority, but which on the other hand were well matched to the gender ideals of a viewing audience whose notions of manners and morals had been shaped by texts like *The Tatler* or *The Spectator*. But what of that same audience's expectations of history painting, and its understanding of the workings of history itself?

In the *Catalogue of Maps, Prints, and Books* published by Bowles in 1728, the "Ten Prints of the Reign of King Charles the First" appear as the first item under the heading of "History Pieces, and other Designs" which he had for sale. The next prints on his list are *The Duke of Marlborough's Victories in Flanders*, done after Louis Laguerre's murals at Marlborough House, followed by Bernard Baron's nine engravings after Rubens's *Story of Achilles*, then by two sets of prints after the Raphael Cartoons. Thus from the standpoint of an early eighteenth-century London commercial publisher and his clientele, "History" as a type of visual imagery seems to have been capable of accommodating portrayals of more or less recent British historical events, represented with a high degree of detailed specificity, alongside idealized portrayals of biblical or mythological narratives—that is, alongside the sort of imagery that had by now come to enjoy the elevated status of "history painting" in the writings of academic art theorists. Neither the Bowleses, nor presumably their buyers, saw any reason to draw any distinctions between one type of history or the other; indeed, one of the striking features of the *Life of Charles I* is the mingling of several different genres, and of two distinct styles pointing in opposite directions: to Italianate "high" decorative painting on the one hand, and Netherlandish "low" print on the other.

As has already been observed, the series begins by trumpeting its affiliation with Rubens's Marie de' Medici cycle of decorations for the Palais de Luxembourg (as George Vertue was quick to recognize);[28] it also ends with an emphatic nod in the direction of another Rubens, the *Apotheosis of James I* on the ceiling of the Whitehall Banqueting House, which appears in the background of the execution scene. Painted in the mid-1630s, the Whitehall ceiling had introduced British viewers to the mode of highly illusionistic decorative imagery then popular across the courts of Europe, but which would only come to enjoy the same dominant position in England with the arrival of Antonio Verrio after the Restoration of Charles II. *The Revolt of the Fleet*, with its framing archway topped by a celestial throng of emblematic figures, was evidently designed to remind the Bowleses' viewers of this extremely distinguished heritage, and of its elevated associations with the houses of the great—though in conjunction with the shipping scene the same architectural *trompe l'oeil* would surely have brought James Thornhill's relatively recent achievements at Greenwich more specifically to mind.[29] Underpinning this kind of imagery, and equally implicit in the Bowleses' artists' use of the conventional trappings of allegory—with its angels, Olympian deities, and the progeny of Cesare Ripa's *Iconologia*, all rendered in the idealized generalities of the classical art tradition—lay a conception of human history, long used to glorify the rich and powerful, as a pattern of events orchestrated by an omniscient God.

In the *Life of Charles I*, however, the grandiose language of "high Baroque" decorative history painting finds itself dignifying and being dominated by a pictorial idiom far humbler in its provenance, which accounted for events in far more earthbound terms, and for a markedly less exclusive audience. The stylistic incoherence of the series speaks for a moment in English history when two regimes of knowledge confronted one another, but when the outcome of that confrontation had yet to be resolved. Although Providential explanations of the workings of history had not altogether lost their capacity to convince, by the early eighteenth century they had ceded much, if not yet all of their authoritative status to a fundamentally different mode of historical understanding—one which appealed to reason, not to faith, and which gave pride of place to "plain" observable "facts". Of these the Bowleses' imagery provided a remarkable plethora, in its meticulous attention to the details of physiognomy, historical costume, settings, and so forth—all of which, as we have seen, asked to be read, duly considered, and in the end judged, both morally and politically. Leo Costello has characterized this emphasis on what John Galt called the "facts of the transaction"[30] as constituting the "informative" aspect of contemporary history painting—an adjective deliberately chosen by Costello for the purpose of linking the appearance of this new art form to "the development of a new public in the eighteenth century", for whom "information held both practical and symbolic importance", as the basis upon which commercial and political decisions were made. To meet this need, the emerging "bourgeois public sphere" depended principally on the press; but painters such as Benjamin West (and Turner, in Costello's account) could also play a significant supporting role.[31]

While I find myself in broad agreement with the gist of Costello's argument, here I'd like to suggest that the invention of history painting in modern dress belongs to a chain of events that in fact were set in motion well before the eighteenth century, in a set of circumstances fittingly signposted by the subject-matter and medium of the Bowleses' *Charles I.* For if we wish to pinpoint the birth of a politicized public in Britain, we need to look back to the period that saw the outbreak of the English Civil War. In 1642—the same year, we may recall, that the king met with open defiance at Hull, and lost control of the nation's fleet—Wenceslaus Hollar marked this recent development with a memorable etching (fig. 96) that lamented the supplanting of proper monarchical authority by the "rule and government" of blind Opinion—a force which Henry Peacham's verse caption identifies as "The fruite [of] those idle bookes and libells [which] In everie street, on everie stall you find"—the fruit, that is to say, of "vulgar" print culture.

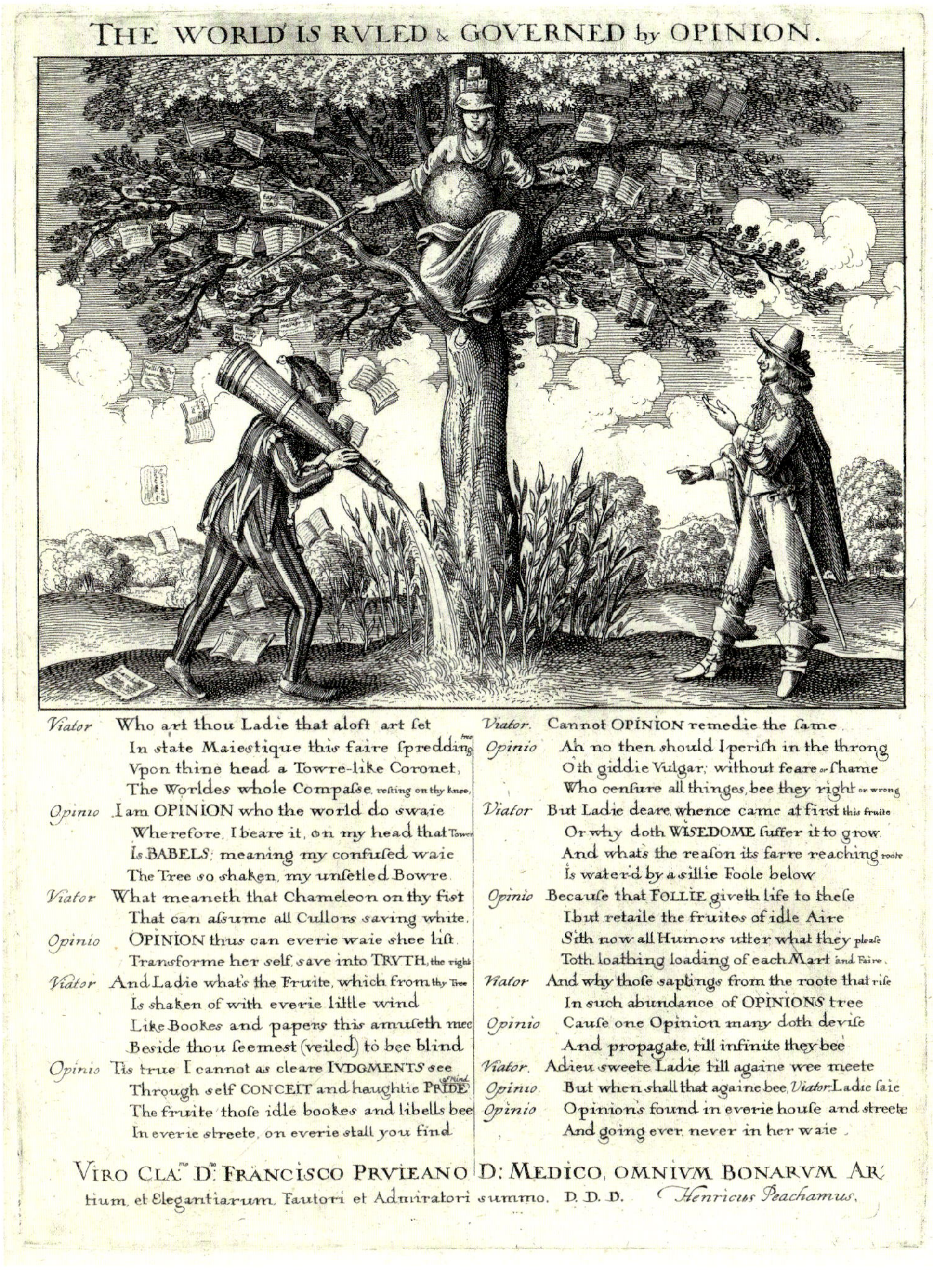

96. Wenceslaus Hollar, *The World is Ruled and Governed by Opinion*, 1642, etching, 11⅛ x 8½ in. (28.3 x 21.5 cm). British Museum, London

As the literary historian Harold Weber has perceptively observed, it was during the early 1640s that England had witnessed its first dramatic explosion in the "production, marketing and consumption of printed matter"—a phenomenon fuelled by the rise of public opinion, and fanning its flames in return. Beyond giving British readers an unprecedented awareness of significant contemporary events, print culture promoted new ways of accounting for those events, in rational rather than Providential terms.[32] Such explanations tended to be formulated in a rhetoric of meticulous specificity that supported their often explicit claims to "truth" or "exactitude"; and while this commitment did find expression in mid- and later seventeenth-century visual culture—at first mainly through the medium of the popular illustrated broadside—its principal outlet was the written word.[33]

This is where the *Life of Charles I* took its narrative, from published histories of the tragic monarch's reign; but its engagements with print culture extended beyond this, and its own engraved medium, to encompass the use of a highly particularized descriptive language, together with the collateral endorsement of a distinctively modern mode of historical understanding that had originated in the era of the martyred king. In his *Catalogue* of 1728, John Bowles drove home this connection when he invited potential buyers to have the prints "bound up in my Lord Clarendon's Folio History".[34] Edward Hyde, Earl of Clarendon, had written his *History of the Rebellion and Civil Wars in England* between around 1650 and his death in 1674, but it only appeared in print in 1702. The text enjoyed immediate popularity, and soon achieved the status of a classic of modern British historiography, thanks mainly to the fame of its noble author, its highly readable style, and its wealth of closely observed detail; by 1732 Clarendon's *History* had gone through at least twelve editions, including eight in folio alone. No wonder, then, that the Bowleses saw its success as a commercial opportunity, nor that they sought to reinforce their series' connection with the book by using paraphrased bits of Clarendon as captions for the majority of their prints.

In so doing the publishers and their artists implicitly embraced the interests of a large target audience of refined cultural consumers, descended from that diverse politically engaged readership that the "English Revolution" had effectively brought into being. It was at that earlier point of crisis that a knowledge of the "facts" had first assumed an inescapably political significance, which eighteenth-century polite society inherited as its legacy from a turbulent era that its genteel members largely wished to consign to the past. But the Bowles series offers us a useful reminder that the origins of the "revolution of history painting" lay in far from peaceful times. Perhaps against all expectations, a revolution may indeed turn out to have been involved after all—but a political upheaval that had much to do with history, little with painting, and nothing whatsoever with West's *Death of General Wolfe*.

1. Leo Costello, *J. M. W. Turner and the Subject of History* (Farnham and Burlington, VT: Ashgate, 2012), 15–60.
2. John Galt, *The Life, Studies and Works of Benjamin West*, 2 parts (London and Philadelphia, 1816 & 1820), ii: 50.
3. Edgar Wind, "The Revolution of History Painting": *Journal of the Warburg Institute* 2, no. 2 (1938): 117–25.
4. The first considered challenge to Wind's arguments was made six years later in Charles Mitchell, "Benjamin West's 'Death of General Wolfe' and the Popular History Piece", *Journal of the Warburg and Courtauld Institutes* 7 (1944): 20–33.
5. This is the title used in the extensive campaign of press advertisements for the series, which appeared in the *Craftsman*, 9 March 1728; *Country Journal*, 9 March 1728; *Mist's Weekly Journal*, 9 and 16 March, 13 and 20 April 1728; *Daily Post*, 14 March and 1 May 1728; *Daily Journal*, 14 and 16 April 1728; *Post Boy*, 4–6 and 16–18 April 1728—and almost certainly elsewhere. In *A Catalogue of Maps, Prints, Books, and Books of Maps, which are Printed for and Sold by John Bowles* (London, 1728), 10, the set is more simply referred to as *Ten Prints of the Reign of King Charles I.*
6. The best discussion of this project may be found in Alan Ide, "Between History and History Painting: *The Life of Charles I* and the London Art World of the 1720s" (unpublished MA report, Courtauld Institute of Art, Univ. of London, 1995). Ide's report served as an invaluable guide to my own research on the *Charles I* series, which has also been the focus of a two part article by Robert Raines and Kenneth Sharpe, "The Story of Charles I", *The Connoisseur* 184, no. 739 (Sept. 1973): 38–46, and 186, no. 749 (July 1974): 192–95. A third and final part was intended but never published. The nine paintings (there was never an oil of *The Revolt of the Fleet*) were all put up for auction at Christie's on 15 Nov. 1996 (lots 10–18), where only three of them appear to have reached their reserve; the current locations of all nine are not known to me.
7. For their acknowledged importance, see, for example, Timothy Clayton, *The English Print, 1688–1802* (New Haven and London: Yale Univ. Press, 1997), 56–57.
8. The passage on which the caption is based can be found in Laurence Echard, *The History of England. From the First Entrance of Julius Caesar and the Romans, To the Conclusion of the Reign of King James the Second, and the Establishment of King William and Queen Mary upon the Throne, in the Year 1688*, 3rd ed. (London, 1720), 419.
9. The crowned man diving to the right of Discord appears to be holding a purse, which may identify him as Greed or Bribery, while to his left (our right) the reclining male figure grasping a spear thrust through a crown may personify Rebellion. Above them both a woman holds out a crescent moon, probably to indicate the darkness that will follow in Rebellion's wake. The two-headed (female?) figure seated in the shadows on the opposite side of the arch may be Fraud. In his *Catalogue* of 1728 (see note 5 above), 11, John Bowles designates these allegorical figures as "hieroglyphicks", following the usage of this term in the first English edition of Cesare Ripa's *Iconologia: or Moral Emblems* (London, 1709), "To the Reader". I am grateful to Richard Johns for his help in trying to decode this allegory, and for the useful reminder that some flexibility over the precise identification of certain figures should be allowed, and almost certainly was, in the early eighteenth century.
10. The speech as given in the caption is paraphrased either from Echard, *History of England*, 545, or more likely from Henry Hyde, first Earl of Clarendon, *The History of the Rebellion and Civil Wars in England, Begun in the Year 1641*, 3 vols. (London, 1720), 2: 16.
11. John Oldmixon, *The History of England, during the Reigns of the Royal House of Stuart* (London, 1730), 367.
12. Clarendon, *History*, 3: 257–58.
13. Gilbert, Bishop Burnet, *Bishop Burnet's History of His Own Time*, 2 vols. (Dublin, 1724), 1: 28.
14. Here it may be worth recalling that in the immediate aftermath of 1688, sermons devoted to the memory of Charles I had taken pains to distinguish him from James II, whose forced removal from the throne was justified on the grounds that he had attempted to rule with absolute power. But with the resurgence of Toryism in the late 1690s and early 1700s, there emerged a virulent cult of the royal martyr, which Whig clergymen sought to counter by stressing the connection between the murdered father and his exiled second son. For an extended discussion of these issues, see Byron S. Stewart, "The Cult of the Royal Martyr", *Church History* 38, no. 2 (June 1969): 175–84.

15. The caption on Bernard Baron's engraving attributes the design to "M" or possibly "Mr" Vanderbank, which may refer to M[r John] Vanderbank, or to his far less well-known brother Moses, who appears to have specialized in history painting.
16. Echard, *History of England*, 661.
17. Burnet, *History*, 1: 28.
18. For an analysis of the Anniversary sermons, which clergymen were required to deliver by an Act of Parliament passed in 1661 (this remained legally binding until 1859!), see Helen W. Randall, "The Rise and Fall of a Martyrology: Sermons on Charles I", *Huntington Library Quarterly* 10, no. 2 (Feb. 1947): 135–67; the same sermons are also extensively discussed in Stewart, "Cult of the Royal Martyr".
19. Ide, "Between History and History Painting", 24–25.
20. This statement reworks a point made in Ide, "Between History and History Painting", 27.
21. Clarendon, *History*, 3: 257–58.
22. Clarendon, *History*, 3: 256–57.
23. Isaac de Larrey, *The History of the Reign of King Charles I*, 2 vols. (London, 1716), 1: 4, 32.
24. Burnet, *History*, 1: 28.
25. Burnet, *History*, 1: 28.
26. Larrey, *History*, 2: 100–1.
27. Ide, "Between History and History Painting", 38, n. 71 dates the Overton and Hoole piracy to 1753, but without providing any supporting evidence; perhaps he found this year inscribed on the single (unidentified) impression he was able to locate. However, none of the three impressions I have been able to trace have a publication date, nor does any make reference to the Copyright Act of 1735—so it may well be that the composite print was first issued prior to that year. This would make it contemporaneous with the set of smaller copies published by Overton on his own, and advertised for sale in the *Craftsman*, 1 Feb. 1735.
28. In 1728, Vertue described "the remarkable storys in ten peices of King Charles the first" as "some kind of Imitation of the History of Mari de Medicis at the Luxembourg"; see "The Note-books of George Vertue VI", *Walpole Society* 30 [1955]: 191.
29. It was the association with the houses of the great that John Bowles aimed to exploit when (in his *Catalogue*, 11) he recommended that the prints be framed and glazed to be "used for Furniture".
30. Galt, *Benjamin West*, 2: 48.
31. Costello, *J. M. W. Turner*, 32.
32. Harold M. Weber, *Paper Bullets: Print and Kingship under Charles II* (Lexington: Univ. Press of Kentucky, 1996), 4–8. Some of the sentences in this paragraph have been shamelessly lifted, with some minor modifications, from David H. Solkin, "Isaac Fuller's *Escape of Charles II*: A Restoration Tragicomedy", *Journal of the Warburg and Courtauld Institutes* 62 (1999): 236.
33. For an example of the printed broadside, see Solkin, "Isaac Fuller's *Escape of Charles II*", 235, fig. 86. The same article focuses on a set of large historical paintings depicting *The Escape of Charles II after the Battle of Worcester*, executed by Isaac Fuller in the early 1660s (National Portrait Gallery, London), which (highly unusually) brought the distinctive "factual" semiotic of mid-seventeenth-century popular print culture into the realm of monumental "high" art. Although the Fullers had no discernible impact on the subsequent development of British art, throughout the later seventeenth century and beyond a meticulous attention to contemporaneous detail remained of central importance to one type of historical art: that devoted to the representation of battles, on either land or sea. Plates 2–5 of the Bowleses' *Life of Charles I* owe much to this (Netherlandish) tradition.
34. Bowles, *Catalogue*, 11.

NETWORKS, SHARED PRACTICES, COMMUNITIES

Lely, Drawing, and the Training of Artists

Diana Dethloff

At some unspecified date in 1661, the young painter Mary Beale and her husband, Charles, a patent clerk, art dealer, and supplier of artists' pigments, recorded their possession of a self-portrait by Peter Lely (fig. 97). In a now lost pocketbook for that year, extracts from which were conveniently transcribed by George Vertue, the Beales noted their ownership of this work, generally accepted to be that in the National Portrait Gallery, London, together with further portraits by Lely of themselves and their family (now untraced), and also paintings by Anthony van Dyck, Peter Paul Rubens, and Adrian Hanemann.[1] The Beales did not record where in their house they displayed Lely's self-portrait, which was painted, in all likelihood, to celebrate his appointment as the King's Principal Painter on 20 June 1660.[2] Given that they were professional acquaintances of the artist, and probably already his friends, it may have hung alongside their own portraits by Lely, all of the same size and format.[3] For visitors to the house, this would have suggested the Beales' close association with the fashionable royal painter, thereby elevating and enhancing their personal and professional standing.

Lely's self-portrait marked an important turning point in his professional life, as he embarked on a new career as royal painter at Charles II's court. Significantly, the historiography on the artist has traditionally assessed and discussed his work within this courtly context. Scholars, in particular Oliver Millar, have concentrated on the artist's considerable output as Principal Painter during this post-Restoration period, and have predominantly focused upon the relationship between his courtly sitters and patrons. The scholarship of Catharine Macleod and Julia Marciari Alexander has had a similar focus, examining Lely's representation of courtly women and the courtly networks of female patronage.[4] But, as this essay will aim to show, there is another side to Lely, and another way of thinking about him. Alongside his royal commissions and his fashionable portrait practice, he remained firmly involved in the artistic community of London during the 1660s and 1670s, pursuing an active and successful career as mentor, teacher, collector, and art dealer. In considering some of these alternative activities, particularly his

emy, and Lely.[13] Building upon this earlier work and upon more recent research into Lely's unrivalled collection of old-master drawings and prints, his working practices, and his use of drawings, we can now make an even stronger case for Lely's involvement with a drawing academy in London, and establish beyond question his commitment to drawing as a fundamental pedagogic tool for artists.

ACADEMIC DRAWING PRACTICE

> The good Draftsman at the academy draws in this Nature Mr F. drew an Academy Figure with a great deal of pains to Shew it to Mr. Lilly, says he looking on it, I had rather see it done without this pains (or wis labour) that is a rude stroke & rare judgment which has the less trouble.[14]

Continental academies considered drawing an essential part of a young artist's training, a point John Evelyn emphasized to readers of his *Sculptura; or, The History and Art of Chalcography* of 1662. He described those "Academies" which "the greatest princes of Europe have erected" in order for the "promotion and encouragement" of the art of drawing.[15] He is referring here to the Florentine, Bolognese, and Roman academies founded in the second half of the sixteenth century, all of which defined drawing—after "old master" works, sculpture, and most importantly the live model—as a central part of a young artist's training. The French Académie Royale de peinture et de sculpture, established later in 1648, placed an even greater emphasis on drawing, with students required to attend life-drawing classes every day for two hours. The practice in the Netherlands, especially relevant to the discussion here, given the number of Dutch and Flemish artists working in England during this period, was less structured, with a number of informal public and private drawing schools developing from the 1580s, often organized by the studio or workshop master. An early example of this was to be found in Haarlem, where in the 1580s Karel van Mander established the "Haarlem Academy", which featured not only drawing from the live model but also drawing from bronzes and casts.[16] We have no record of Lely being part of any such group during his early years in Haarlem, but he would certainly have been aware of this strong graphic tradition. Given this background and his subsequent involvement with an informal academy in London in the 1670s, it is tempting to see Lely as playing some considerable part in the request by members of the Painter-Stainers' Company to its ruling body in 1656, to establish life-drawing classes in the company's hall.[17] Perhaps not surprisingly, given the Painter-Stainers' reluctance to be anything other than a regulatory body, this was refused, with the Court Minute Book recording that; "it is ordered that theyre shall be noe meetinge of any members of the Company or applying to the Guildhall whereby to keepe an Academie in any parte thereof for drawing to the life."[18]

However, as I will argue, by 1673, or possibly earlier, an unofficial academy or drawing school seems to have existed in London, in which Lely was involved. It may have started as an informal gathering of assistants from within his Covent Garden studio, which occupied an upper floor in his house on the Great Piazza, before developing into something more extensive. We can't be sure that this was always the venue but it is likely that the "academy" convened in Lely's studio in those periods after his fashionable sitters had left, with young artists, or artists who had not previously benefited from Continental training, coming and going as their circumstances permitted.

It is not known how often this informal drawing school met or how the teaching was structured. We also do not know whether some charge was imposed on those attending as was the case with Kneller's later Great Queen Street Academy, founded in 1711, for which attendees were required to pay an annual fee of 1 guinea. It seems—as was also the case in Kneller's academy—that Lely called upon other artists to help with instruction. These collaborators may well have included his posture painter John Baptist Gaspars, who later produced drawn copies of Lely's portraits for the mezzotinter Jan van Somer, and whom Bainbrigg Buckeridge praised as an "admirable Draftsman in the Academy". As Bignamini has suggested, another teacher may have been George Freeman, a designer of tapestries who was, Buckeridge claims, "in his Drawings, especially in the Academy, most extraordinary".[19] Lely seems to have been Freeman's friend and mentor. In September 1670 he supported Freeman's petition for the position as royal tapestry designer, noting that he had seen several of his drawings and believed him eminently suited to be "employed in making designs for tapestries, prints or any other inventions belonging to an historical painter". Lely goes on to add that "he would employ him himself before any other on such occasions."[20] In the early 1660s he had also endorsed the private drawing lessons that Freeman was offering to a small number of young artists, offering his opinion on the student drawings which Freeman showed him. As Freeman wrote to Sir William Gawdy, whose son Framlingham was one of his pupils:

> I was at Mr Lilly's about 4 days ago with Mr Fram. & he sayd he liked his drawing very well and that he was much mended but did not doe with freedome enough, wch cannot come but with timed practice . . . I doe intend to tell him to draw from plaster figures, wch will teach him to draw bouldly,

> for there must be a method without intangling of his judgement, wch cannot be done without a greate deal of time and diligence by advancing by degrees and not goeing to the difficult before he doe understand how he should go about it, wch causeth many to follow a bad manor or else to dispare through the difficulties of obtaining to it. Mr Lilly I am certain will certifie you of the same . . . he is very desirous he [Framlingham] should be perfect in his drawing it being the chiefe ground of Painting and the want of it the cause that so few do obtain to Perfection.[21]

Freeman did not teach in his own studio, partly because his large preparatory drawings for tapestries restricted the available space; furthermore, those sitting to the artist for their portraits (which Freeman evidently also produced) apparently disliked "strangers in the Roome".[22] Instead, he lent his drawings for his pupils to copy at home, which in turn led to concerns about the safe keeping of his originals. Perhaps the idea of a drawing academy developed jointly between Lely and Freeman, who together decided to run it from Lely's larger studio. However it originated, it is clear that Lely himself took part in the regular teaching. Gandy reports one occasion when the celebrated master actively demonstrated his method of drawing a figure:

> Mr Lilly draws all things in this manner . . . as suppose it is a Figure. As bodys Armes legs he draws it in angles though there be never so many muscles, only a right stroke in this manner but is pretty sure in drawing of these angles, these are as foundations, then he mends it by degrees, till you see some muscles appear.[23]

Lely's way of drawing, in which the figure was confidently built up through different angles and strokes, offered an exact parallel to the methods he used to begin *painting* a portrait. Paint replaced chalk to mark the body's outline on the canvas in the preliminary stages of a portrait sitting, although a separate chalk drawing, outlining the pose for the sitter's approval, would have been produced first. Gandy recounts a conversation with a fellow member of the academy who noted that "Mr Lilly painted as you and I do draw at ye Academy . . . Mr Lilly did often say to Mr F that painting was nothing else but draft."[24]

LELY'S DRAWINGS

This commitment to drawing remained constant throughout Lely's career, during which he produced various types of drawings in different media, although only around eighty works—a far smaller number than must have once existed—can now be traced.[25] A few landscape studies, together with a couple of presentation drawings for early subject pictures, have survived; the majority of his surviving drawings, however, are preparatory studies for portraits, including hand and arm studies, some of which can be linked to specific pictures. A number of these works are quite crudely outlined, evoking the manner in which Gandy describes Lely building up a drawing through lines and angles; others are much more carefully and delicately rendered (fig. 98). They were presumably intended to help Lely and his assistants complete commissioned portraits, as part of the well-oiled production process that, as we have seen, was characteristic of his studio. The majority of these studies would have been drawn directly from the sitter or model. Lely deployed quick chalk sketches to catch a sitter's likeness at a first sitting—an example of this practice is suggested by the description of a drawing "first in chalk rudely & afterwards in colours" that the Beales witnessed Lely make during his initial sitting with Tillotson. And even though he regularly employed specialist drapery painters, Lely still produced drawn drapery studies. These could serve as

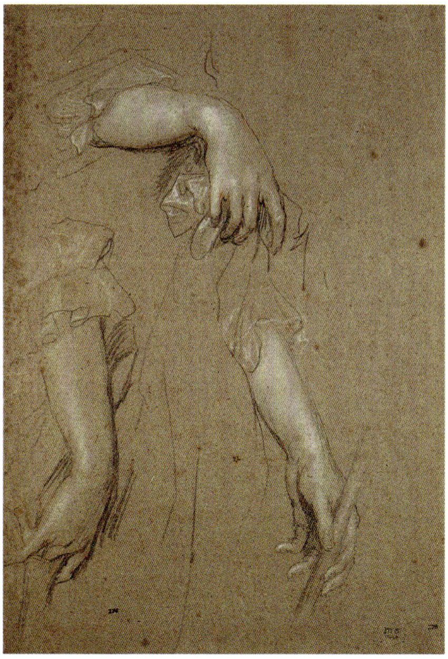

98. Sir Peter Lely, *Studies of Hands*, ca. 1662–5, black, red and white chalk on buff paper, 15 x 10½ in. (38.2 x 26.8 cm). Ashmolean Museum, University of Oxford

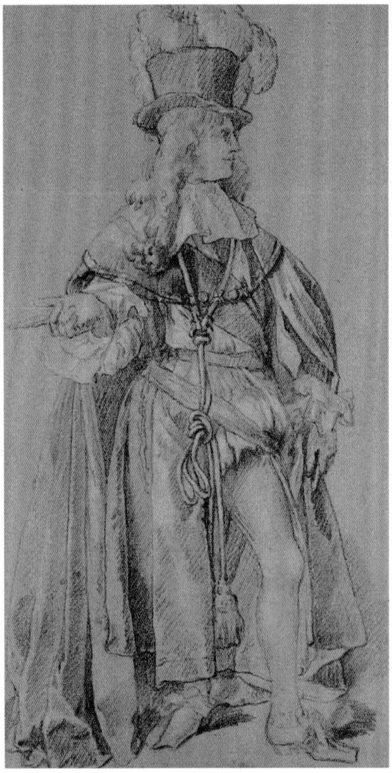

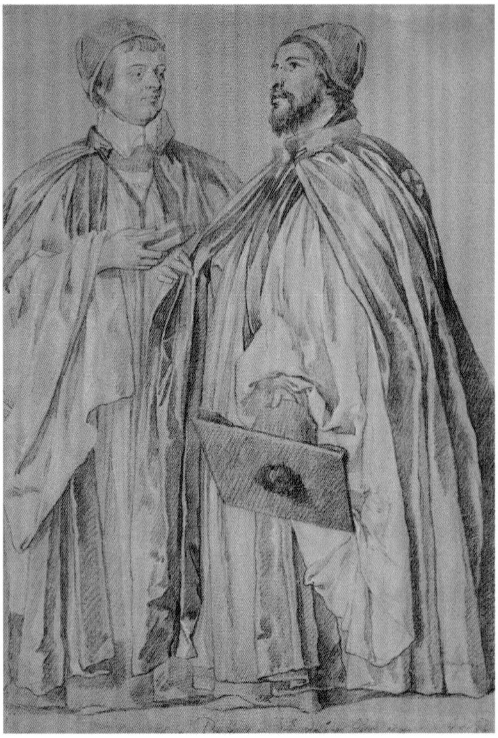

99. Sir Peter Lely, *Knight of the Order of the Garter*, 1663–71, black chalk with white heightening on paper, 19⅞ x 10½ in. (50.4 x 26.7 cm). British Museum, London

100. Sir Peter Lely, *Two Prebends of Windsor*, 1663–71, black chalk with white heightening on paper, 21 x 14⅞ in. (53.2 x 37.8 cm). British Museum, London

a guide to the painter himself, as in the production of Charles Beale junior's portrait in 1672: "Mr Lely dead coloured my son Charles picture . . . took a drawing upon paper after an Indian gown which he had put on his back, in order to the finishing of the Drapery of it."[26] Such drawings could also be made available to his assistants, to be used in conjunction with actual fabric draped over a lay figure.[27]

The drawings that particularly reflect Lely's graphic skill and ability to capture movement and expressive interaction between figures, however, are those depicting members of the Order of the Garter and their attendants (figs. 99 and 100). Why and for whom they were made is unclear, but given their large size and their confident, bold execution—they were drawn in black chalk, heightened with white on blue-grey paper—they seem likely to have been worked up in the studio from rapidly executed eye-witness sketches. They record, very probably, the 1667 Garter procession, held that year at Whitehall in the presence of the Swedish Ambassador in London, who was acting as mediator in the Anglo-Dutch peace negotiations. Given the political sensitivity of the discussions, the Garter ceremony that year was regarded as something of a national showpiece and raised considerable public attention, and not surprisingly was recorded at length in the *London Gazette* for 22–25 April 1667 and by both Samuel Pepys and John Evelyn in their diaries.[28] It has always been thought that these drawings were intended as presentation material for an ambitious decorative scheme intended to celebrate the Garter in this very important year.[29] Furthermore, it has been suggested that Lely's ownership of Van Dyck's Garter oil sketch may have offered a prompt for a royalist-themed celebration. But unlike his father, Charles II does not seem to have been particularly interested in the Garter ceremony, which in fact was only celebrated on five occasions in his twenty-five-year reign.[30] So why then were these drawings made? One possibility may be that the Swedish Ambassador, an important political presence at the ceremony that year, commissioned some visual record of this ceremony, perhaps through the agency of the Swedish Consul Leijonbergh, a neighbour of Lely's in the Great Piazza, which, for whatever reason, never progressed beyond the artist's series of presentation drawings.[31]

The drawings found in the album at Dulwich are very different from these types of drawings. None can be classified as a preparatory work, or work in its own right; most are copies after paintings and other figurative subjects. Nor is it really a sketchbook such as those kept by Van Dyck in the 1620s, in which he made copies of works seen at first hand in Italian collections and churches, or by Kneller during his own Italian visit in the 1690s. It is more accurately a compilation of drawings, made up of a variety of different types and sizes of works, produced in a range of media and on various coloured papers, and of uneven quality, by at least four or five different hands, stuck down onto the pages of a leather-bound book. The album has been assembled with great care and judgment. Similar types and styles of drawings balance each other. Occasionally, if two individual artists have drawn the same subject, their different works—in different media—are highlighted (figs. 101 and 102). The album offers a repository that seems concerned to capture and represent a collective form of drawing, the products of which have been retained and selected by whoever assembled them into the album. We have no idea how they came into this person's possession—whether they were left in an artist's studio, acquired as ephemera, or collected over time and assembled with other drawings owned by the compiler.

The album is generally assumed to have come to Dulwich as part of the 1687 bequest of the actor-playwright manager William Cartwright, whose theatre was in Drury Lane, on the borders of Covent Garden. Cartwright was a patron of John Greenhill, who had initially worked in Lely's studio and a couple of whose works, including his portrait of Cartwright, are copied in the album.[32] He was also a collector, which would have given him contacts on a number of levels with the

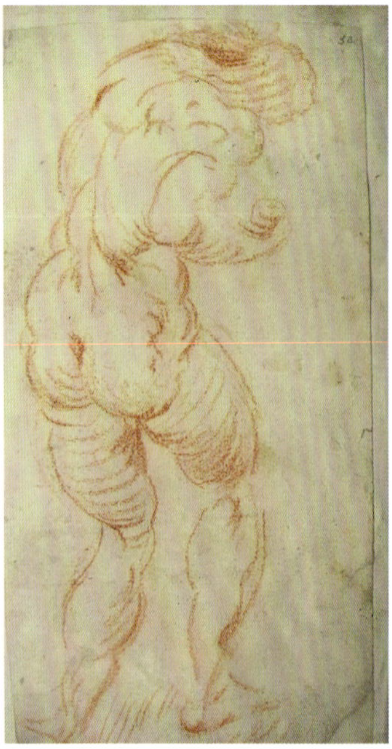

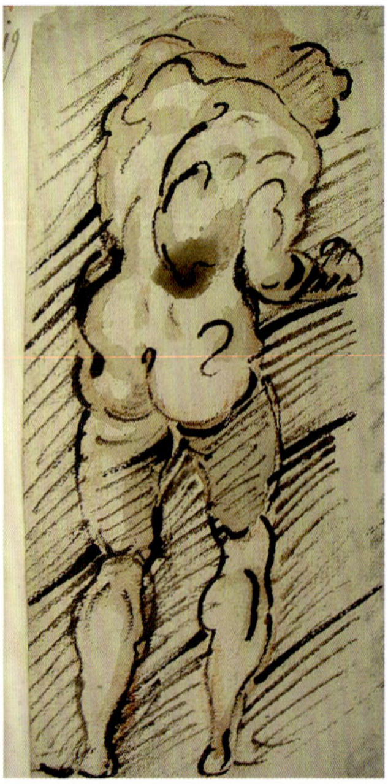

101. *Standing Male Figure*, Dulwich College Album MX XV, fol. 18v, red chalk on paper, 7⅞ x 4⅛ in. (20.1 x 10.5 cm). Dulwich College, London

102. *Standing Male Figure*, Dulwich College Album MX XV fol. 19r, brown ink on paper, 8¾ x 4⅛ in. (22.2 x 10.5 cm). Dulwich College, London

Restoration art world. Some of the works in the album—including paintings of flowers—seem to have little relationship to the kinds of exercises associated with formal academic training; many others, however, are precisely the type of works which suggest such practices. And the fact that, in a number of cases, the same subject-matter is seen being drawn by different hands, and from slightly different angles, does indeed suggest the kind of collective activity associated with an academy of drawing.

When the Library at Dulwich College was catalogued in 1881 by the British Museum's keeper of manuscripts, the album was described as "A Collection of Drawings, apparently students' copies, in various hands, and generally of little merit, together with a few paintings of flowers, coloured coats of arms etc." These "students' copies, in various hands" include copies after paintings, a number after Van Dyck—for example, a detail of crossed arms taken from the painter's portrait of his mistress Margaret Lemon (fig. 103). Significantly, Van Dyck's picture, before being restored to the Royal Collection in 1660, had been bought—and perhaps copied—by Lely's drapery painter, John Baptist Gaspars. The album also contains an offprint of a reduced, drawn copy of Van Dyck's *Anne, Countess of Clanbrassil* and a copy of the head from the same artist's full-length portrait

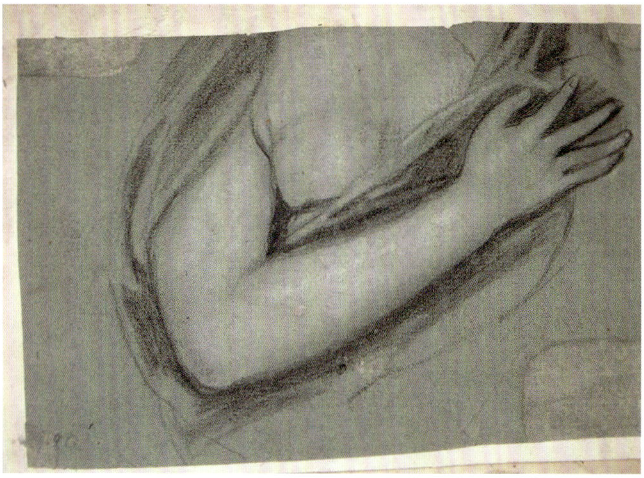

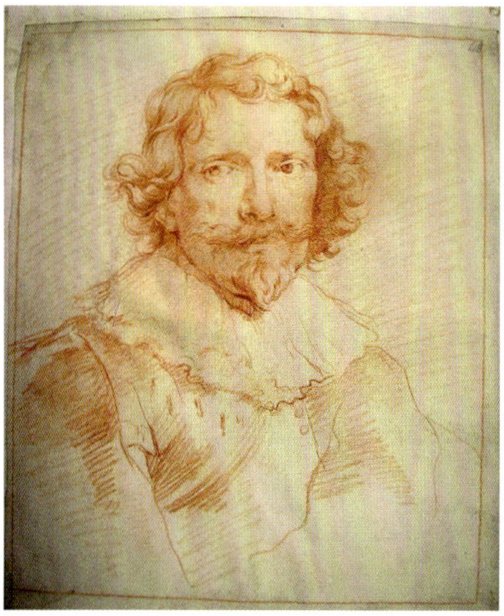

103. *Right Arm from Margaret Lemon*, Dulwich College Album MX XV, fol. 10r, black chalk with white heightening on paper, 6⅝ x 4 in. (17 x 10 cm). Dulwich College, London

104. After Anthony Van Dyck, *Lucas Vorsterman*, Dulwich College Album MX XV, fol. 18r, red chalk on white paper, 7 x 6 in. (18 x 15.3 cm). Dulwich College, London

of the tenth Earl of Northumberland, which had earlier been copied by Lely, perhaps during the later 1640s when he had direct contact with Northumberland's important collection of pictures. There are copies after old-master drawings, for example Raphael's *Mother and Child* (Chatsworth House). There is also a drawing of a putto's head, possibly after Perino del Vaga, which—bizarrely, given the poor quality of the copy—has been pricked for transfer for further copying.

The album also contains copies after prints, including a red chalk drawing after an early impression of the portrait of Lucas Vorsterman in Van Dyck's *Iconography* (fig. 104); a detail from the bottom section of François Perrier's print after Simon Vouet's *Adoration of the Shepherds* (fig. 105); and a pen-and-ink copy after a print from Annibale Carracci's Lascivie series.[33] There are also drawings of sculpture, very probably from casts, as well as copies after antique sculpture known through printed sources, for example the *Farnese Hercules* (fig. 106), which was illustrated in Jan de Bisschop's highly influential *Icones* of 1669. There are also drawings by different hands that seem to show models *posing* in the form of sculpture, following Van Mander's advice (which was standard practice in other and later drawing schools) to draw figures in sculptural rather than natural poses; thus,

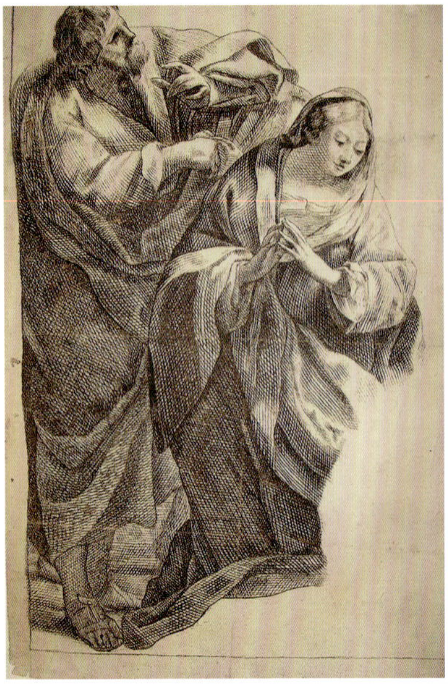

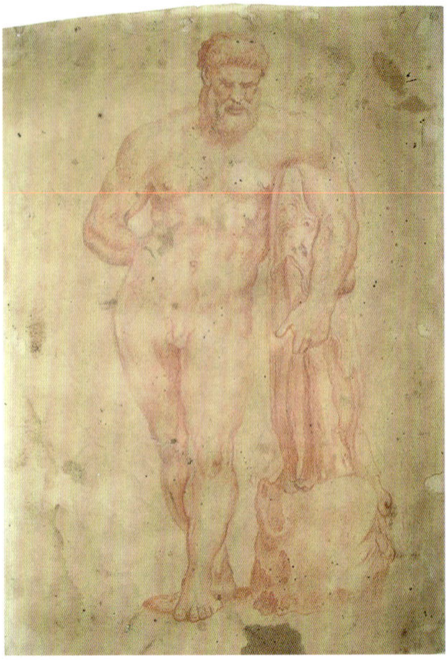

105. After *Vouet's Adoration* (detail), Dulwich College Album MX XV, fol. 5r, black ink on paper, 10⅞ x 7¼ in. (27.5 x 18.3 cm). Dulwich College, London

106. *Farnese Hercules*, Dulwich College Album MX XV, fol. 20v, red and black chalk with white heightening on paper, 9¾ x 7 in. (24.8 x 17.6 cm). Dulwich College, London

the twisting pose adopted in a number of drawings in the album is that of the famous *Crouching Venus* type (figs. 107 and 108).[34]

There are also examples of drawings from the live model, for example of a seated male nude (fig. 109), and two further studies, taken from slightly different angles of a standing male figure, which could be classified as the type of "Academy Figure" referred to in Gandy's comment quoted earlier.[35] Bignamini suggested that a drawing of a female nude, seen from behind, leaning on a column, was a life study; and though it might be a model adopting a sculptural pose, it is in fact more likely to be a copy of a cast after Giambologna's *Astronomy* (fig. 110), perhaps the object described as "A Wax Figure on a Pedistall", sold in Lely's 1682 picture sale.[36] There are, however, a few other drawings which appear to be life studies after the female nude, for example two drawings of a standing nude female figure posing as Minerva, by two different hands, each showing the model in slightly different positions. Drawing the female nude model was not permitted in any of the official contemporary academies, but in the more informal studio or drawing school environment it was allowed. A drawing of a reclining figure, generally accepted to be

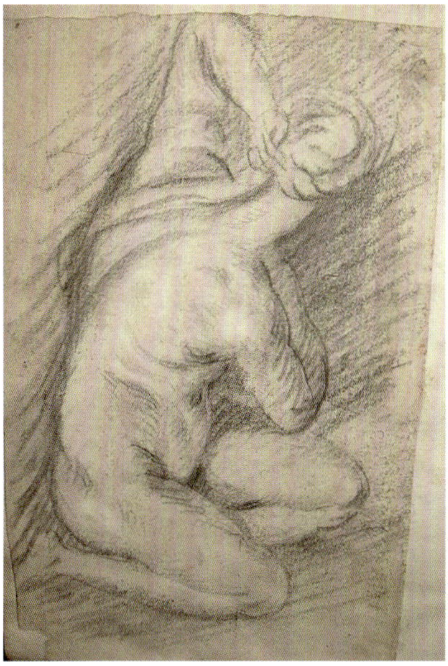

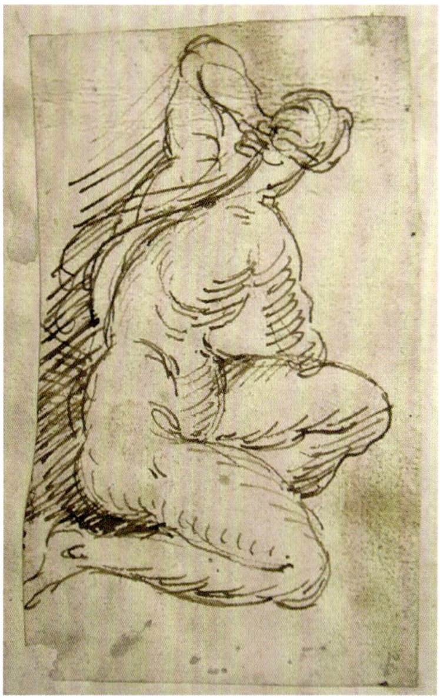

107. *Crouching Venus*, Dulwich College Album MX XV, fol. 9v, black chalk on paper, 6⅞ x 4⅜ in. (17.5 x 11 cm). Dulwich College, London

108. *Crouching Venus*, Dulwich College Album MX XV, fol. 11r, black ink on paper, 5½ x 3¼ in. (14 x 8.2 cm). Dulwich College, London

by Lely, is one of the few known English female nude studies from this period, which reinforces the suggestion that his studio encouraged studies from the naked female model. Finally, the album offers evidence of the use of one of the many printed artist's manuals available at this time—it contains copies of two pages from Abraham Bloemaert's *Artis Apellae Liber* (fig. 111), one of the most successful drawing books produced in the seventeenth century.

Further work will be necessary to identify more of the actual sources for the drawings collected in this album, but even from the relatively limited research carried out so far, it is evident that those who produced the studies it contains had access to a rich and varied source of old-master prints and drawings as well as casts and paintings. It is this evidence that ties the album without question to Lely, and to the contents of his art collection, which he built up over several decades with care, persistence, and determination. For Lely, therefore, the pose of gentleman-collector that he adopts in the Beales' self-portrait was particularly appropriate. At his death, his friend and executor Roger North, using a clever marketing strategy, stamped each of Lely's ten thousand prints and drawings in the collection with the

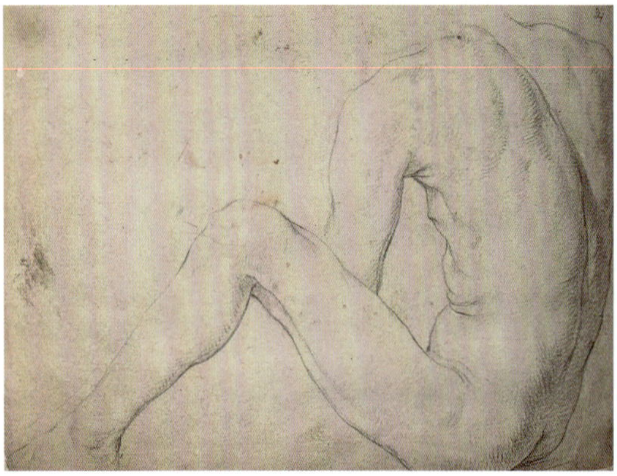

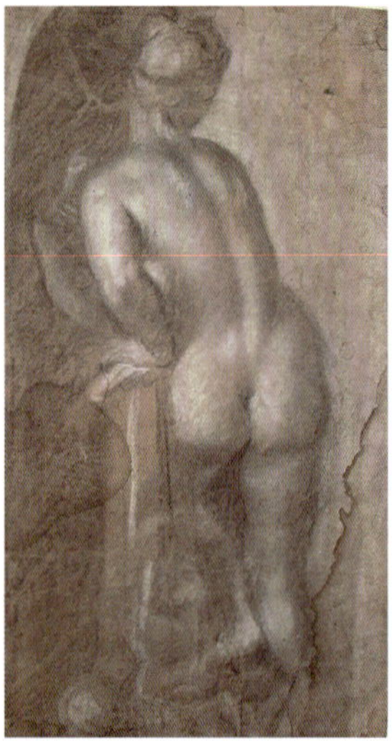

109. *Seated Male Nude*, Dulwich College Album MX XV, fol. 15v, black chalk on paper, 7½ x 5¾ in. (19.3 x 14.5 cm). Dulwich College, London

110. *Female Figure Leaning on Column*, Dulwich College Album MX XV, fol. 21r, black chalk on paper, 11⅞ x 6½ in. (19.3 x 14.5 cm). Dulwich College, London

"PL" stamp, in readiness for their dispersal at auction. Significantly, a couple of drawings in the album were after works which now bear the "PL" stamp, including Raphael's *Mother and Child* (figs. 112 and 113). Other drawings in the album may also have been copies of other works in his collection, perhaps those he sold on before the posthumous "PL" stamping took place.[37]

That Lely saw his collection as having pedagogic as well as connoisseurial and commercial value seems clear. He himself learnt from its contents—a number of sixteenth-century Italian drawings in the collection were a clear source for his own full-length female portraits of the 1670s, which gives his Restoration sitters an earlier aesthetic of grace and beauty.[38] Similarly, his collection of finished chalk portrait drawings by Federico Zuccaro may have prompted him to experiment with his own finished black, white, and red chalk drawings, which are quite unrelated to his larger-scale painted portraits.[39] Offsets from the Zuccaro portraits suggest that these were also copied in Lely's studio. Furthermore, according to Roger North, a drawing from the collection—of a naked woman and a cupid—directly inspired a painting of the same subject by fellow Dutch artist and friend Dirk Freres, which hung as a chimneypiece in Lely's main middle room.[40] In addition to making his own collection available for copying, Lely also borrowed Italian drawings from the Royal Collection for his assistants to copy.[41]

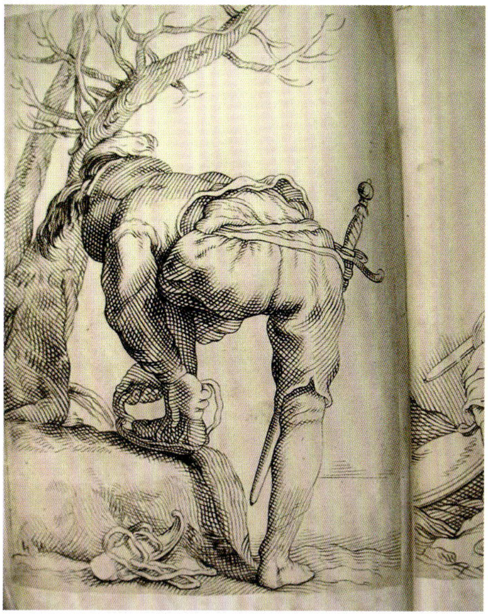

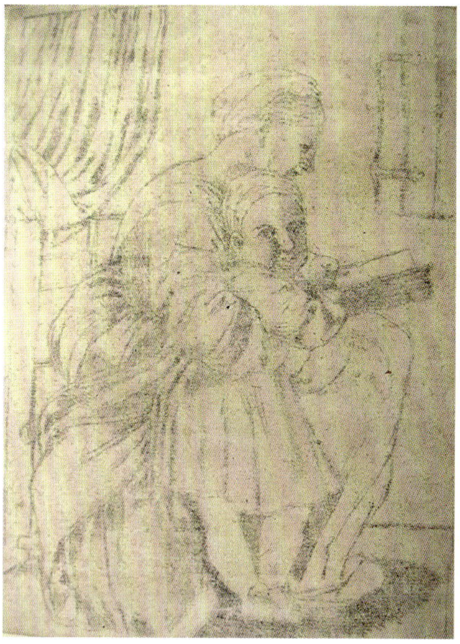

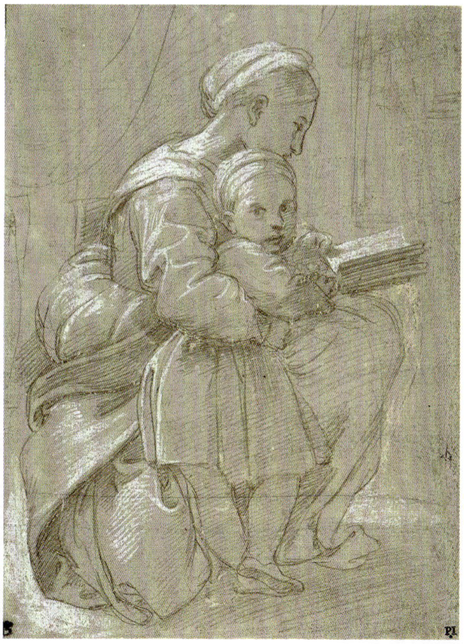

111. *Bending Mercenary Figure Tying Shoe*, Dulwich College Album MX XV, fol. 24v, black ink on paper, 10 x 7 in. (25.5 x 18 cm). Dulwich College, London

112. *Mother and Child*, Dulwich College Album Mx XV, fol. 28v, black chalk on paper, 7½ x 6⅛ in. (19.3 x 15.5 cm). Dulwich College, London

113. Raphael, *Mother and Child*, metal-point with white heightening, 7.5 x 5.5 in. (19 x 14 cm). Trustees of the Chatsworth Settlement

THE ALBUM, THE ACADEMY, AND DRAWING PRACTICE IN LATER SEVENTEENTH-CENTURY LONDON

If, then, the album is a product of a drawing school run by Lely—as seems overwhelmingly likely—what does it tell us about drawing practice in later seventeenth-century London? Though no other artist in Britain had the expertise, experience, or resources to have organized an academy-style drawing school, Lely's enterprise was undoubtedly helped by a growing contemporary interest in drawing. This interest built upon the earlier seventeenth-century writings on the subject by Henry Peacham and upon the accomplished figurative drawings of earlier artists such as Isaac Oliver and Inigo Jones. The proliferation of English art treatises from the mid-seventeenth century—for example, William Sanderson's *Graphice* (1658), Alexander Browne's *The Whole Art of Drawing, Painting, Limning and Etching* (1660), and William Salmon's *Polygraphice* (1672)—also reflects the growing preoccupation with the practice of drawing among both amateurs (the conventional audience for many of these publications) and professional artists.[42] The drawings of experienced professional practitioners such as John Greenhill and Isaac Fuller prove their skill and commitment as draughtsmen, with Fuller's interest actively demonstrated through his *Un Libro da designiare* of 1654, the first English master-model book to be produced.[43] Fuller, whom Buckeridge considered had a "Great genius for Drawing",[44] was considered a sufficient rival to George Freeman to merit a drawing competition arranged by the latter's brother, the collector Colonel Freeman, although the challenge, to draw a figure, was never taken up.[45] Meanwhile, Robert Hooke's experimental drawings for the Royal Society reflect his own considerable ability to use drawing as a way of recording new scientific research.[46] As a young man, he honed his skills as a draughtsman by copying paintings before spending a brief period in the late 1640s working in Lely's studio.[47] He kept in touch with Lely until the latter's death, recording in tantalizingly brief detail a visit to Lely's studio on 27 December 1675 when they discussed "of helping the sight and of picture box" and "drank rare but heady wine".[48] Finally, it is worth stressing the extent to which Lely himself was regarded as a draughtsman by his contemporaries. Hooke supposedly wanted to study with him specifically because of his interest and proficiency in drawing.

We have no idea what happened to the academy after Lely's death in 1680. From Gandy's manuscript we know that some form of drawing school reconvened in the early 1690s, though probably not in Lely's former studio. However, a comment by Gandy about the jeweller and artist Michael Rosse suggests that Lely's influence indeed lived on: when drawing "after a good homely maid", Rosse took "a Choice or positure of one of Sr Peter Lillys Heads in Crayons". However, as

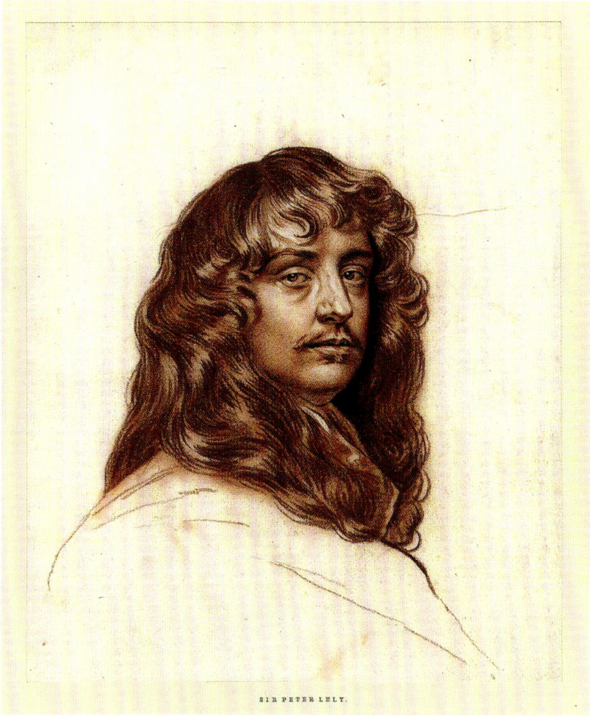

114. Charles Beale after Sir Peter Lely (formerly attributed to Mary Beale), *Head of Peter Lely after Self-Portrait*, 1632–1726, drawing, 8¼ x 6⅞ in. (20.8 x 17.5 cm). British Museum, London

Gandy explains, because Rosse had "drawn so long after Lillys, Handsome Genteel drawings that it was more like Lillys than the Homely Maid".[49] If the character of Lely's academy remains somewhat elusive and enigmatic, so too does that of the album. However, though it is unique in many ways, it can be suggestively compared with a sketchbook kept by Charles Beale the younger, which, though once packed with drawings, has subsequently been dismembered. Beale was old enough to have drawn in the academy in the later 1670s; equally he could have made his studies in his mother's studio, copying works in his parents' collection or borrowed from Lely. There are copies after works in Lely's possession, for example the head of the young boy in Van Dyck's *The Savage Sisters*,[50] as well as copies after portraits by Lely himself, including the head from the self-portrait owned by his parents (fig. 114). Beale also produced copies after small sculptures by François Duquesnoy; copies after casts of hands; a copy after a François Perrier print; and a number of head studies from life of friends and servants.[51] Beale was a competent draughtsman, but although his tightly controlled red chalk drawings display remarkable care and application, they show no interest in experimenting with different graphic techniques, media, or *maniera*, in contrast to the artists whose drawings fill the Dulwich album. As such, Beale's works follow a different agenda for drawing than that suggested not only by the album, but by certain contemporary writers. John Evelyn in his *Sculptura*, for example, advised the young draughtsman learning to engrave that he should aim not so much to make an exact copy of a given work, but to understand its essence: he should proceed "with a certain free and judicious negligence, rather aiming at the ORIGINAL than paining of yourself with overmuch exactness".[52] Evelyn argued that drawing in different media and in a variety of ways would result in greater confidence and competence: "the first principal manner of Drawing is that with the PEN, the next with CRAYON, whither black, white, red or any of the intermediate colours, upon paper either white or coloured."[53] In doing this the young artist would gain knowledge of how different types of handling—of light rapid sketches, a defined pen and ink contour or the soft scumbling of black chalk—could achieve quite different physical and material results. The artists of the Dulwich album seem to have followed such teachings, as opposed to young Beale, who was only concerned with *recording*, albeit very beautifully, the objects he was copying.

CONCLUSION

Alongside his pedagogic commitment, issues of status and legacy must have helped motivate Lely to set up his academy. He was always conscious of his artistic standing, as is clear from the ways in which he presented himself in his self-portraits. The picture owned by the Beales provoked Pepys's acerbic remark that Lely was "a mighty proud man he is, and full of state."[54] A later self-portrait with his friend the architect Hugh May, contrasts Lely's commanding presence with May's more subservient seated pose. The kinds of deference to which Lely clearly felt himself due were certainly expressed within the Beales' notebooks, which show him comfortable in the quasi-paternal role of an experienced and highly respected mentor. Their view of the King's Painter may be partial and one-sided, but it does help us to see him within the context of his Covent Garden studio and the neighbouring artists' community, and not simply within the privileged world of his fashionable and influential sitters.

Lely lived and worked in Covent Garden for almost thirty years, having first moved into the Great Piazza, one of the area's most desirable addresses, in 1651.[55] Many of his neighbours at various times over this period were his fellow artists; by the mid-seventeenth century, Covent Garden and its surrounding streets had become the main artists' quarter in London. Many of these artists became friends or professional contacts, and although Lely could sometimes be difficult in his behaviour—as, for example, when he testily left London to stay in one of his "country" residences at Kew when temporarily threatened by Henri Gascar's success at court—he does for the most part seem to have integrated well with both

English and fellow Netherlandish artists. Tellingly, he never provoked the customary resentment normally directed at "alien" painters. The presence of an artists' community in Covent Garden indicates how socially diverse the area had become, with wealthy residents living alongside a variety of professional and social groups. The fourth Earl of Bedford's original intention in developing Covent Garden had been to create an exclusive residential area, which the Great Piazza mostly remained.[56] But by the 1670s many of the houses in the surrounding streets were subdivided into multiple tenancies, with a socially mixed occupancy that changed quite frequently. However, through its favourable geographical position, approximately halfway between the court and the City and convenient for the Inns of Court, Covent Garden continued to attract many country gentry and titled landowners as a fashionable area to rent property during the winter months. Some of Lely's neighbours became his sitters, and familial ties and social networks, often replicating those in the country, further extended his affluent clientele.[57]

Rather like Covent Garden itself, Lely's studio became a space where different social worlds interconnected, where members of the court, city professionals, and country gentry would attend sittings for their portraits, select suitable poses, browse through the studio stock of famous sitters, and admire or buy from his collection. It provided an environment where sitters and visitors to the studio could exchange news and gossip, where assistants could share experience and skills, and where a collective community of artists could finally come together to receive an important element of Continental academic training—instruction in drawing. In providing this unique opportunity in London, Lely not only assured his legacy; he also elevated the status of drawing and its practical application, prepared the ground for the more formal artists' academies of the early eighteenth century, and made a wider contribution to the seventeenth-century London art world than has previously been acknowledged. In so doing, he is also revealed as having a more complex artistic identity than that suggested by his traditional reputation as the fashionable face-painter of a cynical Restoration court.

1. As is well known, numerous details of the Beales' personal and professional life, including the daily activities in Mary's studio, and Charles Beale's business as a colourman selling artists's pigments, were meticulously recorded by Charles Beale in over thirty notebooks. Only two have survived; that for 1677, now in the Bodleian Library, Oxford, and for 1681 in the National Portrait Gallery, London, although extracts from five other notebooks for 1661, 1671, 1672, 1674, and 1676, are recorded by Vertue.
2. Katharine Gibson, "'Best Belov'd of Kings': The Iconography of Charles II", 3 vols. (unpublished PhD thesis, Courtauld Institute of Art, Univ. of London, 1997), 1: 116, 100 (citing PRO LC3/24).
3. See Jacob Simon's excellent *British Artists' Suppliers, 1650–1950*, http://www.npg.org.uk/research/programmes/artists-their-materials-and-suppliers.php and his *'Three-quarters, kit-cats and half-lengths': British Painters and their Canvas Sizes, 1625–1850*, http://www.npg.org.uk/research/programmes/artists-their-materials-and-suppliers/three-quarters-kit-cats-and-half-lengths-british-portrait-painters-and-their-canvas-sizes-1625-1850.php. Lely's self-portrait and his portraits of Mary and Charles Beale are all listed in the Beale inventory as HL, which was the term given to what we today would describe as three-quarter length (50 by 40 inches, 127 x 102 cm).
4. Catharine MacLeod and Julia Marciari Alexander, eds., *Painted Ladies: Women at the Court of Charles II* (New Haven and London: National Portrait Gallery and Yale Univ. Press, 2001), MacLeod and Alexander, "The 'Windsor Beauties' and the Beauties Series in Restoration England", in *Politics, Transgression, and Representation at the Court of Charles II*, ed. Alexander and MacLeod (New Haven and London: Yale Univ. Press, 2007), 81–120.
5. In the Oct.–Nov. 1637 Minutes of the Haarlem Guild, Lely was listed as a pupil of De Grebber.
6. Painter-Stainers' Court Minute Book, 1649–1723, Guildhall Library MS 5667/2, fol. 221.
7. Painter-Stainers' Court Minute Book, 1649–1723, Guildhall Library MS 5667/2, fol. 22r, 18 Nov. 1652.
8. For an excellent discussion of Lely's studio practice, see Catharine MacLeod, "'Good, but not like': Peter Lely, Portrait Practice and the Creation of a Court Look", in *Painted Ladies*, ed. MacLeod and Alexander, 50–61.
9. Tillotson is probably the version at Elton Hall, and Stillingfleet is only known through a Blooteling mezzotint. See George Vertue, "The Note-books of George Vertue IV", *Walpole Society* 24 (1936): 169–70, and Tabitha Barber with Mary Bustin, *Mary Beale: Portrait of a Seventeenth-century Painter, her Family and her Studio* (London: Geffrye Museum, 1999), 67. They also commissioned another portrait of a relative, Brooke Bridges, untraced, and of their younger son Charles, which was unfinished at Lely's death, purchased by the Beales at Lely's posthumous studio sale in 1681, and completed by Mary Beale. All were closely observed as they were painted and paid for partly in pigments, mainly parcels of ultramarine and red lakes, with delivery of the pigments stretching over a number of years. For a discussion of Charles Beale as a colourman, see Mary Bustin, "Experimental Secrets and Extraordinary Colours", in Barber and Bustin, *Mary Beale*, 43–59.
10. Vertue, "Note-books IV", 169.
11. William Gandy, "Notes on Painting" (1673–1699), transcribed in "The Memorandum Book of Ozias Humphrey", British Library (hereafter BL) Add MS 22,950, and transcribed in parts in Mansfield Kirby Talley, *Portrait Painting in England: Studies in the Technical Literature before 1700* (London: Paul Mellon Centre for Studies in British Art, 1981), chap. 17.
12. Talley, *Portrait Painting in England.*
13. See I. Bignamini, "George Vertue, Art Historian and Art Institutions in London, 1689–1768: A Study of Clubs and Academies", *Walpole Society* 54 (1988): 61; Bignamini and Martin Postle, *The Artist's Model: Its Role in British Art from Lely to Etty* (Nottingham Univ. Art Gallery, 1991), 8; and Lindsay Stainton, "A Seventeenth-century Album", in *Mr Cartwright's Pictures: A Seventeenth-century Collection*, ed. G. Waterfield and others (London: Dulwich Picture Gallery, 1987), 14–15.
14. BL Add MS 22,950, fol. 24v, cited in Talley, *Portrait Painting in England*, 316. Talley identified "Mr F." in the manuscript as the young artist William Fever.
15. John Evelyn, *Sculptura; or, The History and Art of Chalcography*, 2nd ed. (London, 1769), 103.
16. Pieter van Thiel, "Cornelis Cornelisz van Haarlem as a Draughtsman", *Master Drawings* 3, no. 2 (Summer 1965): 128, citing Karel van Mander, *Het Schilder-Boeck, Nederlandtsche Schilders* (1604), fol. 292v.

17. Diana Dethloff, "Reception and Rejection: Lely's Subject Pictures in an 'un-understanding land'", in *Peter Lely: A Lyrical Vision*, ed. Caroline Campbell (London: Courtauld Gallery, 2012), 58.
18. Painter-Stainers' Court Minute Book, 1649–1723, Guildhall Library MS 5667/2, fol. 46r.
19. Bainbrigg Buckeridge, "An Essay towards an English-School of Painters", in R. de Piles, *The Art of Painting and the Lives of the Painters* (London, 1706), 449.
20. From a certificate by Lely endorsing Freeman's work in Calendar of State Papers, Car II. 279, n. 191, 23 Sept. 1670.
21. BL Sloane MS 2717 fol. 246, 18 Nov. 1663.
22. BL Sloane MS 2717 fol. 263, 6 Feb. 1663/64.
23. Talley, *Portrait Painting in England*, 316, citing BL Add MS 22,950, fol. 18r.
24. Talley, *Portrait Painting in England*, 316 citing BL Add MS 22,950, fol. 18r.
25. For an excellent overview of Lely as a draughtsman, see Lindsay Stainton, "Drawing in Late Stuart England", in *Drawing in England from Hilliard to Hogarth*, ed. Stainton and Christopher White (London: British Museum Press, 1987), 30–32. Numerous hand studies and a few figure and drapery studies by Lely were included in the Michael Rosse sale, 26 April 1723, advertised in the *Daily Courant*, 28 March 1723. Michael Rosse was a jeweller and the son-in-law to the artist Richard Gibson, a close friend of Lely.
26. Vertue, "Note-books IV", 172.
27. He also demonstrated his preferred method of painting drapery and adapted and abbreviated the way he painted fabric to help speed up studio production. See MacLeod, "Good, but not like", 60.
28 R. Latham and W. Matthews, eds., *The Diary of Samuel Pepys*, vol. 8, *1667* (London: HarperCollins, 1995), 177, E. S. De Beer, ed., *The Diary of John Evelyn*, 6 vols. (Oxford Univ. Press, 1955), 3: 479.
29. Lely in 1653, with two fellow Netherlandish artists George Geldorp and Balthazar Gerbier, expressed interest in producing a series of decorative schemes for Parliament, which came to nothing. BL Miscellaneous Historical papers, Stowe MS 184, fol. 283.
30. I am grateful to Anna Keay for this information. See also her *The Magnificent Monarch: Charles II and the Ceremonies of Power* (London: Continuum, 2008).
31. Pepys visited the Swedish Resident in London, Baron Leijonbergh, who lived in "one of the great houses" in the Great Piazza, on 21 January 1666/67. See Pepys, *Diary*, 8: 128–29. Given the sociability of the Piazza it is likely Leijonbergh knew or met Lely.
32. Stainton, "A Seventeenth-century Album", suggested that the album may have belonged to and been assembled by John Greenhill.
33. I am grateful to Hugo Chapman and Martin Clayton for helping me identify some of the Italian sources.
34. At some point, Lely gave his *Crouching Venus* to Charles II (now on long-term loan to the British Museum, London). Vertue records it as being saved from the Whitehall Palace fire in 1698; Vertue, "Note-books IV", 77. The drawings in the album are adopting a generic pose of this type, not the specific one in Lely's statue.
35. See also M. Hunter, *Wicked Intelligence: Visual Art and the Science of Experiment in Restoration London* (Univ. of Chicago Press, 2013), 46.
36. BL Add MS 16.174, fol. 39r, bought by Mr Gibson (i.e. William Gibson the miniature painter and artist-dealer friend of Lely) and others.
37. See Diana Dethloff, "Sir Peter Lely's Collection of Prints and Drawings", in *Collecting Prints and Drawings in Europe, c.1500–1750*, ed. Christopher Baker, Caroline Elam, and Genevieve Warwick (Farnham: Ashgate, 2003), 123–41.
38. See Diana Dethloff, "Portraiture and Concepts of Beauty in Restoration Painting", in *Painted Ladies*, ed. Macleod and Marciari, 24–35.
39. See C. Eisler, "Apparatus and Grandeur: Five Portrait Drawings from Clarendon's 'History'", *Master Drawings* 6, no. 2 (Summer 1968): 148–55, 216–18 for a discussion of Lely's technique and the particular recipe for his chalk crayons.
40. BL Add MS 32,507, fols. 36–37.

41. Huygens claimed Lely's assistants returned their copies rather than the originals to the Royal Collection. See "Journal van Constantin Huygens den Zoon", in *Werken van het Historish Genootschap in Utrecht Nieuwe Reeks* 25 (1877): 326. Martin Clayton, in an email correspondence, made the excellent and very convincing suggestion that Lely's assistants made offsets from the originals, which led Huygens to believe they had retained the originals and returned copies made by his assistants.
42. For excellent discussions of English art treatises, earlier courtesy manuals, and the master-model book tradition, see K. Sloan, "*A Noble Art": Amateur Artists and Drawing Masters, c.1600–1800* (London: British Museum Press, 2001), and A. Bermingham, "Drawing and the Courtly Art of Illusion", in Bermingham, *Learning to Draw: Studies in the Cultural History of a Polite and Useful Art* (New Haven and London: Yale Univ. Press, 2000), 3–73. See also Talley, *Portrait Painting in England.*
43. No copy was known until the British Museum purchased one in 1973. See Antony Griffiths, *The Print in Stuart Britain, 1603–1689* (London: British Museum Press, 1998), 173–74.
44. Buckeridge, "Essay towards an English-School of Painters", 420.
45. George Vertue, "The Note-books of George Vertue II", *Walpole Society* 20 (1932): 147–48.
46. For Hooke as a draughtsman, see Hunter, *Wicked Intelligence*, especially chaps. 1 and 2. As a figurative draughtsman, see M. Hunter, "Hooke's Figurations: A Figural Drawing Attributed to Robert Hooke", *Notes & Records of the Royal Society of London* 64, no. 3 (2010): 251–60.
47. Oliver Lawson Dick, ed., *Aubrey's Brief Lives* (London: Secker and Warburg, 1949), 164.
48. Henry Robinson, ed., *The Diary of Robert Hooke* (London: Taylor and Francis, 1935), 204.
49. Talley, *Portrait Painting in England*, 315, citing BL Add MS 22,950, fol. 38r.
50. There is also a drawing of a headless figure after a cast of Giambologna's *Astronomy* (BM Gg.5.38).
51. Young Beale also copied drawings his father had borrowed from the Royal Collection "for his Sonnes to practice by". See "Journal van Constantin Huygens den Zoon", 326.
52. Evelyn, *Sculptura*, 99.
53. Evelyn, *Sculptura*, 99.
54. *Diary of Samuel Pepys*, 8: 129, 25 March 1667.
55. Lely lodged with fellow Netherlandish artist Tobias Flushier. They paid rates jointly in 1651 and 1657. From 1652–6 Flushier was the sole rate payer (in 1656 Lely made his only return trip to his native Holland) and also in 1658–61. From 1662 Lely was the only rate payer in the house. Oliver Millar, *Sir Peter Lely, 1618–80* (London: National Portrait Gallery, 1978), 28, citing Rate Books for the Westminster area, Westminster Public Library.
56. R. M. Smuts, "The Court and its Neighbourhood: Royal Policy and Urban Growth in the Early Stuart West End", *Journal of British Studies* 30, no. 2 (1991): 136–45.
57. S. Whyman, *Sociability and Power in Late Stuart England: The Cultural Worlds of the Verneys, 1660–1720* (Oxford Univ. Press, 1999), 68.

"This Ingenious young Gent and excellent artist": William Lodge (1649–1689) and the York Virtuosi

Helen Pierce

In 1727, the antiquarian George Vertue passed through the city of York on a northern tour with his patron, the Earl of Oxford. At the King's Manor, they called upon the printmaker and potter Francis Place, by then a man of eighty, with whom Vertue had already corresponded regarding information about Place's early mentor, Wenceslaus Hollar. Although Vertue's stay in York was brief, his thoughts and subsequently his notebooks turned upon a number of occasions to the elderly artist and to the intellectual circle with which Place had been associated in earlier decades:

> There were then resideing at York a set of most Ingenious Virtuosos. Martin Lister, John Lambert Esqr, Tho. Kirk Esqr, Mr William Lodge & Mr Francis Place. these frequently met at the house of Mr Henry Gyles ye famous glass painter.[1]

Active between the 1670s and 1720s, this collection of men, largely of independent financial means, included a topographer and antiquarian, a mathematician, several amateur artists, and a member of the Royal Society. Regularly corresponding with each other, and meeting in the city of York on social and intellectual terms, they engaged in activities relating to both the arts and sciences, and the intersections between them, reflecting what Kim Sloan has termed "the omnivorous interests (of which drawing was just one of many) and collecting activities" of the seventeenth-century virtuosi.[2] By the time of George Vertue's visit to York, however, only Place remained in the city, and Vertue's remarks represent a fading awareness of the activities of these once "most Ingenious Virtuosos".[3]

Letters exchanged between members of the Virtuosi date from the early 1670s onwards, and it has been conjectured that their meetings in York began at the house of the glass-painter Henry Gyles on Micklegate from around 1676, following the death of Gyles's father, Edmund, a glazier.[4] Gyles was an exception amongst the Virtuosi in that he was an artisan rather than an independently wealthy gentleman; correspondence between Gyles, commonly referred to as "Honest Harry", and his peers, however, suggests a convivial circle of friends sharing mutual interests, rather than one that felt the need to navigate the intricacies of social hierarchies. That they conceived of themselves as a distinct group of individuals, with particular artistic and intellectual interests, is hinted at not only in Vertue's use of the term "virtuosi"; in a letter to Gyles of 1683, John Lambert significantly predates Vertue as he writes of his warm regard for "ye Virtuosoes".[5]

The word "virtuoso" emerged in English usage in the first decades of the seventeenth century, at this early stage assuming something of a contested status. In George Chapman's tragedy *The Revenge of Bussy D'Ambois*, published in 1613, virtuosi are described as "the poorest creatures", spinning flimsy arguments like spiders building webs; yet Henry Peacham's contrary definition in the third edition of *The Compleat Gentleman* of 1634, a courtesy book encouraging its readers to model themselves on aristocratic courtiers, reveals admiration for the knowledgeable collector of antique statues and coins: "Such as are skilled in them, are by the *Italians* tearmed *Virtuosi*."[6] Towards the middle of the century, the interests of the aspiring English virtuoso were acknowledged as varied, characterized by the accumulation of knowledge across the arts and sciences by leisured, independently wealthy individuals. Noted virtuosi included John Evelyn and Prince Rupert, their own activities being supported and encouraged through the establishment of the Royal Society in Restoration London, granted its royal status in 1662 as an institution "for the promoting of the knowledge of natural things, and useful Arts by Experiments".[7] This practical aspect to the virtuoso's pursuits is underlined by the surfeit of publications in English relating to the technical and instructive rather than theoretical aspects of the study of fine art: from Peacham's *The Art of Drawing with the Pen* of 1607, to Evelyn's printmaking manual, *Sculptura*, of 1662.[8]

As this essay reveals, the artistic activities of certain members of the York Virtuosi, who embarked on sketching tours and engaged in topographical and scientific illustration, placed great emphasis on travel, the acquisition of knowledge, and the recording and categorizing of that knowledge in visual terms. However, these activities were conducted outside of the concerns of European academic art theory, with its hierarchical ordering of genres. Such theory was largely redundant in Restoration England; as Carol Gibson-Wood has noted, it was the tendency of the virtuoso "to stress the importance of pictures for their contributions to empirical, not humanistic, knowledge".[9] Keeping this perspective in mind, this essay will focus upon a less familiar member of the York Virtuosi, the amateur printmaker and gentleman connoisseur William Lodge (1649–1689). Described by Vertue in familiar terms as "this Ingenious young Gent and excellent artist", Lodge was associated, during his relatively short lifetime, with a number of projects which highlight the developing role played by the visual arts in the polite recreations and self-improvement of an emerging urban elite.[10]

William Lodge was born in Leeds on 4 July 1649 into an established and successful family of cloth merchants. Documentary information relating to Lodge's early life is limited, and heavily dependent on notes made by Vertue, in turn based on the brief "Memoirs of Mr William Lodge" sketched by Lodge's relation by marriage, the Leeds antiquarian Ralph Thoresby.[11] Following schooling in Leeds, Lodge was admitted to Jesus College, Cambridge, in 1666; he then proceeded to London to study at Lincoln's Inn Fields. Any pursuit of the law as a serious career was abandoned, however, when the opportunity arose in 1669 to join the retinue of Thomas Belasyse, Viscount Fauconberg, as Belasyse took up the position of ambassador-extraordinary to Venice. Lodge remained in Italy for at least a year longer than his employer and patron, and upon his return to the north of England, by the beginning of 1673, he assumed the role of a leisured gentleman. An independent income of £300 per year had come into Lodge's possession by his early twenties, marking the beginning of a life relatively unburdened by mundane responsibilities. According to one character study noted down by Vertue, "ye ingenious Mr Lodge . . . wh[e]n he was fateagu'd with painting diverted himself with singing. Another of his diversions was Fishing."[12]

Lodge's fishing expeditions were frequently conducted in the company of Francis Place, a "sworn brother" to William Lodge since the mid-1670s when the pair are recorded as visiting London together. Place was an amateur artist of independent means who had experienced early employment as a clerk in the Pipe Office at London's Gray's Inn.[13] A native of Dinsdale in County Durham, Place was active as an artist for over fifty years, with his presence in the Pipe Office in his late teens coinciding with a friendship with, and informal instruction from, Wenceslaus Hollar. According to Place's own words, "Mr Hollar . . . was a person I was intimately acquainted withal, but never his disciple nor anybody's else, which was my misfortune."[14] Place's lack of formal training did not compromise his interests and ambitions in printmaking, however. As well as being a prolific etcher, a skill presumably originating from his friendship with Hollar, he was a notably early English exponent of the mezzotint. At some point between 1666 and 1668, the London print-seller John Overton published a tavern scene after Adriaen Brouwer in this new medium, bearing the address of his premises then in Little Britain, and giving Place's name as its creator (fig. 115). At this time, mezzotint was still a novel and experimental medium in British printmaking. On 13 March 1661 John Evelyn had recorded in his diary that "This after noone his hig[h]nesse Prince Rupert shewed me with his owne hands the new way of Graving call'd Mezzo Tinto"; throughout the 1660s, knowledge of its methods remained largely reserved

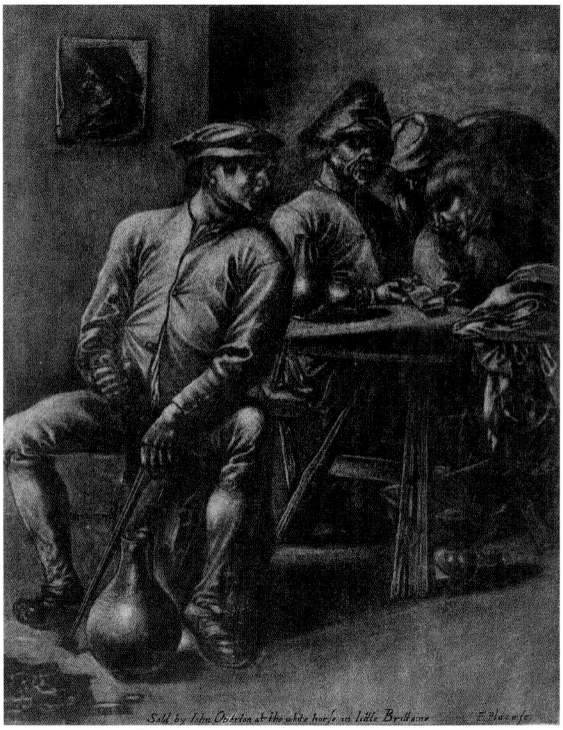

115. Francis Place, *Tavern Scene After Brouwer*, ca. 1666–8, mezzotint, 8⅝ x 6⅞ in. (22 x 17.6 cm). British Museum, London

for a few favoured gentlemen and connoisseurs in Evelyn's mould, with interests aligned to the emerging Royal Society.[15] The appearance of Francis Place's name on a very early British example of this "new way of Graving" suggests a keenness and ability on the part of this young gentleman from Dinsdale to circulate among a group of London virtuosi, perhaps gaining the confidence of Evelyn, or even Prince Rupert, through his association with Hollar. Two later mezzotint portraits by Place, of Henry Gyles and of William Lodge, were undertaken at York during the 1670s, and attest to both practicality and informality. Gyles's likeness (fig. 116) was reproduced as a trade card for his glass-painting business, while the half-length of Lodge in his fur hat appears to be an artistic exercise in the representation of material and texture (fig. 117).

William Lodge's friendship with Francis Place, and Place's links with Hollar, may well have provided the social means through which Lodge would go on to make important contacts within the London print trade, including the publisher John Ogilby and the Yorkshire-born print-seller Pierce Tempest; Place also served, in a more practical sense, as a friend and travelling companion to Lodge on the many sketching tours and fishing trips which took up much of their time during

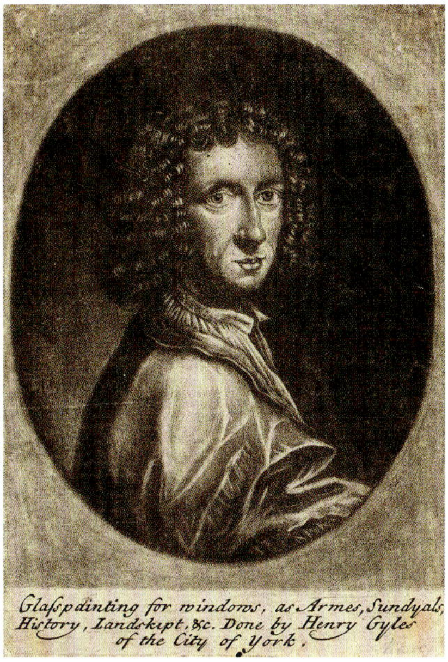

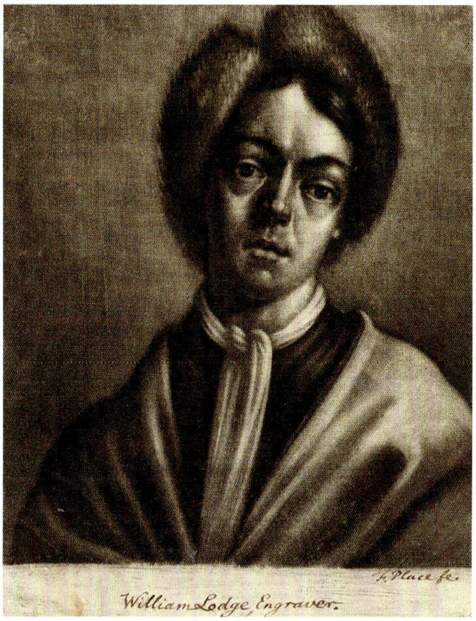

116. Francis Place, *Trade Card for Henry Gyles*, 1670s, mezzotint, 4⅝ x 3¼ in. (11.6 x 8.2 cm). British Museum, London

117. Francis Place, *William Lodge*, 1670s, mezzotint, 6⅛ x 4⅞ in. (15.5 x 12.3 cm). British Museum, London

the 1670s and 1680s. On one such occasion in 1678, journeying through Cheshire and North Wales during a period of public unease occasioned by the discovery of a "Popish Plot" to assassinate the king, Place and Lodge were reportedly arrested following suspicions that these travelling strangers were Jesuit spies.[16]

William Lodge's own practical interest in art appears to have begun following his admission to Jesus College, Cambridge, in 1666. In a letter written to his mother in November of the following year, he explains that he "make[s] painting onely a recreation an hour after dinner or so, no hindrance is it but rather a furtherance to things of greater concernement". Lodge does appear concerned, however, that his painting techniques are not as successful as they could be, particularly when it came to priming his canvas before the application of pigments. As his letter continues: "I shall not scruple to send you downe the best efforts of my limning. If you can but secure me a few directions from Cuz Lambert and enclose them in the next letter you send. I attempted the making a picture the last week: which looks well on the foreside but behind, the colours are sunk through wherefore the cheife directions I desire is onely to know how to order my cloth before I lay on colours."[17]

Family ties between Lodge and "Cuz" John Lambert, another amateur artist and future member of the York Virtuosi (an "exact limner" in the words of Ralph Thoresby[18]) appear to have provided the young Lodge with an important opportunity for social and cultural advancement as well as artistic instruction. Lambert was the son of the Yorkshire-born parliamentarian commander John Lambert, himself the purchaser of "divers raere pictures" from the sale of the Royal Collection during the 1650s, and employer of the Dutch artist John Baptist Gaspars in the role of both practical tutor and picture dealer.[19] The Lamberts were associated through both marriage and political allegiances with a number of important northern gentry families, including the Fairfaxes and the Belasyses.[20] In 1667 Viscount Fauconberg was one of several nobles to successfully petition Charles II for better treatment for the elder Lambert, who had been imprisoned since the Restoration on Guernsey. Despite being married to Mary, one of the daughters of Oliver Cromwell, Fauconberg was a well-regarded and prominent Yorkshire noble, serving the Crown since 1660 as Lord Lieutenant of the North Riding with his family seat at Newbrugh Priory, some twenty miles north of York. William Lodge's familial links to the Lamberts may have provided the opportunity for the twenty-year-old amateur artist to secure a place within Fauconberg's entourage following his Venetian appointment.

Fauconberg's stay in Venice was relatively brief, extending to only four months in the city itself. Quite what William Lodge's role was within the significant ambassadorial party is unclear. According to an account of the embassy published in Amsterdam in 1671, "twenty gentlemen from the finest families of the kingdom, six pages, twenty four footmen, and a great number of attendants" accompanied the Viscount during his tour.[21] Beyond his official duties, one of the ambassador's preoccupations was the purchasing of fine art, and the particular pursuit of works by masters of the Venetian Renaissance, including Titian, Tintoretto, Giorgione, and the Bassano family. An inventory drawn up by Fauconberg in 1684 of artworks housed at his residence near London, Sutton Court, suggests an impossibly stellar list of works by Leonardo, Dürer, Rembrandt, and Caravaggio alongside his Venetian purchases; it is likely that many, if not the majority of the works in this collection were part of the international trade in copies.[22]

The Viscount maintained a keen interest in the visual arts following his Venetian embassy; visiting the Banqueting House at London's Whitehall in May 1689, the diarist Constantijn Huygens noted that while admiring Raphael's tapestry cartoons on display there, "Lord Fauconberg, who is married to Cromwell's daughter, passed us on his way out, but came back in with us, as he is an art lover."[23] Dying without issue in 1700, Fauconberg's will specified that his nephew Henry Belasyse could choose "any one of my best pictures at his own Choice except the great Bassan". This unidentified and now-lost Bassano, which originally hung in the dining room at Sutton Court, had been acquired by the Viscount during the 1680s, in exchange for a painting of the Lord's Supper by the Bassano family, together with an additional payment of £27. Whatever the Viscount's motivations for acquiring and retaining this second "great" Bassano, it is the only work of art specified in Mary Belasyse's will of 1713, having subsequently been displayed "at the upper end of the great room" of her own town house in London's Soho Square, suggesting this painting had some significance to both husband and wife, either in financial or aesthetic terms.[24]

We can only speculate as to whether William Lodge's early essays into painting at Cambridge were the primary reason for his presence in Venice—he may have been taken along as someone with a reputable background and an interest in art who might act informally as an adviser to Fauconberg—or whether the embassy itself provided the catalyst for Lodge's own developing activities as a budding connoisseur. Fauconberg's party also spent time in Florence en route to Venice, where Lodge would have witnessed negotiations for the Viscount's purchase of four bronzes by Giambologna. Further opportunities for connoisseurial study would have been provided by access to the sixty paintings forming the art collection of Sir John Finch, English Resident at Florence, who hosted Fauconberg during his stay.[25]

More tellingly, Lodge did not return to England with the Viscount's ambassadorial entourage in 1670, but remained in Italy for at least another year. A letter from one J. Barker, dated March 1671 and addressed to Lodge care of John Hobson, English consul in Venice, recounts in detail a recent trip taken by Barker and Lodge from Rome to Naples, encountering a medley of ancient and notable ruins as they progressed along the Via Appia.[26] Until now, this letter has not been connected to a series of sketches made by Lodge during his time in Italy, and a number of related etchings later published in London by Pierce Tempest.[27] Executed in pen and ink, these landscape sketches seem largely intended to function as topographical records, rather than as exercises in artistic interpretation, although in one view there is a stylized and fanciful liveliness to the waves which dominate the bay between Formia and Gaeta, and to the ship in the middle ground which appears to dance on the peaks (fig. 118). According to Barker, the pair had broken their travel about halfway along the Via Appia, which had offered them an opportunity for sketching and recording: "to Mola (by ye Sea-side) to dinner: where you saw ye Tombe of M Plancius (who built Lion, in France) on a high hill, above Gaëta . . . ." A further sketch records a similar compositional model, with another ancient ruin set upon a distant peninsula: "As we went from Terracina, you saw Temple Solis, on the Circean Promontory (wch for 3000 yeares, beares its Age well)", noted Barker sagely (fig. 119).

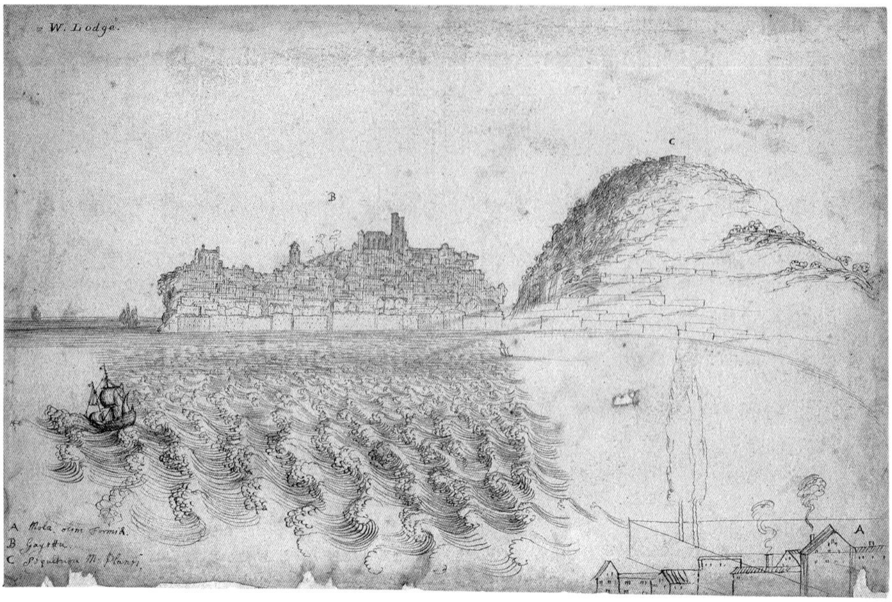

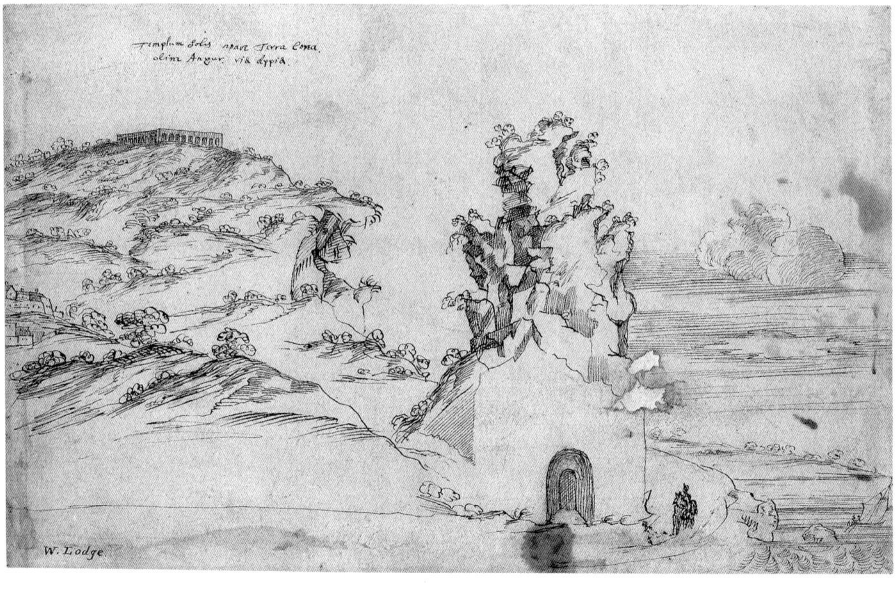

118. William Lodge, *A View of Mola, Gaeta and the Tomb of Munatius Plancus*, ca. 1671, pen and ink. Leeds Public Library

119. William Lodge, *A View of the Circaean Promontory*, ca. 1671, pen and ink. Leeds Public Library

Both of these landscape studies were subsequently revised and developed into small-scale etchings, then published in London by Pierce Tempest as part of *A Book of Divers Prospects Done After the Life* (figs. 120 and 121). Tempest, a fellow Yorkshireman and close acquaintance of both Lodge and Francis Place, set up his print publishing business at premises in The Strand in late 1678, which provides one chronological marker for this publication; Tempest's name, however, only appears on the title page of *A Book of Divers Prospects* from the second state onwards, with the possibility that initial etchings were made by Lodge from his Italian sketches at an earlier point. It is also likely that Lodge produced more sketches and studies than the handful of Italian views which are found in this small collection; Barker mentions their encounter with "the Amphitheatre of old mithurnas as Saturnes temple by ye river . . . Left hand of wch you saw ye old Aquiduct", an etched view of which was subsequently published by Tempest (fig. 122), but for which no preparatory study is known. All of Lodge's etchings relating to his Italian sojourn are notable for the inclusion of several male figures, either on foot or on horseback, admiring the landscape before them. That of the Ponte Nomentano, an ancient bridge spanning the Aniene river just outside Rome (here labelled "Ponte Lamentane"), also features an individual sketching the bridge in the right-hand foreground (fig. 123). These men seem to refer to Lodge and Barker's travels together, and to the first-hand and documentary nature of each etching's content, as well as underlining the polite sociability and gentlemanly conduct associated with the contemplation of the Italian vista and its ancient ruins.

Preserved with Lodge's Italian views are two further signed sketches, both executed in chalk rather than pen and ink, that take the form of nude studies (figs. 124 and 125). The same male figure appears to pose with a rod or narrow staff, and this, together with the manner of shading and shaping, suggests that these are life drawings rather than studies of statues or casts. Here Lodge's approach to his subject is far less assured: although the first sketch is clearly more accomplished than the other, and offers an effective attempt to capture muscle definition and a sense of movement in the model, his landscape studies are comparatively more confident and rhythmical in their execution. Hugh Honour's appraisal is damning: "When he tried figure drawing in a Michelangelesque vein he was very much less successful [than in his landscape sketches.]"[28] Yet the existence of these nude studies, presumably undertaken during Lodge's time in Italy, is suggestive of his exposure to modes of artistic training and learning operating outside the realms of topographic representation.

Correspondence between William Lodge and Martin Lister indicates that Lodge had returned to the north of England by January 1673, and letters exchanged between his circle of friends and acquaintances in York suggest that Lodge's Italian

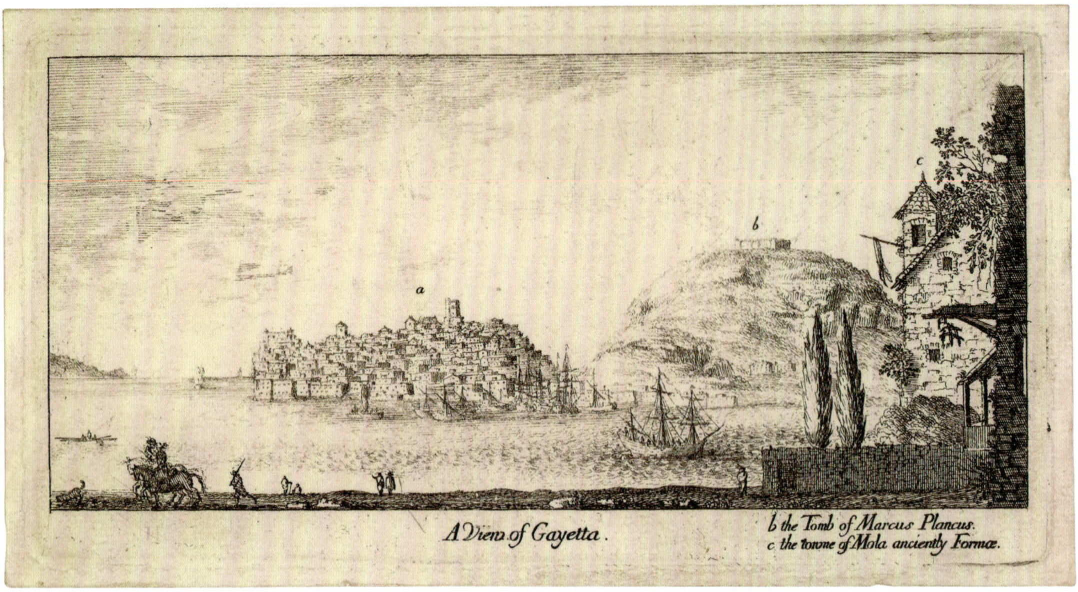

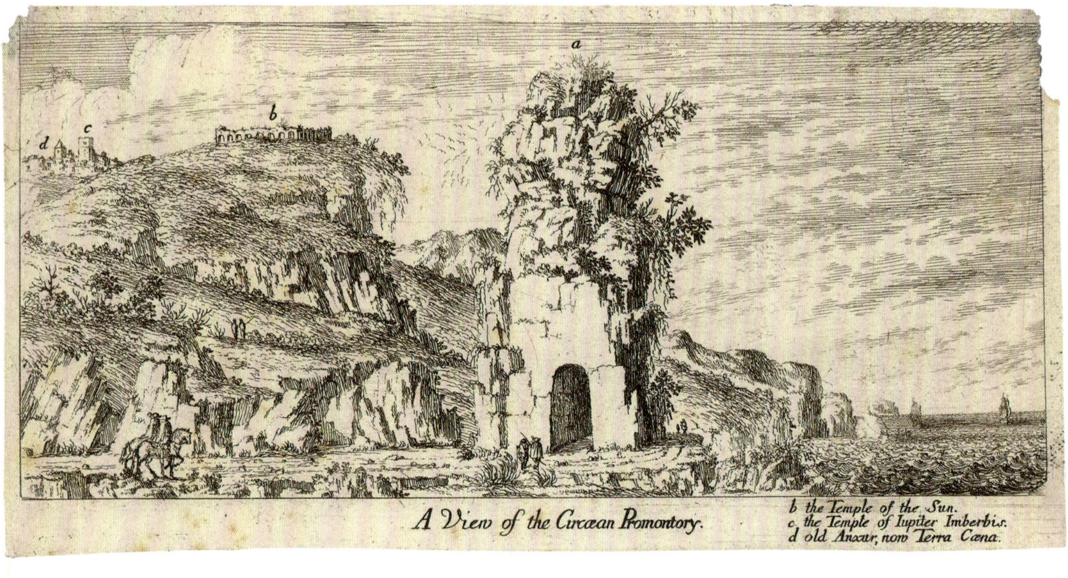

120. William Lodge, *A View of Gayetta*, 1678–90, etching, 3¼ x 6½ in. (8.2 x 16.4 cm). British Museum, London

121. William Lodge, *A View of the Circaean Promontory*, 1670s, etching, 3¼ x 6⅜ in. (8.2 x 16.3 cm). British Museum, London

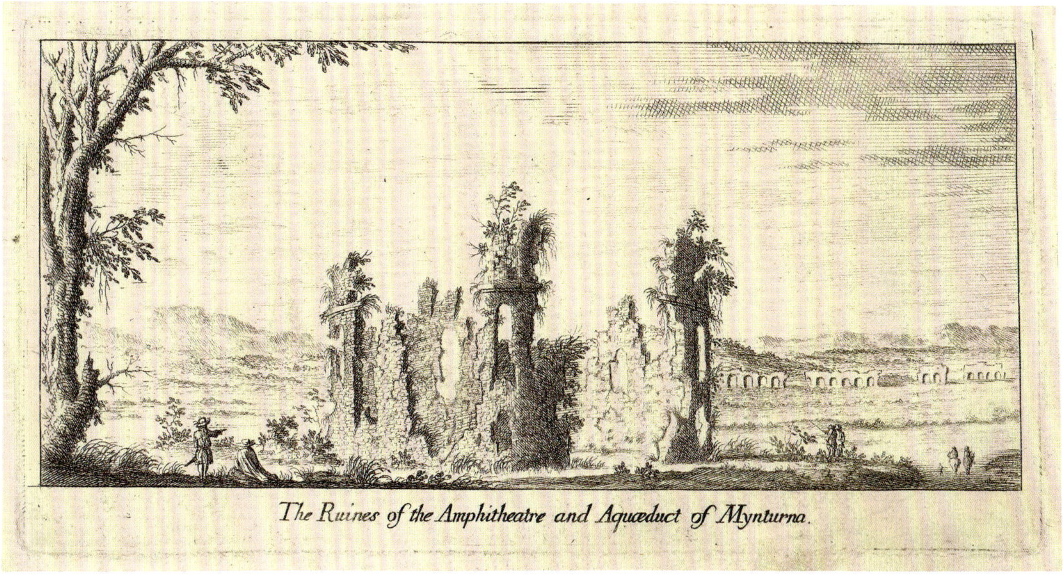

122. William Lodge, *The Ruines of the Amphitheatre and Aquaeduct of Mynturna*, 1678–90, etching, 3¼ x 6½ in. (8.2 x 16.5 cm). British Museum, London

stay had sparked, or further enhanced, his connoisseurial leanings. Writing the following year to Henry Gyles, the mathematician Thomas Kirke confessed:

> I love prints and could wish that I was well with them but circumstances will not suffer me to lye out anything excepting for absolute necessities. You say Mr Lodge will see mee as soone as he comes to towne. I shall be glad to see him and I will goe along with him . . . to see him chuse good things that I may better my judgement that way by him.[29]

Lodge's own particular interests had taken on something of an "omnivorous" tone, and between 1673 and 1675 he was engaged in the production of illustrations for papers on natural history written by Lister, then a York-based physician, which were submitted to the Royal Society in London.[30] As well as illustrating Lister's papers on fossils, snails, spiders, and star-stones, Lodge also collected specimens of rocks, minerals, and shells for the cabinet of curiosities which the physician was assembling in York.[31] Present in London in the early months of 1675, Lodge visited the "Closett of curiosities" of one Captain Hicks, "in company with an ingenious and curious Gentleman, one Captain Fisher"; Lodge and Fisher observed flints and petrified shells, and more exotic exhibits of birds and rattlesnakes, with

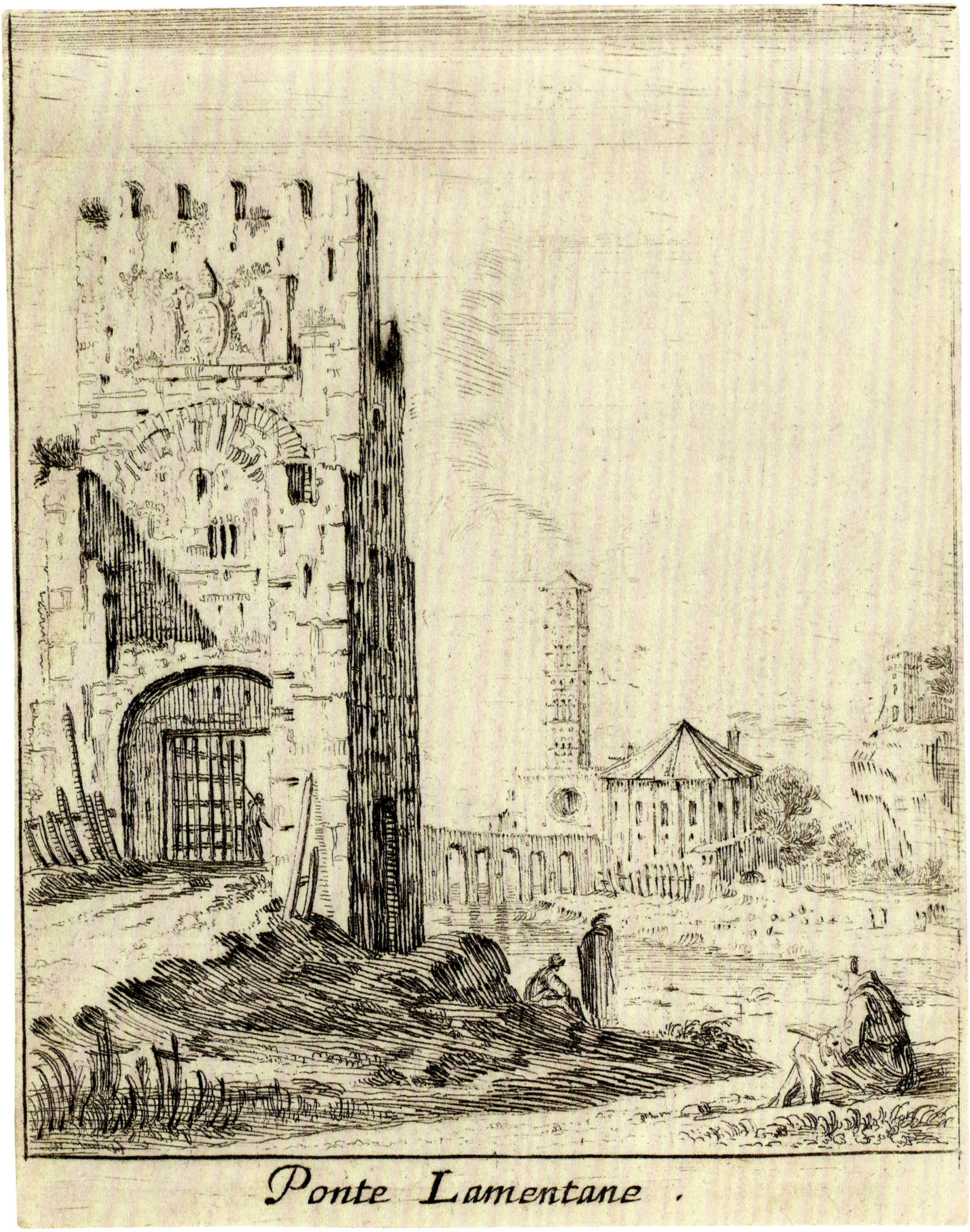

123. William Lodge, *Ponte Lamentane*, 1678–90, etching, 3⅜ x 2⅝ in. (8.5 x 6.8 cm). British Museum, London

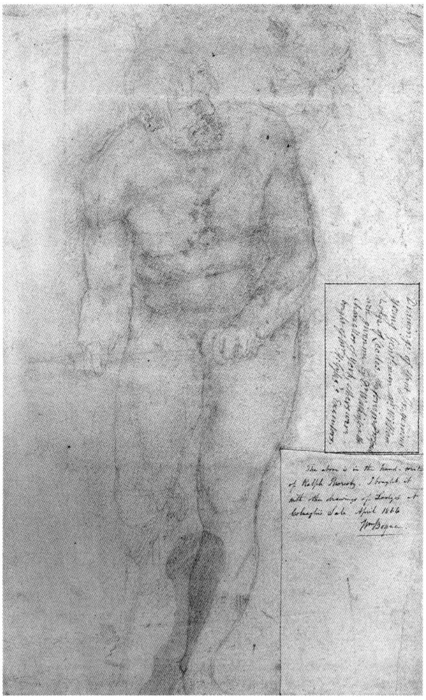

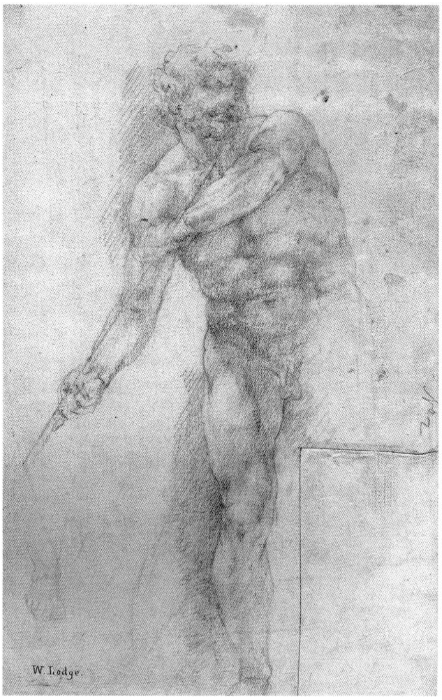

124. William Lodge, *Male Nude*, ca. 1671, black chalk on paper. Leeds Public Library

125. William Lodge, *Male Nude*, ca. 1671, black chalk on paper. Leeds Public Library

intricate stones and a hummingbird sketched in the margin of one letter sent to Lister with an account of the visit.[32] Yet Lodge's focus extended beyond technical drawings of natural history, and he was already planning a summer in York in which he intended to complete an intaglio plate of the city, noting the necessity of taking there "a room or two, for etching is too slovenly an employment for a friends house".[33] Although Lodge's work for Lister represented an important aspect of the latter's scientific investigations, a general tardiness and unreliability on Lodge's part in the supply of drawings and etchings further underlines the varied, rather than fixed and focused motivations of this seventeenth-century virtuoso of independent means. By the early 1680s, Lister had turned to Francis Place to undertake his commissions, including the sketching and subsequent etching of a curious, frog-like creature vomited up by a York baker, Mr Lund. The etching accompanied a descriptive letter sent by Lister to Robert Hooke for the consideration of the Royal Society; the creature itself was preserved in alcohol by the doctor and introduced into his cabinet.[34]

Lodge's status as a connoisseur of fine art was confirmed in the early months of 1679 with the publication in London of *The Painters Voyage of Italy*, his English translation of a little-known text by the Venetian painter and printmaker Giacomo Barri, which forms a summary guide to the locations of a range of old-master artworks in cities across Italy. Barri's *Viaggio Pittoresco d'Italia* had been published in Venice in 1671; its immediate appeal to Lodge, at that point recently relieved of his duties as part of an ambassadorial party, and now an independent traveller seeking cultural edification, is understandable. The opening dedication to *The Painters Voyage*, addressed to Viscount Fauconberg, also hints at more personal motives behind Lodge's subsequent decision to translate Barri's work into English:

> When I had the honour to attend your Lordship in your Embassy to the *States of Venice*, it was my fortune there to meet with a small Piece, entituled *Viaggio Pit toresco d'Italia* . . . I have gratified my self; and I hope not disobliged ingenious Artists in a faithful rendition of it into *English*; which I have done the rather because the Book is rarely to be found in *Italy*, and I can not remember I have seen any *Original* in *England* but that which is in my own hands.

By introducing Barri's text to a wider audience through his translation, Lodge was also taking the opportunity to highlight the role of Fauconberg in his own education and improvement:

> I have taken courage to prefix your Lordships honourable name to this Translation to render it acceptable to the world, under the Patronage of an acurate Judge, and a zealous lover and encourager of the noble *Art of Painting*. If it may serve to put your Lordship in mind of the pleasure you received by a personal view and admiration of those great *Masters* elaborate Pieces when your Lordship was abroad; and in any measure testifie my desires to serve your Lordship, 'tis the greatest Honour and satisfaction can be wished for . . .[35]

This dedication provides retrospective confirmation of Fauconberg's own connoisseurial activities in Venice, and adds weight to the tantalizing possibility that Lodge's role during the embassy, intended or otherwise, was to accompany the Viscount on any personal viewings of important works of art. Lodge's words must, of course, be read through a filter of self-promotion, as he publicly gestures towards the intellectual and cultural qualities of an important patron, and gently downplays Barri's original work as a "small piece . . . rarely to be found in Italy" and thus

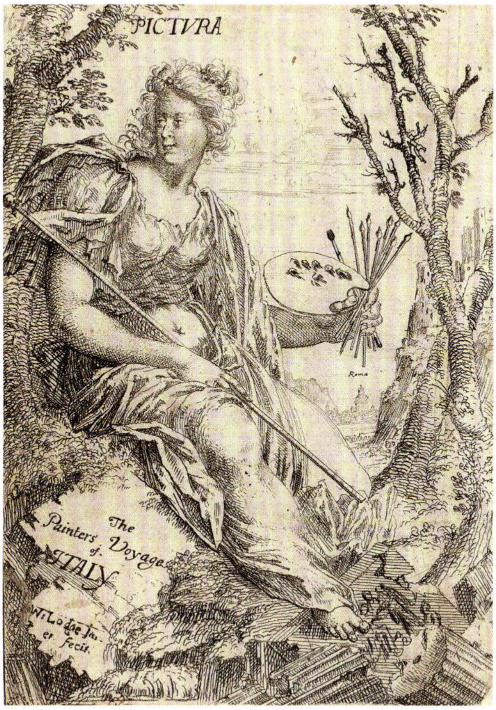

126. William Lodge, *The Painters Voyage of Italy*, 1679, etching, 5½ x 3⅞ in. (13.9 x 9.9 cm). British Museum, London

worthy of his own translation. As well as translating Barri's text, Lodge added in an account of the collection of the Milanese Manfredo Settala (1600–1680), whose famous cabinet of curiosities encompassed both artistic and natural wonders of which the York Virtuosi, with their own budding collections, would have overwhelmingly approved. "This Closet abounds with variety of Rarities, in Nature as well as Art", notes Lodge in *The Painters Voyage*.[36]

Lodge also took the opportunity to add illustrations to his translation, images being absent from the original. The etched title page (fig. 126), prominently signed by the artist, introduces the reader to the allegorical figure of Pictura, with the word "Roma" clearly stated beneath her paintbrushes; this might plausibly be understood as a further reminder of Lodge's own encounter with the Eternal City, extending his cultural knowledge and experiences, rather than gesturing towards Venice and the literary origins of *The Painters Voyage*. Five portraits, including suitable old masters, are dispersed within the text itself: Michelangelo, Raphael, Pietro da Cortona, Titian, and Paolo Veronese. The quality of these illustrations is varied; one caustic modern writer has described them as "messy little engraved portraits of some of the artists mentioned".[37] That of Michelangelo (fig. 127)

No further references are made in Lodge's known correspondence to Ogilby and his London map; however, the reasons why the royal cosmographer might have welcomed the involvement of a Yorkshire virtuoso in his project are not so obscure. Orbiting around this "platforme of London" were a number of individuals linked by degrees to Lodge. Wenceslaus Hollar was the prolific etcher who had forged a strong professional relationship with Lodge's firm friend Francis Place from the mid-1660s; Hollar was also known to Robert Hooke, who recorded in his diary numerous meetings with Ogilby in 1673 and 1674 concerning his "sheets for London", and would go on to correspond with Martin Lister on matters of science and natural philosophy. Meanwhile, the cartographer Robert Morden, who, as Fisher's letter to Lodge goes on to describe, was encountering difficulties in his attempts to produce an accurate panoramic view of London as part of Ogilby's expanding project, would three years later provide the map of Italy which supplements Lodge's illustrations in *The Painters Voyage of Italy*.[40]

Landscape views produced by William Lodge from the late 1670s onwards both allude to his earlier experiences following the Fauconberg embassy, and also justify Ogilby's interest in Lodge's potential contribution towards his "great peece of the platforme of London". Lodge's landscapes, both rural and urban, represent observational rather than interpretive studies, and incorporate clear identifying and labelling elements. The large plate of York, which Lodge had been working on in the summer of 1675, was subsequently printed together with two small-scale city views, both with cherub-borne cartouches bearing the date of 1678 (fig. 130). The panoramic view of "The Ancient and Loyall Citty of York" is paired with two compositionally similar studies: St. Mary's Tower and Fishergate Postern both feature in the left-hand foreground, each structure forming an anchor from which a varied landscape of fields, water, spires, and city walls spills. This compositional approach, with its play on spatial balance and visual distance, allows the smaller etchings both to complement and contrast with the organizational, rationalizing aspect of the larger prospect view, with its prominent keys naming, numbering, and firmly siting significant buildings and landmarks. As found in Lodge's earlier "divers" etchings of ancient Italian ruins, small male figures are present in each compartmentalized York landscape, viewing, gesturing, and engaging in what Mark Hallett has termed "the pleasures of historical meditation and leisured conversation".[41] They also feature in the more ambitious collage of *The Prospects of the Two Most Remarkable Towns in the North of England for the Clothing trade, viz. Leeds . . . and Wakefield* (fig. 131), with a central map framed by panoramas of Leeds and Wakefield, and small-scale views of the ruins of Kirkstall and Fountains Abbey, introduced as further sources for connoisseurial contemplation and discussion. There is also a telling acknowledgment here of Lodge's status, and of the source of

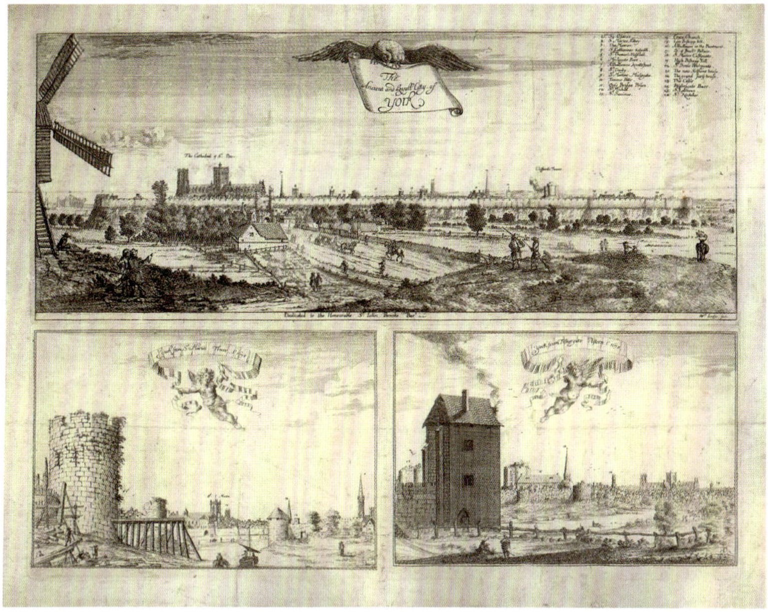

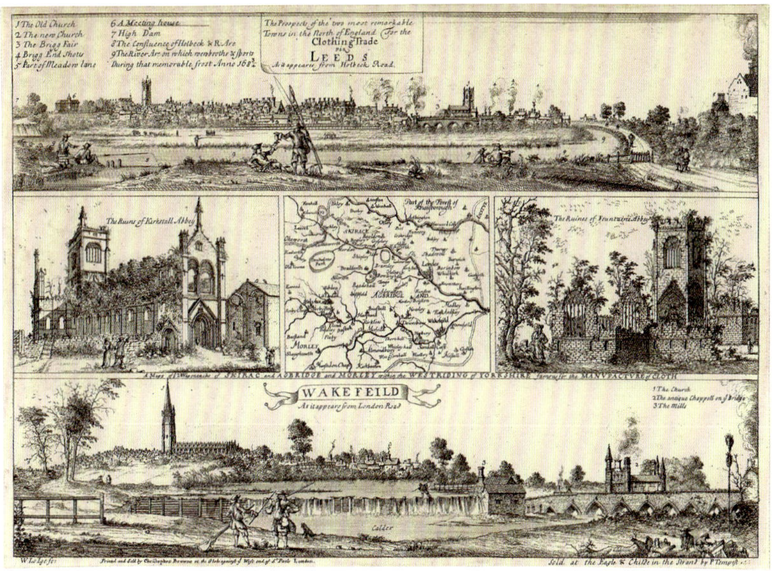

130. William Lodge, *The Ancient and Loyall Citty of York*, ca. 1678, etching on paper, 14¼ x 18⅞ in. (36.1 cm x 48 cm). British Museum, London

131. William Lodge, *The Prospects of the Two Most Remarkable Towns in the North of England for the Clothing trade, viz. Leeds . . . and Wakefield*, ca. 1680s, etching, 11⅝ x 16⅜ in. (29.6 x 41.5 cm). British Museum, London

his wealth, with the central map describing an area "famous for the manufacture of cloth". These conversing figures emphasize each locale's developing identity as a space for the polite activities of the urban elite; they also reflect back favourably, and more specifically, upon the convivial and intellectual pursuits of Lodge and his fellow northern virtuosi, themselves organizing, experimenting, and ordering in both the arts and sciences, through their cabinets, papers, and sketches.

The emergence of the York Virtuosi as a distinct and particular group of independently wealthy gentlemen can be traced to certain social and economic factors of the later seventeenth century. Improvements in travel and communications were enabling greater intellectual engagement with London and its own incipient institutions such as the Royal Society. However, the era of these particular virtuosi also coincided with the beginnings of what Peter Borsay has termed the "cultural refashioning" of York itself into an ideal urban locus for the development of "politeness, and its triple constituents of civility, sociability, and improvement".[42] The physical framework of the city, as the focus of both material and figurative improvements, provided a potent base from which this group of individuals, linked by complementary interests and the more elusive quality of friendship, were able to develop their pursuits.

The careers and practice of William Lodge and the group of York Virtuosi to which he belonged help contribute to our understanding of visual culture in the later Stuart and early Georgian periods. They demonstrate a range of interests operating outside and beyond the discipline-specific barriers of art and science with which we are all familiar today, and serve as an important reminder of the presence and activities of the amateur or at least non-professional artist within cultural and intellectual circles. With the connoisseurial knowledge of art in England not yet bound up in concepts of academic hierarchies, and with a certain focus on the practical and observational rather than creative and intuitive aspects of artistic application, the concerns and activities of the late seventeenth-century virtuoso are representative of a highly distinct approach towards the visual: accordingly, as Carol Gibson-Wood has noted, "the artistic values they register often look incompatible according to later perspectives."[43] Before the values and concerns of the Academy became engrained in the eighteenth-century mind-set, the pursuits of Lodge and his contemporary virtuosi are testament to a rather different perspective on art.

1. George Vertue, "The Note-books of George Vertue I", *Walpole Society* 18 (1930): 120–21.
2. Kim Sloan, *"A Noble Art": Amateur Artists and Drawing Masters, c.1600–1800* (London: British Museum Press, 2000), 80.
3. Attention to the artistic pursuits of the York Virtuosi was revived in a short article by Hugh Honour published in 1957, and Place was the subject of a 1971 exhibition at York City Art Gallery and Kenwood House; the life and work of the glass-painter Henry Gyles has been examined by Trevor Brighton, and Martin Lister's activities in York, involving members of the Virtuosi in the illustration of scientific papers, have been documented in several recent studies. See H. Honour, "York Virtuosi", *Apollo* 65, no. 386 (1957): 143–45; Richard Tyler, *Francis Place, 1647–1728: An Exhibition Representing All Aspects of His Work* (York: H. Morley & Sons, 1971); J. T. Brighton, "The Enamel Glass-Painters of York, 1585–1795" (DPhil diss., Univ. of York, 1978); Robert W. Unwin, "A Provincial Man of Science at Work: Martin Lister, F.R.S., and his Illustrators, 1670–1683", *Notes and Records of the Royal Society of London* 49, no. 2 (July 1995): 209–30; and Anna Marie Roos, *Web of Nature: Martin Lister (1639–1712), the First Arachnologist* (Leiden: Brill Publishing, 2011). On Place and Lodge see also Sloan, *"A Noble Art"*, 32–38.
4. Brighton, "Enamel Glass-Painters of York", 1: 86.
5. John Lambert to Henry Gyles, 27 Sept. 1683, MS3 (87), Yorkshire Archaeological Society, Leeds.
6. George Chapman, *The Revenge of Bussy D'Ambois* (London, 1613), sig. D2v, Henry Peacham, *The Compleat Gentleman*, 3rd ed. (London, 1634), 105.
7. Sloan, *"A Noble Art"*, 11–15.
8. See Henry V. S. Ogden and Margaret S. Ogden, "A Bibliography of Seventeenth-century Writings on the Pictorial Arts in English", *The Art Bulletin* 29, no. 3 (Sept. 1947): 196–207.
9. Carol Gibson-Wood, *Jonathan Richardson: Art Theorist of the English Enlightenment* (New Haven and London: Yale Univ. Press, 2000), 13.
10. Vertue, "Note-books I", 120.
11. Vertue, "Note-books I", 119–20.
12. Vertue, "Note-books I", 120–21.
13. Vertue, "Note-books I", 75; William Lodge to Martin Lister, 5 Jan. 1675, Bodleian Library, Oxford, Lister MS 34, fol. 149; George Vertue, "The Note-books of George Vertue II", *Walpole Society* 20 (1932): 35. See also the annotated drawing of Lodge by Vertue after Alexander Comer, Call Number 49.3664.10, The Lewis Walpole Library, Farmington, CT.
14. Francis Place to George Vertue, British Library (hereafter BL) Add MS 21111, fol. 15.
15. E. S. De Beer, ed., *The Diary of John Evelyn* (Oxford Univ. Press, 1959), 418. See also Ben Thomas, "Noble or Commercial? The Early History of Mezzotint in Britain", in *Printed Images in Early Modern Britain*, ed. Michael Hunter (Farnham: Ashgate, 2010), 279–96.
16. Vertue, "Note-books I", 75.
17. William Lodge to his mother, Elizabeth Aldburghe, 14 Nov. 1667, BL Stowe MS 745, fol. 1.
18. J. T. Brighton, "Henry Gyles: Virtuoso and Glass-Painter of York, 1645–1709", *York Historian* 4 (1984): 9. It has been suggested that Lambert is the artist responsible for a miniature portrait of an unknown man now in the Victoria and Albert Museum, London, but no certain extant work by Lambert is known.
19. David Farr, "John Lambert and the Roots of an Early Modern Art Collection", *Cromwelliana* (2002): 48.
20. David Farr, "Lambert, John (1619–1684), parliamentary soldier and politician", *Oxford Dictionary of National Biography* (Oxford Univ. Press, 2004), http://www.oxforddnb.com/view/article/15939 (accessed 30 June 2014).
21. *Ambassade Extraordinaire de Mylord Fauconberg* (Amsterdam, 1671), 11.
22. "A Note of Pictures taken in November 1684", BL Add MS 41255, fols. 109r–112v.
23. Constantijn Huygens, *Diaries*, 1688–96, National Library of the Netherlands; trans. Sanne van der Schee from Constantijn Huygens, *Journaal van 21 Oct. 1688 tot 2 Sept. 1696* (Utrecht, 1876–77; online edition 2009), in *The Art World in Britain 1660 to 1735*, http://artworld.york.ac.uk (accessed 30 June 2014).

24. Will of Thomas Lord Fauconberg, Baron of Yarom, Viscount Henknowles, and Earl Fauconberg, 21 May 1701, The National Archives, Kew (hereafter TNA) PROB 11/460/265; "A Note of Pictures taken in November 1684", fol. 109v; Will of Mary Countesse Fauconberg, Dowager of Soho Square, City of Westminster, Middlesex, 26 June 1713, TNA PROB 11/533/375.
25. Helen Jacobsen, *Luxury and Power: The Material World of the Stuart Diplomat, 1660–1714* (Oxford Univ. Press, 2011), 78, Sarah Hutton, "Sir John Finch (1626–1682), physician and diplomat", *Oxford Dictionary of National Biography*, http://www.oxforddnb.com/view/article/9439 (accessed 30 June 2014).
26. J. Barker to William Lodge, 28 March 1671, BL Stowe MS 745, fol. 59.
27. These and related sketches by Lodge, now in the collections of Leeds Public Library, are briefly discussed in Terry Friedman, "The Ingenious Mr Lodge's View of Leeds", *Leeds Arts Calendar* 79 (1976): 25–26.
28. Honour, "York Virtuosi", 145.
29. Thomas Kirke to Henry Gyles, 20 June 1674, BL Stowe MS 745, fol. 78.
30. For further detail, see Unwin, "A Provincial Man of Science".
31. Unwin, "A Provincial Man of Science", 219.
32. William Lodge to Martin Lister, 6 Feb. 1675, Bodleian Library, Oxford, Lister MS 34, fol. 151.
33. William Lodge to Martin Lister, 5 Jan. 1675, Bodleian Library, Oxford, Lister MS 34, fol. 149.
34. Antony Griffiths, *The Print in Stuart Britain, 1603–1689* (London: British Museum Press, 1998), 278–79.
35. William Lodge, *The Painters Voyage of Italy* (London: Thomas Flesher for the author, 1679), "The Epistle Dedicatory".
36. Lodge, *The Painters Voyage*, 145.
37. Honour, "York Virtuosi", 145.
38. Captain Fisher to William Lodge, 20 July 1675, Yorkshire Archaeological Society, Leeds, MS4 (131).
39. Shortly after Ogilby's death in September 1676, a large map of London was published and sold at his house in White Friars. "The Survey of London nine feet long and six feet deep" appeared in the *Term Catalogues* for November 1676. This map, partly etched and partly engraved, traces the city north of the Thames and is accepted to be largely the work of Wenceslaus Hollar, with some compositional input from Daniel King; its production was overseen by Ogilby's relative through marriage, William Morgan. The Ogilby–Morgan map, however, is not the elaborately decorated work described by Captain Fisher to Lodge. That project was not completed until 1682, when Morgan published *London &c Actually Survey'd*. This composite work develops the earlier Ogilby–Morgan map, both in terms of the geographic area covered, and through the addition of decorative elements including views of significant buildings and landmarks such as Somerset House and the Royal Exchange, as described in anticipation by Fisher some seven years earlier.
40. *London &c Actually Survey'd* also contains, at the foot of the map, a long prospect of the city as taken from the south bank of the Thames, with an inscription presenting the view as the work of the mapmakers Robert Morden and his one-time apprentice Philip Lea. In 1675 this prospect was a projected exercise for Morden and Lea, and a problematic one at that, as Fisher related in his letter to Lodge: "[Ogilby's] people that do write, worke, collect & travell for him are mightily pressed about a prospect of London, and can find no other but somewhere about the Wind-mill point or the Bank-side which will be but very imperfect they confesse, and are much concerned for it." Captain Fisher to William Lodge, 20 July 1675, Yorkshire Archaeological Society, Leeds, MS4 (131).
41. Mark Hallett, "Pictorial Improvement: York in Eighteenth-century Graphic Art", in *Eighteenth-century York: Culture, Space and Society*, ed. Hallett and Jane Rendall (York: Borthwick Publications, 2003), 28.
42. Peter Borsay, "Politeness and Elegance: The Cultural Refashioning of Eighteenth-century York", in *Eighteenth-century York*, ed. Hallett and Rendall, 7.
43. Gibson-Wood, *Jonathan Richardson*, 13.

"Deceives in an acceptable, amusing and praiseworthy fashion": Still Life, Illusion, and Deception

Tim Batchelor

On Sunday, 11 April 1669, Samuel Pepys noted in his diary a visit to an artist:

> after dinner, my wife and I out by coach, and Balty with us [Balthasar St Michel, his brother-in-law], to Loton [Jan Looten], the landscape-drawer, a Dutchman, living in St. James's Market, but there saw no good pictures. But by accident he did direct us to a painter that was then in the house with him, a Dutchman, newly come over, one Evarelst [Simon Verelst], who took us to his lodging close by, and did shew us a little flower-pot of his doing, the finest thing that ever, I think, I saw in my life; the drops of dew hanging on the leaves, so as I was forced, again and again, to put my finger to it, to feel whether my eyes were deceived or no. He do ask 70*l.* for it: I had the vanity to bid him 20*l.*; but a better picture I never saw in my whole life; and it is worth going twenty miles to see it.[1]

So entranced was Pepys that he returned the following day, again offering the artist £20 for the picture, and although Verelst reduced his price to £50 this was not low enough to tempt him into a purchase and the deal was not completed. This encounter, as told by Pepys, gives us a rare insight into the impact and reception of still life painting in Restoration London—the way that it could beguile and captivate through illusion and deception (see, for instance, fig. 132).

There are instances of still life painting in Britain in the early decades of the seventeenth century, such as in the work of the gentleman amateur-painter Nathaniel Bacon (1585–1627).[2] These, however, are rare examples. Still life painting really becomes established in Britain during the Restoration period and into the early eighteenth century. This new art form was introduced to Britain by artists arriving from overseas, particularly the Netherlands, seeking new opportunities to pursue their art and make their living. Developments in the art market through the introduction of the auction enabled these artists to reach new audiences and sell their work in a way that was not possible before. The images themselves, which

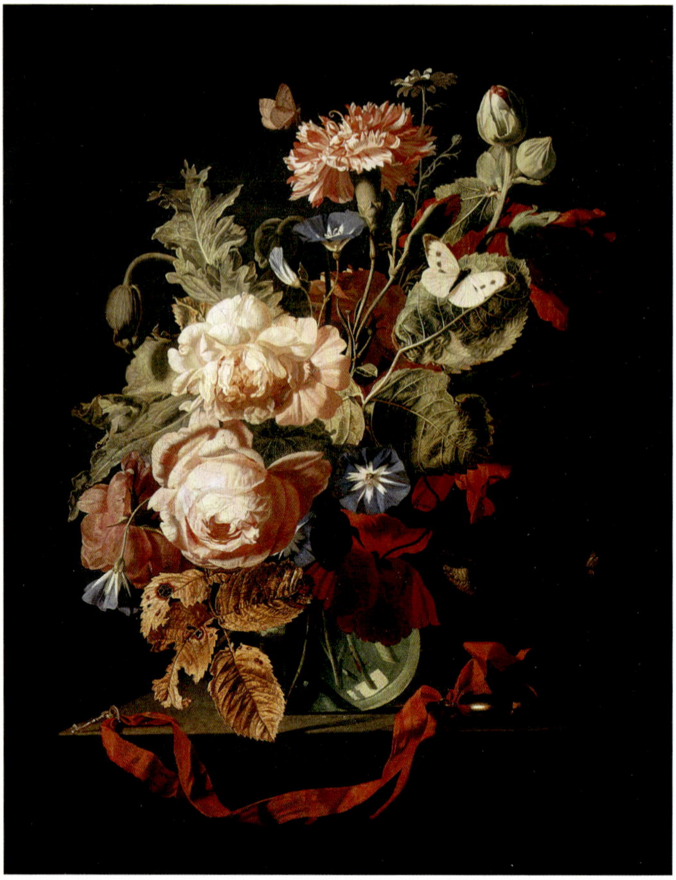

132. Simon Verelst, *A Vase of Flowers*, 1669, oil on canvas, 20⅛ x 16 in. (51 x 40.5 cm). The Fitzwilliam Museum, Cambridge

were often characterized by the kinds of pictorial illusion and deception that so captivated Pepys, proved popular with the art-buying public in an age of uncertain truths and political shams, and the emergence of scientific enquiry through close observation of the natural world. It was these social, economic, and cultural conditions particular to the period 1660–1740 that allowed for the establishment of this new genre in Britain.

Although still life painting existed in pre-classical times, the genre was developed in Europe in the late sixteenth century, reaching its apogee in the Netherlands during the mid-seventeenth century, the "Golden Age". Offering detailed depictions of inanimate objects, artists such as Willem Claesz. Heda (1594–1680), Jan Davidsz. de Heem (1606–1684), and Willem Kalf (1619–1693) produced sumptuous still life paintings of precious jewels and expensive goods, exotic fruit and beautiful flowers.[3] Though considered a lowly genre as an artistic form, these works appealed to Dutch art buyers made rich through economic expansion and overseas trade.[4] However, a faltering of the economic conditions from 1660 saw the United Provinces fall into a deep depression. Demand for paintings weakened drastically, making it difficult for many artists to sell their works. At the same time Britain was benefiting from a period of stability following the restoration of Charles II, and its economy was undergoing a period of growth through increasing international trade and a modernized banking system based on credit. This increase in activity saw London rapidly expanding, becoming the largest city in Europe by 1700. Many of the artists who were struggling in the Netherlands took the short trip by ship to London to seek work and sell their paintings. This form of migration was encouraged by Charles II in 1672 through his Proclamation inviting Dutch citizens of any profession or rank to move to Britain.[5] These migrant artists transformed the cultural landscape of Britain, their work having benefited from sophisticated kinds of artistic training that were far less developed or available in Britain. They also introduced a range of new approaches to painting and new genres, such as landscape and marine painting—and still life painting.[6] Notable still life painters arriving in Britain during this period include Simon Verelst (1644–ca. 1710/17), Pieter van Roestraten (1630–1700), and Edward Collier (ca. 1642–ca. 1708).[7]

Artists were also benefiting from a new development in the art market: the auction.[8] Art auctions had been established in the Netherlands in the earlier part of the seventeenth century and were introduced in Britain in the decades after 1660. Held in taverns, coffee houses, and commercial exchanges, among other places, this new way of selling art began to flourish from the 1670s, reaching a height in the early 1690s. While the traditional, restrictive, practice of artistic patronage by a privileged elite was still desirable, and indeed a viable option for some still life painters, there was now an alternative way for artists to have their paintings seen and sold, reaching a much wider market of prospective buyers at different monetary levels. This was particularly appropriate for the sale of still life paintings, which had a generic aesthetic appeal that was unconnected with any specific family collection or location. The collection of surviving sale catalogues at the British Library, London, covering the period May 1689 to March 1692, reveals the growing taste and appetite for the new genre of still life painting. These have previously been studied by scholars including M. Kirby Talley and Carol Gibson-Wood, but the recent digitization of them on the *Art World in Britain* database has made them more widely accessible.[9] Analysis of the figures shows that still life paintings, along with landscape and genre paintings, were among the most numerous works on offer. Flower paintings and still lifes attributed to Verelst alone number 250 pictures.[10] This is quite a tally for a single artist working over a three-year period; and, even accounting for misattributions and confusion regarding the various members of the Verelst family of painters, it demonstrates the amount of these paintings available for purchase at auction. Yet despite the wealth of materials that are now available regarding the London art market in this period, the information the sale catalogues provide is often tantalizingly brief. For example, lot 78 in the sale, *A collection of paintings by the best masters*, held at the Royal Exchange on 6 November 1689, is listed simply as "A Flower-piece". This summary description is typically brief; however, lot 141 in the same sale gives a bit more information regarding the artist: "A Flower-pot original of young Verelst".[11] Other instances give a sense of scale. Lot 12 in a sale at the Royal Exchange on 16 December 1689, is described as "a small piece of flowers", while lot 67 in the same sale consisted of "a large flower piece".

Larger still life pictures may have served a decorative purpose in an interior setting, such as an over-door. The function of still life flower paintings in this manner can be seen in Charles Philips's *Tea Party at Lord Harrington's House, St. James's* (fig. 133), in which we can see two large flower paintings hanging over the doors in the background of the represented room. This suggests the use and impact of still life paintings in a grand interior of a wealthy household, and their function as decorative items in an interior setting. The role of still life paintings presented in this way, acting as illusionistic imagery for decorative effect, offers a parallel to the use and function of larger painted schemes in the interiors of grand houses.

More everyday insights into the presentation and display of still life paintings in this period can be found in the contemporary press. In October 1710 a certain "M.K." wrote to the *British Apollo* asking advice on the framing and display of a large collection of paintings he had recently bought, including still lifes. A reply is offered from "R.H.", who states that, "but Peices of Still-Life (as they call it) in which are Peices of Plate, must of necessity be always in Black Frames, or the Artificial is destroyed by the Natural."[12] This conveys an awareness of the artifice and deception inherent in such pictures and the best form of display to maintain their effects. The new opportunities provided by the press were also used to promote the producers of still lifes themselves. An advert in the *Collection for Improvement of Husbandry and Trade* on 26 April 1695 listed painters of various genres, including "Mr. Roestrate, King-Str. Cov. Gard" under "Still-Life"; "Mr Bogdan, St Martin's Lane" and "Mr Simon Verelst, Westminster" under "Flower"; and "Mr Van Loon, Long-Acre" under "Flower and Fruit".[13] As well as buying one of the many still life paintings that were regularly appearing at auction sales, prospective buyers could seek out the artist for themselves.

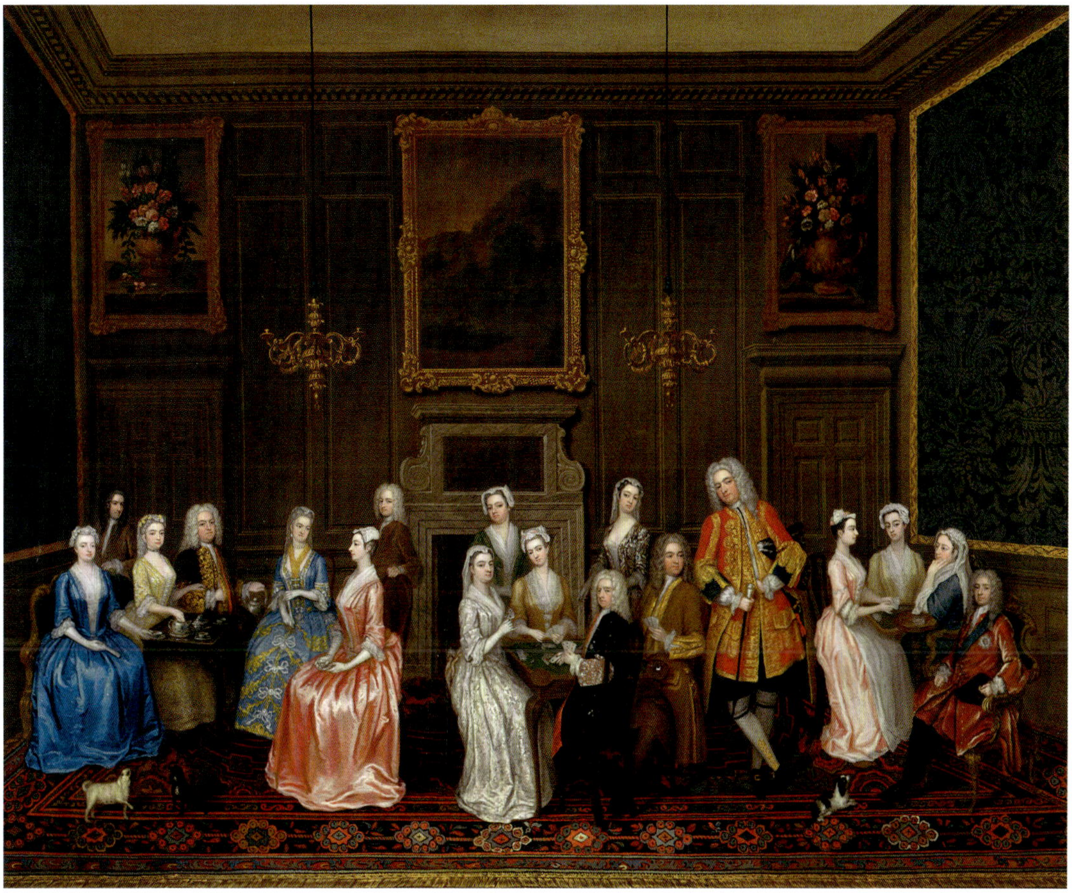

133. Charles Philips, *Tea Party at Lord Harrington's House, St. James's*, 1730, oil on canvas, 40¼ x 49¾ in. (102.2 x 126.4 cm). Yale Center for British Art, Paul Mellon Collection

The Pepys anecdote that was cited at the beginning of this essay is the earliest reference to the presence of Simon Verelst in London—the artist being "newly arrived". Verelst specialized in flower paintings and quickly established himself as a leading still life painter in Britain.[14] The quality of his work was recognized by contemporary commentators and reflected in the high prices he could charge (as found out by Pepys). His paintings typify the approach to flower painting that had developed in Holland, with a rich sumptuous display of flowers conveyed with a pictorial precision that served to suggest an actual vase of flowers in front of the viewer (fig. 132). The inclusion of decaying leaves indicates that this is not a scene of perfection, but one that depicts nature with all its beauties and flaws. The decay may also have symbolic meaning, referring to the passing of time and ultimately to death, and thereby linking the painting to the more obvious "vanitas" still lifes which were being produced at this time.[15] But the overall effect is of a reality frozen in time, as symbolized by the upturned pocket watch. This idea of permanence and of capturing nature's beauty in perpetuity is suggested in the poem *A Flower. Painted by Simon Varelst* by Matthew Prior (1664–1721):

> When famed Varelst this little wonder drew,
> Flora vouchsafed the growing works to view;
> Finding the painter's science at a stand,
> The Goddess snatch'd the pencil from his hand,
> And finishing the piece, she smiling said,
> Behold one work of mine that ne'er shall fade.[16]

However, closer inspection of the flowers in the painting illustrated here shows that the semblance of reality presented by the artist is decidedly false. In showing a variety of spring, midsummer, and late-summer flowers in full bloom, all at the same time, Verelst offers us an impossibility. What the viewer is presented with is not real but an illusion, a deception. Here, the artist pursues a traditional still life approach of seeking to paint a convincing semblance of reality, and of providing an impression that the viewer is looking at the actual object rather than a visual depiction of it. As declared by Philips Angel in his lecture *In Praise of Painting*, delivered to the Guild of St Luke in Leiden in 1641 and published the following year: "If an artist manages to imitate life in such a way that people judge that it approaches real life without being able to detect in it the manner of the master who made it, such a spirit deserves praise and honour and shall be ranked above all others."[17]

The still life painting tradition looks back to the ancient Greeks and the skill of mimesis—the artistic process of imitating life—and often refers to the anecdotes found in ancient literature. One such account is the now legendary tale, as told by Pliny the Elder (Gaius Plinius Secundus, 23/24–79 AD), of the work of the painter Zeuxis (active 435–390 BC) who painted grapes so realistically that it fooled the birds which flew over to eat them. But, as Pliny goes on to add, the great Zeuxis himself was outdone by his artistic rival Parrhasios (active 440–390 BC):

> [Parrhasios] entered into a competition with Zeuxis, who produced a picture of grapes so successfully represented that birds flew up to the stage-buildings; whereupon Parrhasios himself painted such a realistic picture of a curtain that Zeuxis, proud of the verdict of the birds, requested that the curtain

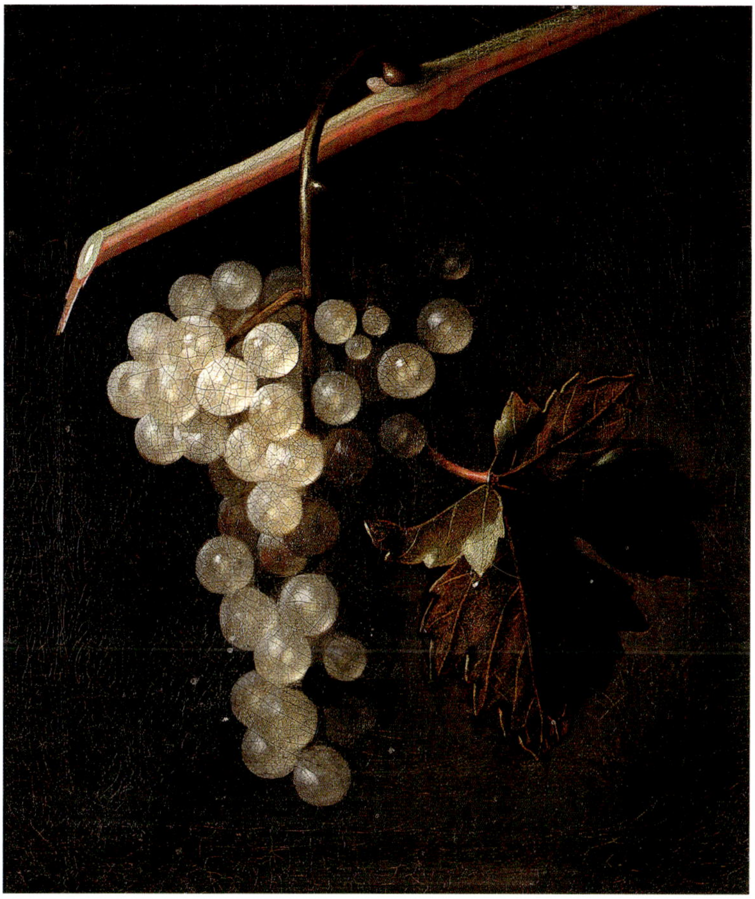

134. Simon Verelst, *A Bunch of Grapes Hanging Before a Stone Wall*, 1709, oil on canvas, 13⅞ x 12¼ in. (35.4 x 31 cm). Private collection

> should now be drawn and the picture displayed; and when he realised his mistake, with a modesty that did him no honour he yielded up the prize, saying that whereas he had deceived the birds, Parrhasios had deceived him, an artist.[18]

Both of these mythical accounts became the standard for still life painters to aspire to. Artists would make reference to these ancient tales in their own work to associate themselves with the great masters, either through depicting the curtain or the grapes mentioned by Pliny—as in Verelst's *A Bunch of Grapes Hanging Before a Stone Wall* of 1709 (fig. 134).

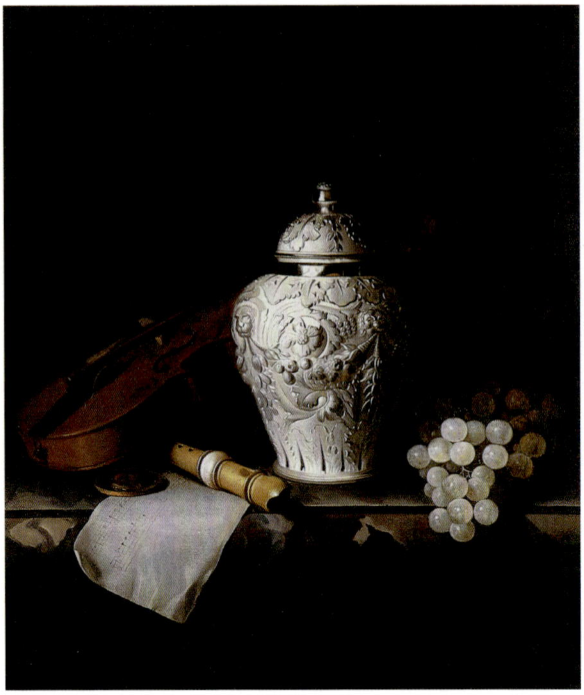

135. Pieter van Roestraten, *Still Life of a Frosted Silver Ginger Jar, Violin, Flute and Grapes upon a Ledge*, oil on canvas, ca. 1680, 20 x 21¼ in. (51 x 54 cm). Private collection

Similar preoccupations informed the work of another Dutch painter of still life active in London in the 1660s: Pieter van Roestraten. Born in Haarlem, Van Roestraten was a pupil of Frans Hals (1582–1666). The young artist married his master's daughter and moved to London at some point in the early 1660s. He produced still life arrangements of luxury objects, developing a specialism for the depiction of silver—reflecting its resurgence during the Restoration.[19] His works often feature a "portrait" of an individual item which forms the centrepiece of the composition surrounded by other related objects. He would later turn his attention to oriental porcelain and lacquered objects, following the new fashion for tea. In his painting, *Still Life of a Frosted Silver Ginger Jar, Violin, Flute and Grapes upon a Ledge* (fig. 135), the central focus is a beautifully rendered silver ginger jar, an object that can be found in other pictures by the artist and similar in design to the jars produced by the British goldsmith Anthony Nelme (active 1679/80–1722). The grapes on the right, along with the musical instruments, may be interpreted as symbolizing the pleasures of life—and the wine that could be made from them. But they may also

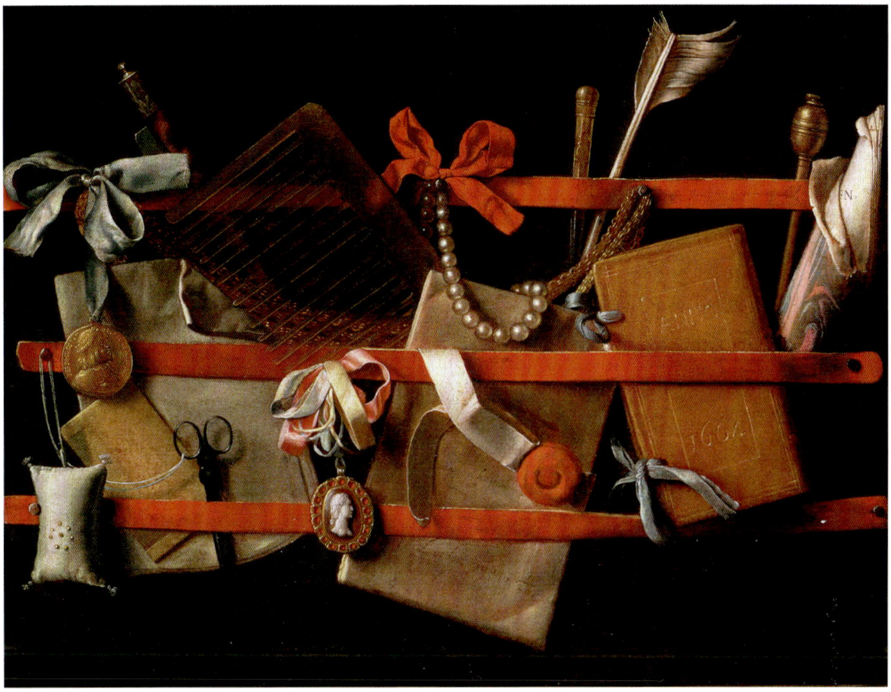

136. Samuel van Hoogstraten, *A Trompe l'Oeil Still Life*, 1664, oil on canvas, 17⅞ x 22⅝ in. (45.5 x 57.5 cm). Dordrechts Museum, The Netherlands

refer back to the story of Zeuxis and the skill of the artist in imitating life so brilliantly that he manages to create the illusion of reality. The ultimate tool in the armoury of the artist for generating an illusion of reality is perspective. The recorder and grapes in Van Roestraten's painting project forward towards the viewer beyond the marble plinth, and the shadowy effect of the objects as they recede into space emphasizes their three-dimensionality. This use of perspective is enhanced through the play of light, which alights upon the objects closest to the viewer but becomes darker as they sink into the background.

In another familiar form of contemporary still life painting—the trompe l'oeil still life—it is the denial of deep perspective that lies at the heart of the artist's success at generating an effect of reality. The trompe l'oeil work tends to distribute a series of pictured objects across a wall or a board; these objects are suggested as occupying a very shallow space in front of this upright support.[20] One of the earliest proponents of this new art was Samuel van Hoogstraten (1627–1678). Born in Dordrecht and trained under Rembrandt in Amsterdam, in 1651 he travelled to

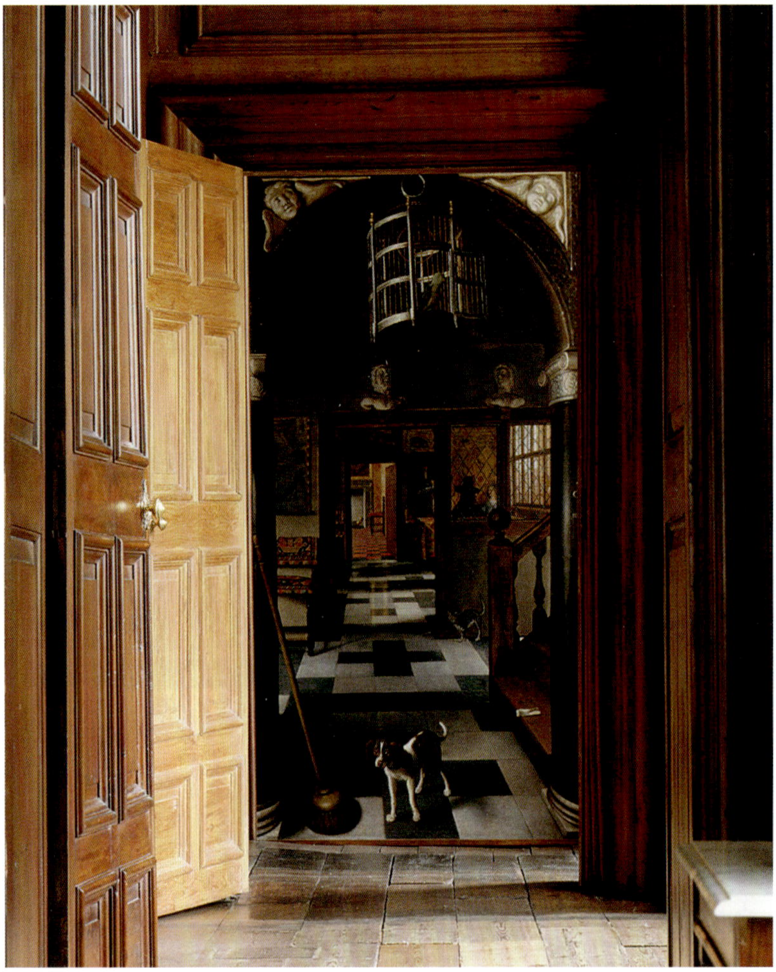

137. Samuel van Hoogstraten, *A View Through a House*, 1662, oil on canvas, 104 x 53¾ in. (264.2 x 136.5 cm). Dyrham Park, Gloucestershire (The National Trust)

the Habsburg court in Vienna. On arrival there he presented Emperor Ferdinand III with a trompe l'oeil still life painting so convincing that it deceived the emperor. Tricking and fooling the most powerful man in the world in public was, perhaps, a risky enterprise for a young artist, but luckily for Van Hoogstraten the emperor was impressed. As Arnold Houbraken recounts: "as the third piece, a still life was shown, the Emperor appeared completely taken with it. He looked at it for a long time and finding himself truly deceived then said, 'This is the first painter to deceive me'. And he went on to say that as punishment for the deception he should not get the piece back; rather he wanted to keep it and cherish it." Subsequently, the emperor bestowed on Van Hoogstraten the highest court honour granted to artists: an imperial gold medallion and chain.[21]

In 1662 Van Hoogstraten moved to London, staying in England for five years. Here he would produce another form of trompe l'oeil still life—the letter rack—one of the first painters, along with his contemporaries Wallerant Vaillant (1623–1677) and Cornelis Gijsbrechts (ca. 1630–after 1683), to produce such works. This art form would be taken up later by Edward Collier, the Dutch artist who was active in London in the 1690s.[22] While the objects appear at first instance to be unremarkable everyday artefacts, Celeste Brusati argues that the trompe l'oeil letter racks by Van Hoogstraten were an assertion of his identity as an artist and of his accomplishments as a practitioner of visual deception.[23] One of his paintings, *Trompe l'Oeil Still Life*, after 1666 (Staatliche Kunsthalle Karlsruhe) includes a poem by the Austrian nobleman Von Stubenberg praising his art and comparing it favourably with that of Zeuxis, as well as displaying the gold medallion and chain. The gold medal can also be seen hanging on the left of another trompe l'oeil letter-rack painting produced when the artist was in London, *Trompe l'Oeil Still Life*, 1664 (fig. 136). Van Hoogstraten gives us a rare insight into his thoughts on art and its effect through his treatise *Inleyding tot de Hooge Schoole der Schilderkonst, anders de Zichtbaere Werelt* (Introduction to the Academy of Painting; or, The Visible World), published in Rotterdam in 1678. In this work he states that: "The art of painting is a science to represent all the ideas, or concepts, that the entire visible world provides, and with contour deceives the eye . . . A perfect painting is like a mirror of Nature, in which things that are not there appear to be there, and which deceives in an acceptable, amusing and praiseworthy fashion."[24]

Van Hoogstraten would employ this skill in deceiving the eye to great effect in his trompe l'oeil architectural perspective works, such as the *View Through a House* (fig. 137). Painted in 1662, this was one of the first works the artist produced after his arrival in London and one of two paintings of a similar nature acquired by Thomas Povey (1613/14–ca. 1705). Povey was a colonial entrepreneur and administrator, and Treasurer to the Duke of York. Successful investments in a range of colonial trading schemes and a profitable marriage to a wealthy widow enabled him to build an elegant house on Arch Row in the most fashionable part of Lincoln's Inn Fields, London. Furnished with fine paintings and the latest fashions, the house was used by Povey to entertain his friends with lavish meals. Van Hoogstraten himself was invited to dine there at a banquet of ten courses and twenty-four varieties of imported wine.[25] Samuel Pepys was a colleague of Povey's (the two men sat on the Tangiers Committee after Povey was made Treasurer of Tangiers) and visited him at his Lincoln's Inn Fields house on several occasions. After an "excellent and large dinner" there on the evening of 19 January 1663, he noted in his diary his admiration for a "piece of perspective" that he saw hanging in a closet off the low parlour. After a visit a week later, on 26 January, he noted that, "above all things I do the most admire his piece of perspective especially, he opening me the closett door, and there I saw that there is nothing but only a plain picture hung upon the wall." Again, of a later visit on 21 September 1664, Pepys writes: "Here I was afresh delighted with Mr Povey's house and pictures of perspective, being strange things, to think how they delude one's eye, that methinks it would make a man doubtful of swearing that he ever saw anything."[26]

This experience of illusion and deception was especially thrilling for Pepys, who delighted in trickery and pranks of this sort. On 28 August 1661, he noted in his diary: "This day I counterfeited a letter to Sir W. Penn, as from the thief that stole his tankard lately, only to abuse and laugh at him." His colleague at the admiralty, Sir William Penn (1621–1670), would later find out about the deception and be angry about it. This was an innocuous "jest" among friends, of course; however, the shams of wits and the "great rascality" of writers and publishers were things that people had to beware of on a daily basis. As Kate Loveman has pointed out, a spectrum of deceit abounded in the period, from the lying news books produced by the "cheating talemongers" and coffee house shams, to a more worrying and serious threat: that of the ideological deceptions of the enemies of Protestantism, who were seen as deceiving people and tricking them out of their religion or political persuasions in order to ruin the nation. This is evident in the prominent national scandals of the Popish Plot (1678), a fabricated Catholic conspiracy against the Crown, and the Warming-pan Scandal (1688) following the birth of the Catholic heir to the throne, James Francis Edward Stuart, and the rumour that the birth was a deception with the child smuggled into the bedchamber in a warming-pan. The same phenomenon can also be recognized in the growth and development of language at this time. From the mid-seventeenth century onwards, new words to describe wit and deception, or a combination of the two, begin to appear in increasing numbers and wider usage. For example, "banter", meaning to make fun of someone, to hold up to ridicule, jest, and rally, is first recorded used as a verb in 1677, the same year that "sham" appears as a verb and noun, meaning to trick, hoax, or defraud. By the end of the exclusion crisis in the 1680s, "sham" was being used to describe not only witty jests and fake stories, but also more serious political conspiracies.[27]

The later Stuart period has been defined as one which saw a new quest for truth as part of the beginnings of the English Enlightenment. Mark Knights has noted that as well as political deception and uncertainty, this was a time when a

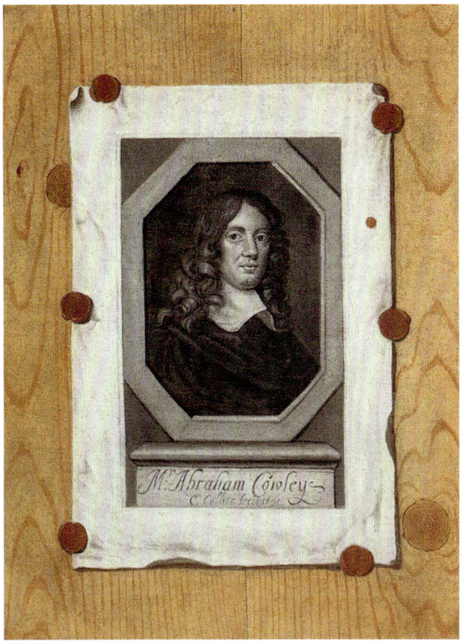

138. Edward Collier, *Tromp l'Oeil with a Portrait of Abraham Cowley*, 1695, oil on canvas, 17⅜ x 13 in. (44 x 33 cm). Private collection

pluralistic religious society was emerging, and the notion of truth was becoming relative but also uncertain. This uncertainty was manifested through dissimulation and hypocrisy, deception and delusion, and with the fictions constructed by people to conceal their true selves. Fragile truths were part of this early Enlightenment culture, a culture which extended to the arts. The still life and trompe l'oeil paintings noted in this essay were thus produced at a time when the kinds of deception that lay at their heart were being recognized as embedded within wider society itself. At the centre of the early Enlightenment debates were the questions: what is a fact?, how do we verify a fact?, and how do we establish how the natural world works? One response to this quest for truth and knowledge was the Royal Society. Founded in London in 1660 under the patronage of Charles II, its members were involved in pursuing "the knowledge of natural things and all useful arts by means of experiment".[28]

The interest in perception and illusion expressed by still life and trompe l'oeil paintings can thus be seen in the context of a wider scientific culture of experimentation and exploration that emerged in this period. This culture was not confined to England, but extended across Continental Europe. As Svetlana Alpers has argued, the still life paintings of the Dutch Golden Age are a product of a society that was itself engaging with a new experimental natural philosophy. They reflect

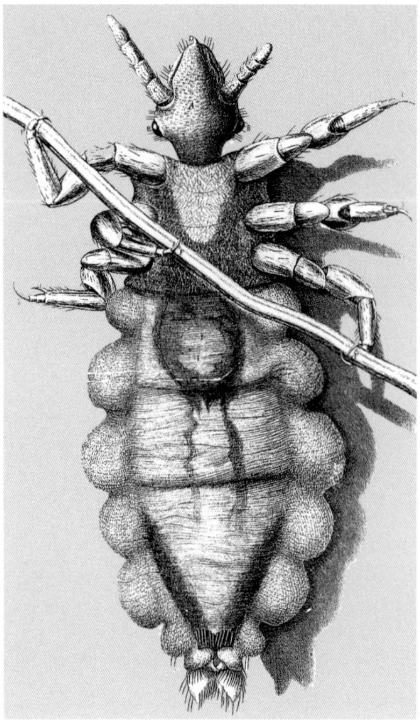

139. Robert Hooke, "Human Louse, a wingless parasitic insect," in Robert Hooke, *Micrographia* (London, 1665), engraving. Universal History Archive

the interest in observing the natural world to gain greater knowledge and understanding, and of the development in optics and methods of close observation in achieving this.[29] This has a particular resonance for Samuel van Hoogstraten. As Celeste Brusati points out, Van Hoogstraten sought out patronage for his art in those places where "a taste for experimental artifice was coupled with aristocratic support for the New Learning". He found this in Vienna at the court of the Holy Roman Emperor in the 1650s, where Ferdinand III's support for experimental art and science was at its height; he also found it in the 1660s in London, which witnessed the formation and development of the Royal Society. The milieu that Van Hoogstraten sought out on his arrival in Britain consisted of Royal Society members such as Thomas Povey, who was a founder member. Povey's own curiosity about the natural world and his interest in art came together when he offered to invite painters to speak to members of the Royal Society on topics such as "the several varieties and curiosities of painting" or to report on "experiments of a new way of laying on colours". Van Hoogstraten's interest in the world of experimentation and natural philosophy also led him to associate with the group around Edward Somerset, second Marquess of Worcester, whose house at Vauxhall acted as a meeting place for experimental engineers and early scientists.[30]

Another figure associated with the Royal Society and with an interest in scientific enquiry was Abraham Cowley (1618–1667). He is best known as one of the leading poets of the Stuart age and an exiled Royalist agent during the Civil Wars and Interregnum. But during the later years of the Protectorate he kept a low profile, studying botany and medicine at Oxford and attaining the degree of doctor of physic in 1657. This interest in early science was expressed in his pamphlet *A proposition for the advancement of learning* (1661), and also the first two books of his poem *Plantarum* (1662), which are based on his botanic studies. Though he was never a member of the Royal Society nor attended its meetings, he was certainly sympathetic to its cause. In 1667, at the request of his friend John Evelyn, he wrote *To the Royal Society* as a prefatory ode to Thomas Sprat's *History of the Royal Society* (1667). The poem acts as a paean to the Baconian spirit of the society and its aims.[31]

The engraving of Abraham Cowley by William Faithorne that illustrated the frontispiece to Thomas Sprat's *The Works of Mr Abraham Cowley* (1668), is the image that Edward Collier used for one of his trompe l'oeil still life paintings (fig. 138). The printed page of the engraving with its curled edges and corners is shown held in place with red wax seals on a wooden board. The grain and knots of the board, a cheap cut of Scots pine known as deal, is painted with such precision as to create the illusion of reality. Collier painted a number of these types of works, but limited the engravings they depict to a small group of figures: Erasmus, Charles I, William and Mary, and Abraham Cowley.[32] Although Cowley was a popular and successful poet, the decision to include him in such elevated company may have a deeper meaning. In his ode to the Royal Society, Cowley conjured the legend of Zeuxis and declared that the observation of nature is the key to both art and science. In including the print of Cowley in his painting, Collier may well have been aligning his own practice with the poet's views regarding the primacy of observation within the visual arts.[33] Whatever the underlying references of such pictures, their ultimate function was to deceive the viewer.

Collier's trompe l'oeil depictions of engravings on wooden board offer a variation on another, similar kind of work, the letter-rack picture, which shows letters and other everyday artefacts secured by straps to a wooden background. It was a picture of this manner that Pepys saw when he noted in his diary on Sunday, 15 March 1667 that he was "mightily pleased with a picture that W. Hewer brought hither of several things painted upon deale board, which board is so well painted that in my whole life I never was so pleased or surprised with any picture, and so troubled that so good pictures should be painted upon a piece of bad deale. Even after I knew that it was not board, but only the picture of a board, I could not remove my fancy."[34]

The close observation and analysis of the natural world espoused by the Royal Society is also exemplified by Robert Hooke's *Micrographia*. Published in 1665, this ground-breaking book contained the results of his examinations of small insects using a new microscope, and his thoughts and conclusions about what he observed.

Although they do not conform to a traditional understanding of the genre, Hooke's illustrations of a magnified flea, louse, and fly could be seen as the ultimate still lifes (fig. 139). Yet for one commentator this new way of looking presented not so much a heightened reality, but rather a distortion of truth. In her *Observations upon Experimental Philosophy,* published in 1666, Margaret Cavendish, Duchess of Newcastle, acknowledges the "wonders" of Hooke's engravings and finds them worthy of admiration; at the same time, she sees the use of these new optical devices as problematic and misleading. She states that the "natural figure may be presented in as monstrous a shape, as it may appear mis-shapen rather than natural. For example; a Louse by the help of a magnifying glass appears like a Lobster . . . The truth is, the more the figure by Art is magnified, the more it appears mis-shapen from the natural, in so much as each joint will appear as a diseased, swell'd and tumid body, ready and ripe for incision." Lady Margaret goes on to argue that she finds such images corrupting, disgusting, and threatening, creating more a "Monster of Art, than a picture of Nature".[35] For other commentators, however, the new ways of looking and the revelations of the natural world that they provided were a wonder and a delight. Samuel Pepys recorded how he sat up until two o'clock in the morning reading *Micrographia*, and described it as, "the most ingenious book that ever I read in my life".[36]

This mirrors the excitement and fascination that observers record in their engagement with still life paintings, and their amusement at the brief deception to which they had been subjected—whether it be Pepys revelling in the experience of a visit to the king's closet and seeing what he thought was a book upon a table, but that was in fact a picture,[37] or George Vertue's account of the surprise viewers felt at seeing the trompe l'oeil painting of a violin hanging on a wooden door (Jan van der Vaart (1647–1727), *Violin Suspended from a Peg*, after 1674, Chatsworth House) when it was revealed at Devonshire House: "fiddles he has painted so deceveingly to ye eye, that all who have seen them were surprizd. the duke of Devonshire has one. done by him. in his collection, that is finely done."[38] Later in the century, Horace Walpole would also take delight and amusement in the effect of deception in still life—though, again, in a form that does not conform to the traditional definition of the genre. In a letter dated 11 May 1769, Walpole recounted the occasion that he dressed to meet a number of distinguished foreign visitors wearing a cravat carved from wood by Grinling Gibbons (produced in about 1690; Victoria and Albert Museum, London), reporting that the French servants "stared and firmly believed that it was the dress of an English Country Gentleman".[39] Walpole's pleasure in the trick he played with his trompe l'oeil carving echoes the sentiments expressed by the Dutch writer Jan de Brune the younger in 1644 when he stated that, "Certainly, it gives one joy without measure when one is deceived by a false likeness of things."[40]

Such pleasures help explain why still life painting became firmly established as a new genre during the post-Restoration period. This was an era, it is worth reiterating, when the attributes of visual illusion and the pleasures of pictorial deception contributed to wider cultural preoccupation with the ways in which one could separate fact from fiction, the real from the fake. These wider concerns about truth and artifice were evident on a political level, particularly in the responses to the various plots, scandals, and shams that served as very real and worrying threats to the stability of the nation. They were evident, too, within the expanding realm of scientific discourse associated in particular with the Royal Society. But they were also evident, I would argue, in the world of art, and helped shape the new interest in pictures that seemed to live up to Samuel van Hoogstraten's aim of deceiving in an acceptable, amusing, and praiseworthy fashion.

1. *The Diary of Samuel Pepys*, http://www.pepysdiary.com/diary/1669/04/11/ (accessed 28 May 2014).
2. For example his painting, *Cookmaid with Still Life of Vegetables and Fruit*, ca. 1620–25 (Tate, London, T06995).
3. See Simon Schama, *The Embarrassment of Riches: An Interpretation of Dutch Culture in the Golden Age* (London: Collins, 1987).
4. See Julie Hochstrasser, *Still Life and Trade in the Dutch Golden Age* (New Haven and London: Yale Univ. Press, 2007).
5. *London Gazette* 685, 12 June 1672, in *17th–18th Century Burney Collection Newspapers* database, British Library, London.
6. Sander Karst, "Off to a New Cockaigne: Dutch Migrant Artists in London, 1660–1715", *Simiolus* 37, no. 1 (2013–14): 25–60.
7. For a short introduction and overview of still life painting in Britain, see Tim Batchelor, ed., *Dead Standing Things: Still Life Painting in Britain, 1660–1740* (London: Tate Britain, 2012) which can be accessed via the University of York website at http://www.york.ac.uk/history-of-art/court-country-city/display2012/.
8. David Ormrod, "The Origins of the London Art Market, 1660–1730", in *Art Markets in Europe, 1400–1800*, ed. Michael North and David Ormrod (Aldershot: Ashgate, 1998), 167–86.
9. M. Kirby Tally, "'Small, usuall, and vulgar things': Still-Life Paintings in England, 1635–1760", *Walpole Society* 49 (1983): 133–23; Carol Gibson-Wood, "Picture Consumption in London at the End of the Seventeenth-century", *The Art Bulletin* 84, no. 3 (Sept. 2002): 491–500; *The Art World in Britain, 1660 to 1735* at http://artworld.york.ac.uk.
10. Karst, "Off to a New Cockaigne", 30–36.
11. "A Collection of Paintings by the Best Masters" [London 1689]; in *The Art World in Britain 1660 to 1735*, at http://artworld.york.ac.uk (accessed 28 May 2014).
12. *British Apollo* 89, 18–20 Oct. 1710, in *British Newspapers 1600–1950* online.
13. *Collection for Improvement of Husbandry and Trade* 143, Friday, 26 April 1695, in *British Newspapers 1600–1950* online.
14. For more details on Simon Verelst, see Frank Lewis, *Simon Pietersz Verelst, 1644–1721* (Leigh-on-Sea: Frank Lewis, 1979); Paul Taylor, *Dutch Flower Painting, 1600–1720* (New Haven and London: Yale Univ. Press, 1995); and Paul Taylor, "Verelst, Simon Pieterszoon (1644–1710/17)", *Oxford Dictionary of National Biography* (Oxford Univ. Press, 2004), http://www.oxforddnb.com/view/article/28222?docPos=4.
15. See Tim Batchelor, "Vanitas", in *Dead Standing Things*, ed. Batchelor, 18–19.
16. H. Bunker Wright and M. K. Spears, eds., *The Literary Works of Matthew Prior*, 2 vols., 2nd ed. (Oxford Univ. Press, 1971), 1: 83.

17. Philips Angel, *Lof der Schilder-Konst (1642)*, translated in *Deceptions and Illusions: Five Centuries of Trompe l'Oeil Painting*, ed. Sybille Ebert-Schifferer (Washington: National Gallery of Art, 2002), 81.
18. Ebert-Schifferer, ed., *Deceptions and Illusions*, 19.
19. For more details on Pieter van Roestraten, see Lindsey Bridget Shaw, "Pieter van Roestraeten and the English 'vanitas'", *The Burlington Magazine* 132, no. 1047 (June 1990): 402–6.
20. Hanneke Grootenboer, *The Rhetoric of Perspective: Realism and Illusionism in Seventeenth-century Dutch Still-Life Painting* (Chicago and London: Chicago Univ. Press, 2005), 3–5.
21. Arnold Houbraken, *De Groote Schouburgh der Nederlantsche Konstschilders en Schilderessen* (Amsterdam, 1718–21), translated in Alan Chong and Wouter Kloek with Celeste Brusati and others, *Still-Life Paintings from the Netherlands, 1550–1720* (Amsterdam: Rijksmuseum, 1999), 221.
22. See Dror Wahrman, *Mr Collier's Letter Racks: A Tale of Art & Illusion at the Threshold of the Modern Information Age* (New York and Oxford: Oxford Univ. Press, 2012).
23. Celeste Brusati, *Artifice & Illusion: The Art and Writing of Samuel van Hoogstraten* (Chicago and London: Univ. of Chicago Press, 1995), 138–40.
24. Samuel van Hoogstraten, *Inleyding tot de hooge schoole der schilderkonst* (Amsterdam, 1678), translated in *Deceptions and Illusions*, ed. Ebert-Schifferer, 81.
25. Brusati, *Artifice & Illusion*, 91–93.
26. *Diary of Samuel Pepys*, http://www.pepysdiary.com/diary/1664/09/21/ (accessed 28 May 2014). The identification of this work is confused by a John Evelyn diary entry of 1 July 1664, which notes a perspective work by Robert Streeter. Yet the Dyrham Park picture has a provenance linking it to Thomas Povey through his nephew, William Blathwayt.
27. Kate Loveman, *Reading Fictions 1660–1730: Deception in English Literature and Political Culture* (Aldershot: Ashgate, 2008), 1.14.
28. Mark Knights, *The Devil in Disguise: Deception, Delusion, and Fanaticism in the Early English Enlightenment* (Oxford Univ. Press, 2011), 4–14.
29. Svetlana Alpers, *The Art of Describing: Dutch Art in the Seventeenth Century* (Univ. of Chicago Press, 1984).
30. Brusati, *Artifice & Illusion*, 93–95.
31. Alexander Lindsay, "Cowley, Abraham (1618–1667)", *Oxford Dictionary of National Biography* (Oxford Univ. Press, 2004), http://www.oxforddnb.com/view/article/6499?docPos=1 (accessed 28 May 2014).
32. The Witt Library, Courtauld Institute of Art, has reproductions of other similar works attributed to Collier, including trompe l'oeil paintings of wooden boards with prints showing Lord Cardross, Samuel Butler, and Reverend Samuel Butler (signed and dated). From the photographs these do not seem to have the same sophistication in handling or technique of the other works mentioned, and are probably in the style of or by followers of the artist rather than by Collier himself, including the one "signed and dated".
33. Joseph Monteyne, *From Still Life to the Screen: Print Culture, Display, and the Materiality of the Image in Eighteenth-century London* (New Haven and London: Yale Univ. Press, 2013), 2–6.
34. *Diary of Samuel Pepys*, http://www.pepysdiary.com/diary/1668/02/15/ (accessed 28 May 2014).
35. Lisa T. Sarasohn, *The Natural Philosophy of Margaret Cavendish: Reason and Fancy during the Scientific Revolution* (Baltimore: Johns Hopkins Univ. Press, 2010), 160.
36. *Diary of Samuel Pepys*, http://www.pepysdiary.com/diary/1665/01/21/ (accessed 28 May 2014).
37. *Diary of Samuel Pepys*, http://www.pepysdiary.com/diary/1660/10/03/ (accessed 28 May 2014): "into the King's closet, where I saw most incomparable pictures. Among the rest a book open upon a desk, which I durst have sworn was a reall book."
38. George Vertue, "The Note-books of George Vertue III", *Walpole Society* 22 (1934): 21.
39. Cited in M. Baker and B. Richardson, eds., *A Grand Design: The Art of the Victoria and Albert Museum* (London: V&A Publications, 1997), 431.
40. Jan de Brune the younger, "Wetsteen der Vernuften" ("Whetstone of the Minds") (1644), 435, quoted in Chong, Kloek, Brusati, and others, *Still Life Paintings from the Netherlands*, 31.

"A Session of Painters": Legacy, Succession, and the Prospects for British Portraiture after Kneller

Jacqueline Riding

Sir Godfrey Kneller (fig. 140) died on 26 October 1723, although according to George Vertue he had been declared "past remedy (nay dead)" as early as May 1722.[1] Alongside the regular bulletins in the London press charting Kneller's declining health, and the tributes in prose and verse celebrating a long and distinguished career, the veteran painter's protracted incapacity focused attention on one issue in particular: his successor as the King's Principal Painter and, more generally, as Britain's most celebrated artist. It was perhaps with this concern in mind that George Vertue, the engraver and contemporary chronicler of the art world, jotted down the "Names of Living painters of Note in London & their pictures by whom painted" sometime in 1723.[2] Commencing with Kneller himself, Vertue itemizes twenty-two painters, including history painters, portraitists, and miniature painters, before turning more briefly to the persons and portraits of three figures working in other fields: the architect James Gibbs, the "Engraver of Gems" Charles Christian Reysen, and the ivory carver David Le Marchand, whose portrait, he notes, is "painted by J[oseph] Highmore". In effect, Vertue's list of painters and portraitists is the roll call from which Sir Godfrey's successor was likely to emerge.

This essay is split into two halves. The first half will seek to suggest what it actually meant to succeed Sir Godfrey Kneller while exploring the public debate that revolved around those who were seen as candidates for such an honour. Here, I will focus in particular on a pamphlet—entitled *A Session of Painters*—that dealt with this issue in some detail. Then, in the second half of this essay, I will focus on the portrait that is mentioned by Vertue at the end of his list—that of David Le Marchand by Joseph Highmore—the creation of which occurred in parallel with Kneller's final illness. This picture, I will argue, served to declare Highmore's own candidacy as a potential successor to Kneller, even though the painter himself was not included in Vertue's initial list of "Living painters of Note in London". Moving between the general debates about British painting stimulated by Kneller's death and the more specific example of Highmore will, I hope, offer a fruitful, two-sided introduction to the tensions and opportunities of the London art world—particularly portraiture—at the end of the period covered by this book.

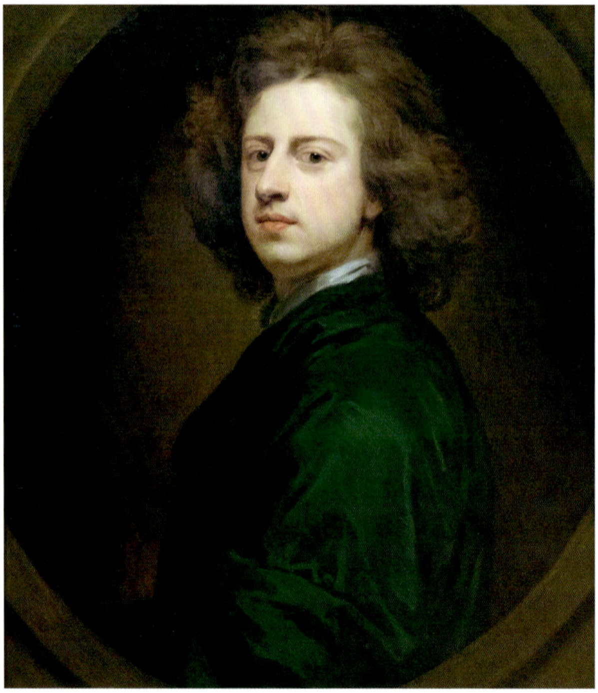

140. Sir Godfrey Kneller, Bt, *Self Portrait*, 1685, oil on canvas, 29¾ x 24¾ in. (75.6 x 62. 9 cm). National Portrait Gallery, London

AFTER KNELLER?

What was at stake in the case of Kneller's death is suggested, at least in part, by the following announcement in the *Daily Post* of 28 October 1723: "On Sunday Morning between 12 and 1, died at his House in Great Queen-Street, Sir Godfrey Kneller, Knt. Principal Painter to his Majesty to which Place is annex'd a Salary of 200 l. per Annum." Kneller's successor as Principal Painter could expect unrivalled access to king and court, with all the associated influence and status, together with a very tidy annual stipend and perhaps even a knighthood. Kneller's career had demonstrated that the position of court painter could provide a significant stimulus for private portrait commissions, as well as for the production and reproduction of official royal imagery in oil on canvas. The artist, as Principal Painter to the King, had also exploited the possibilities of the print market in this regard, acutely aware that engravings after his royal portraits not only served to promote his courtly position, but also helped publicize his London studio. In 1715, soon after the arrival of George I in London, Vertue claims that he [Vertue] had "engravd his Majestys picture from the first Original picture [by Kneller] on a large plate and being first done in print was shown at Court by Sr. Godfrey and much approved on several thousands being Sold of them".[3] This proliferation of the artist's royal imagery, together with the similarly assiduous graphic reproduction of his aristocratic portraits, served to emphasize the ubiquity and dominance of the Kneller "brand" of portraiture, and helped him acquire significant wealth. By the early 1720s Vertue could observe that Kneller "lost 20 thous[a]nd pounds in the South Sea [Bubble]" and "yet has clear 2 thousand a Year income".[4] Kneller's career, in sum, suggested that the vacancy caused by his death offered a career-changing opportunity.

Yet to be considered the true heir to Sir Godfrey Kneller was not only a matter of succeeding him as Principal Painter; it was also a matter of matching the supremacy he had universally been regarded as enjoying in the field of portraiture. Kneller was acknowledged by most observers as the pre-eminent portraitist of his generation, which was confirmed by the panegyrics published around the time of his death. However, there was far less certainty about the quality of the wider community of London-based portraitists, let alone any unanimity as to who, following his demise, was to be regarded as this community's most distinguished practitioner.

Even as Kneller lingered on throughout 1722 and the first half of 1723, opinions regarding the current tranche of portrait painters—and the identity of a possible successor—emerged from the coffee houses and clubs of the city and into a broader more public arena through journal articles and individual pamphlets. One opening salvo was Thomas Tickell's poem *To Sir Godfrey Kneller at his Country Seat*, published anonymously in response to Kneller's illness and brief recovery in the summer of 1722. Tickell's poem commences as a celebration of the artist's illustrious and international career, declaring that the painter had been "Sought by the Kings of every distant land,/ And every Hero, worthy of thy hand." Tickell goes on to dramatize Sir Godfrey's mastery of the intellectual, psychological, and physiological aspects of portraiture:

> A Mind, that grasps the whole, is rarely found . . .
> Few, like thy Genius, at Proportion aim,
> All great, all graceful, and throughout the same.[5]

All this stood in marked contrast to the "Half-learn'd, half-painters, and half-wits" whom Tickell suggests "abound" in the British art world. The poet concludes his eulogy with the hope that Kneller might, despite his recent physical ailments, manage to "Paint on":

Since after Thee may rise an impious Line,
Coarse Manglers of the human face divine,
Paint on, till Fate dissolve thy mortal part,
And live and die the Monarch of thy Art.[6]

That the poem was published by Jacob Tonson, founder of the Kit-Cat club and Kneller's patron, goes some way to explain its general thrust and tone. Tickell refrains from naming the "Coarse Manglers" who, even as he writes, are forming an "impious Line" to replace Sir Godfrey. However, contemporaries would have had no difficulty in putting together their own speculative lists. Vertue's "painters of Note", for example, include a number of figures who enjoyed considerable critical and commercial success in the period: Kneller's one-time assistant Charles Jervas; Michael Dahl; Jonathan Richardson; and a potential young pretender, John Vanderbank. In Tickell's opinion, however, none of these men had any hope of matching Kneller's achievements and abilities, nor of being a worthy Principal Painter to the King.

Nevertheless, on 4 November 1723 the *Daily Journal* reported that "_____ Garvase, Esq; of the Parish of St. James's in the liberty of Westminster, is appointed Principal Painter to his Majesty, with the Salary of 200 l. per Ann. in the room of Sir Godfrey Kneller, decease'd." The short announcement concludes by noting that the position "is in the Gift of his Grace the Duke of Newcastle", inferring that political manoeuvring rather than artistic merit had ultimately influenced the decision. Charles Jervas (ca. 1675–1739; fig. 141) —the artist referred to in the *Daily Journal*'s report—was the favoured painter of Sir Robert Walpole (1676–1745), since 1721 the most important figure within the Whig administration as both Chancellor of the Exchequer and First Lord of the Treasury (and therefore effectively "prime minister"). Thomas Pelham-Holles, Duke of Newcastle (1693–1768) was Walpole's political protégé. Thus, within a week of Kneller's death, the coveted court position had quickly been transferred to an artist who was an adept and successful portrait painter, collector, and man of letters, but who was, apparently, so unfamiliar to the London press that they consistently misnamed him as "_____ Garvase", "Thomas Jervais", "Thomas Jervase", and "Thomas Gervaise" over subsequent days.[7] Even before the appointment had been made, the rumour that Jervas was to replace Sir Godfrey "as the Kings painter" had—according to Vertue—brought him a "great increase of business".[8] Vertue himself is mildly critical in his comments on Jervas's work, noting that "there is something wanting in the truth of the lines the just or good imitation of nature" and, later, that Jervas was "much a mannerist" in his portrait style.[9] For Vertue a "mannerist" is one whose style distracts from or even distorts the "just appearance" of the portrait's

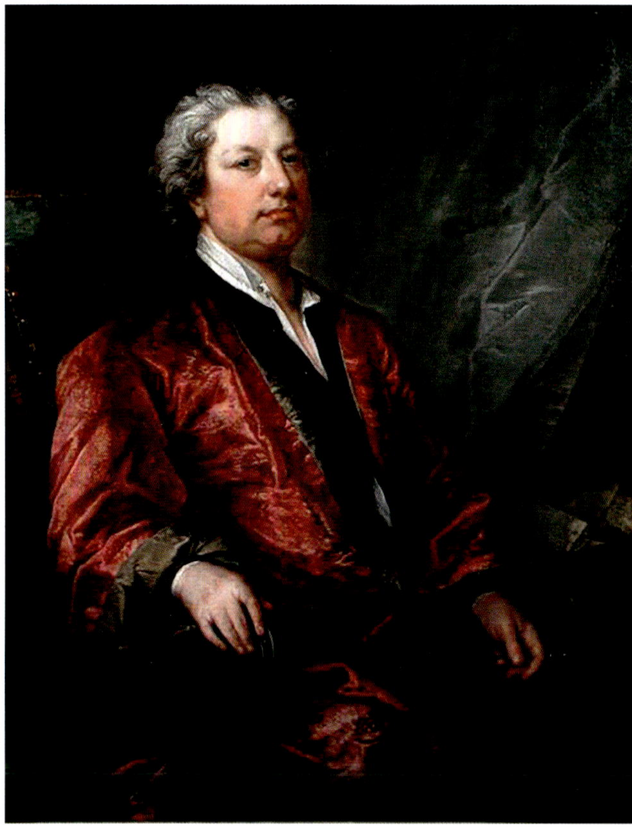

141. Charles Jervas, *Self Portrait*, 1725, oil on canvas, 48⅞ x 39¾ in. (124 x 101 cm). Private collection

subject.[10] We can infer from such comments that for Vertue, Jervas was good, but not good enough.[11]

Others, however, were far less restrained in expressing their negative opinions. Opposition to Jervas's appointment, no doubt triggered in part by the barefaced politicking that lay behind it, began to appear in print prior to his formal installation at St James's Palace in January 1724. On 31 December 1723 even the decidedly pro-government journal, *Pasquin*, could not resist entering the fray with the announcement that:

> on the 18th Day of *January* next, near *St. James's*, to the great Satisfaction of all *Connoiseurs*, will be perform'd a most surprizing Act of Inoculation; it being no less than the Budding or Grafting the Art of Painting on a Man, who never had it before:— But as he believes he hath gone already through it, it is fear'd that the Pustles of the said Distemper will not rise very high on him.[12]

The author is likely to be referring in particular to inoculation against small pox, that is, the infecting of a healthy person with a mild strain of the disease to encourage general resistance. This process had been observed by Lady Mary Wortley Montagu (1689–1762) in the Near East and enthusiastically promoted by her on returning to Britain in 1718. However, the idea of inoculation was not universally accepted or understood and it remained highly controversial. For satirists, the concept of this new, foreign, and potentially dangerous medical process had rich possibilities as a political or religious metaphor. Here, the author of *Pasquin* uses the metaphor in combination with the horticultural terms "budding" and "grafting" to mount a sardonic attack on both the artist and his supporters.

In this period artistic accomplishment was regularly measured both by mechanical ability—derived from a natural "genius" which is then refined through the study of acknowledged masters—and by the possession of a strong and agile intellect. A lesser painter might have one or the other of these qualities, but not both. As described by Jonathan Richardson senior, "a Painter must not only be a Poet, an Historian, a Mathematician, &c. he must be a Mechanick, his Hand, and Eye, must be as Expert as his Head is Clear, and Lively, and well stored with Science." And therefore he must be able to judge "whether what he has drawn is of the same Magnitude with what he pretended to imitate . . . and must have a Hand exact enough to form these in his Work answerable to the Ideas he has taken of them".[13] Distinction in the art of painting, according to such authors, was something that was founded on natural talent, but needed to be developed by assiduous study over time. In contrast, suggests *Pasquin*, Jervas attempts to attain his distinction through unnatural means: for this critic, the ceremony at St James's is lampooned as an experimental operation in which partisan and ill-informed "Connoiseurs"—he may well have had Walpole and Newcastle in mind—aim to forcibly and artificially introduce artistic talent onto and then into Jervas's body. In addition, the author may have been making a sly reference to Alexander Pope's "Epistle to Mr. Jervas", printed with the 1716 edition of Charles-Alphonse du Fresnoy's *The Art of Painting*, wherein John Dryden's original translation was revised by Jervas. Here the portraitist's skill is lauded using horticultural symbolism: "Beauty, frail Flow'r, that ev'ry Season fears,/ Blooms in thy Colours for a thousand Years":[14] an opinion *Pasquin* would obviously dispute.

Pasquin goes on to describe in detail how the hoped-for miracle is to occur at St James's:

> . . . there are great Preparations made for the Experiment: Sir *Godfrey Kneller*'s Thumb and his middle Finger being already sent for to *Twickenham*, where he is inter'd; from which will be then taken a Part both for the

> Patient's Thumb and Finger, which will be splitted on by one of Sir Godfry's Pencil, Sticks; and of all commons, nay un-common Judges, infect him [Jervas] with the said Art of Painting.[15]

So the macabre operation, as described, appears to be more physical or mechanical than intellectual, focused as it is upon the hand that holds the brush, rather than the mind that directs it. The immediate effect is to conjure up a sort of Frankenstein-type assemblage: one part Sir Godfrey, the rest Jervas as passive recipient. Here, the "distemper" of genius that pulses still through Sir Godfrey's thumb and finger will, it is hoped, gradually spread and contaminate its host. *Pasquin* observes, hinting at the grotesque nature of this new configuration, that "in Token of this great Performance, the very next Day, or very soon after, he [Jervas] shall be so improved and acknowledg'd by all true inoculated Knight and Limner, Sir Godfry Ger—se." The operation will therefore create a hybrid, and in so doing, Jervas will not only be transformed into a "true . . . Limner", but also elevated to a "true . . . Knight".[16] Although the analogy is, on a basic level, a medical one, it can also be interpreted in terms of Catholic beliefs concerning the power of saintly relics: the taking of body parts from the corpse of a venerated artist in order to perform a miraculous transformation or transfiguration on a living successor.

A year or so after Jervas's installation another anonymous pamphlet was in circulation, entitled *A Session of Painters . . . occasion'd by the death of the late Sir Godfrey Kneller, inscrib'd to his Widow, The Lady Kneller*.[17] The fact that the pamphlet and poem it contained are dedicated to Lady Kneller masks with a veneer of gallantry what is at times a vicious personal and professional attack on her husband's rivals and successors. The author, who was later revealed to be the aspiring playwright Benjamin Victor (died 1778), declares his wish to reassert the memory of Sir Godfrey, in the aftermath of the inelegant stampede that had taken place to succeed him.[18] The poem begins:

> Mourn, *England*, mourn, since KNELLER is no more,
> Who shall his Place supply?
> What *Genius* can the mighty *Art* restore,
> Or must it vacant lie?
> Alas! Already is the Laurel giv'n,
> Before APELLES can descend from Heav'n.[19]

The poem thus commences with the now familiar vocabulary of a Kneller panegyric. But the fifth line clearly refers to the transfer of Kneller's court office, and therefore the status of pre-eminent portrait painter, to Charles Jervas. And that such an appointment was achieved before Apelles—the ancient Roman painter, now elevated to a deity—could pass judgment himself, continues the line of argument hinted at in the announcement in the *Daily Post* quoted earlier and more directly in *Pasquin*, that artistic ability had had nothing whatever to do with the decision-making process that had brought Jervas to such eminence. In the poem, a clearly irritated Apelles comes down to earth to overturn this presumptuous appointment and "to give the vacant Crown" himself, declaring:

> He must by *Me* be nam'd.
> *He* that usurps it ne'er was known to me,
> *Merit* shall wear the *Wreath*, by my Decree.[20]

It is the outcome as well as the process that is at fault here: Jervas, the usurper, is not only the wrong choice, but—worse still—is an unknown quantity to the great Apelles.

The poem quickly moves on from a veiled critique of political interference and usurpation towards a somewhat bleak assessment of current artistic talent. By the fourth verse, Apelles commands that "*Candidates of Worth* have room to plead;/ None but of *Worth* shall the deceas'd succeed."[21] In the ensuing procession of self-selecting candidates, only ten of the many London-based painters are specifically alluded to.[22] Yet this parade is curiously akin to the feared "impious Line" of "Coarse Manglers" from Tickell's earlier tract. The poet presents each candidate in turn; and though he does not name them explicitly, he offers barely concealed hints to his readers regarding their true identity. In verse nine, for example, he writes,

> A Rich Old *Sage*, to prove his boasted Skill,
> To draw a Portrait try'd;
> When, strange! his Pencil chang'd into a Quill,
> *Apelles*, smiling, cry'd—
> You *Paint* almost as ill as you *Indite*,
> And yet you *Draw* much worse than you can *Write*.[23]

The reference to a "Sage" (suggesting wisdom, experience, and age, and here inferring literary prowess), the inclusion of the word "Rich", and the fact that the said artist, when attempting to produce a portrait, finds his "pencil" or brush transforming into a quill pen, confirms that Jonathan Richardson senior (1665–1745; fig. 142), then a mature fifty-eight years old, is the poet's target. By 1725 Richardson was well known as a theorist and connoisseur through such important published

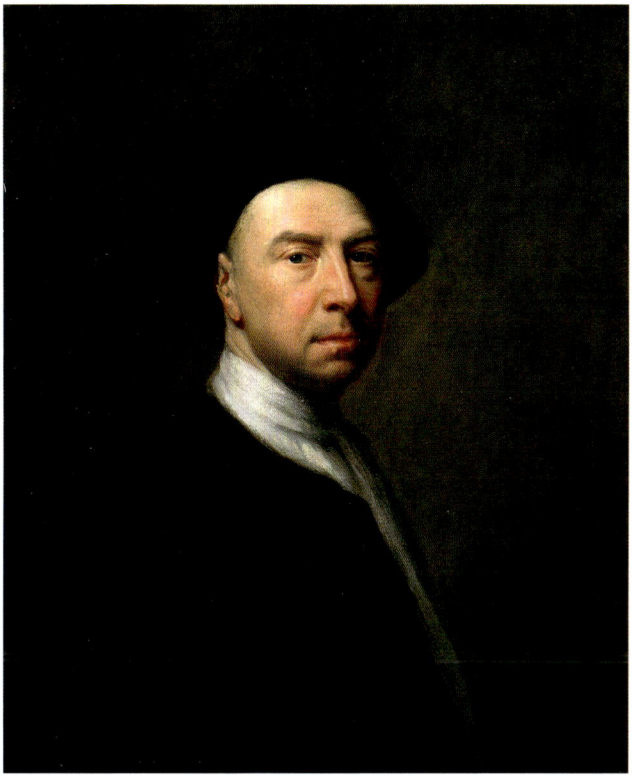

142. Jonathan Richardson, *Self Portrait*, 1729, oil on canvas, 29 x 24¾ in. (73.7 x 62.9 cm). National Portrait Gallery, London

treatises as the earlier-quoted *An essay on the theory of painting* (London, 1715, second edition enlarged and corrected 1725) and *An account of some of the statues, bas-reliefs, drawings and pictures in Italy. &c* (London, 1722). The statement that Richardson writes better than he paints—or rather, that his writing is not as bad as his drawing—is hardly flattering to either of his twin pursuits. The poet refers to another "Sage" in verse twelve:

APELLES wav'd his Hand, with graceful Air,
To an old modest * *Sage*, *D—l.
'Tis just (he cry'd) that I this Truth declare
To this ill-judging Age;
Thy Judgment I approve; go on! be Great:
'Tis sure from Merit well to imitate.[24]

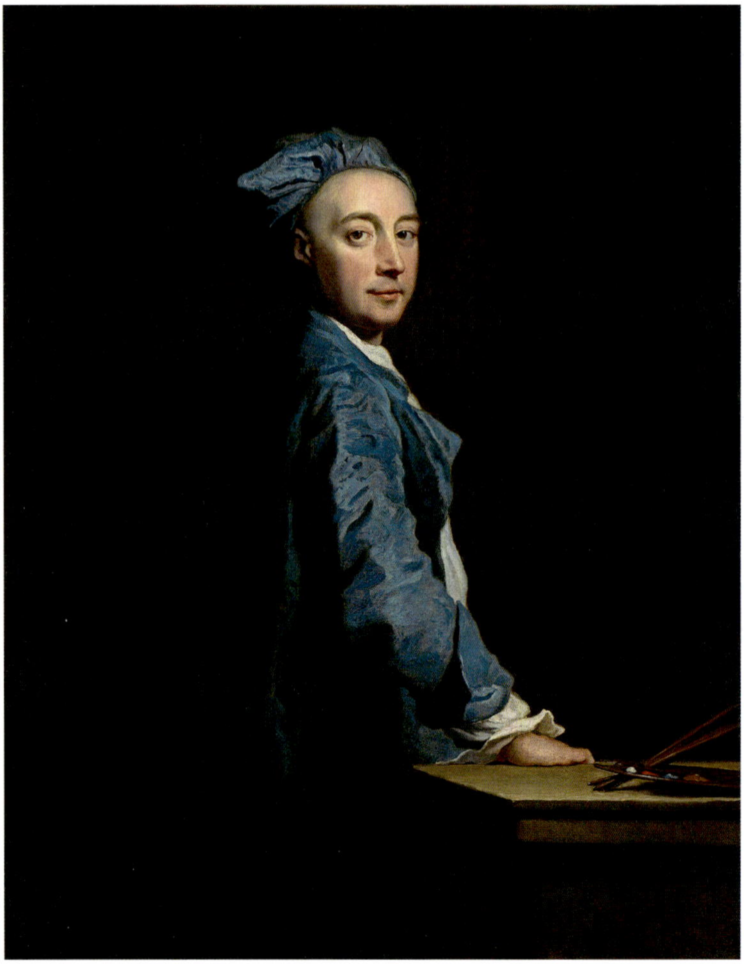

143. Joseph Highmore, *Self Portrait*, ca. 1730, oil on canvas, 49¾ x 39¾ in. (126.4 x 101 cm). Felton Bequest, 1947, National Gallery of Victoria, Melbourne

The cypher "D—l" in conjunction with the reference to age and experience, clearly indicates that the sixty-four-year-old Michael Dahl (1659–1743) is the poet's subject in this instance. Here, the term "Sage" might also refer to Dahl's position as a role model and teacher at the early drawing academies, in particular Kneller's Great Queen Street Academy, founded in 1711. Benjamin Victor, through the figure of Apelles, allows that the Swedish-born artist is deserving of praise, having "Judgment" and "Merit". However, he is not suggested as a suitable replacement for Kneller. Given that both "Sages"—Richardson and then Dahl—have thus been effectively dismissed as Kneller's successors, it can be presumed that the author considers this contest a younger man's game.

In support of this argument, it is worth noting that the majority of the artists alluded to in the poem were either recently established or still emergent. In verse seven, for instance, the following candidate steps forward:

H— r, a Famous City *Candidate*,
Came jutting out his Breech,
Wish not (*Apelles* cry'd) a better Fate,
Thou daubing tasteless Wretch;
Content thyself to please ill-judging Sinners,
To get their Money and devour their Dinners.[25]

From the conceit "*H— r*" it is likely that the poet is referring to Joseph Highmore (1692–1780; fig. 143). This identification becomes even more certain when we note the reference to a "City" candidate. Highmore had launched his portrait practice in 1715 in the City parish of St Swithin, where Vertue observed, "he [had] good employ. amongst the Citizens."[26] Highmore was a native of the City and his local schooling and clerkship in Law provided him with vital early contacts and clients.[27] Tellingly, the poet states that Highmore should content himself in pleasing "ill-judging Sinners" for money and gaining access to their social milieu, which places the artist within a circle of self-made tradesmen and financiers rather than the social elite. There is a sense of Highmore "singing for his supper" in the phrase, "To get their Money and devour their Dinners": in the exchange of art for money and food, the painter becomes undignified and his art discredited. The term "ill-judging", meanwhile, suggests a clientele with no critical faculty in artistic matters and therefore signals an unfavourable critique of Highmore's patrons and practice. Describing the artist as a "daubing tasteless Wretch" clarifies the poet's "anti-City" stance: either Highmore has forfeited his right to replace Kneller by producing "daubed" portraits for undiscerning or gullible patrons, or else he deserves no better status of client in the first place, due to his limited abilities. We can therefore conclude that for the poet, Highmore's lack of aristocratic sitters precludes, once again, his candidacy as Kneller's successor.

Verse thirteen, meanwhile, indicates where the author's support lies and the reason why Highmore, a rival, has been dismissed:

Here paus'd the *God*—and viewing well each rank,
Thus spake with eager Voice,
Why do I miss my Fav'rite *Van—k*?

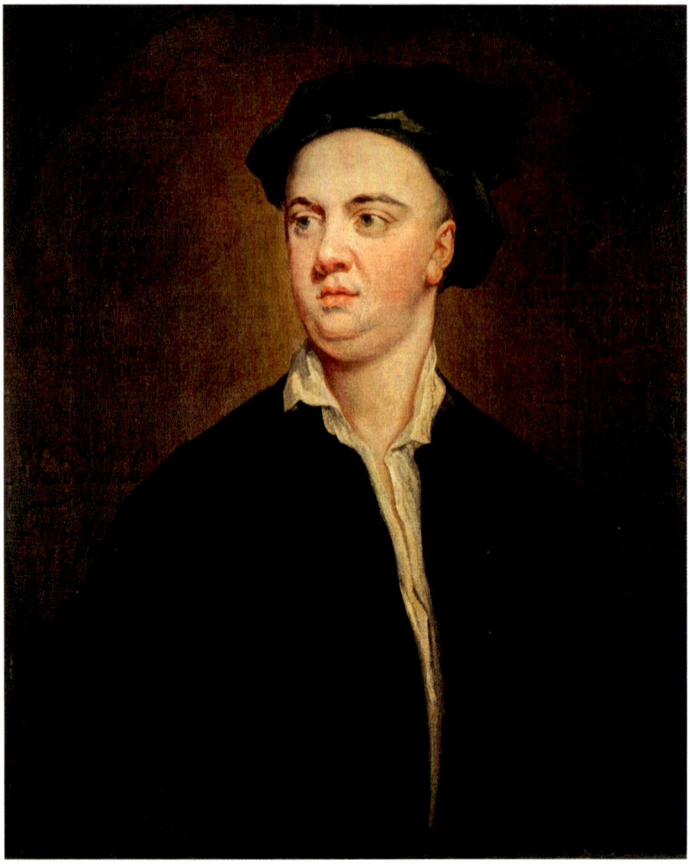

144. John Vanderbank, *James Thomson*, 1726, oil on canvas, 30¼ x 25¼ in. (76.8 x 64.1 cm). Scottish National Portrait Gallery

He long has been my Choice:
Oft have I said, if He with KNELLER's care
Wou'd Progress make, He might His loss repair.[28]

By the early 1720s, John Vanderbank (1694–1739), an artistic prodigy with a private income, was the co-proprietor of the first St Martin's Lane Academy. It was not only Benjamin Victor who thought that Vanderbank had the potential to become the leading portrait painter of his generation (fig. 144). On the painter's premature death in 1739, which was widely attributed to a life of excess and dissolution, Vertue wrote a short assessment of his qualities which included the suggestion that, "after the Death of Sr. Godfrey Kneller—he might have carryd all before him."[29]

But despite all of Vanderbank's obvious artistic talents, his lack of restraint and "the Blemishes of his Vanitys, *of high-living*" proved disastrous to his career, reputation, and ultimately his health.[30] Vanderbank, had he possessed better personal qualities, would—according to Vertue—have been the dominant force in British art. Victor, too, hints that the painter's nonchalant, even careless attitude towards his chosen profession was already evident by the mid-1720s. The fact that Apelles cannot find his favourite within the ranks before him suggests that the artist has not even bothered to present his candidature in person. Apelles declares, with the air of an overindulgent parent, that if only he could emulate Kneller's diligence and focus, then Vanderbank would ably fill the void created by Sir Godfrey's death.

Having assessed the candidates, Apelles returns to the subject of Kneller himself:

> Observe my Kneller, mark his Virtues well,
> How just a *Draught* he drew;
> He strove *Vandike* and *Lilly* to excel:
> His comprehensive View
> Held all the Noble Theory compleat,
> Wise, yet not vain, exalted, yet discreet.[31]

The poet itemizes what made Kneller a great artist: his accuracy of draughtsmanship; his intimate knowledge of the work of his great predecessors Sir Anthony van Dyck and Sir Peter Lely, coupled with his ambition to excel their achievements; his knowledge of the theory as well as the practice of art; and, finally, the character traits which temper the negative effects of his celebrity and status—that is wisdom, modesty, diplomacy, and restraint. Apelles then imparts the following advice:

> My fav'rite Sons peruse his Tracts with care,
> And truly Nature know,
> You must his Taste enjoy, his Judgment share,
> And with his Spirit glow,
> 'Till one thus shines to match the mighty dead,
> The Wreath shall stay on the *De Facto*'s Head.[32]

Having directed his "fav'rite Sons", with Vanderbank as the most prominent, to learn from Kneller's example, Apelles suggests that—as things stand—no one painter is currently good enough to succeed "the mighty dead". Therefore Jervas, the "*De Facto*" occupant of Kneller's position, will have to continue in his place, until such time as a true successor has finally emerged.

Whatever their particular perspectives regarding the future of British portraiture, the writings of Tickell, *Pasquin*, and Benjamin Victor collectively reflect the contemporary sense that there was no single, universally agreed candidate to succeed Sir Godfrey. But Tickell's augury of doom, *Pasquin*'s macabre vision of cross-bodily inoculation, and Victor's blatant partisanship distract from the reality that in 1723 the future for portraiture, from another perspective, could be seen to be particularly bright. Vertue certainly thought so, and seems to have recognized the merits of a situation in which no one portraitist dominated the London and therefore British art scene. Indeed, his various comments on the artists of the day—and his list of "painters of Note"—testify to the emergence of a new generation of painters in the city, a generation which had been nurtured by that older cohort of painters of which Kneller had been a part, and which had been transformed into a coherent corporate body by its shared involvement in institutions such as Kneller's own Academy of Painting. This Academy had not only provided aspirant painters with the means to draw from casts and life models, but was cosmopolitan in its membership and discursive in its character, encouraging conversation about the theories as well as the practices of British and European art. A large number of the artists listed by Vertue, and included in *A Session of Painters*, had been involved at the Academy, either as teachers or students. Dahl, Richardson, and Sir James Thornhill, for example, took the role of elders, while figures such as Vanderbank, the young pretender extolled by both Vertue and Victor, had been students at the Academy from its inception. Following on from this, it can be argued that the death of Kneller did not so much generate a vacuum within British painting, as commentators such as Tickell and Victor were suggesting, but rather marked the moment when a new, locally trained generation of practitioners first saw an opportunity to assert their credentials as ambitious artists, entirely worthy—both individually and collectively—of taking on the mantle of their great predecessor.

THE "CITY" CANDIDATE: JOSEPH HIGHMORE'S PORTRAIT OF DAVID LE MARCHAND

This was certainly the case with another product of Kneller's Academy, Joseph Highmore. As earlier observed, in 1723 Vertue had noted Highmore's signed but undated portrait of David Le Marchand at the end of his list of portraits of eminent living artists.[33] This portrait, as I will now suggest through a detailed reading of Highmore's image, served not only as a striking likeness of a contemporary sculptor; it was also a painting executed to demonstrate that Highmore, too, should now be considered as someone whose practice competed with, and challenged, that of Kneller.

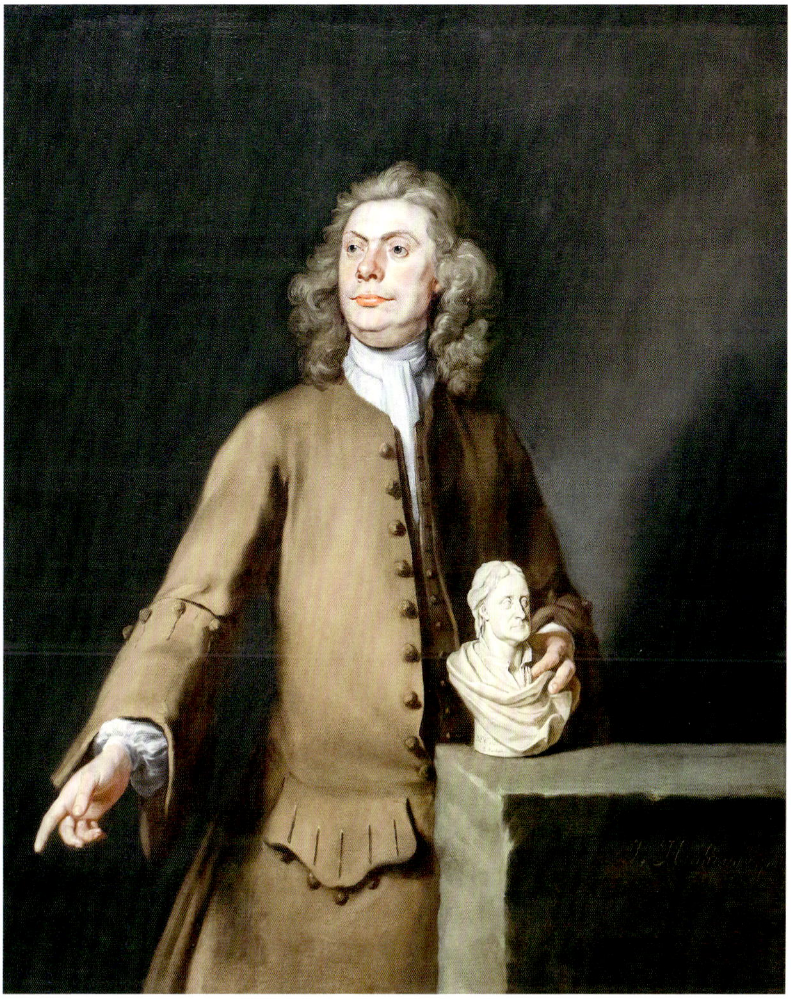

145. Joseph Highmore, *David Le Marchand*, ca. 1723, oil on canvas, 48¾ x 39¼ in. (124 x 99.7 cm). National Portrait Gallery, London

Highmore's portrait (fig. 145), which is now in the National Portrait Gallery, London, was until 1991 in the possession of descendants of Mathew Raper (1665–1748) and Moses Raper (1679–1748), wealthy London silk merchants with close City connections.[34] By 1723 Le Marchand and Highmore had established strong patron-client relationships with the Raper family: they both produced family portraits and, in the case of Le Marchand, ivory portrait busts of close family friends, including Sir Christopher Wren and John Locke. One such portrait bust, of

Sir Isaac Newton (with Le Marchand's signature placed in clear view), appears in the Highmore portrait. Meanwhile, a small ivory relief of Highmore in profile, which was in the collection of Lady King (a Highmore descendant by marriage) in 1930, may be a reciprocal portrait by Le Marchand.[35]

Soon after noting down the existence of the Le Marchand portrait, Vertue composed a short biography of its creator, whom he describes as "an ingenious young painter". In this commentary, Vertue noted Highmore's early law career, his self-directed study and his attendance, from 1713, at the Great Queen Street Academy. Vertue states that Highmore, during his time at the Academy, "fell into acquaintance with most of the ingenious masters" who would have included Kneller himself, and as a result, the young student "turn'd his genius to portrait paintings".[36] Highmore certainly observed and learnt from Kneller's technique. His ownership of eleven paintings by Kneller, including three described in his sale catalogue as "Beginnings of Gentlemens Heads", suggests that Highmore acquired them as models illustrating the various stages of Kneller's painting process.[37] Technically, Kneller was particularly famed for his speed in creating a likeness, which he had used to spectacular effect as a young man at court. Vertue recounts an occasion where Kneller and Sir Peter Lely painted Charles II's portrait at the same sitting, "he [Kneller] having at this first setting almost finished his piece, when Sr Peter had only dead colour'd his picture". Vertue goes on: "After this his reputation daily increased that most noblemen & Ladies would have their pictures done by him."[38] Highmore had clearly noted the sense of immediacy that such technical facility could produce in a portrait; as Vertue later observed in 1731: "M^r^. Highmore paints much, & the faces often at one Sitting as much finisht. as he can—never touches any more. this draws into a Natural way a good likeness."[39] On a practical and financial level, Highmore must also have noted the benefit of speed to the viability of a commercial portrait practice.

Vertue's 1723 biographical note concludes by suggesting that Highmore is "very correct & just in his representations & imitations of nature. with a free masterly manner his pencill free & bold. his colours natural & lively his draparys the habits as worn very natural".[40] As this assessment appears to have been prompted by his recollection of the Le Marchand portrait, which is named just before this entry in the engraver's notebook, Vertue's observations in regard to style and effect will be analysed here as a contemporary response to both Highmore's artistic potential and this portrait in particular.[41]

In Highmore's painting Le Marchand stands behind a roughly hewn block of stone, gazing out to our left and pointing towards the ground with his right hand. He holds in his left hand the small portrait bust, which rests on the stone block. The block and background are rendered in varying tones of brown and

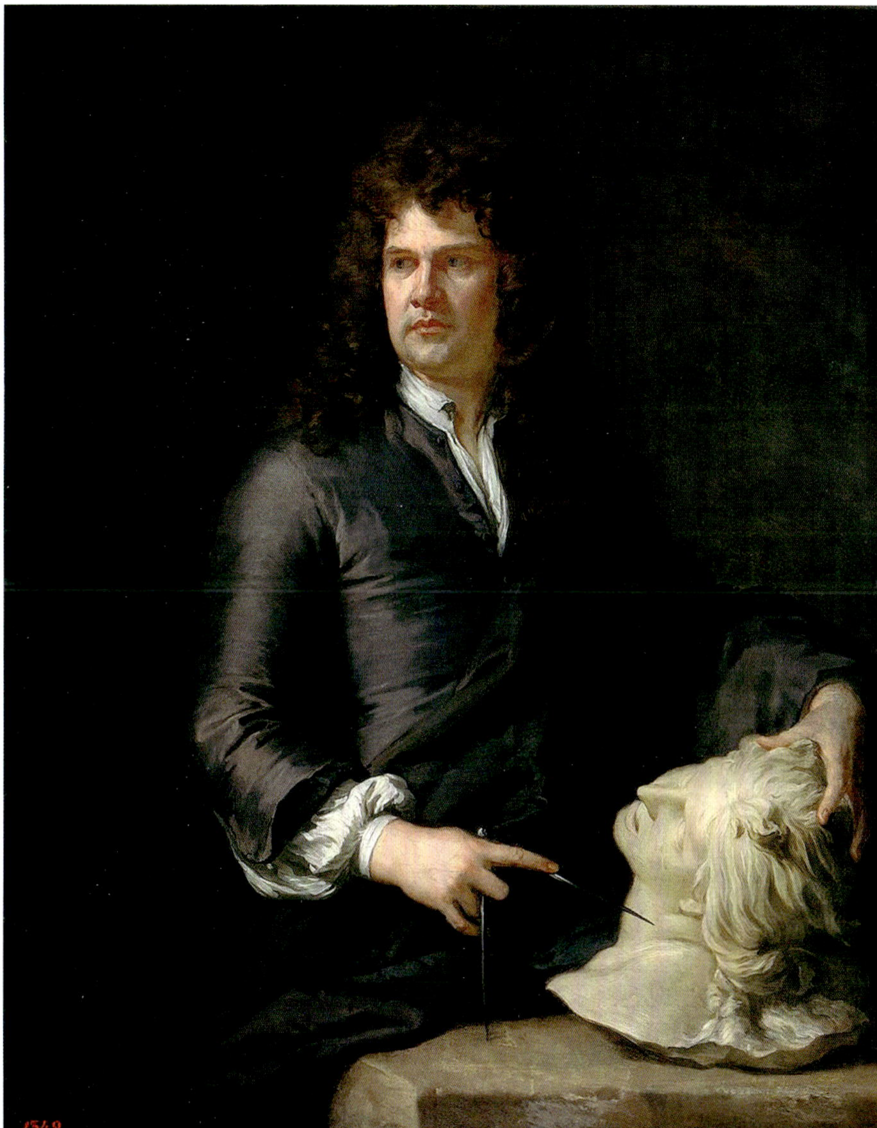

146. Sir Godfrey Kneller, Bt, *Grinling Gibbons*, 1689, oil on canvas, 49¼ x 35⅜ in. (125 x 90 cm). State Hermitage Museum, St. Petersburg

green, which serve to concentrate the eye almost exclusively upon the figure. Significantly, Highmore's composition self-consciously refers to an earlier and well-known prototype. As a carver, Le Marchand obviously had a close professional affinity with the woodcarver and sculptor Grinling Gibbons (1648–1721). Kneller's portrait of Gibbons of 1689 (fig. 146), which by the 1720s was in the collection of Sir Robert Walpole, was widely known through the John Smith mezzotint of 1690. In fact the composition and iconography within Kneller's portrait provided a standard for later portraits of sculptors and carvers during the early eighteenth century.[42]

As in the case of the Le Marchand portrait, Gibbons stands behind a block of stone, holding a sculpted head in his left hand. In his right he holds a pair of compasses, which he is using to measure the bust. James Douglas Stewart identified the bust as a cast from Gian Lorenzo Bernini's *Pluto and Proserpina* of 1621–22 (Galleria Borghese, Rome). He further suggested that Gibbons holds the compass of "Prudence" and "Wisdom" and is shown subduing Proserpina, goddess of the senses.[43] The particular use of a cast after Bernini, a flamboyant as well as highly acclaimed artist, which Gibbons is shown in the process of subduing, is a visual metaphor for Gibbons's command of his art, as well as a pictorial conceit that introduces movement, through the writhing posture of the goddess, within an otherwise still composition. Gibbons looks out to his right, away from the goddess's head, as if gazing at some unknown object or person outside the picture plane. He has perhaps been distracted by a thought. This gesture is mirrored to an extent in the Le Marchand portrait. Gibbons's large dark brown wig frames his face, its loose curls cascading onto his shoulders and the breast of his grey-blue silk robe. The background is plain, and the light—which highlights the sculpted head, stone block, and Gibbons's torso and face—creates a shadow behind him that covers the left half of the canvas, and sharpens the contrast between highlighted figure and surroundings. This formula is again repeated in the Highmore portrait but, it should be noted, with greater exaggeration than is demonstrated in the Kneller painting.

In creating a visual association between Gibbons and Le Marchand, the latter sculptor is aligned with Gibbons both as a sitter and a carver. But the treatment of the two artists is very different. Le Marchand's appearance, in absolute contrast to that of Gibbons, does not attempt to elevate him to the rank of gentleman. Le Marchand is shown, not as wigged, but with his own long hair. He wears brown, woollen, resolutely unfussy artisan's clothing. His robustly fleshy face reveals Highmore's intention to create a true portrait rather than any obvious attempt at flattery. As noted by Vertue, Highmore has produced a portrait which is "natural & lively" and "in the habit as worn".

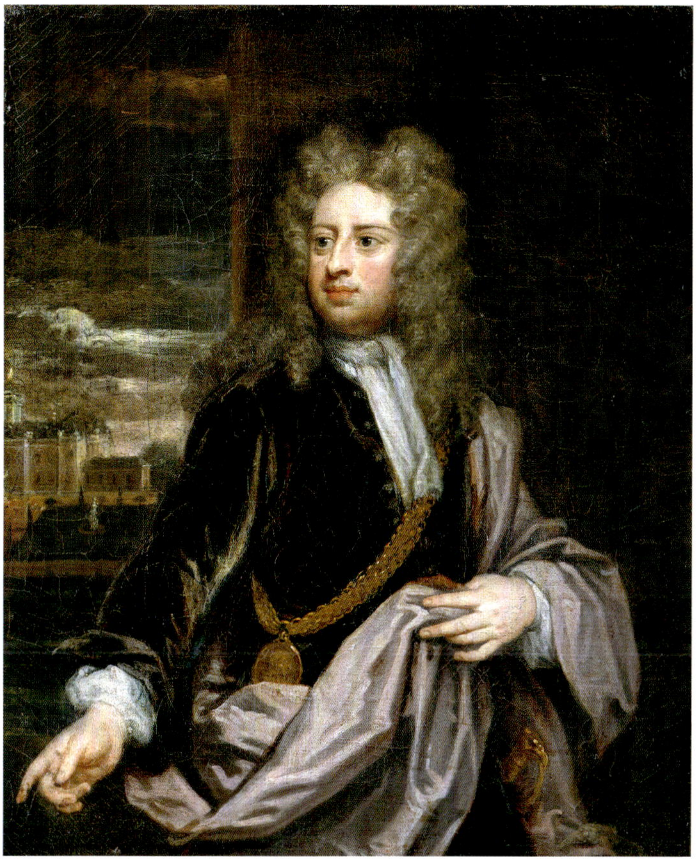

147. Sir Godfrey Kneller, Bt, *Self Portrait*, ca. 1706–11, oil on canvas, 18¼ x 14 in. (46.4 x 35.6 cm). National Portrait Gallery, London

However, one of the most distinctive aspects of the Le Marchand portrait is the pose that Highmore has chosen for his subject. This pose suggests a particularly authoritative masculine archetype. The turn of the right hand with its elegant downward gesture appears to indicate towards some unknown object located on the ground to the viewer's left, an object towards which Le Marchand faces, but with which he does not directly engage. In fact Le Marchand's pose and to some extent gesture can be found in a self-portrait by Kneller. Two versions of this painting exist, respectively dated 1706 (Uffizi, Florence) and ca. 1706–11 (fig. 147). The re-use of this pose in Le Marchand's portrait may well have encouraged the recollection on the spectator's part of Kneller's stellar career and honours.

Whatever its origins and intentions, Highmore's striking portrait begins the transformation of his practice into something more profound and inventive than had been the case beforehand. It is worth noting that this is a portrait not of a merchant—that is, one of Highmore's established clientele—but rather of an artist. The resulting image is as much a celebration of artistic creativity as of Le Marchand himself. Significantly, the carver's attention appears to be directed towards the source of the bright light that bathes his body and the ivory bust, and the effect of the pose he adopts, exaggerated by the particular use of chiaroscuro, is both dramatic and forceful. Rather than depicting him "as seen" in natural daylight, Highmore has chosen to light Le Marchand in this stark manner: perhaps with the intention of suggesting a corresponding boldness or intensity within Le Marchand's character. This is carried through to the figure itself via the almost arrogant lift of the chin, the slightly widened eyes and raised eyebrows, and the self-assured stance. Le Marchand's facial and bodily expression is bold, almost visionary.

In contrast to the Gibbons portrait, Highmore does not include the tools of Le Marchand's trade, but instead depicts a single example of the ivory carver's work: the portrait bust of Sir Isaac Newton (1642–1727) commissioned and owned by Newton himself.[44] This contrasts again with Kneller's portrait of Gibbons, where the carver is represented with a bust by Bernini, rather than with an example of his own work. Indeed, the Highmore portrait can be viewed as a double portrait of Le Marchand and the sitter of the ivory, who by 1723 was one of the most celebrated figures in Europe. In fact, Newton's fame was such that the production of his likeness had become a small industry in its own right. His earliest portrait dates from 1689 and is the first of four images by Kneller, and one of fourteen portrait-types executed during Newton's lifetime.[45] It depicts the natural philosopher and mathematician as a relatively young man of forty-six with his own pale grey hair falling to his shoulders. The simplicity of the composition and palette, as well as the unadorned quality of the sitter's natural shoulder-length hair (which he wears instead of an elaborate wig) does find echoes in Highmore's Le Marchand portrait. James Thornhill's later likeness of 1710 (fig. 148), commissioned and given to Trinity College, Cambridge, depicts the now sixty-eight-year-old sitter in a robe and shirt similar to that seen in the Kneller portrait: now, however, his white hair is cropped short, as seen in the Le Marchand bust. In this instance, Newton turns his head to face a bright light that enters the composition from the left.

Returning to the Le Marchand and Gibbons portraits, the manner in which the sculptor holds the Newton bust is intimate, fraternal, and respectful. Gibbons, in contrast, grasps the hair of the sculpted head before him in the action of mea-

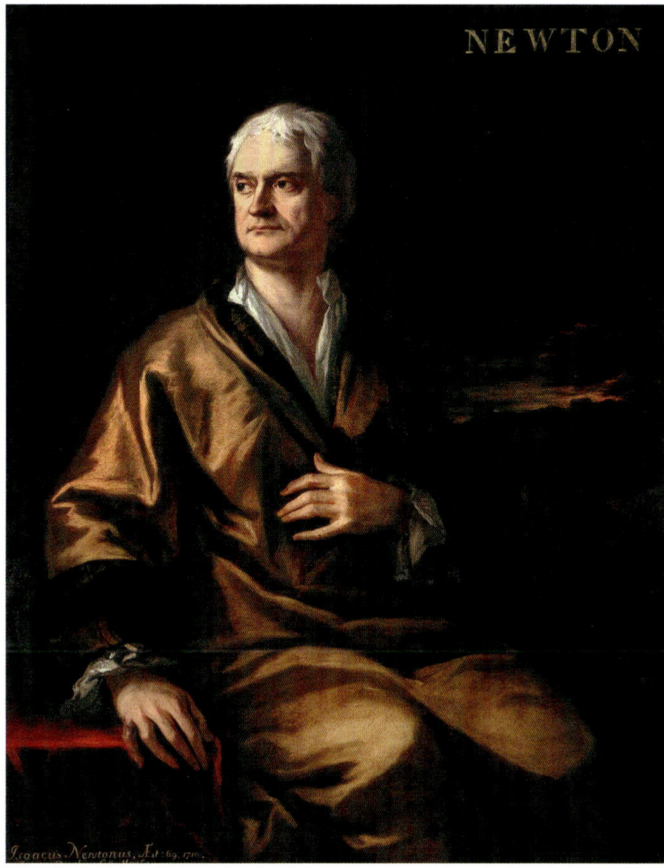

148. Sir James Thornhill, *Sir Isaac Newton*, 1710, oil on canvas, 48 x 40 in. (122 x 101.5 cm). Trinity College, Cambridge

suring—a mechanical process, but also, as suggested by Stewart, one of domination and subjugation. The choice of this particular Bernini head and its contorted features assists in the theatrical, visual conceit that it is Gibbons himself who has wrenched the head back to bare the neck, before pausing in his work. Unlike Gibbons, Le Marchand, with his hand resting on Newton's shoulder, appears to take inspiration from more tender physical contact. The stylistic and physical contrast between Bernini's goddess and Le Marchand's mathematician sets up a corresponding contrast in the nature of the "subject". The expressive physicality of the Bernini bust acts as a counterpoint to the reduced and contained quality of the Newton. If the goddess represents abandonment to the senses, the latter hints at the rejection of sensual pleasure as a prerequisite of spiritual, physical, and mental purity. Some observers viewed Newton in this manner, conspicuously alluding to his physical and spiritual purity. For example, in his *Notes on Newton's character* of about 1727–8, John Conduitt observed that, "Bishop Burnett said he valued him for something still more valuable than all his Philosophy for being the *whitest* soul he ever knew"; and later, "Sir I.N. did not dwell on what are vulgar{ly} called sensual parts of learning but true knowledge which like virtue gives a more solid & lasting satisfaction."[46] The pale creamy white of the ivory, and its brightness against the essentially dark monotone of a greater part of the canvas, lends Newton—in the guise of a portrait bust—an almost ethereal glow.

As I have noted, Highmore's "Newton" is the portrait of a portrait. Furthermore, unlike Kneller's Gibbons, the bust in the Highmore portrait is more than a "work of art". Here the "muse" is not a classical goddess, but a living man of science and an exemplar of logical thought. Yet in this miniature and portable representational form, Newton becomes akin to an amulet or even an idol, bathed in light. This form of representation can be usefully aligned with Newton's writings, and with the ways in which he and they were described by contemporaries. In his *Opticks* and *Philosophiæ naturalis principia mathematica,* Newton set out the physics of light and colour, and a mathematical demonstration of an orderly universe.[47] Such texts influenced poetry as well as science through, as William Powell Jones observes, "the use of new scientific imagery to sharpen old ideas".[48] During Newton's lifetime these included *Death's Vision* by John Reynolds (1667–1727) of 1709 and *The Ecstasy* by John Hughes (1678?–1720) published in 1720. In the latter text, Hughes imagines travelling through the universe, where he encounters Newton's soul—described as "a pointed Flame" and "shining Meteor"—on its daily cosmic voyage in "Search of Knowledge for Mankind below".[49] He begs Newton to let him accompany him "from Orb to Orb", viewing

> Unnumber'd Suns, all Seas of molten Gold;
> And trace each Comet's wand'ring Way,
> And now descry Light's Fountain-Head,
> And measure its descending Speed;
> Or learn how Sun-born Colours rise
> In Rays distinct, and in the Skys
> Blended in yellow Radiance flow.[50]

Finally, Hughes imagines abandoning "Earth and Earthly Things", and "here with native Freedom take my Flight,/ An Inmate of the Heav'ns, adopted into Light."[51]

Thornhill's portrait of 1710 hints at such literary metaphors through its depiction of Newton gazing into a warm light: perhaps the "Sun-born Colours" and "yellow Radiance" that Hughes was later to describe. These references seem amplified in Highmore's *David Le Marchand*. The carver, bathed in a brightness that causes a dark shadow to form behind him, might be described, like John Hughes, as having been "adopted into Light". That Highmore was aware of such Newtonian imagery, and Hughes's work in particular, is indicated by the artist's close friendship with William Duncombe, the friend, biographer, and editor of Hughes's works.[52] Highmore's portrait of Duncombe, dated 1721 (now at Corpus Christi College, Cambridge) depicts the sitter holding a copy of Hughes's celebrated translation of *The Letters of Abelard and Heloise* first published in 1713. Le Marchand's gaze, we can now suggest, extends not just beyond the picture space as seen in the Gibbons portrait, but towards the territory of Newton's life's work.

The astrologer Edmund Halley allows another possible reading of Highmore's distinctive use of light in this portrait. In an *Ode* (originally in Latin) that accompanied the first edition of Newton's *Principia* (1687), Halley writes:

> You who rejoice to eat the heavenly nectar, celebrate in Songs with me the man who reveals such things—Newton unlocking the archives of hidden Truth; Newton dear to the Muses; to whom pure-hearted Phoebus is present and possesses his mind with the fullness of Divinity: nor is it permitted for a Mortal to come nearer to the Gods.[53]

"Phoebus", meaning "shining one" or "God of Light", refers to particular qualities of the classical deity Apollo: that is, light, the sun, truth, and prophecy. The god is "present" to Newton and further "possesses his mind with the fullness of Divinity"—something that is almost suggestive of the relationship between the biblical God and an ecstatic saint. In establishing such an association between Newton and Phoebus, Halley transforms Newton into a visionary demi-god. From such a perspective, the intense light into which Le Marchand stares can be seen as a metaphor for this divinely inspired scientific truth. It is worth remembering in this context that Apollo was God of the Arts as well as of truth and prophecy: his light can be understood as the source of Le Marchand's creativity too, which is elsewhere indicated by his very particular posture and expression.

There is a final way in which the imagery within the portrait might be viewed. If we now reintroduce the commissioners of the portrait—the intimate friends of the natural philosopher as well as the patrons of the ivory carver and painter—it could be argued that Highmore's *David Le Marchand* is also intended to represent a union of art and science under the friendship and patronage of enlightened commerce.

CONCLUSION: "A RISING KNELLER"

The portrait's powerful and insistent reference to Kneller's example can be understood as an advertisement for Highmore's own creativity, and one that deliberately plays his example off against that of the former Principal Painter. Here, we can usefully turn to a poem that made precisely this comparison, written by John Bunce of Trinity Hall, Cambridge, an associate of Highmore's through mutual friends. The poem, which was written at the turn of 1725 and 1726, was published in the *Whitehall Evening Post* in August 1727.[54] Its opening verse offers a ringing endorsement of the artist's merits:

> No more let Britain for her Kneller grieve
> In Highmore see a rising Kneller live
> Whose happy Pencil claims as high a Name
> If equal Merits challenge equal Fame.[55]

The statement that Britain need no longer grieve for the loss of its great artist because Highmore, a "rising Kneller," is at hand, is a direct riposte to the opening line of *A Session of Painters*, in which the nation is urged to mourn the passing of Sir Godfrey and to despair that no suitable replacement can be found. Bunce's poem, in effect, acts as a defence and counter-argument to the vicious critique within the earlier pamphlet. Rather than being described as a daubing, tasteless wretch, Highmore, as a prime practitioner of what Bunce later in his poem describes as "painting's deathless art" is now credited with preserving for future generations the image and therefore the sitter in a sort of perpetual perfection. Bunce restores dignity and honour to Highmore and his portraiture, but importantly this defence is disseminated through the most public forum available: the London press. Significantly, the *Whitehall Evening Post* was not only a newspaper to which Highmore's close friend William Duncombe contributed, but one in which the latter had a financial share. The very public nature of this counter-attack suggests that Highmore and his supporters felt his reputation required defending and exalting. Bunce's poem not only confirms that Highmore required reputational and professional support at this point; it also made a very public declaration that the painter would have been, indeed continued to be, an entirely worthy candidate to succeed the great Sir Godfrey Kneller. In fact Bunce states that Highmore's ability is equal to Kneller's, and that he deserves a corresponding level of reputation and fame.

The consistent references to Kneller and his portraiture within Highmore's Le Marchand portrait can now be understood in parallel to such debates. It becomes clear that the portrait is both a conscious homage to Kneller, whose very public decline in health forms a backdrop to its creation, *and* a declaration of candidacy for Kneller's crown. The Le Marchand portrait is complex in its style, composition, and references but it is important to clarify that it adapts rather than apes Kneller's pictorial prototypes. Strategically then, Highmore has consciously and overtly produced a portrait that offers a considered translation of Kneller's pictorial models. Its conception and execution could be viewed not so much as a straightforward tribute or statement of candidacy, but as a sign of stylistic ownership: Kneller's art is not simply matched, but transformed.

To suggest that 1723 was a crucial moment in British art might be an exaggeration, but it is clear that Highmore himself was preparing for a significant change in his circumstances and career. In March 1724, within six months of Kneller's death, the artist had moved his small family, his studio, and his practice away from the site and patronage base that had supported his early career. As Highmore's son-in-law, John Duncombe (son of William), later observed in the artist's obituary: "His reputation and business increasing, he took a more conspicuous station, by removing to a house in Lincoln's Inn Fields."[56] Therefore, by the time *A Session of Painters* had been published, Highmore had already taken steps to attract Kneller's aristocratic client base and—he must have hoped—to acquire his mantle as Britain's leading portraitist. His ambitious portrait of Le Marchand, I suggest, formed an earlier part of this campaign of artistic aspiration and self-promotion.

1. George Vertue, "The Note-books of George Vertue III", *Walpole Society* 22 (1934): 9. For Kneller's death date see J. Douglas Stuart, "Kneller, Sir Godfrey (1646–1723)", *Oxford Dictionary of National Biography* (Oxford Univ. Press, 2004), http://www.oxforddnb.com/view/article/15710.
2. Vertue, "Note-books III", 12.
3. George Vertue, "The Note-books of George Vertue I", *Walpole Society* 18 (1930): 2.
4. Vertue, "Note-books III", 15.
5. Thomas Tickell, *To Sir Godfrey Kneller at his Country Seat* (London: J. Tonson, 1722), 3.
6. Tickell, *To Sir Godfrey Kneller*, 3.
7. For a rigorous reassessment of Jervas's career, see Caroline Pegum, *The Artistic and Literary Career of Charles Jervas (c.1675–1739)*, 3 vols. (MPhil diss., Univ. of Birmingham, 2009).
8. Vertue, "Note-books III", 17.
9. Vertue, "Note-books III", 17.
10. Vertue, "Note-books III", 29. Here Vertue is referring to Highmore as one who is "not vitiated by mannerists".
11. For Jervas's appointment and career as Principal Painter, see Pegum, *Charles Jervas*, 1: 87–105.

12. *Pasquin*, 31 Dec. 1723, 1; original italics.
13. Jonathan Richardson, *An essay on the theory of painting*, 2nd ed. (London: A.C., 1725), 24–25.
14. Alexander Pope, "To Mr. Jervas, with Fresnoy's Art of Painting, Translated by Mr. Dryden", in *The Art of Painting by C. A. Du Fresnoy: with Remarks*, trans. John Dryden and Charles Jervas (London: Richard Graham, 1716).
15. *Pasquin*, 31 Dec. 1723, 2; original italics.
16. *Pasquin*, 31 Dec. 1723, 2.
17. Anon. [Benjamin Victor], *A Session of Painters* (London: J. Roberts, 1725), title page. All quotations from the poem include original italics.
18. It was included in Benjamin Victor, *Original Letters, dramatic pieces, and poems*, 3 vols. (London: T. Beckett, 1776), 3: 13–20. In the index (299) it is described as "an eulogium on Sir Godfrey, and some strictures on some pretenders; and seems intended to stimulate the then remaining professors of the art to copy such an able master".
19. [Victor], *A Session of Painters*, 3.
20. [Victor], *A Session of Painters*, 3.
21. [Victor], *A Session of Painters*, 4.
22. The order is possibly Charles Jervas, Richard Philips, Joseph Highmore, Thomas Gibson, Jonathan Richardson, John Ellys, John Smibert, John Dyer, Michael Dahl, and John Vanderbank.
23. [Victor], *A Session of Painters*, 5.
24. [Victor], *A Session of Painters*, 6.
25. [Victor], *A Session of Painters*, 5.
26. Vertue, "Note-books III", 29.
27. For details of Highmore's early life and career, see Jacqueline Riding, "Joseph Highmore, 1692–1780", 2 vols. (PhD diss., Univ. of York, 2012), 1: chap. 1.
28. [Victor], *A Session of Painters*, 6.
29. Vertue, "Note-books III", 98.
30. Vertue, "Note-books III", 98.
31. [Victor], *A Session of Painters*, 8.
32. [Victor], *A Session of Painters*, 8.
33. Vertue, "Note-books III", 13. For a full discussion on the context and dating of this portrait, see Riding, "Joseph Highmore", 1: chap. 1, 31–49.
34. See John Kerslake, "Sculptor and Patron? Two Portraits by Highmore", *Apollo* 95 (Jan. 1972): 25–29, and Charles Avery, *David le Marchand, 1674–1726: "An Ingenious Man for Carving in Ivory"* (London: Lund Humphries, 1996).
35. J. W. Scobell Armstrong, "Joseph Highmore, Painter and Author", *The Connoisseur* 86 (Oct. 1930): 208–19, 211; the caption reads "Joseph Highmore Artist Unknown Carved Ivory Plaque". See also Riding, "Joseph Highmore", 2: fig. 15.
36. Vertue, "Note-books III", 17.
37. Abraham Langford, *A Catalogue of the Genuine and Entire Collection of Pictures of Mr. Joseph Highmore* (London: Abraham Langford, 5 March 1762), 3, listed under Kit-Cats, lot 36.
38. Vertue, "Note-books I", 28.
39. Vertue, "Note-books III", 54.
40. Vertue, "Note-books III", 17.
41. For a full discussion on Vertue's references to Highmore in 1723 and their earlier professional relationship, see Riding, "Joseph Highmore", 1: chap. 1, 31–49.
42. For example, John Michael Rysbrack by John Vanderbank of around 1728. For the original composition see John Faber's mezzotint after Vanderbank dated 1734.
43. James D. Stewart, *Sir Godfrey Kneller and the English Baroque Portrait* (Oxford Univ. Press, 1983), 259.

44. This version, now in the British Museum, was purchased from Sir Isaac Newton's nephew and heir and then donated by Mathew Raper III, son of Moses, to the museum in 1765.
45. Milo Keynes, *The Iconography of Sir Isaac Newton to 1800* (Cambridge: Boydell Press, 2005), 2.
46. King's College, Cambridge, Keynes MS 130.07, fols. 1r and 3v respectively; see The Newton Project, www.newtonproject.sussex.ac.uk.
47. Isaac Newton, *Opticks: or, A Treatise of the reflexions, refractions, inflexions and colours of light* (London: S. Smith & B. Walford, 1704), and *Philosophiæ naturalis principia mathematica* (London: The Royal Society, 1687).
48. W. P. Jones, "Newton Further Demands the Muse", *Studies in English Literature, 1500–1900* 3 (1963): 287–306, 288.
49. John Hughes, *The Ecstasy: An Ode* (London: J. Roberts, 1720), 7.
50. Hughes, *The Ecstasy*, 8.
51. Hughes, *The Ecstasy*, 8.
52. William Duncombe, ed., *Poems on Several Occasions . . . by John Hughes*, 2 vols. (London: J. Tonson & J. Watts, 1735).
53. Translated in W. R. Albury, "Halley's Ode on the *Principia* of Newton and the Epicurean Revival in England", *Journal of the History of Ideas* 39, no. 1 (Jan.–March 1978): 24–43, 27.
54. See Anon., "Anthony Highmore's Obituary", *Gentleman's Magazine* 99 (Jan. 1829): 82, "some lines addressed to him by Mr. John Bunce, of Trinity Hall, Cambridge, and published in the Whitehall Evening Post of Aug 12 to 15, 1727". The poem was reprinted in the same volume as Highmore's obituary where the poem's date is given as 6 January 1726. See John Bunce, "To Mr. Highmore", *Gentleman's Magazine* 50 (April 1780): 195.
55. Bunce, "To Mr. Highmore", 195.
56. John Duncombe, "Memoirs of the late Joseph Highmore, Esq.", *Gentleman's Magazine* 50 (April 1780): 176–79, 177.

PROSPECTS, PRINT, EMPIRE

The View from the Gentleman's Seat

John Bonehill

ESTATE landscapes and their representation focused a range of cultural, legal, and political concerns in the years after 1660. With the restoration of Crown authority and the reassertion of the old—if now greatly modified—order, landed property and its improvement became the basis of power and influence for both the aristocracy and the gentry. The apparent resolution of the civil divisions and religious turmoil of the previous century or so, when fear of property being sequestered or broken up had limited development or expansion, encouraged the country's landowners to invest heavily in their formerly vulnerable estates. Landed estates were no longer a loose bundle of assorted customary practices and rights, as they had been into the sixteenth century, but were now legally identifiable and, importantly, measurable extents of owned and controlled private property. New laws enforcing the principle of primogeniture, including the development of entails and strict settlements, helped to ensure continuity of ownership and the undivided maintenance of estates large and small.[1] These legal advances, which had been fashioned over the course of the seventeenth century, reinforced the political victories won in the late 1600s that were to forge a Parliament of the propertied. Given that land was key to the establishment of political and social status, commanding privileges that ranged from the right to hunt to the entitlement to vote and hold high office, its ownership was of wide appeal and significance. Such was the importance of landed property to social standing and position that those who made their fortunes from banking or the law, industry or trade, typically invested their profits in the purchase of a rural or suburban seat.[2] Landownership was a route to gentility and perhaps to Parliament, as well as a reliable investment opportunity.

Landed estates, as they took shape in the decades following the restoration of Crown authority, varied greatly in their geographical distribution, scale, and features. They were remarkably complex in their layout and extent. Some were comprised not only of a house and its formal gardens and parkland but also of an outlying penumbra of agricultural fields, home and tenant farms, industrial sites and buildings, watercourses, woodland and copses for game, as well as a church and housing for workers, zones bounded and linked by networks of hedges, paths, tracks, avenues, and roads.[3] Such far-reaching, large-scale forms of architectural redesign and environmental transformation asserted owners' wealth and power, while also proclaiming their knowledge and taste. Country estates were the regional power bases of families who exerted influence locally, in neighbouring communities and at county level, and on the national stage, at court, and in the capital. Some sites had a national as well as local profile, and were renowned as places of agricultural, industrial, and technological innovation and architectural, artistic, or philosophical pursuit. Estates were thus not discrete entities or communities, despite the long tradition of rural panegyric paying tribute to the insularity and self-sufficiency of the gentleman's seat. Gentry families were no less concerned to maintain a London house and lifestyle or to invest in city projects than aristocratic grandees, whose estates and interests were scattered over several counties and might include properties in the capital as well as lands in the colonies, in Ireland, or the West Indies. They were equally reliant on the mutuality—the cultural, economic, and social interdependence—of country and city.

Estate "improvements"—a term formerly synonymous with land enclosure but applied to a broad range of activity by the second half of the seventeenth century—generated various overlapping associations. Valorized for their aesthetic as well as economic benefits, they were also held to have moral and social effects, bettering the lot of those who lived in, worked, or viewed the landscape.[4] Good estate management, as many an essayist or poet noted, offered a metaphor for effective government. Supervision of a wide extent of variegated land endowed the owner with the independence of means and the capacity for generalizing thought considered essential to participation in government.[5] These ideals, investments, and practices, along with attendant ambiguities and anxieties, found expression in a range of literary and visual forms. Writings on arboriculture, horticulture, and husbandry addressed the improvement of the estate. Works of antiquarian scholarship, travel writing, or poetry detailed its past and present or established its values. Such literary images of the estate were complemented visually, in maps, drawings, paintings, and prints, as well as on the ground, in the design and management of the landscape. While celebratory of landownership and its rights and privileges, these images and texts were also a means of managing its various complexities, vicissitudes, and uncertainties. Indeed, such concerns were central to their making and meaning.

This essay addresses the culture of the country estate in the period through an exploration of the complex and not always harmonious set of exchanges and interactions that existed between the lie of the land and its visual and verbal

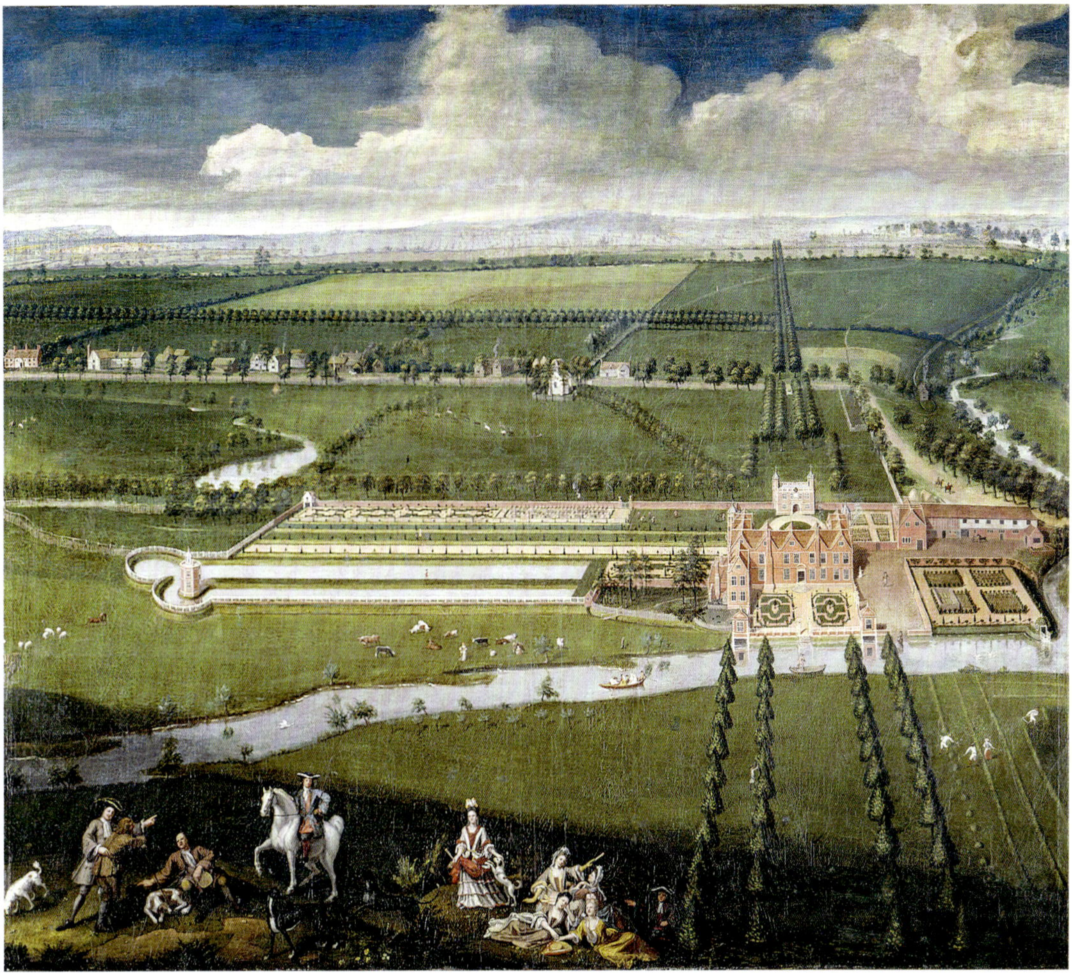

149. Unknown artist, *Charlecote Park, Warwickshire, from the West*, ca. 1696–1700, oil on canvas, 57 x 60 in. (144.8 x 152.4 cm). National Trust, Charlecote Park, Warwickshire

image. These issues are considered with reference to the lives and motivations that shaped the making and meaning of Charlecote, the historic manorial seat of a gentry family situated low on the banks of the River Avon in south-east Warwickshire. Charlecote was an estate of some antiquity, but was greatly improved in the years around 1700. These changes were variously appraised, celebrated, planned, and recorded in an array of written and pictorial statements commissioned by its owners, the Lucy family; these representations included a fine, wide-ranging example of the estate portraiture of the period. Charlecote and the narratives embedded within it were formed from personal attachments and histories, and a variety of practices, skills, and forms of knowledge, if also the wider politics and poetics of the landscapes of lordship and their representation in the years following the restoration of the Crown.

A VIEW OF CHARLECOTE, FROM THE WEST

Sometime around the marriage of Colonel George Lucy to Mary Bohun in 1697, a grand, commemorative oil painting was commissioned showing the couple, with relatives and friends, before the family's historic estate (fig. 149). Though the evidence is only anecdotal, family history records that it was ordered as a gift from the groom's cleric brother, William.[6] Beyond this uncertainty, however, the evident familiarity with the locality and the family's past shown by the unknown artist can presumably only have emerged out of a dialogue with a patron close to Charlecote and its then current custodian. A large and commanding view of the manor and lands beyond, wide-angled and far-reaching, its multiple focal points and mass of precise detail also encourage close scrutiny of its dry and descriptive surface. Charlecote is viewed in the picture from the west, as if from high ground. It is framed by the portrait group on a ridge just below, featuring Colonel Lucy on horseback, accompanied by his new wife Mary and other family members and guests. A fine prospect of the estate and the adjacent country opens up below. Great avenues of trees extend the axial alignments of the old stone and red-brick manor house and the geometry of its garden layout out into the surrounding landscape. A long, straight double avenue of grand common limes, leading out from the monumental castellated gatehouse to the east, appears to cut across the road through the cottages and messuages of the village of Charlecote that edge the estate. It leads the eye out to the tenant farmlands of Coppington and Hunscote, near the ancient settlement of Wellesbourne, the village sited astride the watercourse snaking down the far right of the canvas, and beyond to the landmark escarpment of Edge Hill. Charlecote's gardens and extraordinary ornamental canal system, striding out from the north of the house, were fed by the River Avon, which flows past the west front, and its tributary the Dene, which borders the south. A small pavilion in the southwest corner of a walled vegetable garden to the far right of the painted prospect of Charlecote would have overlooked the confluence of these waters. There are further allusions to the wider locality, as figures travel the road eastward to nearby Stratford-upon-Avon or take boats along the river, perhaps carrying goods and people to and from the market town or to the village of Hampton Lucy, a half mile to the north across the park on the opposite bank, and also in the Lucys' lordship.

A church and manor house, then the seat of the Venour family, are prominent in the view of Wellesbourne, where the Lucys also owned several properties. Charlecote itself is shown surrounded by a complex of courts and yards, terraces and mounts, of precise and geometric order, full of elaborate and particular detail. Charlecote's precincts stage an array of activities, with estate workers harvesting hay in the fertile river meadows, or tending to the livestock in the stables and out in the fields, or making their way along a path out towards Wellesbourne, while the owners and their circle enjoy the pleasures of a country life of good company and rural sports, riding with hounds or else taking in the varied delights of the bucolic prospect. There is space for those who lie and rest alongside those who bend and work in this harmonious rural panorama. Charlecote's extensive and simultaneous activity projects an image of the economic and social well-being of the Lucy estate. It is a scene of abundant plenitude, overseen by a gentleman resident in his "country".[7]

In its imagery and formal organization, the view of Charlecote conforms with the style of prospect art owners in the period commissioned from artist-émigrés from the Low Countries (and some native-born practitioners), who adapted the northern tradition of "bird's-eye" perspectives to the distinctive, newly remade topographies of the British Isles.[8] Estate portraits were commissioned to commemorate a variety of events, not least the improvement of the house or landscape. They were diverse in form and media, drawn and engraved as well as painted, destined for the owner's library folios or walls, in the house depicted or elsewhere, perhaps their London residence. When encountered in the library or on the walls of the house portrayed, with the gardens and wider landscape framed by the view from its windows, the portrait encouraged a series of exchanges between the image of the estate and its material form, between its ideals and its practices.[9] Views of a more narrow, confined scope, where the angle of vision was greatly lowered, were not uncommon. Yet the aerial prospect was to prove a remarkably durable development, still in vogue with artists and their patrons come the middle of the eighteenth century, albeit by then some critics considered "too great an elevation" a "deviation from Nature in landscape-painting".[10]

Widely celebrated in travel accounts and verse as much as the visual arts, commanding, elevated stations, affording wide and unfettered views of the land, whether from high ground, church tower, or the windows of a house, were greatly valued as practically useful and culturally significant. Several recent studies have rightly contended that the country's rivers, pre-eminently the Thames, provided an important focus for late seventeenth-century concerns to (re)imagine the relations or flows between the nation's subjects and its spaces; however, there was a like investment in a network of elevated vantage points affording broad, unconfined views over a series of local but connected landscapes.[11] "Landscape" (or rather "landskip") was not as yet synonymous with a physical tract of land, but rather referred to its artistic depiction, as seen from a particular perspective, arranged and rearranged, ordered and composed into a "picture", a "prospect".[12] A "prospect" encouraged a sense of passage or "progress" through the landscape, opening up views in time as well as space, of past, present, and projected—often improved—future. They invited reflection on a world jointly created by God and man, where nature's bounty was dutifully cultivated, improved rather than preserved.[13] Views of landed property, adopting a seigneurial perspective, accordingly celebrated good husbandry, prudent management and ownership, social harmony and productivity, where the resources of the land were employed to stimulate morality as much as prosperity.[14] Houses were thus often set within a wider landscape, where they contributed to a sense of social order and of an organizing culture overseeing the improvement of the adjacent country.[15]

Such pictures have been largely marginal to accounts of landscape painting in this country, possibly because of their associations with cultures of observation and documentary record, mapping and surveying, rather than high-minded art. Yet, this is arguably to overlook the often considerable cultural ambition and range in evidence. They are views framed by literary references, to the epic pastoral and georgic verse of ancients and moderns, or revered artistic models, sometimes mixing northern and southern landscape modes, all combined with very specific, local knowledge. Classically derived ideals and narratives, as they animated the house and its landscape on the ground as well as on paper or canvas, were given particular inflection by the layered history and present day use of a place. Artists and their patrons thus regarded the topographical specificity of these pictures as critical to their making and meaning. Aerial views out over estates like the prospect of the Lucys' Charlecote allied attentiveness to a local topography, its cultural and imaginative aspects as well as material forms, to a sense of grand spectacle.

Despite there being no documentary evidence for the attribution, family tradition has it that the picture was the work of a "Mr. Stevens", perhaps the Jan or John Stevens otherwise only known for a view of Hampton Court (Herefordshire).[16] Unusually for such paintings, this latter work is signed. Artists were rather rarely named. This may be telling, about a lack of prestige around the genre or its practitioners perhaps, though estate portraiture would on occasion occupy prominent wall space, even forming major decorative schemes.[17] Having said this, while the artist of the Charlecote prospect is obscure, it is unlikely he was local. Highly literate and cultured, the Lucys had always favoured established London-based artists, latterly commissioning portraits of the family from the studios of John Closterman, Godfrey Kneller, and Michael Dahl. Charlecote was mostly managed at a distance under George Lucy, whose absenteeism and preference for the fashionable pursuits of the capital were to have long-term implications for the estate. Yet his cultural ambitions and refinement were most obviously expressed in the laying out of the formal garden areas surrounding the manor house at his ancestral seat—something, of course, that is recorded in detail in the painted prospect of Charlecote. Estate views of the period and later adaptations of the tradition more generally were formed in response to changing approaches to garden and parkland design. A house and its grounds surveyed obliquely, as if from the air or some elevated vantage point, ably conveyed the scale and complexity of the estate landscape, being particularly suited to the geometry and axial alignments of advanced late seventeenth-century garden layouts. Garden designs of the later seventeenth century mixed elements of native tradition with Italianate fashions as well as the French and Dutch styles that Royalists had experienced in exile or military men had encountered on campaign.[18]

Work on Charlecote's canals had begun when the estate was briefly under the stewardship of Sir Thomas Lucy IV, who had inherited in 1677. He introduced to his home county Dutch garden fashions he had viewed when serving on the Continent as a captain in the Royal Horse Guards earlier in the decade.[19] On his sudden death a few years later, these plans were abruptly abandoned when only half realized. Twenty years or so were to pass before George Lucy recommenced the laying out of the elaborate parterre garden to the north-east and the digging of Charlecote's spectacular canals. These long, parallel stretches of water, overlooked at the far end by a banqueting house, are in the view of the estate, complemented by a series of other leisured spaces, including a raised bowling green bordering the gatehouse and a series of pavilions. These areas and features clustering around the house, so precisely delineated in the painted prospect, are shown alongside enclosures of more obviously practical purpose, forming vegetable plots and—just to the side of the riverside terrace—a pen for livestock. Ornamental, recreational, and productive spaces are pictured as happily juxtaposed. Work and recreation are further combined in the areas beyond the courts around the house. Orchards, meadows, and watercourses were sources of pleasure as well as profit. Canals were stocked with fish—carp at Charlecote—while extensive areas of uninterrupted turf grazed by livestock proved a terrain made for riding fast. There was a renewed investment in such traditional symbols of status as the deer park in the years around the turn of the century, with the reassertion of hunting rights and privileges in law, along with the restoration of grounds variously neglected or stripped of their assets—their timber felled and their herds slaughtered—during the war years and after. When the prospect of Charlecote was painted the deer park shown to the west of the canals had been laid out only recently. Deer had long featured prominently in the imagery of the country estate. They animated the landscape, adding colour and movement; they were also important because of their association with the privileges of ownership, with hunting, and with the use of venison in gifts of patronage as well as in the provision of the household.[20] Such use of the land, as it is pictured in the view of Charlecote, signified and was enabled by the control of an extensive area.

Charlecote's tree-lined avenues, extending out east and west from the house, further accentuate the impression of power. Avenues radiating out in long vistas from and continuing the central axes of a house were a distinctive feature of the estate landscape of the period.[21] Some had been planted earlier in the century, with the approach to Charlecote being probably laid out at the time of James I, but they were to become common, as owners—less and less constrained by customary tenure and common rights—consolidated their estates. Decorative or semi-decorative planting, together with the establishment of more obviously commercial stands or management of existing woodland, made for a potent visual statement of an owner's or family's connection with or occupancy and stewardship of a place. Moreover, it activated a rich array of associations and contentions regarding the social order, what it was or ought to be.[22] Indeed, arboriculture and woodland had come to assume a political consequence in the wake of the widespread deforestation of the Civil War and Commonwealth eras. This was expressed most eloquently in John Evelyn's much reprinted *Sylva*, first published in 1664. Structured much like a manual of estate management, giving a step-by-step guide to the cultivation of trees, Evelyn's text was famously prefaced by a plea for planting as an investment in a stable political future, a contribution to "the *Wealth* and *Glory* of this *Nation*".[23] With owners of landed property now more assured of dynastic continuity, they committed large tracts of land to planting and its medium- to long-term rewards. Successive owners of Charlecote had long understood the material and symbolic worth of trees and woodland, enclosing areas of ancient coppice to the north and planting orchards to the south before establishing the groves and avenues of the park.

Charlecote's highly structured, geometric core and the axial alignments of avenues and canals are in the painted prospect viewed to advantage by the Lucys and their guests from their foreground promontory. George Lucy and his circle occupy a literally privileged space, albeit that this is a conceit, the land to the west of the Avon at the site being largely open, gently undulating, and criss-crossed by streams. This platform-like foreground is cast in deep shadow, and the pyramidal grouping of figures is pictured as if in relief against flattened ground, appearing in a different optic to the planar, receding landscape rolling out below, its architecture, roads, watercourses, and hedges forming a series of horizontal bands traversed by the shooting lines of the avenue of trees that extend out from the house. Such a geometric framework, together with this shift in viewpoint, expressed the full extent of the owner's designs on the landscape and the unity of house, garden, and wider estate. It allowed a coherent and ordered display of property, a detailing and enumeration of features that overlaps with the visual inventory of estate maps and plans of the period.[24] There are also parallels with the decorative and symbolic embellishment of contemporary estate maps, the images of plenty—of produce, livestock, haymakers, hunters—that edged or were distributed across more elaborate surveys. Indeed, in their arrangement and placement, the Lucys and their guests resemble the emblematic figures in vignettes attached to cartouche designs. Moreover, views out over estate landscapes of the later seventeenth and early eighteenth centuries engaged with a broader culture of cartography and chorography concerned—since the time of Christopher Saxton's *Atlas* (1579) and William Camden's *Britannia* (1586)—"to make the land visible", and to understand the nation and its constituent counties both spatially and historically.[25] A near obsessive concern with the ancestral past and local history, as registered in the extensive patronage of antiquarian scholarship, genealogy and heraldry, county maps, surveys and topographies, invariably framed the picturing of landed property.[26]

CHARLECOTE'S PROGRESS

Geographically, Warwickshire was traditionally imagined as "divided into two parts . . . sever'd by the River Avon": Feldon lay south of the river, "a champain Country", in Camden's words, a flat, open plain of rich, red clay soils, "fertile fields of corn, and verdant pastures"; Arden, the sandy highlands to the north, was "for the most part clothed with woods" and common waste, a landscape of scattered, isolated farms and few communities.[27] Charlecote and the neighbouring manor of Hampton Lucy were situated along the valley bordering these contrasting terrains of field and forest, a corridor often characterized as a transitional zone. Yet, the county's economy and settlement patterns were far more diverse than those envisaged by writers like Camden. Warwickshire's geography was complex and fragmented, with the county divided into areas that often had more in common economically and socially with neighbouring regions than with other districts in the shire.[28] Development and expansion of industry, of manufacturing and mining, and the emergence of ways of life removed from the traditional rural community, in areas to the north and coal-rich east, added to the diversity. Andrew Yarranton, a tireless advocate of "Englands improvement", argued that making the county's rivers navigable would free farms "lockt up in the Inlands", so forging some sense of arterial connection and unity by bringing together trade and tillage.[29] Circulation and the transportation of goods and produce (especially the flour milled from Feldon's grain) along the Avon would be eased, he maintained, by the establishment of a series of locks and weirs. Work on such a scheme had begun in the 1630s, with the support of local notables including the Lucys. However, the coming of war had brought its progress to an abrupt halt, until Yarranton revived interest and campaigned for further investment in the project in the early years of the Restoration, at a time when Parliament passed a number of bills authorizing the improvement of the nation's inland waterways.[30] Views out over the river from the windows and garden terraces at Charlecote were animated by the sight of laden barges now able to navigate along the reach down to Stratford and its markets.

Most of the county's greater gentry resided in the south, where local communities were close-knit, traditional, and highly manorialized. Although lying at the southern edge of the ancient Forest of Arden, life and land on the Lucys' estates—which were characterized by clustered settlement patterns, arable fields, and rich pastures—had developed in ways largely of a part with the champion lands of the Feldon. Charlecote's development and expansion over the course of the seventeenth century was a slow process of piecemeal consolidation and enclosure characteristic of estate landscapes in and around the south-east of the county. What had been heath and waste along the borders of the adjoining manors was all, by and large, enclosed by the late seventeenth century, made over as tenant farmland on the Hampton Lucy side and parkland on the other. Hampton Lucy was bounded to the north by Fulbrook, the site of a once grand country seat, set amidst an extensive deer park.[31] All but abandoned by 1600, it was gradually remodelled over the next half century or so, once it had come into the possession of the Lucys. They divided what had been enclosed as pleasure grounds into farms, and asserted their claims on the place by taking in an area of adjacent, formerly common, woodland.[32] This series of acquisitions and improvements extended the family's dominion over this corner of Warwickshire and assured its eminence among the "county community"; for all that—given the sketchy, patchwork geography of the shire—this was an idea rather more symbolic than rooted in any actual economic or social ties.[33]

Antiquarian accounts of the county recorded the Lucys as one of Warwickshire's oldest gentry families, resident at Charlecote from the twelfth century.[34] Their standing in the shire had been greatly enhanced and secured in the Elizabethan era by the first Sir Thomas Lucy, whose advantageous marriage to a Worcestershire heiress had augmented the family's estates considerably. He was to sell off some outlying holdings he had inherited, including the site of a ruinous friary, in order to facilitate the purchase of lands close to Charlecote. This concentrated the family's interests and made them easier and more profitable to administer. He was also to rebuild the manor house at Charlecote as a residence befitting his position as a major county figure, who served as sheriff, deputy lieutenant, and knight of the shire. His grandson, another Sir Thomas Lucy, also cultivated a political career, representing Warwickshire in the Commons. The Lucys' spheres of influence were for a time local, regional, and national. Sir Thomas Lucy III made the purchase of the fee simple on Fulbrook, and died holding manors and many other properties across eight counties, allowing him to leave landed endowments to five of his sons and large sums for his daughters. Charlecote itself was then to pass through various hands, successive owners dying unmarried or without male issue.

Gains made under the first three Thomas Lucys were further undermined by the political uncertainties of the mid-seventeenth century and their successors' shifting alliances. Sir Thomas Lucy III's son and heir, Spencer Lucy, allied himself with the king in the early days of the Civil War, his younger brother Robert having then to bribe a way to favour with Parliament during his brief tenure as head of the family. In 1660, Richard Lucy was to declare himself for Charles II; the family's reconciliation with the Crown was eased by the payment of a hefty fine, roughly equivalent to the annual income from their various estates.[35] While the Lucys were to remain leading figures in Warwickshire society, their estates and finances had been greatly reduced by these bequests and reparations. A lengthy dispute over properties in Herefordshire, Gloucestershire, and Worcestershire was to drain the family's resources further.[36] Yet this was not to prevent Captain Thomas Lucy IV, who sold off timber from the estate to finance the project, embarking on the costly improvements close to the house recorded in the painted prospect.[37] These works were the cause of some local resentments and tensions (the damming of the Avon to make the water gardens flooded local grazing fields). Captain Thomas Lucy was the last of the family to hold high office in the county and be returned to Parliament; his successors' ambitions and interests lay elsewhere. On inheriting the now debt-ridden family estates in the mid-1680s, his cousin Davenport Lucy commissioned a review and valuation of Charlecote and the manors of Hampton Lucy, Hatton, and Fulbrook from the local land agent and surveyor James Fish of Warwick, who measured "The Totall of ye whole" at "about 4500 Acres". Fish's terriers took account of acreages, holdings, and income from produce, especially timber, as well as rental values, but also promoted the enlargement of the estates, identifying potential new land purchases or the enclosure of commons and advocating the re-evaluation of tenancies.[38] With the estate proving so "extreamly improveable", Charlecote's new owner declared himself reassured about the "great debts" he had inherited.[39] Davenport Lucy's careful, even frugal management of the estate and his speculative but prudent dealing in the vibrant land market of the period restored something of the family's fortunes.[40] Charlecote then passed to Colonel

George Lucy, whose marriage to the only surviving daughter and heiress of the late John Bohun of Finham—commemorated in the view over the estate—again added to the property portfolio. Her money and that of her cousin Jane Bohun, heiress to the rents of London's Spitalfields, whom Lucy was to marry shortly after the death of his first wife in 1708, would help finance the cost of further improvements to the house and grounds in the years around the turn of the century. When painting Charlecote at the century's end, the artist commissioned by the Lucys surveyed the results of a lengthy, often uneasy, period of alteration and development, shaped by convenience, domestic needs, and fluctuating fortunes as much as fashion.

Charlecote's late seventeenth-century improvements elaborated on the highly literate appreciation of the virtues of rural retreat associated with Thomas Lucy III's stewardship of the estate. While the prospect of Charlecote surveys a much-improved estate, overseen by consciously fashionable new owners of advanced taste, it also comprehends its history, as it centres on the old manor house and draws the eye out towards a site of commemoration and remembrance in the landscape. St Leonard's church is shown situated at the end of an avenue of trees, striking out diagonally across the parkland beyond the eastern gatehouse. It had been locked and its walls whitewashed at the time of the Interregnum; it was then restored and remodelled towards the end of the century, when the bell tower visible in the painting was added. Charlecote's owners had decorated the fabric of their parish church with a sequence of grand sepulchral monuments from the late sixteenth century onwards. These family tombs were documented in a series of fine engravings illustrating an account of the manor published by the noted local antiquary Sir William Dugdale (fig. 150). Sir Thomas Lucy III's canopied monument, with its recumbent effigies of the deceased and his wife Lady Alice (*née* Spencer) in white marble, was the largest and most imposing of these tombs.[41] While the architectural frame of the monument is surmounted by a cartouche bearing the family arms impaling those of the Spencers, it is Lucy's character and education that is celebrated as much as his dynastic lineage. His standing as a learned country gentleman is elaborated in a series of bas-relief panels, including a Latin epitaph praising Lucy's public service and personal piety as well as the hospitable welcome he extended to scholars. Lucy corresponded with a number of notable literary figures, among them the poet John Donne, and had compiled a magnificent library, shaped by his appreciation of classical authors.[42] Books from his library were carved in low relief above his effigy, volumes of Horace and Virgil among them, alongside another panel featuring an equestrian portrait of Lucy riding out on his estate.

Colonel George Lucy's appearance in the painted prospect of the estate commissioned at the century's end echoes this ancestral image. Occupying the ground

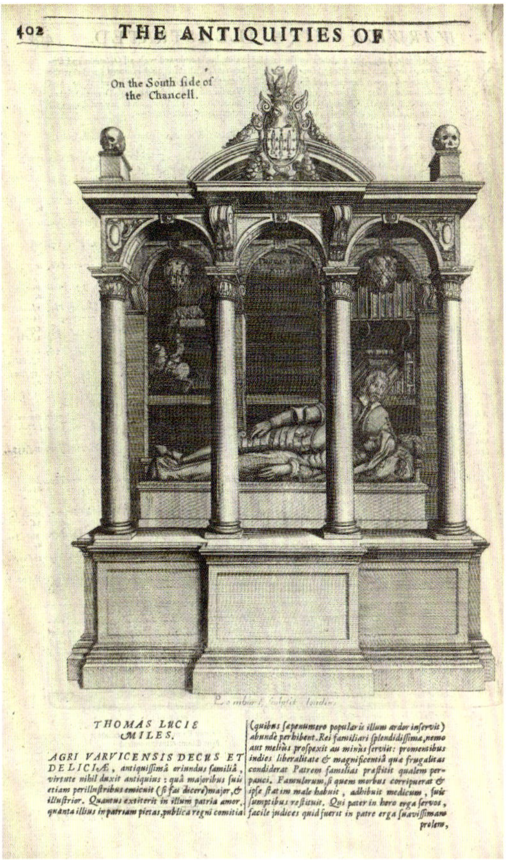

150. Pierre Lombart, "Monument to Sir Thomas Lucy", in William Dugdale, *The Antiquities of Warwickshire Illustrated* (London: Printed by Thomas Warren, 1656), 511. Beinecke Rare Book and Manuscript Library

between a highly animated male group, apparently engaged in some minor, playful squabble, and variously reclining or seated females, and presided over by his new bride, the Colonel is also shown as continuing the tradition of hospitality for which his illustrious forebear was celebrated. Hospitality—a virtuous form of sociability long associated with ideals of country house living—framed the seasonal rhythms of the estate and its occupants.[43] At Charlecote, its imagery and ideals—as they were celebrated by authors ancient and modern—were not only to be found on the shelves of the enviable library bequeathed by Sir Thomas Lucy, but were also literally carved into the fabric of the estate.

Verse that centred on the country house and its landscape, as it developed the early seventeenth-century model of Ben Jonson's poetic tribute "To Penshurst" and his related epistle "To Sir Robert Wroth", would invariably honour friends' or patrons' hospitality as it flowed from the plenitude of the land and its cultivation, celebrating the air, soil, wood, and waters of the estate. Country house poetry celebrated continuity and social hierarchy; the landowner's provision of hospitality—to the local community and guests alike—was demonstrative of this commitment and of the moral responsibility his status entailed upon him. Yet, recent assessments of the country house poem and other literary forms advocating a virtuous rural life, have shown them as rather anxious, fraught statements of stability and hierarchy, shaped as much by contemporary challenges to the values they espouse, both locally and nationally, as by a commitment to the traditional moral economy of the manorial estate.[44] Writings advocating the duties of stewardship and ideals of rural order and prosperity were hedged at various points by a range of anxieties and contesting forces, by religious controversy and the collapse into civil war, by the growth in urban centres and the taking of townhouses, by the ebb and flow of the land market and changing patterns of ownership, and by new conceptions of property and the idea of improvement.

Visual images of the estate, notably as they engaged the imagery of country house and rural poetics, were no less obliged to accommodate these conflicts. A series of such tensions animate and run through the visual survey of the Lucys' Charlecote, not least as the artist attempted to resolve the demand for pastoral ease with georgic energy characteristic of estate portraiture. George Lucy and his circle overlook a landscape of beauty and use, informed by the classical ethos of "pleasure and profit".[45] Charlecote is pictured as a landscape of leisurely, recreational retreat for the owners and their guests, yet—in the array of activity—also a place infused with a georgical vitality. There are exchanges here with the rich "composite mode of rural panegyric" characteristic of much later seventeenth-century writing on "the employments of a Country life", joining much debated ideals of retirement with practical economics in celebrating "the Improvement of something which we call . . . Our Own".[46] Hospitable ideals and their enactment were recast in this period too, in accord with the vision of a "Country life" then taking shape. They were now less concerned with customary duty and social responsibility, becoming more exclusive and leisure focused. Pictorially, they were registered—as in the view of Charlecote—in images of estate plenty or the recreational uses of its spaces, with family members or their guests relaxing in, riding, or strolling the grounds, or else fishing, hawking, shooting, or out on a hunt run. These were activities and pleasures associated with high summer, that time of the year when owners like the London-resident George Lucy tended to return to their estates to avoid the heat of the town and receive guests. Estate portraiture was required to acknowledge the redefinition of such ideals and practices as well as to admit improving change and process in the landscape. Yet, as a vision of idealized prosperity and stability, it was also to celebrate the virtues of historic connection, of accustomed prerogative, privilege, and placement.

A VIEW OF CHARLECOTE, FROM THE EAST

Views of country seats were often interleaved, along with diagrams, elevations, maps, plans, heraldry, and pedigrees, into the sometimes lavishly illustrated county "itineraries", "perambulations", or "surveys" that had begun to appear with greater frequency after mid-century. County surveys compiled family and manorial histories in exhaustive detail, documenting genealogies, heraldry, and the descent of property. William Dugdale's *Antiquities of Warwickshire*, which had documented the Lucys' stone genealogy, was first published in 1656. It was foundational, not least for its innovative and lavish illustration, being richly "Beautified"—so its title page announced—"With Maps, Prospects and Portraictures" contributed by the local gentry as well as professional arms painters, with Wenceslaus Hollar etching its "many curious and chargeable cutts". *Antiquities of Warwickshire* was dedicated to the county's gentry, whose arms and genealogies, grants of land and privilege, burials, effigies, and epitaphs the book assembled and documented. Its author likened his extended paean to the knights and squires of his own native county to a "*Monumentall Pillar*", in the tradition of the grand, roadside tombs established by the great families of Rome to honour their ancestors and commend their example to posterity.[47] Dugdale's great paper monument projected values of continuity, hierarchy, and order, revising the county and its gentry's allegiances, which had been predominantly parliamentarian during the Civil War period.[48] Surveys such as Dugdale's account of Warwickshire were not single-authored texts, but rather a synthesis of ideas and voices, filtered through the insights and abilities of others. They were acts of collective imagination and creative effort, dependent on local and indeed countrywide networks of gentlemanly patronage and social exchange for the compilation and circulation of knowledge and materials.[49] They were ornamented with armorial crests and shields and inscribed with dedications to the illustrious ancestors of the gentlemen and noblemen who paid for the plates. Such men would further constitute much of the intended readership. Still, authors, contributors, and patrons of such texts were also aware that the image of the shire and its landed society that they projected addressed wider worlds, other imagined communities to which they were affiliated beyond their native county lines: regional and national, cultural, political, religious, and social.

Hollar's plates for Dugdale had included a select series of views of Warwickshire seats, a feature which later editions and other county surveys were to greatly expand.[50] William Thomas was to publish a much revised and expanded edition of Dugdale's *Warwickshire* in 1730, with additional plates engraved by Elisha Kirkall after drawings made by the local engineer, mathematician, and surveyor

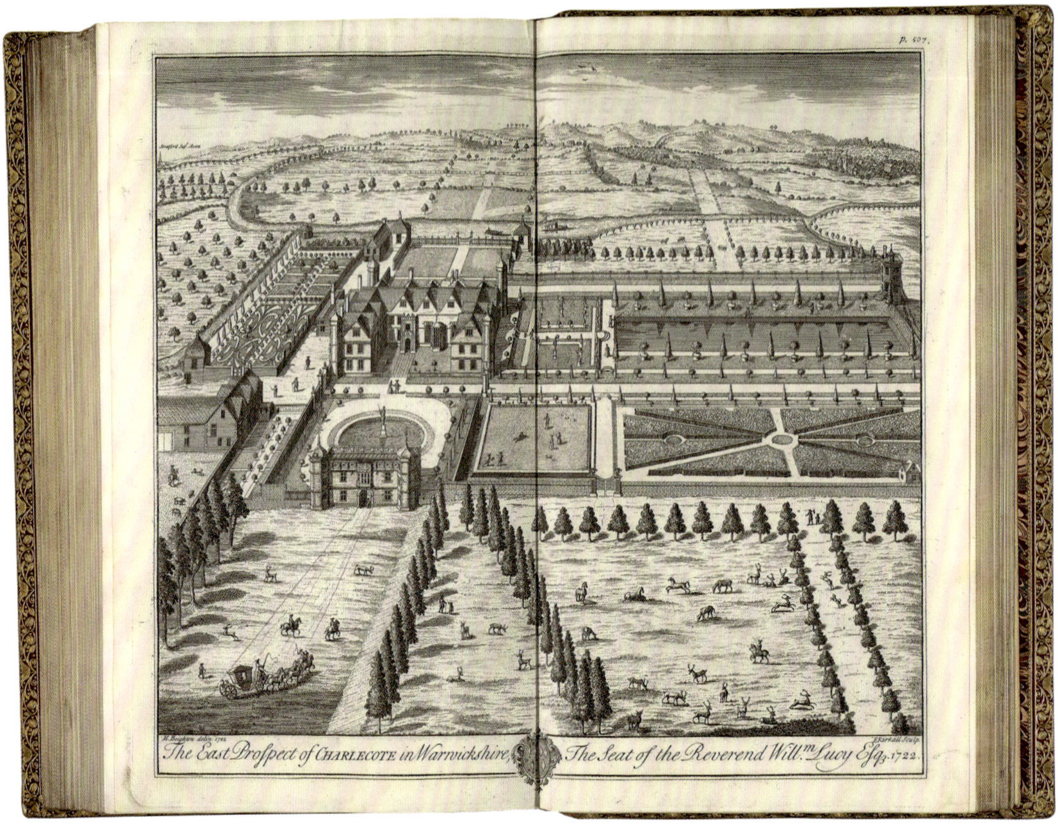

151. Elisha Kirkall after Henry Beighton, "The East Prospect of Charlecote in Warwickshire", from *The Antiquities of Warwickshire Illustrated by William Dugdale* (London: John Osborn and Thomas Longman, 1730), etching and engraving. Yale Center for British Art, Paul Mellon Collection

Henry Beighton, an eastern prospect of Charlecote among them (fig. 151). Beighton's view of Charlecote and its environs was based on drawings made several years earlier, when he was carrying out fieldwork for an ambitious new county map, the first to be based on triangulation (fig. 152).[51] Beighton's map was richly detailed, attentive to the county's natural history and its economic benefits, notably its valuable mineral deposits. It also traced lines of rule and settlement, in the form of ancient landmarks and Roman ways, churches, monasteries, castles and gentlemen's seats, abandoned, depopulated places, and expanding urban centres. A version of the map—along with others detailing the county's hundreds—was included in Thomas's edition of Dugdale's *Warwickshire*. Beighton's maps, along with his views of Warwickshire's estate landscapes, projected an image of a region unified

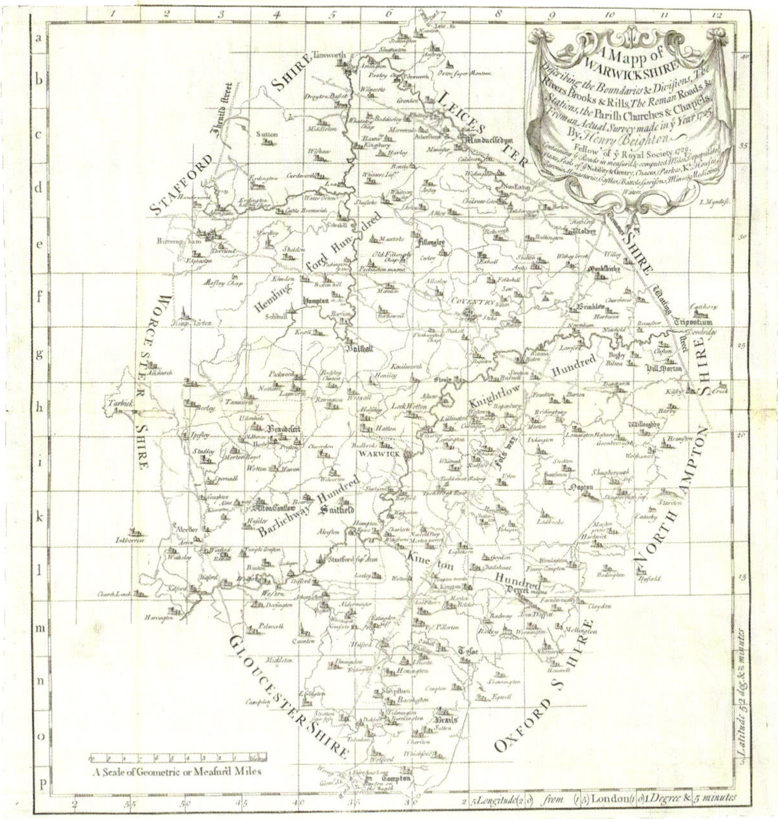

152. Elisha Kirkall after Henry Beighton, "A Map of Warwickshire", from *The Antiquities of Warwickshire Illustrated by William Dugdale* (London: John Osborn and Thomas Longman, 1730), etching and engraving. Yale Center for British Art, Paul Mellon Collection

by history and recent improvement, made ordered and refined; they glossed over its actual diversity. These concerns to trace the lines of connection between the present and that which had endured, as well as to promote the prospective prosperity of the county, were reinforced but also complicated by the antiquarian aspects of the plates and the project as a whole, which documented and so preserved the marks of the past, on paper at least, lest they crumbled or were lost.[52] Beighton's view of Charlecote was indeed consciously commemorative of a time and a landscape already passing into memory when it appeared in print.

According to the credits and the accompanying dedication, Beighton's *East Prospect of Charlecote* showed the estate as it was in 1722, when briefly under the stewardship of the Reverend William Lucy, who had probably commissioned the painting of the estate made some twenty years or so earlier. He had come into the lordship on the death of George Lucy the previous year, only to pass away himself in 1724. Between them, the brothers had over the previous quarter of a century or so overseen a series of improvements to the house, gardens, and wider estate. Francis Smith, a Warwick-based architect-builder, widely favoured by the Midlands gentry, was charged with making various, rather *ad hoc* repairs and alterations to the house from the second decade of the new century onwards. Smith made modest but significant changes to the interior, introducing sash and double-height windows and widening staircases, thereby modernizing the layout of the Elizabethan house. His plans opened up vistas through the house, enabling the freer circulation demanded by the entertainments, lifestyles, and social rituals of the early eighteenth century. He also designed and supervised the building of a new office block, and made plans for additional garden structures, "Drawing Draughts for the Green House".[53]

Beighton's finely observed study of the house shows a regular and near-symmetrical façade flanked by projecting wings, its much-repaired roof punctuated by gables, chimneys, and turrets. There is an elegant, well-dressed couple standing on the gravel path before the house, who the viewer might imagine to be Lucy and his wife, Frances, awaiting the arrival of guests, who approach the fortress-like gatehouse at the end of the avenue of limes on horseback and in a coach-and-six. The addition of such figural incident and narrative—probably by Kirkall—conveys a sense of movement and wider connection, albeit that these are the flows and social affiliations of a leisured world, rather than the ties of local community. There are few estate workers in evidence, and little sense of labour or process. Kirkall's figures dramatize the "playing spaces" of the estate, its pleasure gardens and sporting grounds, as glimpsed and then revealed along the carefully staged approach, as visitors made their way down the processional avenue and were greeted once through the gatehouse by a statue of Diana the huntress at the centre of the circular pool in the courtyard beyond.[54] A shepherd and shepherdess, which had been bought with the Diana from the statuary Edward Hurst of Hyde Park Corner, are also featured in Beighton's delineation of the gardens around the house. Aside from these fashionable additions, however, the layout conforms closely with that of the earlier painted prospect, although a line of trees now shelters the canals and some elements—such as the garden terrace to the west—are shown as less elaborate. A pavilion on the banks of the Dene, overlooking the kitchen garden and a recently planted cherry orchard, may be one of Smith's designs.

Gazing out over the terrain to the east of the River Avon as it bordered Charlecote, Beighton's view encompasses the estate's connections with the communities of the neighbouring lordship of Hampton Lucy and, at its left margin, the market

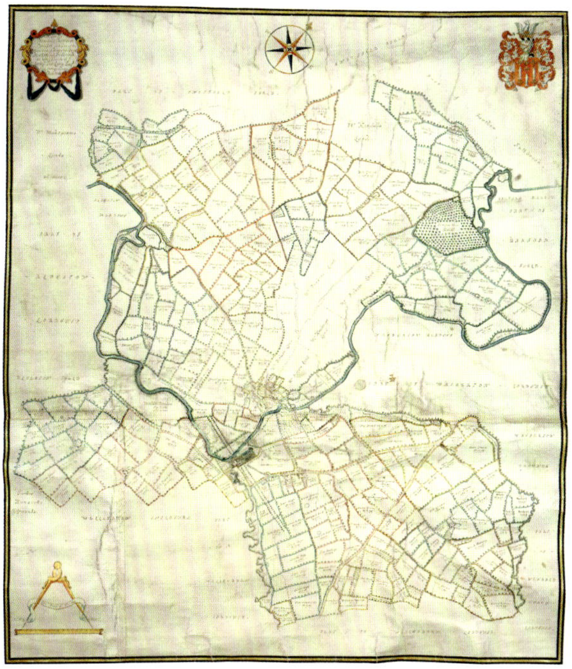

153. James Fish, *Survey of ye Manours of Charlcot and Hunscot with part of the Manours of Hampton Lucy, Hatton and Fullbrook*, 1736, pen, ink, and wash on vellum, 42⅜ x 37¾ in. (107.5 x 96 cm). Warwickshire County Record Office

town of Stratford with the spire of Holy Trinity prominent, the prospect taking in the gentle rises and falls of the country spread out before the distant Welcombe Hills. Hampton Lucy had itself been the site of a series of costly architectural improvements commissioned from Smith, who built the elegant rectory for the Reverend Lucy that is to the fore in Beighton's view of the village. Work on the house had not begun until after Lucy's death, the owner and former rector of the parish having made some provision for the build in his will.[55] Beighton's inclusion of the building in a view of the estate that the draughtsman claimed showed it as it was before this time, paid tribute to Lucy's benefaction and vision. For all the energy he had concentrated on the improvement of the house and grounds, and the image of stewardship projected by the Charlecote prospect, Colonel Lucy had seldom been resident. Although active in the Warwickshire militia at times of crisis, he played no part in the county's administration or politics. Much of his time was spent in the capital, where he rented a fashionable town house on Boulton Street, off Piccadilly. His clergyman brother, as rector of Hampton Lucy, had been far more of a presence locally and in the county as a whole. With William Lucy dying childless, Charlecote passed to a nephew; another Thomas Lucy.

Henry Beighton's principal local rival was the veteran James Fish, whom he grudgingly admitted "a most exact and curious surveyor".[56] A new survey of

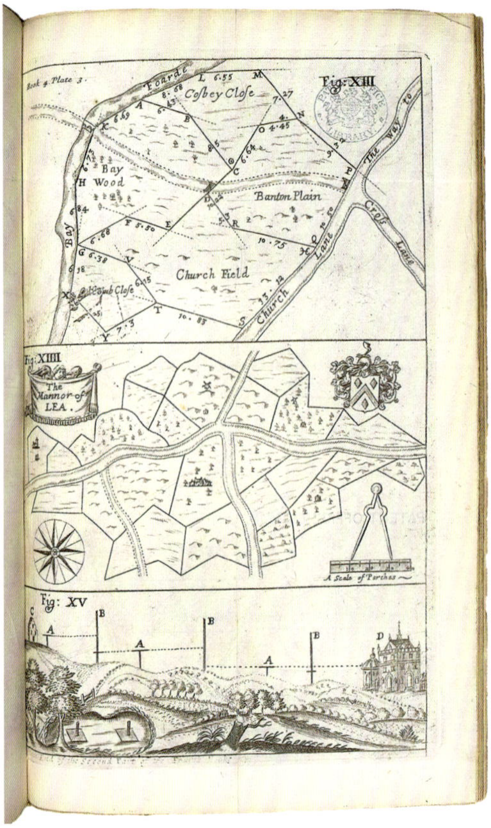

154. After William Leybourn, "Map of Charlecote", in *The Compleat Surveyor Or, the Whole Art of Surveying Land* (London: Samuel Ballard, Aaron Ward, and Thomas Woodward, 1722), plate 3. British Library, London

Charlecote was commissioned on Thomas Lucy's behalf from Fish in 1736 (fig. 153) some five decades after he had drawn up his first account of the estate. Fish's *Survey of ye Manours of Charlcot and Hunscot* conformed closely to well-established models. William Leybourn's *The Compleat Surveyor*, a manual first published in 1653 but still appearing in much revised editions in the early eighteenth century, recommended maps as "a neat Ornament for the *Lord* of the *Manor* to hang in his Study, or other private place; so that at pleasure he may see his *Land* before him, and the quantity of all or every parcel thereof, without any further trouble".[57] Estate maps assumed a variety of forms. Though sometimes the kind of highly wrought "ornament" promoted here, they were also drawn up as strategic working documents, which could be amended and annotated, registering the processes of an estate's improvement and management, and recording its owner's second thoughts and shifting priorities.[58] A model draught, illustrating Leybourn's text, situated the manor house and its surrounding parkland amid a series of irregular but interlocking fields, embellished with indications of the various economies of the estate as well as a church and a series of outlying halls (fig. 154). Such maps traced the projection and material progress of the estate, enunciating ideals and principles as well as recording places. They were documentary and practical, decorative and emblematic. Delicately coloured and decorated, Fish's *Survey of ye Manours of Charlcot and Hunscot* was a fine presentation map of some artistry. Its maker followed the conventions advised by Leybourn, including a compass rose and scale, an elaborate title cartouche, and the family's armorial bearings (which featured three lucies or pikes haurient, in a play on their name as it was understood to derive from the plenty of the waters that bordered Charlecote). Heraldic elements which—as in Beighton's Charlecote prospect—often decorated the edge of views as well as maps, confirmed a family's historic connection with and rights to the possession of the land. Such allusions to the past only reinforce the consciously retrospective tenor of the 1736 map of Charlecote.

Displaying the extent and the complexity of the estate, Fish's map lays out its varied spaces and economies, from the house and its gardens, avenues, park, and orchards to outlying farms and leasows, mills and brickfields.[59] It was a work both practical and commemorative, an inventory of assets and an image of order and prosperity that belied the difficulties that beset the owner of the estate, which had been mortgaged out the previous year. Given to violent seizures, William Lucy's heir was effectively excluded from the control of Charlecote. Thomas Lucy's ill health and the neglect of the estate during his tenure accentuated a sense of unease and decline that had long been evident, despite the extensive investment in its improvement. Colonel Lucy had died in 1721, without leaving a son and heir or will. His successors were left with a catalogue of debts, however. Having ventured a substantial sum in South Sea Company stock, the Colonel suffered near ruinous losses in the financial crash of the previous year.[60] While William Lucy did manage to discharge some of the "many long and large summs" his brother had left owing, and to resolve a fractious dispute over the inheritance the Colonel's widow had brought to the estate, some debts were to remain unsettled.[61] Francis Smith, for one, had gone unpaid for the building he had supervised; indeed, the architect held a bond on the Lucys for a sizeable loan, on which the interest was still outstanding as late as the 1740s. Smith was to further his interest by purchasing the mortgage on the Lucy estate offered in 1735.[62] Charlecote's grand canals and formal gardens, which had been the spectacular focal point of views of the estate from the prospect commissioned at the close of the century to Fish's late survey, fell into neglect. Out of fashion and too expensive to maintain, they were swept away by Thomas Lucy's younger brother, another George Lucy, who came into the estate in the mid-1740s. He was eventually to contract "Capability" Brown "to fill up all the ponds on the north front of the house, to alter the slopes and give the whole a natural, easy, and corresponding level with the house on every side".[63]

The surveys made of Charlecote by Fish and Beighton, as that of the latter was to appear in Dugdale's *Warwickshire*, were overshadowed by William Lucy's passing and the uncertainty of his heir's tenure. They upheld the same sense of good management and order that had underwritten the pleasures of a country life on a warm summer's day enjoyed so blithely by the party pictured in the view of Charlecote commissioned when William Lucy and his brother were still young men. But the outlook was now more reflective, less carefree perhaps, about a need to consolidate and take stock rather than invest and develop. They were commemorative of a time as well as a place, additions to the archive of family history and estate papers held in the muniment room.

CHARLECOTE'S PROSPECTS

Greater investment in the country's estates in the decades either side of 1700, with increasingly large and elaborate ornamental gardens and parks at their core, was aided by and in turn promoted the development of a rich and varied range of literary and visual forms, given over to the improvement of the landscape. Whether concerned with its planning or commemoration, these activities invariably overlapped and enhanced each other, in ways characteristic of so much of the culture of the period. With the arts and sciences associated with the estate and its representation themselves understood as now "improved" or at least "improvable", they were indeed emblematic of broader developments. Now extended beyond the land (and its enclosure), the idea and the ideals of improvement came to be applied to ever-widening fields of knowledge and practice.[64] A work like Johannes Kip and Leonard Knyff's *Britannia Illustrata* (1707) may be understood as both contributing to and emerging out of these processes. A project of national imagining, collecting together engraved views of nearly a hundred of England's foremost seats, it afforded subscribers to the series the opportunity to admire improvements in the quality and the patronage of the visual arts as well as the reformation of the country's landed estates. *Britannia Illustrata* incorporated the properties engraved into a general framework; the attentiveness to topography and the sense of spectacle characteristic of the "bird's-eye" view fashioned into a national style. A scheme originating in the capital's increasingly vibrant artistic community, it was also very much the product of its often overlooked ties with the culture of the regions. With *Britannia Illustrata*, the interests and achievements of men of landed property, in terms of their collective authority over and impact on a series of local landscapes, were conflated with those of the country as a whole, projecting shared tastes and values. Bespoke, commissioned drawings or oils (often crafted for specific architectural spaces) addressed a relatively select viewer, and in terms so often dependent on very particular forms of local knowledge. Despite the lack of such attachments, those whose only encounter with the site was in reproduction might still be expected to recognize and respond to the display of ideals. Various narrative associations or "plot[s] of [his] owne contriving" were mobilized by these images.

"Landskip" converted the country's topography into a dazzling artefact, a "Deceptive vision", in Edward Norgate's much recycled words, "counsing or cheating your owne Eyes . . . by a plot of your owne contriving".[65] While offering an attractive, orderly, and wide-ranging view of life and land, it also had the capacity to dissemble and distort the world.[66] Visual and verbal celebration of landed property as a "landskip", a "prospect", a "view"; arranging, rearranging and so "improving" the lie of the land in accord with rules of scenic composition; accentuating some features and screening out others; conflating the observed and the imagined; all of this was of course a powerful means of addressing, if not always entirely resolving, the play of conflicting forces vivifying the estate and its representation. Views adopting the controlling, organizing perspective of the owner were adapted to a range of sites, whether the grand, noble seats featured in Kip and Knyff's series or the concerns and resources of a county gentry family like the Lucys of Charlecote. They (re)framed the relation between land and lord, asserting the primacy of individual rights over the ties of community, by insisting on the harmonious accommodation of the old and the new, past and present, ancestry and continuity, pleasure and profit, process and progress, local, regional, and national interests. Views and visions of the estate landscape were shaped by a range of shifting ideals and priorities, at a local and personal level as well as more widely, investments that were variously conflicting or combined, upheld with greater or lesser force.

On occasion these contests and their attendant concerns were addressed directly, in scenes of decay or desertion. In other instances, the more familiar insistence on rural plenty and virtue was troubled by circumstances that lay outside the frame, not registered in the image except in as much as any such state of completion and plenitude occasions the anticipation of its loss. Views of Charlecote's late seventeenth- and early eighteenth-century improvements, as they were displayed in maps, painting, and print, for all that they projected assured, confident images of good order and plenty, were edged by unease and uncertainty about the maintenance of the estate, about its "prospects". There were anxieties and failures as well as the expectation of pleasures and profits framing the view from the gentleman's seat.

Thanks to Steve Daniels, Nick Grindle, and the editors for their comments on earlier drafts of this essay.

1. Tom Williamson and Liz Bellamy, *Property and Landscape: A Social History of Land Ownership and the English Countryside* (London: George Philip, 1987), 122–23. See also David Sugarman and Ronnie Warrington, "Land Law, Citizenship and the Invention of 'Englishness': the Strange World of the Equity of Redemption", in *Early Modern Conceptions of Property*, ed. John Brewer and Susan Staves (London: Routledge 1996), 111–43.
2. Richard Grassby, *The Business Community of Seventeenth-century England* (Cambridge Univ. Press, 2002), 374–82.
3. On the problems attending even the most general of definitions of an estate, see Tom Williamson, "Archaeological Perspectives on Landed Estates: Research Agendas", in *Estate Landscapes: Design, Improvement and Power in the Post-Medieval Landscape*, ed. Jonathan Finch and Kate Giles (Woodbridge: Boydell Press, 2007), 1–16.
4. Stephen Daniels and Susanne Seymour, "Landscape Design and the Idea of Improvement, 1730–1900", in *An Historical Geography of England and Wales*, ed. R. A. Dodgshon and R. A. Butlin, 2nd ed. (London: Academic Press, 1990), 488–520; Paul Warde, "The Idea of Improvement, c.1520–1700", in *Custom, Improvement and the Landscape in Early Modern Britain*, ed. Richard W. Hoyle (Farnham: Ashgate, 2011), 127–48.
5. John Barrell, "The Public Prospect and the Private View: The Politics of Taste in Eighteenth-century Britain", in Barrell, *The Birth of Pandora and the Division of Knowledge* (Basingstoke: Macmillan, 1992), 41–61; Tim Fulford, *Landscape, Liberty and Authority: Poetry, Criticism and Politics from Thomson to Wordsworth* (Cambridge Univ. Press, 1996), 3–6, *passim*; Donna Landry, *The Invention of the Countryside: Hunting, Walking and Ecology in English Literature, 1671–1831* (Houndmills: Palgrave, 2001), 4–5, 129–30.
6. Alice Fairfax-Lucy, *Charlecote and the Lucys* (Oxford Univ. Press, 1958), 176. This draws on a family history compiled in the nineteenth century by Mary Elizabeth Lucy.
7. On the several connotations of this term at the time, see R. A. Butlin, "Regions in England and Wales c.1600–1914", in *An Historical Geography*, ed. Dodgshon and Butlin, 223–54.
8. Studies of estate portraiture of the period include: John Harris, *The Artist and the Country House* (London: Sotheby's, 1979); M. Spivy and others, *Country Houses in Great Britain* (New Haven and London: Yale Center for British Art, 1979); Julius Bryant, *Finest Prospects: Three Historic Houses: A Study in London Topography* (London: English Heritage, 1986); Stephen Daniels, "Goodly Prospects: English Estate Portraits, 1670–1730", in *Mapping the Landscape: Essays on Art and Cartography*, ed. Nicholas Alfrey and Stephen Daniels (Univ. of Nottingham, 1990), 9–12; Nicholas Grindle, "The Wise Surveyor: Surveying and Representation in British House and Estate Portraiture, c.1675–1715" (unpublished PhD thesis, Univ. of London, 2002); and David Jacques, "Netherlandish Topographical Artists and English Gardens", in *Dutch and Flemish Artists in Britain, 1550–1800*, ed. Juliette Roding and others (Leiden: Primavera Pers, 2003), 177–88. See also Gregory Rubinstein, "Artists from the Netherlands in Seventeenth-century Britain: An Overview of their Landscape Work", in *The Exchange of Ideas: Religion, Scholarship and Art in Anglo-Dutch Relations in the Seventeenth Century* (*Britain and the Netherlands* 11), ed. Simon Groenveld and Michael Wintle (Zutphen: Walburg Instituut, 1994), 163–95.
9. While the prospect of Charlecote now hangs in the entrance hall to the manor house, alongside a fine collection of family "heads", it is not clear where it was originally placed. It may well have been intended for George Lucy's London residence.
10. *The Spendthrift*, 28 June 1766.
11. For an important recent discussion of circulation in relation to seventeenth-century discourse on rivers, attentive to conflicting perceptions of land as property on the one hand, and a nation imagined in terms of vital lines of connection on the other, see Andrew McRae, *Literature and Domestic Travel in Early Modern England* (Cambridge Univ. Press, 2009), 21–66.

12. There is not space here to consider the range of variously complementary and conflicting ways these terms were employed. Indeed, the association and variety of meanings accumulating around "landskip" in English culture of the period is bewildering. Its relation to an array of cultural debates and practices, not only as it featured in writings on "the arts of picture", visual and verbal, but in political and religious tracts, rendered the category and its vocabulary still more imprecise. See James Turner, *The Politics of Landscape: Rural Scenery and Society in English Poetry, 1630–1660* (Cambridge, MA: Harvard Univ. Press, 1979), and, most helpfully, the same author's "Landscape and the 'art prospective' in England, 1584–1660", *Journal of the Courtauld and Warburg Institutes* 42 (1979): 290–93; and Denis Cosgrove, *Social Formation and Symbolic Landscape*, rev. ed. (1984; Madison: Univ. of Wisconsin Press, 1998), 192–96. Henry V. S. and Margaret S. Ogden, *English Taste in Landscape in the Seventeenth Century* (Ann Arbor: Univ. of Michigan Press, 1955), remains the only extended survey of the topic.
13. Robert J. Mayhew, *Landscape, Literature and English Religious Culture, 1660–1800: Samuel Johnson and Languages of Natural Description* (Houndmills: Macmillan, 2004), 41–47.
14. While the focus here is on prospects of landed property and the adoption of the owner's perspective, elevated views were of course also applied in other contexts where the politics were subtly different. See Christine Stevenson, "Vantage Points in the Seventeenth-century City", *London Journal* 33, no. 3 (Nov. 2008): 217–32; and McRae, *Literature and Domestic Travel*, 199–200.
15. Daniels, "Goodly Prospects", 10–11, Nigel Everett, *The Tory View of Landscape* (New Haven and London: Yale Univ. Press, 1994), 42.
16. Jan or John Stevens, *The South Prospect of Hampton Court in Herifordsheir* (ca. 1705–10; Yale Center for British Art, New Haven): see Fairfax-Lucy, *Charlecote and the Lucys*, 176. A careful study of surviving estate papers has not uncovered any evidence to verify this attribution.
17. An example would be the suite of views of estates in Monmouthshire commissioned from Thomas Smith by Henry Somerset, first Duke of Beaufort for Badminton, ca. 1685–90: see Harris, *The Artist and the Country House*, 123–24.
18. John Dixon Hunt and E. de Jong, eds., essays on "The Anglo-Dutch Garden in the Age of William and Mary", in *The Journal of Garden History* 8, nos. 2–3 (1988), Tom Williamson, *Polite Landscapes: Gardens and Society in Eighteenth-century England* (Stroud: Sutton, 1995), 24–31.
19. Work on the gardens and the development of the wider estate is best traced through the estate and family papers held at Warwickshire County Record Office, Warwick (hereafter WCRO) L6: see references below.
20. Daniels and Seymour, "Landscape Design", 492.
21. Williamson and Bellamy, *Property and Landscape*, 143.
22. Stephen Daniels, "The Political Iconography of Woodland in Later Georgian England", in *The Iconography of Landscape*, ed. Denis Cosgrove and Stephen Daniels (Cambridge Univ. Press, 1988), 43–82.
23. John Evelyn, *Silva, Or A Discourse of Forest-Trees, And the Propagation of Timber in his Majesty's Dominions*, 5th ed. (1664; London: John Walthoe and others, 1729), 256.
24. Daniels, "Goodly Prospects", 10, Sarah Bendall, *Maps, Land and Society: A History with a Carto-bibliography of Cambridgeshire Estate Maps, c.1600–1836* (Cambridge Univ. Press, 1992), 6, 177.
25. Richard Helgerson, *Forms of Nationhood: The Elizabethan Writing of England* (Univ. of Chicago Press, 1994), 145.
26. Daniel Woolf, *The Social Circulation of the Past: English Historical Culture, 1500–1730* (Oxford Univ. Press, 2003), Jan Broadway, *"No historie so meete": Gentry Culture and the Development of Local History in Elizabethan and Early Stuart England* (Manchester Univ. Press, 2006).
27. William Camden, *Camden's Britannia*, rev. ed. (London: F. Collins and A. and J. Churchill, 1695), 499, 503.
28. Joan Thirsk, "The Farming Regions of England", in *The Agrarian History of England and Wales*, vol. 4, *1500–1640*, ed. Thirsk (Cambridge Univ. Press, 1967), 91, T. R. Slater and P. J. Jarvis, eds., *Field and Forest: An Historical Geography of Warwickshire and Worcestershire* (Norwich: Geobooks, 1982).
29. Andrew Yarranton, *Englands Improvement by Sea and Land*, 2 parts (1677–81; London: Thomas Parkhurst, 1698), i: 123, 156.

30. T. S. Willan, *River Navigation in England, 1600–1750* (London: Frank Cass, 1964), 8, 28, 46.
31. Chris Dyer, "A Landscape for Pleasure: Fulbrook, Warwickshire and John, Duke of Bedford in the Fifteenth Century", *Warwickshire History* 15, no. 6 (Winter 2013/14): 239–50.
32. Fulbrook was first leased by the Lucys around 1609, and was in the family's possession by the middle of the century: see WCRO L6/223, 224.
33. See Alan Everitt, *The Community of Kent and the Great Rebellion, 1640–60* (Leicester Univ. Press, 1966), and the various challenges to and revisions of his model of the "county community", helpfully summarized in Jacqueline Eales and Andrew Hopper, eds., *The County Community in Seventeenth-century England and Wales* (Hatfield: Univ. of Hertfordshire Press, 2012).
34. Sir William Dugdale, *The Antiquities of Warwickshire Illustrated* (London: Thomas Warren, 1656), 398–403.
35. On the Lucys' political affiliations in this period, see Ann Hughes, *Politics, Society and Civil War in Warwickshire, 1620–1660* (Cambridge Univ. Press, 1987), *passim.*
36. For the conflict over the estates in the late 1650s, see WCRO L6/86, 1157.
37. Work on the canals is recorded in a surviving volume of accounts for Charlecote [1683–90]: WCRO L6/1009.
38. James Fish, letter to Davenport Lucy, 4 May 1685; Fish, "Survey of the Charlecote lordship" (ca. 1685); Fish, "Survey of the manors of Hampton Lucy, Hatton and Fullbrook" (ca. 1685), WCRO L6/1010, 1032, 1033.
39. Davenport Lucy, letter to Sir William Underhill, 12 April [1685], WCRO L6/1249.
40. On the late seventeenth-century land market in the county, see Geoffrey Tyack, "Warwickshire Country Houses in the Age of Classicism, 1650–1800", *Warwickshire Local History Society Occasional Papers* (1980): 4–5.
41. This was commissioned from Nicholas Stone's workshop, the figures by John Schorman. See Nigel Llewellyn, *Funeral Monuments in Post-Reformation England* (Cambridge Univ. Press, 2000), 165, and Broadway, *"No historie so meete"*, 190.
42. Hughes, *Politics, Society and Civil War*, 45.
43. Felicity Heal, *Hospitality in Early Modern England* (Oxford Univ. Press, 1993); John Trevor Cliffe, *The World of the Country House in Seventeenth-century England* (New Haven and London: Yale Univ. Press, 1999); Kari Boyd McBride, *Country House Discourse in Early Modern England: A Cultural Study of Landscape and Legitimacy* (Aldershot: Ashgate, 2001).
44. There is an extensive literature on the country house poem including, notably, McRae, *Literature and Domestic Travel*, 55–60; Martin Elsky, "Microhistory and Cultural Geography: Ben Jonson's 'To Sir Robert Wroth' and the Absorption of Local Community in the Commonwealth", *Renaissance Quarterly* 53, no. 2 (2000): 500–28; Andrew McRae, *God Speed the Plough: The Representation of Agrarian England, 1500–1660* (Cambridge Univ. Press, 1996), 285–90; Alistair Fowler, *The Country House Poem* (Edinburgh Univ. Press, 1994); Don E. Wayne, *Penshurst: The Semiotics of Place and the Poetics of History* (Madison: Univ. of Michigan Press, 1984); and Raymond Williams, *The Country and the City* (London: Chatto and Windus, 1973), 26–34.
45. There was of course a strong tradition in English culture of writing in a Georgic mode, there having been several vernacular translations of Virgil's verse by the time of John Dryden's celebrated edition of 1697. See McRae, *God Speed the Plough*, 198–200.
46. McRae, *God Speed the Plough*, 290; Abraham Cowley, *The Works of Mr. Abraham Cowley* (London: J. M. for Henry Herrigman, 1668), 98, 114.
47. Dugdale, *Warwickshire*, "To my Honoured Friends the Gentrie of Warwick-Shire".
48. Jan Broadway, "'The honour of this Nation': William Dugdale and the *History of St Paul's* (1658)", in *Royalists and Royalism during the Interregnum*, ed. Jason McElligott and David L. Smith (Manchester Univ. Press, 2010), 194–213.
49. It is worth noting in this context that Sir Thomas Lucy III was one of the contributors to Dugdale's county history: see Broadway, *"No historie so meete"*, 160.
50. Marion Roberts, *Dugdale and Hollar: History Illustrated* (Newark: Univ. of Delaware Press, 2002), 18–45.

51. William Lucy's account book for 1722 records a payment of £4 4s. being made to "Mr. Beighton in full for ye Draught & prospect of Charl-House": WCRO L6/1257. On the surveyor's county survey, see Shelley Costa, "Marketing Mathematics in Early Eighteenth-century England: Henry Beighton, Certainty and the Public Sphere", *History of Science* 40, no. 2 (2002): 211–32.
52. On concerns to render the past "visible" in this period, see Woolf, *Social Circulation of the Past*, 183–220, and Broadway, "*No historie so meete*", 207–36.
53. Bromley-Davenport muniments, John Rylands Library, University of Manchester, Box 114, Andor Gomme, *Smith of Warwick: Francis Smith, Architect and Master-Builder* (Donington: Shaun Tyas, 2000), 55–56.
54. A receipt for the purchase, dated 16 Sept. 1718, survives: WCRO L6/1099. For readings of the theatrical spaces of the house and garden and their use, which have interesting implications for the visual imagery of the estate, see Alison Findlay, *Playing Spaces in Early Women's Drama* (Cambridge Univ. Press, 2006), 66–109, and Julie Sanders, *The Cultural Geography of Early Modern Drama, 1620–1650* (Cambridge Univ. Press, 2011), 101–32.
55. Smith's work at Hampton Lucy can be traced through correspondence in the Bromley-Davenport muniments, John Rylands Library, University of Manchester, Box 114; and by way of accounts in the Lucy papers at WCRO L6/1257. For the master-builder's often strained relations with the Lucys, see Gomme, *Smith of Warwick*, 45, *passim*.
56. *The Ladies Diary: Or, The Women's Almanac* (London: A. Wilde, 1728), 39. Beighton was the editor of this annual periodical devoted to mathematics.
57. William Leybourn, *The Compleat Surveyor: Or, the Whole Art of Surveying the Land*, 5th ed. rev. (1657; London: Samuel Ballard, Aaron Ward, and Thomas Woodward, 1722), 114.
58. On the various modes of estate mapping in the period, see P. D. A. Harvey, "English Estate Maps: Their Early History and Their Use as Historical Evidence", in *Rural Images: Estate Maps in the Old and New Worlds*, ed. David Buisseret (Univ. Of Chicago Press, 1996), 27–62.
59. Fish also compiled a terrier and survey book to accompany the map: WCRO L6/1035–36.
60. WCRO L6/1013, fol. 1277. On the increasing integration of landed and moneyed interests in the period, see Lawrence and Jeanne Stone, *An Open Elite? England, 1540–1880* (Oxford: Clarendon Press, 1986).
61. William Lucy, letter to John Hammond, Aug. 1721, WCRO L6/1684.
62. For the assignment of the mortgage, dated 24 Dec. 1735, see WCRO L6/298.
63. For Brown's work at Charlecote, see WCRO L6/1476. Brown's first thoughts for the redesign of Charlecote are sketched on the reverse of a plan for Packington Hall, WCRO Z143/1(L).
64. Warde, "The Idea of Improvement", 143–48.
65. Edward Norgate, *Miniatura or the Art of Limning*, ed. Jeffrey M. Muller and Jim Murrell (New Haven and London: Yale Univ. Press, 1997), 87. Circulated in manuscript from ca. 1627–28, Norgate's text first appeared in print as part of William Sanderson's *Graphice. The use of the Pen and Pensil, Or, the most excellent art of painting* (London: Robert Crofts, 1658).
66. Turner, "Landscape and the 'art prospective'", *passim*.

Thirty different Drafts of Guinea: A Printed Prospectus of Trade and Territory in West Africa

Emily Mann

A LENGTHY advertisement in the London *Daily Journal* in March 1728 announced proposals for engraving by subscription "Thirty Different Pieces" after drawings by William Smith, surveyor to the Royal African Company of England.[1] The advertisement stressed the surveyor's great pains in making "Draughts, Plans, and Prospects of all the Rivers, Islands, Bays, Capes, Castles, Forts and Factories belonging to the said Company on the Coast of Africa", and his hope that these prints of "remote Parts" would "oblige the Ingenious and Curious Part of Mankind".[2] Their target audiences were more than casually curious, however. The announcement suggested that the maps and profiles of capes and headlands "may be very useful to all who use the Guiney Trade"—a diverse yet interconnected group including company men and private slave traders, merchants, mariners, money-lenders, and insurers—and that the prospects, framed under glass, would make handsome ornaments for rooms and closets as well as the cabins of ships.[3] The published set of prints, which appeared in May 1729 with the title *Thirty different Drafts of Guinea* (fig. 155) and included views juxtaposing English and Dutch settlements, was re-advertised in February 1730 as "At this Time very proper for all Members of Parliament".[4]

By uncovering the motives for Smith's survey and its publication, this essay shows how printed visual culture was drawn into one of the longest and most bitter economic and political controversies of the late seventeenth and early eighteenth centuries, which emerged in the years following the incorporation of the Royal African Company in 1672 and endured up to and even beyond the company's dissolution in 1752.[5] Smith's plans, profiles, and prospects (see, for example, figs. 157–160) are not tame delineations or transcripts of a given spot, as Henry Fuseli later regarded topographic representation of the landscape.[6] The territory that is visualized and the trade carried out there—the form as well as the object of trade—were contested, not just along Africa's shoreline, but in Britain's Privy Council and parliamentary chamber, in its country houses, in coffee houses across London and other cities, and in the colonies too. The purpose of *Thirty different*

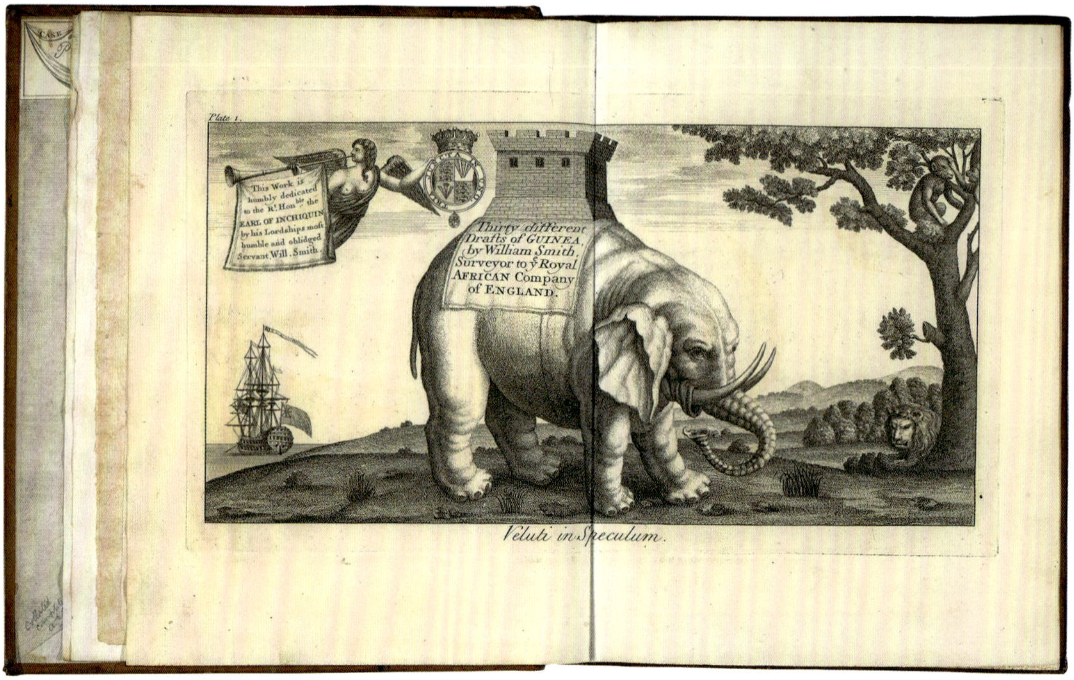

155. John Gray after William Smith, "Veluti in Speculum", in William Smith, *Thirty different Drafts of Guinea* (England, 1727–9), title page, engraving with etching, 11 x 16½ in. (28 x 42 cm). Yale Center for British Art, Paul Mellon Collection

Drafts of Guinea was not merely to bring English settlements in West Africa into wider view (and, indeed, into close-up view within English closets), but to influence public opinion and political decisions on the nation's presence and activity there. It was an intervention in a debate that shaped imperial policy and imagination, ultimately reconceptualizing the interests of an English joint-stock company as British concerns and escalating Britain's slave trade. The publication of Smith's images in 1729 thus provides an early example of topographical imagery born of British imperial imperatives and responding to "imperial issues in metropolitan political controversy", which John Crowley has associated mainly with the period following the Seven Years' War (1756–63).[7]

While the focus here is on the visual representation of the Royal African Company's built settlements, their material construction and condition are necessarily part of the story. It was because control of the physical settlements was at stake, this essay argues, that the survey was commissioned and the set of prints

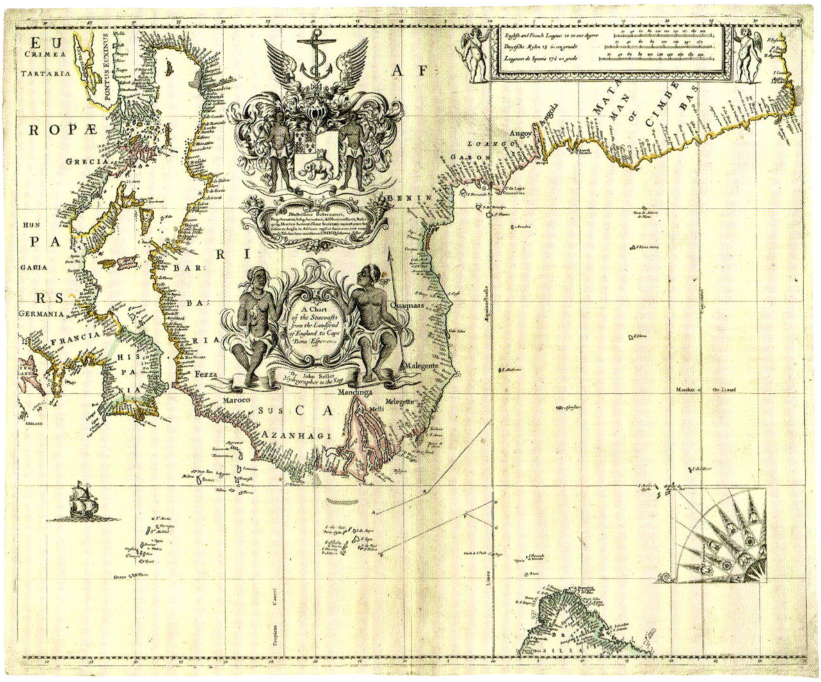

156. John Seller, *Chart of the Seacoasts from the Landsend of England to Cape Bona Esperanca*, 1672–5, hand-coloured engraving, 17⅞ x 22⅝ in. (45.5 x 57.5 cm). John Carter Brown Library, Brown University

published. Smith boasted that his draughts were "true" reflections—the motto on the title plate, *Veluti in Speculum*, translates into "As in a mirror"—yet they are unreliable evidence for what he saw on the ground.[8] Two centuries later, in the 1950s, A. W. Lawrence (otherwise known as the brother of T. E. Lawrence, or Lawrence of Arabia) scrutinized individual plates while directing the repair or restoration of eleven fortifications during the last years of British rule in Ghana; the preserved remains today form a UNESCO World Heritage Site, a "collective historical monument", stretching the length of the country's coastline. In his subsequent book, *Trade Castles and Forts of West Africa*, Lawrence questioned the trustworthiness of some of the printed views, which gave the "impression of having been fudged up from sketches", and suggested other "mistakes" were an inevitable consequence of translating drawings into engravings.[9] However, Lawrence's critical assessment of their accuracy missed the point of the published prints, and likely the drawings too.[10] The historical value of Smith's "map-work" may be found

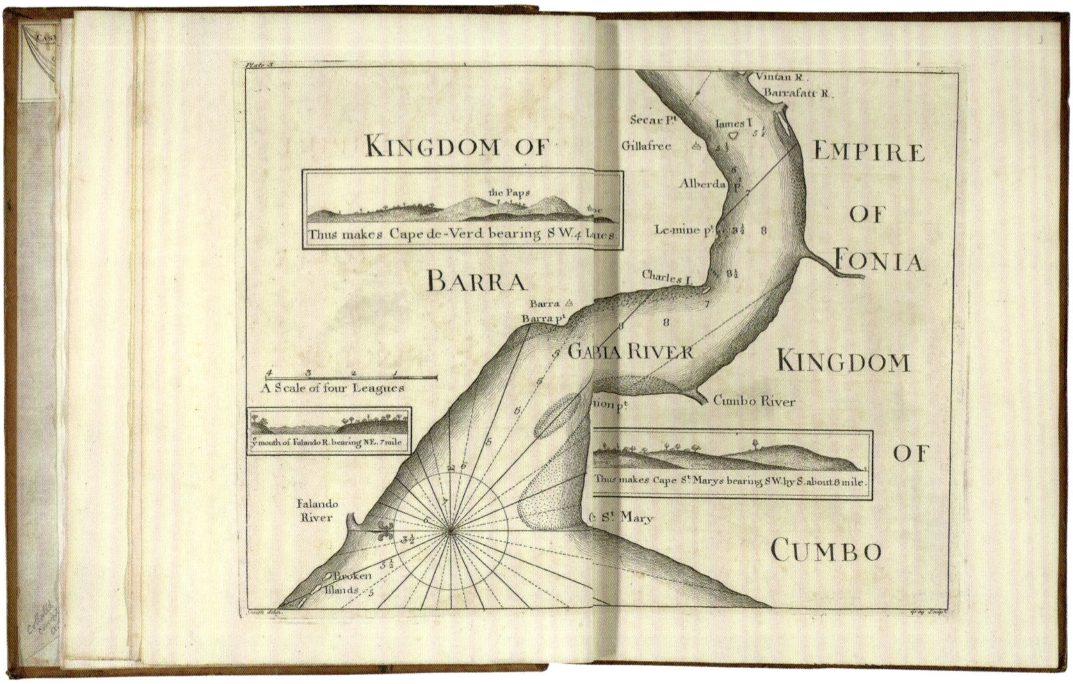

157. John Gray after William Smith, Map of the Gambia River with a profile of Cape Verde, in William Smith, *Thirty different Drafts of Guinea* (England, 1727–9), plate 3, engraving with etching, 11 x 16½ in. (28 x 42 cm). Yale Center for British Art, Paul Mellon Collection

less in the information it delineated than in the ideas it communicated about British interests in Africa, ideas whose contemporary currency was increased because enmeshed in the surveyor's eyewitness testimony.[11] By his own admission, Lawrence provided "an archaeologist's sidelight on history" and was "only indirectly concerned with the history, political or economic, of European endeavour".[12] In contrast, this essay contends that Smith's *Thirty different Drafts*, as with the built settlements they represent, are inseparable from European endeavour in Africa—European endeavour being a polite term for what was, from the start, a scramble.

"ALL GUINEA IN MY POCKET"

It was August 1726 when the Royal African Company's directors gathered at Africa House in Leadenhall Street in the City of London to draw up the commission for a full survey of their settlements. These bases had been acquired or built by the company over the previous half-century and formed part of an expanding trade network connecting Britain, Ireland, Africa, Asia, America, and the Caribbean. William Smith provided a transcript of his commission from the company and a description of his travels in *A New Voyage to Guinea* (1744), which included his return journey to Britain via Barbados.[13] Judged by company officials to be "fitly qualified", he was given detailed instructions both for his passage and the production of the survey, wished health and success, and sent swiftly on his way.[14] Nine days later, the surveyor embarked the *Bonetta* at Gravesend, and within two days the ship had sailed.

Smith's journey can be traced on John Seller's *Chart of the Seacoasts from the Landsend of England to Cape Bona Esperanca* (fig. 156), which was printed shortly after the company's establishment in 1672 and dedicated to its officers and members (a copy was filed with the company's charter in the office of the Council of Trade and Foreign Plantations).[15] Oriented to the east, with England and Brazil on its fringes, the map focused attention on the extensive limits laid out in the company's charter, from Salé, south of Tangier, to the Cape of Good Hope, and suggested the company's assumed prerogative and ambition by subsuming North and West Africa under its coat of arms. It took just over a month to sail from Gravesend to the Gambia River (south of Cape Verde, the westernmost point on mainland Africa); from James Fort, located on a small island in the Gambia, Smith continued to Sierra Leone, then eastwards along what European traders called the Gold Coast, the location of the majority of the company's forts including its headquarters at Cape Coast.

The journey from Gravesend to Gambia was enlivened by many sightings of flying fish and of dolphins chasing them—the dolphins did not "in any Way resemble what our Heralds or Sign-Painters describe!"—but especially by the sighting of land at Cape Verde.[16] It was the lie of the land that particularly excited Smith and the ship's crew: two round hills, he remarked, "at a Distance appear like a Woman's Breasts".[17] The view inspired his first "exact draught" in the service of the company (fig. 157, inset top left): a profile of Cape Verde, dutifully marking "the Paps" (as the sailors called them).[18] The feminization of this foreign landmass in the gaze of the European men is suggestive of the company's territorial claims and commercial exploitation, as well as the close encounters that individuals sought with African women. (Smith included a long and lascivious account from the company's agent Charles Wheeler in which he dwelt upon the "jetty Breasts" of his "Black Lady", whose complexion he soon forgot about when they went to bed.[19]) Smith's casual visual pleasures were short-lived, however, as indeed were many Europeans who voyaged to the West African coast. The great pains Smith took to complete his survey included wading across the Gambia River to measure the distance between its banks, and finding his life in the hands of a group of local people who feared he meant to bewitch them, or worse, with his measuring tools: "How dangerous an Expedition I had undertaken", Smith reflected, "which had cost so many ingenious Men their Lives."[20] There is more than a hint of bravura and self-congratulation in the line. And yet he had a point. Later invited to dine at Elmina Castle, the Dutch headquarters on the coast (only after convincing the Dutch general that, had he come as a spy, he would at least have sneaked in some drawing tools), Smith was shown some plans begun by Dutch surveyors given a comparable commission to his; their "prettily begun" plans, as Smith described them, were left half-finished because the surveyors, "like many others before them", had died on the job.[21]

The physical challenges of such a survey give some credence to the advertisement's claim that Smith, on his return to London, found "few or no true Draughts of those remote Parts extant, except his own".[22] The most recently published images based on drawings made "on the spot" appeared in Willem Bosman's *Nauwkeurige Beschryving van de Guinese Goud–, Tand– en Slave-kust,* first published in Dutch in 1704 (see, for example, fig. 161), and in English as *A New and Accurate Description of the Coast of Guinea* in 1705 (with modified plates).[23] This book appeared in successive Dutch editions, was reprinted in English in 1721, and was also translated into French. Bosman had served the Dutch West India Company in Africa from 1688 to 1701; he was appointed chief merchant in 1698 and began work on his book while on the coast. For some time he was troubled "that there was not a Man on the Coast that could draw and design", so as soon as one "vers'd in that Art" arrived, Bosman set him to work.[24] He was to be disappointed, however, when the artist fell ill. "In a few Days time he was well and dead", Bosman wrote, "and so left me provided only with the half of what I design'd."[25] The images that were printed, in the Dutch topographical tradition, place the fortifications in a commanding position centre stage. The built forms are cast as a dominant yet benign presence—the focal point, as Crowley puts it, of "exquisite scenery".[26] Yet the partial view they provide, cropped by a life cut short in Africa, quietly undermines the apparent beauty and tranquility, suggesting instead a fragility to the European presence.

Bosman had used his book to criticize the governance and business strategy of the Dutch West India Company, but he was hardly complimentary about its English counterpart either. One English company agent at Cape Coast damned the author's "disingenuity, partiality, and malice" (Smith later accused the Dutchman of speaking ill of Cape Coast Castle "as if he was sorry for speaking well of any Thing that belong'd to the *English*") and recommended that the company publish a refutation.[27] Indeed, Bosman commented in his second edition that he had heard "that the English are greatly disturbed about the first edition . . . [and]

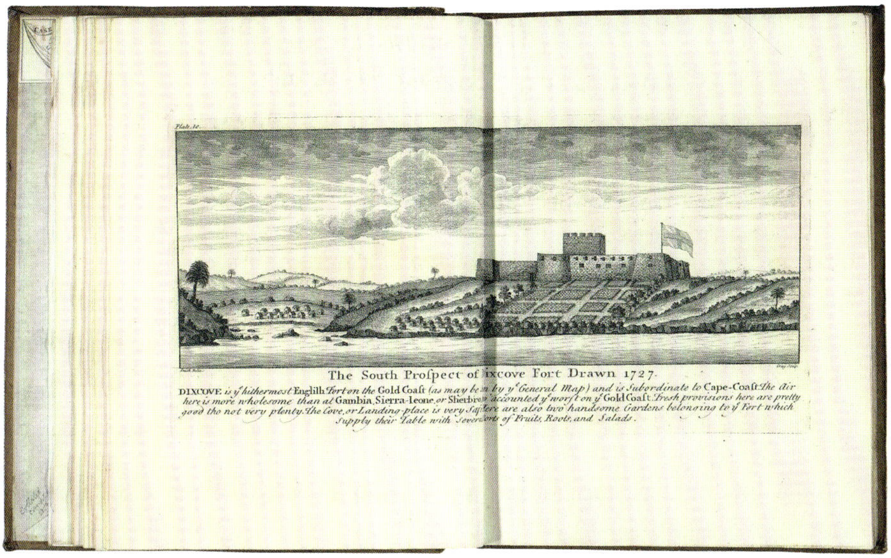

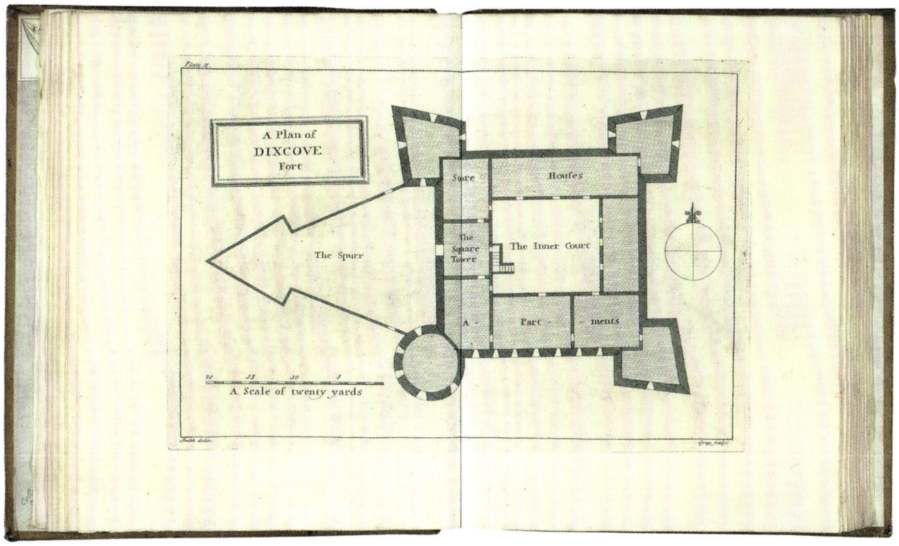

158. John Gray after William Smith, "The South Prospect of Dixcove Fort", in William Smith, *Thirty different Drafts of Guinea* (England, 1727–9), plate 10, engraving with etching, 11 x 16½ in. (28 x 42 cm). Yale Center for British Art, Paul Mellon Collection

159. John Gray after William Smith, "A Plan of Dixcove Fort", in William Smith, *Thirty different Drafts of Guinea* (England, 1727–9), plate 11, engraving with etching, 11 x 16½ in. (28 x 42 cm). Yale Center for British Art, Paul Mellon Collection

are now engaged in the writing of a book to disprove mine, I must say that I am looking forward to it, and I wish it were already in print."[28] Smith's *Thirty different Drafts* served as a visual refutation, albeit about two decades overdue: it was because his draughts had given "entire Satisfaction" to the company and "all others" who had seen them that he was encouraged to publish them for the benefit of a wider audience.[29]

The title plate certainly flatters the Royal African Company, with *Thirty different Drafts of Guinea* inscribed in the sash of a sturdy tusked elephant carrying a castle on its back—the company's emblem. Next comes a fold-out map of the coast on which the English and other European forts are distinguished by the use of key letters: D for Dutch, E for English, F for French. The twenty-eight plates that follow represent the forts in prospects and plans—see, for example, figs. 158 and 159—and these plates are arranged in the order in which they would typically be encountered by English ships (from west to east). Beneath each prospect is what the advertisement described as a "concise Description" of the fort's position, defences, local surroundings and inhabitants, and trading benefits. The encyclopaedic combination of maps, profiles, plans, prospects, and text creates a seemingly comprehensive view of the company's settlements, reflecting Smith's commission to obtain a "compleat Knowledge" of what he found and the company's reach. The incorporation of diverse imagery into a single set also suggests a shared aim.

Early European written accounts of Africa tend to emphasize difference, but Smith's visual images do not make the unknown known so much as look strangely familiar—aesthetically pleasing and thus imaginable as British. The "wholesome" castle air of Dixcove Fort (fig. 158) is exaggerated by the rugged-looking masonry on what were typically rubble walls given successive coats of whitewash to help keep them standing up. The town nestling beneath these walls suggests a feudal-like relationship between the company and the local people. The situation of the town "under shelter . . . of the Fort Guns", as the text puts it in another prospect, had special significance: the company committed to protecting the townspeople who lived within range of the guns in exchange for their assistance and loyalty in the business of trade; the inhabitants also provided construction labour and helped defend the forts. The English flag would have been sizeable—similar to ship flags from the period, which could measure five metres or more across—but is nonetheless enlarged for effect. As Geoff Quilley has argued, the prospects "present the forts as neat, clean, efficient and impersonal structures within an overall commercial system marked by its clarity and order".[30] In effect, the forts stand for the company. Daniel Defoe, an outspoken supporter of the Royal African Company, employed this metaphor in his eulogy of the company as "a noble Fabrick".[31] The

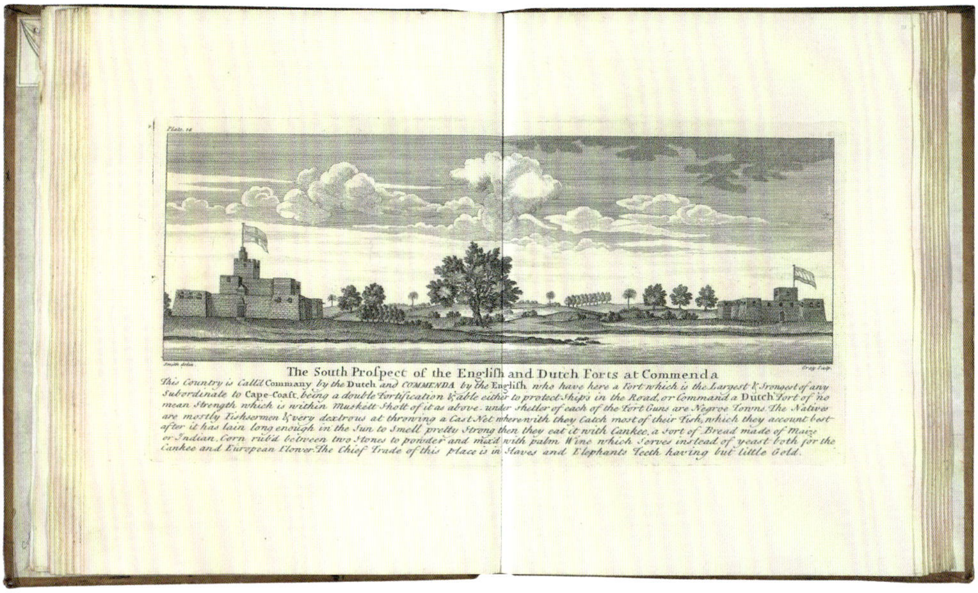

160. John Gray after William Smith, "The South Prospect of the English and Dutch Forts at Commenda", in William Smith, *Thirty different Drafts of Guinea* (England, 1727–9), plate 14, engraving with etching, 11 x 16½ in. (28 x 42 cm). Yale Center for British Art, Paul Mellon Collection

calm coastal waters and clouds, the gentle hills and cultivation of clearings, gardens, and trees (in Quilley's view, the imposition of the English countryside upon the African terrain) draw a veil over the coastal trade in slaves, who are itemized as just another commodity in the texts below.[32] The reassuringly pleasant and fertile backdrops also mask the vast unknown territory inland, where the relationship between the company and the African peoples it relied on for trade was volatile and often aggressive. Images and texts together seem amply to illustrate Beth Fowkes Tobin's analysis of colonialism as a process of both "extraction" and "abstraction".[33]

The landscapes are notably lacking in human figures, yet the English and Dutch guns—ranged at each other and over the "Negroe Towns belonging to each of them"—powerfully draw attention to their interaction in what were, in reality, deeply entangled spaces. The proximity of the English and Dutch settlements is dramatically staged not just in the volume's fold-out map, where the European forts jostle for position, but in four of the plates where the competing forts lay "within Muskett Shott" of each other—for example, at Komenda [Commenda] (fig. 160). It was part of Smith's commission to observe, as he made his way along the coast, "the Number, Strength and Situation of such Forts and Factories as belong to any other Nation".[34] The Dutch general at Elmina therefore had some grounds to suspect Smith of espionage, warning him that "tho' I came abroad to carry home all *Guinea* in my Pocket, yet I shou'd not carry home *Elmina* Castle with me."[35] The second Anglo-Dutch war of the previous century had a long-lasting effect on the coast, and each nation warily watched against encroachments by the other. Yet the residents of the forts, typically far fewer in number than the scale of the buildings might suggest, also saw advantages in having a well-armed neighbour and were not averse to collaborating in a policy of divide and rule. Smith recounted how two of the towns at Accra (where there was a Danish fort, as well as English and Dutch) "almost join together" and the inhabitants "can never well agree, each distinguishing themselves by the Titles of either *English Men*, or *Dutch Men*".[36] Relations between the English and Dutch easily turned sour. Smith told a story of how an English chief at Komenda, "having had some Words of Dispute with the *Dutch* Chief, was unhandsomely and unwarily attack'd by him under a great Tree between the Two Forts, where he bravely defended his own at the Expense of the unhappy *Dutchman*'s Life".[37] The said tree is presumably the one Smith placed at the centre of his prospect (fig. 160), significantly taller than the Dutch fort (and even the English fort, were it not for the proud St George's flag).

Smith surely intended his images to trump those printed in Bosman's book (fig. 161). Other Dutchmen offered more refined models for turning a first-hand survey into print, such as Wenceslaus Hollar in his engraved views of the fortifications at Tangier, which included the set of six *Divers Prospects in and about Tangier* (1673), and the military engineer John Slezer in his *Theatrum Scotiae* (1693, fourth edition 1719). Smith may also have been aware of a series of prospects of European forts drawn by the Huguenot exile Jean Barbot and engraved by Johannes Kip in the first decade of the eighteenth century. These had not yet been released in print, but were finally published in 1732 with Barbot's *Description of the Coasts of North and South-Guinea*, which also included a composite engraving by Kip of the views in Bosman's book.[38] Kip was probably commissioned to work on this project on the basis of the prestigious and commercially successful *Britannia Illustrata,* a collaboration with Leonard Knyff that was published in one volume in 1707. Smith certainly would have been familiar with this collection of high-quality engraved and etched bird's-eye prospects of palaces and country house estates, and was likely inspired by their "intimate combination of fidelity and a feeling for the spectacular".[39] Once the preserve of royal palaces and manor houses, proprietary prospects of this kind were growing in popularity among City merchants as they accrued wealth and assets in and outside London.

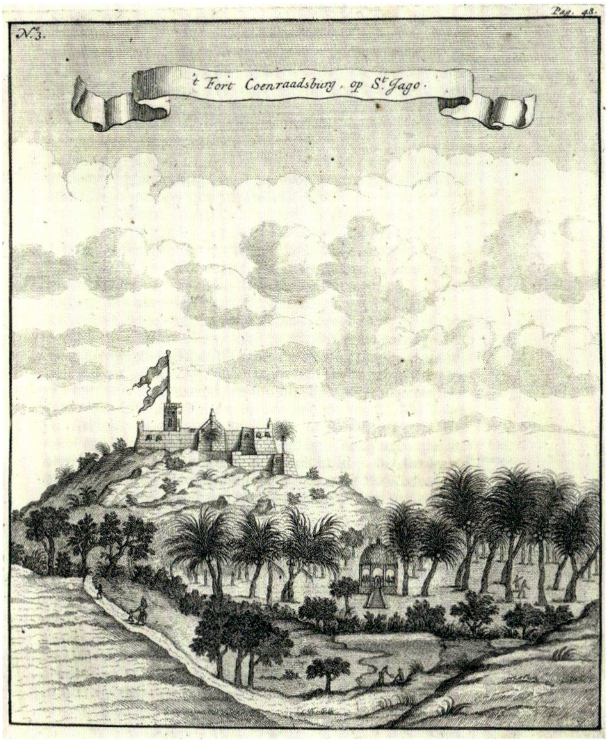

161. Dutch Fort Coenraadsburg, in Willem Bosman, *Nauwkeurige Beschryving van de Guinese Goud–, Tand– en Slave-kust* (Utrecht: Anthony Schouten, 1704), plate 3. Beinecke Rare Book and Manuscript Library

Smith followed Kip and Knyff's model of financing and promoting their work by subscription. Subscriptions were taken by Smith as "author", by Thomas Bowles at his print shop in St Paul's Churchyard, and by Thomas Jemson, proprietor of Lloyd's coffee house on Lombard Street—the coffee house of choice for dealers in maritime trade—where a catalogue of the drawings was available to view alongside the daily domestic and foreign news. Interesting questions are raised by the list of subscribers printed with *Thirty different Drafts*. These subscribers paid 15s. down, and 15s. on delivery, and those who bought six sets got another one free. Two of the four subscribers who splashed out on six sets appear to have been Smith's relatives: Peter Smith, surveyor of the Cove of Cork, and John Smith, rector of Kilmore. A third major patron, to whom Smith dedicated the publication, was the fourth Earl of Inchiquin, whose grandfather, the second earl, had served as colonial governor in Tangier and Jamaica, and whose seat at Rostellan overlooked the Cove of Cork.

Little has ever been written about William Smith because little is known, but it may reasonably be inferred from his circle of subscribers that he came from Ireland, and probably from the County of Cork or neighbouring Waterford, in Munster province. An Irish background would make sense of a passage in *A New Voyage to Guinea* which recounts a friendly exchange outside a French warehouse at Whydah (Ouidah, in present-day Benin): "the Mate who had the Charge of the Goods there, happening to be a Native of *Ireland*, desir'd me (in the *English* Language) to accept of a Dram."[40] Perhaps Smith was the son of the Cove of Cork surveyor, a revenue position in a prized harbour of great and growing significance in transatlantic trade, provisioning the Caribbean and American colonies in particular (note John Seller's inclusion of southern Ireland on the left edge of his map, fig. 156); that certainly might have made Smith "fitly qualified" for the task of giving a full and exact account of the Royal African Company's trading posts.[41] Other eminent customs officials were among the subscribers: two commissioners of his majesty's customs—Brian Fairfax and Alan Brodrick, second Viscount Midleton (the town of Midleton lying about fifteen miles from the city of Cork)—and William Maynard, collector of Cork. Other Cork dignitaries on the list include Robert Bettesworth, Jonas Morris, and Richard Newman (three sets).

Smith secured subscriptions from fellow employees of the Royal African Company, men who had exercised power on the coast and for whom the condition of the forts was a matter of professional pride. They include the aforementioned Charles Wheeler; John Tinker, former general of Cape Coast, and Jeremiah Tinker, former governor of Whydah (both of whom moved on to top jobs in the Bahamas); and John Brathwaite, who a couple of years later was engaged in the company's efforts to build settlements further south on the African coast. Smith also used his connections in Barbados. In his account of stopping at the island in 1727, he wrote of being "kindly entertained" by "several of my old Acquaintance", and he took the opportunity of showing the governor his draughts.[42] Three subscribers "of Barbadoes" invested in two sets. One was Smith's "learned and ingenious Friend" Dr Henry Warren; another was John Bennett, who later published a pamphlet on the indivisibility of the West Indies plantations and the "Guinea trade".[43]

Not on the subscriber list but the owner of an advance copy was Edward Deane, governor of a number of the company's forts between 1729 and 1733.[44] It appears Deane got hold of his set, which included only twenty of the final thirty prints, in time to take it with him on his voyage to the African coast, just as the advertisement suggested. He died on his passage home. Manuscript amendments on the plan of Dixcove Fort (possibly in the hand of his son James, who inscribed his name beneath his father's in the front endpapers in 1734) mark the "improvements" made under Deane's governorship, a duck pond amongst them. These notes offer a glimpse of how the images were engaged with by their most invested audience. A list of subscribers in this copy—dated 13 July 1728, and with Edward Deane's name added—included the following note: "There are several other Noblemen and Gentlemen who have promised my friends to subscribe, whose Names I hope to be honour'd with speedily, in order to perfect the list that is to be prefix'd to the work. Above twenty of the plates are actually finish'd, and the Rest are in Hand, so that the publication of them will not exceed the next month."[45] The implication is that Inchiquin and other influential acquaintances of Smith and his family had been busy rustling up subscribers, which helps to explain the predominance of Ascendancy nobility, gentry, and clergy on the list, such as Richard Boyle, third Earl of Burlington and fourth Earl of Cork, the Lord High Treasurer of Ireland; Charles Calvert, fifth Lord Baltimore (proprietor and soon-to-be governor of Maryland in North America); Henry Boyle, MP for County Cork; Henry Maule, Lord Bishop of Cloyne, and his brother, James Maule (six sets).

Research into these individuals quickly reveals the manifold relations between them—and therefore the workings of early eighteenth-century networks of patronage—rather than direct investments or involvement in the English company, or even the African trade. Irish ports were banned from launching direct voyages to Africa, yet the growing fortunes of Ireland's elites depended on increasing flows of goods related to the slave trade, and these elites were gathering strength in defence of their economic interests in England.[46] More generally, the significant Irish interest generated in Smith's project, notably from Ascendancy landlords, invites consideration of the parallels between English encounters with Ireland and with Africa (and with America and the Caribbean too). Such a connection was implicitly made by Jonathan Swift in *A Modest Proposal* (1729), in which the proposer refers to the Irish as "*Savages*" who might "sell themselves to the Barbadoes" (Swift's curate, Reverend Stafford Lightburn, was another of Smith's subscribers).[47] For Charles Smith, who wrote a series of Irish county histories in the 1740s and 1750s with a view to producing a great work along the lines of "HIBERNIA; or the present State of Ireland", the country was "*Terra Incognita* to the greater part of *Europe*", just as Africa was.[48] (As the preface to William Smith's *New Voyage to Guinea* remarked, "There is no Part of the World with which we are less acquainted than the interior Part of Africa."[49]) It was partly Ireland's "great remoteness from the continent of Europe" that made it "very little known"—remaining in obscurity like the "*ultima Thule* of the ancients".[50] Charles Smith aimed to dispel the "many gross misrepresentations" that had been made of the country, singling out the recent *Present State of Great Britain and Ireland*, which claimed that the Irish people were "uncivilized, rude and barbarous" and delighted in eating "Flesh without Bread; but which they eat raw, having first pressed the blood out of it".[51] He pointed out the "additional lustre" that Ireland, with the commitment of its nobility and gentry to the place, "will be to the diadem of the British empire, both abroad and at home, in beauty, strength, and glory".[52] There are grounds to suspect a family connection between William Smith and Charles Smith, who, finding existing maps deficient, set about surveying the landscape on his researches, accompanying his accounts with several plates depicting Irish castles and tower houses (such as Kanturk, Co. Cork) that bear comparison with the prospects in *Thirty different Drafts*.[53]

Other names that stand out on the subscriber list include the London Assurance Company director George Hatley (no doubt signed up at Lloyd's coffee house); the Lombard Street goldsmith John Barker, whose shop sign was the Morocco ambassador's head; Launceston Oglethorpe, likely a relation of James Oglethorpe, soon-to-be director and subgovernor of the Royal African Company and founder of the colony of Georgia; and three men by the name of Penn, each presumably related in some way to the founder of Pennsylvania, William Penn, who had become a Quaker in Cork. In short, Smith's subscribers represent an extensive and highly interconnected imperial commercial network with shared and symbiotic interests, in which West Africa, aided by the printed publication of Smith's survey, was being positioned as a central part.

MARKS OF POSSESSION

Why might *Thirty different Drafts of Guinea* have been of interest to *all* members of Parliament "At this Time"? Two weeks after the advertisement making this suggestion appeared in February 1730, Robert Sutton, a Nottinghamshire MP and subgovernor of the Royal African Company, presented a petition to Parliament seeking a government subsidy to support the maintenance of the forts.[54] There followed a vigorous debate over the company's motives and the consequences of approving such a request. The Anglo-Irish politician Viscount Perceval (of Kanturk, Co. Cork) recorded both sides of the debate in his diary. The arguments for receiving the petition and referring it to a committee were, he wrote:

> that it was a matter deserved consideration, for if they are not able to support their forts and settlements, and England will not give money towards it, those forts must fall into the hands of a neighbouring state, Holland, France or Portugal; that if we lose our property there, we shall lose the African trade, which is the most valuable one we have; that if another nation should possess

> themselves of the forts we shall abandon, we must enter into a war to regain them, which would cost us a hundred times more than a little money, suppose twenty thousand pounds a year, to secure them.[55]

It is no coincidence, it seems, that the text beneath Smith's prospect of Elmina and Cape Coast remarks that the Dutch forts "are far better arm'd and mann'd than the English who have not such good Encouragement to Support a Trade of so great importance To their Nation". Opponents of the petition dismissed it as a ploy to boost a beleaguered company's value, and argued:

> that some may sell out, and draw other unwary persons to buy, which may be the ruin of many families. That the company had broke more than once, and are now not worth a shilling; that there is no need of any forts at all there; those that are, are but only wooden ones, and therefore of no defence against an enemy if attacked, without the help of our men-of-war, and therefore our fleets will be sufficient security for our trade. That this trade is at present . . . in an exceeding flourishing way, but to restore the company to vigour is to put them in a power to be hard upon the separate traders.[56]

The petition was rejected by 134 to 90 (Perceval among the latter number), but a debate was set for the following week to consider the trade in general. It was a debate that had erupted repeatedly over almost half a century, dividing the defenders of the company's chartered monopoly and the supporters of a free trade (the "separate traders"), and it centred around the question of whether the forts were necessary or not. And if so, who should pay?

The 1672 charter granted the company a monopoly on the African trade provided it sent all gold home to the Royal Mint, supplied quotas of slaves to the American colonies, and built and maintained forts. Its monopoly was immediately challenged and in 1698 an Act of Parliament opened up the trade, but with a 10 percent duty to finance the forts. From 1705, the company campaigned for the restoration of its monopoly, arguing that the duty (frequently evaded anyway) did not cover the cost of the forts, but the expanding interest group of separate traders and their supporters held sway. The expiration of the 1698 act in 1712 left the trade entirely deregulated, with far-reaching implications for the nation's economic and political affairs.[57] It was a very public and protracted dispute, generating as much, if not more, literature as any other economic controversy during the period.[58] According to one pamphleteer writing in 1710, it was "the daily Occasion of our Coffee-house Contests and Debates".[59] Barely a debate was heard or an essay published on the subject that did not assert or question the necessity, cost, and condition of the Royal African Company's forts, which came to represent monopoly even as the company failed to enforce it, and for long after the monopoly ended. It puts in a different light the company's insignia of an elephant bearing the weight of a castle on its back.

In this "War", as Defoe described it, the separate traders had begun to "appear on the Coast of *Africa* in Defiance of the Company's Forts"—they had even been known to sail under the protection of the Dutch—and as a result the company had "less Security for the Possession of their Properties".[60] The separate traders dismissed the forts as mere "Baubles and Trifles"; but if they were of such small value, Defoe demanded, "Why so many subtle Endeavours to get them out of the Company's Hands?"[61] The private traders were carrying out "an Open Invasion" of the company's trade, he wrote, and in effect "blowing [it] up". Defoe was skilled in hyperbole, but his words reflect the explosiveness of the debate, which was still raging in 1726, in the months leading up to Smith's departure for Africa. By this point the company had been forced to bring a halt to its trade and to petition for a subsidy to maintain the forts. The Board of Trade's repeated requests for "an account of the nature, number, strength and situation of the company's forts and settlements" help to explain the urgency with which the Royal African Company despatched Smith in August—and the critical importance of the result of the debates for the company's future must have influenced the decision to translate the survey into print. The series of views of well-built, well-maintained forts suggests a company secure in its property and busy protecting the trade in the interests of the nation: these are, the advertisements assert, *English* settlements.

Whether the company was to survive and maintain responsibility for the forts or whether the forts would be bought using the public purse and the company dissolved, the company's interest was to suggest the highest possible value for its property against those who saw it as dead stock: "the real value", in its own view, "may be said to exceed all price or estimation."[62] If, as Adam Jones has commented, "reporting on the Gold Coast became almost like writing a prospectus for potential investors", *Thirty different Drafts* was designed to be the most visually persuasive prospectus of all.[63] The East India Company, facing challenges to its own monopoly in Asia—and accused of keeping "Forts abroad, at a great Expence to colour the Necessity of such Monopolies, and to oppress and rob the Natives there with security"—likewise responded with a visual defence.[64] In 1731, George Lambert and Samuel Scott received a commission to paint six views of company settlements for the court of directors' room at the rebuilt East India House (near Africa House on Leadenhall Street).[65]

Did Smith's images have the effect that was being sought? In March 1730, the government gave the company a lifeline with an annual subsidy of £10,000 to

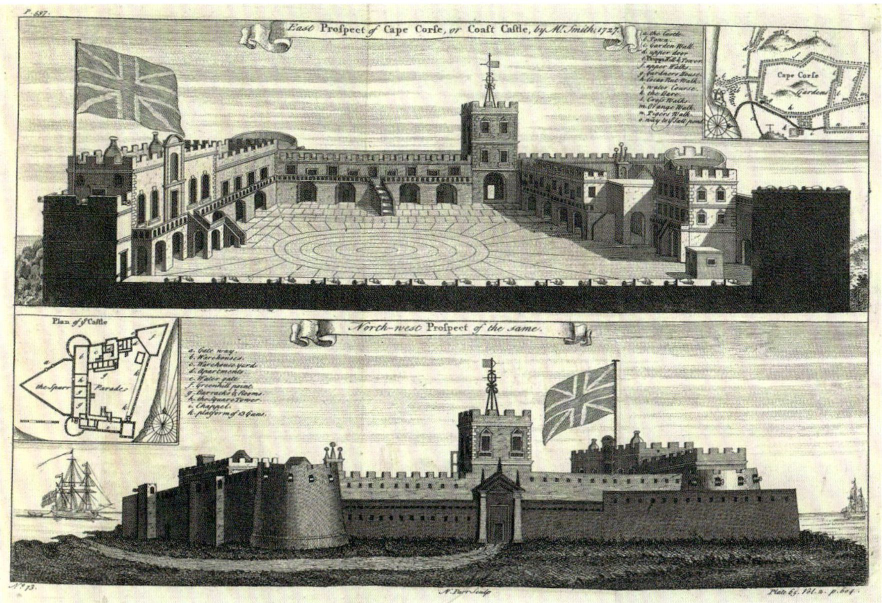

162. Nathaniel Parr (engraver), Compilation of prospects and plans of Cape Coast Castle, in William Smith, *Thirty different Drafts of Guinea*, from *A New General Collection of Voyages and Travels* (London: Thomas Astley, 1745–7), vol. 2, plate 65. Special Collections, University of Virginia, Charlottesville

maintain the forts; it also passed a resolution that defined them as "marks of the possessions of Great Britain in those parts".[66] In 1744 the subsidy was doubled, only to be reduced again in 1745 and removed altogether the following year. In 1749, amid a further flurry of pro-company literature, John Millan reprinted *Thirty different Drafts*.[67] The company, however, was doomed. The cost of the forts (and with it, much control over them) was transferred to the government, which compensated company shareholders.[68] Like the forts, Smith's images had other incarnations. Thomas Astley had the "elegant draughts" reworked for the second volume of *A New General Collection of Voyages and Travels* (1745); one plate combines four of Smith's images relating to Cape Coast Castle: two prospects and two plans, one of the fortification and another of the adjacent gardens (fig. 162).[69] Astley hoped "the Reader will be the better able to judge of the Importance of the African Trade, and the Necessity of supporting the Forts and Settlements of the Company; a Matter which of late has been much the Subject of Enquiry and Conversation."[70] Smith's images were reworked yet again with the translation of Astley's volumes into French as part of Antoine François Prévost's *Histoire générale des Voyages* (Paris, from 1746), and into German in Johann Joachim Schwabe's *Allgemeine Historie der*

Reisen zu Wasser und Lande (Leipzig, from 1748). Here Smith's forts appear artistically aged, with vegetation sprouting from the soft-edged masonry so that the structures blend harmoniously, almost romantically, with the surrounding landscape, becoming a part of nature. It is as though the forts had always been there.

By investigating the construction of William Smith's printed images and their involvement alongside the printed word in the business of empire formation, I have aimed also to recover some of the meaning of architectural construction in Africa from a British point of view. A list of "Rules for Fortifications and Settlement at the Coast of *Guinney*, observed by all that trade thither", printed in *The Golden Coast* (1665) a few years before the establishment of the Royal African Company in 1672, made clear the architecture had meanings that the African people might not accept.[71] Rule eight directed that the King of Haban "be moved about the building of some forts, so as that he may not understand our meaning".[72] The fortifications and their representation in print were for British onlookers statements of intent, staking out a wider claim, serving an imperial vision that did not dissolve with the company in 1752. Successive publications urged the company to extend the trade inland (which the company itself gave as a function of the forts), and Smith's images—not least his plan of the cultivated yet boundless gardens at Cape Coast (reworked in fig. 162)—constituted a visual argument for colonial ambition and appropriation.[73] The existence of the forts may have depended in reality on careful and continuous diplomacy with African leaders (by "little gifts, and a noble appearance", as the author of *The Golden Coast* put it), but their visualization in print sought to persuade an interested early eighteenth-century British public of uncontested ownership and the potential for expanded settlement and control.

1. *Daily Journal*, 18 March 1728.
2. *Daily Journal*, 18 March 1728.
3. *Daily Journal*, 18 March 1728. Europeans in the early modern period used the word "Guinea", with diverse spellings, to refer broadly to the West African coast.
4. *Daily Journal*, 12 May 1729 and 5 Feb. 1730. The latter advertisement invited customers to the exclusive seller of the prints, John Clark in Gray's Inn, to have their portraits made at the same time, "in Miniature, Pastels or Crayons, By Monsieur T. Thevenard, From Paris". Clark was an engraver as well as print-seller, but the engraver of Smith's drawings was John Gray. Gray's connection to Clark was John Pine, to whom Gray was bound in 1720 and who was for a short time in partnership with Clark. The professional relationship between Clark and Monsieur Thevenard ended badly, judging by a later advertisement that accused "a certain French Painter in Miniature" of leaving Clark's lodgings with "a Silver-hilted Sword, and a Cane with a Gold wrought Head": *Daily Journal*, 29 May 1730.
5. For accounts of the company's history and failure, see K. G. Davies, *The Royal African Company* (London: Longmans, Green and Co., 1957); Ann M. Carlos and Jamie Brown Kruse, "The Decline of the Royal

African Company: Fringe Firms and the Role of the Charter", *Economic History Review*, new ser., 49, no. 2 (May 1996): 291–313; Robin Hermann, "Money and Empire: The Failure of the Royal African Company", in *The Empire of Credit: The Financial Revolution in Britain, Ireland and America, 1688–1815*, ed. Daniel Carey and Christopher J. Finlay (Dublin: Irish Academic Press, 2011), 97–120; and William A. Pettigrew, *Freedom's Debt: The Royal African Company and the Politics of the Atlantic Slave Trade, 1672–1752* (Chapel Hill: Univ. of North Carolina Press, 2013). See also Pettigrew, "Free to Enslave: Politics and the Escalation of Britain's Transatlantic Slave Trade, 1688–1714", *William and Mary Quarterly*, 3rd ser., 64, no. 1 (Jan. 2007): 3–38.

6. Fuseli cited by Malcolm Andrews in *Landscape and Western Art* (Oxford Univ. Press, 1999), 91.
7. John E. Crowley, *Imperial Landscapes: Britain's Global Visual Culture, 1745–1820* (New Haven and London: Yale Univ. Press, 2011), 1–2.
8. The word "true" is used in the initial advertisement: *Daily Journal*, 18 March 1728.
9. A. W. Lawrence, *Trade Castles and Forts of West Africa* (London: Jonathan Cape, 1963). For the brief chapter on images as evidence, see 96–99.
10. Lawrence compared the engravings to a manuscript volume then held by the United Africa Company, now by Unilever Archives & Records. The drawings look more like presentation drawings or preparatory works for the proposed set of engravings than "on the spot" sketches.
11. "Map-work" is Fuseli's term, cited by Andrews in *Landscape and Western Art*, 91.
12. Lawrence, *Trade Castles and Forts of West Africa*, 17.
13. William Smith, *A New Voyage to Guinea* (London: John Nourse, 1744). A second edition was published in 1745. For Smith's commission, see 1–6. Adam Jones argues that Smith's account was published posthumously, as the preface comments that the manuscript had been deposited in a library: "William Smith the Plagiarist: A Rejoinder", *History in Africa* 7 (Jan. 1980): 327–28. It is also worth noting that Smith is referred to in the past tense.
14. Smith, *New Voyage*, 1.
15. Charter and chart appear together in Colonial Entry Book, vol. 1: see http://www.british-history.ac.uk/cal-state-papers/colonial/america-west-indies/vol7/pp404-417 (accessed 24 Aug. 2015). The map shown in fig. 156 is part of a collection known as the Blathwayt Atlas, compiled by William Blathwayt, Secretary to the Lords of Trade and Plantations, in the late 1670s and early 1680s.
16. Smith, *New Voyage*, 7–8.
17. Smith, *New Voyage*, 8.
18. Smith, *New Voyage*, 8–9.
19. Smith, *New Voyage*, 252–54.
20. Smith, *New Voyage*, 16–18.
21. Smith, *New Voyage*, 130–31.
22. *Daily Journal*, 18 March 1728.
23. Willem Bosman, *Nauwkeurige Beschryving van de Guinese Goud–, Tand– en Slave-kust* (Utrecht: Anthony Schouten, 1704), and Bosman, *A New and Accurate Description of the Coast of Guinea* (London: J. Knapton and others, 1705). Citations in this essay from the English translation have been checked against Albert van Dantzig's series of articles comparing the English and Dutch texts: "Willem Bosman's *New and Accurate Description of the Coast of Guinea*: How Accurate is It?", *History in Africa* 1 (Jan. 1974): 101–8; and subsequent volumes of the same journal.
24. Bosman, *New and Accurate Description*, preface (n.p.).
25. Bosman, *New and Accurate Description*, preface (n.p.). The second Dutch edition, reprinted several times between 1709 and 1737, was "illustrated with many new copper engravings", but these do not appear in the 1721 English edition.
26. Crowley, *Imperial Landscapes*, 36.
27. The Cape Coast agent is cited by A. W. Lawrence in "Some Source Books for West African History",

Journal of African History 2, no. 2 (July 1961): 227–34 (230). See also Van Dantzig, "Willem Bosman's *New and Accurate Description*", 105 and 108, n.9. For the accusation from Smith (who nonetheless borrowed much material from Bosman in his own account), see *New Voyage*, 128.

28. Albert van Dantzig, "English Bosman and Dutch Bosman: A Comparison of Texts", *History in Africa* 2 (Jan. 1975): 208 and 215, n. 52.
29. *Daily Journal*, 18 March 1728.
30. Geoff Quilley, "The Lie of the Land: Slavery and the Aesthetics of Imperial Landscape in Eighteenth-century British Art", in *Representing Slavery: Art, Artefacts and Archives in the Collections of the National Maritime Museum*, ed. Douglas Hamilton and Robert J. Blyth (Aldershot: Lund Humphries, 2007), 120–35 (124).
31. *Atlas Maritimus & Commercialis; or, A General View of the World, so far as relates to Trade and Navigation* (London: James and John Knapton and others, 1728), 251. Defoe is thought to have written parts of the *Atlas* and certainly seems the likely author of the pages dealing with the Royal African Company.
32. Quilley, "Lie of the Land", 124. The Royal African Company's charter of 1672 itemized negroes and slaves as commodities alongside redwood, elephants' teeth, hides, wax, and grains.
33. Beth Fowkes Tobin, *Picturing Imperial Power: Colonial Subjects in Eighteenth-century British Painting* (Durham, NC: Duke Univ. Press, 1999), 6, 25, 202.
34. Smith, *New Voyage*, 4.
35. Smith, *New Voyage*, 130.
36. Smith, *New Voyage*, 135.
37. Smith, *New Voyage*, 121.
38. Jean (or John) Barbot, *A Description of the Coasts of North and South-Guinea* (London: John Walthoe and others, 1732), vol. 5 of *A Collection of Voyages and Travels* (vols. 1–4, London: Awnsham Churchill, 1704). For Kip's background and career, see Nicholas Grindle, "Kip, Johannes (*b.* before 1653, *d.* 1721?)", *Oxford Dictionary of National Biography* (Oxford Univ. Press, 2004); online ed., Oct. 2006, http://www.oxforddnb.com/view/article/15640 (accessed 24 Aug. 2015).
39. Renzo Dubbini, *Geography of the Gaze: Urban and Rural Vision in Early Modern Europe*, trans. Lydia G. Cochrane (Chicago and London: Univ. of Chicago Press, 2002), 41.
40. Smith, *New Voyage*, 168.
41. Peter Smith is named as Richard Toler's predecessor in *The Case of Richard Toler, Esq; Late Surveyor of the Cove of Cork in Ireland* (London, 1757), 38. Toler succeeded Smith in March 1733.
42. Smith, *New Voyage*, 272–73.
43. Smith, *New Voyage*, 272; John Bennett, *Two Letters and Several Calculations on the Sugar Colonies and Trade* (London: R. Montagu, 1738). Bennett refers to the African forts on 2–3, casting the sugar colonies as their foundations.
44. This copy, inscribed "Edw. Deane Esq. his Book", was sold at Bonhams, New Bond Street, London, 23 March 2010, sale number 17807, lot 134.
45. From Edward Deane's copy (see above). Comparison of the final list of subscribers with the names contained in the bound volume of *Thirty different Drafts* at the Yale Center for British Art—this list dated 13 July 1728, as in Deane's copy—reveals no additions were made, though the layout of the list was changed to a horizontal format to fit with the other plates. The lack of new names may suggest the urgency to complete the published set rather than a lack of interest.
46. On Ireland's involvement with the slave trade, see Nini Rodgers, *Ireland, Slavery and Anti-Slavery, 1612–1865* (Basingstoke and New York: Palgrave Macmillan, 2007). For the role of Cork in particular, see Mark McCarthy, "The Forging of an Atlantic Port City: Socio-economic and Physical Transformations in Cork, 1660–1700", *Urban History* 28, no. 1 (May 2001): 25–45. On Irish efforts to influence British policy and legislation in the period 1700–40, see Francis G. James, "The Irish Lobby in the Early Eighteenth Century", *English Historical Review* 81, no. 320 (July 1966): 543–57.
47. Jonathan Swift, *A Modest Proposal for Preventing the Children of Poor People from being a Burthen to their Parents or Country, and for making them Beneficial to the Publick* (Dublin: S. Harding, 1729), 6, 9. For Swift's

connection between Ireland and Africa, and the influence of a "culture of enslavement" on his work, see John Richardson, "Swift, *A Modest Proposal* and Slavery", *Essays in Criticism* 51, no. 4 (Oct. 2001): 404–23 (406). Smith uses the word "savages" in relation to cannibalism in Africa, noting of Cape Palmas: "The Inhabitants of this Place are Savages, exceeding covetous, and delight in Human Flesh, when they can come at it" (*New Voyage*, 110).

48. Charles Smith, *A Topographical and Chorographical Survey of the County of Down* (Dublin and London: Thomas Boreman, 1740); Smith, *The Antient and Present State of the County of Down* (Dublin: Edward Exshaw, 1744); Smith, *The Antient and Present State of the County and City of Waterford* (Dublin: Printed by A. Reilly for the Author, 1746); Smith, *The Antient and Present State of the County and City of Cork*, 2 vols. (Dublin: Printed by A. Reilly for the Author, 1750); Smith, *The Antient and Present State of the County of Kerry* (Dublin: Printed for the Author, 1756). Smith mooted the title "Hibernia" in his *Topographical and Chorographical Survey*, preface (A2). For his description of Ireland as terra incognita, see Smith, *County of Kerry*, iv.
49. William Smith, *New Voyage*, iii.
50. Charles Smith, *County and City of Cork*, 1: xvi, Smith, *County of Kerry*, xii.
51. Smith, *Topographical and Chorographical Survey*, preface (A2), Smith, *County of Down*, vi.
52. Smith, *County and City of Cork*, 1: xxi.
53. For Charles Smith's comments on surveying the County of Cork, "which will be found to be of a considerable extent", see Smith, *County and City of Cork*, 1: xviii. Several views in Smith's works were drawn by Anthony Chearnley, but the plates showing individual buildings are unnamed. The two Smiths shared a number of subscribers including, possibly, Richard Newman, purchaser of three sets of *Thirty different Drafts*.
54. Romney R. Sedgwick, "Sutton, Sir Robert (?1671–1746), of Broughton, Lincs.", in *The History of Parliament: The House of Commons, 1715–1754*, ed. Sedgwick (Martlesham, Suffolk: Boydell and Brewer, 1970), http://www.historyofparliamentonline.org/volume/1715-1754/member/sutton-sir-robert-1671-1746 (accessed 24 Aug. 2015).
55. Historical Manuscripts Commission (hereafter HMC), *Manuscripts of the Earl of Egmont*, 3 vols. (London: HMSO, 1920), 1: 51. Perceval was made Earl of Egmont in the peerage of Ireland in 1733.
56. HMC, *Manuscripts of the Earl of Egmont*, 1: 51–52.
57. For a detailed study of the implications for the slave trade, see Pettigrew, *Freedom's Debt*. See also Pettigrew, "Free to Enslave" and "Parliament and the Escalation of the Slave Trade, 1690–1714", in *The British Slave Trade: Abolition, Parliament and People*, ed. Stephen Farrell, Melanie Unwin, and James Walvin (Edinburgh Univ. Press for the Parliamentary History Yearbook Trust, 2007), 12–26.
58. See Tim Keirn, "Monopoly, Economic Thought and the Royal African Company", in *Early Modern Conceptions of Property*, ed. John Brewer and Susan Staves (Oxford: Routledge, 1996), 427–66.
59. Anon., *A True State of the Present Difference Between the Royal African Company and the Separate Traders* (London, 1710), 3.
60. [Daniel Defoe], *An Essay Upon the Trade to Africa, In Order to Set the Merits of That Cause in a True Light and Bring the Disputes between the African Company and the Separate Traders into a Narrower Compass* (London, 1711), 5, 11–12. See also Charles Davenant's pamphlet, *A Clear Demonstration, from Points of Fact, that the Recovery, Preservation and Improvement of Britain's Share of the Trade to Africa, is wholly owing to the Industry, Care and Application of the Royal African Company* (London, 1709).
61. Daniel Defoe, *A Review of the State of the English Nation* (London, 1711).
62. The National Archives, Kew (hereafter TNA, T70/172 (*Entries of petitions, establishments and papers delivered into the House of Commons by the Royal African Company of England*, vol. 1, *February 15, 1725–October 24, 1732*, fol. 15.
63. Adam Jones, "Semper Aliquid Veteris: Printed Sources for the History of the Ivory and Gold Coasts, 1500–1750", *Journal of African History* 27, no. 2 (July 1986), 215–35 (218).
64. *A Collection of Papers Relating to the East India Trade: Wherein are shewn The Disadvantages to a Nation, by confining any Trade to a Corporation with a Joint-Stock* (London: J. Walthoe, 1730), ix.

65. See Brian Allen, "The East India Company's Settlement Pictures: George Lambert and Samuel Scott", in *Under the Indian Sun: British Landscape Artists*, ed. Pauline Rohatgi and Pheroza Godrej (Bombay: Marg, 1995), 1–16.
66. 26 March 1730, *Journal of the House of Commons*, 21, no. 522. See also TNA T70/172, fol. 104.
67. Before his death in 1746, John Clark had issued *Fifteen different Drafts of Guinea*, presumably spotting a market for a smaller version at the more modest price of 5s., though surviving sets of fifteen seem even rarer than the sets of thirty.
68. For a reading of British and other European forts in Africa as part of the world of fiscal-military (or fiscal-naval) states, see Helen Julia Paul, "The Maintenance of British Slaving Forts in Africa: The Activities of Joint-Stock Companies and the Royal Navy", in *The Spending of the States: Military Expenditure During the Long Eighteenth Century: Patterns, Organisation, and Consequences, 1650–1815*, ed. Stephen Conway and Rafael Torres Sánchez (Saarbrücken, Germany: VDM Verlag, 2011), 213–36.
69. *A New General Collection of Voyages and Travels*, 4 vols. (London: Thomas Astley, 1745–46). Astley includes a list of the thirty plates before a summary of Smith's account of his voyage (2: 464–85).
70. *New General Collection*, 2: vii.
71. Anon., *The Golden Coast, or A Description of Guinney* (London: Printed for S. Speed, 1665). The original source for the rules, being "Certaine Articles delivered to M. John Lok . . . touching a voyage to Guinie", were drawn up in 1561 and printed in *The Principal Navigations, Voyages, Traffiques, and Discoveries of the English Nation*, ed. Richard Hakluyt, 2nd edn, 3 vols. (London: Printed by George Bishop and others, 1598–1600), vol. 2, part 2: 52–53.
72. *The Golden Coast*, 52.
73. See, for example, *Atlas Maritimus & Commercialis*, 251. Also Pettigrew, *Freedom's Debt*, 205.

Dialogues in Paint and Print: Mezzotint Portraiture and Intermedial Exchange

Peter Moore

In his 1662 treatise on the history of copperplate engraving, *Sculptura*, John Evelyn introduced British readers to a "new way" of printing, which he called "Mezzo Tinto".[1] Having been "universally approv'd of" and "admired" by all who had "consider'd the effects of it", this new technique, Evelyn suggested, represented a "Rare" and "Extraordinary" development in the history of art.[2] For Evelyn, a defining characteristic of this form of engraving was its ability to "accurately resemble" and "emulate even the best of *Drawings, Chiaro e Scuro*, or (as the Italians term it) pieces of the *Mezzo Tinto*". Translated as "half tone", the "Mezzo Tinto" drawings referred to here by Evelyn were characterized by the dramatic depiction of light and shade; similarly, "Mezzo Tinto" engraving's forte was its capacity to create the impression of shadow, tone, and texture with remarkable fluency and dynamism. While creating these effects was a laborious task in the traditional method of line engraving, this new kind of engraving—which, following modern usage, I shall henceforth call "mezzotint"—allowed them to be achieved in an "expeditious" manner, with "the greatest facility" and "so little Curiosity".[3] Yet, as Evelyn emphasized, this kind of engraving could "not succeed" unless the engraver was "an accomplished *Designer*" and had "a competent talent in *painting*".[4] Though clearly keen to extol the virtues of this innovative new way of printmaking, Evelyn was decidedly guarded about fully explaining the mechanics of its production and chose to leave his account "*Ænigmatical*".[5] This, he explained, was in order to prevent "an *Art* so curious, and (as yet) so little vulgar" being "prostituted at so cheap a rate" by the commercial print trade.[6]

However, despite his best efforts to preserve the medium as an exclusive or privileged art form, by the beginning of the eighteenth century mezzotint had evolved into one of the most widely produced forms of print in Britain.[7] When it came to reproducing the effect of paint on canvas, mezzotint was superior to all other modes of engraving, and so it was generally exploited for this purpose. Moreover, it was well suited to the naturalistic representation of the human form, the softness of flesh, and the texture of fabric.[8] It was for this reason that mezzotint became the favoured mode of reproduction for portrait painters, whose clients often required multiple copies of their likenesses to circulate among friends and family, or to promote their celebrity. The technique's close association with the genre is underscored by the fact that nearly two-thirds of the eighteenth-century British mezzotints held by the British Museum are portraits.[9]

While the relationship between high-end studio portraits and mezzotint reproductions is today typically seen in one-directional, binary terms, this essay seeks to recover some of the more complex ways in which mezzotint portraits mediated exchanges between paint and print during the period. In particular, it examines how, as a result of their commercial success and mass distribution, reproductive mezzotint portraits acted as catalysts for a range of other artistic practices in the early eighteenth century. A series of case studies will trace the dispersal of mezzotints from the metropolitan publishing centre of London to the peripheral domestic British provinces, and further afield to the North American colonies. In each of these situations it will be demonstrated how these prints performed a didactic purpose for artists, acting as visual sources which could be carefully observed and reconfigured into something "new". Identifying examples of this practice from different times and different contexts allows us to reconnect art objects which, through the passage of time, have followed separate trajectories into disparate categories, art-historical traditions, or national histories, and have therefore become seen as wholly distinct from one another. However, through their mutual relationship with British mezzotints, these various forms of imagery may be reconceptualized as part of a shared, albeit fragmented, visual tradition.

As London was the primary centre of mezzotint production during the period, the capital can be identified as a constant source of influence, providing a steady stream of prints from which a range of vernacular derivatives were borne. "Like the hub of an eccentric wheel or the off-center core of an incomplete spider's web", Charles Clark explains, the capital "sent off spokes, as it does today, to every part of the kingdom." Furthermore, "just as all the main roads fanned out from London, so did the principal sea lanes of the empire . . . providing London's link with the American ports of Portsmouth, Boston, Newport, New York, and Philadelphia."[10] Along with many other commodities and export products, mezzotints traversed these road and sea routes and made their way into the hands of people living in all parts of the empire. In time, these prints were followed by printmakers themselves, both across the British Isles and within the Americas.

Examining mezzotint portraits within a provincial and circum-Atlantic arena marks a departure from earlier studies of eighteenth-century British graphic art, which have tended to adopt a narrower geographic perspective. Seminal works by Tim Clayton and Antony Griffiths, for example, have been extremely helpful in suggesting how British print culture operated as part of an "international system of print publishing, distribution and collecting", underpinned by the "huge business of importing printed impressions".[11] However, these studies have largely focused on London and its engagement with a pan-European market. Alternatively, this essay suggests that the early eighteenth-century British mezzotint demands to be understood in terms of a "plural" or "multi-contextual history" which looks beyond the metropolis to the British regions, and also encompasses the nation's former territories in the Atlantic world.[12] Integrating the North American colonies into this narrative allows us to confront images that are not normally studied in the context of British art, but are more commonly associated with the disciplines of "colonial" or "early American" art history. As recent art-historical debates have challenged the uses and usefulness of the term "British", we may, perhaps, similarly problematize these designations and their normative periodization.[13]

THE KNELLER EFFECT: THE MEZZOTINT AND PROVINCIAL PORTRAITURE

As the relationship between portrait painting and mezzotint engraving grew ever stronger in Britain towards the end of the seventeenth century, it became increasingly common for painters and printmakers to form commercial partnerships. The most notable collaboration of this type was between Godfrey Kneller and John Smith: a pairing which saw the leading portraitist of the day matched with a man who was widely regarded as the foremost producer of mezzotints.[14] This symbiotic relationship, which saw painter and printer play a central role in advancing each other's reputation, lasted from 1688 until the mid-1720s. During this time, Smith engraved vast numbers of portraits by Kneller, typically of figures associated with the court, or of aristocratic landed gentry. By the turn of the eighteenth century, Kneller's portraits were becoming increasingly pared-down in their visual character, and exhibited a restricted range of compositions. This shift, J. Douglas Stewart has suggested, was a deliberate decision on the part of the artist to cultivate a "sensible" kind of portraiture that reflected "the moral changes which occurred in English society" during the period.[15] Here, Stewart obliquely refers to the establishment of a "polite society", which David Solkin has powerfully argued gave rise to "an entire propertied class" which hoped to embrace the virtues of politeness as "the defining hallmark of its own self-image".[16]

Kneller's "polite" style, geared in the first instance to the painter's London clientele, quickly found itself, through the means of the mezzotints made after his works, shaping the character of the portraits commissioned by refined provincials.

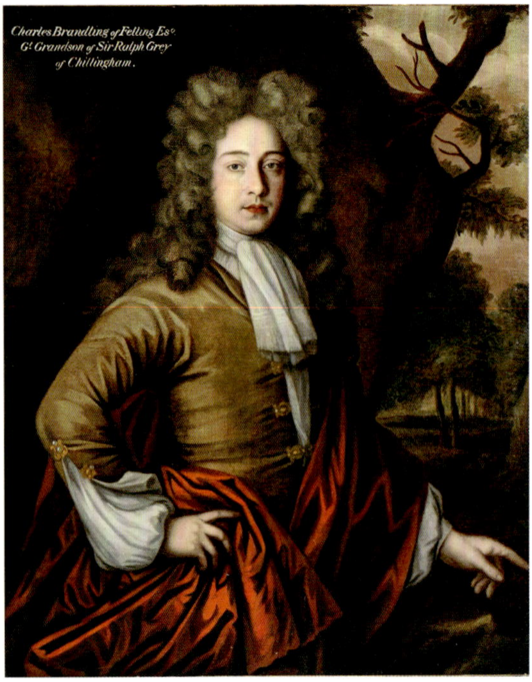

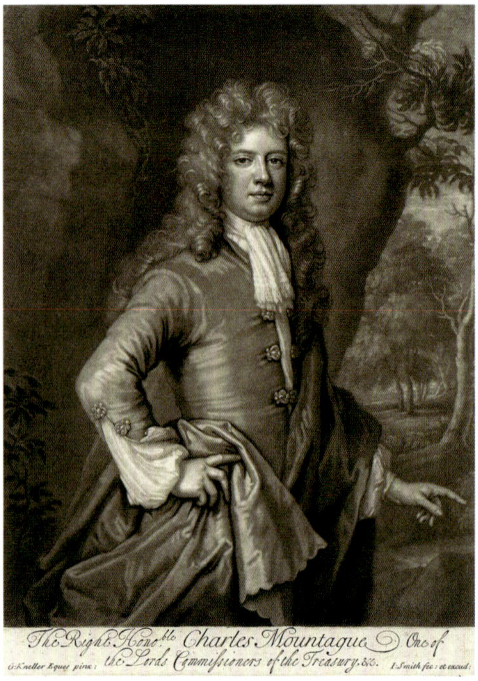

163. John Verelst, *Charles Brandling*, 1698, oil on canvas, 50 x 40 in. (127 x 101.6 cm). Leeds Museums and Galleries, Temple Newsam House, Gift from Lord Halifax, 1948

164. John Smith, after Sir Godfrey Kneller, Bt, *Charles Montagu*, ca. 1693, mezzotint, 13¼ x 9¾ in. (33.6 x 24.7 cm). National Portrait Gallery, London

More particularly, the regionally based painters who fulfilled the provincial demand for portraits repeatedly looked to Smith's mezzotint reproductions as guiding sources. Though written documentary evidence of this practice is scant, if not non-existent, pictorial comparison allows us to make a compelling case for its existence. In the collection of Leeds Museums and Galleries, for instance, is a portrait of Charles Brandling, a land-owning coal merchant from Newcastle, which is dated 1698, and signed by a twenty-two-year-old artist named John Verelst (fig. 163). The image is clearly a replication of Smith's mezzotint after Kneller's portrait of Charles Montagu, first Earl of Halifax (fig. 164). From the sitter's pose, to the hang of the drapery, to the rocky outcrop and wooded scene beyond, each detail has been observed with quite deliberate precision. Additionally, the artist's handling of paint, which exhibits a striking tonal variation between light and dark, seems to be influenced by the visual quality of mezzotint, and stands in contrast to the softer feel of Kneller's original work (fig. 165). A pendant portrait by the same artist, depicting Brandling's wife, Margaret, displays similar characteristics, as well as a distinct flatness. While no mezzotint prototype for this portrait has yet been identified, these qualities perhaps also indicate a work copied from a two-dimensional printed source, rather than taken from a figure observed in the flesh.[17]

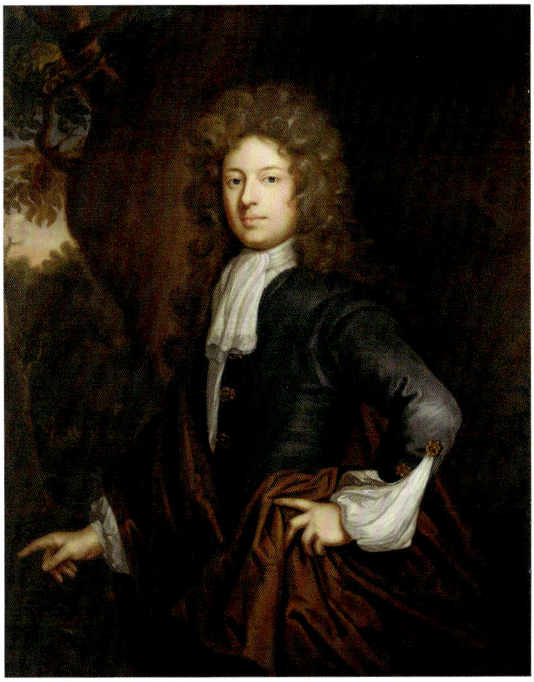

165. Sir Godfrey Kneller, Bt, *Charles Montagu (1661–1715), 1st Earl of Halifax, Founder of the Bank of England (1694), Chancellor of the Exchequer*, oil on canvas, 48½ x 38½ (123 x 98 cm). Trinity College, University of Cambridge

Though very little is known about John Verelst, he is best remembered for his portraits of the so-called "four Indian Kings", who visited London in 1710.[18] We can therefore pinpoint him to the capital at this time. Prior to this, he is virtually undocumented. However, there are a small number of portraits by the artist in public collections, dating from around 1700, when he was in his early twenties. These depict sitters from towns such as Skipton and York, which suggests that he was active in the north and north-east of England during these years.[19] There is no indication he had received any formal or academic training by this point, but he had certainly spent some of his youth living in London with his father, Harman Verelst, who Bainbrigg Buckeridge later noted "educated several sons and one daughter in the same way of drawing".[20] After arriving in England in 1683, Harman became a relatively well-established painter in the capital, producing history scenes, flower pieces, and portraits for private clients as well as supplying works to a burgeoning auction trade. In the earlier part of his career he had developed a reputation as an itinerant artist, working in Amsterdam, The Hague, Ljubljana, Rome, and Vienna.[21] Perhaps encouraging his young son to develop a similarly peripatetic practice, this time within the context of the British regions, we might imagine that Harman equipped John with some rudimentary artistic training

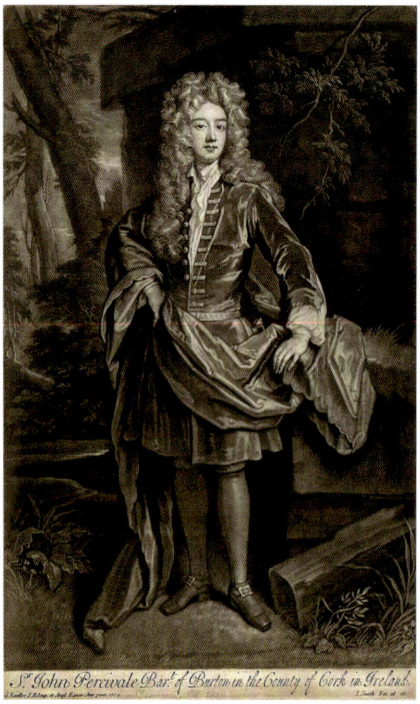

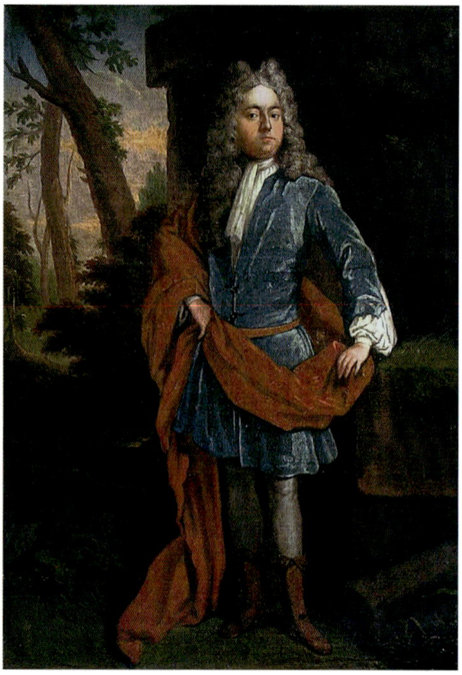

166. John Smith after Sir Godfrey Kneller, Bt, *Sir John Perceval Bart. of Barton*, 1708, mezzotint, 16⅝ x 10½ in. (42.3 x 26.7 cm). British Museum, London

167. Unknown artist [attributed to Edward Byng], *Portrait of a Gentleman*, ca. 1704, oil on canvas, 15 x 10½ in. (38 x 27 cm). Private collection

before sending him away to refine his craft in a less competitive provincial environment where he was more likely to gain commissions from members of the elite. Evidently, during this period of artistic immaturity, mezzotint reproductions of fashionable portraits informed at least part of his practice.

Similar examples of provincial portraits based on mezzotint models further suggest how these printed sources facilitated intermedial dialogues in British portraiture during the period. An unsigned portrait of a young Hamphire lady, Mary Chute, for example (National Trust, The Vyne), is clearly based on Francis Kyte's mezzotint after Godfrey Kneller's portrait of the Countess of Godolphin. Like Verelst's portrait of Charles Brandling, this portrait not only mimics the entire posture and compositional framework of its mezzotint source, but displays brushwork which seems to replicate the distinctive tonal quality of the printed image. Likewise, an anonymous portrait thought to depict William Molyneux of Croxteth, Liverpool (National Museums Liverpool) is an almost direct copy of John Smith's mezzotint reproduction of John Closterman's portrait of Thomas Maxwell, Commander of the Royal Regiment of Dragoons. A further unsigned example of this practice, which depicts an unidentified gentleman, not only reproduces the form of Godfrey Kneller's portrait of Sir John Perceval, but is painted on exactly the same scale as John Smith's 1708 mezzotint after this work (figs. 166 and 167). This reduced format perhaps offered a more economical and portable option for an artist working itinerantly in the provinces.

THE MEZZOTINT IN THE AMERICAN COLONIES

A portrait of Johannes de Peyster, painted by the colonial artist Nehemiah Partridge in 1718, allows us to trace the dispersal of the same mezzotint across the Atlantic, where it was employed for a similar purpose (fig. 168). Here, the top portion of the print has been recycled to create a half-length likeness of the son of one of the Hudson Valley's most renowned tycoons. The artist, who was the son

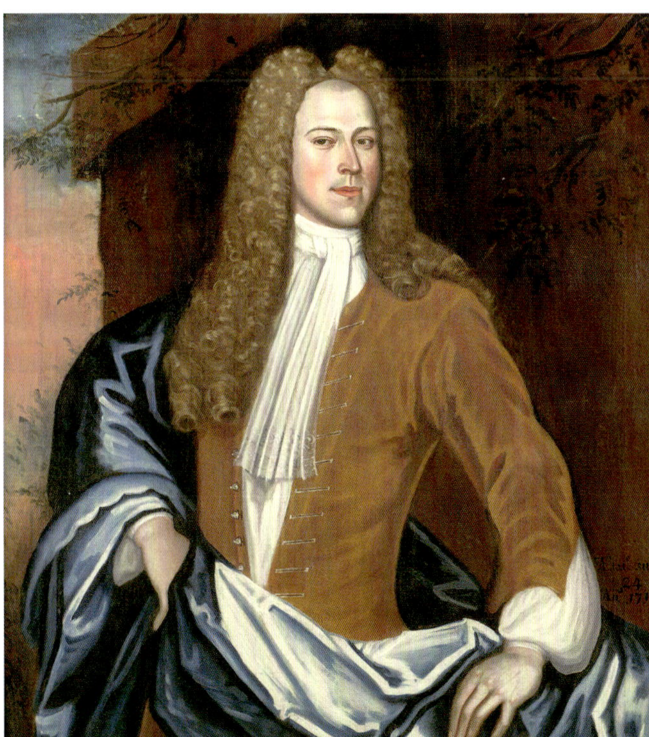

168. Attributed to Nehemiah Partridge, *Johannes de Peyster III*, 1718, oil on bed ticking, 44 x 38¼ in. (111.8 x 97.2 cm). New York Historical Society

of British settlers, is not known to have received any formal training, and in the early part of his career traded in all kinds of commodities in the port of Boston.[22] Through piecemeal, contemporary records relating to Partridge, we can build up a picture of him as a versatile entrepreneur who imported the latest fashionable goods, and was also able to turn his hand to a variety of manual labours, handicrafts, and decorative arts.[23] Collectively, the products in which he traded, and the portraits he painted, contributed to a material culture that was inextricably "integrated into the British consumer economy".[24] For the inhabitants of towns like Boston, Julie Flavell suggests, "their colony was their home" but "their nation was Britain. And London was their capital city."[25] In this circum-Atlantic commercial milieu, mezzotints like those engraved by Smith after Kneller could easily be obtained from dealers such as Samuel Gerrish, who sold a "great Variety of . . . Prints", which he routinely advertised in Boston's newspapers as being lately "Imported from London" and "very Cheap".[26]

Partridge's reconstructive use of John Smith's mezzotint in his portrait of Johannes de Peyster is typical not only within his own oeuvre, but is indicative of the working methods employed by almost all portrait painters active in colonial America before the mid-eighteenth century. The breadth of British mezzotint portraiture's influence in this regard is underscored by the posthumously published notes of the American art historian, Waldron Belknap, in which he exposes the "slavishly imitative" way in which colonial painters used these sources, and how the mezzotint acted as "the major factor in transmitting . . . the pictorial elements of Old World culture to the New".[27] While imported British mezzotints offered untrained artists a kind of tutelage, they also allowed the upper ranks of colonial society to adopt the modern pictorial language of English gentility as a "social insulator" which distinguished them from lower-ranking colonists.[28] Partridge's work for such patrons took him beyond Boston to a variety of towns and provinces in Massachusetts, New Hampshire, and New York—all locations within a two-hundred-mile radius of Boston. Later subjects can be placed within communities in Maryland and Virginia, some four to six hundred miles south of Boston. As Mary Black has suggested, the painter's connections with merchant traders who had financial interests in Virginian tobacco plantations were critical in allowing him to travel by sea to these parts where new clients awaited.[29] In each of these contexts, mezzotint sources for Partridge's portraits can be identified.[30] Our ability to identify these blueprints allows us to imagine Partridge picking and choosing visual elements from a whole cache of imported prints, like an improvised pattern book which he carried with him on business-getting ventures.

In spite of the apparent connections between portrait painting (and specifically the influence of mezzotints) in Britain and America during this period, artists like Partridge have often been seen as distinctively colonial in their output. Yet, for a man whose portraits so clearly reflect an awareness of high-end London studio models, it seems illogical that Partridge should be included in a book titled *American Naive Paintings*, in which "naive" is defined as denoting a "freshness of vision".[31] In the catalogue accompanying the American National Portrait Gallery's 1987 exhibition *American Colonial Portraits*, the artist's technical flaws were similarly read as signs of a "disarming honesty that places directness above flattery".[32] The suggestion that Partridge and his clients valued candidness above beauty seems highly unlikely. On the contrary, the mode of portraiture he was attempting to replicate was polished, refined, and unquestionably aimed to flatter the sitter. Similarly, it has been suggested that "whereas Europeans expected painters to idealize their features to conform with prevailing concepts of beauty, American Colonists required their portraits to capture a true likeness of the sitter."[33] More convincing is the suggestion that "beauty . . . figured into the calculus of consumption" as much in the case of portraits as it did in other manufactured goods.[34] In recent years, indeed, scholarship has begun interrogating these kinds of images within the larger framework of the British Atlantic world. Notably, Margaretta Lovell has positioned the didactic use of mezzotint portraits within a system in which "ideas, pigments [and] conventions" were routinely derived from British "source cultures". "New England experience", she argues, "was conditioned and culturally bracketed" by this market.[35] Likewise, as Joseph Roach's seminal paradigm of "circum-Atlantic" culture suggests, portraits based on mezzotint models must be understood as "self-referential" expressions of "memory and substitution", and demand to be approached holistically within a broad geographic framework.[36] This model of "circum-Atlantic" pictorial exchange, we might argue, not only encourages new perspectives on colonial American art, but suggests how historians of eighteenth-century British portraiture might similarly adjust the scope of their gaze.

LEARNING TO PAINT

As we have seen, the distribution of mezzotint portraits across a swathe of dislocated British territories fuelled forms of artistic expression that, despite being scattered over a vast geographic space, were fundamentally embedded in the same "network of material practices".[37] It is important to note, however, that while mezzotint offered a critical insight into London's studio practices, fashions, and the codes of deportment associated with "politeness", it lacked one critical element: colour. For those who mimicked mezzotint sources in paint, and who had not enjoyed the benefits of an apprenticeship to a painter, at least a very basic understanding of draughtsmanship and colour mixing was required. A variety of printed manuals provided this knowledge. Texts like *Albert Durer Revived* (1698), for instance, which described "the names and mixtures of colours used by the picture-drawers", performed a critical role.[38] Educating readers in "the art of painting", the book provided directions on "How to make . . . A Flesh Colour", "Colours for Landskips", "Colours for the Skie", and "Colour in Garments".[39] Further instructions "for the Compounding of Colours" recommended which colours should be used to complement one another, suggesting that "Blews" should be "set off with Reds, Whites and Browns".[40]

Perhaps acting on such advice, almost all of Nehemiah Partridge's portraits adhere to these combinations. Likewise, the British portraits copied from mezzotints examined in this essay employ colour palettes that are balanced in a similar way. Other manuals, such as *Art's master-piece* (1701), provided checklists of the tools and equipment necessary for a portraitist, and advocated the development of artistic skill through a series of practical exercises, beginning with simple shapes and building up to "Humane Faces and Bodies, wherein lies the excellency of this Art".[41] Critically, the author suggests that until one's "Mind can well frame such Ideas" it is necessary to have pictorial sources "to imitate".[42] William Salmon's *Polygraphice* is another such text that was widely known in Britain, and one that we can be certain was also available in the colonies, as it appeared at Samuel Gerrish's auction of "Curious and Valuable Books" at Boston's "Crown Coffee-House" in 1719.[43] In this treatise, Salmon describes two means by which one can develop as a proficient draughtsman: "Imitation of the Life" or "Imitation of Draughts". In order to master "Imitation of the Life", he states, "it will be necessary . . . to choose a good Master, with whom you may spend two Days in a Week at least; or else a Society of about half a score or a dozen young Men, who are experienced to draw after the Life, by the Advice and Example of whom, and your own diligent Observations and Care, you may come not only to mend one anothers Faults, but also one anothers Judgments."[44] Alternatively, should this not be possible, one may cultivate artistic skill through "the imitation of Draughts"—a process by which "the Learner must, by many and often Trials, get a Habit of Imitation" by "drawing after a Print or Picture".[45] In copying a draught, one must "first observe the thing in general, in respect of the circumferent stroaks . . . then consider in like manner the parts, and supposing the parts each to be a whole, you may come to represent the parts of parts, and by the same means to express the whole of any Draught whatsoever."[46] Salmon also explains how an "excellent pattern or print" might be copied as a rescaled image in "other proportions"—a piece of advice we can well imagine being heeded by those who chose to imitate mezzotint portraits on a larger scale in paint on canvas.[47] In light of this text, we might surmise that in the context of a colonial or domestic British provincial society, devoid of drawing masters, societies of art, academies, or portrait painters to whom one could be apprenticed, learning to paint portraits through the use of mezzotint models was less of a personal choice than an autodidacticism made mandatory by the prevailing socio-artistic and economic climate.

THE EXAMPLE OF PETER PELHAM

While this essay's case studies have so far demonstrated the way in which the distribution of mezzotint portraits (and other forms of print) had the potential to motivate homogenized forms of artistic expression across Britain's domestic and imperial provinces, the introduction of mezzotint as a locally produced art form in the colonies prompted a quite distinct arena of graphic consumption and appreciation. The pioneer of this development, Peter Pelham, arrived in Boston in 1728. He had started his career as a commercial mezzotint engraver in London, after serving an apprenticeship with John Simon, one of the capital's leading practitioners of the art. Like others who specialized in mezzotint production in the English capital at this time, Pelham operated almost exclusively as a copyist, reproducing painted portraits by fashionable artists such as Kneller, Michael Dahl, and Hans Hysing.[48] Surviving examples of his work suggest that he was active in London throughout the early 1720s, but in 1726 he disappeared from the London art world forever in circumstances that remain unexplained. Two years later, when he is first noted as living in Boston, he had set up shop as the first practitioner of mezzotint in the colonies. In February of that year, he advertised in the *Boston Gazette*, "PROPOSALS, For Making a Print in *Metzotinto*, of the late Reverend Dr. Cotton Mather, by *Peter Pelham* . . . done after the Original Painting after the Life by the said *Pelham*" (figs. 169 and 170).[49] His subject, the most venerated Puritan minister of his generation and a leading Doctor of Divinity at Harvard College, had died just a week earlier. When this mezzotint was completed some weeks later, it became the first to be published in colonial America.[50]

Though this development did not abate the mass importation of mezzotint portraits from Britain, it did create an additional facet to the way in which prints (and particularly printed portraits) were understood and used. Had Pelham produced such a print in London, where numerous reproductive mezzotint engravers supplied a thriving trade, his status as "a skilled but subordinate craftsman, dutifully responding to the demands of the more powerful institutions of the print market" would have remained unchanged.[51] But by emigrating to New England,

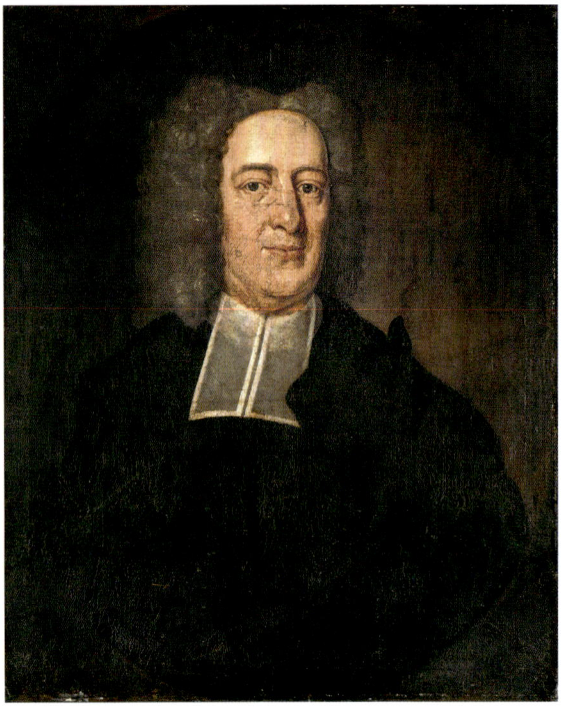

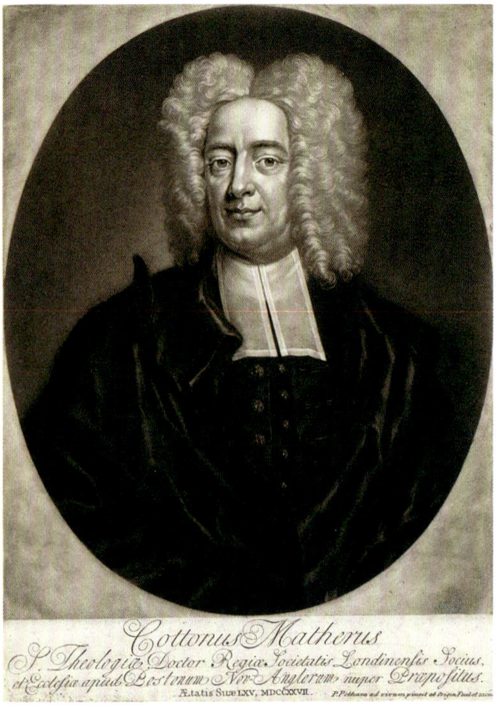

169. Peter Pelham, *Cotton Mather*, 1727, oil on canvas, 32 x 27¼ in. (81.3 x 69.2 cm). American Antiquarian Society, Worcester, MA

170. Peter Pelham, *Cottonus Matherus*, 1728, mezzotint, 14¼ x 10⅜ in. (36.1 x 26.2 cm). The Metropolitan Museum of Art, New York, Bequest of Charles Allen Munn, 1924

and independently inaugurating mezzotint portraiture as a local form of artistic production, he became an esteemed member of the urban community to which he belonged, and a leading figure within this community's cultural development. As a result, he is today remembered in the United States as a man whose "activities helped to transform the provincial town [of Boston] into a leading cultural center of colonial America".[52] In contrast, he is largely unknown in British art-historical scholarship and remains entirely unstudied.

However, a closer inspection of Peter Pelham's different oeuvres on both sides of the Atlantic can productively destabilize the parochial way in which the early eighteenth-century "British" mezzotint has been conceptualized in recent years. Pelham did not seek to establish mezzotint portraiture in New England as an import replacement for British prints; nor did he endeavour to generate a market for mezzotints that was analogous to London's. Rather, it was his intention to foster a separate graphic culture with its own specific character, in which printed images of eminent local sitters enjoyed an altogether different status. For the Puritan literati with whom Pelham became so closely associated in New England, the relative restraint of his monochrome bust-length portraits, engraved on an intimate scale, offered an antidote to more ostentatious forms of portraiture, favoured by those whom one Puritan columnist described as being "more eager after what glitters and dazzles upon their Imaginations, than what instructs their Reason".[53] Moreover, with the colony's pre-existing history of printed portraits centring on local theologians, and being allied with an associated literary culture of printed sermons and tracts at the Harvard press, Pelham's inauguration of mezzotint was seen as a direct perpetuation of this tradition.[54]

The first public announcement made by Pelham in Boston offers us a clear indication of his ambitious intentions upon arriving in the New World. The detail in which he described his plans contrasted greatly with the way in which imported prints were normally advertised in the colonies, and by choosing to sell his work by subscription he imbued his undertaking with an air of gravitas not normally associated with rudimentary mezzotint portraits in Britain. On a more practical level, this method of selling also allowed him to test the water and ascertain whether enough interest could be generated to make his proposed venture a profitable one. With a population roughly 2 percent of London's, there were far fewer potential buyers for any one print in Boston, and so with a smaller print run a greater profit margin was required to recoup costs. Consequently, Pelham's print came with a hefty price tag of 5s.—a sum that was "three times that of an equivalent print published in London".[55] Recognizing that this might be perceived as a steep price to pay, Pelham assured potential subscribers that he could "prove the Charges" involved in producing the work would "run high", and so the substantial cost was unavoidable.[56] Though Pelham's print was publicly available for purchase, there does seem to be a suggestion that the work was privately commissioned (or at least privately encouraged) by a small group of local Puritans who had been close acquaintances of Cotton Mather. As Pelham's advertisement explained, "some of the late Doctor's Friends" had expressed a "particular desire" to have a "Print in Metzotinto" made of their recently deceased companion.[57]

In view of this evidence, it seems likely that it was the same friends of Cotton Mather who had enlisted Pelham to record his likeness in paint some months earlier, during a period in which the ageing minister was suffering with increasingly ill health and his death was seemingly inevitable.[58] The imminence of Mather's death may well have been a motivating factor in the production of his portrait, and the choice of Pelham to carry out the task may also suggest that the idea to produce a mezzotint in memoriam was conceived at this time too. As far as can be gathered, Pelham had not been employed as a painter at any point earlier in his career, and there is no record of him painting portraits while he was living in Britain, so it is unlikely that he was tasked with recording Mather's likeness on the merit of his ability with brush and paint alone. Indeed, it seems notable that when advertising his mezzotint, Pelham did not invite potential buyers to inspect the original painting from which his print derived, but offered other "Prints in Metzotinto . . . by way of Specimen" to demonstrate his work.[59]

It has been suggested that Pelham was simply forced to paint the model he needed because the colony had "no portrait painters whose works were suitable for mezzotint reproduction".[60] Yet, while reasonably competent, Pelham's talent in painting does not seem remarkably superior to other portraitists active in New England at the time. More critically, this assumption negates the idea that Pelham made a deliberate choice to paint his own prototype—perhaps for financial reasons, but also ideological ones. While this would have allowed him to maintain commercial independence, it would also have provided an opportunity to propagate new ideas about authorship and the perceived value of prints. He was evidently keen to promote his mezzotint as part of an independent creative project, boldly stating in a caption beneath the print: "P. Pelham ad vivum pinxit ab Origin, Fecit et excud" (Painted from the life, engraved and printed by Peter Pelham). By publicizing the fact that his mezzotint derived from a work that he had drawn from the life, Pelham re-established the engraved portrait as the end product in a sequential creative process, rather than an ancillary medium that could be transformed into new painted contexts and then casually eschewed.

Despite elevating New England's native graphic culture to a new level of sophistication, Peter Pelham did not go on to become a prolific printmaker in Boston, ultimately finding that the small size of the population was too much of a barrier to commercial success. Though he remained in Boston for the rest of his life, he engraved only a dozen more mezzotint portraits over a period of twenty-three years before his death in 1751, mostly of Puritan ministers, in the same manner as his portrait of Cotton Mather. Produced sporadically, according to the ebb and flow of local life, but changing very little in style or method over time, Pelham's colonial mezzotints relate to a slower process of artistic evolution, antithetical to the status of mezzotint portraiture in Britain as a proliferating, rapid form of print production. Their history offers a warning against identifying essential, inherent qualities of the medium, as such properties were actively generated through economic and cultural exchange. Mezzotint was not fundamentally or necessarily a medium of mass production and rapid dissemination, inevitably tied to the expansion of a commercialized public realm: it could, in another context, be exclusive, and limited in its reach, and valued as such.

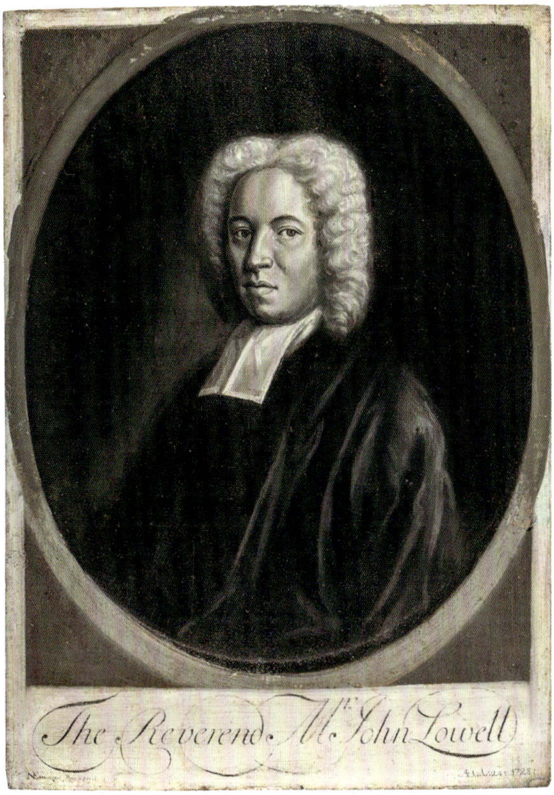

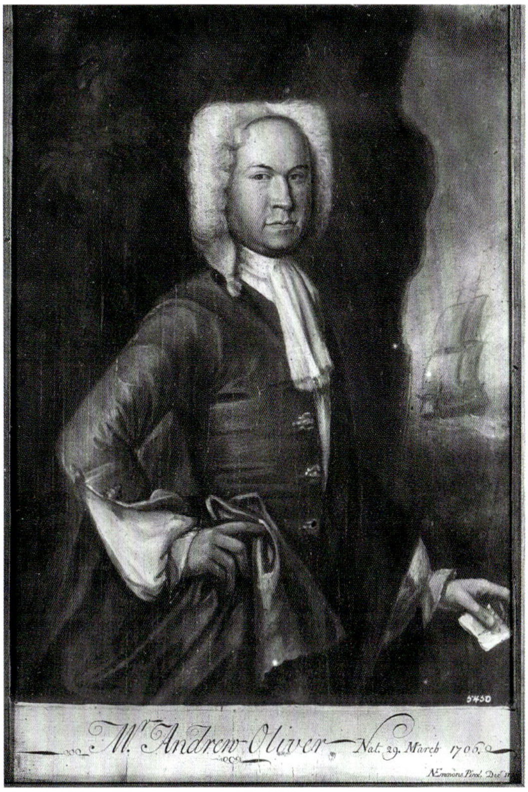

171. Nathaniel Emmons, *The Reverend Mr John Lowell*, 1728, oil on panel, 14½ x 10⅜ in. (36.7 x 26.5 cm). Harvard University Portrait Collection, Gift of the Estate of Ralph Lowell, 1978

172. Nathaniel Emmons, *Mr. Andrew Oliver*, 1728, oil on panel, 13 x 10¼ in. (36.8 x 26 cm). Private collection

PAINTING IN MEZZOTINT

Though Pelham's initial impact as a mezzotinter in Boston may have been short-lived, and did not fuel a rapid surge in the production and consumption of local portrait prints, it did seem to have a surprising and almost immediate effect on local approaches to portrait painting. In the same year that his mezzotint of Cotton Mather was published, a new kind of painted imagery, directly imitative of mezzotint, began to appear in Boston. Rather than using mezzotints as models for larger paintings in colour, these works made a virtue of mezzotint portraiture's intimate size and monochromatic aesthetic. It has so far been possible to trace five examples of this short-lived genre of New England portraiture, each dating from around 1728.[61] Each is painted in oil on board, and closely corresponds with the dimensions of "14 Inches by 10" which Pelham publicized in the *Boston Gazette* as being the "Common Size" of mezzotint portraits by him.[62] Though three are unsigned, two bear the signature of Nathaniel Emmons. One of these depicts the Boston Puritan minister John Lowell; the other is of Andrew Oliver, a local merchant and public official (figs. 171 and 172). Each is dated 1728 and includes "mock-print" script denoting the sitter's name and age, with the inscription "N Emmons Pinx" playfully referring to an imagined painted model by Emmons on which each "print" is based. While the portrait of John Lowell clearly perpetuates the conventions used by Pelham to depict Cotton Mather, Andrew Oliver's likeness derives from Smith's mezzotint of Charles Montagu after Kneller.

Though very little is known about Emmons, there are a few clues relating to him which suggest how these painted imitations of mezzotints might have operated in a nascent New England visual culture. Notably, his will cites him as a "painter stainer", implying that his employment as an artist extended to house and sign painting.[63] His obituary, published in the *New England Journal* on 27 May 1740, describes him as "the greatest Master of various Sorts of Painting that was ever Born in this Country", and notes that as well as painting "Faces" he was renowned for his "Rivers, Banks and Rural Scenes".[64] The kinds of contrived landscape scenes to which this seems to refer were routinely used in the colonial period to decorate fireboards, overmantel panels, and walls, and were typical of the "fancy architectural painting" employed to enliven plain domestic interiors.[65] A range of other imitative painting techniques were also commonly used in these spaces: walls painted to imitate wood grain or marble; emulations of drapery painted around covings; stencilled patterns on staircases to mimic carpet runners; images of vases painted above shelves; and furniture in imitation painted styles like japanning were all typical features.[66] Within these interiors, utterly concerned with artifice and illusion, a clear logic for portrait paintings imitating mezzotints can be conceived. Indeed, further study of Emmons's obituary helps us to understand the centrality of imitation to the nascent colonial artistic culture of which he was part. "Some of his pieces", it explains, "are such admirable imitations of nature . . . that the pleased eye cannot easily leave them. And some [of his works] are so exquisite, that tho' we know they are only paints . . . they deceive the sharpest sight while it is nearly looking on them."[67] Herein lies Emmons's (and by implication, other colonists') fascination with the reproductive mezzotinter's craft: for the ability to demonstrate one's skill as a copyist or imitator was essentially what distinguished a good reproductive mezzotint artist from a poor one.

There are certainly British precedents for paintings which imitate prints; in the surviving auction catalogues of picture sales from late seventeenth-century London, we occasionally find examples of "A Mock-Print on a Deal-board" or "a painting in imitation of a print, on board".[68] However, as these descriptions suggest, such images were not intended as surrogates for prints but were positioned as knowing imitations whose interest and effect depended not on the absolute effectiveness of their illusion but rather their exposure as illusions. It was a convention of the genre to introduce elements which drew attention to the image's illusory status: a curling corner, a tear, a fly, or broken glazing. Edward Collier's trompe l'oeil paintings of mezzotints, which were popular in London at this time, exemplify this practice.[69] Unlike the paintings of prints produced in and around Boston in the late 1720s, there is a desire here to convey a sense of three-dimensionality: the print in the painting is an object within the image, rendered illusionistically. In contrast, Emmons's painted imitations of mezzotints do not represent the graphic image as an object per se, but stand in for the graphic image. Purporting to represent locally produced mezzotints, they position their subjects as esteemed figures, worthy of such a limited and exclusive colonial art form. Paradoxically, they acknowledge mezzotint's empowering quality as a repeatable statement through the means of a single visual gesture, to be viewed by a limited number of people in a single context. Like Peter Pelham's colonial mezzotint portraits, they might be understood as antithetical to the "depersonalized world of prints" represented by Boston's import trade in British impressions.[70] Yet, by bringing "local identities, as well as a global angle" simultaneously together "in sharp relief", they are bound up in an inherent sense of ambiguity.[71]

In conclusion, we might recall Adrian Johns's plea that, when thinking about print, we should "consider fixity not as an inherent quality, but a transitive one", and that we should always be mindful of the manifold ways in which "print culture might emerge from print."[72] Indeed, we might extend this idea and also consider how print culture might emerge from paint, or how painted culture might emerge from print. A proper understanding of mezzotint's intermedial function in this regard demands that we interrogate a diverse range of images—some of which may seem marginal, but which are nevertheless important in recovering a more complete sense of mezzotint's cultural and artistic impact. Necessarily, we must look across and beyond media, adopting a kaleidoscopic view which oscillates from the centre to the periphery, from court and city to country and colony. From this perspective, the early eighteenth-century mezzotint portrait may be conceptually rehabilitated as one of the most dynamic, complex, and contradictory art forms of its time.

1. John Evelyn, *Sculptura: or, the History, and Art of Chalcography and Engraving in Copper* (London, 1662), 145.
2. Evelyn, *Sculptura*, 145.
3. Evelyn, *Sculptura*, 146. As Louise Siddons eloquently puts it: "Instead of offering a sign for texture and tone, mezzotint engravers presented their audiences with the textures and tones themselves." Siddons, "'An English Art': Nationalist Rhetoric and Civic Virtue in Valentine Green's Mezzotint of John Boydell, 1772", *British Art Journal* 14, no. 1 (Autumn 2013): 74.
4. Evelyn, *Sculptura*, 148.
5. Evelyn, *Sculptura*, 148.
6. Evelyn, *Sculptura*, 147–48.
7. As Ben Thomas notes, contemporary sources reveal a "recurring theme of secrecy associated with mezzotint". Thomas, "Noble or Commercial? The Early History of Mezzotint in Britain", in *Printed Images in Early Modern Britain: Essays in Interpretation*, ed. Michael Hunter (Farnham: Ashgate, 2010), 279.
8. As John Chaloner Smith wrote in his seminal catalogue of mezzotint portraits, "no other style of engraving is so well suited" to the representation of the human form. "It is unequalled in its power of giving softness to the carnations, delicate distinctions of textures, the very touches of the painter's brush, and general richness and brilliancy of tone with consequent life-like effect." Smith, *British Mezzotinto Portraits*, 4 vols. (London: Henry Sotheran & Co., 1878–84), 1: vii.
9. Of the museum's 21,449 eighteenth-century British mezzotints, 14,248 are qualified as portraits.
10. Charles Clark, *The Public Prints: the Newspaper in Anglo-American Culture, 1665–1740* (New York: Oxford Univ. Press, 1994), 55.
11. Timothy Clayton, *The English Print, 1688–1802* (New Haven and London: Yale Univ. Press, 1997), xii, Antony Griffiths, *The Print in Stuart Britain, 1603–1689* (London: British Museum Press, 1998), 19.
12. John Pocock, "The Limits and Divisions of British History: In Search of the Unknown Subject", *American Historical Review* 87, no. 2 (1982): 320.
13. Of particular note is the University of York's 2014 symposium, "There's no such thing as British Art", giving rise to the short papers published online at *British Art Studies* 1 (Nov. 2015), http://www.britishartstudies.ac.uk/issues/issue-index/issue-1/conversation
14. As Walpole later proclaimed, Smith was "The best mezzotinter that has appeared, who united softness with strength, and finishing with freedom . . . in the portraits of Kneller." Horace Walpole, *A Catalogue of Engravers who have been born, or resided in England* (London, 1763), 105–6. More recently, Antony Griffiths has suggested that "More than anyone else, John Smith, whose working career spanned nearly fifty years from 1683 to 1729, raised the quality of mezzotint." See Griffiths, "Early Mezzotint Publishing in England—I: John Smith, 1652–1743", *Print Quarterly* 6, no. 3 (Sept. 1989): 243.
15. J. Douglas Stewart, *Sir Godfrey Kneller and the English Baroque Portrait* (Oxford: Clarendon Press, 1983), 45.
16. David Solkin, *Painting for Money: The Visual Arts and the Public Sphere in Eighteenth-century England* (New Haven and London: Yale Univ. Press, 1992), 27.
17. This painting is also in the collection of Leeds City Council.
18. These portraits are now in the collection of Library and Archives Canada (LAC). For further reading, see John Garratt and Bruce Robertson, *The Four Indian Kings* (Ottawa: Canadian Government Publishing, 1985), and Peter Moore, "British Graphic Art, 1660–1735: An Atlantic Perspective" (PhD diss., Univ. of York, 2013), chap. 4.
19. See, for example, portraits of Elizabeth and Henry Iveson (Leeds City Museum) and Mary Compton (National Trust, Beningbrough Hall). It has not been possible to identify mezzotint blueprints for these works. There may well be other unknown or unattributed works by Verelst in public and private collections, though further research is required to identify these. Further examples of mezzotint portraits being re-used by provincial painters are identified in Moore, *British Graphic Art*, chap. 4.
20. Bainbrigg Buckeridge, "An Essay towards an English-School of Painters", in Roger De Piles, *The Art of Painting and the Lives of the Painters* (London, 1706), 474.

21. Paul Taylor, "Verelst, Harmen (b. 1639, d. in or after 1691)", *Oxford Dictionary of National Biography* (Oxford Univ. Press, 2008), http://www.oxforddnb.com/view/article/28220. Taylor notes that John Verelst was most likely the son of Harman Verelst, though he is often incorrectly described as his brother. This confusion seems to have arisen because another John Verelst (profession unknown) was also living in London at the time. It is this John Verelst, not the portrait painter, whom Taylor suggests was Harman's brother.
22. *Boston News Letter*, 31 March 1712, 21 Sept. 1713, 7 March 1714.
23. As Richard Saunders notes, "the tenuous nature of colonial painting made any sensible person prepare to do a variety of tasks." Thus it "was the rule, rather than the exception" to find painters advertising a range of other commercial services. Saunders, "The Portrait in America, 1700–1750", in *American Colonial Portraits, 1700–1776*, ed. Saunders and Ellen Miles (Washington, DC: Smithsonian Institution Press, 1987), 1.
24. T. H. Breen, "An Empire of Goods: The Anglicization of Colonial America, 1690–1776", *Journal of British Studies* 25, no. 4 (Oct. 1986): 486.
25. Julie Flavell, *When London Was Capital of America* (New Haven and London: Yale Univ. Press, 2010), 4.
26. *New England Weekly Journal*, 12 Feb. 1728, *New England Courant*, 17 July 1725.
27. Waldron Phoenix Belknap Jnr., *American Colonial Painting: Materials for a History* (Cambridge, MA: Harvard Univ. Press, 1959), 274–75.
28. Ian Steele, "The Empire and Provincial Elites: An Interpretation of Some Recent Writings on the English Atlantic, 1675–1740", *The Journal of Imperial and Commonwealth History* 8, no. 2 (1980): 19.
29. Mary Black, "Contributions toward a History of Early Eighteenth-century New York Portraiture: Identification of the Aetatis Suae and Wendell Limners", *American Art Journal* 12, no. 4 (Autumn 1980): 4–31.
30. Partridge's portrait of Elizabeth Brodnax (Virginia Museum of Fine Arts, Richmond, VA), for example, is derived from Smith's 1720 mezzotint after an earlier portrait by Kneller of Princess Anne. Likewise, his portrait of Catryna ten Broeck (Philadelphia Museum of Art) is modelled on Kyte's early eighteenth-century mezzotint reproduction of Kneller's portrait of the Countess of Godolphin.
31. Deborah Chotner and others, *American Naive Paintings* (Washington, DC: Princeton Univ. Press, 1992), xi. For entries on Nehemiah Partridge see 334–35.
32. Saunders, "The Portrait in America", 5.
33. Carol Wax, *The Mezzotint: History and Technique* (London and New York: Harry N. Abrams, 1990), 91.
34. Breen, "An Empire of Goods", 496.
35. Margaretta Lovell, *Art in a Season of Revolution: Painters, Artisans, and Patrons in Early America* (Philadelphia: Univ. Pennsylvania Press, 2005), 1.
36. Joseph Roach, *Cities of the Dead: Circum-Atlantic Performance* (New York: Columbia Univ. Press, 1996), 4.
37. H. Aram Veeser, ed., *The New Historicism* (London: Routledge, 1989), 14.
38. Anon., *Albert Durer Revived, or, A book of drawing, limning, washing, or colouring of maps and prints* (London, 1698), title page.
39. Anon., *Albert Durer Revived*, 13–14.
40. Anon., *Albert Durer Revived*, 14.
41. C. K., *Art's master-piece: or, A companion for the ingenious of either sex* (London, 1701), 8–9.
42. C. K., *Art's master-piece*, 9–10.
43. British Library Microfilm, reference BL.Mic.F.863/Evans.39701. Only a handful of colonial book auction catalogues from this period survive, so we can't be sure how many other copies of Salmon's text were imported, though it seems likely there would have been more than this sole example.
44. William Salmon, *Polygraphice: or, the arts of drawing, engraving, etching, limning, painting, vernishing, japaning, gilding*, 2 vols., 8th ed. (1672; London, 1701), 1: 13.
45. Salmon, *Polygraphice*, 1: 16, 10.
46. Salmon, *Polygraphice*, 1: 18.
47. Salmon, *Polygraphice*, 1: 9.
48. For a comprehensive list of Pelham's "British" mezzotint portraits, see Smith, *British Mezzotinto Portraits*, 3: 964–78.

49. *Boston Gazette*, 19 Feb. 1728.

50. Pelham's mezzotint of Cotton Mather was probably also the first to be made anywhere outside Europe.

51. Mark Hallett, *The Spectacle of Difference: Graphic Satire in the Age of Hogarth* (New Haven and London: Yale Univ. Press, 1999), 17.

52. Georgia Barnhill, "Pelham, Peter", in *American National Biography* (2000), http://www.anb.org/articles/17/17-00663. Despite being heralded in this way, Pelham has received little scholarly attention.

53. *New England Weekly Journal*, 5 Aug. 1727.

54. For more on this, see Moore, *British Graphic Art*, 258–77.

55. Timothy Clayton, "Pelham, Peter (1695?–1751)", *Oxford Dictionary of National Biography* (Oxford Univ. Press, 2006), http://www.oxforddnb.com/view/article/21796.

56. *Boston Gazette*, 19 Feb. 1728.

57. While the specific identity of these "friends" remains unknown, and no comprehensive subscription list for the mezzotint can be traced, a single receipt in the name of the Reverend Benjamin Colman survives. This is owned by the Massachusetts Historical Society, Boston. See Andrew Oliver, "Peter Pelham (c.1697–1751) Sometime Printmaker of Boston", in *Boston Prints and Printmakers, 1670–1775*, ed. Walter Whitehill and Sinclair Hitchings (Boston: Colonial Society of Massachusetts, 1973), 133–73.

58. Robert Middlekauf, *The Mathers: Three Generations of Puritan Intellectuals, 1596–1728* (Oxford and New York: Oxford Univ. Press, 1971), 367.

59. *Boston Gazette*, 19 Feb. 1728.

60. Oliver, "Peter Pelham", 135.

61. Those not illustrated in the present essay include Samuel Sewall, a Boston judge and noted philanthropist, dated 1728 (American Antiquarian Society, Worcester, MA); and Samuel Prince and Mercy Hinckley, husband and wife (Massachusetts Historical Society, Boston, MA)—Prince was a merchant and son of a local pastor and academic, Hinckley the daughter of a Massachusetts governor. Prince died in 1728 and Hinckley is shown wearing mourning dress, so it seems likely that both paintings were produced at this time as an act of memorial.

62. *Boston Gazette*, 19 Feb. 1728.

63. Cited by James Flexner, *History of American Painting*, vol. 1, *First Flowers of Our Wilderness (The Colonial Period)* (New York: Dover, 1969), 287.

64. *New England Journal*, 27 May 1740.

65. Nina Fletcher Little, *American Decorative Wall Painting, 1700–1850* (New York: E. P. Dutton, 1989), 25.

66. Little, *American Decorative Wall Painting*.

67. *New England Journal*, 27 May 1740.

68. Lot 145 in "A Sale of paintings at the Long Dog in New Palace Yard", 6 Nov. 1691; lot 151 in "A Sale of paintings and furniture next to Bedford Gate in Covent Garden", 2 Dec. 1690. Transcriptions of these sale catalogues can be accessed in *The Art World in Britain, 1660 to 1735* at http://artworld.york.ac.uk.

69. For a further discussion of this and other such paintings of prints in London, see Joseph Monteyne, *From Still Life to the Screen: Print Culture, Display, and the Materiality of the Image in Eighteenth-century London* (New Haven and London: Yale Univ. Press, 2013), 1–3.

70. Lovell, *Art in a Season of Revolution*, 23.

71. Uriel Heyd, *Reading Newspapers: Press and Public in Eighteenth-century Britain and America* (Oxford Univ. Press, 2012), 2–3.

72. Adrian Johns, *The Nature of the Book: Print and Knowledge in the Making* (Chicago and London: Chicago Univ. Press, 1998), 19.

THEORY, ARTWORDS, PERIODIZATION

A Royal Subject: William Sanderson's Guide to Painting on the Eve of the Restoration

Caroline Good

"It is an Art I never professed", wrote William Sanderson (ca. 1586–1676), in the preface to his *Graphice. The use of the Pen and Pensil. Or the most excellent art of painting* (1658); "these Readings are gathered at my Study, accompanied with observations which I met with beyond Seas, and other Notions, pickt up from excellent Artizans abroad, and here at home; not without some experience by my own private practise, and altogether suiting my Genius."[1] Containing practical instruction, connoisseurial advice, theoretical reasoning, and an incipient notion of a canon of master painters, *Graphice* is an ambitious publication that combines material on painting drawn from the literature of the previous sixty years with original observations and ideas. Presented in two parts, it sets out in the first instance to persuade readers of the power of art, and to guide them in the collection, judgment, and display of pictures.[2] The second part of *Graphice*, meanwhile, divulges the practicalities of painting itself, using a body of material pirated from a previously unpublished manuscript by the courtier and painter Edward Norgate (1581–1650).[3] The overall effect is that of a guidebook intended for the budding art lover, geared to those who enjoy the art of painting, but who know little of the social expectations or critical concepts that go with it.

Up until this point, Sanderson's major literary contribution had been that of a Royalist historian; and in the same year that *Graphice* came to print, his final historical work, *A Compleat History of the life and raigne of King Charles from his cradle to his grave*, was also published.[4] Though the son of a merchant, Sanderson is here styled as having been "bred up at court", and described as someone who distinguished himself through his loyalty to Charles I at the time of the Civil War.[5] Based at least in part on Sanderson's personal knowledge of court life, the writing of *A Compleat History* is partial and polemical.[6] The ode "To the Author", by his friend and contemporary James Howell (ca. 1594–1666), sums up the flavour of the work as affording the king "a Burial, a Monument, and a Resurrection".[7] In Sanderson's *Graphice* we find a text formed in much the same manner. Presented as the work of a Royalist gentleman, its pages resound with references to the experiences

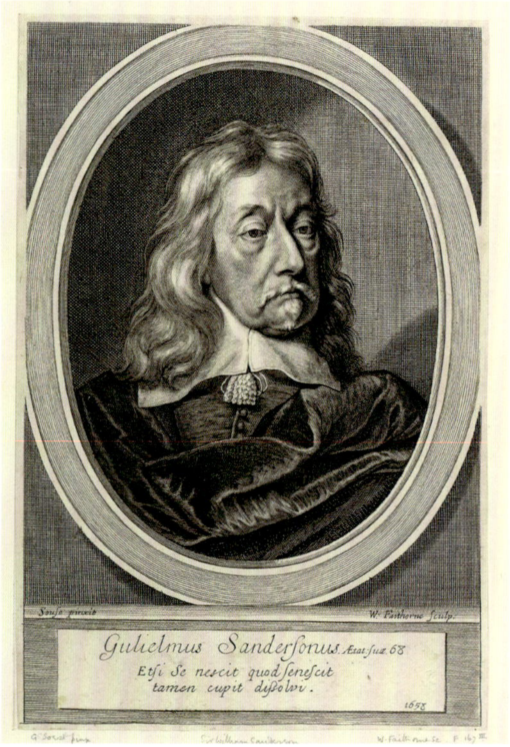

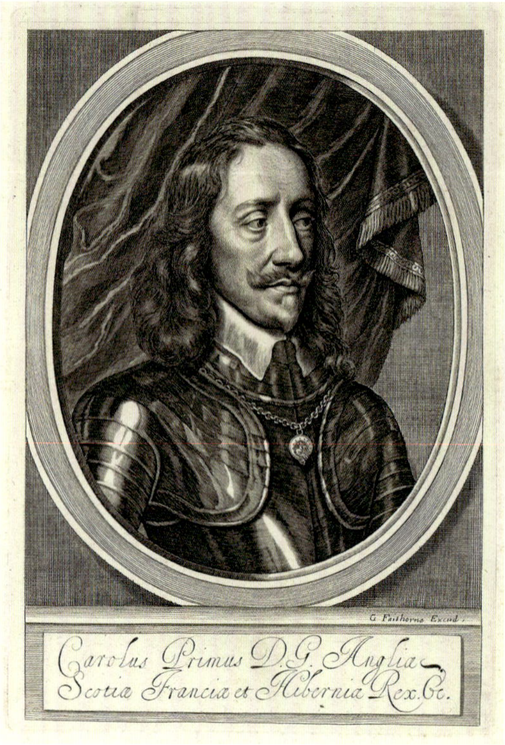

173a. William Faithorne after Gerard Soest, *Portrait of William Sanderson*, 1658, engraving, 9⅞ x 6¾ in. (25.1 x 17.2 cm). The Fitzwilliam Museum, University of Cambridge

173b. William Faithorne (printmaker), *King Charles I Carolus Primus D.G. Angliae Scotiae Franciae et Hiberniae Rex. Etc.*, 1658, engraving, 14⅝ x 11⅛ in. (37.3 x 28.3 cm). The Fitzwilliam Museum, University of Cambridge

of a past era, and to the author's loyalty to the Stuart dynasty. Especially telling in this respect are two portrait engravings that precede the text proper within the pages of *Graphice*, both by William Faithorne (1616–1691). The first depicts the refined elderly figure of the author himself (fig. 173a), shown bust length in an oval frame, with long greying hair. The second presents the late Charles I (fig. 173b), whose portrait was accompanied, on the facing page, by an epitaph to the martyred monarch written by the Church of England clergyman William Morehead (1637–1692). Morehead, along with the miniaturist Thomas Flatman (1635–1688) and Royalist satirical poet Edmund Gayton (1609–1666), all contribute a number of dedicatory verses at the outset of Sanderson's text. Morehead and Flatman are identified in *Graphice* as former Fellows of New College Oxford, something that adds further weight to the book's Royalist stance, the college having supported the exiled king when he resided in the town during the Civil War.[8]

As has been well documented, the decades prior to the Civil War had witnessed a renaissance in the arts in England, as elsewhere across Europe, forged by the burgeoning literary and collecting activities of the country's aristocratic elite.[9] Charles had sought to establish a royal collection in common with other notable European courts of the time, and had surrounded himself with advisers who could satisfy his passion for the connoisseurship of the visual arts.[10] In *Graphice* Sanderson comments on the king's "Repository of Rarities", stating that "Our late King Charles, had many most rare Originalls, Collections, both of Painting and Sculpture. He being the most of fame, for his incouragement, and Patronage of Arts and Honour."[11] Evidently, the historian had not set aside his Royalist sympathies, and in *Graphice* he developed a guide to art appreciation and art history that had its ideological roots in a belief in the superiority of the English aristocracy, with the monarchy at its head. The significance of this politicization of artistic dialogues must not be overlooked. The author's occupation as a Royalist historian and the timing of *Graphice*'s appearance on the market—after almost a decade of Republican rule in England, and in the same year that saw the death of the Lord Protector, Oliver Cromwell (1599–1658)—suggest that his publication was designed to offer something more than an attempt to educate its readers in the art of painting. In this essay I will demonstrate how this Royalist historian uses *Graphice* to outline a distinctive agenda of taste and sensibility on the part of the English art lover, and to promote a critical vocabulary about painting that is born directly out of the culture of the court.

AN ART LOVER'S GUIDE

As has been noted, Sanderson's historical writing indicates that he was familiar with court life, and the little more that is known of his career suggests something of the milieu that he may have been keen to emulate and capture within the pages of *Graphice*. He served as secretary to the courtier Henry Rich, Earl of Holland (1590–1649) in the late 1620s. A favourite of Queen Henrietta Maria, Holland had in 1626 been sworn bedchamber servant to the king. He was one of the numerous art lovers with whom Charles surrounded himself, the painter Peter Paul Rubens singling him out for criticism, along with the Earl of Carlisle, for their excessive expenditure and an extravagance that had left the court hopelessly in debt.[12] The artistic enthusiasms of these courtiers prompted frequent informal discussions on the subject of painting within the royal household, such as that which took place in 1626 upon the arrival of some pictures sent to the king from the Vatican. The gift included works attributed to Leonardo, Andrea del Sarto, and Giulio Romano, the reception of which was recorded by Gregorio Panzani, the papal envoy:

> The King came rushing to see the pictures the moment he was informed by the Queen that they had arrived and called Inigo Jones the architect, a great connoisseur of pictures, the Earl of Holland, and the Earl of Pembroke to be present. The very moment Jones saw the pictures he greatly approved of them and in order to be able to study them better he threw down his riding cloak, put on his eyeglass, took a candle and, together with the King, began to examine them very closely, admiring them very much . . . They let the Earl of Arundel know the paintings had arrived in court and he came immediately to see them.[13]

Later, Charles was said to have playfully removed the labels and had Jones guess the artists' identities in order to demonstrate his expert connoisseurship.[14] Guessing the hand and style of different artists was a favoured amusement at his court.[15] The king was even rumoured to have taken up the brush himself in order to "supply the defects in art" he found in the works of the artists' studios he visited.[16] Although the veracity of these individual anecdotes is in doubt,[17] such accounts usefully suggest an emerging interest in style and attribution within elite culture that is echoed in *Graphice*.

Through guidelines on the "Choyce of Pictures", the merits of "Originalls and Copies", and the subject of how to know what is "Well Designed" and "Well Coloured", Sanderson advises his readers on the novel and increasingly fashionable pastime of art appreciation. While suggesting a growing interest in taste, value, and attribution, Sanderson's suggestions and explanations also betray the difficulty of expounding such judgments in writing. His attempts to articulate the merits of originals and copies demonstrate this problem most explicitly: original works supposedly possess "a Natural force of Grace Rising; which copies only 'seem to have'"; meanwhile, copies are produced without "natural genius in the Workeman" and for that reason exhibit only "an imperfect and borrowed comeliness".[18] Applying such ambiguous definitions in practice would presumably have been difficult for his readers. Sanderson, however, is insistent that copies always come short of the unique original: "An imitator, does never come neer the first Author . . . a similitude ever more, comes short of that truth, which is in the Things themselves: the Copier being forced to accommodate himself, to another mans intent."[19] Paralleling his ideological position as a celebrant of the blood purity of the aristocracy, Sanderson concludes that a copy, no matter how good, can never serve as more than a poor imitation of another man's idea.

While the copyist can never hope to succeed in capturing the spirit of the original, he is also faced with another problem as far as direct duplication is concerned. Time ages pictures, and a painting's colours are especially affected during this process. "It is the opinion of many Masters of this Art concerning Ancient Originalls; that the ayre, by time and age works so much upon the Colours, that the Oilynesse thereof, being vaded, the Colour becomes more fleshy, more Naturall than at the first. So they say of Tytians, and of Jurgiones [Giorgione] being his Master."[20] In order to reproduce faithfully the changed colouring of the original, "the workeman must alter the manner of his colurs by a mixt tempering; otherwayes then the Modern Naturall way of Painting admits."[21] Sanderson here appears to be acknowledging the concept of the "Old Master" that had emerged in seventeenth-century Italy, stating that "Garish Colours, in new Pieces, take the eye at first; but in old Pictures we are delighted with their decaying, horridnesse of the Colours . . . Old Pictures, in a wonderfull simplicity of Colours, draw their chief Commendations, from a more accurate, and gracefull designe."[22]

More practical advice is also given by Sanderson to his reader regarding an ideal programme of pictorial decoration. This is given such headings as "How to dispose of Pictures and Paintings" and how "To place the Pictures within Doors", as well as "Of Grotesco" and "Of Fresco". Written to instruct readers not only how to collect works of art, but also how to present and interpret them, these passages acknowledge the growing importance of art collecting in England in the first half of the seventeenth century. Sanderson's advice points to a concern to integrate works of art into the social life of the house. He begins with some general advice, "not to Clutter the Room with too many Pieces, unlesse in Galleries and Repositories, as rarityes of severall Artizans intermingled; otherwise it becomes only a Painters-Shop, for choyce of sale".[23] He goes on: "place your best Pieces, to be seen with single lights: Thorough Lights on both sides, or double windows at each end, are Enemies to the view of Painting."[24] This is followed by a discussion of particular picture-hanging areas within the house: thus, staircases were intended to welcome and delight the visitor, with works "to be seen and observed at a view passing up"; meanwhile, the ceiling over the top stair should be filled with figures "looking downwards out of Clouds, with Garlands and Cornucopia's". Dining rooms were to be hung with portraits of the king and queen so that the householder could toast their health, "forbearing to put any other Pictures of the life, as not to being worthy to be their Companions unless at the lower end, two or three of the chief nobility, as attendants of their Royal persons". Portraits of the women of the family were placed away from public view, "lest some wanton and libidinous guest should gaze too long on them, and commend the work for her sake". Reserved for the gallery are "Histories, grave stories, and the best works . . . where any one may walk, and exercise their senses, in viewing, examining, delighting, judging and censuring".[25] As a discursive space, the gallery demanded that those who enter it perform as individuals with a knowledgeable authority about the subject, signifying not only a love of art, but a reverence regarding its worth, signification, and function.

Sanderson's ideal programme of display is a far more detailed and exhaustively expanded version of remarks on the same subject by Sir Henry Wotton (1568–1639) in his *The Elements of Architecture* of 1624.[26] Wotton writes that:

> Lastly, that they [i.e. paintings] bee as properly bestowed for their quality, as fitly for their grace: that is, chearefull Paintings in Feasting and Banquestting Roomes; Graver Stories in Galleries; Land-schips, and Boscage, and such wilde-workes in open Terraces, or in Summer Houses (as we call them) and the like.[27]

Among Wotton's contemporaries, architecture was a frequent topic of discussion, particularly on the part of those wealthy enough to plan the design of a country house and its interior, and concerned with the concept of decorum or appropriateness that provided the principal theme in architectural literature at this time.[28] English palaces and country houses built after 1580 often contained long galleries for displaying paintings and sculptures. Unlike the Italian *studioli*, the gallery was a larger, more public space, one in which the householder's collection was displayed both for their own delight and also for the edification of others.[29] Francis Junius (1589–1677), the Earl of Arundel's librarian, notes how "out of his [Arundel's] noble and art-cherishing minde, doth at present expose these jewells of arte to the publicke view in the Academie at Arundell House".[30] Opening his gallery to travellers, scholars, connoisseurs, and artists, the earl cultivated a form of public display that signalled the owner's participation in an international collecting culture, but also his promotion of art collecting as "an education in taste for the nation".[31]

A novel sense of cultural nationalism is explicitly articulated by Sanderson in several further passages on "Particular Masterie" from *Graphice*, in which the author includes an account of "English Modern Masters".[32] This was the first time an English writer had articulated such a group of artists,[33] and speaks of the author's desire to characterize native painters as a coherent body of practitioners which could be measured against the dominant European schools of art and artists. The relevant passage in *Graphice* follows a discussion of the ancient and modern painters of Europe, which treats first the Italians, then the Northern schools, and concludes with the French. Whilst reinforcing the familiar argument that the Italian school demonstrated a superiority in painting, Sanderson also notes the Northern painters (he refers to them as "Dutch" although many were German or Flemish) coming to prominence in the late fifteenth and early sixteenth centuries. Of contemporary painters, he held "the most excellent" French history painter Nicolas Poussin in particularly high regard. Sanderson then discusses the painters of particular note from throughout Europe, organizing them by genre: "Life", "Landskip", "Flowers", "dead-standing-things" (i.e. still life), "prospective Sea Pieces", and "Hunting and Beasts of Prey".[34] Sanderson's outline of a putative English school follows this account. His enumeration of native "masters" includes a number of foreign-born painters, as well as a handful of gentlemen and gentlewomen amateurs. Around forty figures are named, although no individual biographical particulars or details of distinguishing painterly styles are included. Professional artists are grouped together in relation to the genres or practices in which they excelled, with the non-professionals divided by gender. Sanderson's articulation of genres does not directly follow those laid out in his discussion of the European schools: for example, for what we would call still life, he doesn't repeat the term "dead-standing-things" but groups "Flowers and Fruits" together, separated from "Fish and Fowl". These rather ambiguous and interchangeable terms exemplify how attempts to define the discussion of painting in England trailed behind examples already being set in Continental Europe. Sanderson grapples with a vocabulary of specialist terms that had yet to be properly defined.

Sanderson's account also tells us something of the art worlds that existed in England at this time. Robert Streeter is singled out twice by Sanderson as "a compleat Master" who excelled in history, landscape, still life, and portrait painting as well as etching and engraving, architecture, and works of perspective. Portrait painters dominate among the professional artists he describes, with familiar names such as Peter Lely, John Michael Wright, Anthony van Dyck, and Robert Walker presented alongside the less familiar figure of John Hayls,"de Grange" and "Shepheard". As well as Streeter, Isaac Fuller is also singled out as an exemplary history painter, with Francis Barlow given the same status for works in "Fish and Fowl". Henry Stone and Michael Cross are described as the leading copyists, as is "Marshall" for "Flowers and Fruits", and "Flesher" for "Sea Pieces". In the categories of limning and engraving, a handful of names are given, something which suggests that these categories, like portrait painting, were already well established by 1658, with a longer English history than is sometimes thought. For limning, three father-and-son pairs—the Coopers, Hoskins, and Hilliards—underscore this established artistic tradition, together with Richard Gibson the "court dwarf" and the now unfamiliar "Cary", "Reurie", and "John Baptista". Similarly for the practice of engraving, six or so names are given, with Robert Vaughan, Wencelaus Hollar, his pupil Richard Gaywood, the same Michael Cross listed earlier as a master copyist, and the unidentifiable "Father Lambert" and "Trevethen", all pointing to a lively and multifarious print culture.

Sanderson does not restrict himself to a discussion of professional painters, but also includes a selection of gentleman and gentlewoman practitioners of note. Mary Beale, now recognized as a commercially important painter of the period, is not only featured here, but placed amongst a milieu of distinguished female painters. Amongst the gentlemen, Sir John Holland is indicative of a different kind of practitioner, one known to be an enthusiastic art lover who practised privately and for his own amusement.[35] These varied and intriguing figures bring into question how we understand and define the identity of the "English artist" in the seventeenth century. While Sanderson distinguishes between professional and genteel practitioners, his inclusivity is of particular note. *Graphice* constructs English painting as a thriving and cosmopolitan realm of practice, attracting painters from across Europe while also nurturing and recognizing the talents of its native male and female artists.

This early rhetorical effort to identify a national artistic school—a school which Sanderson proudly describes as "tantamount with any now beyond Seas"[36]—has been understood as evidence of a growing movement within Stuart England to carve out a "political terra firma" and to define a more rigidly bound and inherently "nationalist" artistic identity comparable to those associated with the Continent.[37] Utilized in this manner, artistic practice is coupled to values of political and cultural progress, where art becomes collectively or symbolically a sign of cultural capital and national well-being. The desire to define a collective of notable native contemporary practitioners is certainly at the heart of Sanderson's enterprise; for him, however, the English school of painting articulated in the pages of *Graphice* was also one that sustained the glorious memory of Charles I as the great patron of the arts who had enabled, for the first time, a body of painters—professional and private, male and female—to form what could be comprehended as a coherent body or school.

SANDERSON'S VISUAL LANGUAGE OF CRITICISM

Sanderson's recommendation of the values associated with a pre-Civil War court culture is even more apparent in the detailed discussion of four paintings that is one of the most intriguing components of *Graphice*. His critical analyses are given as templates "to teach the Gallant by such Artificiall Patterns, how to ascribe due praise to a deserving person".[38] What Sanderson makes explicit here is the possibility of learning the connoisseurship of pictures not only from paintings themselves, but directly from text and prints; and although only one illustration was included in the final publication, we can assume he had intended there to be engraved copies of all four paintings to accompany his analysis.[39] Sanderson's suggestion that "the Practitioner may be furnished at Mr. Fatherns, [William Faithorne] (a Graver, without Temple-bar) and at other Print-sellers, with such Cuts and Prints, as may serve his own private use for this whole Book", underscores his intentions about how *Graphice* was to be approached—as an illustrated guide.[40]

Beginning with a portrait by Peter Lely of a now unknown female sitter, Sanderson's case study for a pictorial critic notes her "lively Spirit and good Grace. Well wrought; Round, and Neatly painted . . . A beautious blushing Browne." In his analysis, he works his way down the portrait, beginning with "Her haire proper to the complexion; neatly put into Curles and folds". He then treats the face, "made up of excellent parts", at length:

> A quick Eye and full, amends the defect in the Colour; and yet the circled brows gracefully big and black. Her Nose not over-Romane, with Nostrils fair enough. A full mouth: the largenesse of the Lipps commendable, because plump and Red. I like well the deepned shadow stroak, which parts them, and almost shews her Ivory teeth, as if to appear; and altogether seems to be speaking. The very dimple by the Cheek, with a wanton touch of the Pensil, singly sets out her looks, most lovely: Somewhat long visage; and it may be in true measure to the Life, and sufficient Symmetry.[41]

He moves on to "her Noble Neck: roundrising full and fat", and her "Ample Brests interlined with River'et Vanes See, see; the swelling Papps like fair Pome-waters. The Nipples too, like Rasberry fountains, in true center to their circles . . . Her brawny Arms of good flesh, and pure colour", and "A Hand well drawn; the fingers spread, and yet not forced." He concludes that "Her Body well fed, not too fat" is "An Italian Don's delight".[42]

The tone that the critical analysis takes is a sensual one, that of the male admirer of a beautiful woman; the subject's physical beauty is the viewer's primary concern. Moreover, the analysis appears to address the portrait in line with certain established notions of ideal beauty, and as we see in the three further pictorial analyses found in Sanderson's text, a particular vocabulary of beauty emerges, in which similar terms and phrases are reiterated, and in which similar physical features are highlighted and analysed repeatedly. Contemporary literature, such as Louis Guyon's *Miroir de la beauté et santé corporelle* (1643), claims that a clear complexion was the most important attribute of beauty, along with brilliant sparkling eyes and a small mouth; almost as important as the face were the white and polished neck and shoulders, and the breasts which should be like two beautiful apples (an analogy, as has been seen, that is used by Sanderson himself).[43]

Sanderson's marriage of established notions of ideal beauty and critical pictorial analysis is extended further in his second critical discussion. This examines Anthony van Dyck's portrait of his wife, Mary Ruthven (fig. 174), and is the only analysis that is accompanied by an engraving in the text (fig. 175).[44] He begins by noting, in a similar fashion to his analysis of the Lely portrait, that the subject has "A goodly Plump, Fat, well Favoured, well formed Figure" and a "firm, fair, and noble Neck; full and fat fleshed shoulders, plump breasts, well coloured skin". Her hair is "a well chosen mingled Colour, (as you may say) of all into one. Not brown, nor black, and too too [*sic*] gracefull she was, to produce a flaxen . . . a lovely pure bright Aburn; with which the darkned folds, set out each Circle, sufficient to enchant a man into those Mazes." Her eyes are "full black and rouling" and hold the viewer transfixed in rapturous wonder, "only, you might have leave to steal to her Cheek and Lippe, and there to dine and sup, and sip."[45] In this analysis Sanderson's connoisseur takes on the role of the lover or gallant, making explicit a dialogue between the art lover and the male lover. By using a portrait of Van Dyck's wife he sets up the painter's gaze as one that identifies with the gaze of the husband. This sensual voyeurism aligns the ideal beauty of a woman with ideal beauty in art, further evidence that for Sanderson the visual arts were not an entirely distinct cultural category. When he comes to discuss the subject's mode of dress, this particular connoisseurial position is further enforced:

> Her Habit put into a Garment, call it a Petty-coate, and Wast-coate, or morning dresse . . . But ile say so much for this Piece, not overcurious (it seems) to set out her self . . . the Bodies tackt together before, with four Jewells set into buttons of Diamonds; on each side thereof an Orient Pearle, and a fift Jewel more faire, the pendant to the other four, in fashion alike; only, the lowest pure Pearle, so large, (such is the Painters Art to make it) inestimable. These but untacked, (with little paines, but much passion) you come to the smock, which peeps out between them; and at the hand-wrest carelessely purfled of purest Holland . . . A goodly Rope of Pearle surrounding her firm, fair, and noble Neck; full and fat fleshed shoulders, plump breasts, well coloured skin, and altogether, able to indure a mans handling.[46]

Sanderson, framing the painter's depiction of his subject's bodice as artfully and enticingly "untacked", and the string of pearls about her neck drawing the eye to her alluring neck, shoulders, and breasts, uses the costume to underscore his argument for the consumption of the picture as a highly sensual and evocative experience. The use of the terms "overcurious" and "carelessly" in this passage is also significant, highlighting the extent to which observations upon costume in paint-

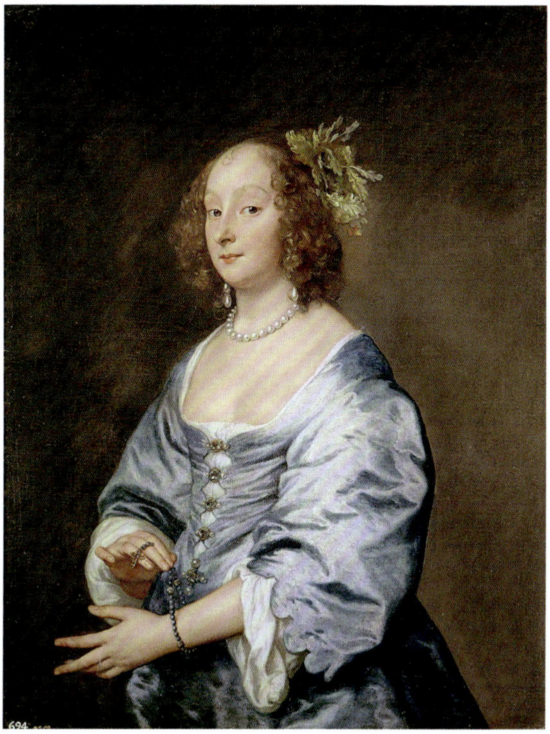

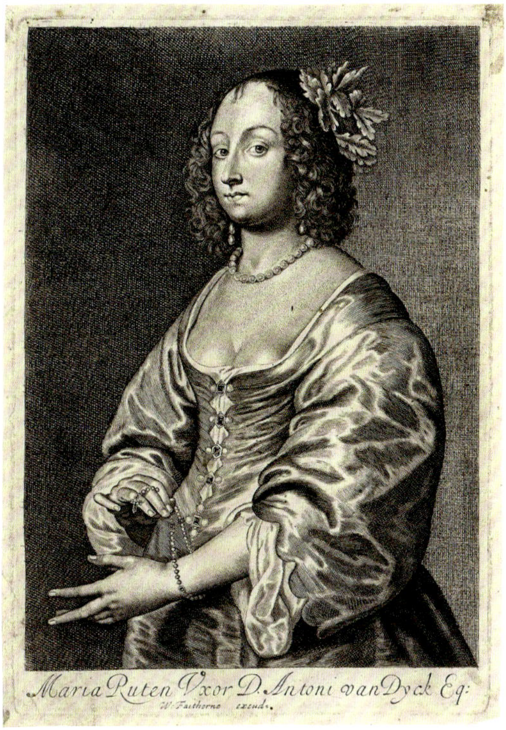

174. Antony van Dyck, *Portrait of the Artist's Wife, Mary Ruthven, Lady van Dyck*, ca. 1640, oil on canvas, 41 x 31⅞ in. (104 x 81 cm). Museo Nacional del Prado, Madrid

175. William Faithorne after Anthony van Dyck, *Lady Mary Ruthven, Maria Ruten Vxor D. Antoni van Dyck Eq*, 1639-58, engraving, 11¼ x 7⅞ in. (28.7 x 19.9 cm). The Fitzwilliam Museum, University of Cambridge (transferred 1876 Cambridge University Library)

ing were beginning to be informed and even theorized. Francis Junius had offered an explanation of the meaning of such terms in his *The Painting of the Ancients* (1638), recommending that painters avoid overly "curious"—highly descriptive and precise—painting in favour of a degree of deliberate abandon: a "Picture must follow a bold and carelesse way of art, or it must at least make a shew of carelessnesse in many things."[47] Junius's arguments regarding "carelessness" and "overcuriosity" stem from a central preoccupation with the quality of grace as a principal part of painting, as much as invention or perspective. Junius understands the effect of grace on spectators to be one of amazement, carrying them "into an astonished extasie, their sense of seeing bereaving them of all other senses"; it "doth sweetly enthrall and captivate the hearts of men with the lovely chain of due admiration and amazement".[48] He therefore warns against excessive care and polishing, and recommends ease and facility as making grace more graceful.[49]

A similar set of preoccupations are again observable in Sanderson's final two critical readings, one of a female portrait by Van Dyck, which has been identified

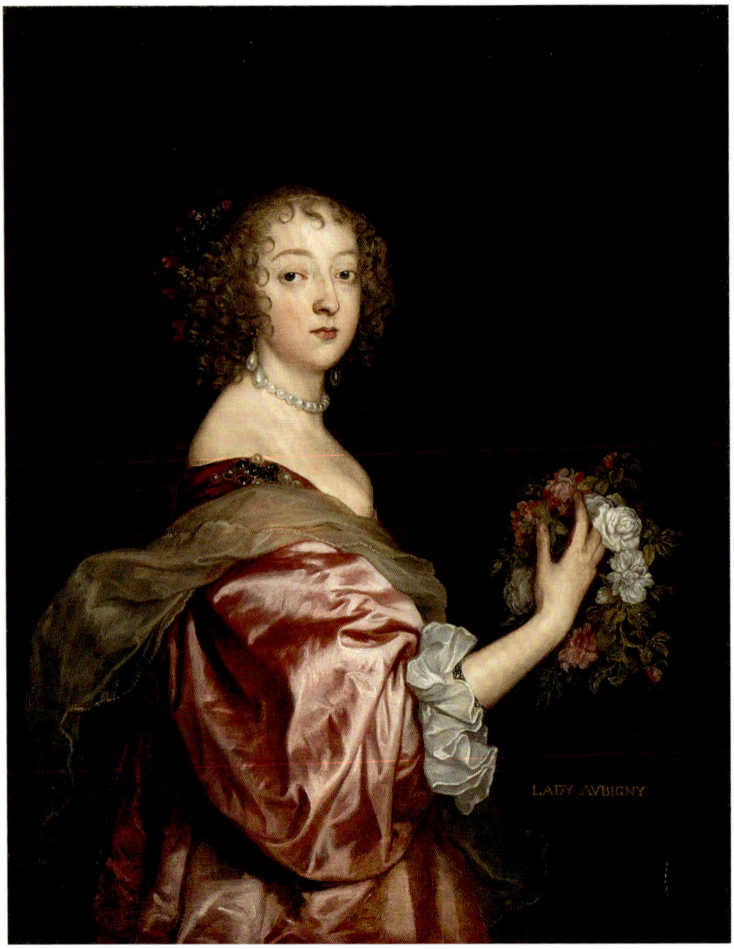

176. Anthony van Dyck, *Catherine Howard, Lady d'Aubigny*, ca. 1638, oil on canvas, 42 x 33⅝ in. (106.7 x 85.4 cm). National Gallery of Art, Washington DC, Widener Collection

as that of Catherine Howard, Lady d'Aubigny (fig. 176),[50] the other of "A Picture of the Husband and his Wife" identified as a double portrait of Lord and Lady Fairfax by Gilbert (traditionally known as "Gerard") Soest (fig. 177).[51] The critical discussion of Lady d'Aubigny follows much the same pattern as Sanderson's previous two discussions of single portraits; she is described as "fair and full, not fat; plump enough, and with good features to her length; Not over-tall, nor too slender", with "light brown hair; handsomely curl'd; not too forward upon the face . . . A Cherry lip and full, which does invite you . . .".[52] The final discussion, of the double portrait by Soest, is worth quoting at greater length, however, so as to demonstrate the comparable critical framework that Sanderson sets in play when discussing a double portrait:

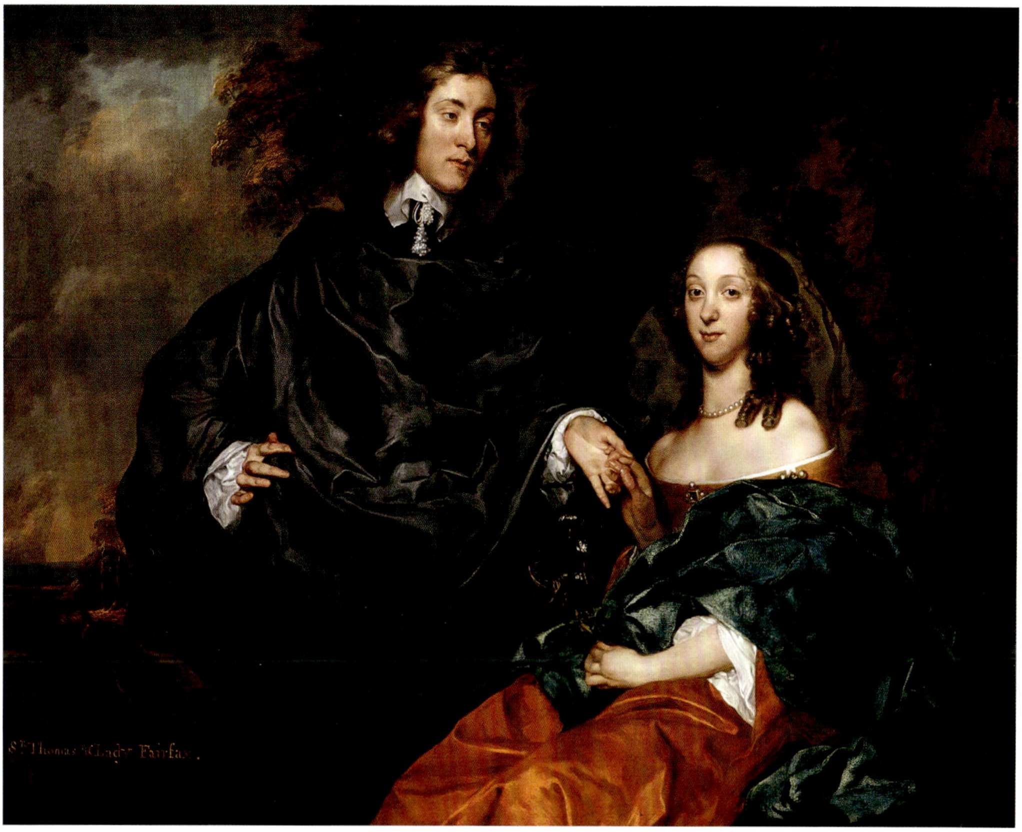

177. Gilbert Soest, *William Fairfax, 3rd Viscount Fairfax of Emley; Elizabeth (née Smith), Viscountess Fairfax of Emley (later Lady Goodricke)*, 1645–48, oil on canvas, 54¾ x 68¾ in. (139 x 174.6 cm). National Portrait Gallery, London

> Her Head was well set on (as Artists use to say) supported by a round necke, down behind to her rising shoulder, full and plump, and meeting before with a fair breast, well proportion'd, interlaced with Riveret-azur-veines. See, see, the swelling paps like ripe Pome waters, well grown and fit for her Husband's gathering. The ruddy nipples, two if seen, would seem Rasbery fountaines in true Center to their Globy-Orbs . . . Her body well fed not fat, fitted onely for his delight.[53]

Once more the female subject is understood through the sensual masculine eye; but here we also have the male lover included in the portrait, which serves to emphasize the parallels between two ways of looking—that of the husband and

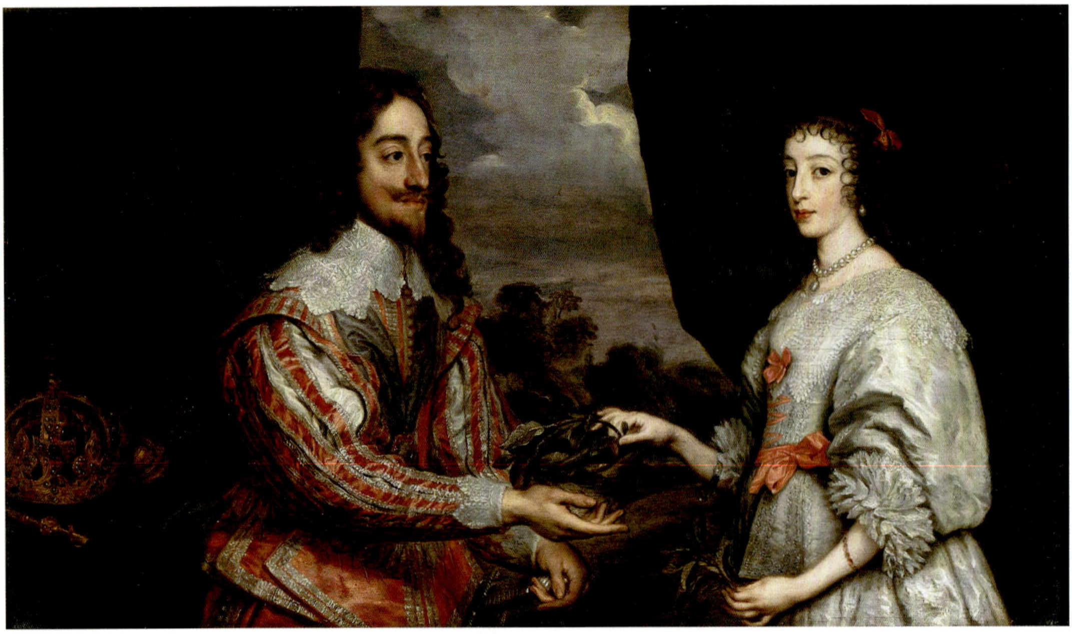

178. Gonzales Coques, after Daniel Mytens, *Charles I of England and Queen Henrietta Maria*, 17th century, oil on oak panel, 17⅞ x 30⅞ in. (45.5 x 78.5 cm). Victoria & Albert Museum, London

the spectator—which are seemingly presented as one. Within the portrait itself, Lord Fairfax looks directly at his wife while she looks out towards the viewer, and Sanderson goes on:

> The designe sets it out, as after Mid-Noon Summer, when heat hath influence on hearty affections. A new Bed-Bridall went out a walking, led by the way into a well-grown Wood, where, under the branched boughes of an ample Oak they two sat billing: and after all, in the close of the Even, the Married Man starts up, and looketh wishly on Her . . . Her Skarfe of Azure skye, opened with the wind to let in Aire, or to uncover her beautious breasts to her Husbands beholding . . .[54]

Here Sanderson conceives the gaze of the young husband on his wife and her casual undress, as a sensual tool that reinforces his argument for a type of masculine voyeurism in which the art lover and male lover become one and the same.

This configuration of a double portrait appears elsewhere in well-known courtly works from the period, as is demonstrated by Gonzales Coques's double portrait of Charles I and Henrietta Maria after Daniel Mytens (or Mijtens; fig. 178) and Van Dyck's depiction of Buckingham and his wife in a seminal reimagining

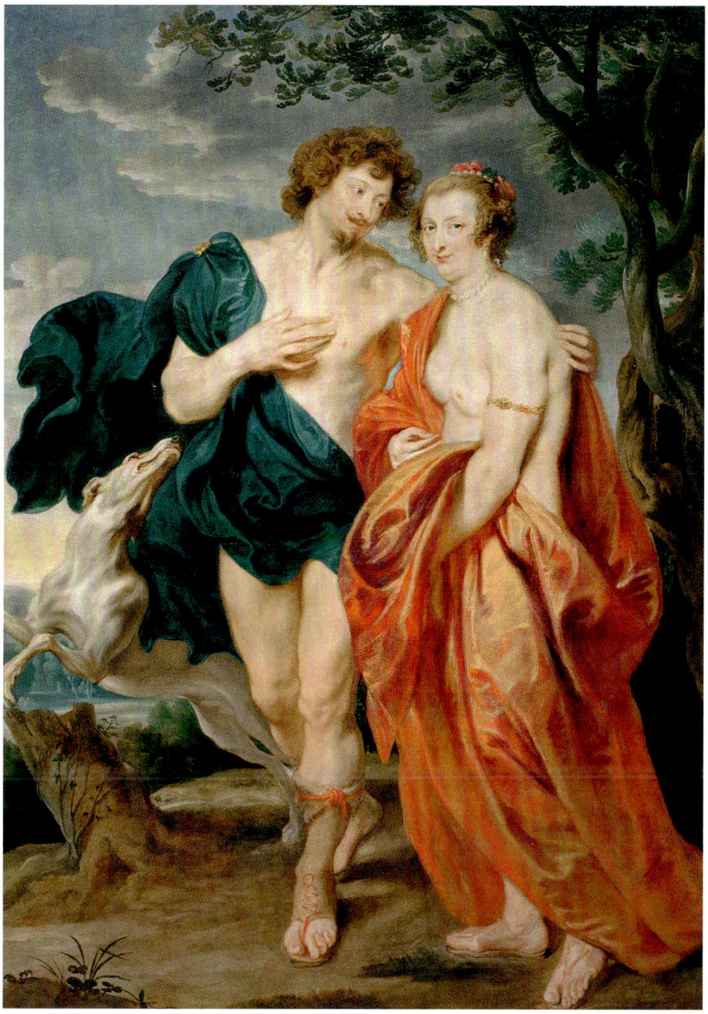

179. Anthony van Dyck, *Lady Manners and Lord Buckingham as Venus and Adonis*, ca. 1620–1, oil on canvas, 87⅞ x 63 in. (223 x 160 cm). Private collection

of Venus and Adonis (fig. 179), both depicting the same triangular gaze. The "undressed" appeal of Lady Fairfax's attire also has its parallel in other forms of contemporary courtly culture. Plays and poetry patronized by the same courtiers responded to and expressed a similar range of ideas. Some poets ventured into the sensual, even openly erotic realm when describing their mistress's undress. Thus, the court poet Robert Herrick (1591–1674) detailed the attraction of his mistress Julia's clothes: "Whenas in silks my Julia goes,/ Then, then (methinks), how sweetly flowes/ That liquefaction of her clothes."[55] In another poem, Herrick is more explicit about his delight in loosely flowing garments:

A sweet disorder in the dresse
Kindles in cloathes a wantonnesse:
A Lawne about the shoulders thrown
Into a fine distraction:
An erring Lace, which here and there
Enthralls the Crimson Stomacher:
A Cuffe neglectfull, and thereby
Ribbands to flow confusedly:
A winning wave (deserving Note)
In the tempestuous petticote:
A carelesse shooe-string, in whose tye
I see a wilde civility:
Doe more bewitch me, then when Art
Is too precise in every part.[56]

Herrick's description of a shawl thrown about the shoulders, or an "erring lace", evokes the sort of costume that Sanderson remarks upon in his own pictorial analyses. In *Graphice* he offers an important definition of the evolution in portrait dress that had unfolded in England in the previous decades. Singling out Van Dyck, Sanderson describes him as "the first Painter that e're put Ladies dresse into a careless Romance."[57] In doing so he himself becomes the first writer to articulate this new approach to dress in portraiture from Van Dyck onwards.[58]

Significantly, the preoccupation with defining female beauty that we find widely exemplified in these written sources from the period, as well as in Sanderson's *Graphice* itself, are founded upon the Neoplatonic ideas that had circulated widely at the court of Charles and Henrietta Maria. In a broad sense, Neoplatonism had provided the court with a fundamental conception of the role and function of art.[59] Images were understood to reflect a truth that lies within. Visual material could therefore take on a crucial significance, for it was assumed to carry an underlying meaning. This concept came to the fore in the court masques of the period.[60] Music and dance enhanced the spectacle, and the same group of courtiers engaging in these courtly spectacles witnessed and commissioned portraits from the trio of painters that *Graphice* examines.

Tracing these links to an established notion of ideal beauty exposes the extent to which Sanderson applied the culture of the court to pictorial criticism. His suggested model for pictorial engagement operated through a perceptive and responsive attempt to apply a variety of established ideas to the description of four portraits. Uncovering the ambitious but uncertain viewing "model" that is constructed through these forms of close readings offers a new perception of the complex practices and identities being cultivated in critical art writing from the mid-seventeenth century. Using a vocabulary that responds to current developments in pictorial theory and practice, Sanderson's remarks represent a new development in English literature on painting. His commentaries are not merely indulgent anecdotes, but convey, if in microcosm, some of the wider narratives and conflicts of English culture on the brink of the Restoration.

CONCLUSION

> Great Artist,
> When I saw thy ROYAL STORY,
> (That Theater erected for thy glory)
> I stood amaz'd at each Majestick line,
> And deem'd each syllable therein Divine,
> Thinking Thee All-Historian: But now,
> Thy Protean Pen constrains me to allow,
> The Diadem of Arts and Sciences to Thee;
> Their vanquish'd depths confesse Thy Soveraignty:
> Whose absolute Dominion can dethrone
> The Rest, and fix supremacy in One
> (Rare MINIATURE) whose glitt'ring Trophies stand,
> Rear'd by the learn'd endeavours of Thine hand.
> Thy Water-Colours shall out-brave the Fire,
> And dare couragiously confront Jove's ire.
> Your fame shall (spite of Proverbs) make it plain,
> To write in Water's not to write in vain.
>
> Anonymous dedication to William Sanderson, *Graphice* (1658)

These words of praise for Sanderson and his "Protean Pen" appeared at the very end of his career as a writer. For the author was never to publish again on painting, history, or any subject for that matter, during what remained of his lifetime. With the Restoration of Charles II in 1660, Sanderson was knighted, made gentleman of the privy chamber, and finally bestowed with a grant of the Paddock Walk in Windsor Park, which had earlier been promised by the Earl of Holland. It seems his rallying effort had paid off, and by looking back to events of the recent past he had secured his own future, gaining the recognition he believed he deserved and so desperately wished for. With that, he abruptly set down his tireless "pen" for the last time. In his characterization of a lover of art, Sanderson had evidently enhanced his reputation; and the return to monarchical rule now set the stage for the transformation of English art and culture, as begun by Charles I. Sanderson could not have known that the courts of the Restoration would never again resemble that of the former monarch, nor that the cultural heart of painting in England would never again be tied so singularly to the patronage of its king and his immediate social milieu. The impact of these factors meant that *Graphice*, and all it had championed, was destined to fail as a voice of critical authority in the Restoration era, its ideological fabric outmoded by the new ideas being forged for a transforming state.

The literature of post-Restoration England echoed the ambiguities and uncertainties of a society poised between tradition and change, helping validate contemporary shifts towards a politics of party and a society of looser social arrangements. The differences that needed to be negotiated were not merely those of past civil conflict, but also of contemporary political and cultural life. As dramatists and poets began to point up their failings, Charles II's governments saw the need to recruit loyal pens to answer their attacks, with official organs like *The Current Intelligence* including loyalist and Royalist verse.[61] By the late 1660s, however, voices critical of the king and court—particularly those articulated within the thriving genre of satire—were increasingly excoriating the corruptions of courtiers and the failings of a king so weakened by debauchery that he could not defend his realm against Dutch invasion. In these conditions, Sanderson's connoisseurial vocabulary, rooted as it was in ideas of sensuality, ideal beauty, and feminine "undress", could no longer be applied and accepted unquestioningly as representative of inner virtue.

1. William Sanderson, *Graphice. The use of the Pen and Pensil. Or, the most excellent art of painting: In Two Parts* (London: Robert Crofts, 1658), "Preface".
2. What constituted a "picture" or "painting" was still relatively undefined for Sanderson. They appear throughout *Graphice* to refer to pictorial representations that could range in form from watercolour miniatures and oil paintings, to print engravings, drawings, and even tapestries. The term "graphice" is itself Greek, and appears to have been used first in this manner by Henry Peacham for his *Graphice, or The most auncient and excellent art of drawing and limning* (1612). Peacham's equation of writing and drawing stems back as far as Aristotle for whom "graphice", the use of the pen (a term which actually referred to a paintbrush, not a pencil) in writing, painting, and drawing, constituted one of the four parts of his curriculum: "Aristotle designing foure principall exercises, wherein he would have all children in a well governed Citie or Commonwealth, brought up and taught, as namely Grammatice or Grammer; Gymnastice, or exercising the bodie by wrestling, running, riding, &c. Graphice or use of the Pen in writing faire, drawing, painting, and the like; lastly, Musick". Peacham, *Graphice*, "To the Reader".
3. Edward Norgate, *Miniatura or the Art of Limning*, ed. Jeffrey M. Muller and Jim Murrell (New Haven and London: Yale Univ. Press, 1997).
4. William Sanderson, *Aulicus Coquinariae, or a Vindication in Answer to a Pamphlet entitled "The Court and Character of King James"* (London, 1650); *A Compleat History of the lives and reigns of, Mary Queen of Scotland, and of her son and successor, James the Sixth, King of Scotland, and (after Queen Elizabeth) King of Great*

Britain, France, and Ireland (London, 1656); *A Compleat History of the life and raigne of King Charles from his cradle to his grave* (London, 1658).

5. James Howell, "To the Author", in Sanderson, *Compleat History of the life and raigne of King Charles.*
6. See D. R. Woolf, "Sanderson, Sir William (1586–1676)", *Oxford Dictionary of National Biography* (Oxford Univ. Press, 2004), http://www.oxforddnb.com.ezproxy.york.ac.uk/view/article/24630 (accessed 31 May 2014).
7. Howell, "To the Author", in Sanderson, *Compleat History of the life and raigne of King Charles.*
8. Although not acknowledged in *Graphice* in the same manner, Gayton was also at Oxford during the Royalist occupation where he served as a captain in the Duke of York's company.
9. See Edward Chaney and Timothy Wilks, *The Jacobean Grand Tour: Early Stuart Travellers in Europe* (London: I. B. Tauris, 2013); Stephen Orgel, "Idols of the Gallery: Becoming a Connoisseur in Renaissance England", in Peter Ericson, ed., *Early Modern Visual Culture: Representation, Race and Empire in Renaissance England* (Philadelphia: Univ. of Pennsylvania Press, 2000), 251–83; and R. Malcolm Smuts, *Court Culture and the Origins of a Royalist Tradition in Early Stuart England* (Philadelphia: Univ. of Pennsylvania Press, 1987).
10. As well as aristocrats such as Endymion Porter (1587–1649), Sir Kenelm Digby (1603–1665), George Villiers, Duke of Buckingham (1592–1628), and Thomas Howard, Earl of Arundel (1585–1646), the king also enjoyed the company of artists such as Daniel Mijtens (1590–1647/48), Inigo Jones (1572–1652), Orazio Gentileschi (1563–1639), Peter Paul Rubens (1577–1640), and Anthony van Dyck (1599–1641). For more, see Francis Haskell, *The King's Pictures: The Formation and Dispersal of the Collections of Charles I and His Courtiers* (New Haven and London: Yale Univ. Press, 2013); Fiona Donovan, *Rubens and England* (New Haven and London: Yale Univ. Press, 2004); and Smuts, *Court Culture.*
11. Sanderson, *Graphice*, 14–15.
12. Donovan, *Rubens and England*, 65.
13. Translated and quoted in Edward Chaney, ed., *The Evolution of English Collecting: The Reception of Italian Art in the Tudor and Stuart Periods* (New Haven and London, Yale Univ. Press, 2003), 58–59.
14. Donovan, *Rubens and England*, 53.
15. Smuts, *Court Culture*, 122.
16. Smuts, *Court Culture*, 122.
17. This anecdote appeared in a martyrological work of the Restoration era by R. Perrinchief, *The Royal Martyr* (London, 1676), 253; quoted in Smuts, *Court Culture*, 158.
18. Sanderson, *Graphice*, 16.
19. Sanderson, *Graphice*, 16.
20. Sanderson, *Graphice*, 16–17.
21. Sanderson, *Graphice*, 16.
22. Sanderson, *Graphice*, 16.
23. Sanderson, *Graphice*, 25.
24. Sanderson, *Graphice*, 25.
25. Sanderson, *Graphice*, 26–28.
26. Henry Wotton, *The Elements of Architecture* (London, 1624).
27. Wotton, *Elements*, 109–10.
28. Graham Parry, *The Seventeenth Century: The Intellectual and Cultural Context of English Literature, 1603–1700* (Abingdon and New York: Longman, 2014), 42–79. See also John Onians, *Bearers of Meaning: The Classical Orders in Antiquity, the Middle Ages, and the Renaissance* (Princeton Univ. Press: 1988).
29. For more on the origins and development of the gallery, see Rosalys Coope, "The 'Long Gallery': Its Origins, Development, Use and Decoration", *Architectural History* 29 (1986): 43–84.
30. Quoted in Jane Roberts, "Thomas Howard, the Collector Earl of Arundel and Leonardo's Drawings", in *Evolution of English Collecting*, ed. Chaney, 257–58.
31. Orgel, "Idols of the Gallery", 251–83.
32. Sanderson, *Graphice*, 20.
33. There is an earlier generalized reference in Nicholas Hilliard's *The arte of Limning* (ca. 1600) to the need for the Crown to support the visual arts or risk damaging the national reputation.

34. Sanderson does not use the term "still life" because the term did not yet exist, and the genre now known as "still life" had yet to receive a recognizable English name. For more on this, see Caroline Good, "From 'dead-standing-things' to 'still life': Defining a New Genre in British Art", http://www.york.ac.uk/media/historyofart/ccc/images/display2012/Dead-things-standing-Good.pdf (accessed 12 Aug. 2013).
35. Muller and Murrell, in Norgate, *Miniatura*, 16.
36. Sanderson, *Graphice*, 20.
37. Catharine MacLeod and Julia Marciari Alexander, *Painted Ladies: Women at the Court of Charles II* (New Haven and London: National Portrait Gallery and Yale Univ. Press, 2001), 69.
38. Sanderson, *Graphice*, 39.
39. Other contemporary texts often simply assumed their readers would have access to the prints analysed within their pages. For example, John Evelyn in his translation of Roland Fréart de Chambray's *Idée de la perfection de la peinture* as *An Idea of the Perfection of Painting* (London, 1668) chose to rely on his readers' own collections rather than publish images alongside the text.
40. Sanderson, *Graphice*, "To the Reader".
41. Sanderson, *Graphice*, 35.
42. Sanderson, *Graphice*, 35–36.
43. Quoted in Aileen Ribeiro, *Fashion and Fiction: Dress in Art and Literature in Stuart England* (New Haven and London, Yale Univ. Press, 2005), 338, n. 102. A "Pomewater" was a variety of apple known for being particularly large and juicy. Another example in this vein is Sir Kenelm Digby's description of his wife Venetia in his *Loose Fantasies* (London, 1627), 85.
44. In being illustrated with an engraving by William Faithorne (fig. 174), the account of Van Dyck's portrait of Mary Ruthven seemingly stands as a unique example of an illustrated explanation of a portrait in English seventeenth-century literature on the visual arts.
45. Sanderson, *Graphice*, 37.
46. Sanderson, *Graphice*, 37.
47. Francis Junius, *The Painting of the Ancients* (London, 1638), 288.
48. Junius, *Painting of the Ancients*, 329, 332.
49. S. H. Monk, "A Grace Beyond the Reach of Art", *Journal of the History of Ideas* 5, no. 2 (April 1944), 143–46.
50. Mansfield Kirby Talley, *Portrait Painting in England: Studies in the Technical Literature before 1700* (London: Paul Mellon Centre for Studies in British Art, 1981), 235.
51. Talley, *Portrait Painting*, 235.
52. Sanderson, *Graphice*, 39.
53. Sanderson, *Graphice*, 41–42.
54. Sanderson, *Graphice*, 41–42.
55. Robert Herrick, "Upon Julia's Clothes", in *The Complete Poetry of Robert Herrick,* ed. Tom Cain and Ruth Connolly, 2 vols. (Oxford Univ. Press, 2013), 1: 246.
56. Herrick, "Delight in Disorder", in *Complete Poetry of Robert Herrick,* ed. Cain and Connolly, 1: 28.
57. Sanderson, *Graphice*, 39.
58. How such a dramatic change of aesthetic preference could occur in less than half a century has, however, only recently begun to be addressed, studies in English art at the turn of the seventeenth century having tended to scrutinize portraits of Elizabeth I, and then proceed directly to the study of Van Dyck's canvases for Charles I. See Christiane Hille, *Visions of the Courtly Body: The Patronage of George Villiers, First Duke of Buckingham, and the Triumph of Painting at the Stuart Court* (Berlin: Akademie Verlag, 2012), especially "Introduction".
59. See Erin Griffey, ed., *Henrietta Maria: Piety, Politics and Patronage* (Burlington, VT, and Aldershot: Ashgate, 2008), and Karen Britland, *Drama at the Courts of Queen Henrietta Maria* (Cambridge Univ. Press 2009).
60. This has been discussed in detail by Emilie Gordenker, *Anthony van Dyck (1599–1641) and the Representation of Dress in Seventeenth-century Portraiture* (Turnhout, Belgium: Brepols, 2001), 17 and n. 118.
61. Kevin Sharpe, *Reading Authority and Representing Rule in Early Modern England* (London: Bloomsbury, 2013), 205.

Engraving's Third Dimension

Martin Myrone

GRADUALLY, and with little in the way of fanfare, John Evelyn's monograph on the history and techniques of intaglio printmaking, *Sculptura: or the History, and Art of Chalcography and Engraving in Copper. With An ample enumeration of the most renowned Masters, and their Works. To which is annexed A new manner of Engraving, or* Mezzo Tinto, *communicated by his Highness* Prince Rupert *to the Authour of this Treatise* (London, 1662), has emerged as a significant reference point in the cultural history of the late seventeenth century (fig. 180). For a range of commentators on the intellectual and artistic worlds of the period, the book, and most especially the brief but fascinating announcement it contains of the invention of the technique of mezzotint, flagged up on the title page and illustrated practically by the inclusion of a plate executed by Prince Rupert (fig. 181), may be more worthy of scrutiny than has previously been allowed.

This essay is not intended primarily to further this rehabilitation, although its very presence in the context of this volume, along with Peter Moore's essay, may mean that it seems to do so, if only incidentally. Rather, it addresses Evelyn's text and the conception of engraving it relays as a problem, and reflects on the difficulties of interpretation and value Evelyn's work has presented and continues to present to many readers. This essay proceeds with an eye to the specific historical dynamics of art historiography, but also to suggest how Evelyn's text might be situated at the moment of post-Restoration political, cultural, and economic transformation. That moment is quite properly the object of enquiry for many of the essays included here, whether these touch on the post-1660 reconstruction of court and royal identity, post-1666 architectural rebuilding, post-1688 political, intellectual, and commercial enterprise, or on the themes of Dutch and Flemish cultural migration, technological innovation, developing ideas of nationhood and empire, the art market, and urban change which have pertinence for the period 1660–1735 as a whole, and which underpin a sense of the era's nascent modernity. Evelyn's *Sculptura* may, and sometimes has been folded into an account of an emerging modernity, its intellectual style matched to novel ideas about natural

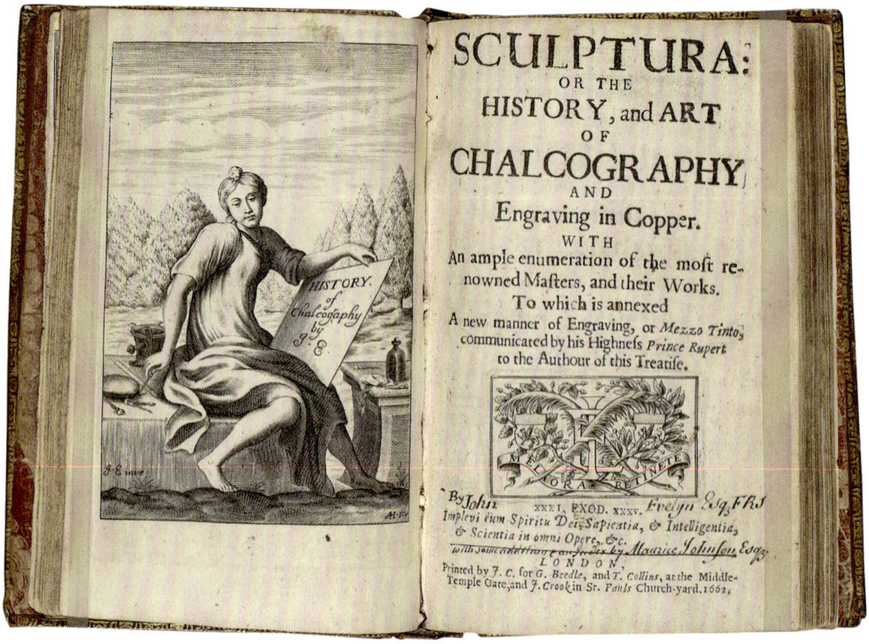

180. John Evelyn, *Sculptura: or the History of Art, and Chalcography and Engraving in Copper. With An ample enumeration of the most renowned Masters, and Their Works. To which is annexed A new manner of Engraving, or* Mezzo Tinto, *communicated by his Highness* Prince Rupert *to the Authour of this Treatise* (London, 1662), title page. Beinecke Rare Book and Manuscript Library

philosophy and the history of trades, and its revelation of mezzotint identified as a prime document of the appearance of this exemplary modern and commercial medium. But, as I hope to show, the text can be accommodated only partially to the dominant narratives of cultural change in the period; it also stands aside from, even against, the idea of progressive change, at least in so far as this involves a complete correspondence of modernity and commerce, and exhibits misapprehension and anxiety about the dawning of the modern even as it bears witness to it.

Several of the scholars who have over the last twenty years transformed our understanding of the graphic arts of the seventeenth century have made us aware of and had something to say about *Sculptura*, even if they have sometimes approached the task as a necessity rather than a thing of pleasure. In one of his magisterial studies of the Stuart print, Antony Griffiths endeavoured to give Evelyn's text its due, but also termed it "a book that has been more often cited than read", and asserted that "it is not easy to get through from beginning to end."[1] This renewed recognition of *Sculptura* has a context in the wider reassessment of the seventeenth-century print, greatly supported by the digitization of the British Museum's collections (surely one of the defining initiatives of contemporary art-historical research) and Michael Hunter's *British Printed Images to 1700* database.[2]

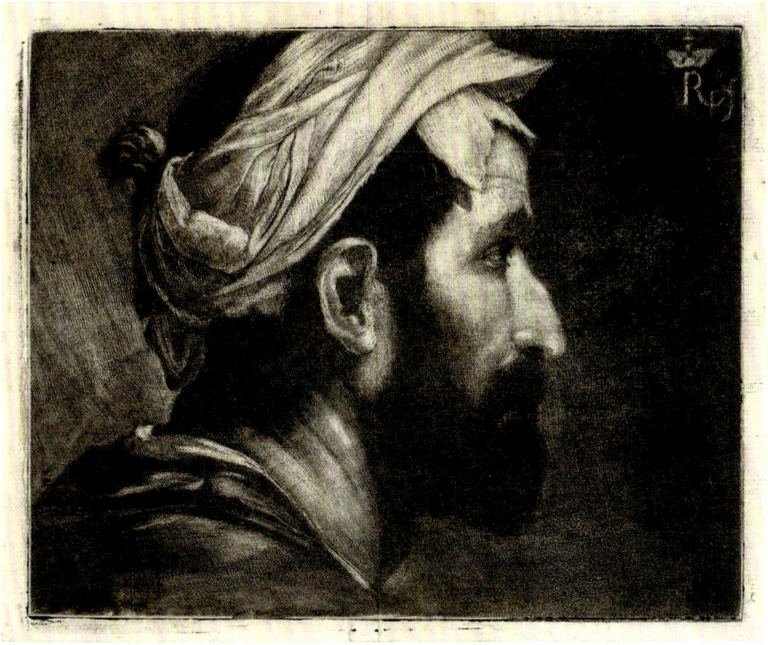

181. Prince Rupert of the Rhine after a follower of José de Ribera, *The Little Executioner*, 1658, mezzotint, 5⅛ x 6½ in. (13.1 x 16.4 cm). British Museum, London

Further focused studies, notably Ben Thomas's account of early mezzotint, have deepened our knowledge of the circumstances of the production and reception of Evelyn's text.[3] Historians of the literature on art and on Restoration intellectual cultures have also given *Sculptura* a context, although the analysis of the text is still routinely marked by reticence about its relevance and literary quality. Johannes Dobai, in his mammoth but routinely overlooked survey of early English art-historical writing, described the book and noted its "diffuse" character.[4] More recently, Craig Ashley Hanson has tried to be yet more generous towards the text, recuperating it as part of an antiquarian intellectual culture and as a "starting point in the literature of prints" and even "an entirely logical starting point for English art-historical writing in general."[5] At the time of writing, Hanson is promising as a future publication "an annotated edition of John Evelyn's 'Sculptura'—one of the first histories of European prints ever published".[6] If he has sought to overcome modern prejudice against the text—and a new edition would surely complete its rehabilitation—he still sees the genealogies of print it contains in terms of "peculiarities" and admits that "Evelyn's narrative buckles under the massive weight of information."[7]

Such reservations have a long history. The publication history of the book does not in itself suggest that there was extensive market interest. After being first published in 1662, the book remained long out of print. There was some talk of republication even within Evelyn's lifetime, but this came to nothing. In 1668 Evelyn was urged by John Beale to publish a new edition with illustrative plates, and in 1689 Evelyn himself said he had made "some Collections" towards this new edition, but was not now sure where those manuscripts were, which hardly suggests he was greatly focused on the project.[8] By 1697 Evelyn recorded that "I had been importun'd to make a second edition of my Chalcography (now grown very scarce)"; but as Griffiths notes, whatever new he might have had to say about engraving had been channelled instead into his *Numismata* (1697).[9] A second edition did not in the event appear until 1755, although when it did it was welcomed by *The Monthly Review*: "This work was originally published in the year 1662, since when its deserved reputation had chiefly confined it to the libraries of the more curious among the learned, so that it has been very scarce."[10] A "Third Edition" was issued with the date 1759 (published by T. Jefferys, Charing-Cross) and a reprint of the 1755 "Second Edition" appeared in 1769 (published by J. Murray, "successor to Mr Sandby"). In Joseph Strutt's dictionary of engravers (1785), *Sculptura* was counted among the handful of published books on engraving, all of which, including Evelyn's, were counted as "defective".[11] A republication appeared within the edition of Evelyn's miscellaneous works edited by William Upcott in 1825, but after that date the book was unavailable until the 1906 Clarendon Press edition.[12] This last remains standard, notwithstanding the reticent introductory commentary by the editor, C. F. Bell, which in the present context is worth considering in itself.

Bell, the first Keeper of Fine Art at the Ashmolean Museum, Oxford, and among other things mentor to Kenneth Clark, has been reckoned "a died-in-the-wool [*sic*] documentary art historian who disliked poetic effusion and admired those who attempted to put art history onto a scientific footing".[13] His brief commentary introducing Evelyn's text reflects a sense of intrigue on his behalf but also a desire to create a sense of distance between the modern editor, as art historian, and the seventeenth-century writer, as antiquarian of miscellaneous, diverse, and sometimes apparently idiosyncratic interests. Bell entertains the possibility that it is only the fame of the author which has saved the treatise being binned as an example of "superannuated technical literature" (xiv). He makes efforts in his introduction to acknowledge an intellectual and historical context for Evelyn's text, and to retrieve it as something worthy of consideration, but his emphatic language registers the struggle felt in coming to terms with, for instance, the "incomprehensibly irrelevant eulogy" of the Italian author Giacomo Maria Favi (vii) which appears at the front of the volume, and, of particular interest here, "the fanciful linking together of sculpture and engraving in this treatise" (xvi) together with the "indiscriminately Catholic" range of historical and technical references (xv) which overwhelm almost every page. Bell was able to conclude that *Sculptura* is an interesting but deeply flawed attempt to "bring art criticism within the sphere of Natural Philosophy" (xx); however, such a positive outcome has evidently been something of a struggle to achieve.

In similar terms, Geoffrey Keynes announced it "a dull, if useful, compilation of names and authorities [which] does not make good reading at the present time", while, reviewing Bell's edition, *The Burlington Magazine* ("for Connoisseurs", as the full title insisted) asserted that "His [Evelyn's] purpose was honourable, and his dry, curious scholarship gives the book a certain literary value; but the part of it which would really be of use to a serious student was just that which he published in a hopelessly cryptic form, or never published at all", that being the translation of Abraham Bosse's practically detailed account of printmaking (which became, instead, the basis of William Faithorne's *The Art of Graveing and Etching*, 1662, often treated as a partner volume to *Sculptura*). The review does concede, if grudgingly, that "the book will have a permanent interest for lovers of engraving from the fact that it contains the earliest announcement (absurdly vague though it is) of the process of mezzotint."[14] This art-historical view of the text has become orthodox: that it is dry, obscure, and largely irrelevant, and that its singular redeeming feature is the glimpse it offers of the emergence of a new print medium. In accounting more generally for its author's life and many, varied intellectual and practical interests, his biographers have offered nothing more in the way of enthusiasm or clarity: Gillian Darley dismisses the whole text as "muddled" and John Bowle describes it as "elaborately pedantic".[15]

Bell's position in effect replays the overriding of antiquarianism which defines the emergence of modern modes of historical writing in the eighteenth century.[16] It echoes, tellingly, Horace Walpole (who has, rightly, been reckoned "always sympathetic to Evelyn").[17] Admiring of Evelyn's learnedness, Walpole nonetheless complained of the cryptic brevity of his account of mezzotint. Evelyn, he perceived:

> was so dazled with the honour of the confidence, or with the curiosity of the new art, that after encouraging the world to expect the communication, he checked his bounty, and determined not to prostitute the Arcanum, but to disclose it only to the elect . . . Thus, as he owns, he leaves it enigmatical.[18]

Elsewhere, he complained of the limitations of Evelyn's style: "Mr Evelyn, who loved to know, was too fond of telling the world all he knew . . . one wishes he had written with a little more judgment."[19] While mild, Walpole's criticisms of his hero are telling, for they mark the limits of his appreciation by defining a boundary between the modern writer of art history, who organizes his material with judgment and decision, and the antiquarian whose output is, however deeply informed and fascinating, disorderly and lacking in self-awareness. Walpole's poising of a fluent, transparent, historically narrated history of art and of printmaking against the "dry", awkward, unreflexive methods of George Vertue (his main source, and target, in this enterprise), helped mark the emergence of the discipline of art history.[20]

What I want to do in this essay is neither simply to challenge the traditional prejudices against *Sculptura* as a piece of writing about art, nor simply to extend our sense of the direct relevance of the text as evidence about the chronology of printmaking in Britain. I propose instead thinking around the challenges of *Sculptura*, and see it as problematizing some key elements of the established narratives of print history. In particular, I want, through this text, to perform two connected, and similarly counter-intuitive manoeuvres: to think about how we can extract "the print" (the printed image) from the larger scholarly discourse around print culture, and to suggest how we might think about printmaking as a three-dimensional rather than a "simply" or self-evidently graphic medium. *Sculptura* draws attention to a sense of dimensionality which is so thoroughly ingrained in modern culture that to expose it at all appears (outside of any highly rarefied scientific or philosophical context) counter-intuitive, even eccentric. The acceptance of the printed image as constituted in two dimensions has compelling disciplinary power.

Making such a claim with respect to a rather technical and narrowly focused treatise may in itself seem rather ambitious, but the genesis of Evelyn's *Sculptura* was inextricably tied to a much larger philosophical project, as well as to a much more particular and practical experiment with the new medium of mezzotint. Evelyn's nineteenth-century editor, Upcott, stated: "He had conceived and planned another work, almost too comprehensive even for his universal genius; this was 'A General History of all Trades' . . . His 'Sculptura' was only one portion of this vast project; he had also prepared treatises on the several arts of painting in oil and in miniature; annealing in glass; enameling; and making marble paper. But none of these were published."[21] This larger project had been conceived in the wake of his Grand Tour in 1652, and worked up by at least 1657. A plan of the whole was developed enough to be presented in outline to the nascent Royal Society in January 1661. In his diary he reported:

> I went to the *Philosophic Club*: where was examin'd the *Torricellian* experiment. I presented my Circle of *Mechanical* Trades, & had recommended to me the publishing what I had written of *Chalcography*.[22]

With this encouragement Evelyn proceeded to draft a full history of engraving. A year and a half later the book was published: on 10 June 1662 he noted: "I returned to Lond: &: presented my *Historie of Chalcographie* (dedicated to Mr *Boyle*) to our *Society*."[23] The final text included, of course, the announcement of the "discovery" of mezzotint. The chronology of Evelyn's exposure to the new medium has been described well before, most recently and carefully by Ben Thomas.[24] Mezzotint must, in fact, have been on Evelyn's mind from the outset. The first documentary reference to the introduction of mezzotint into Britain is the reference in the outline document, "The History of Art Illiberall and Mechanick", dated 16 January 1661, to "Pr: Rupert's new way of ingraving". Famously, Evelyn noted witnessing a demonstration by Prince Rupert of the "new way of ingraving" in a retrospective entry in his diary for 13 March 1661: "This after noone his highnesse Prince Rupert shewed me with his owne hands the new way of Graving, call'd *Mezzo Tinto*, which afterwards I by his permission, I publish'd in my history of *Chalcographie*."[25]

Sculptura is dense with references and allusions, forbidding to modern readers and, given its record of publication and reception, apparently not particularly welcome to many readers in the past. Broadly, *Sculptura* provides an account of the printed image which by taking account of the material specificity of the copperplate as a three-dimensional object (capable of creating an image because it is incised) and of the image as a form of communication (conveying meaning through a conventionalized array of lines and marks) connects the narrower history of the modern print (i.e. the familiar one which starts in the Renaissance) with the history of writing itself, which in originating with incised marks (exemplified in the Mosaic tablets but also pre-dating these) takes us back to the very beginnings of human history. The narrative which we can pick out from all those references is unfamiliar, ungainly, and even preposterous. Printmaking, by being sculpture, is integrated into a massive, totalizing vision of human enterprise over history back to the beginning of time. In chapter II we read:

> We shall not, with *Epigenes* in *Pliny*, depose that this Art had its being from Eternity, because it is not sence, and would contradict its invention; but, if that may passe with St *Augustine* affirmes, that the *Protoplast*, our father *Adam*, or his good *Genius* the *Angel Raziel*, were as the first inventor of Letters, *Sculpture* may derive its pedigree from the infancy of the World, and contend for its Pre-eminence with most of the Antiquities which it so much celebrates . . . whoever was the inventor of *Letters*, was also doubtless the father of *Sculpture*.[26]

What we might reasonably consider as a conventional history of engraving, with its starting point in the introduction of intaglio printmaking for specifically artistic uses in the fifteenth century, is only initiated in chapter IV of *Sculptura*, and as the single extended quote given here should make clear, Evelyn has covered a huge amount up to this point. When Horace Walpole covered the same ground in the opening lines of his *Catalogue of Engravers*, such speculation was simply cast aside in favour of a definitive sense of chronology: "printing was not discovered till about the year 1430: in thirty years more it was applied to the multiplication of drawings."[27]

The technical history of what we would recognize as a print is, then, in Evelyn's account, only an episode in the longer history of human communication. Printmaking is, rather than a specifically technical matter, fundamentally about how knowledge can be retained and relayed. William B. MacGregor asserted in his 1999 essay on the early modern print, that "the key cognitive metaphor of the period [was] borrowed from the language of printmaking to explain the creation and storage of mental images."[28] Thus, in Locke: "There seems to be a constant decay of our minds, even of those which are struck deepest and in minds the most retentive: so that, if they be not sometimes renewed by repeated exercise of the senses or reflection on those kind of objects which first occasioned them, the print wears out and at last there remains nothing to be seen."[29] Evelyn's *Sculptura* conceives of the relation between print and the mental image as less than metaphorical, and rather more literal. The physicality of sculpture appears in Evelyn to be a guarantor of value: it is sculpture (engraving) which preserves the "sacred person" of the monarch, while it is "vile *copies* multiplyed from an ill Painting" which defiles the royal image.[30] "*Copies*", states Evelyn, in a passage strikingly counter-intuitive to a modern reader, "are in *Prints* much more easily detected, then in *paintings* . . . to discern an *Original print* from a *Copy-print* . . . is a knack very easily attain'd; because 'tis almost impossible to imitate every *hatch*, and to make the stroaks of exact and equal dimensions, where every the least defect, or flaw in the Copper itself, is sufficient to detect and betray the Imposture."[31] As Adrian Johns has noted of *Sculptura*, in such passages the treatise served as a means of helping elite readers understand and test out images as sources of reliable information, something that was key to the self-image of modern intellectual circles associated with the Royal Society, separating them as modern, Protestant, progressive thinkers from their superstitious and tyrannized Catholic forbears.[32]

But if Evelyn's account of print as sculpture sits well with contemporary philosophical attitudes towards the nature of mind, and could therefore be accounted for as part of a modernizing secularization of knowledge, there is still an older and contrary set of associations in play here as well. As Charles Talbot explored in a 1986 essay on the early print:

> The element of physical contact in printmaking, which resulted in one thing transferring its image to another, had connotations of its own. It accounted for the fact that the impression, like a fingerprint, was a one-to-one replication of the original form in mirror image, and therefore was a true and reliable image. But there was also a symbolic, perhaps mysterious side to this. Since the print had pressed against the form-giving object, some invisible quality of that former presence might be thought to remain attached to the impression. This phenomenon is akin to the meaning of the touch in certain other situations. Authority and rank were conferred with gestures of touching, and clothing could acquire the status of a sacred relic when it had been worn by a saint.[33]

Michael Gaudio has extended the idea considerably (perhaps beyond breaking point): "While engraving, of course, cannot be classified as a sculptural work in the round like the cult statue, its early modern practitioners and collectors still considered it to belong to the same art form that had catalysed the Reformation's controversy over religious images in the first place."[34] Evelyn, most forcibly in connection with his fears about the royal image, retains a sense of this sacred conception of the image as materially impressed with value. It is, in this account, the physical character of the material object of engraving which helps provide its value.

Half a century after Evelyn, the engraver and art chronicler George Vertue brought Evelyn's terminology into play in unpublished notes prepared for a prospective book on printmaking which he never completed. As deployed by Vertue, there is a sense of valiant defensiveness, of battling against history and the irresistible forces of commerce in the physical sense of the engraved plate:

> Of these works of the Graver cut in, may be properly expressed by the word Burin-Sculpture, Burination, the Burinator, or burinavit, from the Greek work, Burim—or plowing—or plough share, for it is properly and naturally a plowing in brass or metal of any kind—like furrowing—in all degrees necessary.[35]

This is contrasted with etching "done with the point or needle on grounds and eaten in with Aquafortis . . . an invention for Expedition", and mezzotint, a process of "scraping on the copper" which takes "one fourth the time". This shift from the material to the immaterial, the deep to the shallow, the sculptural to the graphic, is fundamental to this transformed understanding of print in this period. The triumph of William Hogarth as model of autonomous engraver-artist-publisher, and of print as fluid commodity, protected by law, pivoted on this change: "It is in connection with the Engraver's Act, I think, that we can find the earliest explicit recognition of the immateriality of the commodity created by intellectual property law—that is, the clear distinction between the artist's invention or design and the piece of paper on which it is imprinted."[36] To apprehend such is to do more than the habitual linking of Hogarth with consumerism, and to register instead the epistemic break necessary for the "silent revolution" of print capitalism.[37] We might jump forward to the introduction of aquatint, vaunted by Peter Perez Burdett in the early 1770s: "It is by a chemical & not a mechanical operation these superior beauties are imitated" (1771).[38] He exhibited aquatints in 1773 with the note that they are printed "from a plate wrought chemically, without the use of any instrument of sculpture".[39] Sculpture is "old school", the physical is old school, the hand and tool belong to a world which is passing; the new world is chemical, beyond human; the artisan has given way to the scientist, the physically unique to the multiple. Evelyn apprehends the advent of a normative definition of sculpture, enshrined in the Oxford English Dictionary entry:

> *Originally*, the process of carving or engraving a hard material so as to produce designs or figures in relief, in intaglio, or in the round. *In modern use*, that branch of fine art which is concerned with the production of figures in the round or in relief, either by carving, by fashioning some plastic substance, or by making a mould for casting in metal; the practice of this art. Now chiefly used with reference to work in stone (esp. marble) or bronze (similar to work in wood, ivory, etc. being spoken of as *carving*), and to the production of figures of considerable size. Thus to apply the term, e.g. to die-sinking or to stone-carving on a small scale would now be considered as a transferred use.[40]

Definition "3", marked as "obsolete", has "A picture or illustration printed from an engraving plate or block; and engraving; engravings collectively", which is illustrated with quotes mainly from the late seventeenth century.

This is not a matter of precise and definitive historical changes in language. There are any number of later technical treatises and dictionaries where sculpture and engraving are linked; and you can of course find a limitless supply of prints inscribed "Sc" or "Sculp" from later centuries, making absolutely conventional a continued use of that affiliation. Abraham Bosse had anticipated (and doubtless informed) Evelyn in proclaiming engraving's liberal identity on the basis of its relationship with a range of inscribed communications going back to Moses, and the use of "Sculpture" as a term for printed images appears, in fact, to have been continuous and casual in English-language publications throughout the period

1660–1735.[41] But if the title of an example of a later treatise on the art of engraving, *Sculptura-Historico-Technica and the Art of Ingraving* (London, 1747), seems to continue Evelyn's usage, it also draws a sharper line between printmaking and "Sculpture" and provides a historical account of the practice which, taking as its starting point fourteenth-century Florence, is (from our modern perspective) normalized. When Evelyn's editor remarked in 1906 that his linking of sculpture and engraving in a shared history was "fanciful", he was reflecting a significant shift in usage. A modern commentator like Joseph Levine seems genuinely surprised to discover that *Sculptura* is largely about engraving, and seems almost to suggest that Evelyn himself was simply misled in talking about print rather than three-dimensional art: "Apparently", he says, "he [claims] any form of carving or molding as a kind of sculpture."[42]

The main body of Evelyn's text provides an account of printmaking which stands against our assumptions of print's modernity. There may be a parallel here to the shift Lisa Maruca traces between Joseph Moxon's manual on typography (1683), produced like *Sculptura* from the orbit of the Royal Society as a contribution to the History of Trades, and a later (1755) treatise on printing by Joseph Smith:

> In Moxon's manual . . . the body of print emerges as a working body, a laborer whose physical construction of print is every bit as, if not more, important than the writer who supplies text. Indeed, the print worker is understood as a *collaborator* in the construction of the meaning of the print text. By the time Smith wrote his manual, however, the working body had dissolved into the subject writing, the transcendent Author, whose disembodied intellect is privileged over the physical book.[43]

Maruca asserts that even if the outlook represented by Smith became dominant, to the point that it is hard to read Moxon, "to adopt these notions as an 'essential' aspect of the print medium is to accede too swiftly or readily to this regime."[44] I would contend that, accounted for historically, Evelyn, like Moxon, can be positioned as a point of (perhaps already belated) resistance to the disembodying or dissolution of print as a symptom of modernity. Our dismay, frustration, and confusion at Evelyn's text stems, to some extent, from the degree to which it fails to accord with the accepted idea of a print revolution which was (as the phrase itself suggests) more sudden, traumatic, and progressive than Evelyn could possibly allow for. An account of the print which goes back to pre-history, which is dignified by divine associations, and which stresses the sculptural solidity and stature of the engraving process, seems irredeemably alien.

Now, clearly, a great deal of the best work on print history has made its intellectual advances through thinking about prints in a larger cultural context, as part of a wider realm of print. However, we can still ask whether by folding the graphic image into the "print revolution" of the late seventeenth century—what Dror Wahrman has recently termed "Print 2.0"—we are complicit with print capitalism's defining narratives, pivoting as they do around acceleration, expansion, penetration, efficiency, and extent.[45] Evelyn's conception of print as sculpture is resistant to such complicity; his reticence about the technical character of mezzotint exposes his anxieties. If these characteristics constitute *Sculptura*'s oddness in our eyes, they also register its sense of modernity, not as a fixed condition but as a "conviction of historical *difference*".[46] For all its antiquarian erudition, Evelyn's text was deeply tied to a sense of historical change, and he several times alluded to his perception that the art of engraving was changing, improving, and growing: prompted to think about a new edition in 1697, he reflected on "so greate an improvement of Sculpture" which he had seen in the intervening thirty-or-so years.[47] In his own copy of *Sculptura*, he noted at some unknown date: "this [mezzotint] is since the publishing of this, arriv'd to the utmost curiosity."[48]

Evidently there is no denying a print revolution, and one which involved the graphic image quite centrally. The material evidence is overwhelming, indicated for instance in the fact that F. G. Stephens was able to get through the British Museum's collection of satires dating from 1320 to 1733 in two volumes, while M. Dorothy George took ten thick volumes for the next century's worth of material.[49] How that material evidence is interpreted and characterized is another matter. It is, quite understandably, conventional to think of the print revolution as an upsurge, a flood or avalanche. Mark Hallett, for instance, writes that in the early eighteenth century:

> print shops had become fluid centres of visual culture in the city, selling both high and low forms of graphic art. As their numbers increased, and as the passage of prints across their counters became ever more hurried, they emerged as ubiquitous, bustling, and highly visible centres of the print trade. Engravings would not only crowd the interior of such shops, and be put on display in their windows, but frequently would also spill haphazardly into the street itself, pinned to the door or window frame, and hung on boards standing outside.[50]

Hallett has exposed how the genre of the medley print exemplified a new world of commercial print production, quite literally graphically interweaving news, gossip, art, and polemic in densely layered images (fig. 182). The first words of Michael

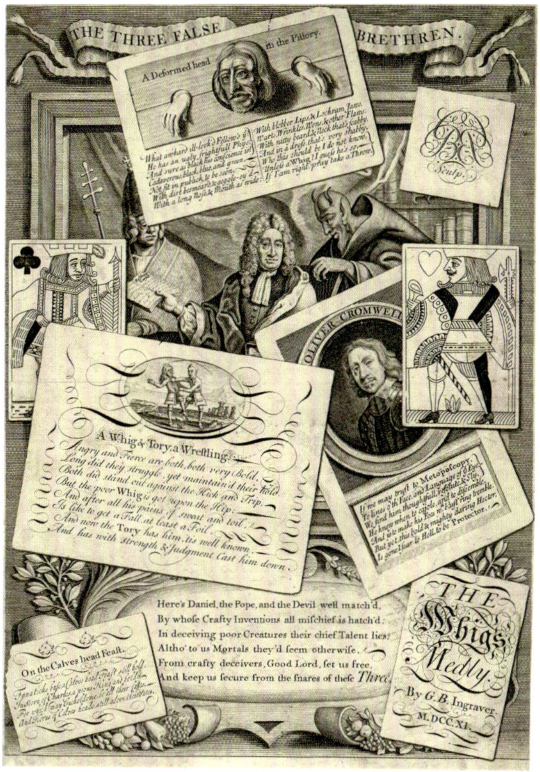

182. George Bickham the Elder, *The Whig's Medly / The Three False Brethren*, 1711, etching and engraving, 15⅛ x 10¾ in. (38.5 x 27.3 cm). British Museum, London

Hunter's essay collection, *Printed Images in Early Modern Britain*, announce that: "Printed images were ubiquitous in early modern Britain . . . Wherever they were to be found, they served a multiplicity of purposes in people's lives, from the functional to the recreational or decorative."[51] Wahrman's account of "Print 2.0" builds excitedly on such observations: "The key to the qualitative difference of Print 2.0 was ephemerality . . . it was a true breakthrough, in terms of sheer scale, staying power, reach, ubiquity . . . London was abuzz with the new possibilities—and possible dangers—of an unfettered flood of cheap, ephemeral information pouring from the press."[52]

Evidently, many contemporaries bore witness to the material changes in print and its circulation, in terms which support this characterization. Outside of *Sculptura*, Evelyn himself was well aware of the changes around him, in the range and availability of graphic products. Mezzotint has an important role to play in these narratives of commercial expansion. The capacity of the medium to render tonal and textural effects with greater illusion and immediacy than line engraving meant that it became associated with sensational, sensual, and therefore commercial,

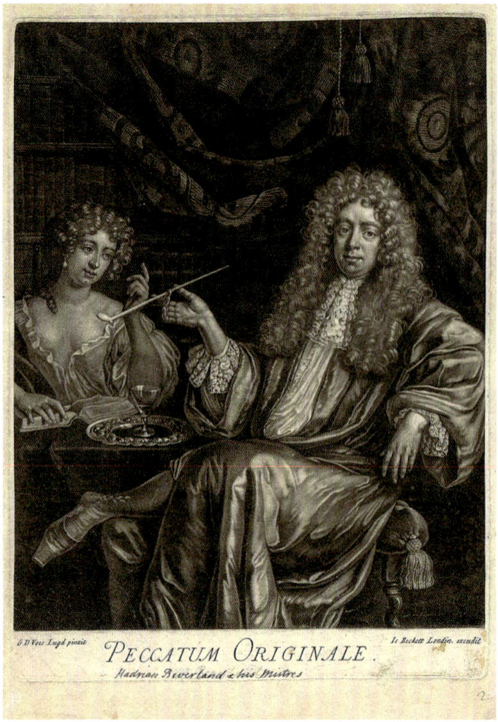

183. Isaac Becket after Arie de Vos, *Peccatum Originale (Hadrian Beverland & his Mistres)*, 1686, mezzotint, 13½ x 10 in. (34.2 x 25.5 cm). British Museum, London

subject matters. The print-seller Pierce Tempest wrote tellingly to Francis Place in 1686, remarking that mezzotints "doe sell a little, especially fancy's Heads and bawdy".[53] In his influential *Groot schilderboek* (1707), Gérard de Lairesse recommended it for "portraits, night and candle-pieces, spectres and enchantments, apparitions, flowers, fruits, silver, gold, china-ware, crystal, arms and herbs".[54] Images like Isaac Beckett's mezzotint portrait of the licentious writer Adrian Beverland, tellingly labelled *Peccatum Originale* ("Original sin") (fig. 183), or Robert Robinson's mezzotint still lifes (fig. 184), make the most of the velvety luxuriousness of the medium in representing subjects which by their nature are about the theme of luxuriousness itself, about sensuality, the body and its gratification, produced in an era of expanding materialism.

These specific images, and mezzotint as a medium more generally, might readily be folded into a larger narrative about modernity, equated with the ascent of materialism, commercialization, private pleasures, and accelerated communication networks. But we may need to pause when considering this. Writing in relation to the emergence of the literary market in seventeenth-century France, Geoffrey Turnovsky has insisted that the transformations which we identify as

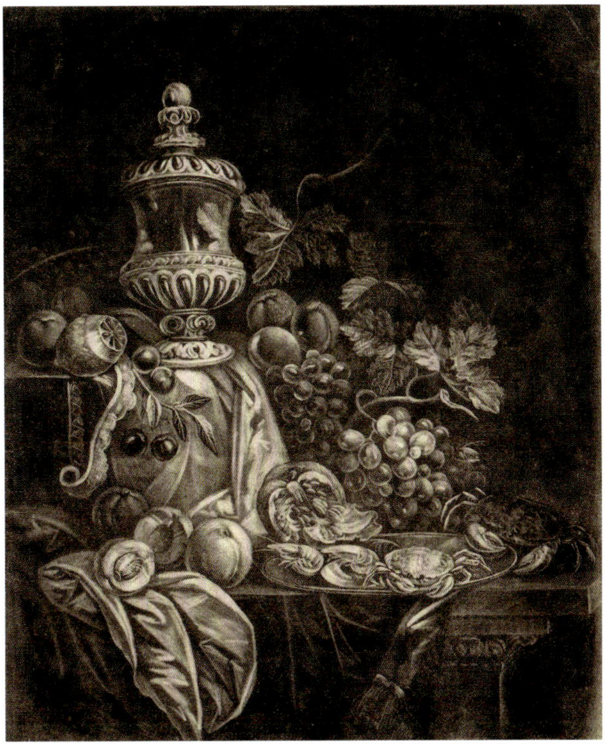

184. Robert Robinson, *Banquet Piece with Tobacco Jar*, undated, mezzotint, 8¾ x 7½ in. (22.2 x 19.1 cm). Yale Center for British Art, Paul Mellon Fund

modernization were not simply, self-evidently, or inevitably the result of an "'objective' expansion of the print trade": while the material conditions of production evidently did change, that need not be assumed as co-extensive with "modernity".[55] Modernity instead arises within polemical battles which are founded in and refer to material circumstances rather than being absolutely and directly defined by those circumstances in a utilitarian or functionalist sense. Even if there are any number of late seventeenth-century witnesses to the upsurge of the printed image, as part of a wider expansion of print, the question of whether we are simply right to identify in the form of specific technical developments (new media, marketing, and the expansion of production) the advent of "modernity" may be more moot.

Firstly, there are ways of thinking around print (the printed image) aside from this wider print culture. Compared to type, the printed image could be slow, expensive, and inconvenient in its preparation and production. Bibliographers give quite another story about the engraved image to that presented by "Print 2.0". Copperplate printing and the printing of type were distinct activities, generally undertaken with different equipment and skills in different physical locations. Copperplate printers and letterpress printers worked to quite different scales and paces: 3,000 printed pages could be produced in raised type in one day; as few as 180 intaglio prints might be produced in the same period. Writing on the technical details of the printing house and engraving shop in the period, Roger Gaskell surmises that the production of one engraved sheet cost the same as three letterpress sheets, so that adding one illustrational plate to a quarto of 240 pages in an edition of 500 would add 5 percent to the overall costs.[56] In the context of the printed book at least, the printed image was far from simply being part of an accelerating, ever more efficient print world. Mezzotint itself, for all its fluency in rendering tonal effects and making newly available to viewers the manifold sensual associations of texture, was not well suited to mass production: the finely textured surface of the prepared copperplate was simply too vulnerable to allow very large editions without reworking. The famous mezzotint plate for *Sculptura* could only be printed one hundred times without the need for renewal, and the format of the print meant that it had to be folded in (the pristine impression illustrated here must not have been included in the book itself).[57] Evelyn himself acknowledged that the major drawback of this new medium was the limited print run it allowed, noting that "the plates last not so long under the rolling-press."[58]

The new studies of the post-Restoration print have endeavoured to break down "some of the technical and disciplinary boundaries" which have separated media, formats, and visual and textual productions, in an effort towards "doing justice to the overall significance of early printed images".[59] Such studies are allied to a conception of print culture underpinning the commercial or public sphere, wherein text and image were in intimate and dynamic dialogue, exemplified in the productions of William Hogarth, posited as the figure who heralds a new model of the artist-entrepreneur. "All of these media forms", asserts John Bender, "could serve the easy flow between inwardness and open exchange among the informed public that Habermas describes", being part of "a burgeoning commercial market purveying the clothing, images, books, furniture, objects of use, and even the taste that marked membership in its domain".[60] There may nonetheless be a need for reasserting those boundaries, or at least recognizing the historicity of those boundaries and therefore the historically bounded characteristics of our own efforts. As Joseph A. Dane has observed, the term "print culture" has proliferated in scholarly literature since around 1980, becoming, in his view, dangerously imprecise and misleading.[61] For Dane the turning point came with the newly illustrated, abridged edition of Elizabeth L. Eisenstein's study of the growth of print, issued as *The Printing Press as an Agent of Change* (1979), in which "print culture, is no longer dependent on material books as were earlier studies on the early history of printing. Print culture is something different from the institution and procedure of printing, and something different from print or what one finds in books." In fact,

Eisenstein herself latterly recoiled from the overuse of the term: "the term 'print culture' is being employed in so many diverse contexts that it is in danger of becoming a meaningless cliché."[62]

Reading Evelyn now might lead us to rethink our own assumptions about the nature of print's relationship with modernity and with capitalism (and even whether these two latter terms can properly be identified with one another). Intaglio printmaking in *Sculptura* is not quick, easy, novel, commercialized, secularized, eminently reproducible, or even two-dimensional in the way that we might imagine it to be from the perspective of modern "print culture". It is ancient, difficult, unique, mysterious, allied to the sacred, and, above all, sculptural. In this it edges towards becoming, as many commentators from subsequent eras recognize, absurd. In its intellectual context, *Sculptura* was part of a collective effort towards experiment, "lifting the limits of the thinkable", without the certainties of disciplinary knowledge, or of disciplinarity itself, as these subsequently took shape; in these circumstances, as Adrian Johns highlights, the "criteria for discriminating the rational from the ridiculous were themselves likely to prove violently contentious".[63] Like Robert Hooke, with the famous illustration included in *Micrographia* (1685) of a printed dot of ink revealed, under magnification, to have the gross physicality of a "great splotch of *London* dirt", Evelyn exposes the printed image as having a materiality contrary to our expectations or immediate perceptions.[64]

Evelyn was not, though, making an empirical observation of the material world with primarily philosophical implications. He was writing about a set of image-making activities that were professionalized and commercial, and he knew it. As Johns notes: "what to men like John Evelyn seemed a self-evidently worthwhile subjection to rational inquiry was to [artisans] an economically disastrous revelation of valuable and proprietary techniques."[65] Responding to Robert Boyle's encouragement to undertake the writing of a full history of trades in the 1650s, Evelyn expressed reservations given the political context at that time, "least by it, should also disoblige some, who make those professions their living; or at least, debase much of their esteeme, by prostituting them to the vulgar".[66] In thinking about putting together a series of treatises on artistic techniques, Evelyn in 1657 wrote that: "I have since been put off from that design, not knowing whether I should do well to gratify so barbarous an age (as I fear is approaching) with curiosities of that nature."[67] Seeing on the one hand new knowledge and new techniques, and, on the other, a political and economic environment which looked to be assuming (from his perspective) potentially unmanageable new forms, Evelyn was not sure in himself whether the publication of knowledge could be justified. In *Sculptura* Evelyn elaborates in (to us) excruciating detail an antiquarian account of printmaking history which is rooted in a sense of the depth (even physical depth), slowness, and skilfulness of intaglio printmaking. Yet he also announces and celebrates a medium which in some regards seemed to be on the point of superseding intaglio—mezzotint. As he announces, he also withdraws. He states that he has full technical information on this new technique, but "I did not think it necessary that an *Art* so curious, and (as yet) so little vulgar (and which indeed does not succeed where the *Workman* is not an accomplished *Designer*, and has competent talent in *painting* likewise) was to be prostituted at so cheap a rate, as the more naked describing of it here would too have expos'd it to."[68] This selective dissemination of knowledge was matched in practice. As Griffiths has noted, Evelyn was prepared to demonstrate the mezzotint process to Samuel Pepys but not to the professional printmaker William Faithorne.[69]

Evelyn's reticence has been the source of complaint for almost every commentator from Walpole onwards. We can begin to make sense of Evelyn's equivocation in biographical terms—he was at the time of preparing and writing *Sculptura*, in Michael Hunter's phrase, "a Virtuoso in Quest of a Role", uncertain of his place in a changing world.[70] Darley personalizes it entirely, identifying it as "a release from bewildering political realities . . . a very personal subject . . . its strengths and weaknesses were those of its author, by turns well informed and perceptive, prolix and discerning".[71] Even Griffiths sees it as "a form of exorcism. By draining himself dry of everything he knew about prints, he could put them behind him, and start afresh on new paths."[72] But beyond the specificity of biography, there is a broader sense in which Evelyn registers the ambivalence of intellectual culture at this moment—compelled to publicity, yet also tied to a sense of rank and social exclusion. Under the aegis of the Royal Society and the new philosophy, knowledge may be validated by public scrutiny, but the definition of that public was moot in the extreme. And we might make an even bolder and bigger claim—that Evelyn's equivocal apprehension of modernity in printmaking exposes the limits of that modernity. Or, rather, that it embodies a sense of modernity, in apprehending historical difference—the same sense of historical difference that Thomas Sprat exposed contemporaneously in his 1667 history of the Royal Society: "now the World is become more *active and industrious*", the nobility "more apply themselves to *Traffic and Business than ever* . . . It is now most certain that in those Coasts, whither the greatest Trade shall constantly flow, the greatest *Riches and Power* will be establish'd."[73] The shift from Commonwealth ("barbarous" in Evelyn's terms), to restored monarchy had not simply and completely re-established an old order; even as ancient and dignified an activity as engraving (as conceived in *Sculptura*) could be pursued only in a radically novel environment of fluid commercial and social relations.

In *Sculptura* Evelyn sets out to give an account of intaglio printmaking as a fundamental feature of human progress, given to mankind by divinity as a form of communication, and practised with distinction over an extended history. Based on its material fixity, printmaking, as a form of sculpture, embodies and relays knowledge, in a more reliable and accurate way than any other medium, certainly painting or drawing. Mezzotint, as a new technical development, is positioned historically as a climax of this history (as he said elsewhere, it has "arrived at the utmost curiosity and accurateness"), but in an environment which provided little regulation on its use or dissemination. He puts a limitation on technical progress by, rather unexpectedly, evoking sexual proprieties: the spread of print becomes, suddenly, a matter of morality. In historical perspective, standing against the "prostitution" of print on the marketplace opened Evelyn to the accusations of eccentricity, other-worldliness, and irrelevance which have been the constant in commentaries on *Sculptura*. As Craig Ashley Hanson has detailed most recently, the figure of the virtuoso was a target for satire, particularly for engaging in experiments which seemed useless or absurd—like, you might say, weighing air, the very experiment Evelyn witnessed before presenting his paper on the "Circle of Mechanical Trades" in January 1661.[74] Evelyn's conception of print as having three-dimensional objectivity is not, clearly, about the print itself as an artefact (commodity): it is about the fact that the process of printmaking itself is a spatial practice: it involves cutting, scratching, the removal and impressing of hard matter. It was more like Hooke's surprising apprehension of the printed full stop as a physical thing, a tiny dot of ink becoming, under magnification, a material thing of (comically) unexpected proportions (fig. 185). Establishing a print as a sculptural artefact, or measuring the relative surface depth of engraving, aquatint, or mezzotint, as Vertue subsequently did, might be counted alongside such apparently extravagant experimentation.

What Evelyn's text does above all, in its impenetrability to modern readings, in what it leaves out and keeps secret, in its irrelevance and illegibility, is tell us how deeply the values of commercial modernity have penetrated, so that it is almost impossible to think of print as sculpture. It is similarly difficult to think of the print away from the sense of graphic avalanche or flood that defines the meta-narrative of the emergence of modern print culture (to the near exclusion of other models), with Hogarth at its heart: "All commentary on Hogarth begins in want and ends in surfeit. His images filled the blank slate of modern consciousness to overflowing with their antic inventiveness, moral urgency, and keen humour."[75] Accordingly, if we are able now to read Evelyn and to see print as sculpture, we might also find a way to think around and away from that commercial modernity and to historicize our understanding of the emergence of a public sphere as some-

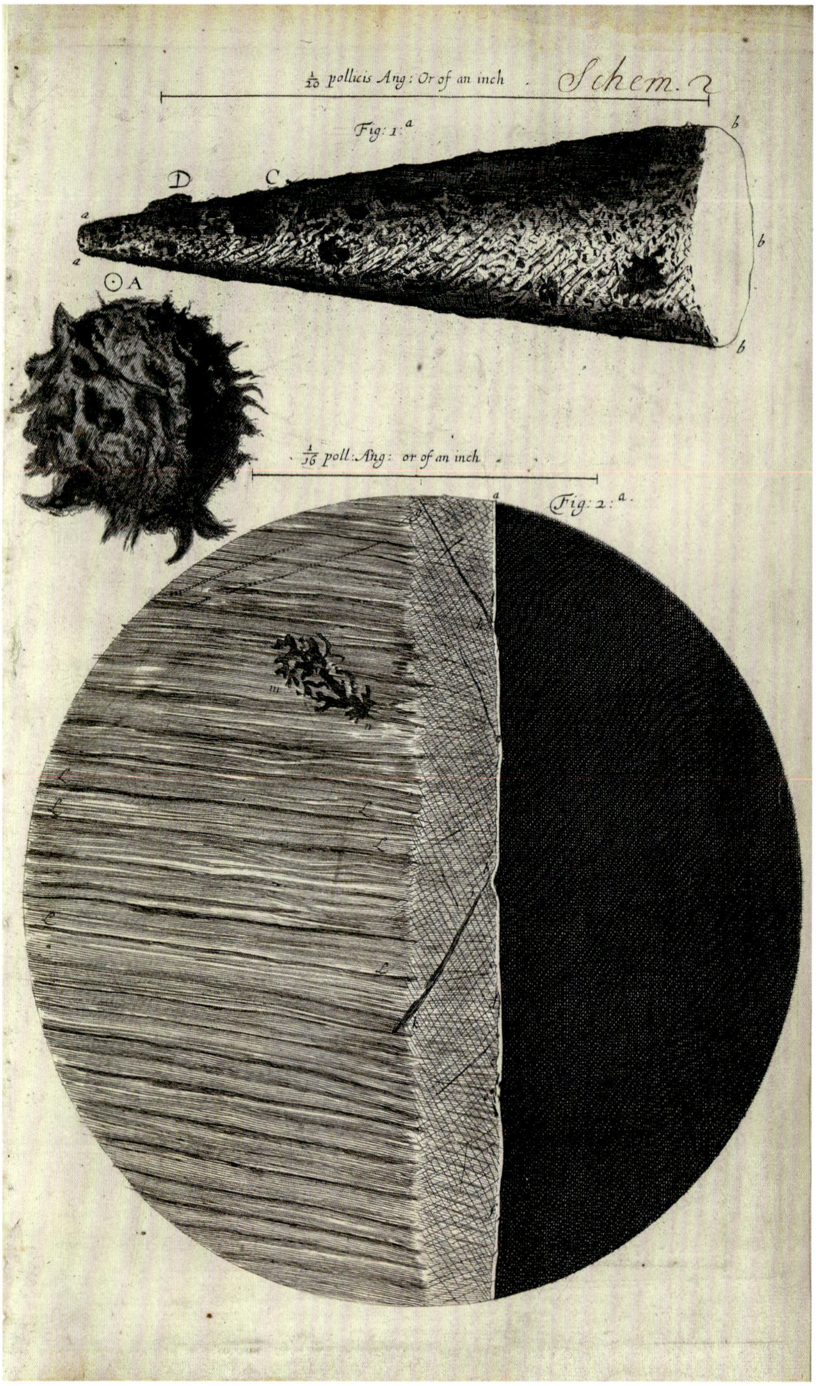

185. Robert Hooke, "Schem. II: Illustrations showing microscopic views . . .", in Robert Hooke, *Micrographia: or Some Physiological Descriptions of Minute Bodies Made by Magnifying Glasses with Observations and Inquiries Thereupon* (London, 1665), engraving, 12 x 6¾ in. (30.5 x 17 cm). The Royal Society, London. This schematic illustrates microscopic views of the point of a needle (Fig. 1); a printed period [a "full-stop"], original size and magnified (A); and the edge of a razor (Fig. 2).

thing that was actively brought into being rather than arising inevitably from technical and economic change. The naturalizing language which characterizes attempts to understand the emergence of a modern print culture in the period 1660–1735 ("flood", "avalanche", "outpouring", and so on) may have a descriptive force, but it may also convey a greater sense of inevitability than was the case; or, rather, it adds to the difficulty of interpreting resistance to or alternatives from that historical development.

It is surely no accident that an at least half-serious modern-day bid to revive the term "chalcography" took place in the context of writing about the visionary printmaker and poet William Blake, in the knowledge of Evelyn's precedent.[76] Blake, as Morris Eaves has detected, is Evelyn's heir with regards to understanding the sculptural materiality of intaglio printmaking, and bestowing value (even spiritual value) on it accordingly.[77] How Evelyn conceives of printmaking, and the historical narratives he connects it to, are alien to us. In the simplest terms, we find *Sculptura* a hard read. But this difficulty is worth dwelling on: it indicates the bounds of the normative being put into place, the functional limits on thinking imposed by commercial modernity. If those limits are hardly in reality to be actively disregarded now—to do so wholeheartedly is to risk social exclusion in one way or another—neither is it that they have inevitably to be left unexamined.

1. Antony Griffiths, "John Evelyn and the Print", in *John Evelyn and his Milieu*, ed. Frances Harris and Michael Hunter (London: The British Library, 2003), 95.
2. Antony Griffiths, *The Print in Stuart Britain, 1603–1689* (London: British Museum Press, 1998); Tim Clayton, *The English Print, 1688–1802* (New Haven and London: Yale Univ. Press, 1997); Malcolm Jones, *The Print in Early Modern England: An Historical Oversight* (New Haven and London, Yale Univ. Press, 2010); Michael Hunter, ed., *Printed Images in Early Modern Britain: Essays in Interpretation* (Farnham: Ashgate, 2010). *The British Museum Collection* database is at http://www.britishmuseum.org/research/collection_online/search.aspx; *British Printed Images to 1700* is at http://www.bpi1700.org.uk/index.html.
3. Ben Thomas, "Noble or Commercial? The Early History of Mezzotint in Britain", in Hunter, ed., *Printed Images*, 279–96. See also Ben Thomas's exhibition catalogue, *The Paradox of Mezzotint* (Museum of Canterbury, 2008), and his "John Evelyn's Project of Translation", *Art in Print* 2, no. 4 (2012): 28–34.
4. Johannes Dobai, *Die Kunstliteratur des Klassizismus und der Romantik in England*, vol. 1, *1700–1750* (Bern: Benteli, 1974), 702.
5. Craig Ashley Hanson, *The English Virtuoso: Art, Medicine, and Antiquarianism in the Age of Empiricism* (Chicago and London: Chicago Univ. Press, 2009), 83.
6. http://www.calvin.edu/academic/art/about/faculty/hanson/.
7. Hanson, *English Virtuoso*, 80–83.
8. Gillian Darley, *John Evelyn: Living for Ingenuity* (New Haven and London, Yale Univ. Press, 2006), 179. On the publication history, see Geoffrey Keynes, *John Evelyn: A Study in Bibliophily and a Bibliography of his Writings* (Cambridge Univ. Press, 1937), 116–19, and also Howard C. Levis, *Extracts from the Diaries and Correspondence of John Evelyn and Samuel Pepys Relating to Engraving* (London: Ellis, 1915).
9. Levis, *Extracts*, 94, Griffiths, "John Evelyn and the Print", 107–8.

10. *The Monthly Review* 12 (May 1755): 390–91.
11. Joseph Strutt, *A Biographical Dictionary; Containing an Historical Account of all the Engravers, from the earliest period of the art of engraving to the present time*, 2 vols. (London, 1785), 1: v–vi.
12. *The Miscellaneous Writings of John Evelyn*, ed. William Upcott (London: Henry Colburn, 1825), *Evelyn's Sculptura with the Unpublished Second Part*, ed. C. F. Bell (Oxford: Clarendon Press, 1906).
13. Jon Whitely, Aug. 2009, quoted in the article on Bell appearing online at https://dictionaryofarthistorians.org/bellcf.htm.
14. Keynes, *John Evelyn*, 116, *The Burlington Magazine* 10, no. 46 (Jan. 1907): 266.
15. Darley, *John Evelyn*, 179, John Bowle, *John Evelyn and his World: A Biography* (London: Routledge and Kegan Paul, 1981), 102.
16. See the classic article by Arnaldo Momigliano, "Ancient History and the Antiquarian", *Journal of the Warburg and Courtauld Institutes* 13 (1950): 285–315.
17. Austin Dobson, ed., *The Diary of John Evelyn*, 3 vols. (London and New York: Macmillan, 1906), 1: liii.
18. Horace Walpole, *A Catalogue of Engravers who have been born, or resided in England* (Strawberry Hill, 1763), 74.
19. Horace Walpole, *Anecdotes of Painting in England*, 4 vols. (Strawberry Hill, 1762), 2: 38.
20. See Martin Myrone, "Graphic Antiquarianism in Eighteenth-century Britain: The Career and Reputation of George Vertue (1684–1756)", in *Producing the Past: Aspects of Antiquarian Culture and Practice, 1700–1850*, ed. Martin Myrone and Lucy Peltz (Aldershot: Ashgate, 1999), 35–54.
21. Upcott, ed., *Miscellaneous Writings of John Evelyn*, xxi. On the intellectual context of the History of Trades, see Walter E. Houghton, "The History of Trades: Its Relation to Seventeenth-century Thought", *Journal of the History of Ideas* 2, no. 1 (Jan. 1941): 33–60, and Kathleen H. Ochs, "The Royal Society of London's History of Trades Programme: An Early Episode in Applied Science", *Notes and Records of the Royal Society of London* 39, no. 2 (1985): 129–58.
22. E. S. De Beer, ed., *The Diary of John Evelyn*, 6 vols. (Oxford Univ. Press, 1955), 3: 268.
23. De Beer, ed., *Diary of John Evelyn*, 3: 325.
24. See note 3 above.
25. De Beer, ed., *Diary of John Evelyn*, 3: 274.
26. Bell, ed., *Evelyn's Sculptura*, 11.
27. Walpole, *Catalogue of Engravers*, 1.
28. William B. MacGregor, "The Authority of Prints: An Early Modern Perspective", *Art History* 22, no. 3 (Sept. 1999): 390.
29. Quoted in MacGregor, "Authority of Prints", 416.
30. Bell, ed., *Evelyn's Sculptura*, 25.
31. Bell, ed., *Evelyn's Sculptura*, 129.
32. Adrian Johns, *The Nature of the Book: Print and Knowledge in the Making* (Chicago and London: Chicago Univ. Press, 2009), 434.
33. Charles Talbot, "Prints and the Definitive Image", in *Print and Culture in the Renaissance: Essays on the Advent of Printing in Europe*, ed. Gerald P. Tyson and Sylvia S. Wagonheim (London and Toronto: Associated Univ. Presses, 1986), 200–1. In this context, the renewal of the Royal Touch by Charles II is suggestive, indicating a continued faith in the sacred power of physical contact; see Jane Shaw, *Miracles in Enlightenment England* (New Haven and London: Yale Univ. Press, 2006), 64–73.
34. Michael Gaudio, *Engraving the Savage: The New World and Techniques of Civilization* (Minneapolis and London: Univ. of Minnesota Press, 2008), 100. The whole of the chapter from which this quote is taken, "Flatness and Protuberance: Reforming the Image in Protestant Print Culture", has pertinence to the present arguments.
35. Quoted and discussed in Myrone, "Graphic Antiquarianism", 44.
36. Mark Rose, "Technology and Copyright in 1735: The Engraver's Act", *The Information Society* 21, no. 1 (2005): 63.

37. Ronan Deazley, *On the Origin of the Right to Copy: Charting the Movement of Copyright Law in Eighteenth Century Britain (1695–1775)* (Oxford and Portland: Hart Publishing, 2004), 88–94. See also J. G. A. Pocock, *Political Thought and History: Essays on Theory and Method* (Cambridge Univ. Press, 2009), x–xi, on 1688 as a paradigm shift after which politics can only be understood as the politics of a commercial society.
38. Quoted in Martin Hopkinson, "Printmaking and Print Collectors in the North West, 1760–1800", in *Joseph Wright of Derby in Liverpool*, ed. Elizabeth E. Barker and Alex Kidson (New Haven and London: Yale Univ. Press, 2007), 88.
39. Society of Artists, London, catalogue of the annual exhibition of 1773, no. 4, quoted in Algernon Graves, ed., *The Society of Artists of Great Britain, 1760–1791, The Free Society of Artists, 1761–1783: A Complete Dictionary of Contributors and their Work from the Foundation of the Societies to 1791* (London: G. Bell and Sons, 1907), 43.
40. "sculpture, n." OED Online. June 2015. Oxford Univ. Press. http://www.oed.com/view/Entry/173877?rskey=424EHc&result=1 (accessed 16 July 2015). Emphases added.
41. Carl Goldstein, *Print Culture in Early Modern France: Abraham Bosse and the Purposes of Print* (Cambridge Univ. Press, 2012), 23–25. A term search on *The Art World in Britain, 1660 to 1735*, http://artworld.york.ac.uk (6 Aug. 2012) threw up 121 uses of the term in the historical materials—mainly newspapers—then transcribed in the database. At least 33 were unequivocally references to printed images, books "Adorned with Sculptures" or "Books of Sculpture", distributed across the years 1665–1729. A further search on 4 June 2015 brought up 191 references, with around 40 unique references clearly referencing printed images, including occasional references which acknowledged the equivalence of the terms print and sculpture. See, for example, *London Post*, 6 Nov. 1699: "At the Exchange Coffee-House, in Cornhill over against the Royal Exchange, will be Sold by Auction a Collection of Excellent English Books in Divinity, Histories, Voyages, Travels, Lives, Sculptures or Prints, &c."
42. Joseph M. Levine, *Between the Ancients and Moderns: Baroque Culture in Restoration England* (New Haven and London: Yale Univ. Press, 1999), 19.
43. Lisa Maruca, "Bodies of Type: The Work of Textual Production in English Printers' Manuals", *Eighteenth-Century Studies* 36, no. 3 (2003): 321–43.
44. Maruca, "Bodies of Type", 338.
45. Dror Wahrman, *Mr. Collier's Letter Racks: A Tale of Art & Illusion at the Threshold of the Modern Information Age* (New York and Oxford: Oxford Univ. Press, 2012).
46. Kathleen Wilson, "Citizenship, Empire, and Modernity in the English Provinces, c.1720–1790", *Eighteenth-Century Studies* 29, no. 1 (1995): 71.
47. Levis, *Extracts*, 94.
48. The British Library, London (hereafter BL), *Sculptura or the History, and Art of Chalcography and Engraving in Copper* (London, 1662), Eve.a.19.
49. *Catalogue of Prints and Drawings in the British Museum. Division 1. Political and Personal Satires. (Catalogue of political and personal satires, etc.)*, vols. 1–4 by Frederic George Stephens, vols. 5–11 by Mary Dorothy George (London: British Museum, 1870–1954).
50. Mark Hallett, *The Spectacle of Difference: Graphic Satire in the Age of Hogarth* (New Haven and London: Yale Univ. Press, 1999), 17.
51. Hunter, ed., *Printed Images*, 1.
52. Wahrman, *Mr. Collier's Letter Racks*, 20–21.
53. Quoted in Harry M. Hake, "Some Contemporary Records Relating to Francis Place, Engraver and Draughtsman, with a Catalogue of his Engraved Work", *Walpole Society* 10 (1922): 65.
54. Quoted in Thomas, *Paradox of Mezzotint*, 5. See Gerdien Wuestman, "The Mezzotint in Holland: 'Easily Learned, Neat and Convenient'", *Simiolus* 23 (1995): 63–89.
55. Geoffrey Turnovsky, *The Literary Market: Authorship and Modernity in the Old Regime* (Philadelphia: Univ. of Pennsylvania Press, 2010), 5.

56. Roger Gaskell, "Printing Press and Engraving Shop: A Mysterious Collaboration", *Book Collector* 53 (2004): 213–57.
57. Griffiths, *The Print in Stuart Britain*, 212. Accordingly, a new copy of the print was produced, by Richard Houston, for the 1755 edition.
58. Annotation in his own copy of *Sculptura*, BL Eve.a.19.
59. Hunter, ed., *Printed Images*, 2.
60. John Bender, *Ends of Enlightenment* (Stanford Univ. Press, 2012), 63.
61. Joseph A. Dane, *The Myth of Print Culture: Essays on Evidence, Textuality, and Bibliographical Method* (Toronto, Buffalo, and London: Univ. of Toronto Press, 2003), 10, presenting figures from an MLA Bibliography Search for "print culture" which revealed 249 entries from 1963 onwards, 1,991 from as recently as 1996–2001, and only 2 from before 1980.
62. Elizabeth L. Eisenstein, "AHR Forum: An Unacknowledged Revolution Revisited", *The American Historical Review* 107, no. 1 (Feb. 2002): 87–105.
63. Adrian Johns, "Identity, Practice and Trust in Early Modern Natural Philosophy", *The Historical Journal* 42 (1999): 1137. See also Steven Shapin, *A Social History of Truth: Civility and Science in Seventeenth-century England* (Chicago and London: Univ. of Chicago Press, 1994).
64. See Matthew Hunter, "The Theory of the Impression According to Robert Hooke", in *Printed Images*, ed. Hunter, 167–90.
65. Johns, "Identity, Practice and Trust", 1144.
66. Quoted and discussed in Thomas, "Noble or Commercial?", 281. On the contemporary image of the prostitute as a "dystopic symbol of democracy", see Melissa M. Mowry, *The Bawdy Politic in Stuart England, 1660–1714: Political Pornography and Prostitution* (Aldershot: Ashgate 2004).
67. Quoted and discussed in Michael Hunter, "John Evelyn in the 1650s: A Virtuoso in Quest of a Role", in Hunter, *Science and the Shape of Orthodoxy: Intellectual Change in Late Seventeenth-century Britain* (Woodbridge: Boydell & Brewer, 1995), 80.
68. Bell, ed., *Evelyn's Sculptura*, 147–48.
69. Griffiths, *The Print in Stuart Britain*, 194.
70. Hunter, "John Evelyn in the 1650s".
71. Darley, *John Evelyn*, 149.
72. Griffiths, "John Evelyn", 108.
73. Thomas Sprat, *The History of the Royal-Society of London, for the Improving of Natural Knowledge* (London, 1667), 407–8.
74. On contemporary satire specifically involving the Torricellian experiment, see Marjorie Hope Nicolson and David Stuart Rodes in Thomas Shadwell, *The Virtuoso*, ed. Nicolson and Rodes (London: Edward Arnold, 1966), xx–xxii.
75. Timothy Erwin, "William Hogarth and the Aesthetics of Nationalism", *Huntington Library Quarterly* 64, nos. 3/4 (2001): 383.
76. Robert N. Essick, "William Blake, William Hamilton, and the Materials of Graphic Meaning", *ELH* 52 (1985): 834.
77. Morris Eaves, *The Counter-arts Conspiracy: Art and Industry in the Age of Blake* (Ithaca and London: Cornell Univ. Press, 1992), 110.

A Taxonomy for the Invisible: Categories for English Funeral Monuments

Nigel Llewellyn

Growth, diversification, and innovation were key trends in art and architecture in England in the years 1660–1735, and they combined to create what is coming to be recognized as a distinct art world with some recognizably modern features.[1] The essays collected in this book have illustrated, amongst other things, how art institutions and cultures of understanding about visual art started to develop in the unified British state (from 1707), with new forms of artistic practice and patronage taking hold and—despite political and economic uncertainties—marked increases in buying and selling.[2] In parallel with this activity and partly dependent on it, art criticism emerged as a recognized literary genre.[3] Despite the new understandings that are being reached about this art-historical period, the impression remains that it has not been identified by academic art historians as one of great interest.[4] In fact, the hitherto somewhat sparse art history of late Stuart and early Hanoverian Britain has tended to fall back on standard models and systems, devised originally to explain the art of quite other times and places, and which are deployed rather indiscriminately to promote a description of these years as an intermediate or fallow era.[5] If the outcome of the political events of 1688–9 was the triumph of a modernizing faction (the Whigs) and the subsequent and profound transformation of the British state, should we not also expect there to be a significant cultural share—to include the visual arts—which would be touched by those dramatic changes? Do such perturbations in the body politic rob artists of opportunities, or do they create them, or perhaps do they do both? Art historians have shied away from such questions, and from exploring the artistic impact of the extraordinary changes that took place in the social, political, and economic life of the period.

Furthermore, the art history dealing with this era has hesitated to recognize the consequences of two longer and slower contextual "revolutions" that were under way in Britain around 1700—those in science and in sexual behaviour.[6] To take the former as an example, art history has been slow to enquire about the issues that were posed for the visual arts by the distinction made in contemporary science between "primary" qualities that could be measured mathematically such as size, position, and weight, and "secondary" qualities, which were perceived through the senses—colour, order, taste, and so on. What effect did the stress on the utilitarian encouraged by science have on the visual arts in an age of strikingly ornamental styles such as the Baroque and the Rococo? Should scientific principles be applied to works of religious art? In sum and with few exceptions, art history has declined to operate on such levels and our critical expectations of British art around 1700 have been modest: it has invariably been described simply as an age of transition. Instead of asking how art should be understood in a society dominated by Lockean ideas about monarchical rule governed by consent and contract, art history has in the past tended to fall back on such assumptions as that the Commonwealth was a complete Dark Age for the visual arts—a reasonable enough view in some senses but no longer as certain as once it was—and has concentrated on whether or not classicism and other Continental styles were able successfully to migrate to Britain from their points of origin.

As for art-historical accounts of the three visual arts of design—which was itself a conception just starting to find acceptance in this period—sculpture is clearly the poor relation in comparison with painting and architecture. Elsewhere in this collection, Van Hensbergen draws attention to how weakly the theme of the public function of sculpture has been addressed in the historiography. It is the painters and architects about whom authoritative books have been written and exhibitions curated, not the sculptors.[7] Sculpture remains less visible, regarded as a medium defined with reference to the free-standing marble statue and a poorly defined genre with its boundaries little understood. As Malcolm Baker has pointed out, we need to see the sculpture of this period both as a category within the luxury arts (which, I would argue, should include a good deal of church art) and as an art form defined by its intermediality. The category "sculpture" needs to be understood as embracing a range of effects and materials such as the coin, the ivory, the wax figure, plasterwork, ships' figureheads, work in lead and in gardens and on buildings.[8] Of sculptors active in England alongside better-known architects and painters such as Nicholas Hawksmoor or Godfrey Kneller, only the virtuoso woodcarver Grinling Gibbons has received much attention. The general art-historical silence about sculpture in late Stuart and early Hanoverian England has been particularly telling in the treatment of what was then the most important of all sculptural categories, the particular hybrid that we now know as the tomb or funeral monument, which in terms of scale, cost, and number dominated stone sculpture at this time. This essay suggests ways of rescuing these tombs from their current state of near invisibility and proposes a set of categories determined by their social context to bring them more clearly into the mainstream and to illuminate historiographical and methodological issues of still wider resonance.

THE FUNERAL MONUMENT AS A CASE STUDY

The standard account of funeral monuments after 1660 is that the rate of increase in their number dropped off following the great expansions of the early seventeenth century, but that their sculptural quality improved. This improvement is usually explained by reference to the availability of better materials and to the activities and influence of incoming foreign and increasingly well-travelled indigenous sculptors. Indeed, funeral monuments were carved and set up in large numbers over the seventy-five-year period covered by this book and thousands of examples still survive; however, they have been little studied by scholars and are not recognized by a wider public since, by token of their commemorative function, they are very widely dispersed and very obscurely housed in countless parish churches. But important though this physical obscurity is, the fact that art historians working on this period can hardly imagine, let alone discuss, post-Restoration funeral monuments in interesting ways is because we do not have an appropriate language to use when discussing them. This conceptual and linguistic gap needs to be filled by a richer analytical vocabulary deployed alongside a new and more accommodating set of categories. What is needed are both new ideas and new terms. As is made apparent by Mark Hallett's introduction to this volume, the vocabulary of such commentators on the arts as George Vertue became increasingly sophisticated by the 1730s; he had terms such as History Painter, cupola and "from the life" at his finger-tips. The period literature on tombs is far less obviously forthcoming. The sparse antiquarian and other surviving evidence suggests that at the time tombs were valued by both patrons and makers but—as is so often the case in cultural history—the shortage of relevant written sources means that we know little in detail about what their audiences expected of them. Funeral monuments cost very significant sums of money and were the subject of comprehensive legal contracts whose wording does reveal some of the then-current terminology. Rather than making the most of such clues, art historians have tended to employ only unhelpful variants and adaptations of standard art-historical categories and labels—both stylistic and historical—a failing which has left English funeral monuments of around 1700 in a state of art-historical obscurity that matches their physical isolation.

We should start by considering the people who made these tombs: who were they and what were they called? In the years around 1700, the "artist" and the "sculptor" were not words or concepts applied to tomb-makers in their modern senses. Instead, contemporaries used a range of other terms such as carvers, masons, free-masons, stone-cutters, lapidaries, statuaries, image-makers, or even picture-makers. When he was buried in Paddington in 1703, John Bushnell, who had travelled extensively in Italy and had invented a new category of monumental dramatic tableau, appears in the parish register as an "image-maker".[9] In her path-breaking survey of the Restoration period in *Sculpture in Britain, 1530–1840* (1964), Margaret Whinney sought to differentiate classes of sculptors on the grounds of their varying levels of artistic ambition and quality of execution. She distinguished between what she called "statuaries", a term that privileged the expert handling of the carved human figure by members of an elite group, and the master masons or "mason-sculptors", who were professional stone workers occupying a lower rank. This second group made figures but they also turned their hands to architectural decoration and other ornamental work, activities that Whinney thought lowered their standing.[10] Malcolm Baker has drawn attention to the baleful tyranny of this term "mason-sculptor".[11] Amongst even the higher beings, the statuaries, Whinney was hard-pressed to identify "artists", especially those of that discriminating turn of mind associated with canonical painters such as Anthony van Dyck. Despite the increasing and enlightened curiosity about technique, technology, and making, evidenced by John Evelyn's *Sculptura* (1662), there has been an assumption that Restoration sculpture continues to be covered by Henry Peacham's earlier maxim from the 1630s, in which he suggests that the mechanical arts could never be noble.[12]

Finding the right term to describe a group of makers within historical, visual culture is in essence a problem in historical sociology, and it is precisely in contextual areas such as this that the historiography of British art around 1700 has been so deeply flawed. Cutting across these class-based distinctions between one tomb-maker and another—on the grounds of competence or quality—is a second major question, that of the native-born artist versus the incomer. Historiographically, this is tied into the notion of the British Baroque, an idea that has long troubled architectural historians but which became visible in the discourse of art at least as early as the publication of the first volume of Colen Campbell's *Vitruvius Britannicus* (1715). In his apologia, Campbell describes the Baroque style and its proponents as capricious, affected, licentious, extravagant, and lacking in proportion, symmetry, and grace. In short, the book's influential readers are told that the Baroque style is Italian, papist, and inappropriate to the British context.[13]

The existing literature on the art of this period is desperately weak on the serious analysis of social context. For example, in relation to tombs, political change and tensions between the social classes are usually seen as a distant backdrop to patronage, rather than as an essential framing condition. This is an important failing and one which is limited to art-historical discourse, since we find that the early antiquarian commentators do have important things to say on exactly these issues. William Bird's *The Magazine of Honour* (published in 1642 but reissued in the 1650s by Doderidge) describes how nobles should behave and how they are created and ranked; the terms that he uses are relevant since funeral monuments were to remain vehicles for heraldic display during our period. Bird states that entry into the class of "the Gentry, or civill Nobility" is denoted by the bearing of heraldic arms either because the person's "beginning [is] in blood . . . or [because] they had expedited something worthy in peace or warre, whereby they deeserve [*sic*] to have armes".[14] Bird is open in his explanation that heralds will offer arms for payment, for example, for inventing a lineage or "for virtue . . . for the merits . . . and certaine qualities that he do see in him, and for sundry noble acts which he hath performed",[15] for heraldry has become the visible sign of "gentle" status: "in these dayes he is a Gentleman, who is so commonly taken and reported . . . whosoever studieth in the Universities, who professeth the liberall sciences, . . . who can live idly, and without manual labour, and will bear the Port, charge, and Countenance of a Gentleman, he shall be called Master." This definition resembles a blue-print for a monumental representation or portrayal: the challenge to the tomb-maker was to show the armigerous subject with what Bird calls "the Port, charge and Countenance of a Gentleman". Passages such as this explain the universality of coats of arms on monuments in the years around 1700, and suggest that it is the appropriate portrayal of the individual, supplemented by heraldry, that is taken as a sign of gentle status. If the subject of the funeral monument, portrayed in effigial form, has the appearance of a gentleman or gentlewoman, he or she is assumed to be just such a one and we should apply this simple rule to our reading of funerary portraiture in relation to their displays of effigial statuary in all its facets, including pose and costume.

A second area of context and change relates to the fundamental questions about the constitution and national identity that were asked of the British polity in this period. Although the restoration of Charles II was very widely celebrated, deep-rooted economic and political tensions were left unresolved, only to be brought to the fore during the reign of his brother James II. In England, the events of 1688/9 returned matters to the 1660 consensus. However, no such consensus was possible in either Scotland or Ireland, where there were clear winners and losers and where many were driven to Jacobitism or other forms of opposition. Under these circumstances, we cannot talk in simple terms about a single hegemonic "British" sculpture. Given the primary commemorative function of monuments, which was to represent continuity and to create a monumental body in perpetuity, these challenges and changes to political authority and to the nature of the newly united kingdom create another important context for tombs in this period.

Furthermore, questions of religious difference and the doctrinal tensions within the established Church, in whose buildings the monuments stand, need to be added to this list of contextual circumstances. The monarchs so often referred to in monumental inscriptions were also going through a period of change, their powers increasingly limited—a limit exacerbated by absence in warfare (William III) or ill health (Queen Anne)—as cabinet government was steadily evolving. What is more, the economic conditions of the age were turbulent in the extreme. The national debt was invented, an economic device that required taxation to pay off interest, which is why its renewal led to the regular calling of parliaments and the establishment of parliamentary control over the court via the setting up of Civil List payments. Finally, there was the economic context represented by the City of London—with a Bank of England at its heart from 1694—and its network of links with Britain's ever-expanding trading and colonial interests. As Richard Stephens has shown earlier in this book, the Palace of Westminster was a centre for the art trade and the members of both Houses and the City of London merchants (often one and the same) were precisely the kinds of individuals and family members represented by funeral monuments.

Although around 1700 there was no sophisticated language available with which to discuss funeral monuments, there is clear evidence that the lexicon was in a state of development.[16] The itinerant antiquaries were the literary class most actively engaged in such work. Elias Ashmole (1617–1692) represents the older-fashioned tendency and his writing conveys the general impression that monuments are merely framing constructions to support the display of portraits and other forms of representation. He uses the words "decumbent" and "recumbent" interchangeably and clumsily describes figures as lying "against" or "in" the wall or "within the arch". In general, Ashmole struggles in the absence of an adequate set of technical terms: "the Figure of a Man to his Middle" or "the statue . . . of a Woman to the middle" could have been more neatly expressed had the term "bust" been available.[17] Dignity and, by implication, antiquity is, however, something that Ashmole *is* able to suggest through language: "the Proportions of a Man and Woman, lying along, holding up their Hands in a devout Posture of Prayer".[18] A shortage of epithets means that his descriptions of monuments tend to be very bland: either "stately", "fair", or "handsome". From the aesthetic standpoint he is bereft of any sense of the idealizing function of the nude figure: "On one side . . . is the Figure of a Woman, to the Breasts naked . . . On the other . . . another . . . somewhat naked, though with a Scarf thrown loosely round her."[19] Allegorical functions are, however, signalled and such representations differentiated from portraits by the simple use of the word "Figure", as in the "Figure of Time".[20]

By contrast, Ashmole's slightly younger contemporary John Aubrey (1626–1697) displays a richer lexicon. His multi-volume account of the antiquities of Surrey (published in London in 1719, the same year as Ashmole on Berkshire) had its origins in work undertaken many years beforehand.[21] Intriguingly, Aubrey understands the concept of the portrait bust. The Bentleys at Richmond appear as "two large Bustos",[22] and he also knows enough about the subject to be able to make helpful interpretative points about sculpted details: "the dead being distinguished from the living by the Sculls [*sic*] in their Hands", or "Finials (which is a term in Carving, implying an Emblem of the End of Life, as Boys holding extinguished Torches or Sculls)".[23]

In none of the antiquarian literature is there any evidence of an authoritative understanding of the technical and material qualities of statuary marbles. Even amongst the specialist writers of a scientific bent, such as Nehemiah Grew (1641–1712), sculptured stone was a mineral and treated only as a petrological specimen. In his treatise, *Museum Regalis Societatis, or, a Catalogue and Description of the Natural and Artificial Rarities belonging to the Royal Society And preserved at Gresham College* (London, 1681), Grew includes a section entitled "Of Stones Irregular" where the only reference to sculpture comes in an observation about "BASTARD-ALABASTER", that it is *Gypsum variegatum* which can be made into "*Statues* of any desirable bigness, yet very light". We are left unconvinced of Grew's ability to discuss sculpted art with any real insight or understanding.[24]

This same lack of certainty is a feature of the way that the style-period labels are deployed in the historiography. The years around 1700 are generally regarded as the period when the Baroque has its moment in the English sun, but the Baroque is a label that can operate on two levels: either in the full sense theorized by Heinrich Wölfflin, that is, as a complete compositional and aesthetic system, or alternatively as a set of decorative forms.[25] Monuments in our period rarely embrace the Baroque in the first of these senses but they habitually adopt the second; for example, in heraldic cartouches where exaggerated size, colour, and eye-catching ornamental forms draw attention to shields of arms as signs of status.

In short, the thousands of funeral monuments erected in England in the years around 1700 are complex hybrid objects that have not yet been classed into adequate typological categories. The style categories that have been used to describe them have been applied only patchily, and often lack critical purchase. Contemporary sources provide no evidence that fully developed autonomous styles—as recognized in modern art history—were valued or recognized in late Stuart and early Georgian England or that they set patterns to be emulated or striven for. Furthermore, thought needs to be given to the inherent intermediality of funeral monuments, and in fact to the relationship between sculpture and the other arts of design. For example, the coat of arms and the portrait bust in their ornamental frames are features not only of monuments but also of portrait engravings. But more than anything, the demanding historical and social contexts for these works of art that we have briefly explored need to be given serious attention, rather than being ritually cited and then ignored. The iconographic programmes of funeral monuments were often dominated by secular material yet they were located in churches and they signalled the resurrection of the righteous; their stress on loyalty to the Crown, to the realm and to the established Church was being signalled at a time of unprecedented turbulence for all those institutions; and their mix of dignity, playfulness, pathos, luxury, learning, solemnity, and sentiment can only be understood as a response to the social changes of the period.

Having identified some of the difficulties, what possible solutions might be worth applying? What is argued here is that what is needed is an alternative set of terms or categories to be applied to the vast body of sculpture represented by funeral monuments. In order to classify and measure change amongst works in their fields, historians of painting and of architecture have adopted the system of genres—the many variants of portraiture, for example, or of building types, such as the country house, the villa, the castle, the town hall, the town house, and the palace. What would a set of "types" for funeral monuments look like? They could be based on contextual and functional characteristics in stark contrast to the loose stylistic categories traditionally used in art history. They nevertheless need to take stylistic difference into account, as well as questions of commemorative function, scale, and iconography. However, in a period of heterodox sculptural practice, style categories do not represent an exclusive, simple formula. Indeed, certain issues tend to recur across these proposed categories, for example the tendency for monumental subjects to be commemorated near to their country seats or to have themselves portrayed in Roman dress as part of a timeless convention. In general, component parts tend to be standardized across the new categories that I will propose here, following some general observations on funeral monuments over this seventy-five-year period, themselves set out under two headings: those of the monumental economy and the monumental content.

THE MONUMENTAL ECONOMY

What were the broad trends in the pattern of monument building between 1660 and 1735? First, geography: in England it is clear that the home counties were growing in importance as the location for significant monuments. Essex has more than a dozen important monuments from the period, reflecting the increasing need of the patron class to have easier access to London for its law courts, political institutions, and the City of London itself, the latter of which served an ever-expanding commercial centre. Indeed, the monument trade seems to have been increasingly centred on London, with few if any non-metropolitan English monument manufacturing centres of more than local significance and with an attendant increase in the rate of imported monuments.

A second factor relates to the "revolution" in sexual behaviour alluded to earlier in this essay: this was the age of Aphra Behn and Daniel Defoe and the period that formed Lady Mary Wortley Montagu. Distinctive women's voices start to be heard more prominently in the public spaces of the theatre and read on the pages of popular literature. In relation to monuments, there was an increase in the numbers of tombs commemorating women in their own right and of monuments showing women as active partners rather than simply as appendages to their menfolk. As we shall see towards the end of this essay, widows are not distinguished on tombs simply by their hooded head-gear as once they were; increasingly they are exemplary monumental subjects in their own right.

Next—and of enormous significance for commercial practice—is the fact that these years see the start of monuments designed by architects but made by sculptors. For example, at Westminster Abbey in the 1720s and 1730s we can find James Gibbs and William Kent working with a range of makers on monuments for dominant intellectual and political figures of the age: Isaac Newton (1731) designed by Kent and carved by John Michael Rysbrack; the Duke of Newcastle, designed by Gibbs, carved by Francis Bird and erected in 1723; Matthew Prior (died 1721), designed by Gibbs and made by Rysbrack and Antoine Coysevox; and James Craggs the younger, politician, designed by Gibbs and carved by Giovanni Guelfi in 1727. This new way of working in partnership demonstrates the increasing importance accorded by patrons to monuments: their detailed programmes and the quality of the cutting are too important to be left to a single maker.

Furthermore, the ramifications of the Reformation continued to have an impact.[26] In the very early Restoration, in the immediate aftermath of the Commonwealth period, there was a severe falling away of the numbers of monuments being erected. A Puritan legacy remained in the form of lingering concerns over the legitimacy of church imagery of any kind, including monuments. It is noteworthy that a good number of bishop's monuments after 1660 are non-figural: Bishop Monck (died 1661), at Westminster Abbey, with an obelisk but no effigy; Bishop Laney (died 1675) at Ely Cathedral; and a group at Worcester: Bishop Blandford (died 1675) and—using the simple Tuscan order—Bishops Fleetwood (died 1683) and Thomas (died 1689). In the 1650s, designers, patrons, and tombmakers seem often to be playing safe, steering away from effigial portraiture in church monuments and finding other ways of symbolizing the monumental body. At Winterbourne Stickland in Dorset is the black column or "*statua sepulchri*" erected for Rachel Sutton (died 1653) and her children, and in the same county at

Iwerne Courtney is a large monument to Sir Thomas Freke that spurns effigial representation in favour of a central mass of shields of arms, carved symbols, and quotations from the biblical books of Psalms and Proverbs. This pattern is continued in other Dorset monuments, from that to Anthony Ettrick (died 1693) at Wimborne through to General Charles Churchill's (died 1714) at Minterne Magna. Although the dominant mood is dignified, communicated by various means—pose, scale, location, and so on—inventive and sometimes even playful narrative becomes more readily—perhaps surprisingly—acceptable, for example, in William Stanton's drawing for the monument at Sutton, Surrey, to Lady Brownlees who died in 1700.[27]

Since monuments are so very much concerned with repairing a social fabric damaged by the death of the individual, and since in earlier seventeenth-century England monuments had been so closely identified with a social and ecclesiastical hierarchy with the monarch at its summit, the regicide and the lack of an anointed prince between 1649 and 1660 must have had a destabilizing impact on the continuities of practice accepted by patrons, designers, and makers of complex monuments. Perhaps there was a sense that church art could, as it were, safely begin again with the Restoration? But we do not yet know how quickly these views evolved. It was perhaps not always easy for the previous widespread practice of putting up funeral monuments to be picked up. John Cosin (1594–1672) was created Bishop of Durham in 1660 having spent seventeen years in exile in France. A high church former Master of Peterhouse, Cambridge, and Vice Chancellor of Oxford, he ordered some important late Baroque fittings for Durham Cathedral including a forty-foot-high (12 metres) wooden font cover, but did not organize any monuments.[28] On a purely political level, the accession of Charles II made it easier to commemorate supporters of his late father and to make a point about their loyalty. William Master (died 1662) was a supporter of Charles I, who is commemorated in a monument at Circencester, Gloucestershire, possibly by Jasper Latham (ca. 1636–1693), which has twisted columns and numerous draped marble statues. It is very doubtful that such a showy statement for a Royalist would have been set up in the 1650s. Even so, it is hard to isolate a collection of monuments relating to a court group; indeed, there were radical changes at the court under Charles II from the early 1660s to the early 1680s, which make it hard even to describe such a grouping.

Any changes in the appearance of monuments could be brought about only because they were encouraged by a changing patronage base and, on the supply side, permitted by an increasingly international culture of provision. From the standpoint of the market, the years around 1700 marked a turning point, the decisive beginning of a long-term trend in English sculpted monuments that was continued well into the nineteenth century. If we take a long view on the market for monument-making between 1500 and 1800, in the centre of which our period 1660–1735 falls, the significant points of international engagement can be identified in a number of phases.

In the early sixteenth century (Phase 1), itinerant Italian sculptors (Pietro Torrigiano, Benedetto da Rovezzano) worked for the court elite but had limited influence nationally. There followed an enormously influential and far-reaching wave of involvement (Phase 2), based on the migration of Protestant refugees from north-west Europe from the 1560s, all of whom were assimilated by around 1600. Then, in the early seventeenth century, there appeared as Phase 3 a second elite, court-based, group of French and Italian sculptors (Francesco Fanelli, Hubert Le Sueur), who, like their forebears in Phase 1, were of limited influence. From the Restoration through to the early eighteenth century (Phase 4) there were increasing signs of international engagement, operating mainly, but not only, at the top end of the market. This international engagement was highly influential and not as elitist as in Phase 3. From around 1730 right through to about 1800 (Phase 5), there was an increasing domination of the tomb market by international artists, working in England but mostly trained abroad and using foreign materials. In the preceding Tudor and early Stuart periods, the ranks of foreign tomb-makers had, with a few notable exceptions, been filled with Netherlanders.

The period around 1700 was marked by the employment of a broader range of international tomb-makers, more diverse in terms of ethnicity and style. Netherlanders—a broadly defined geo-social group—continued to be employed and to establish careers in England, but the novelty now lay in the growing numbers of Italian and French artists (Antoine Coysevox, Giovanni Battista Guelfi) working in the English market. In addition, that market was increasingly international since foreign sculptors often worked here as part of an international practice. The impact of the sixteenth-century Netherlandish tomb-makers—many of them refugees—had been migratory and after a while they had tended to become naturalized: the Jansens became the Johnsons. This pattern was repeated in the Restoration period, as evidenced by the brief career of Artus "Arnold" Quellin (1653–1686). Arriving in London from the Low Countries in 1678, he worked in a subsidiary capacity and was a fellow assistant alongside John Nost the elder (died 1729); he then joined Grinling Gibbons (1648–1721), who was extending his sculptural practice in wood to include stone monuments, for which he had detected increasing and substantial demand. After a few years Quellin split from Gibbons in 1683. Once free, Quellin looked around for trusted assistants and chose his old colleague Nost, who became his foreman. When Quellin died in 1686, Nost continued his workshop.

In the early eighteenth century, the market was to become more mobile with entrepreneurial foreign tomb-makers increasingly attractive to British patrons. The British practitioner Francis Bird (1667–1731) appears to have gained an extensive knowledge of contemporary art in Rome and was available to receive commissions from visiting British aristocrats; however, when visiting that city on his fourth Grand Tour of 1695–1700, John Cecil, fifth Earl of Exeter, ordered a monument to be shipped to Stamford church from the Frenchman Pierre-Etienne Monnot (1657–1733). In parallel with these trends, British-based tomb-makers operating outside London found it increasingly hard to diversify their practice geographically and to secure commissions beyond their immediate local markets. In fact, the market reach of such tomb-makers stayed very limited: Thomas White of Worcester (at Birtsmorton) and John Hunt of Northampton (at Newbold-on-Avon, Warwickshire) are two documented names on quite a short national list.

MONUMENTAL CONTENT

In relation to the appearance of the monuments, we can propose five important trends during this period, across locations and makers, all of which need to be thoroughly researched and verified. First, there was a steady stream of very large-scale monuments, usually erected against a wall rather than free-standing and often filling whole sides of church buildings. These created tableaux filled with life-sized figures. Second, there is a decrease in the use of emblematics in favour of figural allegory, with those allegories sometimes replacing the effigial body.[29] Third, for the whole of our seventy-five-year period, genuine portraits in bust form are consistently and increasingly deployed as the centrepieces in monumental compositions.[30] Fourth, there was a steady interest in the open portrayal of emotion and intimacy and the use of rhetorical gesture, evidenced by the steady decline of the recumbent effigy in favour of animated semi-recumbent and standing figures; these figures are often shown in *all'antica* Roman or ceremonial robes, intended to convey timelessness, reclining in meditation or on their feet and making strong gestures. The scale and visual prominence of these figures must in many cases have had a remarkably enlivening effect on church spaces. Fifth and finally, we find many monuments confidently restating a belief in the central Christian mystery of the resurrection of Christ and the eventual resurrection of the blessed, but also a parallel increase in monuments of a secular portrait type that make almost no reference to religion or death.

DIFFERENT TYPES OF MONUMENTAL BODY

In earlier studies, I have argued that tombs create for their subjects a monumental body, a permanent replacement for the natural body that is abandoned at death.[31] The tomb categories that will be proposed below—which are, again, five in number—reflect the main constituent parts of the monumental body, namely: a strong arm; reproductive fecundity; a lively mind; a beating heart; and the soul eternal. They also take as their starting point the notion of *purpose*—that is, the commemorative functions that are intended for monuments. As we shall see, these functions tend to cut across social rank or station and are not determined by the art historian's habitual stand-by categories of pose or style.

1) The Strong Arm

This category is concerned with political, military, and legal power and it is, of course, an extensive one. Such monuments create an impression of authority and maintain it through references to loyalty to the Crown and the independent strength of justice as well as to force of arms. The standing figure of William, second Lord Maynard (1622–1696) at Little Easton, Essex, proclaims his pragmatic loyalty to the Crown. Grandson to Sir Henry Maynard, the founder of the family fortune, he was made Baronet by Charles II and also employed by James II.[32] The sculptor (probably Edward Pierce) presents him in Roman costume with the cardinal virtues represented allegorically on a relief.

In the many monuments for soldiers and sailors, visual symbols are often present: for example, Sir Mark Milbanke (died 1680?) at Croft in Yorkshire, with its bold and direct military still life set on the huge tomb-chest, or Sir Metcalfe Robinson (died 1688), portrayed at Topcliffe in an oval medallion in civilian wig and lace cravat with a military style still life below. A relief set below the portrait bust of Edward Wynter (died 1686) at Battersea (perhaps by Bushnell?) shows his military feats while the inscription records that "Alone unarmed a Tigre he opprest . . . Thrice-twenty mounted Moors he overthrew, singly on foot." Narrative panels are especially important on the tombs of sailors such as Gibbons's Admiral Sir Cloudesly Shovell (died 1707) at Westminster Abbey or Sir John Narborough (also died 1707) at Knowlton, Kent, erected by Shovell's widow with a relief showing the wreck on the Isles of Scilly.[33]

Given the shattering changes in constitution, regimes, and governance that had overtaken the realm, the judiciary also had to appear strong. Lawyers are shown as pillars of authority within the state, using different means to accentuate the legitimacy of judicial processes—for example, by portraying the subject in

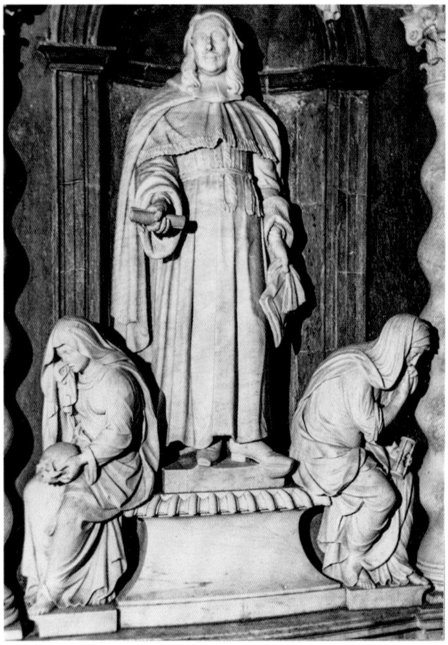

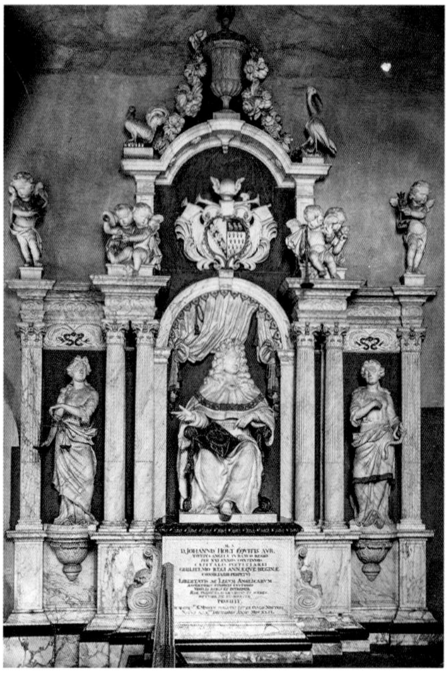

186. John van Nost the Elder, *Monument to Sir Hugh Wyndham*, 1692. Church of St. Nicholas, Silton, Dorset. Conway Library, Courtauld Institute of Art, London

187. Thomas Green, *Tomb of Sir John Holt, Lord Chief Justice*, ca. 1710. St. Mary's Church, Redgrave, Suffolk. Conway Library, Courtauld Institute of Art, London

judicial robes or in the act of sentencing. Examples are John Nost's monument of 1692 to Sir Hugh Wyndham at Silton, Dorset with its standing figure in robes and wig against a reredos and flanked by twisted columns (fig. 186), or Scheemakers's life-sized figures of Sir Francis and Lady Page (she died 1730) at Steeple Aston, Oxfordshire, with the judge in legal robes and periwig and his lady in déshabillé, both portraits propped up on one elbow on bolsters with Sir Francis placed above and behind his wife in time-honoured manner.[34] A second means of emphasizing judicial strength lay in monumental inscriptions: for example, the unshakable self-confidence of Thomas Strode, at Beaminster, Dorset (died 1698) who is described as "juris prudentia, pietate & Consolio, insignis" and shown flanked by weeping putti. A third method is to use allegory: for example, the figures of Justice and Vigilance on Thomas Green of Camberwell's Holt monument at Redgrave, Suffolk, dated 1710, which also deploys a powerful "*ex cathedra*" seated figure (fig. 187). Judges are rarely shown in less formal semi-recumbent poses and where soldiers are shown in such poses, the widow is often the patron.[35]

2) Reproductive Fecundity

Monuments of this type concentrate on recording procreation, growth, and consolidation in relation to dynasties and worldly riches. The establishment and sustaining of a dynasty through marriage and the production of heirs was a dominant preoccupation amongst the elites, not only the hereditary aristocracy but increasingly amongst the merchants. In such tombs, rank tended to outweigh the personal qualities of the individual. In 1682, the third Marquis of Worcester (died 1699) was created first Duke of Beaufort, and his tomb for the Garter Chapel of St George's at Windsor Castle (attributed to Gibbons and moved to Great Badminton in 1875) includes the ducal coronet on a cushion set a good deal higher than the main figure group. The duke is in his garter robes, reclining on a sarcophagus with a relief of St George and the Dragon (a reference to the garter) and the figures of Truth and Justice and parted curtains showing the heavenly host in the form of a troop of cherubim.[36] In the case of Thomas Stayner's tomb of 1717 at Steeple Bumpstead, Essex, for Sir Henry Bendyshe, the monument replaces the dynasty since it had by then failed. Bendyshe was the last baronet and is shown with his deceased heir Henry, who died an infant, alongside him with the lineage proclaimed in huge letters.

The arriviste was as eager as the longest established aristocratic family to use tombs to create a dynastic impression; unlike their counterparts amongst the soldiers and sailors, they do not use relief and symbols to retell narratives but tend to emphasize conservative choices of imagery. An example of this is John Nost's powerful mercantilist monument (after 1699; fig. 188) commemorating Sir Josiah Child (1630–1699) at Wanstead, the parish church for Epping Forest in Essex, which was where Child built his grand Palladian seat, having come suddenly into money through his position at the East India Company (he was a Director in 1677, the Deputy-Governor, then Governor in 1681). Child was an advocate of Dutch commercial and economic principles that he expounded in a series of publications, and was highly critical of the lack of business skills amongst MPs, whose knowledge and experience he did not respect. His monument continues an existing tradition of painted portraiture best exemplified by the work of John Riley, who captured Child soberly, without the use of allegory, in his robes, against a backdrop of the Corinthian order.[37]

In 1705, Sir William Gore (died 1707) acquired the manor at Tring, Hertfordshire, from a courtier of Charles II's. The patron of his remarkable monument, just a few years later, was Gore's eldest son, also William, who was a rare thing, a Tory Governor of the Bank of England. Sir William had been Lord Mayor of London, an honour made prominent on the monument through the City arms displayed

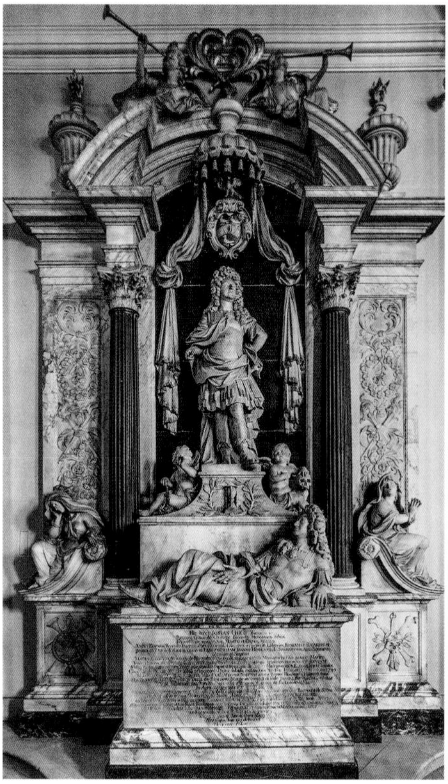

188. Attributed to John van Nost the Elder, *Monument to Sir Josiah Child*, 18th century. St. Mary the Virgin Church, Redbridge, Wanstead. Conway Library, Courtauld Institute of Art, London

in the pediment and the insignia of sword, mace, and beaver hat set on the black marble back-plate. The sumptuous composition—possibly also by Nost—which greets visitors as they enter the church, shows Gore and his wife, semi-reclining, on the opposite ends of a segmental top to a sarcophagus.[38] The arrangement gives equal prominence to Lady Gore (Elizabeth Hampton, the daughter of a City merchant) and signals the main purpose of the tomb. The inscription, which must have been composed by the patron, includes a phrase explaining that her family name is not "repeated" on the tomb "because she wanted no borrowed lustre; being adorned wth all Graces & perfections of Body and mind".[39] The key issue here is the arriviste status of the Gores, a point of sensitivity for the patron, who was wealthy but who married into the aristocracy and was not allowed to forget his lower station.[40]

Sir Henry Furnese (1658–1712), knighted in 1691 at The Hague and raised to a baronetcy in 1707, is an example of the successful merchant with Whiggish political interests.[41] His monument at Waldershare, Kent (his place of origin) is by Green of Camberwell and was made between 1715 and 1717 at a cost of just over

£400. Both of Furnese's marriages were to the daughters of merchants: "having by ye Blessing of Providence, acquired a plentifull Estate . . . Being early distinguished by ye Favour of our Great Deliverer King William he faithfully adhered to the Cause of Liberty & ye Protestant interest with a steady and indefatigable Zeal." The monument is remarkable and rare in its conception and execution: free-standing in the centre of a chapel, it is very tall for its space, centrally planned, and designed on three stories: below, there are inscriptions and seated female mourners; in the middle, standing putti with symbols of mortality and coats of arms; and, above, a top-knot with an urn on colossal decorative scrolled volutes. More rarely shown on monuments are the actual means of generating wealth, the merchants' trading ships, the civil equivalents of the vessels on the naval tombs. An exception is the relief on John Bennett's spectacular tomb at Barking of 1706, where his lively portrait bust is entirely surrounded by such nautical and trading references.

3) The Lively Mind

Monuments for intellectuals cut across the ranks of the nobility, embracing not only professional intellectuals but also gentleman scholars and clerics. By the late seventeenth century, Nicholas Stone's invention of the pile of books as an architectural and monumental motif, so well suited to small epitaphs on college chapel walls, had been current for two generations and was still in use.[42] More explicit recognitions of intellectual contributions rise in popularity under Queen Anne.

The tomb at Wimborne St Giles, Dorset, to Anthony Ashley Cooper, third Earl of Shaftesbury (1671–1713), distinguished moral philosopher and leading pupil of John Locke, takes the form of a sarcophagus-shaped wall monument with a niche over it containing a female allegory representing "Polite literature mourning the death of her most distinguished votary." Shaftesbury having died at Naples, his body was returned to Dorset for burial five months later. He was an innovative thinker about the didactic power of the visual arts, having commissioned Paolo de Matteis to paint an exemplary *Choice of Hercules* (1712; now Ashmolean Museum, Oxford). In his published commentary on this picture, Shaftesbury remarks on the inadequate English vocabulary for the discussion of the visual arts, a point that I touched on at the start of this essay: "by the word Tablature (for which we have yet no name in English besides the general one of Picture we denote . . . a Work not only distinct from a mere *Portraiture*)."[43] The Wimborne monument is appropriate in its emphasis on allegory rather than portraiture.[44]

But intellectuals' tombs could be more anecdotal and less austere. Edward Stanton's monument to Sir Robert Atkyns (1647–1711) at Sapperton, Gloucestershire, shows the author of a local history, *The Ancient and Present State of Glouces-*

tershire (published posthumously in 1712 and described in the inscription as a more durable monument than the tomb itself), reclining in his wig and consulting a reference book. Overall, the monument is eccentric, with its four pairs of Ionic columns matched by the design of the wrought-iron screen and the sizeable superstructure with its vast achievement of arms and niched allegories. The monument to Isaac Newton (1642–1727) designed by Kent, carved by Rysbrack, and erected in 1731 at Westminster Abbey, is playful and theatrical with a near total absence of dignity (fig. 189). Now nearly hidden beneath Edward Blore's nineteenth-century additions to the choir screen, the monument includes a panel of relief on the front of the sarcophagus showing a team of putti acting out Newton's discoveries in the fields of gravity, optics, and the fixed coinage standard. On the sarcophagus itself, Newton is portrayed robed, semi-reclining with one arm propped up on his books on divinity, chronology, optics, and mathematics. At his feet and to his scale stand two more putti displaying a manuscript. Above and behind and showing another abrupt change of scale is a huge zodiacal globe marked with the course of the 1680 comet under the watchful eye of the personification of Astronomy.

4) The Beating Heart

This category of monuments is intended to represent the emotions, to represent affection and bereavement and to speak directly to the sensibilities of the viewer. It is a novelty in our period. In the 1670s, a small and remarkable pair of monuments in East Sussex by John Bushnell and Caius Gabriel Cibber exploit the dramatic potential of tableaux to communicate the sorrow of the bereaved: Cibber's Thomas Sackville monument at Withyham (erected 1678), which is about parental loss, and Bushnell's Jane, Countess of Marlborough and William Ashburnham monument (erected 1675) at Ashburnham, which is about matrimonial affection.[45] Also about affection within marriage is the tomb showing the Wysemans holding hands at Great Canfield, Essex (by William Stanton and dated 1684), and the pair of portrait busts for Sir John and Lady Keyt (he died 1662) at Ebrington, Gloucestershire. Pulling the heart strings in other directions is the monument at Great Barrington in the same county, perhaps by Francis Bird, to the two Bray children, both dead of smallpox by 1720, which shows them in everyday clothes following the lead of their guardian angel traversing the clouds of heaven.

Rather than focusing on a person or a single family, some monuments sought to generate sympathy for humankind more widely. The monument to Edward Colston (died 1721, All Saints, Bristol) is an exercise in decorous sensibility for a subject whose wealth was substantially based on the slave trade but who was also

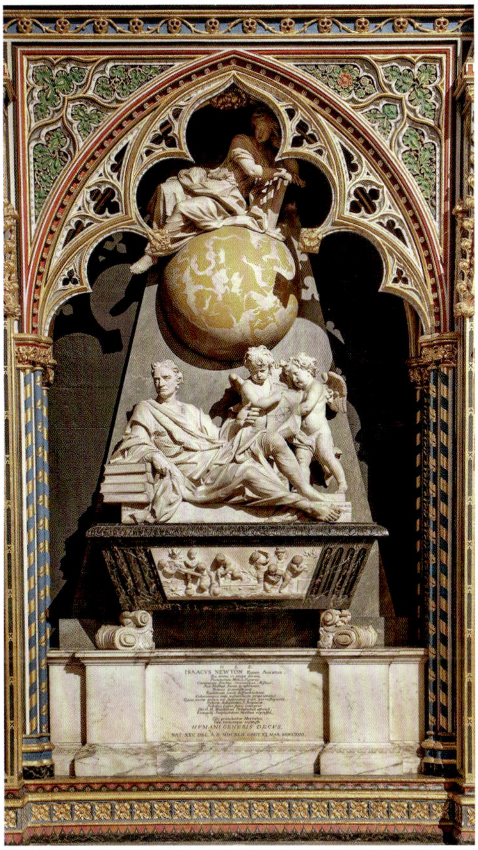

189. Michael Rysbrack after William Kent (designer), *Isaac Newton*, 1731, marble. Westminster Abbey Library, London

a very significant philanthropist in Bristol and elsewhere. His monument takes the form of an elegant, Ionic frame, designed by James Gibbs (a governor of St Bartholomew's Hospital in London as were Colston's executors) but carved by Michael Sidnell of Bristol. The composition is dominated by two things; first, the enormous length of the inscription, which completely fills the tall back wall and simply lists Colston's benefactions and their value in pounds sterling, and second, by the humility of Colston's semi-recumbent gesture—his finger-tips humbly touching his breast—on the effigy by Rysbrack, who has carved a figure that is both dignified and exemplary. The engraved text ends with the words: "This great and pious Benefactor was known to have done many other excellent Charities, and what He did in Secret is believed, to be, not inferior to what He did in Publick."[46] Long inscriptions like this are a feature of monuments that appeal to the sensibilities of onlookers by recording charitable dispositions; for example, Thomas Stayner's tomb of Dr Thomas Turner (1645–1714) at Stowe Nine Churches, Northants, who was President of Corpus Christi, Oxford, and whose bequests established a charitable foundation, the Corporation of the Sons of the Clergy, which was funded from the income of this manor.[47] Turner is, in fact, buried at Oxford rather than in Northamptonshire, and the long, laudatory Latin inscription—the choice of language indicative of whom the readers of this text were thought to be—is cut into a simulated textile as the centrepiece of the tomb, under a baldacchino, so honouring the word rather than the person. The subject stands on a terrestrial globe on the left flank of the work and to the right is Fides, on a celestial globe and holding a model of a church.

5) The Eternal Soul

This final type of monument was erected in the expectation of the resurrection and it functions conventionally by recording a good death and setting an example. In our period, the visual and doctrinal traditions of the *memento mori* and the dying of a good death continue to be referenced on monuments, and lingering fears of dying a bad death encouraged the marked inventiveness of a master such as Edward Pierce (1630–1695), resulting in works such as the skulls in relief on the Withers monument of 1692 at Arkesden in Essex. Nicholas Stone's monument to John Donne (1631) playing on the image of the shrouded figure, continued to be influential; for example, Thomas Burman's signed and dated (1661) monument for John Dutton (died 1656) at Sherborne, Gloucestershire, upright, shrouded, and pious, with few of the military references one might have expected from a Royalist colonel. More dramatic is Joshua Marshall's monument to Edward Noel, Viscount Camden, and his wife Juliana, erected in 1664, many years after their deaths, in Chipping Campden in the same county, which includes two upright alabaster shrouded figures, their macabre forms revealed by the open doors of the monument itself.

The funerary urn is increasingly deployed as a reference to the *memento mori* tradition; for example, in the tomb of Sir Richard Ryves (died 1671) at Yateley, Hampshire, with its odd-shaped urn in a recess, and that of Dorothy Clarke at Fulham (died 1695) with its large draped urn on a bulging sarcophagus. References to the resurrection abound: from 1674 Dr Edmund Castell (died 1684/5) was rector at Higham Gobion, Bedfordshire, where he was buried and was also Professor of Arabic at the University of Cambridge. "He elected to be buried in this spot in hopes of a better", states the inscription in Arabic.[48] As has been suggested, it is the "sober life and conversation" of Edward Goddard (died 1724) that accounts for the restraint and the lack of the usual swagger of his monument at East Woodhay, Hampshire.[49]

Tombs to exemplary women, nobles, widows, and other exemplars of piety and virtue increase in number and come in many forms. Bridget Peck (died 1712) at Little Sampford, Essex, has a monument with no theological references to speak of: she reclines on a sarcophagus and in the midst of reading she gazes into the middle distance and, lowering her book, contemplates the mysteries contained within. The Duchess of Somerset (died 1692) at Westminster Abbey is shown by Gibbons semi-reclining on a couch like a sarcophagus, with her eyes to heaven and making a pleading gesture. Two charity boys attend her, marking the generosity of her donations. Lady Williamson (died 1684) at Loddon, Norfolk, has a tomb-chest with a massive gadrooned edge on which she reclines, head on elbow, prayer book in hand and gazing heavenwards. She was a generous contributor to the costs of rebuilding the City churches after 1666.[50] The monument to Clare and Elizabeth Talbot (died 1681 and 1689) at Salwarpe, Worcestershire, has no effigies but shows two charity girls leaning mournfully up against the inscription which cites Acts 9: 36, 37 and 39.[51] Indeed, there are countless examples in various modes of didactic monuments to women commemorated within the overriding patriarchal context in ways that stress their individual qualities and contributions: Judith Strode (died 1662) at Knebworth, Hertsfordshire, takes the form of a restrained Italianate bust, while Mary Markham (died 1673, and possibly by Edward Stanton?) at Ardeley, Hertfordshire, is a lively half figure in a niche, making strong gestures with a baby on a ledge before her. Dame Frances Earle (died ca. 1687) at Sturton-le-Steeple, Nottinghamshire, has an upright, life-size figure of a Roman matron against an altar background with columns and a segmental pediment, while Mrs Bovey (erected 1726/7) in the South aisle at Westminster Abbey, designed by Gibbs and carved by Rysbrack, juxtaposes allegories of Faith and Wisdom with a portrait medallion.

CONCLUSION

I have restricted my discussion to major funeral monuments without attempting to take into account the local cultural circumstances that determined so many smaller epitaph-like mural monuments, floor monuments, and other memorials. In the absence of a full national survey of monuments we can at this stage only arrive at impressions rather than at definitive explanations. What is needed next—not just for funeral monuments but for the wide range of artistic materials covered in this volume—is an approach that goes into deeper quantitative detail, that takes serious account of the major historical, cultural, and artistic developments of the era, and that is attentive to the functions of different kinds of object. The era needs to be considered from a British perspective, the new country constituted in law but not always in reality as a single nation, but made up of different countries and peoples, regions, factions, and social groupings. An argument that monuments represent the body politic has to be based on historical factors such as the fundamental changes in gender relations and scientific understanding that took place in this period, and the increasing social and geographical mobility of the artist. Meanwhile, the categories for monuments that have been proposed here derive directly from a close attentiveness to the *primary* function of this form of sculpture: to create a monumental body (or sculpted body politic) perpetually replacing the natural body as it decays in the grave. Attending to the language of art and to the terms and categories needed to describe different kinds of art object, and different kinds of artistic effect, will be enormously helpful in better understanding such objects, as will a prioritizing of function and historical and social context over the lazy use of ill-suited and misleading style-period labels.

1. Some of the ideas presented here were first shared with colleagues in the form of a paper entitled "Nation and Religion in the History and Historiography of post-Reformation Funeral Monuments" given at *The British School of Sculpture: Rethinking Sculptural Practice c.1650–c.1830* conference held at the University of York in November 2009.
2. There is a general but not universal acceptance for the proposition that new art markets developed in Britain in the late seventeenth century; see Mireille Galinou, ed., *City Merchants and the Arts 1670–1720* (London: Corporation of London, 2004), and the critical reception for Dror Wahrman, *Mr Collier's Letter Racks: A Tale of Art & Illusion at the Threshold of the Modern Information Age* (Oxford Univ. Press, 2012). For the older literature see Lorna Weatherill, *Consumer Behaviour & Material Culture in Britain, 1660–1760* (London: Routledge, 1988), and John Brewer and Roy Porter, eds., *Consumption and the World of Goods* (London: Routledge, 1992). For the expansion of the art world in these years, see too Mark Hallett's introduction and Richard Stephens's essay in this volume.
3. William Aglionby, *Painting Illustrated in … Dialogues … with an Explanation of the Difficult Terms* (London, 1685).
4. For example, I cannot recall seeing that the period 1660–1735 was being offered as a special subject.
5. See the debates generated by the publication of Steven Pincus, *1688: The First Modern Revolution* (New Haven and London: Yale Univ. Press, 2009).
6. For the latter, as a starting point, see Faramerz Dabhoiwala, *The Origins of Sex: A History of the First Sexual Revolution* (London: Penguin, 2012).
7. See the bibliography in Lisa Jardine, *On a Grander Scale: The Outstanding Life of Sir Christopher Wren* (New York: HarperCollins, 2002), and see too the survey included in Mark Hallett's introduction to this volume.
8. Baker is the leading scholar in this field; see his key-note lecture to the *Court, Country, City* conference at York in September 2012 and several publications, especially *Figured in Marble: The Making and Viewing of Eighteenth-century Sculpture* (London and Los Angeles: V&A Publications and J. Paul Getty Museum, 2001).
9. Mrs A. J. K. Esdaile, "The Sculptor and the Brass", *Transactions Monumental Brass Society* 7, Part 2 (Dec. 1935).
10. Margaret Whinney, *Sculpture in Britain, 1530–1830* [Pelican History of Art] (Harmondsworth: Penguin, 1964), see chap. 8, 63–66.
11. Malcolm Baker, key-note lecture cited at note 8.

12. Henry Peacham, *Compleat Gentleman* (London, 1634), 12–13; in the rhetorical tradition of the *paragone*, there were of course many seventeenth-century attempts to lift painting from the mechanical category.
13. The text is conveniently reprinted in E. G. Holt, ed., *A Documentary History of Art*, vol. 2, *Michelangelo and the Mannerists: The Baroque and the Eighteenth Century* (1963; Princeton Univ. Press, 1982).
14. William Bird, *The Magazine of Honour* (London, 1642), sig. N6r.
15. Bird, *Magazine of Honour*, sig. N6v.
16. The importance of language in relation to the visual arts in their historical context was a constant interest of Michael Baxandall's, see his publications from *Giotto and the Orators: Humanist Observers of Painting in Italy and the Discovery of Pictorial Composition, 1350–1450* (Oxford Univ. Press, 1971 onwards).
17. Elias Ashmole, *The Antiquities of Berkshire*, 3 vols. (London, 1719), 1: 98 and 2: 396.
18. Ashmole, *Berkshire*, 1: 185.
19. Ashmole, *Berkshire*, 2: 359.
20. Ashmole, *Berkshire*, 3: 147.
21. John Aubrey, *The Natural History and Antiquities of the County of Surrey. Begun in the Year 1673*, 5 vols. (London, 1719).
22. Aubrey, *Surrey*, 1: 72–73.
23. Aubrey, *Surrey*, 5: 29 and 177.
24. Nehemiah Grew, *Museum Regalis Societalis, or, a Catalogue and Description of the Natural and Artificial Rarities belonging to the Royal Society And preserved at Gresham College* (London, 1681), 319.
25. M. Snodin and N. Llewellyn, eds., *Style in the Age of Magnificence, 1620–1800* (London: V&A Publishing, 2009), especially chap. 2, "The Baroque Style".
26. See N. Llewellyn, *Funeral Monuments in Post-Reformation England* (Cambridge Univ. Press, 2000).
27. Victoria and Albert Museum, London, D.1104-1898.
28. Indeed County Durham has almost nothing from our period except M[. . .] Smith's stylistically heterodox monument for Michael Matthew (died 1689) at Whitburn.
29. See, for example, Sir Nathanial Napier (died 1708) at Minterne Magna, Dorset, by Robert Taylor, 1725, or the third Earl of Shaftesbury at Wimborne St Giles, Dorset.
30. From Bushnell's animated and negligent portrayal of Mrs Pepys (died 1669) at St Olave Hart Street, City of London, to Christopher Horsnaile I's accomplished bust of William Rogers (died 1734) at Dowdeswell, Gloucestershire.
31. See N. Llewellyn, *The Art of Death: Visual Culture in the English Death Ritual, c.1500–c.1800* (London: Reaktion, 1990), and *Funeral Monuments in Post-Reformation England.*
32. Other standing soldiers are Colonel John Birch MP (died 1691) at Weobly, Herefordshire, in armour in a niche; gesturing authoritatively with a baton of command flanked by architecture and military trophies of arms in relief. It is attributed to William Stanton (see Alan Brooks and Nikolaus Pevsner, *The Buildings of England: Herefordshire* (Newhaven and London: Yale Univ. Press, 2012), 652 and plate 86); Colonel Edmund Soames (died 1706) at West Dereham, Norfolk, by Robert Singleton of Bury St Edmunds; General George Monk, Duke of Albemarle (died 1670), erected 1730 in the South Aisle, Westminster Abbey, designed by William Kent, made by Peter Scheemakers as a black obelisk—the *columna rostrata*—with the duke in armour.
33. Admiral Sir George Rooke (died 1709) in St Michael's Chapel, Canterbury Cathedral, also has ships in relief. Admiral Priestman (died 1712) at Westminster Abbey, by Francis Bird, is the earliest example of the type with medallion head against an obelisk. The tomb of Admiral Caldwell (died 1718) at Birtsmorton, Worcestershire, attributed to White of Worcs., shows his flagship on the tomb-chest with nautical instruments on the reredos behind.
34. Another robed Scheemakers judge is the Serjeant-at-Law John Turner (died 1688) with his wife at Kirkleatham, Yorkshire; erected years later in about 1740.
35. See Robert Jennens (died 1725) at Acton, Suffolk, who was adjutant to Marlborough. He reclines before his reredos monument, in its own chapel, with his mourning wife seated at his feet.

36. Examples of other aristocratic tombs include those of John Digby, third Earl of Bristol (died 1698), Sherborne, Dorset, by John Nost; Denzel Lord Holles, 1699, Dorchester, Dorset (not in its original location).
37. The portrait attributed to Riley is at the National Portrait Gallery, London, NPG 5932.
38. As Pevsner points out, not unlike the arrangement of Giacomo della Porta's monument to Pope Paul III in San Pietro in Vaticano.
39. For some outstanding photographs, see www.flickr.com/photos/erichardyuk/6231303964/in/set-72157627738150857. For other monuments to Lord Mayors of London, see Sir Thomas Foot (died 1688) and Sir James Smyth (died 1706), both at West Ham.
40. See http://www.historyofparliamentonline.org/volume/1690-1715/member/gore-william-1675-1739 (accessed 5 May 2015) for Gore's son. Relating the design at Tring to della Porta's Paul III must have been Nost's idea, not Gore's. The Gores do not seem to have visited Italy until this Sir William's grandson, Charles, did in 1734. See John Ingamells, *A Dictionary of British and Irish Travellers in Italy, 1701–1800* (New Haven and London: Yale Univ. Press, 1997), 412.
41. As with Gore, Furnese's son was in Italy as his father was being raised to the Baronetcy; it seems that Sir Henry himself wasn't a tourist (Ingamells, *Dictionary*, 385).
42. For example, the monument of John Martin (died 1680) and his wife in the crypt at St Paul's Cathedral, City of London, with two figures kneeling against a reredos and a pile of books between them, cherubs and babies below.
43. Conveniently reprinted in Holt, ed., *Documentary History of Art*, 2: 243.
44. S. O'Connell, "Lord Shaftesbury in Naples, 1711–1713", *Walpole Society* 54 (1988): 149–219. Also rich in allegory is the tomb of Dr Hugh Chamberlain in the North Aisle at Westminster Abbey (died 1728; erected 1731), carved by Peter Scheemakers, assisted by Laurent Delvaux; Chamberlain is shown semi-reclining with Physic and Longevity personified alongside him.
45. On these two monuments, see N. Llewellyn, *East Sussex Church Monuments, 1530–1830* (Lewes: Sussex Record Society, 2011), 20, 413, and plates 5–7, 195–196); Llewellyn, "'The Happy Preserver of his Brother's Memory': From Monumental Text to Sculptural Figure in Early Modern Sussex", in M. Dimmock, A. Hadfield, and P. Quinn, eds., *Art, Literature and Religion in Early Modern Sussex: Culture and Conflict* (Farnham: Ashgate, 2014), 221–54; and Llewellyn, "Baroque Sculpture: Materiality and the Question of Movement", in David Gaimster, Tara Hamling, and Catherine Richardson, eds., *Research Companion to Early Modern Material Culture* (forthcoming).
46. The church was the established burial place of the Colstons: there is an earlier monument there to Colston's mother, Sarah (died 1701), attributed to William Woodman the Elder.
47. Stayner (born 1665), had recently served as Master of the Mason's Company.
48. Charles O'Brien and Nikolaus Pevsner, *The Buildings of England: Bedfordshire, Huntingdonshire and Peterborough* (New Haven and London: Yale Univ. Press, 2014), 184. Compare with Joshua Barnes (died 1712) at Hemingford Abbots, Hunts, who was Regius Professor of Greek and whose inscription is partly in that language. See O'Brien and Pevsner, *Bedfordshire, Huntingdonshire and Peterborough*, 510.
49. Nikolaus Pevsner, *The Buildings of England: Hampshire and the Isle of Wight* (New Haven and London: Yale Univ. Press, 2002).
50. Nikolaus Pevsner, *The Buildings of England: Norfolk* (New Haven and London: Yale Univ. Press), 2: plate 45.
51. Nikolaus Pevsner, *The Buildings of England: Worcestershire* (Harmondsworth: Penguin, 1968), plate 66. Their face types are not unlike those of Reeves the carver operating at Gloucester in the 1660s.

Notes on Contributors

Tabitha Barber is Curator of British Art (1550–1750) at Tate Britain, London. Her recent projects include the exhibition with accompanying catalogue, *Art under Attack: Histories of British Iconoclasm*, on display at Tate Britain (2013) and curated with Stacy Boldrick, Ruth Kenny, and Sofia Karamani.

Tim Batchelor is Assistant Curator of British Art (1550–1750) at Tate Britain, London. His recent projects include the exhibition with accompanying catalogue, *Dead Standing Things: Still Life 1660–1740*, on display at Tate Britain (2012).

John Bonehill teaches art history at the University of Glasgow. He is currently researching and writing a book-length study of estate portraiture and the landscape arts in Britain, ca. 1660–1832.

Diana Dethloff is a member of the faculty in History of Art at University College London. Her ongoing research on Peter Lely, which will result in a full catalogue raisonné and exhibition (with co-author Catharine MacLeod), has also recently appeared in the catalogue accompanying *Peter Lely: A Lyrical Vision*, on display at the The Courtauld Gallery, London (2012). Diana is a member of the editorial board for the *The Art World in Britain, 1660 to 1735* (http://artworld.york.ac.uk) and a Fellow of the Society of Antiquaries.

Sebastian Edwards is currently Deputy Chief Curator at Historic Royal Palaces, where he has contributed to projects including the exhibition *Secrets of the Royal Bedchamber* displayed at Hampton Court Palace (2013).

Anthony Geraghty is Professor of the History of Art at the University of York, and Chairman of the Society of Architectural Historians of Great Britain. His recent publications include *The Sheldonian Theatre: Architecture and Learning in Seventeenth-century Oxford* (Yale University Press, 2013).

Caroline Good is a postdoctoral research fellow at the University of Oxford, currently working on an art historical analysis of human wildlife conflict, with the Wildlife Conservation Research Unit. She served as a project assistant on the AHRC-funded project *Court, Country, City: British Art, 1660–1735*.

Mark Hallett is Director of Studies at the Paul Mellon Centre for Studies in British Art, London. In addition, he is currently a Visiting Professor at the Courtauld Institute of Art and also serves on the International Advisory Panel of the Courtauld's Research Forum. His many publications include *Reynolds: Portraiture in Action* (Yale University Press, 2014).

Lydia Hamlett is a Leverhulme Early Career Fellow at the University of Cambridge. She is working on a monograph on mural painting in the context of British visual culture of the late seventeenth and early eighteenth centuries.

Matthew Hargraves is Chief Curator of Art Collections and Head of Collections Information and Access at the Yale Center for British Art, and the author of *Varieties of Romantic Experience: British, Danish, Dutch, French, and German Drawings from the Collection of Charles Ryskamp* (Yale University Press, 2010).

Claudine van Hensbergen is Senior Lecturer in Eighteenth-century English Literature at Northumbria University at Newcastle. Her research focuses on the literary marketplace and British culture from the Restoration period to the mid-eighteenth century. In 2014 she edited and contributed to a special issue of *the Journal for Eighteenth-Century Studies* marking the tercentenary of Queen Anne's death, and she recently finished editing the late plays of Nicholas Rowe for publication as Volume III of *The Plays and Poetry of Nicholas Rowe* (forthcoming 2017).

Richard Johns is Lecturer in the History of Art at the University of York, where his research is focused on art and visual culture in Britain during the long eighteenth century, with a special interest in grand-scale decorative history painting. Recent projects include the exhibition co-curated with Christine Riding, together with accompanying catalogue, *Turner & the Sea* at the National Maritime Museum, Greenwich (2013).

Nigel Llewellyn is the former Head of Research at Tate. He previously taught at the University of Sussex, where he also served as Dean and Pro-Vice-Chancellor. He is currently a member of the AHRC Advisory Board, where he chairs a number of subcommittees on Science and Heritage.

Emily Mann recently defended her doctoral thesis "Architecture and the Negotiation of Empire in the Early Modern Atlantic World" at the Courtauld Institute of Art. She has taught in the Department of History of Art at the University of Cambridge and the University of York, and currently is Research Associate at the Centre for the Political Economies of International Commerce, University of Kent.

Anya Matthews is an architectural historian and has recently completed a PhD at the Courtauld Institute of Art on the architecture and political uses of London's seventeenth-century livery halls. She is currently Research Curator for the Painted Hall at the Old Royal Naval College, Greenwich.

Peter Moore's current research focuses on the development of landscape and its subgenres in eighteenth-century British art. He has recently published articles on John Collett and John Wootton, and is working a on a number of research projects relating to Thomas Gainsborough, particularly his early career in London and Suffolk. He is Research Curator at Gainsborough's House, in Sudbury, Suffolk.

Martin Myrone is Lead Curator, pre-1800 British Art, at Tate Britain. In addition to serving as co-investigator on the AHRC-funded project *Court, Country, City: British Art, 1660–1735*, his recent noteworthy projects include the exhibition *British Folk Art*, on display at Tate Britain (2014) and featuring an accompanying catalogue co-authored with Jeff McMillan and Ruth Kenny.

Helen Pierce is a Lecturer in British Art at the University of Aberdeen, Scotland. She is the author of *Unseemly Pictures: Graphic Satire and Politics in Early Modern England* (Yale University Press, 2008), and is currently researching the patronage and production of art in England and Scotland during the 1650s.

Jacqueline Riding specializes in Georgian and Jacobite history and visual culture, and is the author of *Jacobites: A New History of the '45 Rebellion* (Bloomsbury Publishing, 2016) and the forthcoming *The Angel of Mercy: Joseph Highmore and the Foundling Hospital* (Paul Holberton Publishing, 2017). She was the consultant historian and art historian for Mike Leigh's award-winning film *Mr. Turner* (2014) and is an Associate Research Fellow in the School of Arts, Birkbeck College, University of London.

David H. Solkin is Walter H. Annenberg Professor of the History of Art and Dean and Deputy Director of the Courtauld Institute of Art. His numerous publications include *Art in Britain 1660–1815* (Yale University Press/Pelican History of Art Series, 2015).

Richard Stephens is editor of the online database *The Art World in Britain, 1660 to 1735* (http://artworld.york.ac.uk). In 2016 he curated the exhibition *Light, Time, Legacy: Francis Towne's Watercolours of Rome* at the British Museum, and his catalogue raisonné of Towne was published at www.francistowne.ac.uk.

Christine Stevenson is Professor of Early Modern Art and Architecture at the Courtauld Institute of Art. Her many publications include *The City and the King: Architecture and Politics in Restoration London* (Yale University Press for the Paul Mellon Centre for Studies in British Art, 2013).

Credits and Sources

Every effort has been made to credit the photographers and sources of all illustrations in this volume; if there are any errors or omissions, please contact Yale University Press so that corrections can be made in any subsequent edition.

Photo: akg-images: fig. 179

By permission of the Warden and Fellows of All Souls College, Oxford: fig. 7

Courtesy American Antiquarian Society: fig. 169

© The Art Institute of Chicago: fig. 6

© Ashmolean Museum, University of Oxford: figs. 85, 86, 87, 88, 89, 90, 91, 92, 93, 95, 98

Beinecke Rare Book and Manuscript Library, Yale University: figs. 2, 37, 38a, 38b, 47, 150, 161, 180

Blenheim Palace, Oxfordshire, UK / Bridgeman Images: figs. 58, 67

© The British Library Board: fig. 154

© Trustees of the British Museum: figs. 5a, 5b, 10, 11, 12, 15, 16, 18, 19, 28, 52, 55, 68, 94, 96, 99, 100, 114, 115, 116, 117, 120, 121, 122, 123, 126, 127, 128, 129, 130, 131, 166, 181, 182, 183

John Carter Brown Library, Brown University: fig. 156

By kind permission of the Duke of Buccleuch & Queensberry KBE: fig. 72

Charlecote Park © National Trust: fig. 149

Château de Versailles, France / Bridgeman Images: fig. 48

Reproduced by permission of Chatsworth Settlement Trustees: fig. 113

© Country Life Picture Library: figs. 40, 41

© The Courtauld Institute of Art, London: figs. 20, 186, 187, 188

David Cronin: fig. 76

With kind permission of the Governors of Dulwich College: figs. 101, 102, 103, 104, 105, 106, 107, 108, 109, 110, 111, 112

© The Fitzwilliam Museum, Cambridge: fig. 132

© The Fitzwilliam Museum, University of Cambridge / Bridgeman Images: figs. 173a, 173b, 175

Image courtesy of Frick Art Reference Library Photoarchive: fig. 172

Collection of Anthony Geraghty: figs. 39, 43

Imaging Department © President and Fellows of Harvard College: fig. 171

© Historic England: fig. 71

© Historic England / © David Bowie: fig. 80

© Historic Royal Palaces: fig. 34

Houses of Parliament, Westminster, London, UK / Bridgeman Images: fig. 4

Houses of Parliament, Westminster, London/ Photo © Christie's Images / Bridgeman Images: fig. 3

Reproduced with the kind permission of the Masters of the Bench of the Inner Temple: fig. 69

Knole © National Trust / Jane Mucklow: fig. 31

By kind permission of Leeds Library and Information Services: figs. 118, 119, 124, 125

Leeds Museums and Galleries (Leeds Art Gallery), UK/ Bridgeman Images: fig. 77

Photograph courtesy of Amanda Lillie: fig. 44

London Metropolitan Archives, City of London: figs. 21, 26

© Look and Learn / Peter Jackson Collection / Bridgeman Images: fig. 25

The Metropolitan Museum of Art, New York: fig. 13

The Metropolitan Museum of Art. Image source: Art Resource, NY: fig. 170

© Mike Kipling Photography: fig. 35

© Miles Barton - Period Paintings, London: fig. 167

Museo Nacional del Prado, Madrid, Spain / Bridgeman Images: fig. 174

Museum of Dordrecht, The Netherlands / Bridgeman Images: fig. 136

Museum of London, UK: fig. 8, front cover

National Gallery of Art, Washington D.C., Widener Collection: fig. 176

National Gallery of Victoria, Melbourne, Felton Bequest, 1947: fig. 143

© National Maritime Museum, Greenwich, London: figs. 49, 81

National Portrait Gallery, London, UK: figs. 57, 142, 147, 164, 177

© National Portrait Gallery, London, UK / © Stefano Baldini / Bridgeman Images: figs. 1, 97, 140, 145

©National Trust Images/Andreas von Einsiedel: fig. 137

© Collection of the New York Historical Society, USA / Bridgeman Images: fig. 168

© Norwich Castle Museum and Art Gallery / Bridgeman Images: fig. 9

Nottingham City Museums and Galleries: fig. 29

© Peter Scholey / Alamy Stock Photo: fig. 79

Private Collection / Photo © Christie's Images / Bridgeman Images: fig. 134

Private Collection / Photo © Philip Mould Ltd, London / Bridgeman Images: figs. 45, 141

Private Collection / ©Tate, London 2016: figs. 135, 138

© RIBA Library Drawings and Archives Collections: fig. 27

© RMN-Grand Palais (Château de Versailles) / Gérard Blot: fig. 42

Royal Collection Trust / © Her Majesty Queen Elizabeth II 2016: figs. 33, 34, 50, 53, 54, 61, 64, 66, 73, 84

Royal Collection Trust / © Her Majesty Queen Elizabeth II 2016 / Bridgeman Images: fig. 46

Royal Collection Trust/© Her Majesty Queen Elizabeth II 2016 / © Historic Royal Palaces: fig. 32

Royal Collection Trust / © Her Majesty Queen Elizabeth II 2016 / Lydia Hamlett: figs. 60, 63, 65

© Royal Hospital Chelsea, London, UK / Bridgeman Images: figs. 14, 56

© The Royal Society: fig. 185

Salisbury Diocesan Board of Finance / Gerry Lynch: fig. 83

Scottish National Portrait Gallery: fig. 144

State Hermitage Museum, St. Petersburg, Russia / Bridgeman Images: fig. 146

Fotograf: Oberhofmarschallamt / Verwaltung der Staatlichen Schlösser und Gärten (1927-1945) / Stiftung Preußische Schlösser und Gärten, Berlin-Brandenburg: fig. 70

Temple Newsam House, Leeds, West Yorkshire, UK / Bridgeman Images: fig. 163

The Master and Fellows of Trinity College, Cambridge: fig. 165

The Master and Fellows of Trinity College, Cambridge / Bridgeman Images: fig. 148

UIG / Bridgeman Images: fig. 139

Special Collections, University of Virginia, Charlottesville: fig. 162

Collection of Claudine van Hensbergen: fig. 78

© Victoria and Albert Museum, London: figs. 17, 30, 62, 178

Virginia Historical Society: fig. 75

Warwickshire County Record Office: fig. 153

Welbeck Abbey, The Portland Collection, Harley Gllery Collection / Derek Adam: fig. 74

Copyright: Dean and Chapter of Westminster: fig. 189

Winchester City Council, UK: fig. 82

The Provost and Fellows of Worcester College, Oxford: fig. 59, back cover

© World History Archive / Alamy Stock Photo: fig. 51

The Worshipful Company of Brewers / London Metropolitan Archives, City of London: fig. 22

© The Worshipful Company of Stationers and Newspaper Makers: fig. 23

Yale Center for British Art, Paul Mellon Collection: figs. 24, 36, 133, 151, 152, 155, 157, 158, 159, 160

Yale Center for British Art, Paul Mellon Fund: fig. 184

Index

Note: Page numbers in *italics* refer to illustrations.